The Tootin' Louie

The Tootin' Louie

A History of the Minneapolis & St. Louis Railway

Don L. Hofsommer

University of Minnesota Press
Minneapolis • London

Published by the University of Minnesota Press
111 Third Avenue South, Suite 290
Minneapolis, MN 55401-2520
http://www.upress.umn.edu

Library of Congress Cataloging-in-Publication Data

Hofsommer, Donovan L.
The Tootin' Louie : a history of the Minneapolis & St. Louis Railway / Don L. Hofsommer.
p. cm.
Includes bibliographical references and index.
ISBN 0-8166-4365-2 (hc : alk. paper). — ISBN 0-8166-4366-0 (pbk. : alk. paper)
1. Minneapolis & St. Louis Railway—History. I. Title.
HE2791.M663H64 2005
385'.0977—dc22
2004014189

Printed in the United States of America on acid-free paper

12 11 10 09 08 07 06 10 9 8 7 6 5 4 3 2

For Charles A. Brown
and all who worked for the Minneapolis & St. Louis

Contents

PREFACE

CUSTOMS OF DRESS IN THIS COUNTRY HAVE CHANGED over the past several decades. We have become more casual. My own standards reflect this. Yet I maintain one small tradition of style. Each Christmas Eve I don my finest three-piece suit, wind and set the old Hamilton Railway Special, and dig through a now-little-used jewelry box to find a cherished fob and chain given to me long ago by Charles A. Brown. With watch ticking bravely in the right vest pocket and chain and fob swinging gently to my movements, I feel ready to present myself for the early evening worship service. My thoughts, I know, should be focused otherwise, but wearing that old fob and chain inevitably diverts my mind to happy memories of early youth—to Charlie Brown and his fellows, and to the Minneapolis & St. Louis Railway (M&StL) for which they labored.

"When are you going to Fort Dodge with us?" Charlie blithely inquired of me one day in the spring of 1952 as we stood together on the station platform at Spencer, Iowa. I stammered some meaningless reply, dumbfounded at the possibilities suggested by his question, but when I saw him again the next day I was categorically direct: "June 16," I said. "June 16?" he replied, a quizzical look on his face. "Yes, it's a Tuesday," I said. "I'll come back with you Wednesday on 57." There was a pause as Charlie studied this curiously one-sided conversation. Then he recalled his question of the previous day and his oblique invitation, smiled, and said, "Fine." Years later, I wonder if his invitation was extended in jest. But my affirmative response left no doubt where I stood. And at the moment, I had no doubt about his veracity. After all, Charlie was conductor on M&StL's triweekly freight from Estherville through Spencer to Fort Dodge. He was the "boss." Why would I not take him seriously?

Charlie Brown was hardly the first M&StLer to befriend me. My father had managed the S. Hanson Lumber Company yard at Callender, Iowa, during my earliest years. The yard was next to M&StL's house track on the back side of the depot, the center pivot on Callender's "metropolitan corridor," which included grain elevators, bulk plants, and a stock yard to the north, more elevators to the south. It was in that depot (Oh, the mysteries of that place!) and along that corridor that I was indulged by John Dallman, foreman of the Gowrie section crew, who often worked his men with the Callender crew as they unloaded and piled grain door boards, changed out and tamped cross ties, or—most exciting of all—obliterated the vegetation that infested the track with a flame-spewing monster called the weed burner.

We moved to Fort Dodge in 1944, but to a home that was in easy proximity to M&StL's line that made its way along Soldier Creek out of the Des Moines River valley toward Albert Lea, a splendid place to watch the noonday drama of train 51 assaulting the grade with a shiny 400-class steamer throwing smoke heavenward with an ear-shattering exhaust that must have nearly awakened the dead in a nearby cemetery. And puttering along behind came a timid-sounding and anemic-looking General Electric forty-four-ton diesel-electric that presumably was providing assistance by shoving against the caboose with its handsome cupola—although, given the ferocious display of the 2-8-0 ahead, I was never quite convinced. Occasionally I heard the cackling report of gas-electric cars heading train 3 toward Minneapolis, but that train and its counterpart were confined to nocturnal schedules, so I was not to see them in that location.

In 1948 we moved again, this time to Spencer, shortly after M&StL had removed passenger trains 17 and 18. But depot personnel—John G. Benson, agent; Jake Fritz, cashier; and Edward F. Pierce, operator—were gracious and tolerant, letting me hang around, responding to endless questions, and even permitting me to help load and unload less-than-carload lots (LCL) of freight from Brady trucks that ran daily except Sunday between Fort Dodge and Estherville. The depot was also a fine place to overhear railroad gossip, to wonder at the banter of office personnel and trainmen, and to witness fierce arguments over train orders, the book of rules, national politics, the evils of management, or how the yard should be switched. My worldly knowledge and my vocabulary were greatly enriched by all of this. In addition, I was always welcome in the caboose when train 57 arrived from Fort Dodge and tied up, and on Saturday mornings I was frequently an unauthorized, nonrevenue passenger on the locomotive of 56, detraining at Ruthven, Iowa, thirteen miles east, returning as a legitimate, fare-paying customer on Chicago, Milwaukee, St. Paul & Pacific (Milwaukee Road) number 11, the westbound Sioux. And on one Friday afternoon 57 came up with two cabooses. There would be ample bed space in them if I wanted to ride along to Estherville and come back the next day. Would I like to go? Does a bear like honey?

Charlie was good to his word. On June 16 I went to Fort Dodge with him on 56, stayed overnight as a welcome guest of Charlie and his marvelous wife, Bess, and returned with him the next morning on 57, waving to Bess from the caboose as we left the yard. It was one of many trips I took with Charlie and several others—one, incidentally, with Max A. Sedelmeier, another M&StL conductor, on the caboose of a "snow plow extra," with two unsuspecting officials riding ahead in the Russell plow. "Stay out of sight," Max told me. I did, but I saw plenty, and the officials did not see me.

Later on, before I discovered athletics, automobiles, schoolwork, the female gender, and other impediments to all things railroad, I spent a summer working on the local section gang. It was good pay ($1.49 an hour), and I worked forty hours a week, with Saturdays off. And I was working for "my" railroad. Indeed, I had long since taken a proprietary interest in M&StL. All I wanted to do, I told myself, was spend my life working for the railroad—and the only railroad I wanted to work for was M&StL, a company saved from certain oblivion by its president, Lucian C. Sprague, and thoroughly enshrined for me by Frank P. Donovan Jr. in *Mileposts on the Prairie*. But when Ben Heineman "stole" M&StL from Sprague, I decided that I certainly did not want to hitch my star to any nefarious outfit that would suffer his ilk—and maybe I did not want to work for any railroad if Heineman was an example of the kind of person who led such enterprises. Instead I wandered into teaching, and soon into higher education, where, I assured myself, one would find only unselfish gentility, collegiality, courtesy, and civility, and where one would never have to worry about one's backside—in sum, the very opposite of the business world. It was not the last time I made a serious error in judgment.

My affection for and my interest in M&StL did not dissipate, however, and, fortunately for me, a fourteen-day leave from the army corresponded with M&StL's last days in October 1960. I was on hand to see the end. With the military behind me and teaching ahead, I determined to get a master's degree, and, for whatever strange reason, Dr. Leland L. Sage at what was then the State College of Iowa agreed to work with me. So did Dr. Erma B. Plaehn. And both agreed that a history of the Iowa Central Railway was a worthy thesis topic. In Minneapolis, Frank P. Donovan Jr., with whom I had long corresponded and in whose home I had been a guest, offered encouragement, as did Paul H. Stringham in Peoria, Illinois, and former Iowa Central employees at various locations. I completed my thesis in 1966. By that time, however, I had ridden over M&StL lines on trains or had driven to every outpost from Leola to Peoria, talking to employees or former employees who universally responded with generosity and grace to my endless requests for materials or recollections. Their sense of devotion to M&StL was palpable—it made no difference what craft they were in or had been in. Later on I would have the privilege of working on histories of other railroad companies, and I would be struck by employee loyalty and devotion to railroading in general, but I never witnessed it anywhere to the degree I found at M&StL, where long, tedious years of desperation forged inseparable bonds between workers and employer that became M&StL's greatest single asset.

More than four decades have passed since M&StL perished in 1960, nearly five decades after Charlie Brown asked when I would join him in a trip to Fort Dodge. Virtually all of the men who generously shared themselves and "their" railroad with me are gone. But I remain the lucky one. In my memory those great friends of yesteryear still wave to me with cheery greetings from locomotive cabs and little red cabooses that glide effortlessly along ghost rails, and from bay windows of depots long removed. And I wave back at them.

Minneapolis & St. Louis was a hard-luck railroad from the beginning. It is a great wonder that it lasted as long as it did; its longevity is powerful testimony to the company's managers and its rank-and-file employees.

My thesis when I began working on this volume was that Minneapolis millers and other entrepreneurs and land speculators, with brilliant insight into the future, formed the railroad as a tool of urban economic imperialism to hold a significant hinterland subservient to those same Minneapolis interests—moving raw materials inbound, finished goods in return. There is some validity to that argument. But in the main, those Minneapolis interests did not have that gift of

Figure P.1. "And I wave back at them" (in this case, conductor Albert L. Pickett). Photograph by the author.

foresight. Instead, they were reacting to the growing power and influence of Chicago and Milwaukee and their several railroads, which were spewing their way west and northwest to claim huge chunks of domain that threatened the hopes and aspirations of the Minneapolitans. When they formed M&StL, they did not act in advance, guided by a vision of the future; they reacted.

This tardy response and the concomitant lack of local capital were deadly. M&StL's purposes were sound—seeking to break the power of Chicago and Milwaukee roads with an alternative route to the attractive St. Louis gateway, tapping Iowa coal fields to aid the fuel-starved north country and sending lumber from Minnesota pineries in return, providing an all-season highway from a huge wheat-producing empire to the hungry mills at Minneapolis and using that same thoroughfare as a chute for flour into a wide marketing area, and, incidentally, laying out a route to Duluth, Minnesota, and the Great Lakes chain as a safety valve. But the timing was terrible. When Minneapolis promoters finally got around to founding M&StL, and by the time they had built a bit of track, the awful panic of 1873 was upon them; once the depression had passed and M&StL wheezed into Albert Lea in 1877, the power of the Lake Michigan roads was nearly at its peak. Bum luck followed bum luck. M&StL had strategic importance for Northern Pacific (NP) and subsequently for Chicago, Rock Island &

Pacific (Rock Island) and as part of Edwin Hawley's expansive plans, but NP coughed up M&StL during the panic of 1873, Rock Island jettisoned M&StL later, and Hawley's dreams died with him in 1912. By that time M&StL had merged with Iowa Central to form a curiously configured vertical-axis route structure with a significant westward branch to Le Beau, South Dakota, which, from a strategic point of view, was orphan to the rest of the system. Restricted to a four-state area (Minnesota, Iowa, South Dakota, and Illinois) highly dependent on agriculture, crossing east-west roads often in a way that encouraged customers to use M&StL for short hauls, the road enthusiastically and successfully sought overhead or bridge traffic (business that merely moved over M&StL rails, neither billed to nor coming from M&StL stations) for its longest haul, Minneapolis to Peoria; the *St. Louis* in *Minneapolis & St. Louis* was never attained.

Financial distress was part and parcel of the M&StL experience. The road nearly died during the Great Depression, and, from a strictly economic point of view, dismemberment was likely the appropriate prescription. But through the leadership of Lucian C. Sprague and others, M&StL dodged that bullet to bask a few years in the pleasure of relative prosperity. In 1954 Sprague was unceremoniously unseated by Ben W. Heineman through a nasty proxy fight, and M&StL later failed to acquire Toledo, Peoria & Western as a means of extending its line hauls. In the end, none of this mattered. Shadows lengthened throughout the 1950s as modal competition—water, highway, and pipeline—relentlessly ate away at railroad traffic and as public policy failed to realize that the age of railways was long since past. Mergers became the favored elixir, and in 1960 M&StL shareholders determined to get out of the railroad business while M&StL was still financially and physically attractive. Whether Chicago & North Western was the best home for it is a question without purpose; that is where the road ended up, and no amount of second guessing will change the outcome.

This, then, is a study of the Minneapolis & St. Louis—a game if unlucky old railroad—and, by extension, its four-state service area, from the dawn of the steamcar civilization to the post–World War II period of the national railroad era. Hang on; it's a bumpy ride.

> Hail and Farewell
> Old M. and St. L.
> Eighty as your depot
> A good life, you say?
> History says, "Nay,
> You were sickly from
> The start."
> —*Author unknown*

I have examined the Iowa Central experience more thoroughly in *The Hook & Eye: A History of the Iowa Central Railway,* and M&StL's early context is a large part of *Minneapolis and the Age of Railways* (both published by the University of Minnesota Press).

Without ever dreaming that I would one day write a book on the Minneapolis & St. Louis, I began collecting photographs, memorabilia, and memories even before I was an adolescent—a pattern that continues to this moment. A nearly endless list of generous persons have helped, a fact that gives me much pleasure, but because this work has been done over a protracted period of time and because I occasionally neglected to keep records, I fear that I shall fail to give proper credit where it is due.

Because no appreciable block of M&StL corporate records exists, I was forced to "grub in strange places" for information. Archival materials do exist in bits and pieces among collections from larger roads such as Great Northern and Northern Pacific. In this search I have been helped by many people, and I wish to thank W. Thomas White, James J. Hill Reference Library, St. Paul; Joyce W. Koeneman, Association of American Railroads, Washington, D.C.; Robert A. McCown, University of Iowa Libraries, Iowa City; Lida Lisle Green, State Historical Society of Iowa, Des Moines; Harry F. Thompson and Ronelle F. H. Thompson, Augustana College, Sioux Falls; Mark J. Cedeck and Gregory P. Ames, Mercantile Library, St. Louis; and Susan Motin and Joan O'Driscoll, St. Cloud State University, St. Cloud, Minnesota.

From trainmen at Watertown to engine crews at

Fort Dodge I was warmly received by all hands in every department at Minneapolis & St. Louis and Chicago & North Western. Of course Charles A. Brown endeared himself to me by carrying me up and down the line, but the same can be said of Max A. Sedelmeier, James W. Murphy, Albert L. Pickett, Walter J. O'Connor, and many others. John A. Dallman, Dan N. Knight, William F. Arp, Virgil W. Peterson, Albert M. Ramnes, and Vaughn R. Ward all contributed in one way or another. John G. Benson, the agent at Spencer for many years, has a special place in my heart. Former officers William W. Landmesser, Manford J. Reitan, H. E. Herington, Charles W. Stone, and James R. Sullivan were unstinting in their cooperation. At Chicago & North Western, Robin Bourne-Caris and Penny Menchy graciously made available M&StL minute books and other essential information.

Still others helped in assorted ways. Robert E. McMillan and George Pacocha opened Toledo, Peoria & Western records to me, and when Frank P. Donovan Jr. died in 1970, Jan, his widow, gave me Frank's M&StL files. Others who provided data, guidance, encouragement, and assistance include Laverne W. Andreessen, John L. Hodson, Lorenz P. Schrenk, James Mischke, Paul Stringham, Dennis E. Holmes, Evelyn M. O'Day, Alfred E. Tietel, Henry M. Larson, Harold Fisher, Gene Green, Dorothy Mills, John Willand, Thomas T. Taber, Roger B. Natte, William F. Armstrong, Hudson Leighton, Jerry Masters, Arthur D. Dubin, John Paul, Stephanie Paul, John S. Gutteter, Lisa D. Hanson, Yvette Villeneuve-Ezell, Timothy M. Hoheisel, Paul B. Kattner, Patrice C. Bass, Michael J. Hargesheimer, and Edward W. Solberg. Throughout, Janice Schlangen and Ann Anderson turned my messy copy into clean manuscript.

Several persons from the academic world and the railroad industry read all or parts of the manuscript and offered their own special insights and constructive criticisms. In this area, special thanks go to Robert W. Downing, James R. Sullivan, Georges C. Denzene, Frank P. Donovan Jr., Leland L. Sage, Erma B. Plaehn, H. Roger Grant, John C. Kenefick, Robert E. McMillan, and James A. Ward.

I was pleased to receive research grants from the James J. Hill Reference Library and St. Cloud State University, which I happily acknowledge.

Finally, I am grateful to my parents, wife, and children, whose tolerance for my interests in and devotion to all things M&StL and to the railroad industry generally must have taxed their sensibilities.

To all of those mentioned, and to others whom I have regrettably overlooked, I am deeply grateful. For errors of fact, and for infelicities of style that remain, I alone am responsible.

Don L. Hofsommer

Acronyms and Shortened Names

A&C	Albia & Centerville
Alton	Chicago & Alton
AT&SF	Atchison, Topeka & Santa Fe
B&W	Burlington & Western
BCR&M	Burlington, Cedar Rapids & Minnesota
BCR&N	Burlington, Cedar Rapids & Northern
Burlington	Chicago, Burlington & Quincy
C&A	Chicago & Alton
C&NW	Chicago & North Western or North Western
C&O	Chesapeake & Ohio
C&RI	Chicago & Rock Island
CB&P	Chicago, Burlington & Pacific
CB&Q	Chicago, Burlington & Quincy or Burlington
Cedar Rapids	Chicago & North Western
Central	Central Iowa or Iowa Central
CF&M	Cedar Falls & Minnesota
CGW	Chicago Great Western or Great Western
CI	Central Iowa
Clover Leaf	Toledo, St. Louis & Western
CM&A	Centerville, Moravia & Albia
CM&StP	Chicago, Milwaukee & St. Paul or Milwaukee Road
CMStP&P	Chicago, Milwaukee, St. Paul & Pacific or Milwaukee Road
CR&MR	Cedar Rapids & Missouri River
CRCI	Central Railroad Company of Iowa
CRI&P	Chicago, Rock Island & Pacific or Rock Island
CStP&KC	Chicago, St. Paul & Kansas City
CStPM&O	Chicago, St. Paul, Minneapolis & Omaha or Omaha
D&SC	Dubuque & Sioux City
DM&CI	Des Moines & Central Iowa
DM&FtD	Des Moines & Fort Dodge
DMV	Des Moines Valley
ER&CC	Eldora Railroad & Coal Company
FtDDM&S	Fort Dodge, Des Moines & Southern
G&M	Grinnell & Montezuma
GN	Great Northern
Great Western	Chicago Great Western
IC	Illinois Central
IC&NW	Iowa Central & Northwestern
ICC	Interstate Commerce Commission
LCL	Less-than-carload lots

LS&M Lake Superior & Mississippi
M&D Minneapolis & Duluth
M&NW Minnesota & Northwestern
M&StL Minneapolis & St. Louis
MI&N Missouri, Iowa & Nebraska
Milwaukee Road Chicago, Milwaukee & St. Paul or Chicago, Milwaukee, St. Paul & Pacific
MK&T Missouri, Kansas & Texas
MNU&SW Minneapolis, New Ulm & Southwestern
MStP&SSteM Minneapolis, St. Paul & Sault Ste. Marie or Soo Line
North Western Chicago & North Western
NP Northern Pacific
Omaha Chicago, St. Paul, Minneapolis & Omaha
ORT Order of Railroad Telegraphers
P&F Peoria & Farmington
PRR Pennsylvania Railroad
Railway Transfer Railway Transfer Company of the City of Minneapolis
RDC Rail diesel car
Rock Island Chicago, Rock Island & Pacific
RPO Railway Post Office
Santa Fe Atchison, Topeka & Santa Fe
Soo Line Minneapolis, St. Paul & Sault Ste. Marie
SP Southern Pacific
StL&CR St. Louis & Cedar Rapids
StP&D St. Paul & Duluth
StP&SC St. Paul & Sioux City
TOFC Trailer-on-flat-car
TP&W Toledo, Peoria & Western
TStL&W Toledo, St. Louis & Western
USRA United States Railroad Administration
WM&P Wisconsin, Minnesota & Pacific

Chapter 1
EXPECTANCY

We are firmly of the opinion, without equivocation, or mental reservation, that no city in Minnesota offers so great inducements to the capitalist, as the city of St. Anthony.
—*St. Anthony Weekly Democrat,* June 3, 1870

"We are a state of the Union," boomed the *Saint Paul Daily Minnesotan* on May 14, 1858. "No longer outside barbarians," exclaimed the editor, "[we] have donned our freedom suit." Indeed, predicted the *Daily Minnesotan,* the new state would shortly have a population of a half million persons and would post great advances in "wealth, manufacturers, agriculture, and the mechanic arts." Typical Western boosterism, yes, but pardonable since the state did hold great potential. Yet the nasty panic of 1857 and a regional "Indian menace" had thrown a distressing pall over the region. Moreover, Minnesota, for the most part, remained a raw wilderness that was mostly devoid of modern comforts and betterments. To be sure, news that on May 11 President James Buchanan had signed legislation admitting Minnesota to statehood had been wired to the nearest telegraph office—Prairie du Chien, Wisconsin, 190 miles downstream on the Mississippi River—from whence the message was relayed northward by a St. Paul–bound steamboat. News of Minnesota's statehood had taken forty-eight hours to reach the new state. It was galling.[1]

The need for advanced communication and modern transportation was fully apparent. "We must have an outlet, *and an outlet by rail,* and this as speedily as possible, or we are nowhere," screamed the *St. Anthony Express.* Liberal grants of land in support of railroad development had, in fact, poured from the federal government to Minnesota Territory, which had chartered a number of important enterprises and doled out to them blocks of the public domain. One of these was the Minnesota Western Rail Road, which in 1853 was authorized to build a road "from some convenient point to be selected on Lake St. Croix, or St. Croix River" to St. Paul and nearby St. Anthony and on to the western boundary of the territory, with a branch on the west to the Red River and another on the east to the St. Louis River (where it emptied into Lake Superior). But neither Minnesota Western (the earliest corporate ancestor of Minneapolis & St. Louis) nor other of the roads chartered by the territory proved active, and in fact, all were projected ahead of reasonable demand. "Minnesota wants these roads commenced at once," cried the *Sauk Rapids Frontiersman.* Nevertheless, investment capital remained extremely scarce and very competitive—a problem greatly magnified by the panic of 1857. Roads "commenced at once" would be delayed. Not surprisingly, pulling and hauling was accompanied by angry finger pointing and bad feeling. In time some of the early companies were rechartered to take up important responsibilities for developing railroad transportation in the fledgling state. Not among them, curiously, was Minnesota Western, which inexplicably went into eclipse.[2]

Elsewhere rails pushed the transportation frontier to the nation's interior. Already in 1848 a predecessor of Chicago & North Western (C&NW or North Western) pushed out from Chicago to the west. It was much the same just eighty-five miles up the Lake Michigan shore, where Milwaukee interests promoted two predecessors of Chicago, Milwaukee & St. Paul (CM&StP or Milwaukee Road) on individual routes to the Mississippi—one to Prairie du Chien and the other to LaCrosse, Wisconsin. Each of these roads represented bold urban economic impulses of community leaders in Chicago and Milwaukee, and each one, in time, would be a primary player in the railroad affairs of Minnesota.[3]

St. Louis, another important interior aspirant, would rank seventh among American cities in terms of population by 1860. Strategically located on the Mississippi River just south of its confluence with the Illinois and the Missouri and above its junction with the Ohio, St. Louis earned early dominion over a huge hinterland. Its claim to be the Gateway City was difficult to refute, with its shoreline levees a constant fever of activity as riverboat cargoes were loaded, unloaded, or transloaded. As early as 1840, St. Louis met about half the marketing and supply needs of Illinois, and St. Louis denizens took pride in the trade inroads made in what would become the states of Iowa, Wisconsin, and Minnesota. St. Louis would find itself in great competition with the two youthful Lake Michigan contenders—locally and across a huge swath of the prairies and plains of the West.[4]

Gradually—ever so gradually, it seemed to Minnesotans—the age of railways dawned in their state. A combination of government land grants and private investments ended the long gestation. One of the grantees, Minnesota & Pacific, regained its authority, then stumbled again, and was restyled as St. Paul & Pacific. It was this road's handsome *William Crooks* that steamed out of St. Paul on June 28, 1862, over spindly rails to St. Anthony, ten miles distant, and in the process exposed Minnesota to the steamcar civilization.[5]

St. Paul, from which this pioneer train had departed, quickly emerged as the region's urban center. It stood at the head of navigation on the Mississippi, trade centered there, and it was the state capital. But St. Paul was hardly the only regional urban oasis. Chief among other contenders were nearby St. Anthony and Minneapolis, both hard by a thundering sixteen-foot cataract on the Mississippi, St. Anthony on the east side and Minneapolis on the west. An immense forest stretched northward from the falls, and, in fact, two-thirds of the state was overlaid with commercially valuable timber. Most of the remaining third, to the south and west, was rolling prairie with rich soil. The Falls of St. Anthony was strategically located to profit from these marvelous nearby resources. Logs from the forest and wheat from the prairies could be brought to the falls for milling; finished products—beyond those necessary for local consumption—could move to distant markets down the Mississippi.[6]

Together St. Anthony and Minneapolis seemed destined for a bright future in manufacturing, made possible in large part by water power at the falls. But the falls and its environs proved a mixed blessing. On the one hand, Mother Nature had blessed St. Anthony and Minneapolis with the falls as a premier source of natural power, but on the other hand, Mother Nature had played a mean trick on them by giving the downstream Mississippi a torturous, crooked, and rock-filled channel that defied navigation before broadening and slowing at St. Paul. Consequently, passengers and freight alike were forced to move overland to and from rival St. Paul. That meant expense and delay in transloading, and, for that matter, relying solely on the Mississippi for transport substantially restricted options for movement to and from the falls, especially in a time of railway ascendancy fully embraced by eager competitors along the shores of Lake Michigan to the east.[7]

Even before angry assaults in 1861 ushered in the awful Civil War, four Chicago-based railroads had thrust themselves out to the Mississippi River. One of these, Chicago & Rock Island (an early ancestor of Chicago, Rock Island & Pacific, CRI&P or Rock Island), became the first road to link the Great Lakes chain with the Mississippi, reaching Rock Island, Illinois, in 1854. Another of these, Chicago, Burlington & Quincy (CB&Q or Burlington), true to its corporate namesake, pushed westward from Chicago to Galesburg, Illinois, where one leg tilted southwestward to strike the Mississippi at Quincy, Illinois, and the other leg drove westward to East Burlington, Illinois, reached on March 17, 1855. Equally energetic was Chicago & North Western, which reached Fulton, Illinois, across the river from Clinton, Iowa, in 1855. Illinois Central likewise pressed its nose against the Mississippi, at Dunleith, Illinois, opposite Dubuque, Iowa. Friends or associates of these several Chicago roads already had fingers extending into Iowa, and Chicago & Rock Island and its Iowa ally boasted a bridge at Davenport (Iowa)–Rock Island to facilitate through movements. Others would not be far behind. And the race across Iowa would be accelerated as candidates vied for traffic to and from Union Pacific's central overland route, which would be completed on May 10, 1869. Not a part of this race, but greatly important to Minnesota, was the Milwaukee-sponsored route from Milwaukee to Prairie du Chien, already in place, and its Iowa counterpart, McGregor & Western, which lifted itself out of the Mississippi valley opposite Prairie du Chien to reach Calmar, Iowa, in 1866; its route then turned tantalizingly northwestward toward Minnesota. In every instance, however, these lines represented intense impulses of urban mercantilism or urban economic imperialism of the Lake Michigan cities, already claiming, as their "natural territory"—as against St. Louis and all others—huge chunks of Illinois, Wisconsin, Iowa, and even Minnesota. Would this help or hurt those with their own instincts of urban mercantilism at the Falls of St. Anthony?[8]

In the short run, business and community leaders of Minneapolis and St. Anthony were captivated by St. Paul & Pacific, the pioneer road that in 1862 had linked St. Paul with St. Anthony, and, after a lengthy pause, inched out of Minneapolis with two lines: one proceeding northward up the east side of the Mississippi to Elk River in 1864 and to East St. Cloud in 1866, and the other westward to Willmar in 1869. These twin lines were bound for the Red River valley and eventually would open huge chunks of domain that would be tributary to Minneapolis, St. Anthony, and St. Paul. At about the same time, predecessors of the future Chicago, Milwaukee & St. Paul were active severally. One of these, Minnesota Central, gradually pushed southward from St. Paul, and, when joined with McGregor & Western's line in Iowa from Marquette and Calmar, gave Minnesota its first direct rail link with the East over a crescent-shaped route to Milwaukee through Austin and Prairie du Chien. An extension from Milwaukee to Chicago, coupled with a new line up the west bank of the Mississippi to St. Paul from LaCrosse, Wisconsin, and LaCrescent through Winona and Hastings, all completed in 1872, taken together with its existing line from Milwaukee to LaCrosse, gave Milwaukee Road two strategic options in the vital Chicago–St. Paul/Minneapolis corridor. Other of Milwaukee's predecessor roads were locking up substantial portions of Minnesota's farm belt, one building westward from LaCrosse through the southern part of the state to Austin and Albert Lea toward Dakota Territory, and another moving westward from Hastings on an alignment south of St. Paul and Minneapolis to Chaska and beyond.[9]

One other principal railroad concern envisioned an operation from St. Paul southwestward along the Minnesota River to Mankato and eventual construction of connections to Sioux City and Omaha. St. Paul & Sioux City, ultimately styled Chicago, St. Paul, Minneapolis & Omaha (CStPM&O or Omaha), opened service from St. Paul to Shakopee in 1866, to St. Peter in 1868, and to Sioux City in 1872. Other elements eventually to be associated with the Omaha in Wisconsin joined powerful Chicago & North Western in ways that in 1872 would grant Chicago-based North Western an important through route to St. Paul in close competition with Milwaukee Road.[10]

A company that would connect with the Omaha and one soon to fall into North Western's widening orbit was Winona & St. Peter. In the years 1864–1871, this firm completed a line westward from the Mississippi at Winona through Waseca to the Minnesota River at St. Peter before stretching out in 1873 to Lake Kampeska in Dakota Territory. Elsewhere, work began during the war, if haltingly, on the Lake Superior & Mississippi (LS&M) between St. Paul and the Head of the Lakes. Track reached northward to White Bear Lake in 1868, and during the summer of

1870 the entire 156-mile line to Duluth would open for business.[11]

No railroad venture in the state held more allure or drew more attention in this country and abroad than did Northern Pacific (NP), chartered by Congress on July 2, 1864, to construct and operate a line of road all the way from Lake Superior to Puget Sound. The project languished until banker Jay Cooke took a personal and then a financial interest, however. Cooke and his associates also invested in properties in and about Duluth, ensuring, in effect, that it would become the eastern terminus of NP. Ground was broken on Lake Superior & Mississippi on February 15, 1870, at Thompson Junction, twenty-four miles west of Duluth. (NP acquired use of LS&M into and out of Duluth, avoiding unnecessary duplication). Rails pushed into Brainerd in 1870 and then were extended toward the distant Red River valley.[12]

The railroad era had finally come to Minnesota. A total of 766 miles of line were completed during the 1860s, and the state boasted a population of 434,706, of whom 20,300 lived in the capital city of St. Paul. But, just as important, St. Paul had become the state's transportation capital—its hub, in fact, with spokes of water and rail heading in all directions to a vast hinterland.[13]

By comparison to St. Paul, Minneapolis and St. Anthony had a combined population of 18,079, but claimed only marginal transportation services, and these, city leaders tartly admitted, had a distinctly "foreign" flavor. St. Anthony had served briefly as end-of-track for St. Paul & Pacific, but that road quickly scurried off west and northwest. In addition, in 1865 a CM&StP predecessor had spiked down a spur from Mendota on the original St. Paul–Milwaukee route to tap Minneapolis. These companies as well as LS&M and Omaha all focused on St. Paul; St. Anthony and Minneapolis, however, were mere way stations on one road, and Minneapolis was at the stub end of another's branch.[14]

Minneapolis, to which St. Anthony soon would be joined, had one conspicuous shortcoming as the 1870s dawned: what it needed, and needed desperately, were railroads and more railroads—forged and locally owned, tightly focused on the needs of Minneapolis industry and commerce, and certainly not pets of St. Paul or powerful economic tentacles of far-off Chicago and Milwaukee.

Chapter 2
LETHARGY, EUPHORIA, AND PANIC

If completed, M&StL will be controlled by our citizens and run in the interests of our cities, bringing competition and reducing the tariff on both freight and passengers.
—*ST. ANTHONY WEEKLY DEMOCRAT,* FEBRUARY 11, 1870

DURING THE YEARS FOLLOWING THE CIVIL WAR the United States was hard at the business of transforming itself from a decentralized agrarian republic into an urban and industrial nation. The value added by manufacture leapt by an astonishing 82 percent between 1869 and 1879. The modern factory concept, with large numbers of workers managed or supervised in central shops, was an essential element of the new order. Those factories needed at once a massive labor force and a massive body of consumers. Mass production, of course, required mass consumption, with railroads and the telegraph the twin maidens providing the essential transportation and communication linkage. Predictably, sites of mass production and mass consumption were cities; just as predictably, the growth of cities and the dramatic expansion of the American railroad network led to the creation of large vertically integrated business concerns.[1]

Minneapolis was bound to be a player in all of this; the lumbering and flouring mills at the Falls of St. Anthony would be at center stage. So believed the political and business elite of Minneapolis. And with fair reason. Marvelous stands of white pine had characterized a huge domain that extended westward from Maine; Minnesota was the last outpost. By 1856 there were six lumber mills on both sides of the cataract that were producing twelve million board feet of lumber annually. By 1870 the aggregate value of production was $4.3 million and the mills employed three thousand men. Among those who invested in or were actual entrepreneurs in lumber milling at the falls were R. P. Russell, Isaac Atwater, Henry Titus Welles, R. J. Mendenhall, W. W. Eastman, J. R. Sidell, and William D. Washburn.[2]

Many of these same men were also involved in flour milling. The first grist and merchant flouring mill was established in 1851, and the production of wheat in the countryside and the milling of flour at the falls accelerated in the decade following. In Minnesota, the percentages of tilled area sown to wheat grew from nearly 54 percent in 1860 to 62 percent in 1868; a significant portion of this production flowed to the falls, where 30,000 barrels of flour were milled in 1860, growing to 98,000 barrels in 1865. And profit from flour milling drew the talents and capital of lumbermen such as John S. Pillsbury, Curtis H. Pettit, William P. Ankeny, John Martin, and William D. Washburn and his brother, Cadwallader C. Washburn, as well as others, Paris Gibson and William W. Eastman among them. By 1870, thirteen mills at the falls operated by as many firms produced 193,000 barrels of flour valued at $1.125 million. Of the several

Figure 2.1. The Falls of St. Anthony, a thundering sixteen-foot cataract on the Mississippi, promised a rich future for St. Anthony and Minneapolis. Author's collection.

independent merchant mills, easily the most impressive was that owned by C. C. Washburn.[3]

Flouring centers had moved westward across the nation with the wheat culture. St. Louis claimed a marvelous hinterland served by the Mississippi, Ohio, Illinois, and Missouri Rivers, and even some of Minnesota's early wheat production moved to St. Louis for milling and then downstream as flour to various southern destinations. That pattern was jolted by the Civil War, and then the amounts were severely reduced by rails emanating from Chicago and Milwaukee, where railroad companies and others built, owned, and operated large grain elevators. Even before Chicago-based rails reached Minnesota, grain from the Minnesota area had moved to Chicago by water and then rail. Cars loaded with grain arriving at Chicago were reloaded with lumber and finished goods for the interior; moving loads in both directions was a formula for financial success that favored Chicago and its railroads alike. And Milwaukee interests were no less enthusiastic advocates of this type of urban mercantilism.[4]

All of it was vexing and even harmful to the flour millers—and even indirectly to lumber interests—at the falls. Moreover, the growing power and influence of railroads and grain handlers based in Milwaukee and Chicago also irritated farmers in southern Minnesota, who complained of heavy tariffs and high storage charges for wheat moving eastward. These urban and rural forces came to believe that the development of alternative railroad service to give them marketing options was the right and proper way to satisfy their needs. The *Minneapolis Tribune* of January 7, 1868, blustered that Minneapolis was "already the acknowledged railroad center of the upper Mississippi and the state." But this was nonsense. Rail service at Minneapolis was modest in the extreme, and none of it emanated from or even focused on that city. St. Paul & Pacific had built a line to St. Anthony and then through Minneapolis to the west and northwest; Minneapolis was served only by a Milwaukee Road spur; Lake Superior & Mississippi had studiously avoided both St. Anthony and Minneapolis in choosing St. Paul as its sole southern outpost on the line from Duluth; and St. Paul & Sioux City likewise had ignored the two communities at the falls. It was downstream rival St. Paul that truly was "the acknowledged railroad center"—or, as one chronicler put it, "the point where merchandise is concentrated and distributed, where great railroad systems meet and connect, and where travel halts and is transferred."[5]

Leaders at the falls glared enviously downstream at St. Paul, but a more serious problem was the rapidly increasing power of Chicago and Milwaukee, with their well-muscled railroads that increasingly cut into what Minneapolis saw as its "natural territory." The division of wheat with points to the east was particularly irritating and meant, of course, that Minnesota-grown wheat was competitive and that local millers had to pay a premium for what they got. And as millers at the falls increased their capacity beyond local flour demand, they were forced to seek additional and distant markets for their product. This, in turn, meant that for the first time they had to pay close attention to rates of transportation. What they learned to their dismay was that railroads based at the Lake Michigan ports of Chicago and Milwaukee set very clear policies in favor of those cities and against all others. Local millers and their supporters finally realized that they were depen dent on "foreign" railroads that had the power and ability to strangle them by rendering their investments valueless. It was an epiphany.[6]

The milling interests and other leaders at the falls were inexplicably slow to see the reality of the new transportation order and to embrace railroads—locally based railroads—as requisite tools of their own urban economic purposes. St. Paul had stolen the march close at hand; Chicago and Milwaukee already had lines well placed to serve the interior. Finally, however, a curious mixture of fear and determination gripped the millers and others, who belatedly saw the need for independent action. And, as it developed, their campaigns, their dreams, and their desires would commingle with the campaigns, dreams, and desires of others in Iowa and Missouri. Indeed, St. Louis, smarting acutely from Chicago's abrupt rise, looked northward to Iowa and pledged support for an assortment of north–south rail propositions that might be linked to the Gateway City.

One of these emerged as the Burlington, Cedar Rapids & Minnesota, which projected and then built an angular line from Burlington through Cedar Rapids to Cedar Falls in 1870–1871 and on to Plymouth Junction, in north central Iowa hard by the Minnesota boundary. Another Iowa operation, Cedar Falls & Minnesota, was chartered in 1858 with authorization to build from Cedar Falls to the Minnesota border, about seventy-five miles. The owners did some grading in 1860 and 1861, but the war came on, contractors could not be paid, and in 1864 the road was leased to an Illinois Central predecessor, Dubuque & Sioux City, which in the same year completed the line to Waverly under the Cedar Falls & Minnesota flag. By the end of 1869, rails were pushed on to Lyle, Minnesota, seventy-six miles from Cedar Falls. And the next year Milwaukee Road would drive a line forty miles southwestward from Austin through Lyle and Plymouth Junction to Mason City, Iowa, giving Cedar Falls & Minnesota as well as Burlington, Cedar Rapids & Minnesota northern connections to Austin and on to St. Paul and Minneapolis.[7]

The same Cedar Falls & Minnesota, in conjunction with a Missouri road, was to have been an integral element of what one booster blithely called "the Grand Trunk Railway of the West" and another breezily labeled "the grandest railroad project of the age." This was the ill-fated Iowa Central Railroad, which pledged to link up with North Missouri on the south and Cedar Falls & Minnesota plus Minnesota Central (the Milwaukee predecessor between St. Paul and Austin) on the north to create "the new trinity—Minnesota, Iowa, and Missouri." Chartered in 1865,

Iowa Central's local boosters saw in it a means by which to bypass Chicago and circumvent the increasingly powerful Chicago-based horizontal-axis roads, to tap St. Louis as an alternative or competitive outlet, and to funnel Iowa coal to northern markets and Minnesota lumber to Iowa consumers. Cooperation and assistance among the several parties seemed sure. Several factors militated against the Iowa Central venture, however, and in the end it perished, as did so many other "paper railroads" of the time.[8]

Ever so curiously, it was not Iowa Central *Railroad,* "the grandest railroad project of the age," but rather a most humble operation nicknamed "the plug," that eventually metamorphosed into the Iowa Central *Railway* and became an essential north–south artery in the heartland. It was the presence of coal banks in the valley of the Iowa River in Hardin County that prompted organization of the Eldora Railroad & Coal Company early in 1866 for the purposes of extracting that coal and operating a road from Eldora through the coal beds to Ackley, sixteen miles north, where traffic could be interchanged with the newly built Dubuque & Sioux City, soon to be leased to Illinois Central, and part of the important cross-Iowa line from Dubuque to Sioux City. In that way Eldora coal could be distributed broadly to the fuel-starved upper Midwest. But even as "the plug" went into service during the summer of 1868, the Eldora Railroad & Coal Company dissolved to become the more important Iowa River Railway, with power to extend down the Iowa River valley to Marshalltown and beyond. Rails reached Marshalltown in 1869, but in the next year further corporate reorganization resulted in formation of the Central Railroad Company of Iowa, which integrated existing properties from Ackley through Eldora to Marshalltown, and in 1871 would extend the road from Marshalltown through Grinnell and Oskaloosa to Albia, one county short of Missouri, and from Ackley northward to Mason City, Manly, and Northwood, four miles shy of Minnesota, at the point of a triangle southeast of Albert Lea and southwest of Austin.[9]

Since the dawn of the railroad era, advocates had asserted that an American system of roads, "if advantageously applied and sufficiently extended," would serve to unite "remote sections" of the country so as to perfect and preserve the Union. Such sentiments were particularly prevalent in the West and were given practical application as promoters sought to stitch one area to another, creating, ultimately, a national mosaic. Railroads would at once unlock the land's ultimate potential; generate bountiful harvests of minerals, timber, and agricultural products; and profit individuals and society alike in generous measure. Certainly this thought informed and eventually animated Henry Titus Welles and William Drew Washburn, among others at the Falls of St. Anthony, who studied the changed and changing railroad maps of Missouri and Iowa and scrutinized wild rumors and mature plans in those parts to discover any or all that might provide an advantage for St. Anthony and Minneapolis. They had followed with interest the efforts of Cedar Falls & Minnesota promoters, but were dismayed when that property fell into the clutches of those associated with Chicago-based Illinois Central, and they had watched with mixed emotions as Iowa Central Railroad blossomed, only to wither. They were pleased to see Burlington, Cedar Rapids & Minnesota (BCR&M) crews bring that road from southeast Iowa to the north central boundary of that state. Yet they wondered as to BCR&M loyalties and traffic alliances with Chicago roads it connected with or crossed, especially Chicago, Burlington & Quincy (at Burlington), Chicago, Rock Island & Pacific (at West Liberty), and Chicago & North Western (at Cedar Rapids). Of particular interest to them was the emerging Central Railroad Company of Iowa. Surely, they concluded, a combination of symbiotic interests could be welded in such a way as to simultaneously advance individual and collective purposes in Iowa and Missouri and at the falls. What of their own intentions? It was time for action, declared both W. D. Washburn and Henry T. Welles. A rail outlet to Lake Superior was absolutely essential, but at the same time they pledged themselves to another line of road striking southward from the falls.[10]

During the late summer of 1869 several prominent men of the area were summoned to the office of Franklin Steele, then an aging entrepreneur who had been president of the Minnesota Western Rail Road, moribund since 1854. In short order they agreed to dust off that old charter and seek amendatory rights from the Minnesota legislature, which would give them permission to form a new company or new companies adequate for their needs. All of it was accomplished in 1869 and 1870, when the legislature authorized the Minneapolis & St. Louis Railroad (M&StL), giving it rights to build and operate a line from some point on the Lake Superior & Mississippi through Minneapolis to the Iowa boundary. Even before this authority was given, W. D. Washburn pledged considerable personal support for the enterprise and purchased substantial properties for terminal facilities and trackage to and about the mills on the west bank of the falls that would give M&StL sole entrance. The first board of directors was a "who's who" of leadership at the falls: Henry T. Welles (president), William D. Washburn, John S. Pillsbury, R. J. Baldwin, R. P. Russell, W. W. McNair, Isaac Atwater, and Levi Butler. That fine directory, boasted the *Minneapolis Tribune,* made the business "a Minneapolis road . . . controlled by the citizens of this place, and kept from the hands of outside parties." These men, said the *Tribune,* most assuredly would keep "the road true to the interests of this city."[11]

Figure 2.2. Henry Titus Welles, M&StL's first president. Author's collection.

Finance remained the bugaboo. Money was tight. The old Minnesota Western was to have received land grant support, but that enterprise had languished, and those rights had been effectively picked up by others. For that matter, public sympathies regarding land grants had ebbed and then stopped. Nevertheless, special legislation did authorize communities to bond themselves in support of rail projects. Interest in such assistance was especially strong in St. Anthony and Minneapolis, where newspaper support was intense. Meanwhile, M&StL issued two thousand special shares that were taken by Henry T. Welles and W. D. Washburn to pay for construction of a line northeastward from Minneapolis to White Bear Lake, about fourteen miles away. M&StL's board authorized Welles and Washburn to form a new company, Minneapolis & Duluth Railroad (M&D), to own and operate that line; articles of incorporation were filed on May 16, 1871.[12]

The whole matter was curiously ad hoc, but at least modest financing had been arranged and Chief Engineer J. B. Clough's survey had been approved. For that matter, construction had begun even before legal niceties were in place. By February 1871 the *Minneapolis Tribune* reported that one hundred men were working on cuts and fills. On the Minneapolis side, M&D would own (with M&StL) trackage securing the mills on the west bank and would gain access to St. Anthony by means of rights over St. Paul & Pacific's bridge. In July workmen were completing most segments of the road.[13]

Minneapolitans smiled proudly at all of this. On July 22 about five hundred of them took particular pleasure in boarding a special eight-car train for a gala opening run to White Bear Lake. Excursionists exclaimed at the new cream-colored station on the outskirts of St. Anthony and the "foot-deep" lettering proclaiming "MINNEAPOLIS & DULUTH R.R." W. D. Washburn said he had never known a prouder day since arriving in Minneapolis fourteen years earlier, and he gloated when recalling that a representative of Milwaukee had told him that he was "insane" for promoting M&D and M&StL. "This road is everything to us," said Washburn. "It will make Minneapolis the great railroad and commercial center west of Chicago." Welles was less euphoric, but still expansive. "This connection with Lake Superior," he observed, "puts us upon a par with all other points in the state, and by giving us completed lines of railway, makes us comparatively independent." Regularly scheduled service from Minneapolis began on August 7.[14]

While extolling the profound value of the White Bear line to the welfare of Minneapolis, Washburn likewise took note of "the St. Louis road," saying, "Upon this enterprise more than any other hangs the future destiny, for good or for evil, of our young city." Typical boosterism of the time, yes, but Minneapolis did hang its hat on M&StL to provide an independent outlet for its flouring and lumbering interests and to bring a large and predictable flow of wheat from southern Minnesota and northern Iowa. To that end Washburn and Welles had repaired to Mason City early in 1870 to talk with representatives of the Central Railroad Company of Iowa, who pledged to provide a cross-Iowa bridge between M&StL and the North Missouri road.[15]

Progress was slow. Chief Engineer Clough suggested a route southwestward from the west bank mills in Minneapolis toward Cedar Lake and beyond. That would require the good humor and even cooperation of St. Paul & Pacific, which already owned land and operated its line toward Willmar in that corridor. A contract was drawn on May 10, 1871, leasing rights to construct and operate a line parallel to StP&P from near that company's Minneapolis station (Holden Street) to its Cedar Lake station. From there Clough's survey continued southwestward through what later became the village of Hopkins, then gingerly down a brow of bluffs into the valley of the Minnesota River through Chaska to a crossing of the Minnesota River at Carver, and then more or less south to meet St. Paul & Sioux City's line that extended from St. Paul toward Iowa. Bids for grading were solicited in mid-1870, and some heavy work was done yet that year.[16]

Tracklaying began August 14, 1871. Construction already had started on a six-stall roundhouse "in the lower part of the city," and on a two-story office building–passenger station–freight house "at the corner of Second and Marshall" streets. On November 14, a special train was run to end-of-tracks, one mile south of Carver, for the purpose of allowing members of the Minneapolis City Council to conduct a personal examination of the road prior to issuance of municipal bonds in support. The mood was celebratory, and after a lunch sponsored by townspeople of Carver, "a heavy fire from champagne corks was commenced," as one reporter observed. The return trip of twenty-five miles was made in a mere fifty-five minutes.[17]

Even in this moment of euphoria, change was afoot. It was the intention of M&StL to push the road on south to Iowa "as rapidly as possible," said President H. T. Welles, but "its further completion was dependent somewhat on circumstances." What did that mean? In short, it meant that despite the inflated rhetoric of building the two roads with only local money—private investment plus municipal aid from Minneapolis ($250,000) and Carver ($20,000)—and despite the constant admonition that the roads were to be locally owned and locally operated, the reality was otherwise. Local boosters, frankly, were either unwilling or unable to carry the burden. As early as March 1870, Welles had said: "We have behind us the whole Northern Pacific Company." That expansive and tantalizing statement was less than completely true, yet it was accurate in part. In fact, the life and times of Jay Cooke & Company, Lake Superior & Mississippi, Minneapolis & Duluth, and Minneapolis & St. Louis were to be linked with those of Northern Pacific.[18]

The fabled Northern Pacific enterprise had languished until Jay Cooke took an interest. He already knew much about Duluth, had invested heavily there, and with other Philadelphia interests was much involved with Lake Superior & Mississippi (LS&M). In a sense Northern Pacific (NP) was a natural interest for Cooke. In any event, in 1869 Cooke agreed to get money for building the road, and, even as construction crews inched west toward the Red River valley, Cooke gathered in St. Paul & Pacific and placed its existing twin lines leading out of Minneapolis to the west and northwest under NP's flag. Then, early in 1871, NP purchased a half-interest in LS&M's line from Duluth west to Thompson. NP was a colossus—

the biggest single business enterprise undertaken in the United States to that time.[19]

M&StL's star would be part of NP's constellation. On May 1, 1871, M&StL's board heard a proposal from LS&M for lease of M&StL, and two days later they agreed to a "Philadelphia proposition" on the line from Minneapolis to Sioux City Junction, Minnesota. "They [the Philadelphians] helped us" with M&D, said W. D. Washburn, and, he went on, "they are going to help us build" M&StL "to Carver, and then on to the state line." He was ready to drop the other shoe. "We shall transfer the road to them, and I can assure you . . . that they will run it on liberal principles." Even that was unclear, for he spoke of M&D and M&StL as one. The picture soon cleared. In the end M&D, like M&StL, was leased to LS&M. Washburn would serve nominally as M&D's president, and Welles would be on its board, but the three remaining members—a majority—were Philadelphians.[20]

The situation for M&StL was rather more complicated, but had the same result. The company was responsible for placing its own bonds, which earned 7 percent and were endorsed by LS&M, to which M&StL was leased on October 24, 1871. But the arrangement was unlike the M&D agreement; M&StL retained its full complement of officers and directors—all local—and, said the *American Railroad Manual,* "this company maintains an independent organization." M&StL, nevertheless, was very much in NP's camp through LS&M. Over the next two years Welles, as president of M&StL, worked diligently with Charles C. Gilman of Central Railroad Company of Iowa to coax Cooke and Northern Pacific into a massive plan to finish the missing links in the Minneapolis–St. Louis route, to consolidate the corporate entities, and to have NP take the entire completed package. But to no avail.[21]

Figure 2.3. William Drew Washburn would put his own personal stamp on M&StL. Author's collection.

Washburn, Welles, and others of M&StL persuasion had done a volte-face, at least on the vaunted matter of local operation by local ownership. Perhaps they had reached the limits of their financial abilities; perhaps they had no stomach for managing companies in an industry with which they had no experience; perhaps they had planned all along to build critically important lines and then dispose of them as best they could. In any event, they had met short-term needs—gaining access to St. Paul & Sioux City on the south and access to Lake Superior on the north.

As summer turned to fall in 1872, the air was abundant with rumor regarding M&StL under NP's broad canopy. The local press reported that NP had authorized one survey from Sioux City Junction southward to Albert Lea and another from the Central Railroad of Iowa at Northwood, Iowa, to Albert Lea. The shorter section, from Northwood to the Southern Minnesota Rail Road at Albert Lea, would be rushed to completion yet in 1872, said the *Minneapolis Tribune;* the longer segment would be done "within a year."[22]

Then, sadly, it all began to unravel. NP did not reach the Missouri River at Bismarck, 455 miles from Duluth, until June 3, 1873. "All that this country needs now," Milnor Roberts had told Cooke a few days earlier, "is settlers." True. But there was no time. Cooke's legendary colonization campaign to populate such a vast domain in such a short time was doomed to failure. Neither had Duluth developed as fast as Cooke had hoped, nor had traffic on LS&M grown in a profitable way. LS&M sought shelter by offering itself for sale to NP early in January 1872, but NP agreed only to lease the road. On September 13, 1873, NP's executive committee considered a curious request from W. D. Washburn, who offered to "rent" M&StL to NP. Washburn feared that Cooke's house of cards would collapse. It did, the next day, precipitating the awful panic of 1873.[23]

Not surprisingly, these circumstances quickly embraced Northern Pacific and those around it. On November 1, 1873, NP defaulted payments on M&D's bonds; LS&M bondholders met the same fate. NP tried to hold on, and, in the case of M&D, asked for new leases—with financial obligations guaranteed personally by Henry T. Welles, W. D. Washburn, and C. C. Washburn—a burden totally unacceptable to those men. NP shuddered. It would surrender its lease of LS&M on February 1, 1874, and give up stock control of the larger St. Paul & Pacific later that year. Receivership would follow on April 22, 1875.[24]

The fallout for M&StL and M&D was swift. A special meeting of the M&D board was held in Philadelphia, and the LS&M agreement was terminated. NP formally turned over M&StL and M&D to their owners on December 11, 1873. M&D then was leased "in perpetuity" to M&StL, with M&StL promising to pay interest on M&D's bonds. In the process, M&D effectively—if not legally or corporately—lost its identity, with the entire operation from White Bear Lake to Sioux City Junction henceforth identified as M&StL.[25]

M&StL's bubble had burst. It had succeeded in securing a rail outlet for the milling and manufacturing interests of Minneapolis and St. Anthony (which was joined to Minneapolis in 1872), an outlet to the Great Lakes chain via LS&M, and a connection to St. Paul & Sioux City (which by now had completed its line through rich country to Sioux City, Iowa). But the great goal of reaching St. Louis remained unmet. Moreover, absent Cooke and Northern Pacific there seemed no white knight to salvage that dream. Those who had given birth to M&StL and M&D now had those properties back in their laps; they would be obliged to play the part of owner-operators in the swirl of the worst depression to hit the American people to that time.

Chapter 3
Albert Lea at Last

Minneapolis greets St. Louis . . . the metropolis of the upper Mississippi and the "Queen City" are separated by but 26½ hours time.
—*Minneapolis Tribune,* November 13, 1877

Even as fiscal calamity rained down about him, W. D. Washburn boldly reasserted that the Minneapolis & St. Louis would be driven southward to meet the Central Railroad Company of Iowa and in that way realize his much-longed-for but sadly delayed Minneapolis–to–St. Louis dream. Yet the Iowa road itself remained without connection to the North Missouri road, and in truth was little more than an isolated vertical axis route across Iowa. It stumbled into receivership in mid-1874. Another attractive candidate, Burlington, Cedar Rapids & Minnesota, also stood beckoning at the Iowa border, and, in fact, had joined with Chicago, Milwaukee & St. Paul and others in 1872 to provide through if doglegged service between St. Louis and Minneapolis. Nevertheless, early in 1874 BCR&M continued to woo Washburn, promising to guarantee M&StL's construction bonds on an extension from Carver to Albert Lea, Minnesota. Like the Central Railroad Company of Iowa, BCR&M was itself desperate for traffic and, like Central Railroad, offered M&StL impressive synergies. But, also like the other Iowa road, BCR&M was financially embarrassed, defaulting on interest due late in 1873 and headed for receivership in 1875.[1]

Meanwhile, there was a railroad to run. When M&StL and Minneapolis & Duluth (M&D) properties had been returned to the owners, there was but one officer of the company, A. H. Bode, who received $1,500 per year for performing his duties as secretary, superintendent, general ticket agent, and general freight agent. Bode was in charge of forty-two miles of railroad, the engineering for which had been "economically done," with a track structure that was innocent of ballast except for dirt and very light (forty-nine pounds per yard) iron rail. Equipment consisted of two M&D locomotives and two others leased from Northern Pacific as well as five cars for passenger business plus sixty-eight pieces of freight equipment, likewise leased from NP. Even before the panic neither M&D nor M&StL had earned income over operating expenses—explaining, no doubt, why NP (through Lake Superior & Mississippi) had been so eager to end the leases. For instance, in the last five months of lease (July–November 1873), M&StL had operating expenses totaling 134.9 percent of its earnings—a dismal record, indeed. M&StL's operating revenues for fiscal 1875 exceeded its operating expenses by 20 percent, but after paying taxes and interest on bonds, the road was in the red by nearly $30,000. The next two years proved no better.[2]

Casual is the word that sums up early M&StL operations. Under NP's banner, M&StL and M&D

had operated two mixed trains (freight and passenger) daily except Sunday from Minneapolis to White Bear Lake and from Minneapolis to Sioux City Junction. That pattern continued under independent management. For a while M&StL trains utilized the St. Paul & Pacific station in Minneapolis, but to save money M&StL moved to meager quarters across from the Milwaukee Road station on Second Street in 1874. Boardings were modest: 7,858 in 1873, but rising to 30,866 in 1875 and to 40,709 in 1876. Passenger hauls were short, 15.4 miles on average in 1875, and revenue thin, $24,570 for the same year.[3]

Freight was and always would be most important at M&StL. Daily switching was necessary in and about the mills, but except for extras when demand required, billings were handled by the regularly scheduled mixed trains. Lumber and wood led all commodities in volume, followed by grain, flour, and merchandise. In 1875 M&StL moved 136,958 tons, earning $98,186 in revenue; the record for 1876 was marginally higher. Wheat moved to Minneapolis from Lake Superior & Mississippi at White Bear Lake, from on-line stations, and from St. Paul & Sioux City at Sioux City Junction. Minneapolis-milled flour, on the other hand, moved mostly northbound to Duluth for transshipment; indeed, in 1876 every barrel of it billed on M&StL moved in this direction.[4]

Of the eight stations from White Bear Lake to Sioux City Junction, Minneapolis was clearly the largest and the best established. Others, like Eden Prairie

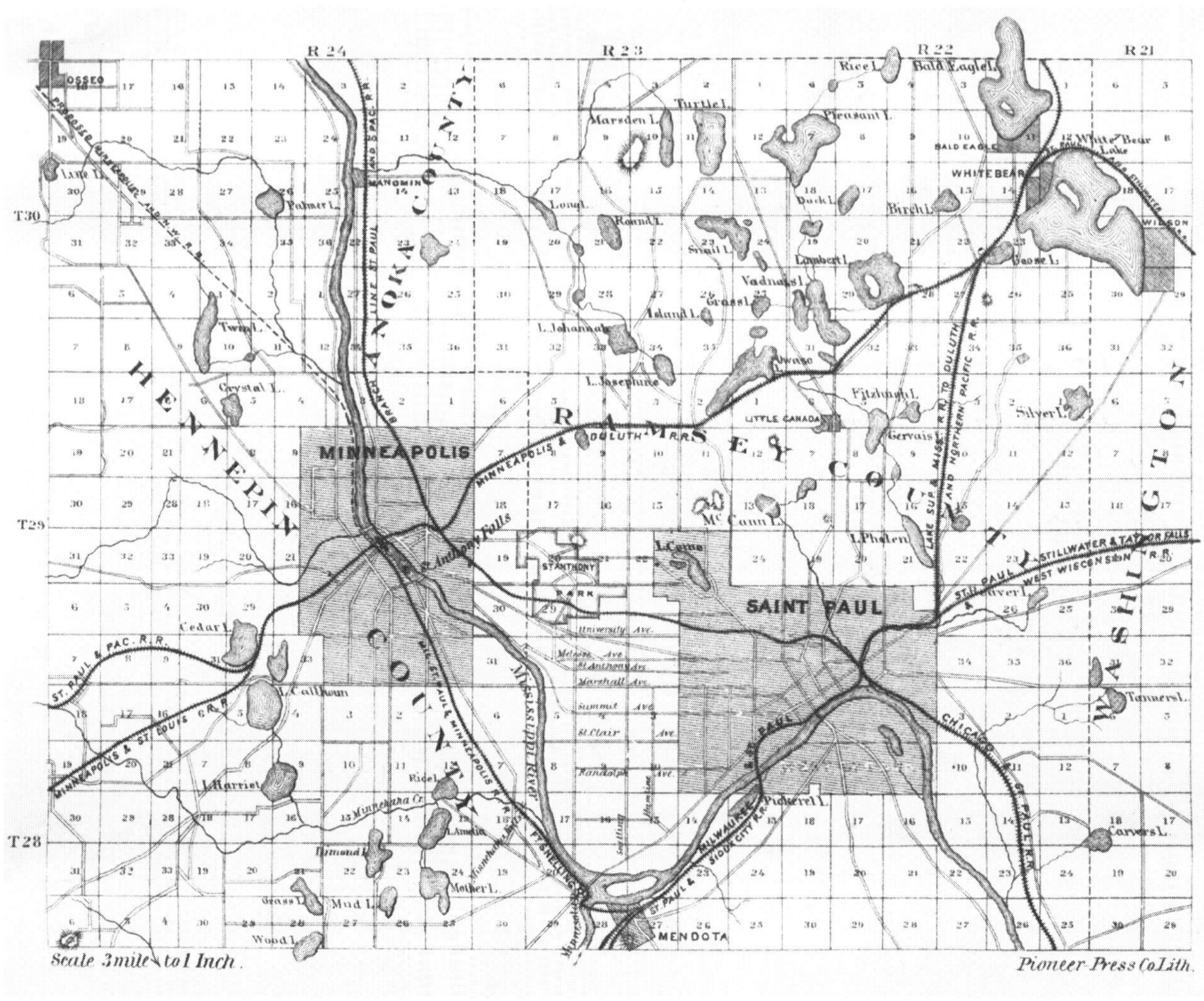

Map 3.1. Minneapolis, St. Paul, and vicinity, 1876.

and Hopkins, were given life by the railroad, and still others, Chaska and Carver, for example, were nourished by the new service. Carver had been platted as early as 1857, but did not thrive until the coming of the railroad. By 1875 it claimed about one thousand inhabitants, and area farmers used M&StL to ship an average of 187,406 bushels of wheat to Minneapolis for the 1875 and 1876 seasons. Carver also shipped brick in carload lots, much of it to Minneapolis and St. Paul. Three hotels, including the Railroad House, "convenient to the Minneapolis & St. Louis depot," served the needs of the traveling public, while other local entrepreneurs met local express and omnibus requirements. The strong and growing commercial ties between Minneapolis and Carver as part of the larger community's hinterland was typical. So, too, were the railroad and its trackside cohabitant, the telegraph line, providing the necessary umbilical cord.[5]

What M&StL needed was more traffic on that umbilical cord. An increase in traffic *from* Minneapolis, with flour as the easy example, depended on an increase *to* Minneapolis, with wheat as the corollary example. But M&StL's tiny service area could not, of itself, generate adequate additional traffic. "The Minneapolis & St. Louis is now in the hands of gentlemen of Minneapolis whose first thoughts are for the best interests of the city," intoned the *Minneapolis Tribune* when reporting that the road had been returned to its owners late in 1873. To make good on that great claim, however, M&StL was obliged to expand. And the owners boldly claimed that they had a plan "to extend their railroad . . . to a connection . . . with the Central Railroad Company of Iowa . . . this making a direct line . . . from Duluth, Minneapolis and St. Paul, to St. Louis and New Orleans." A bold plan, to be sure. The panic held otherwise. The Iowa concern remained dormant at Northwood, just south of the Iowa-Minnesota border, and M&StL was utterly without ability to complete its own leg.[6]

But M&StL would finally build south. By 1876 there were modest signs of financial recovery, investment capital began to seek outlet, and the Washburns took on a new resolve. They had given up on linking with Central Railroad Company of Iowa, which remained in receivership, with competing groups of eastern bondholders squabbling over its control and direction. Rather, the Washburns turned to Burlington, Cedar Rapids & Minnesota, which also had fallen on hard times, but which was reorganized by bondholders, sold, and on June 27, 1876, restyled Burlington, Cedar Rapids & Northern Railway (BCR&N). The old company had financial and traffic support from large and powerful Chicago, Burlington & Quincy (CB&Q), with which it connected at Burlington, Iowa, and ownership of the new company was mostly in the eastern hands of investors who had substantial stakes in CB&Q as well as Chicago, Rock Island & Pacific. Although bitter rivals in a later time, in the mid-1870s to the end of the decade these two strong roads had harmonious relations. BCR&N reflected this harmony and was, as noted railroad historian Richard C. Overton observed, a joint project of Burlington and Rock Island. The latter fed and received traffic at West Liberty, Iowa, west of Davenport and northwest of Burlington, and the former reciprocated at Burlington. Moreover, CB&Q had been picking up lines in Illinois, Iowa, and Missouri. One of these was the Rockford, Rock Island & St. Louis, a vertical axis road that intersected CB&Q's main line from Chicago to Burlington at Monmouth, Illinois, and provided CB&Q a long-mile but nevertheless important access to St. Louis. BCR&N traffic to and from St. Louis had used this route previously, and that continued now on an all-Burlington route. Elsewhere, CB&Q was building or buying line segments that, when stitched together, would eventually create a direct route down the west side of the Mississippi from Burlington to St. Louis.[7]

The old BCR&M had urged M&StL southward in 1874 to no avail, but W. D. Washburn maintained negotiations and even jockeyed BCR&M into guaranteeing that it would pay principal and interest on bonds to build a line from the Iowa boundary to Albert Lea under M&StL's authority. That had not been possible in the short term, but early in 1877 the reorganized and rejuvenated BCR&N extended its line in northern Iowa from Plymouth to Manly, five miles, from whence it secured operating rights over crestfallen rival Central Railroad Company of Iowa's tracks to Northwood, eleven miles away and only four miles from the state boundary. As these developments were unfolding, W. D. Washburn was in New York City making arrangements with BCR&N President Fred Taylor for construction and lease of a twelve-mile stub from the Iowa boundary to Albert Lea and for joint traffic programs. (BCR&N would build the short link from Northwood to the border on its own account.) Washburn was also on the east coast to forge bonding and mortgage contracts with several large financial houses.[8]

On April 11, 1877, M&StL asked for bids on grading a line from Merriam to Albert Lea. "The company means business," reported an exultant *Minneapolis Tribune.* The route selected lifted out of the Minnesota River valley to traverse young glacial plain typified by lakes and moraines through established yet small communities—Jordan, New Prague, Waterville, Waseca, Hartland, and Manchester—and it led to the creation of the new villages of Montgomery, Kilkenny, Palmer, Otisco, and New Richland. By late August tracklayers were south of Montgomery; two months later iron adequate to complete the project was reported "afloat" on the Great Lakes and construction crews had reached New Richland.[9]

On the south end, BCR&N crews pushed across the Iowa state line in mid-August, and, having completed not quite seventeen miles of construction from Northwood, reached Albert Lea on September 6. Two days later the first revenue freight arrived, and on September 9 BCR&N inaugurated daily-except-Sunday passenger service featuring "Palace sleeping cars owned by this line."[10]

Finally, on November 12 workmen laid the last rail and drove the final spike at Albert Lea on the M&StL segment from the north—shortly before arrival of a splendidly appointed excursion train from Minneapolis, which stopped only briefly before hurrying on to ceremonies at the state line and then returning to a "sumptuous repast" and jovial "speech-making" at the Hall House. W. D. Washburn exclaimed that "it was the happiest day of his life." He also praised BCR&N's Fred Taylor of New York, and, in a most interesting admission, said that M&StL could not have been built except for "the valuable assistance rendered at a critical time."[11]

The equipment for the Albert Lea excursion and regular service that began three days later was brand new and much admired. Late in 1877 Baldwin Locomotive Works of Philadelphia supplied seven American Standard 4-4-0s, and, typical of the time, these were named for M&StL directors. Ohio Falls Car Company supplied four new coaches, named for stations along the Albert Lea extension—Jordon, Waterville, Waseca, and Albert Lea—with *Minneapolis & St. Louis Railway* painted in gold across the letter board of each. The interiors were finished in natural woods, with trimmings of silver plate and bronze. A strip of carpet extended the length of each aisle. All cars were equipped with "self-couplers and with the Westinghouse improved air brake." Said the *Minneapolis Tribune:* "They make the handsomest passenger train that ever graced a western road." Seven additional coaches were on order, as were 125 boxcars, 40 flats, and 3 cabooses.[12]

Additions and improvements to property continued through the winter and into 1878. Pens and chutes for livestock, as well as depots, spurs, sidings, passing tracks, water facilities, and tool houses appeared. A joint passenger depot with Chicago & North Western at Waseca was placed in service, a seven-stall roundhouse took shape at Albert Lea, and plans for machine shops and attendant repair facilities were on the drawing board at Minneapolis.[13]

The new order was heady stuff, and M&StL's advertising reflected as much: "Minneapolis & St. Louis Railway. The Shortest and Most Direct Line to St. Louis, New Orleans and Galveston. Making Quicker Time than by any other Route, and Carrying the Great Southern Mail." Two express trains daily, "With Pullman's Palace Sleeping Cars," plied the Minneapolis–to–St. Louis route daily via M&StL/BCR&N to Burlington, thence via CB&Q to Monmouth and St. Louis, a total of 571 miles. (The beleaguered Central Railroad Company of Iowa simultaneously joined with Chicago, Milwaukee & St. Paul and St. Louis, Kansas City & Northern to form another through car route on a dog-legged path via Austin and Ottumwa, 589 miles.)[14]

Not nearly as flashy and appealing as express train passenger service, freight nevertheless paid most of the bills. As soon as the line to Albert Lea was open, M&StL dispatched daily "flour express" trains from the milling district eastward over BCR&N, to the immense satisfaction of the two railroad companies and shippers alike. In 1877 M&StL moved more than half of the Minneapolis flour production. Moreover, the many new country elevators built along the Albert Lea extension soon disgorged thousands of bushels of wheat, billed to the hungry mills at the Falls of St. Anthony, and as on-line communities grew, so did their need for lumber and other building materials as well as the full range of mercantile goods, which were supplied by Minneapolis industrialists and wholesalers.[15]

The Washburns found no opportunity to rest on their oars. Completion of the road to Albert Lea and into the waiting arms of Burlington, Cedar Rapids & Northern opened new vistas for M&StL, but simultaneously activated determined hostility from powerful quarters. M&StL found itself in an exciting but utterly volatile environment. For the Minneapolis road, Chicago, Milwaukee & St. Paul always represented a distinct and disturbing thorn in the side. A relative newcomer, Chicago & North Western (C&NW), also stirred the pot. These two roads had once briefly shared common management and directory, but more usually—as was now the case—they were fierce competitors. C&NW had pushed westward and northwestward from Chicago by construction for its own account, through acquisitions, and through clients. For instance, in a bold strategic move, in 1868 C&NW had acquired Winona & St. Peter, which had built through Waseca and New Ulm, Minnesota, before dashing on to Lake Kampeska in Dakota Territory. C&NW was no less active in Wisconsin, where it went head to head with Milwaukee Road and even claimed certain portions of the state for its own. Indeed, in 1872 the West Wisconsin Railway and a friendly associate had completed a line into St. Paul and with C&NW commenced through operations to Chicago.[16]

Much speculation surrounded the question of the ownership and allegiance of several prominent area railroads. West Wisconsin, for example, often was considered a client for Chicago & North Western, and West Wisconsin did connect with C&NW and had a traffic agreement with C&NW bearing on business between Chicago and St. Paul. Furthermore, control of West Wisconsin and its neighbor, North Wisconsin, had passed to a syndicate headed by H. H. Porter, a Chicagoan on the board of C&NW, and the Porter clique was rumored to have its eye on St. Paul & Sioux City. Did all of that confirm that C&NW was orchestrating events from behind the scenes? Many Minnesotans thought so.[17]

These unstable variables were swiftly manifested at M&StL. In fact, serious problems had surfaced earlier, when millers in competition with the Washburns, and even some who were friendly, worried over M&StL's practical monopoly in the west bank milling district and over M&StL's modest route structure, which they felt restricted the supply of wheat as well as their ability to move finished product to expanding markets. They were motivated variously by jealousy and by legitimate fears and were egged on by powerful Chicago, Milwaukee & St. Paul and those behind plans for St. Paul & Sioux City and West Wisconsin, plus opportunistic surrogates. In any event, the dissidents, led by Joel Bassett, a man long hostile to the Washburns, discovered and dredged up an old charter that had given Minneapolis Eastern Railroad authorization to build and operate a line between Minneapolis and St. Paul. Articles of incorporation claiming those rights and using that name were filed on June 17, 1878. On the surface Minneapolis Eastern appeared nothing more than an unnecessary nuisance, but there was more here than met the eye, and for M&StL the stakes were enormous. Indeed, as a consequence of difficult and contentious legal proceedings, Minneapolis Eastern was awarded property rights in the west bank milling district and M&StL was forced into "the exchange and leasing of tracks." It was a stinging loss for the Washburns and M&StL.[18]

M&StL's strong position in the west bank milling district was effectively broken; bad news would follow bad news. Minneapolis Eastern built about three miles of track in and about the milling district, but never more. In fact, that is all its promoters ever wanted. M&StL expanded its own switching network, and in the future would still handle a plurality of line hauls to and from the district. But for M&StL the worst news was yet to come: early in the fall of 1878, Minneapolis Eastern announced that it was owned in equal parts by Chicago, Milwaukee & St. Paul (CM&StP) and by Chicago, St. Paul, Minneapolis & Omaha (West Wisconsin's successor). The camel's nose would be forever more under M&StL's tent. Operations began in midsummer 1879 and included both plant switching and interchange of cars to and from CM&StP. In another numbing blow to M&StL, Minneapolis Eastern gained track connection with St. Paul, Minneapolis & Manitoba (successor to St. Paul & Pacific), allowing interchange with that major road as well. Moreover, St. Paul & Sioux City was enthusiastically agitating for rights to run its trains directly to Minneapolis from Merriam, just as West Wisconsin was gaining running rights over Manitoba from St. Paul to Minneapolis.[19]

Meanwhile, traffic arrangements for M&StL's outlet to Duluth became confused. Lake Superior & Mississippi was always a close working partner, and after Northern Pacific's lease of that road ended early in 1874, M&StL poured even more flour over LS&M to Lake Superior. The Lake Superior road stumbled through the panic of 1873 as a stand-alone carrier still controlled by Philadelphia interests. Finally, in 1876 LS&M bondholders announced intentions of foreclosing, a process culminated in 1877 by creation of the St. Paul & Duluth Railroad (StP&D) as successor. The "new" road had several former LS&M directors, a clear Philadelphia flavor, and continuing if less tangible financial linkage to Northern Pacific.[20]

By mid-1879 rumors circulated to the effect that control of St. Paul & Duluth had changed. The rumors proved founded. New directors included persons closely connected with Chicago & North Western; Chicago, Rock Island & Pacific; and Chicago, Milwaukee & St. Paul. The potential impact on M&StL, was obvious; StP&D interchanged more freight with M&StL than with any other road, and M&StL was hostage to it for any movement to and from the White Bear Lake line. Cadwallader Washburn was irritated and frustrated, for M&StL's relationship with LS&M and StP&D under previous owners had been mutually advantageous if not always cordial. Furthermore, with historic agreements between them, M&StL, never financially robust, had been spared the need to consider its own expansion beyond White Bear Lake to Duluth. Now, however, Cadwallader Washburn leaked rumors that M&StL would make surveys to the northeast. At the same time, William Drew Washburn and John Martin quietly purchased shares of Taylor's Falls & Lake Superior Railroad, a company that had its own aspirations but that the Washburns thought might be useful in levering M&StL's strategic options. (This stock was held in trust for M&StL.)[21]

There seemed no end of concerns. During the first three days of 1878, M&StL delivered to the mills 35,000 bushels of wheat from along its line; during one April day alone, 18,000 bushels were dispatched from on-line stations. Yet demand exceeded supply, and those millers friendly to Washburn—and others, too—worried even more openly and loudly that the country tributary to M&StL was inadequate to meet their needs. Like it or not, M&StL's owners had to confront reality: expansion was essential.[22]

Iowa beckoned. That state had been well blessed by Ice Age gifts—especially rich soils abroad the earth's rolling crust that proved utterly irresistible to the plowman. Agriculture produced significant tonnage in rye, barley, and oats, but corn flourished everywhere, and wheat, the eager millers noted, was the leading staple crop and was especially popular in northern counties. Coal, of which Minnesota had none, was found near Fort Dodge and among other locations to the south. What Iowa had, Minnesota needed. Conversely, much of Iowa was without timber from which to produce milled lumber, and the state's merchants complained that they were dependent on goods supplied from Chicago and, to a lesser extent, from St. Louis. Minnesota—and particularly Minneapolis—could meet Iowa's needs. The potential synergies were obvious: coal and grain could move northbound, lumber, flour, and merchandise southbound—loads in both directions.[23]

None of this was new to the Washburns, who long had been alert to possibilities in Iowa. As early as 1872, they had taken an interest in the Albert Lea & State Line Railroad, a paper outfit, and a year later they gathered up its charter rights for M&StL. Then, after M&StL reached Albert Lea in 1877, Cadwallader Washburn made a personal reconnaissance of the territory southwest of Albert Lea and declared that the Clarion-Webster soils in the headwaters country of the Cedar and Iowa Rivers held great promise.[24]

Iowans, too, saw great potential in vertical-axis lines that would connect their state with Minnesota, and several local dreams and schemes took form at least on paper. One of these, the Minnesota & Iowa Southern Railroad, made up of men from Forest City, Iowa, but backed by the Washburns, was incorporated in May 1878, for the purpose of acquiring right-of-way and building a line from "some point on the Minnesota" border (with Albert Lea clearly in mind) to a junction with another Iowa organization, the romantic-sounding Fort Dodge & Fort Ridgely Railroad and Telegraph Company. That road had gained charter rights on July 22, 1876. Its inception had derived from fears of Fort Dodge business leaders who perceived that they would be disadvantaged by another proposed railroad designed to link Ames, Humboldt, and Rutland. If completed, that line would bypass Fort Dodge to the east and north and surely would drain commerce away from the capital of Webster County. They responded with Fort Dodge & Fort Ridgely, which held vague authorization to construct and operate a road to the Minnesota border. Although Fort Ridgely was above Mankato, on the Minnesota River, the immediate goal was more reasonable—Humboldt County, just north of Fort Dodge. Moreover, Humboldt County residents had voted $35,000 in aid plus seven thousand acres of swampland; Webster County had already pledged $38,000.[25]

Work advanced slowly from Fort Dodge. It was not until late summer of 1878 that crews worked through the rough contours of Soldier Creek, lifting the line out of the Des Moines River valley to the northeast. After completing twelve miles, the road "rested" at the county line of Webster and Humboldt, its financial condition desperate. The company owned one locomotive, eight pieces of rolling stock, and one handcar, all underutilized, with the line ending in a pasture.[26]

The property passed to Angus McBane of Fort Dodge on July 9, 1879, but one month earlier, Cadwallader and William Drew Washburn had pledged that they were "ready and willing to advance necessary funds" to gain "the terminus in Humboldt County." In effect, the Washburn brothers agreed to bankroll those behind Fort Dodge & Fort Ridgely in order to get the line completed through the village of Humboldt to Livermore, Iowa, 28.4 miles north of Fort Dodge, a task that would be completed by Christmas 1879. C. C. Washburn and four others from M&StL's directory went on the local road's board of directors, and the company's stock was conveyed to Washburn; John Martin of Minneapolis was named president. Then the road was leased to M&StL, which purchased all equipment owned by the Fort Dodge firm.[27]

On the north end, construction was slow, in part for want of rail, which was in short supply because of nationwide demand, with crews in 1879 driving the line slowly southwestward from Albert Lea over the state boundary to Lake Mills (October 28) and to Forest City (December 10). The latter community was predictably elated when M&StL officials and others arrived aboard the first passenger train for a "Grand Jubilee." It was cold and stormy on December 10, but when the train showed up at 3:40 p.m., "all the business houses in town were locked up and the streets deserted." When all the whoops and hollers subsided, the entire entourage marched off to the Congregational church, "where a great reception and banquet was held." For Forest City, dreams were finally realized. "Now it had a railroad! No more long drives over poor roads and through swamps to get supplies. No more winter snow blockades."[28]

M&StL moved to close the forty-mile gap between Forest City and Livermore. Ostensibly construction was on behalf of Minnesota & Iowa Southern, and local Iowans were listed as officers and directors, but John Martin was president, the Washburn brothers were in control, and the whole thing was under M&StL's canvas, with bonds issued at the rate of $10,000 per mile and the mortgage held by Central Trust Company of New York. There could also be no doubt that the Washburns controlled M&StL; by the end of 1879, the board was made up completely of Minneapolis men, but between them Cadwallader, with 5,742 shares, and William Drew, with 5,926, had a huge majority of M&StL stock. Contracts were awarded late in March 1880 for the forty-mile section. Crews worked southwestward, building a crossing over CM&StP at Britt and installing a boxcar depot at that station before moving on to the new town site of Corwith, where the depot was the second building put up after Gaylord's Hotel, named for E. W. Gaylord, M&StL's superintendent, who owned the town-site company. By midsummer 1880 rails were joined at Livermore and the 210-mile route from Minneapolis to Fort Dodge was complete.[29]

The new line from Albert Lea to Fort Dodge spawned communities including Twin Lakes, Norman, Leland, and Corwith and prospered already established centers including Forest City and Humboldt. Four dray lines were supported at bustling Lake Mills, Iowa, and Corwith soon sported two each blacksmith shops, livery stables, drugstores, and other business houses that were supported by a population of eight hundred. The case of Leland was especially instructive. Given life by M&StL in 1879, the lonely depot there soon was joined by a lumber yard, a creamery, a hotel, a manufacturing plant, a hardware store, three grain elevators, a drugstore, a bank, and two churches. There followed establishment of a post office, mail routes, a telephone system, and even a lutefisk processing plant to satisfy urgent needs for that commodity among citizens of Norwegian extraction.[30]

Construction crews regrouped at Fort Dodge, where local observers predicted they would continue their work down the east side of the Des Moines River to or at least in the direction of Iowa's capital city. In fact, however, bridge builders took M&StL to the west bank and a more immediate destination—coal fields in and around Kalo, about eight miles southeast of Fort Dodge. The presence of coal-bearing rocks exposed along the river in Webster County, Iowa, had excited early interest. In 1880 Webster County mines produced 128,712 tons—some of it billed to coal yards at new M&StL stations such as Corwith, some to Northwestern Fuel Company of Minneapolis, and more of it to M&StL as locomotive fuel. But the supply was sadly inadequate to meet the need. "There is not half-coal enough on our line to supply the demand," admitted M&StL's Charles F. Hatch, general manager. "The wonderful growth and extension of railroads throughout the West in the last year, and the opening up and settlement of a large amount of new territory," said Hatch, "have caused a largely increased demand for fuel and particularly coal."[31]

At Albert Lea M&StL now had an acceptable connection with BCR&N for traffic to and from the east and southeast as well as its own new artery into a fertile and productive hinterland. To the north, however, M&StL faced a growing dilemma, with its only outlet, St. Paul & Duluth, in the hands of a consortium representing rivals Chicago and Milwaukee. The Washburns were in a tough spot. William Drew had made investments in Taylor's Falls & Lake Superior, of course, but that may have been merely a feint. Now, however, the two brothers were forced on the issue of an independent route to Lake Superior. Cadwallader dispatched surveyors into the field northeast from Taylor's Falls, Minnesota, across Wisconsin.[32]

In February 1880 came word that Taylor's Falls had voted $23,700 in aid of M&StL and that William Drew had successfully arranged for additional financing from Central Trust of New York. Work began initially above the rocky escarpment near Taylor's Falls on what M&StL confidently labeled its "Lake Superior Extension." The line was to be built by Taylor's Falls & Lake Superior under M&StL's supervision; on May 1, 1880, William D. Washburn assumed full stock ownership of the Taylor's Falls road. St. Paul & Duluth cried "Uncle." Negotiations followed. A covenant was made with StP&D whereby M&StL agreed to terminate construction on its "Lake Superior Extension" except the heavy work in the rock-walled gorge near Taylor's Falls; M&StL and StP&D would jointly construct and operate a line from Wyoming to Taylor's Falls; and M&StL would enjoy perpetual running rights over StP&D from White Bear Lake to Wyoming. Moreover, StP&D grudgingly agreed to give M&StL overhead or operating rights for three years all the way to Duluth from White Bear Lake. The contract spoke to "common benefits," which were obvious, but the news came as a shock and a great disappointment in both Minneapolis and St. Paul, where leaders had pinned their hopes on M&StL to provide a new outlet to Lake Superior.[33]

During the ensuing spring and summer, work progressed on the new route from Wyoming to

Taylor's Falls, and M&StL commenced through freight operations, actually mixed trains with very little passenger business, to and from Duluth. Several factors militated against timely completion of the new line, but finally the twenty-mile route serving the villages of Chisago City, Lindstrom, Center City, Shafer, and Franconia was opened. Ringing church bells and the boom of cannon greeted the first passenger trains to creep into the Dalles of the St. Croix and roll to a stop in the picturesque community of Taylor's Falls. The date was November 8, 1880, and it was a perfect Indian summer day, by one account. Nine carloads of "railroad dignitaries" and other "honored guests" from Minneapolis and St. Paul quickly adjourned to Folsom's Building on First Street to enjoy a meal of chicken pie and listen to the long-winded speeches that always seemed to attend such festivities. Guests eventually reboarded the cars, and the trains chugged upgrade and out of sight, but locals danced the night away at the Dalles House.[34]

Figure 3.1. The Taylor's Falls line was picturesque. Would it generate profitable traffic volumes? This view is from about a mile and a half west of the Taylor's Falls, Minnesota, depot. Northern Pacific photograph.

Chapter 4
Optimism and Realism

Here is the art of God and the art of man commingled.
—A St. Louis newspaperman in referring to the states of Iowa and Minnesota, 1878

From the very beginning of the company back in 1870, the Minneapolis & St. Louis had been the tender handmaiden of the Minneapolis flour millers, the Washburns in particular and, by extension, those whose fortunes were tied in one way or another to those flour millers. There was a distinct symbiosis that all could see and understand. Flour millers needed a constant and reliable source of wheat, and they needed constant and reliable avenues along which to move flour to market near and far. Flour millers also needed favorable rates on both raw material and finished product. Indeed, favorable rates were crucial to their financial success. Fortunately, the millers had an ace in the hole in this regard—moving flour to hinterlands that produced the very wheat they milled. Another head haul, lumber, likewise protected the back haul, wheat, through indirect subsidy. The same effect might be had by shipping merchandise billed to Minneapolis wholesalers in cars that carried flour outbound. All of this explained M&StL's early plan to link up with St. Paul & Sioux City at Merriam, to reach the Great Lakes chain at Duluth, to push on to Albert Lea and a grand union there with Burlington, Cedar Rapids & Northern, and finally to drive into Iowa with a line to Fort Dodge.

Each one of these campaigns had mirrored the flour millers' need for supply as well as outlet, and a need for balance of traffic that would provide the lowest possible rates on both wheat and flour. But the decline of lumber milling at the Falls of St. Anthony threatened this delicate arrangement. Small wonder that the Washburns and those associated with them looked so often and so longingly to the country northeast of Minneapolis toward Lake Superior—not merely to guarantee a seasonal Great Lakes chute for flour, but also to tap immense stands of commercially valuable timber that could provide lumber shipments offsetting those lost as the era of sawmilling at the falls gradually tailed off. Flour millers also had to confront another troubling reality: the locus of the wheat belt was shifting. In fact, the shift was ongoing. The "old" wheat belt had been in Ohio, Indiana, and Illinois, but as the westering process had accelerated, the wheat culture had moved west and north, to Iowa and southern Minnesota. And the shift continued. In its wake came the corn belt, or, more correctly, the corn and hog belt. Increasingly wheat production moved to western and northwestern Minnesota and into Dakota Territory—away from M&StL's service area and into the areas of comparative giants, all of which, it seemed, were constantly expanding their reach.

None of this was lost on the Washburns and other

Figure 4.1. Industry at the Falls of St. Anthony, Minnesota, was crucial to M&StL interests. Author's collection.

business leaders at Minneapolis. They understood that loads leaving Minneapolis needed to be matched by loads arriving from the hinterland. That would keep rates down; that would tie surrounding areas to Minneapolis; that would profit manufacturing, jobbing, and banking interests; and that would make M&StL viable as a "home" road. More easily said than done. The prescription was accurate in all its parts, but the administration of it would be difficult in the best of circumstances, and even more so in the 1880s, as the big roads were fastening their grips on service areas with blankets of branch lines.

As Cadwallader Washburn considered all of this, he must have shaken his massive head in growing consternation, but he saw what had to be done: M&StL had to expand, again. It was a gamble, especially when the giants were venting their imperial instincts, but the Washburns were in too deeply to get out, and once more they would be required to step forward in order to protect earlier investments of time, talent, and treasure. Plainly stated, M&StL needed a greater range over which to disperse products and goods of Minneapolis and to gather in a greater volume of grain. There was another element in this mix. The winter of 1880–81 was unusually brutal, with blizzards and bitter cold setting in early and staying long. Rail lines were blocked, cleared, then blocked again by capricious and vicious storms. All served to exacerbate the area's chronic fuel scarcity; railroads themselves were forced to cancel runs for want of coal. Of course one of the reasons given for building the road on to Fort Dodge had been to tap Webster County coal fields. Some shipments were made that hard winter, but those billings were inadequate to meet the need, and, furthermore, the Webster County fields were not large. The M&StL managers considered both strategic and immediate options. Kansas City, Kansas, was an attractive point; so was Council Bluffs, Iowa. Articles of incorporation for the old Fort Dodge & Fort Ridgely were brought out, dusted off, and amended to allow extensions to both places. But for the moment the M&StL managers focused only on additional coal beds southeast of Fort Dodge.[1]

Money for M&StL construction was arranged for early in 1881 though Central Trust Company of New York, but work progressed slowly. The new line crawled southward out of the Des Moines River valley near Kalo, Iowa, found seams in the rolling countryside beyond, and passed through or gave life to the Iowa communities of Otho, Burnside, Dayton, and Pilot Mound before crossing Chicago & North Western's Chicago–Council Bluffs artery at Ogden, Iowa, early in November. Thirteen miles and another month of labor saw the line through Berkeley to Coaltown—in 1883 to be renamed Angus, honoring R. B. Angus, one of Hill's associates—259 miles from Minneapolis. Financial documents and the trade press asserted that the line would be further extended in "the coming season" 52 miles to a Chicago, Burlington & Quincy line at Greenfield, Iowa, "for a direct and short connection with Kansas City, which will open up an immense trade in lumber for southwestern points, and for coal and course grains for northern" destinations. In this way, read the mortgage, M&StL would "be able to run through trains from Kansas City to Duluth."[2]

The Iowa extension met the needs of M&StL's equity holders, providing an artery for outbound milled lumber, merchandise, and to a lesser extent flour, as well as a means to deliver grain and coal northbound. But as the wheat belt shifted west and northwest, to be replaced by the corn and hog belt, Minneapolis millers had to alter their own buying strategies. So, then, did M&StL need to shift. Actually there was nothing new in M&StL's looking westward. The law of 1853 authorizing predecessor Minnesota Western and that of 1869 modifying the road's purposes had called for a cross-state route from the St. Croix River on the east to the Red River valley on the west. These particular rights rather mysteriously evaporated, as did those vested in Minneapolis & St. Cloud, which James J. Hill's Manitoba eventually picked up for its West Side line and other endeavors. Yet M&StL still had authorization under special laws passed in 1874 and 1875 for westward branches. Hard times and preoccupation with other matters had diverted M&StL's energies, but in 1879 something finally was afoot. Early that year the road secured precise authority to build to the south shore of Lake Minnetonka, the largest body of water in the greater Minneapolis area and one early embraced by those eager to avail themselves of its beauty and recreational gifts. Although rail service to the area along the north shore had obtained since August 24, 1867, when locals saluted arrival of a pioneer train on the St. Paul & Pacific route extending toward Willmar and beyond, agitation had surfaced a decade later for additional service to the south shore. For a quarter century wealthy southerners had journeyed by steamboat and more recently by rail to enjoy the sights and especially the cooler summers of Minnesota. Lake Minnetonka, so close to Minneapolis and St. Paul, stood to capitalize on such seasonal traffic. So, too, did M&StL with its route to St. Louis via connections.[3]

In January 1880, W. D. Washburn announced plans to build to the lake. Others had anticipated as much and made investment decisions accordingly. The splendid Lake Park Hotel, for instance, had been completed in 1879. The local press followed all of this with great eagerness and enthusiasm, and soon began to report rumors that M&StL actually had two engineering teams in the field—one working between Hopkins, on the main line to Albert Lea, and Lake Minnetonka, and another pushing west of Minnetonka toward Redwood Falls or New Ulm. In fact, Washburn did have two crews in the field, but owing to problems regarding right-of-way and preoccupation with the extension to Fort Dodge, little other than surveying and modest grading was accomplished in 1880. The public speculated endlessly as to Washburn's purposes beyond the lake, but he kept his own counsel and would say little except that the road looked to the boundary of Dakota Territory as its objective.[4]

Motivations for the move west were much the

same as for the extension to Iowa—to establish marketing areas for Minneapolis wholesalers and lumbermen and to claim wheat-bearing territory for the millers—but with differences, too. Iowa offered coal and was rather more established than western Minnesota, but the recent economic panic had been a reminder of opportunities in the American West, and with recovery had come a surge of newcomers from older states and from Europe as well. Timing was an important consideration. The shifting wheat belt was another. Strategic circumstances represented another variable. The big roads—Chicago & North Western, Chicago, Milwaukee & St. Paul, Manitoba, and Northern Pacific—all were about the business of expanding in western Minnesota, and each one had moved into or had stated plans to move into nearby Dakota Territory. M&StL had either to move or to be left out of this race to establish territorial dominion. Finally, during the late 1870s Minneapolis commercial and business interests developed an acute self-confidence that translated into renewed interest in urban economic imperialism reflected in M&StL's campaigns.[5]

Talk was replaced with action in 1881. Financial arrangements were made in New York for 92 miles of "Pacific Extension" and 1.5 miles of a Lake Park Branch to serve resorts at Lake Minnetonka. Steel was laid from Hopkins, and the new line opened to Excelsior, in mid-July. Meanwhile, graders took up their work following engineering stakes to a crossing of Chicago, Milwaukee & St. Paul's Hastings & Dakota at Norwood and then along a wonderfully chosen alignment lying below the Hastings & Dakota and above the Minnesota River—a crescent-shaped route through an area certain to provide bountiful movements of wheat and other grains inbound to Minneapolis with a rural customer base sure to demand heavy shipments of lumber, coal, and manufactured goods. So Washburn believed, and so M&StL's board agreed. Tracklayers followed the grade to Arlington, where a depot was located late in July, to a place soon to be named Gaylord, after M&StL's superintendent, by October, and the next month to Winthrop, sixty-nine miles from Minneapolis, where they laid up for the winter. To the west stretched a nearly completed grade into the valley of the Minnesota River; to the rear lay several new Minnesota communities—Deephaven, Minnetonka Beach, Green Isle, Victoria, Hamburg, Arlington, Gaylord, and Winthrop among them.[6]

By the end of 1881, Minneapolis & St. Louis as an operating entity had been around for a full decade, and although it was tiny in comparison to the region's giant carriers, it was nevertheless a force to be reckoned with. Its 363-mile route structure looked at first blush to be categorically irrational, with the 20-mile Taylor's Falls Branch stubbing to the northeast and disjointed from the old Minneapolis & Duluth line to White Bear Lake, a single artery southwestward into Iowa, and now the "Pacific Extension" west to Winthrop. But there was a logic to it. The Taylor's Falls Branch anticipated further construction in Wisconsin to Superior or Bayfield, maybe both, for a seasonal passage to the Great Lakes with ample timber stock en route; the line to Albert Lea was a conduit to Burlington, Cedar Rapids & Northern and its crucial links to Chicago and St. Louis gateways; the Iowa route extended the range for Minneapolis lumbermen and merchants while guaranteeing a flow of cereal grains and coal northward; and the new route west promised a nice balance of traffic to and from the Minneapolis hub. The company's stock had been issued at the rate of $8,888 per mile and bonds at $10,688, respectable on both counts. Its modest roster of rolling stock included 638 pieces of freight equipment plus eight passenger cars, three baggage and mail cars, and one new "directors' car" from Ohio Falls Car Company that the local press thought "the handsomest thing of its kind ever placed on wheels." Motive power consisted of 4-4-0 American Standard locomotives, twenty-seven in all, plus four 0-4-0 switchers. Locomotives and cars alike were maintained at the new roundhouse and shop at Cedar Lake, about three miles from the milling district and five miles from Hopkins.[7]

Passenger trains provided for the necessary and important movement of people, baggage, mail, and express, but they also performed a valuable public relations function: passenger service was always a crucial yardstick by which a railroad was measured. M&StL's

early offerings were humble in the extreme, although the company did have a contract as early as 1878 with Pullman Palace Car Company to move and utilize Pullman's cars on its trains. In 1879 M&StL handled 81,067 passengers who rode an average of 33.3 miles, paid an average of $1.06 per ticket, and generated $86,954 in revenues. To this was added $7,988 for hauling mail and $3,894 for express. Collectively passenger service contributed about 21 percent of total revenues.[8]

Regular passenger listings featured the daily St. Louis Express, with "Pullman Palace Car Sleepers to St. Louis without change," plus mixed (freight and passenger) runs to White Bear Lake and Duluth and to St. Paul & Sioux City at Merriam. Offerings were expanded by late 1880 to include the Chicago Express, which represented through service via Burlington, Cedar Rapids & Northern (BCR&N) at Albert Lea, but also handled cars for Fort Dodge. All trains utilized the St. Paul, Minneapolis & Manitoba depot at Minneapolis, but tickets also could be had from the City Ticket Office, at No. 8 Washington Avenue, opposite the splendid Nicollet House. In 1881 round-trip service was added to Excelsior, on what was briefly called the Minnetonka Branch, and by the end of the year express and mixed trains were scheduled daily except Sunday for the Pacific Division as far as the temporary end-of-tracks at Winthrop. Another train was added to the Iowa route, and both trains were extended to Angus when service began to that place on January 1, 1882.[9]

Additional passenger revenues derived from special movements, especially excursions, of which there seemed to be an endless procession over the next many years. These included a Gethsemane Parish picnic excursion to White Bear Lake, a full train that traveled to Waseca for the Turner Society annual gathering, forty-four persons from Albert Lea who went to Minneapolis simply to "do the city," sixty persons from northern Iowa who arrived in Minneapolis on a

Figure 4.2. M&StL could not gracefully resist the new municipal passenger station. A diminutive Minneapolis Eastern 0-4-0 is in the foreground; an unidentified passenger train awaits departure in the background. Photograph courtesy of the Minnesota Historical Society.

warm July afternoon "for a season of pleasure," untold numbers from along the Albert Lea line who took advantage of M&StL's "half fare" rates to go to the Minnesota State Fair, and others who plunked down $20 for round-trip tickets from Minneapolis to the St. Louis Exposition and Fair in 1878. And on July 21, 1880, happy residents of Britt, Iowa, bought tickets at the new boxcar depot for the first excursion from Fort Dodge to Minneapolis. But the grandest excursion of M&StL's early days was likely that hosted by the company itself during mid-July 1878, when "sixty ladies and gentlemen" from St. Louis and "twenty-five businessmen from Cedar Rapids" were delivered to Minneapolis by a special train headed from Albert Lea by an M&StL locomotive elegantly "dressed with evergreens and national colors." W. D. Washburn freely admitted his purposes in staging the event. He thought there was a lamentable ignorance among leaders of St. Louis "as to this vast and beautiful region of the Northwest," which he sought to redress while at the same time showcasing M&StL as "the short and comfortable way to reach" this "magnificent empire." Guests toured Minneapolis, St. Paul, and Lake Minnetonka before going on to Duluth, again aboard a special train, this one pulled by M&StL's *Isaac Atwater,* a splendidly groomed 4-4-0. Upon their return to Minneapolis guests were feted to a gala dinner and then reboarded the cars for home. "The party was preeminently a jolly one, enjoyed by all," reported the local press, adding, significantly, that "denizens" of St. Louis had, as Washburn hoped, exclaimed enthusiastically at the wonders of the country they had beheld. One of those "denizens," a reporter from Missouri, was especially taken by what he had seen from his window as the train passed through Iowa and southern Minnesota. Both states, he contended, were "wealthy and populous, with many thriving cities, towns, and villages," along "with boundless farm country crowned" by "waving wheat and corn fields bathed in yellow light . . . as far as the eye can reach." And, he concluded in benediction, "Here is the art of God and the art of man commingled."[10]

M&StL freight volumes grew as the road expanded and as the shipping public matured in productive capacity. The number of ton miles increased from 13,841,921 in 1878 to 19,042,053 in 1879; freight revenues rose in the same period from $303,811 to $372,507. In 1880 M&StL's traffic mix included lumber (24.7 percent), grain (21.9 percent), flour (17.5 percent), merchandise (11.2 percent), coal (9.1 percent), livestock (1.7 percent), and assorted other goods (3.9 percent). M&StL remained the premier carrier of lumber and flour from Minneapolis. In 1878 it handled nearly forty-nine million board feet of lumber from the mills, although billings slipped to thirty-five million board feet in 1880, nearly all moving south to BCR&N at Albert Lea or to line stations in Minnesota and Iowa. About half of all flour milled in Minneapolis moved out on M&StL rails; in 1878 billings were nearly equal, north and south, to Duluth for transshipment or all-rail to eastern points, but in 1880 nearly 65 percent went south. Shipments of coal were modest early, with delivery by way of lakes through Duluth, but with linkage to Iowa after 1877, more cars came from BCR&N than from the north. The coal volume would jump in 1880 to 34,189 tons (up from 1,830 in 1878) as M&StL's own line reached mines in Iowa's Webster County.[11]

In 1879 more of M&StL's total freight business rolled southbound (54 percent to 46 percent), and more than three-quarters of its business originated on or terminated on another railroad. That year the most important connections in terms of revenue were, in order:

1. Burlington, Cedar Rapids & Northern at Albert Lea
2. St. Paul & Duluth at White Bear Lake
3. St. Paul & Sioux City at Merriam
4. Chicago, Milwaukee & St. Paul at Chaska

Of these, BCR&N offered M&StL its longest haul, but that was only 107 miles, from Minneapolis to Albert Lea. M&StL clearly suffered from short hauls. This liability could be offset, at least in part and in the short run, by captive business directed from outlying stations to Minneapolis. That pattern developed early and would last into the next century, particularly from stations with no other rail outlet to offer an alternative urban magnet, such as Chicago & North Western and

Chicago. Producers of wheat from noncompetitive points certainly sought Minneapolis as their natural market, but so did producers of oats, barley, and corn. Forest City, on the line to Iowa, for example, posted outbound billings of wheat, beans, butter, tallow, hides, live hogs, and empty barrels plus receipts of machinery merchandise and building materials. Dressed hogs, eggs, butter, and lard were billed from nearly every station, almost all consigned to Minneapolis. Poultry moved from New Prague and Waterville, apples from New Richland and Albert Lea, beer from Jordan, brick from Chaska, and even ice from White Bear Lake and Jordan.[12]

The decade of the 1880s was the golden age of railroad expansion. It was during the same explosive decade that huge interregional systems developed, many of them in the trans-Chicago West. The breath-taking expansion of route miles and emergence of giant operations also was traumatic. In an earlier era, railroad owners and managers had made alliances and established cartels as means of maintaining at least a semblance of stability. But in the aftermath of the panic of 1873, railroad managers and then railroad investors and speculators succumbed to instincts of aggression. Overbuilding resulted in increased competition, rate wars, and corporate consolidations. All of it was bound to impact M&StL sooner or later.[13]

It was in this increasingly fluid and Darwinian environment that W. D. Washburn charted a course for M&StL. Its lines reached BCR&N at Albert Lea for important Chicago and St. Louis connections; coal moved in promising volumes from the pits around Angus; and grain moved from and lumber moved to virtually all stations in Iowa and Minnesota. The route west to Winthrop was open—rails would reach Morton by November 1882—and of course the line to White Bear Lake gave access to Duluth by trackage rights over St. Paul & Duluth as well as means to gain the stub to Taylor's Falls. Frankly stated, though, it was inadequate. There were so many unrealized aspirations—an independent avenue to Lake Superior through rich pinelands to feed the hungry lumber mills at Minneapolis, for example. And what of the line west? Was it destined to stay forever stuck in the valley of the Minnesota River at Morton? Was it likely an ultima Thule? What about Angus to the south? Would it be the road's farthest outpost?

There was little that the Washburns could do. Money had flowed generously to all sorts of investment after the panic of 1873 had run its course, but the shooting of President James A. Garfield in July 1881 and his death on September 19 cast a growing pall. Optimism soured; sober-minded investors talked darkly about overexpansion in the railroad industry. Nevertheless, early in 1882 W. D. Washburn talked boldly of taking M&StL beyond Angus. *Railroad Gazette* reported that M&StL surveyors would examine "about 50 miles" of country from near Des Moines to Creston, Iowa, and in April Minneapolis newspapers optimistically repeated a story from the *Chicago Tribune* referring to the Angus line as the "Kansas City extension," saying that upon completion it would "be the shortest and most direct route between Minneapolis and Kansas City." Graders, however, failed to follow surveyors.[14]

An important diversion and also a personal investment for William D. Washburn attended M&StL's line to the west at Excelsior, nineteen miles from Minneapolis, along the south shore of Lake Minnetonka. Even before M&StL rails reached there in 1881, the Hotel St. Louis was in place near what became the Deephaven station; not far distant at Sunrise Point above Gideon's Bay stood the Lake Park Hotel. The St. Louis Hotel—"accommodations for 500 guests"—had been erected in 1879 by Charles Gibson of the place's namesake city, and the Lake Park—"every room opens onto a veranda"—had been put up in the same season. M&StL took a half interest in the Lake Park, likely at Washburn's behest, and Washburn himself was the initial owner of the $57,000 *City of Saint Louis,* a beautiful 150-foot steamer capable of handling one thousand passengers that was placed on the lake during the early summer of 1881. Modern in every way, the *City* was the first inland vessel in the country to be lighted with electricity. The striking sidewheeler met all trains (two daily and two daily except Sunday by August) and when not thus engaged offered eager vacationers excursions over the lake's broad expanse. Minnetonka became a favored watering spot for southerners, mint julep–drinking planters and businessmen and their wives, fair southern belles, and their servants, who arrived to enjoy Minnetonka's sparkling blue water and its marvelous sandy beaches as well as splendid social life at the hotels.[15]

The year 1882 is generally acknowledged to have marked the beginning of Minneapolis's reign as the premier flour milling center—the world leader in flour production. As it turned out, 1882 would also prove to be a pivotal year for the railroad industry in Minnesota and for M&StL in particular. As always, the trail to important change was long and complex. During the summer of 1879 had come those unsettling reports of significant changes in ownership of St. Paul & Duluth, with which M&StL had had a long and usually friendly association. W. D. Washburn had hurried to New York City to investigate. There he learned the awful truth: control of StP&D had passed to a consortium of persons clearly connected in the affairs of North Western and, curiously, Rock Island. This was serious, indeed, for M&StL had a valued alliance with StP&D for trackage rights that gave it outlet to the Great Lakes chain as its means of levering rate advantages against the Chicago roads. Ownership and management of St. Paul & Duluth also was of critical interest to the cities of Minneapolis and St. Paul and, really, to Minnesota at large; it was not merely the parochial concern of M&StL and the Minneapolis flour millers. StP&D's president, J. P. Ilsley, claimed that the Duluth road would run in competition to the Chicago and Milwaukee companies, but when StP&D forthwith raised rates on flour by 14 cents a barrel there was a general sense that the company, controlled by a coalition clearly and powerfully connected to eastern interests, was engaged in larceny.[16]

Figure 4.3. W. D. Washburn himself was the initial owner of the handsome *City of Saint Louis.* Author's collection.

W. D. Washburn was outraged, as was most of the state's press and a majority of Minnesotans, who already brooded about the power of the great railway systems and their owners. "The value of the products of Minnesota are to a greater extent than almost any of the states dependent upon transportation," Washburn had argued earlier in the decade. The problem, he went on, was that railroad transportation was controlled "by a set of sharks and speculators, men who have amassed fortunes not in legitimate business but by a systematic robbery of the people." Of course the matter of ownership and control of St. Paul & Duluth was what earlier had provoked the Washburns to respond with the Taylor's Falls & Lake Superior project, but construction of that road, jointly owned with StP&D, plus operating privileges to Duluth, had produced only a mixed blessing.[17]

For M&StL, circumstances only deteriorated. As if to erase all pretense, Alexander Mitchell joined St. Paul & Duluth's board in 1880, as did another Milwaukee senior manager, William C. Van Horne, in 1881. H. H. Porter, large in the affairs of Chicago & North Western and Omaha, also went aboard in 1881. The Washburns and M&StL had had a love-hate relationship with the predecessors of Porter's Omaha, itself formed on May 26, 1880, and into which were poured franchises and assets formerly held by North Wisconsin Railway, West Wisconsin Railway, and St. Paul & Sioux City. The latter road had provided M&StL considerable sustenance by means of interchange of traffic at Merriam, but West Wisconsin, physically connected to Chicago & North Western at El Roy, Wisconsin, often was seen as a surrogate of Chicago and opposed to the best interests of Minneapolis. The driving force at the two Wisconsin companies and then at Omaha was Henry H. Porter, a native of Maine who had entered railroad service with a predecessor of C&NW and served as a director of that road from 1870 to 1878. Allied with Porter were David Dows and others from New York financial circles plus, among others, Ransom R. Cable, usually associated with Chicago, Rock Island & Pacific. Indeed, Cable was with Rock Island; by 1880 he was a vice president, and he had been on the board since 1877.[18]

Elsewhere, since the fall of 1877, Burlington, Cedar Rapids & Northern had provided M&StL's vital outlet to the south and east. BCR&N bondholders had taken over a substantial part of M&StL's debt, and the two roads had executed a "perpetual contract of unison" regarding traffic. BCR&N maps of the time showed a solid through route from Minneapolis to St. Louis via M&StL and BCR&N, with Chicago, Burlington & Quincy from Burlington, Iowa, to Monmouth, Illinois, and then Rockford, Rock Island & St. Louis. M&StL schedules were included in the *Official Guide,* although subordinated to those of BCR&N. Yet BCR&N had other alliances, with C&NW via Cedar Rapids and with CB&Q via Burlington, both favoring Chicago over St. Louis. BCR&N, to be sure, had complex and often conflicting loyalties, as reflected in its directory and in its management. H. H. Porter, who in 1878 sat on the boards at C&NW and Rock Island, also had a seat on BCR&N's board, and Judge John Tracy of Burlington, former president of both Rock Island and C&NW and a personal friend of CB&Q president Charles E. Perkins, was BCR&N's lawyer and became its president in 1880.[19]

Eventually Rock Island took a lease on the entire BCR&N, but as matters settled out, Rock Island and Burlington were in joint control, with Chicago, Rock Island & Pacific as the dominant partner. It was a useful arrangement for both roads. BCR&N clearly expanded Rock Island's domain to the northwest, and CB&Q, which earlier had failed in an independent sortie to the northwest, could at least content itself with an established if jointly controlled through route from St. Louis toward Minneapolis–St. Paul. The arrangement would divide territory, ensure friendly connections, maintain rate stability, and guarantee that BCR&N did not fall into unfriendly hands.[20]

Rock Island was known as a solid, prosperous, and well-managed company; its stock and bonds commanded premium prices. Perhaps its one liability had been inadequate branches to drain traffic from country contiguous to its road. Control of BCR&N reflected a more aggressive posture in that regard, and, in fact, Rock Island was becoming more aggressive in general, reflecting, in great part, the instincts of Ransom Reed Cable. Would Cable use this line to make good on the "Pacific" in Rock Island's corporate title? Perhaps. After all, Cable, like most managers of the time, saw the need to defend existing "natural territory," to stake out new service areas, to use expansion as a defensive as well as an offensive strategy, and to engage all of this through construction, consolidation, or both.[21]

It was against this backdrop that the Washburns and their associates who had birthed M&StL and seen it to adolescence were required to formulate decisions as to the future of the enterprise. In reality, M&StL was caught in the jaws of changed and changing circumstances as the big roads increased in size and power. Where did M&StL fit in? The road had long been the favorite of Minneapolis, the local road, locally managed. But compared to Manitoba, Northern Pacific, C&NW, Milwaukee, Omaha, and now Rock Island, it was not much. Expansion on its own to Lake Superior or even to an Omaha connection in Wisconsin, on to Des Moines or Kansas City, or from Morton to Dakota Territory might be possible, but only with a management and directory with a heart for it. That was not the case for M&StL. William Drew Washburn often was absent attending to political aspirations and responsibilities, and brother Cadwallader had wearied of bailing his brother out and of the M&StL project in general.[22]

In the end, the formerly vigorous but now very weary Cadwallader shook his massive head and, through eastern bankers and investors, agreed along with several others to dispose of their stock in a way that would bring "foreign" control to M&StL's board. Out were Cadwallader Washburn, W. D. Hale, R. J. Baldwin, Paris Gibson, John Martin, John S. Pillsbury, and Henry Titus Welles, most of whom had served from the beginning in 1870; in were H. H. Porter, J. F. Withrow, H. R. Bishop, and Benjamin Brewster. Porter and Brewster were on Rock Island and Omaha boards, Brewster was an Omaha director, and Bishop was a lawyer for Rock Island. Which road, if any, now had control of M&StL? It was not clear. Nevertheless, it was clear that tired and sick Cadwallader Washburn was no longer a factor at M&StL, and his brother's influence had been tightly curtailed. (Cadwallader suffered a paralyzing stroke in February and would die in May 1882.)[23]

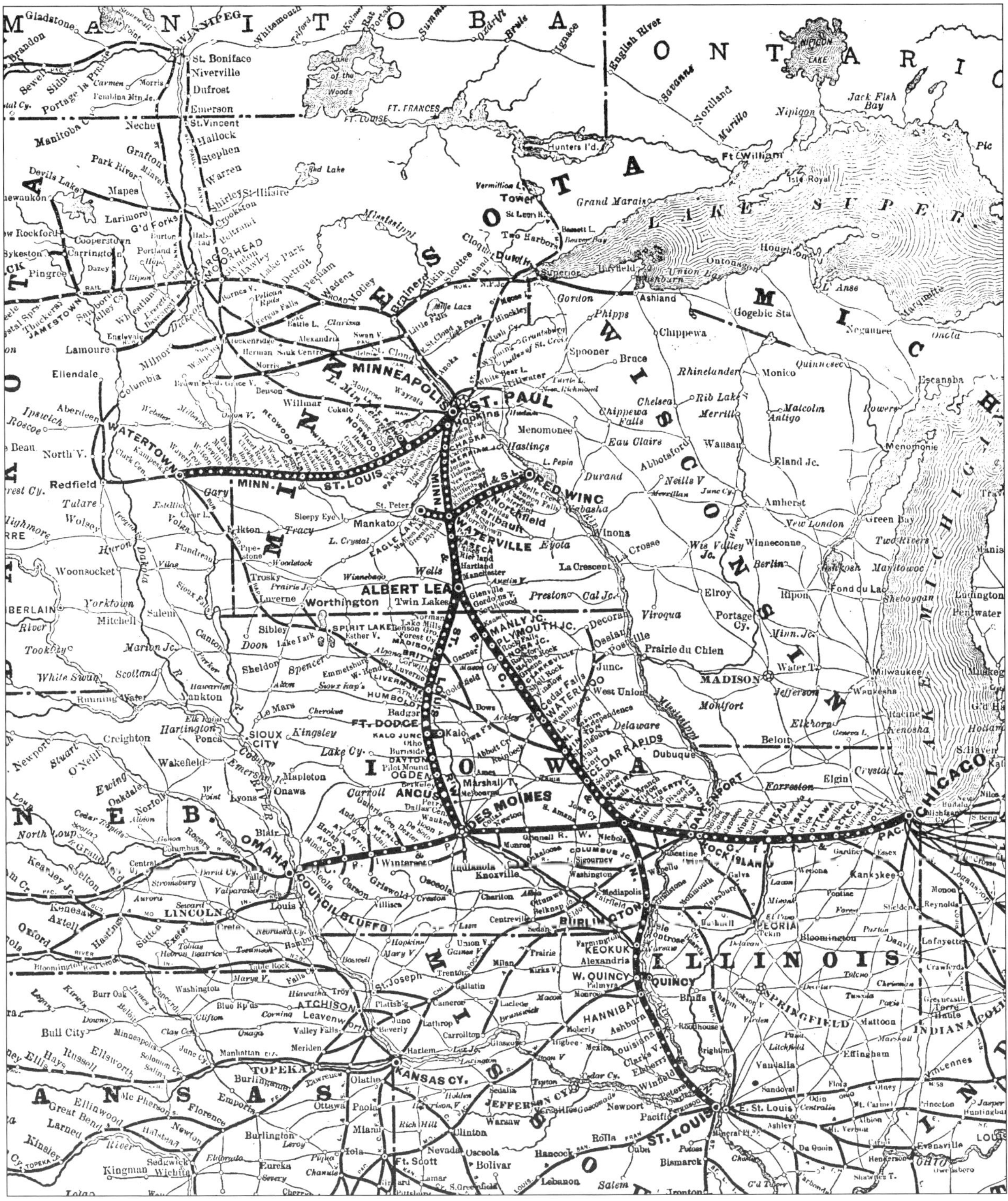

Map 4.1. The Albert Lea Route at once demonstrated the symbiotic association of the M&StL, BCR&N, and CRI&P, as well as competitive routes along the Twin Cities–Chicago and Twin Cities–St. Louis corridors.

Certainty gradually emerged from uncertainty. Several more new and "foreign" directors were elected in October 1881. These included three men from St. Paul—W. R. Merriam, A. B. Stickney, and C. D. W. Young—all of whom had been in one way or another associated with Omaha or its predecessors; also added was Ransom Cable who, like the others, had an Omaha connection as well as a distinct tie with Rock Island. Then, in April, a joint announcement was made by M&StL, BCR&N, CRI&P, and CB&Q that an improved through passenger service would be instituted between Minneapolis and St. Louis. Even earlier, Rock Island had begun to advertise Chicago–Minneapolis service over what it trumpeted as the "Albert Lea Route." Furthermore, Rock Island stockholders were told that "a considerable traffic destined to and from Minnesota, Dakota and Manitoba" had begun to move over the "continuous line from Chicago to Minneapolis."[24]

Matters came to a head in May 1882. "Minneapolis & St. Louis has passed through the process which awaits every local road on the American continent," intoned the *Minneapolis Tribune* on May 2: "the process of virtual absorption by older, stronger and wealthier corporations controlling great through lines of traffic." The *Tribune* was referring in this instance to a major transfer of stock and management control to "a syndicate of railway managers and capitalists" headed by Ransom Cable and H. H. Porter. *Railroad Gazette* maintained that CRI&P and Omaha would manage M&StL for their own interests, and Cable, now president of M&StL, said as much. M&StL would maintain headquarters in Minneapolis and would enjoy an independent management, in an arrangement much like that with BCR&N. W. D. Washburn stayed on the board and retained his stock in M&StL (for a while as the largest single shareholder), and, although Cadwallader earlier had disposed of his stock, at his death he still held a heavy investment in M&StL bonds. In late summer, M&StL passenger trains were running into Des Moines (to Rock Island's station) via trackage rights over Des Moines & Fort Dodge from Angus, and effective August 1, 1882, M&StL passenger trains originated and terminated in St. Paul. By September, contracts were in place facilitating M&StL freight service into Des Moines.[25]

There was much brave talk in Minneapolis and abroad in M&StL's service territory as to the impact of "foreign control." But there also was much regret and even anxiety in the wake of the Cable-Porter conquest. "There is no railroad touching this city which is so distinctively a Minneapolis road as the M&StL," the *Tribune* had correctly asserted in 1877. "It had its origins here, and was built by our people, and it belongs to them and will always be run for their benefit." The state's railroad commissioner put it bluntly: "The Minneapolis & St. Louis has been alienated from state ownership." Others were plainly bitter, seeing betrayal in the actions of the Washburns and their associates who had sold out the M&StL project. "I propose to be loyal to Minneapolis interests, first, last, and all the time," William Drew Washburn had promised nearly a decade earlier. Now those words had a hollow ring for critics who always had seen him as arrogant and presently judged him also as duplicitous. "W. D. Washburn whenever he retired from anything left trouble, as well as maledictions, behind," contended one very uncharitable historian of the flour milling industry. Would that be the case with regard to M&StL?[26]

Chapter 5
The Great Rock Island Route

[Minneapolis & St. Louis penetrates] the very heart of the agricultural paradise of the Continent [where] the civilization, wealth and culture of American farm life are seen at their best—a land like that which gladdened the prophetic vision of Moses, "flowing with milk and honey."
—Chicago, Rock Island & Pacific, 1886

In the 1860s and 1870s Chicago, Rock Island & Pacific (CRI&P) had been slow, probably too slow, in extension of its lines, main arteries and feeders alike. Its management had chosen to err on the side of caution; its shareholders, after all, were not prone to speculation. As other roads moved to solidify service areas against "invasion," however, Rock Island was forced to reassess what it saw as its "natural territory." But again Rock Island chose a conservative path. Its alliance with Chicago, Burlington & Quincy in the Burlington, Cedar Rapids & Northern matter was an apt application of the strategy of gaining territory already occupied by an existing road. So was the plan of Ransom R. Cable and Henry H. Porter regarding Minneapolis & St. Louis. Nevertheless, Rock Island needed to move more expansively—and on its sole account.

Cable and associates unveiled for Rock Island's board of directors an aggressive plan to reach the Pacific Coast by a northern route. The board members pondered the idea. Cable pressed them, reminding that by gathering in BCR&N and M&StL, Rock Island had gained precious and constant sources of traffic, had gained valuable access to Minneapolis–St. Paul, and had significantly extended Rock Island's frontier westward toward tidewater. For example, M&StL's "Pacific Division" already had reached Winthrop, would be extended into the Minnesota River valley at Morton before 1882 was out, and was in position to be pushed on to a junction with BCR&N's "Pacific Division," which by the summer of 1882 would be built to Spirit Lake, Iowa, 235 miles northwest of Cedar Rapids, and a bit beyond, and would be on a line to intercept an M&StL extension in Dakota. From that point Rock Island could press westward.[1]

Another important variable in Cable's overall strategy was the little-remarked Wisconsin, Minnesota & Pacific Railway (WM&P), which was to be something of a holding and management company for the vast project. WM&P, not to be established until August 13, 1883, would be the successor to Minnesota Central and the Cannon River Improvement Company, each with valuable land grants and franchises as well as a sixty-six-mile line of railway finished in 1882 from Waterville, an M&StL station a bit more than halfway to Albert Lea from Minneapolis, eastward through Faribault, Northfield, and Cannon Falls to Red Wing, on the Mississippi River below St. Paul. Franchise rights also permitted construction to the western boundary of the state. A. B. Stickney, already well established in area railroad circles, briefly vice president at M&StL, and an important intermediary

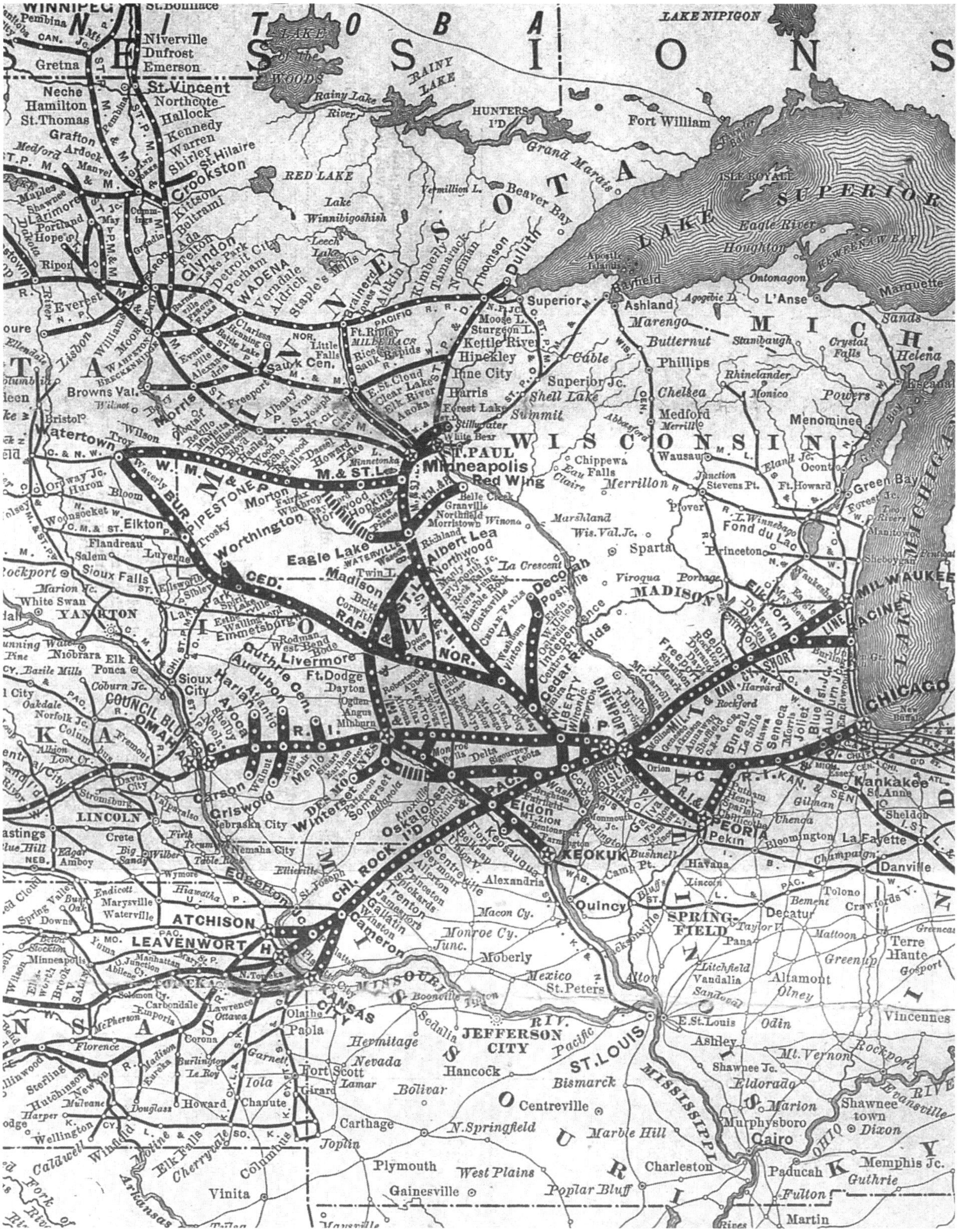

Map 5.1. Would Ransom Cable use M&StL and BCR&N to launch a westward path to the Pacific? Author's collection.

between Cable and W. D. Washburn in conveying M&StL to Rock Island control, had taken charge of construction, and nobody would be surprised early in 1883 when WM&P was turned over to operation by M&StL as its Cannon Valley Division. Behind all of this, however, was Ransom Cable and powerful Rock Island.[2]

At the same time Cable had little interest in Taylor's Falls & Lake Superior, which M&StL had operated on its own since December 1, 1881, with trains out of Minneapolis utilizing Minneapolis & Duluth to White Bear Lake, St. Paul & Duluth (StP&D) overhead to Wyoming, Minnesota, and Taylor's Falls & Lake Superior to the end of the line at Taylor's Falls. That ended on July 31, 1882, when M&StL ceased operation of the branch and also terminated operation over StP&D to Duluth. On the next day StP&D took sole lease of both Taylor's Falls & Lake Superior and, quite surprisingly, M&StL's historic Minneapolis & Duluth. The Taylor's Falls operation had been strategically important to M&StL during the Washburn years, of course, but frankly had been marginal as a business venture. Operation to Duluth since May 17, 1880, had cost $50,000 annually in rentals, but in 1881 had yielded revenues of about $140,000 from Duluth (mostly from carriage of wheat, lumber, and merchandise; one hundred passengers added a paltry $481.75). In February 1883, M&StL would sell its half interest in Taylor's Falls & Lake Superior to St. Paul & Duluth.[3]

The relationship between Cable and Porter, between Rock Island and Omaha, and among all of them and M&StL was at best blurred during most of 1882. During the summer the trade press reported that M&StL was "under the control of the Omaha," an understandable conclusion given the collaborative efforts of Cable and Porter and the presence on the Omaha board of W. D. Washburn and Henry T. Welles. Rumors of union were further fanned when M&StL and Omaha entered a lease agreement on September 25 that gave Omaha rights over M&StL from Merriam into Minneapolis; Omaha already had trackage rights over Manitoba from St. Paul to Minneapolis. Together these contracts gave Omaha overhead privileges by which to connect its eastern and western lines right through the Twin Cities and, incidentally, gave it the ability to reach its jointly owned Minneapolis Eastern in the heart of the milling district from both directions. For its part, M&StL gained access to St. Paul over Omaha from Merriam, a marginal gain at best.[4]

Late in 1883, a new—and, from M&StL's point of view, patently ironic—variable burst onto the regional railroad scene when the Minneapolis, Sault Ste. Marie & Atlantic Railway was organized under the laws of Wisconsin. Strategic purposes were implied in its very name: to link Minneapolis with Atlantic ports via Sault Ste. Marie, bypassing Chicago in the process. It all sounded so familiar. The specific idea had been broached as early as 1873 in a speech by Israel Washburn, it had percolated in the minds of others who associated the concept with purposes of Northern Pacific, and it finally had taken root when "a number of prominent citizens" of Minneapolis were summoned to the office of William Drew Washburn, whose mixture of genius and boyish enthusiasm quickly won them to the daring enterprise. Included in the directorate were Washburn, J. K. Sidle, Henry T. Welles, John Martin, and W. W. Eastman—every one an incorporator of M&StL in another age—as well as W. D. Hale, C. A. Pillsbury, and Charles Martin, all of whom had been members of M&StL's board at one time or another. Even at that very moment Washburn was on the board at M&StL and at Omaha; the idea of conflict of interest was not yet mature.[5]

The "Washburn Road" (that, too, sounded familiar), or "Soo Line," as it became popularly known, elbowed out M&StL, now under Rock Island domination, as the favorite local road, but, like M&StL at the time of its birth and later, Soo was strapped for cash, and the road would not gain its Sault Ste. Marie goal until 1887. Meanwhile, however, in 1884 a satellite, also a "millers' enterprise," the Minneapolis & Pacific, was to be organized for the purpose of building west from Minneapolis. Taken together, these predecessors of Minneapolis, St. Paul & Sault Ste. Marie were designed to bring wheat into Minneapolis and take flour from it—at the expense of Duluth on the one hand and Chicago on the other—all of which sounded very much like the original purposes of M&StL and was led by the same cast of characters. "The importance to this section, and especially to Minneapolis, of this enterprise can hardly be overestimated," observed the *Minneapolis Tribune.* Déjà vu. Nevertheless, Soo, if a latecomer, would have to be reckoned with locally and, as it developed, in the grand scheme of railroad strategy as well.[6]

Railroad construction in the United States had continued apace in 1881 and 1882, but Cable continued to move cautiously, probably because of the severe national recession that took hold in 1883 and would not yield to recovery until 1886. Investors and most railroad managers, including Cable, believed in general that the country's rail net had expanded too far compared to demand and that adding more mileage at the moment would waste capital. To that rule was an exception, however: the "Dakota boom" continued; it had slowed to be sure, but was not yet exhausted. Cable could justify expansion there, to stake out territory, to share in a growing traffic from a region not yet saturated with lines, and to position Rock Island for its planned drive to the Pacific.[7]

The "boom mentality" in Dakota was not matched nationally and certainly was not reflected in financial centers where gloom precluded issuance of the large blocks of securities necessary for major construction. Cable put his group's transcontinental plans on hold, but scoured endlessly for funding to take Rock Island clients into Dakota. He remained conservative and constrained, moving by indirection. After an M&StL board meeting in October 1883, the press reported that "the company at present prefer to say nothing relative to an extension of their road into the country of the Red River valley." But on November 30, articles of incorporation for Cedar Rapids, Iowa Falls & Northwestern, a BCR&N subsidiary in charge of constructing and operating that company's "Pacific Division," were altered to allow further movement in Iowa, Minnesota, and Dakota Territory. At about the same time, articles pertaining to Wisconsin, Minnesota & Pacific were changed to give that enterprise rights to build by "a most feasible route in the direction of the Great Bend of the Missouri River." Plans jelled during the winter of 1883–84. WM&P surveyors studied the country west of Waterville on the stub from Red Wing, and local press reports promised track work "as soon as this work is completed." Cable settled on another plan, however, one that used WM&P's general authority for expansion but hitched it to M&StL's existing line west from Hopkins into the Minnesota River valley. In that way WM&P could leapfrog ahead, leaving a gap between Waterville and a connection with M&StL's Pacific Division at some yet unidentified location that could be decided on later. On April 1, 1884, Rock Island purchased all of WM&P's securities, stocks and bonds alike, advancing that road monies for construction of an extension from the M&StL line at Morton "to some point on the Northern Pacific, probably Jamestown, Dakota," opined *Railway Age.* On the same date, BCR&N sold bonds adequate to push a new line of road from Lake Park, in northwestern Iowa, in a "northwesterly direction, to the city of Bismarck."[8]

This news was not received kindly by the owners and managers of Northern Pacific and Manitoba, and, in truth, it represented a revocation of what Cable had promised earlier. "We will make some extension either from the Minneapolis & St. Louis, or Burlington, Cedar Rapids & Northern in a westerly or northwesterly direction in the territory now occupied by the North Western and Milwaukee roads," he had confided to Manitoba's James J. Hill on May 14, 1883. But, he went on, "we have no intention of going north of points already held by them, knowing very well," he said, "that the Northern Pacific and your company are disposed to give our interest at St. Paul and Minneapolis a full share of business from the territory covered by your respective lines." In other words, Cable had pledged not to transgress into the service areas of NP and Manitoba west of Minneapolis if each maintained favorable traffic relations in the Twin Cities. Failing that, Cable implied retaliation. What explained the move now? Perhaps Hill or NP managers had irritated Cable, but more likely he was pursuing his own instincts in pressing on toward the Pacific.[9]

Construction began west of Morton in the early spring of 1884. Chicago & North Western threatened retaliation by lengthening a branch northwestward from Redwood Falls across the WM&P survey "to prevent encroachment on its territory," but it did not do so. WM&P surveyors soon located a line out of the river bottoms onto the rich, undulating prairie, for seventy miles following the northwestward angle of the Minnesota River but diverging from it gradually before turning abruptly west to cross the boundary of Dakota Territory and assault a range of hills known as the Couteaux des Prairie that would require heavy excavation, long fills, tight curves, and high trestles before dropping into the broad drainage basin of the Big Sioux and James Rivers. By early May it was clear that Cable had selected Watertown as an intermediate destination with confluence of WM&P and BCR&N. The latter, meanwhile, had chosen a route from Lake Park, Iowa, that crossed the extreme southwest corner of Minnesota and then continued along the west side of Couteaux des Prairie northward in the fertile valley of the Big Sioux River through Dakota's easternmost counties before angling northwest to Watertown.[10]

As WM&P and BCR&N construction crews labored through the summer of 1884, Cable's lieutenants considered plans by which the two companies would "build jointly to Bismarck," a distance of about 225 miles from Watertown. C. F. Hatch, president of WM&P, and C. J. Ives, president of BCR&N, pointed out that when completed a year hence, the route to Bismarck would "secure a large traffic," benefiting Chicago via BCR&N and CRI&P as well as Minneapolis via WM&P and M&StL. Meanwhile, by early fall WM&P announced plans to fill the gap between Waterville and M&StL's Pacific Division at Gaylord. That news had been expected, but WM&P added, mysteriously, "and thence westerly into Dakota." In addition, and even more mysteriously, WM&P announced plans for "bridges for an eastern extension" at St. Paul, Minneapolis, or Red Wing "and over the St. Croix and Chippewa rivers at points yet to be named." These ambiguous assertions set off a predictable wave of rumors, among them that Cable's real goal was to build a line parallel with Manitoba to Winnipeg, that WM&P would build from Gaylord to a junction with the joint WM&P-BCR&N line to Bismarck somewhere above Watertown, and—most expansively—that Rock Island was out to "scoop" Milwaukee and Manitoba alike by gathering in the new or planned Washburn roads east and west of Minneapolis and, not so incidentally according to one observer, furnishing "healthy competition where it will be needed."[11]

Elsewhere, facts and not rumors marked progress toward Watertown. Tracklayers for WM&P and BCR&N, in spirited rivalry, pressed toward that mutual destination. Substantial bridge and trestlework over the Minnesota River west of Morton was completed on July 3, and as quickly as surfacing was completed beyond, the line was opened to operation under lease by M&StL—to Wood Lake on August 18, to Hanley Falls a few days later, to Marietta by early September, and to Revillo before the month was out. BCR&N rail went down at the rate of two miles per day; tracklayers were north of Pipestone by early August and near Elkton at month's end. WM&P, however, won the race; its rails were put down in Watertown on October 27, a few days before BCR&N arrived. M&StL initiated passenger service from Minneapolis on November 1.[12]

In driving westward to Watertown, WM&P would pass through or give birth to North Redwood, Delhi, Belview, Echo, Wood Lake, Hanley Falls, Hazel Run, Clarkfield, Boyd, Dawson, Madison, and Marietta—all in Minnesota—and Revillo, Strandburg, Troy, and Waverly—in Dakota. Hanley Falls took its name from J. A. Hanley, an M&StL official, but initially was called Cable, after Ransom Cable, who for some reason declined the honor. It was laid out in an unusual diagonal pattern, with a large park in the center and streets radiating from it. By Christmas 1884, Hanley Falls claimed several small business houses. The cooperative creamery there may have been the first of its kind in Minnesota, and the Hanley Falls Bottling Works became a major supplier of soft drinks for the entire area. Farther west, Madison bid fair to become "the future metropolis of Lac qui Parle County," and before the summer of 1885 it had fourteen businesses along its streets. Revillo, just across the boundary in Dakota Territory, in 1886 featured several stores and shops, the usual grain elevator and lumber yard, and the Fleming Hotel. The dramatic growth at these three places was typical of those west of Morton.[13]

The *Minneapolis Tribune* called Rock Island's twin

thrusts to the northwest "a significant event in railroad circles," because until that time that part of Dakota Territory had been the province of C&NW and Milwaukee. And the *Tribune* looked forward to 1885, when "a new road will be pushed on toward Bismarck, and the upper territory of the Northern Pacific Railroad will be invaded by the redoubtable Rock Island." Surveyors had problems in the hill country east of the James River, but before winter closed in they found a favorable route with easy grades leading toward Bismarck.[14]

M&StL's life under the great protective shield of Ransom Cable and Rock Island during the remainder of the 1880s proved a mixed blessing—much like the relationship of a younger sibling with a "big brother." There were times when M&StL was sheltered and nurtured by the arrangement; there were times when the road suffered from inattention and from an inability to act unilaterally on its own merit. In any event, it was often heady business being an integral part of CRI&P's well-known and highly respected railroad empire. Rock Island's "Albert Lea Route" was composed of M&StL, BCR&N, and Rock Island—a thoroughfare pointing "Toward the Rising Sun" from Minneapolis and St. Paul to "Chicago . . . and . . . all Eastern points in the United States," over which in 1884 were carded through passenger trains in each direction. One set, M&StL trains 5 and 6, which

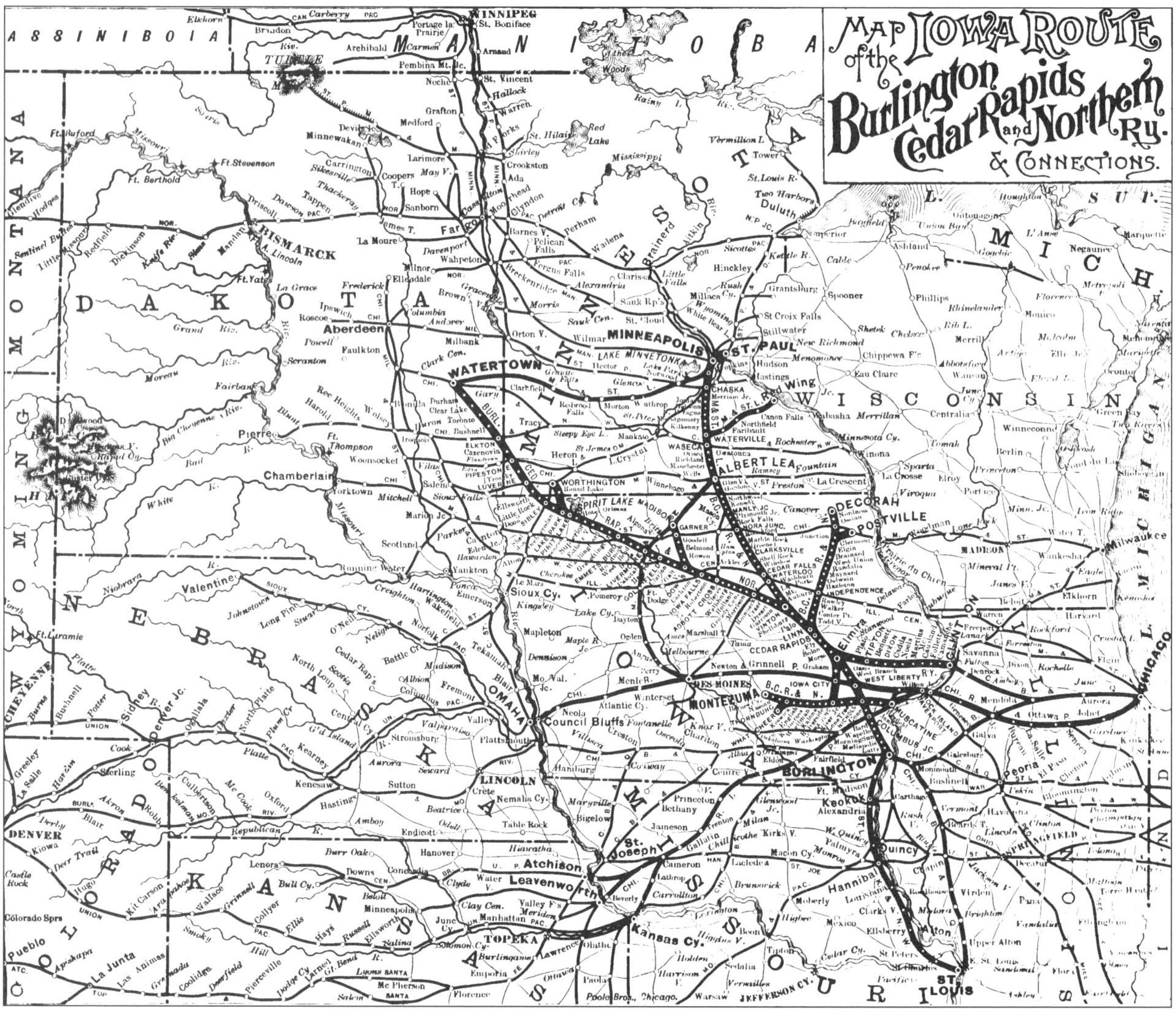

Map 5.2. The Albert Lea Route was a great advertising ploy in the hands of M&StL's Samuel F. Boyd and Rock Island's E. St. John. Author's collection.

took the name the Cannon Ball Express, consisted of head-end cars, coaches, a diner, and Pullman sleepers, and stopped only at Hopkins, Merriam, Waterville, and Waseca, Minnesota. Another set, trains 1 and 2, offered more pedestrian services to and from Chicago, while a third set, trains 3 and 4, provided daily "solid trains" of coaches and sleepers to St. Louis via M&StL, BCR&N, and CB&Q.[15]

In addition to trademark service to and from Chicago and St. Louis, M&StL offered options west and southwest. In 1883 one passenger and one mixed train daily worked the line to and from Morton; service extended to Watertown a year later. M&StL's "Des Moines Air Line," however, received more attention, providing, "the only direct line to Central Iowa Points," as well as access to Rock Island in Des Moines for connections beyond. Two trains daily ran as far as Fort Dodge, only one beyond, to Des Moines. Mixed train service from Fort Dodge to Angus supplemented the "varnish." Mixed train service also sufficed on the Cannon Valley Division between Waterville and Red Wing.[16]

In all cases, Minneapolis and St. Paul were center stage from M&StL's perspective. By 1883 about 100 passenger trains moved in and out of Minneapolis each day; even more, 155, served St. Paul. During the Washburn years, St. Paul had played second fiddle in M&StL's strategy, but Cable thought Rock Island's empire incomplete without service to Minnesota's capital city. St. Paul was, without question, vastly important in commerce, jobbing, government, and transportation. Cable was right to seek avenue to St. Paul; he gained it with the Omaha contract (a modest advantage in carriage of freight), and temporarily wedged access to St. Paul Union Depot for passenger trains over Manitoba.[17]

Demand for passenger service grew as M&StL expanded its domain and as the population increased throughout the growing service area. In 1881, 145,510 passengers boarded M&StL's cars, traveling an average of 34.9 miles and generating $131,335 in revenue. In 1889, however, 510,569 passengers traveled only an average of 25.5 miles and paid $384,029 for the privilege. Mail receipts jumped from $8,902 in 1881 to $42,933 in 1889; the same was true of express receipts, rising from $6,846 in 1881 to $23,418 in 1889. Passenger, mail, and express revenues collectively increased as a percentage of total revenue from 17 to 28 percent, and of course the company's equipment roster had to be expanded accordingly—from ten coaches and six baggage and mail cars in 1881 to eighteen coaches and eleven baggage and mail cars eight years later. Diners and sleepers were operated by Rock Island and Pullman, respectively.[18]

Freight, as always, brought in the greatest revenue. Loadings increased predictably with expanded mileage, with favored linkage to BCR&N and CRI&P, with growing population in the service area, and with Cable's "purchase" of tonnage through rate wars. The number of ton miles jumped from 19 million in 1880 to 110 million in 1886; revenues from freight rose similarly, from $472,785 in 1880 to $1,205,252 in 1886. The percentage of tonnage by commodity shifted according to weather conditions affecting agriculture, demand for building materials, competition, and the economy at large. In 1880 lumber led, with nearly a quarter of all loadings, followed in order by grain, flour, merchandise, and coal. Six years later coal led, with a quarter of all tonnage, followed by lumber, flour, grain, and merchandise. M&StL also hauled significant volumes of cement, brick, and lime; livestock tonnage more than doubled between 1880 and 1886.[19]

Cable's focus on the Twin Cities during the first half of the 1880s, coupled with M&StL's historic position in Minneapolis, was reflected statistically. In 1884 M&StL handled 44,264 loads in and out of Minneapolis, was the clear leader in lumber billed out of the city (40 percent), and led all roads in delivery of coal (140,377 tons). Two years later, M&StL hauled 25,926 cars into Minneapolis (18.6 percent) and stood fourth behind Manitoba, Milwaukee, and Omaha in delivery of wheat, third in tonnage of flour taken from the mills (14.5 percent), second behind Milwaukee in delivery of merchandise (26.0 percent), and first in coal (30.0 percent).[20]

Ransom Cable was president of M&StL from late 1882 until 1888, but early in 1883 he placed a talented and trusted friend in charge of local operations, retaining ultimate control from Chicago. William H. Truesdale, late of employ by Omaha, was the man

Figure 5.1. Heavy tonnage derived from Minneapolis shippers, but M&StL was also very dependent on outlying stations. Here a tiny 4-4-0 is spotting cars or setting out on the house track at Fairfax, Minnesota, an important point on the West End. Author's collection.

chosen as assistant to the president of M&StL. Born at Youngstown, Ohio, on December 1, 1851, Truesdale had moved west with his family to Rock Island, Illinois, where he had received a common school education before gaining employment as a clerk for the Rockford, Rock Island & St. Louis Railroad. Cable had met him there and nurtured his career. Indeed, shortly after arriving in Minneapolis, Truesdale was named vice president.[21]

Competition for business to and from Minneapolis and St. Paul had gotten more intense with each passing year, and that intensity had been greatly accentuated when newcomers—Wisconsin Central, Minnesota & Northwestern (soon to become Chicago Great Western), and Chicago, Burlington & Northern (a CB&Q surrogate)—appeared on the scene. The entire scenario perplexed Rock Island and thoroughly vexed M&StL. The press fully expected and generally predicted that Cable's irritation and frustration would be vented variously. In far-off Boston, the *Transcript* claimed that there was "an abundance of room in the great Northwest for thousands of miles of new railways" and asserted that the owners of Rock Island, through BCR&N and M&StL, "have on foot three extensions in Dakota." Those at the *Commercial & Financial Chronicle* thought similarly, contending that "Rock Island we may rest assured would not fail to use its Minneapolis & St. Louis and Burlington, Cedar Rapids & Northern to advantage." Early in 1886, the *Chicago Tribune* argued that M&StL had acquired right-of-way from Minneapolis to Anoka and shortly would survey a new line to Duluth. At the same time, Rock Island unveiled a new campaign advertising the advantages of Dakota "for young men of active health and brains," who no longer had to "stay in the over-crowded, slow-moving Eastern communities" and compete there with "the accumulated capital of ages." To put its money where its advertising was,

Rock Island announced plans for a thirty-two-mile BCR&N branch to Sioux Falls from that road's line to Watertown, to be completed later in the year. "Rock Island is striking out in all directions," exclaimed a banker close to Manitoba, "and I am well advised have Bismarck in view as one of their objective points, and I believe they will soon be there!"[22]

In 1886 Rock Island promoted the "Favorite Albert Lea Route" with gusto, bragging that "its astonishing success and well earned popularity" were "attributable solely to superior management and the excellence of accommodation provided for transportation of both passengers and freight." Furthermore, said Rock Island, "this combination of different lines" penetrated "the very heart of the agricultural paradise of the Continent," where "the civilization, wealth and culture of American farm life are seen at their best"—"a land like that which gladdened the prophetic vision of Moses, 'flowing with milk and honey.'" Rock Island would continue to advertise the Albert Lea Route and its productive countryside over the next several years, but not again with the same intensity or purpose. "I think the Rock Island has seen its best days," James J. Hill told a member of Manitoba's board during the summer of 1886, "and will not go to Bismarck." Furthermore, Hill speculated, "M&StL was not a financial success for that company whatever it might have been for the individuals" who had acquired M&StL securities—"Flowers, Cable, Brewster and possibly Bishop."[23]

Hill's perception was correct. Cable and Rock Island lost interest accordingly, in fact throwing in the towel on its attempt to reach the Pacific by northwest passage. The reasons likely were several, but two stand out: competition and strategic checkmate. Rivalry for the crucial Chicago–Twin Cities business had been intense after Rock Island cobbled together the Albert Lea Route, but increased maddeningly when Wisconsin Central, Minnesota & Northwestern and Chicago, Burlington & Northern entered the fray. With the long-mile route (532 miles versus 407 for Omaha-C&NW, the shortest) among several options, Rock Island's margins were thinner than others'. In 1886 M&StL was first among carriers delivering coal to Minneapolis, second in merchandise, fourth in wheat; was first in hauling away lumber and third in flour billings; and handled nearly 20 percent of all cars into the city. Two years later the numbers were much less impressive. In 1888 M&StL remained number one in lumber, dropped to third in merchandise, retained fourth place in wheat, dropped to fourth place in coal and third place in merchandise, but plummeted to seventh place in flour and handled a mere 8.7 percent of all inbound cars. (The car count also was down precipitously, from 25,926 in 1886 to only 14,526 in 1888). Drawing business away from M&StL were Omaha and St. Paul & Duluth, which handled greater consignments of waterborne coal from Duluth, and newcomers Soo Line and Chicago, Burlington & Northern, both of which cut rates to gain premier status as flour carriers. Indeed, M&StL would carry a tiny 2.2 percent of Minneapolis flour when the decade ended.[24]

Rock Island also lost out in the strategic race, with M&StL checkmated at Minneapolis and M&StL and BCR&N together halted at the lonely Watertown outpost, while Wisconsin, Minnesota & Pacific crawled westward from Waterville only a few miles to Eagle Lake, although the company puffed that it shortly would move on to Mankato and New Ulm, the prospective destination of M&StL's Pacific Division at Gaylord, already on the scrap heap. Cable had failed to move quickly in 1882 and 1883, had moved inadequately in 1884 and not at all in 1885, and by 1886 Rock Island's options in the entire region were tightly circumscribed. Beyond Watertown, C&NW drove a line northward through Aberdeen to meet a Northern Pacific branch from Jamestown to Oakes, Manitoba was infesting much of Dakota Territory, with lines to towns including Watertown and Aberdeen, and the Washburn Road sealed other options.[25]

Cable always strongly preferred expansion through acquisition or control of established roads such as BCR&N and M&StL, and in 1887 he used that technique to gather in Des Moines & Fort Dodge, with which M&StL connected at Fort Dodge and Angus, and used that acquisition to gain access for M&StL to Des Moines. Small potatoes. Although Rock Island earlier had explored merger with C&NW, Burlington, and more recently NP, nothing came from these high-stakes adventures, and smaller candidates were few and reluctant. Meanwhile, Burlington had reached Denver and was known to be considering further expansion to Salt Lake, perhaps beyond. C&NW already had several hundred miles of line west of the Missouri River and was known to have even more expansion in mind. By 1888 Milwaukee rail would touch the Missouri River at three locations—Chamberlain, Council Bluffs, and Kansas City. Even Illinois Central (IC) was a player at Sioux City, and by now Sioux Falls; rumor had it that IC soon would extend to the Black Hills. Others had stolen the march on Rock Island.[26]

Cable saw no choice but to expand Rock Island—through construction. Burlington's Charles Perkins had anticipated as much in 1883, and was pleased when Cable became preoccupied with the Albert Lea Route, because then he would "be less likely to break out elsewhere, and the Rock Island must break out somewhere." And break out it did, in 1888, with a breathtaking program that took CRI&P from the Missouri River at St. Joseph, Missouri, to Colorado Springs and, through trackage rights to Denver, to far southwestern Kansas at Liberal, to El Reno in 1888–89, and on to Fort Worth in 1893. Rock Island would never make good on the *Pacific* in its corporate namesake, but early in the next century it would link up with Southern Pacific to create the Golden State Route, and it would also extend all the way southward to Houston. Nevertheless, in the "march of the Four Armies," as *Railway Age* once phrased it, Rock Island proved the weakest and least able compared to C&NW, Milwaukee, and Burlington.[27]

Truesdale's morale must have sunk as he saw Rock Island's interest in the Albert Lea Route slacken. There were other problems. Indeed, one matter that Truesdale and virtually all other railroad managers brooded about was government regulation, public support for which had ebbed and flowed for nearly three decades, but in the late 1880s flowed with a vengeance. Farmers and businessmen in rural areas complained often about rail rates, but tariffs actually had gone down, drastically and demonstratively, the result of competition and other factors. Facts aside, many Americans had come to fear and despise railroads as giant corporations, seeing in them a perversion of private enterprise embodying liberty, freedom, and individualism. Critics also saw railroad leaders as flaunting their riches and selfishly increasing their own private power and fortune. They further equated the practice of basing rates on "all that traffic will bear" with outright gouging.[28]

The debate heightened. In 1885 Minnesota replaced its office of a railroad commissioner with a three-member Railroad and Warehouse Commission, two years later adding greatly to that body's power by giving it rate-making authority. Iowa was no less vigorous. "The transportation of the products of a great agricultural state like Iowa is of too great importance to her people and their general prosperity to be left unregulated," said that state's railroad commission in 1878. Nine years later Iowa, like its Minnesota neighbor, strengthened the commission, authorizing it to hold investigations, to file suits, and to declare against special rates or privileges as well as pooling. The Iowa regulatory agency also undertook to determine the value of each road in the state, that is, the aggregate of all capital put into individual companies. M&StL and all others had yet another headache; on April 5, 1887, the Interstate Commerce Commission Act took effect, placing the federal government squarely in the regulatory arena. Its consequences could only be guessed at.[29]

By coincidence, the great Dakota boom came to an end just as federal regulation of the rails began. Several factors converged, among them an economic contraction that began late in 1886, the virtual disappearance of free land, trouble between the federal government and various tribes of Indians, slowed railroad construction in the area, and devastating drought that dragged into the next decade. The hardest-hit areas in what soon would become South Dakota were west of Watertown, between the James and Missouri Rivers; if Ransom Cable had any lingering ideas of expanding to the northwest, they were quashed by increasingly dreary reports from that region.[30]

William H. Truesdale, now M&StL's president, must have slumped deeply in his chair at the company's thinly appointed offices in the Boston Block of Minneapolis at Hennepin Avenue and Third Street. There was simply no good news as 1887 ended; nor did the new year promise relief. Heavy snows early in

1888 added substantial costs to operations. In March the line west was plugged for ten days before a plow accompanied by one hundred shovelers broke through from Gaylord to Winthrop; spring floods would follow in April. By comparison to news brought to him from the treasurer's office, that news was good. Even before Christmas 1887, the hearty, bluff Truesdale had been forced to tell Cable that M&StL could not pay interest on bonds due in January. It was an awful humiliation, and the usually unflappable and judicious Truesdale took out his frustration on the Minnesota railroad commissioners, whom he accused of ruining "the business of this railroad." The state's regulatory authority was increasingly cavalier and worthy of scorn, it was true, but Truesdale's blast was off the mark in explaining M&StL's embarrassment. In addition to regulatory woes, M&StL suffered greatly from an inadequate route structure, from intense competition not only in Minneapolis but at many locations (Chaska and Waseca, for example) where traffic could be bled off by one of the stronger roads (short hauling M&StL in the process), from inability to meet low rates on critical tonnage during most of 1887, from absentee principal owners no longer vigorous in their support, and even from Mother Nature, it seemed.[31]

On May 26, 1888, the large, handsome Truesdale straightened his back, drew in a deep breath, gritted his teeth, and bluntly told M&StL bondholders that during the first five months of the year "net earnings fell short of the interest on the company's bonded indebtedness." Monies due on June 1 could not be paid out of earnings; M&StL's board declined to borrow for that purpose. Shortly thereafter a demand for payment was made by certain holders; the road demurred, foreclosure followed, M&StL fled to protection of the courts, and Truesdale was named receiver.[32]

Chapter 6
INDEPENDENT AGAIN

Sale of Minneapolis & St. Louis must be regarded as a good thing for this city and the Northwest, as it indicates that the road will remain independent and a competitive factor in transportation.
—*MINNEAPOLIS TRIBUNE,* OCTOBER 12, 1894

WILLIAM HAYNES TRUESDALE WAS ONE OF THE most able managers Minneapolis & St. Louis ever had. Bright, sagacious, and a born leader, Truesdale was well on his way to a distinguished career in the railroad industry. But at M&StL his considerable talent was constantly under test. No longer the local favorite in its home city, merely a part of the "Great Rock Island Route," M&StL was rather viewed as just another of the oft-despised Chicago roads. Moreover, its principal owners were distant and distracted. Truesdale and M&StL usually had to fend for themselves. Growing government regulation was a constant vexation, as were periodic rate wars in which M&StL was the universal loser; if it went with the crowd, it lost money on traffic gained or retained, and if it did not go along, traffic assuredly went elsewhere. At particular risk was M&StL's powerful position in the Minneapolis milling district, where stronger roads increased pressure and from which location the lumber industry was making a precipitous exit. Erosion of lucrative traffic volumes from that rich base meant that M&StL would have to make up the difference elsewhere. But how? Expansion of lines was doubtful in the extreme, and the company's circumscribed service area was essentially settled and already subject to harsh competitive attack by larger roads. Finally, there was the awful embarrassment of receivership and the constant cloud of ambiguity accompanying that painful circumstance.

Truesdale was acutely perplexed by the "extremely slow and tedious" nature of "foreclosure proceedings." He thought it a pity that "the different interests" had not been able to find an amicable reorganization strategy. Meanwhile, he seethed, business was lost "for want of passenger cars and boxcars" and "certain other facilities"—a circumstance, Truesdale noted acidly, "most discouraging to the entire official staff of the road." As long as the affairs of the company were administered by the court, or until its finances "were arranged or adjusted on some permanent basis . . . all interests" were bound to suffer, concluded the dejected receiver in 1890.[1]

Some of Truesdale's irritation may have been reserved for Ramsom Cable's attention to Chicago, Rock Island & Pacific interests elsewhere, although he said nothing in that regard for public consumption. For his part, the vigorously frank Cable indeed was preoccupied with integrating and prospering Rock Island's new lines west and southwest of the Missouri River, paid scant attention to M&StL, and plainly had given up on a "northwest passage." To be fair, however, the "Albert Lea Route" was still advertised as a fully coordinated effort by Rock island in combination with Burlington, Cedar Rapids & Northern and M&StL; M&StL and

BCR&N shared facilities at Watertown, Minnesota; and, a BCR&N branch in Iowa northward from Dows used M&StL trackage for a few miles into Forest City. Early in 1890, furthermore, a trainload of Rock Island passenger agents making a systemwide swing arrived in Minneapolis from Watertown on M&StL, gaily toured that city and St. Paul, then departed for Chicago via Albert Lea, Minnesota. And a few months later Cable himself brought Rock Island's entire board of directors and other prominent shareholders on a trip from Chicago to Minneapolis over M&StL that returned by way of Des Moines.[2]

Haulage of lumber remained an essential component of M&StL's traffic mix, but always it was subject to competitive attack and machinations of government rate makers. The road's curiously configured route structure actually favored the movement of lumber out of Minneapolis at a time when the market for Minnesota white pine was shifting south and west as Michigan's supply diminished. M&StL proved favorably located to serve the needs of Iowa and, by connections, those of Nebraska and Kansas as well. The road also profited from new marketing techniques reflected in "line yards"—several retail lumber yards at individual stations operating under common ownership and management. As Minneapolis became "lumber emporium of the Northwest," it also became headquarters for millers and for many line yard companies. On M&StL, C. A. Smith Lumber and J. N. Queal Company were pioneers—the latter, for instance, with yards on the Watertown line at Hanley Falls, Clarkfield, Dawson, and Madison. It was to these locations and others that M&StL wheeled car after car of lumber spewing from the Minneapolis mills. Indeed, it hauled more lumber out of Minneapolis in the years 1888, 1890, and 1891 than any other carrier, despite the fact that by now the mills were "off line" in the northern part of the city.[3]

The story of flour and wheat volume became less satisfactory as M&StL's relative position among Twin Cities' carriers floated downward even as the prominence of Minneapolis as a great wheat exchange and flour milling center went up. In 1888 M&StL delivered 4.9 percent of the wheat received in Minneapolis, but during one particular week of the year the percentage of flour billed out on M&StL was a minuscule 0.5. The reasons for M&StL's awful slippage from premier status were many and included the continuous shift of the wheat culture to the northwest and away from its lines, loss of support from the Washburn interests, ruinous rate wars brought on for the most part by new contenders, by rail-water movement of export flour via Duluth and East Coast ports by more favorable routes, and by Rock Island's preoccupation with other interests. M&StL remained a bit player even in 1891, when a bumper harvest of fifty-eight million bushels required the court to grant Truesdale's request for two hundred new boxcars to help move wheat to the hungry mills. Truesdale, however, saw no reason to throw in the towel. M&StL retained extremely valuable access and egress in the west bank milling district, Minnesota stood first in the production of wheat, nearly 90 percent of the milling capacity at St. Anthony Falls now was held by only four companies (Pillsbury and Washburn-Crosby the top two), and the decade of the 1890s would prove profitable for millers who would respond by doubling capacity.[4]

In order to protect and enhance its valuable properties in the milling district, M&StL had seen to incorporation of the Railway Transfer Company of the City of Minneapolis (Railway Transfer), a wholly owned subsidiary, on March 31, 1883. Railway Transfer was authorized to buy, lease, construct, and operate a system of transfer tracks "between the different lines of railroad and the mills and factories within Minneapolis." To this end, M&StL leased Railway Transfer up to twenty-five tracks with four leads, including two main tracks—about twelve track miles in all. Locomotives leased from M&StL performed switching duties, and M&StL and Northern Pacific used the main tracks as part of their joint operation between Minneapolis and St. Paul.[5]

M&StL had little capital for improvements, and in any event all expenditures were overseen by the court. Truesdale was not parsimonious, just cautious. A new freighthouse in Minneapolis at Third Street and Fourth Avenue and a new passenger station at Washington Avenue were followed by a modest overflow freight yard at nearby Kenwood. Truesdale also obtained permission from the court to replace the wooden machine shop at Cedar Lake—"a dangerous fire trap"—with "a substantial building of stone, brick, and iron." In addition, the physical plant of the road was enhanced with strengthened bridges, ballast, and more telegraph capacity. And, to alleviate congestion, to serve a growing body of local shippers, and to upgrade commuter operations to and from Lake Minnetonka, the receiver gained permission to double track five miles between Kenwood and Hopkins, a task completed in July 1892. To clear those and other tracks following winter storms, in 1889 the road also acquired a fine rotary snow plow, which, Truesdale predicted, would "save the cost of the plow several times over in a winter such as we are likely to have in any year." Finally, late in 1890 M&StL moved its headquarters to the Guaranty Loan Building, taking the entire eleventh floor. Offices there, said one newspaper, were "tastefully furnished in oak," that is, spartan.[6]

Much of M&StL's available capital was expended in and about Minneapolis, seat of its management and clearly the most important single location in terms of production of tonnage and revenue from local customers and connections. By 1890 the city claimed 164,738 residents—ahead of St. Paul, with a population of 133,156. Minneapolis had become the country's largest primary wheat market; it still produced monumental stacks of milled lumber, and was increasingly important in the production of linseed oil, farm machinery, and other manufactured goods. St. Paul, by comparison, was the state capital, the center of transportation, an established manufacturing city, and a vastly important jobbing center. Small wonder that M&StL—and through it Rock Island—had wanted a presence there. In 1888 an average of 221 trains moved in and out of St. Paul Union Depot and the city received 158,892 carloads of freight while dispatching 92,006 cars. M&StL admittedly stood last among ten roads serving the city in terms of carloads handled, but Truesdale and Rock Island's Ransom Cable both recognized that the need was there.[7]

M&StL's managers recognized the danger in being too tightly wedded to the Twin Cities, however, and increasingly looked to the country tributary to its lines to supply a larger portion of resources. M&StL's three-state service area—aside from Minneapolis and St. Paul—remained much as it had been: rural and agricultural. For example, Iowa's population had swelled to 1.9 million by 1890, but Des Moines, its capital, claimed only 50,093 of those residents. Iowa's railroads reflected as much, with grain making up 20 percent of all tonnage and merchandise a tiny 6 percent in 1890. Three years later, M&StL's system percentages for grain and merchandise were 22 and 6.5; for neighboring Chicago Great Western they were 28.8 and 8.9, and for Milwaukee Road 22.5 and 9.0. For the "Granger Roads," as Midwestern carriers came to be called, changing the numbers in any appreciable way was problematic. During the crop year M&StL station agents were made to submit regular reports as to local conditions regarding wheat, corn, oats, flax, barley, rye, potatoes, and hay. Reports of blight, rust, hot winds, heavy rains, and early frost drew frowns, just as news of positive growing conditions and bumper crops brought smiles. As early as 1890, Truesdale told stockholders, "Only in the development and up-building of its local traffic can this road . . . hope to earn even a moderate return upon the capital invested in it." He would "encourage by all reasonable means the establishment of local industry"—mills, creameries, brick yards, grain elevators, and the like. These might be as remote from Minneapolis as Delhi, Minnesota, or Dayton, Iowa, but they could be as close as St. Louis Park, established in 1886 as a railroad suburb and named after "the St. Louis Road," as M&StL often was called. Such local development certainly was the case for Hopkins, where several industries and supply houses flourished by the 1890s. Among them was Minneapolis Threshing Machine, predecessor of Minneapolis-Moline.[8]

But M&StL, for better or for ill, was tied irrevocably to agriculture, celebrating, as in 1891, when good crops and high markets allowed farmers to pay off debts and make improvements, "erecting new houses, barns, fences, etc." and "adding machinery, blooded stock and articles of consumption . . . never equaled before in a like period." Moreover, said M&StL management to company owners, "The country through which this road passes is showered with all of Nature's blessings . . . good soil, water, and diversified crops," with a "population that is thrifty and takes advantage of natural conditions." Puffy rhetoric, yes, but not far from the mark in describing M&StL's rich and productive domain—a domain worth expanding, if possible, one clearly coveted by others, and one well worth protecting.[9]

As always, there were rumors composed of mere wind, but also there were rumors predicated on substance. One frightening but fortunately stillborn project was the Minneapolis, St. Paul & Southwestern, a paper road, which would have paralleled M&StL, as well as A. B. Stickney's very real Chicago Great Western. Another road that was partially completed and eventually fell into Stickney's orbit was Winona & Southwestern, which promised a diagonal route between Winona, Minnesota, and Omaha, Nebraska. From the west came rumblings of lines within South Dakota from Sioux Falls to Watertown, Sioux Falls to Pierre, and Watertown to Aberdeen. To the south, Stickney remained on Iowa Central's board, and rumors continued to link that property with him, but Iowa Central instead formed a close traffic alliance with Chicago, Milwaukee & St. Paul, which provided through passenger and freight service between Minneapolis–St. Paul and Kansas City, if by a circuitous route. Closer to home, a St. Louis Park syndicate dreamed unsuccessfully of a "belt line" to serve that community, and in 1889 Congressman John Lind of New Ulm, Minnesota, urged linkage of that community with M&StL at Winthrop, not quite twenty miles north.[10]

M&StL's interest in traffic via Duluth, Minnesota, historic but nearly moribund during the mid-1880s, rekindled as M&StL and St. Paul & Duluth together attempted to blunt the growing influence of James J. Hill throughout the region and to drain off some of Omaha's impressive lake business via Duluth or Washburn, Wisconsin. At stake were prodigious volumes of coal, cement, and merchandise inbound; grain, flour, and lumber outbound. In 1888 M&StL agreed to provide StP&D terminal facilities in Minneapolis (Lower Yard) on an annual rental basis, giving M&StL much-needed cash and a friendly connection northward once more. For the years 1890–94, M&StL stood either first or second among several carriers interchanging freight with StP&D.[11]

There was, of course, a constant swirl of activity involving the larger roads—all of it, fact and rumor alike, reported in newspapers. One bit of quite correct information that the press did not pick up on was Hill's quiet attempt in 1888 and 1889 to acquire M&StL. Just as the road headed into the dungeon of receivership, Hill wrote to banker John S. Kennedy in New York, saying: "I think we can probably make some arrangement that will give us control of the reorganization of the company without the necessity on our part of paying out much money." Hill was particularly covetous of M&StL's Minneapolis properties, observing that "next to our own they are the largest and most valuable in that city." Indeed, said Hill, M&StL "is almost invaluable to us as it would give us permanent control of all the valuable terminals in Minneapolis except those of the" Milwaukee Road. To those ends, Hill ordered the company treasurer to begin buying M&StL debt and equity "to be covered up in the account of 'Bills Receivable,'" in a way that would not allow "anyone examining the books to know what it was." Truesdale learned early to be wary of the wily Hill; he had ample reason.[12]

Handsome, capable, and well liked, Truesdale had been the unanimous choice of creditors to manage their affairs, and he discharged his receiver's duties with skill. "None of the diverse interests have made any complaint regarding his management policy," observed one Minneapolis newspaper in 1891. But he was forty years of age that season and was predictably anxious to have broader opportunity, and he reportedly entertained several "brilliant offers made by Eastern roads." He did resign his position with M&StL in June of 1891 amid a swirl of reports as to a new appointment elsewhere. Local speculation centered on consolidation of M&StL and BCR&N with Rock Island and hinted that with that accomplished, Truesdale would replace R. R. Cable as president of Chicago, Rock Island & Pacific. Another story had Hill dangling a position at Great Northern. In the end, however, Truesdale stayed on, likely at Cable's request, and vowed to remain until M&StL was out of receivership.[13]

But the man of "exceptional ability," as the *Minneapolis Tribune* called him, must have been antsy.

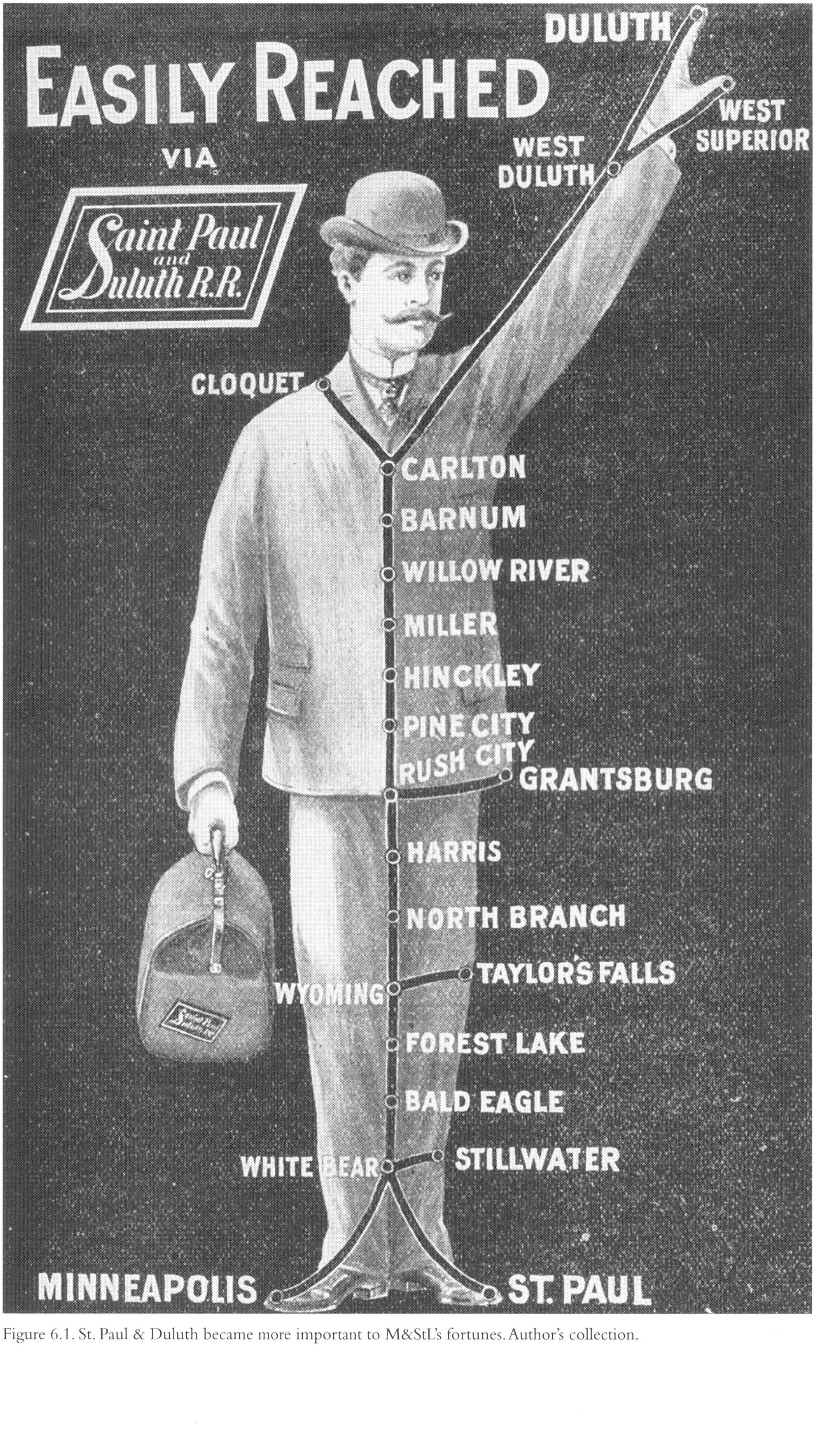

Figure 6.1. St. Paul & Duluth became more important to M&StL's fortunes. Author's collection.

M&StL had to expand. But where? And how? Geographically, options were few—farther into Iowa or, in what by now had become the state of South Dakota, beyond Watertown. Yet there is no evidence that Truesdale made efforts to push beyond Angus to Des Moines, to Council Bluffs, or anywhere else in the Hawkeye State. And, while Watertown presented itself as a "marvelous city" and railroad hub (for M&StL, BCR&N, Chicago & North Western, and Great Northern), the bloom was off the "great Dakota boom." A terrible drought set in during 1889–90, and many persons were in dire want; the governor of the state frankly admitted that some were absolutely destitute and threatened by starvation. Irrespective of conditions in Dakota, and despite any allure in Iowa, Truesdale would have had to overcome opposition from the court and from the several constituencies represented in the receivership action.[14]

In any event, dreams of broadening M&StL's reach in any way were dashed irrevocably by the onset of the terrible panic of 1893. The national economy had been vibrant in the late 1880s, and in April 1891 *Bradstreet's* had reported that Wall Street was "in a fairly healthy condition." But the economy softened during the summer of 1891, and international investors increasingly shied away from American securities, especially railroads. This plus growing political hostility toward the industry at large slowed expansion of the national network in 1891 and 1892. Developments moved in train. Demand for pig iron eroded, residential construction slumped, immigration dropped, weak and overextended banks stumbled, financial failures increased, and the stock market plunged. In 1893 alone, owners of one-sixth of American rail mileage entered bankruptcy. Additional misery followed in 1894, with massive strikes in the soft coal and railroad industries and crop failures in many parts of the country. Those unemployed numbered in the thousands and often were unrooted; tramps commandeered trains with regularity. The number of freight ton miles bottomed out in January 1894, but recovery would prove halting and awkward.[15]

"There is no competition so mischievous as that of a bankrupt road with no dividends or coupons to pay," J. M. Forbes of Chicago, Burlington & Quincy had groused in 1879. However accurate Forbes's assessment in general, it did not apply to M&StL, which never had the muscle itself or the impetus from Rock Island to do more than maintain stability during its long season of receivership. M&StL was not "ruined" by overzealous state regulation, as Truesdale had once shrilly complained (although well-intentioned but wrongheaded regulation hardly helped), nor was it grossly overcapitalized, poorly managed, or badly maintained. It simply generated too little compensatory traffic in a highly competitive region; its margins were predictably thin.[16]

Reorganization rocked along at a painfully slow pace. "But little progress seems yet to have been made in adjusting the affairs of the road by means of an amicable reorganization," Truesdale sorrowfully complained in 1891. The next year brought increased revenues, and the receiver rejoiced in M&StL's "handsome showing," which, he thought, would "serve to restore confidence in its value, and create a belief that it has a future of much promise." Truesdale also pointed proudly to betterments of the road's property and to effective management that kept train mile expenses low while driving up gross revenues—that is, producing more net profits from its operations. In a difficult 1893, however, the road produced only modest net profits, but with all line segments except the Fort Dodge–Kalo line "in the black." Indeed, despite serious rumblings of depression, Truesdale found money adequate for the court to approve paying out interest on several issues of bonds, and at the end of the year the road was free of floating debt.[17]

Finally there was movement. In 1892 Frederic C. Olcott, president of Central Trust Company, had taken the lead in establishment of a stockholder protection committee that included him and four other prominent New Yorkers—William A. Read, August Belmont, William L. Bull, and J. Kennedy Tod. This was agreeable with Rock Island interests until the redoubtable H. H. Porter, long associated with CRI&P's Ransom Cable in various ventures and a principal M&StL bondholder, broke ranks, "completely disconcerting the present management of the Minneapolis & St. Louis Railway as well as the plans of the Rock Island Company," according to the *New York Times.*

This development clearly threatened to derail Rock Island's purposes in M&StL and led to a predictable if curious reaction near at hand. Olcott and Central Trust were close to Hill and Great Northern, and rumors quickly flew again that Hill would find a way to grab M&StL—something, incidentally, that Northern Pacific's senior management privately believed was imminent. "I beg to say that neither our company, nor anybody connected with it, that I know of, has any interest in the Minneapolis & St. Louis," Hill told Truesdale when challenged on the matter. That was hardly the case. In any event, change was afoot. In October 1892, Read, Belmont, Bull, Tod, and another but rather more obscure New Yorker, Edwin Hawley, replaced a like number of Minneapolitans on M&StL's board. The change was not cosmetic. Rock Island maps presently showed M&StL as a friendly connection, not as an integral part of CRI&P as it had been in the past, although Wisconsin, Minnesota & Pacific's Red Wing–Mankato and Morton–Watertown line segments continued to be shown as part of (if disconnected from) the Rock Island system. Wall Street insiders still believed, however, that Rock Island expected "to buy the Minneapolis & St. Louis Road at forced sale for a low figure," which, most likely, had been Rock Island's intent from the beginning. That seemed to be the case in May 1893, when the press reported a successful reorganization of M&StL, with Truesdale made president. Truesdale himself confirmed the story, adding that M&StL was very valuable and "well worth fighting for." But there was no reorganization in 1893, probably "owing to the severe and widespread financial and business depression existing throughout the country," as Truesdale put it.[18]

On June 6, 1894, Rock Island held its annual meeting in Chicago, where William H. Truesdale was named third vice president of the company. Reorganization of M&StL was at hand, and Rock Island was confident of the outcome because that road and its friends—including Porter, who meanwhile had been mollified—owned a substantial chunk of M&StL bonds, and bondholders, not stockholders, usually came out ahead in such proceedings. Truesdale could at once be a senior manager at Rock Island and head of M&StL. But it did not work out that way. Henry Siebert, on behalf of CRI&P, had rolled the dice in 1888 with the view of forcing M&StL fully into Rock Island's web. But the dice failed Siebert and Rock Island. Stockholders and the New York syndicate composed of August Belmont & Co., J. Kennedy Tod & Co., and Vermlye & Co. that had grown out of Olcott's protective creation, levered itself into ultimate control, and Rock Island, not the power it had been less than a decade before, came up short. When the sheriff's sale was held in Minneapolis on October 11, 1894, Ransom Cable and William Truesdale were on hand to represent CRI&P, as was C. J. Ives on behalf of BCR&N, but they were there only to ensure that the sale would bring in enough to pay the bonds held by their respective roads, not to make competing bids. In the end, \$5.01 million was adequate to win the property.[19]

The new Minneapolis & St. Louis *Railroad* assumed the rights and properties of the Minneapolis & St. Louis *Railway* of Minnesota and Iowa, itself an amalgamation in 1881 of Minneapolis & St. Louis, Minneapolis & Iowa Southern, Minneapolis & Duluth, and Fort Dodge & Fort Ridgely. Shareholders of the old Minneapolis & St. Louis *Railway* paid a \$25 assessment per share and received in exchange one share of common stock and one share of second preferred stock; for every \$100 in assessment paid, they also received one additional share of first preferred stock. The new company also issued consolidated bonds to cover payment of \$4.7 million on all earlier bonds. In the process, M&StL's debt per mile moved up slightly, stock per mile up substantially, with debt and equity combined totaling \$58,418 per mile by the end of 1894. (BCR&N, by comparison, had debt and equity of a mere \$21,288 at the same time.) Officers of the new company included William L. Bull, president; Edwin Hawley, vice president; Richard B. Harshorne, treasurer; Joseph Gaskell, secretary; William Strauss, general counsel; and A. L. Mohler, general manager. Gaskell and Mohler, the latter recently arrived from Great Northern, were holdovers and the only officers from Minneapolis; the rest were New Yorkers, as was the entire board of directors. Gone was Truesdale, who went to Rock Island and then to Delaware, Lackawanna & Western, where he finished his distinguished career.[20]

The *Minneapolis Tribune,* which long had followed M&StL's fortunes, thought sale to New Yorkers "must be regarded as a good thing for this city and the Northwest, as it indicates that the road will remain independent and a competitive factor in transportation." The *Tribune* also noted with satisfaction that the new owners had said the road was purchased "as an investment and not for speculation," and that "the same friendly relations would exist between the road and the Chicago, Rock Island & Pacific." Curiously, the *Tribune* said nothing of the categoric absence of Minneapolis influence from the board. Even William Drew Washburn had been vanquished, ending a tenure begun in 1870. Clearly M&StL had passed over the threshold into a new era.[21]

But what did that era hold for the company? What were the true intentions of the new owners? Ransom Cable and those of Rock Island persuasion might pay lip service to "friendly relations," but losing Minneapolis and St. Paul as endpoints in the highly competitive domain of the Chicago roads clearly disadvantaged CRI&P against Burlington, Milwaukee, and North Western. The loss must have smarted. How would Rock Island finally respond? Furthermore, railroad systems were either growing through or disappearing by consolidation. By the 1890s the greatest systems were the largest enterprises not only in this country but in the world. Among the giants, where did M&StL fit in?[22]

For persons living in the Minneapolis & St. Louis service area during the mid-1890s there was nervousness as to the purposes and intentions of the road's new owners and management. Every member of the directorate was from New York, as was William L. Bull, president, and Edwin Hawley, vice president. Albert L. Moehler, already a seasoned and respected railroader and destined to be president of Union Pacific some years later, remained as general manager; Joseph Gaskell of Minneapolis, secretary and treasurer since 1883, and William Crooks, chief engineer and long associated with Minnesota railroads, each provided links to the past and a sense of continuity. Yet concerns were understandable. Union Pacific's Charles F. Adams Jr. complained that William Bull was part of "a Wall Street gang," and indeed Bull and Hawley—like fellow directors W. A. Read, J. Kennedy Tod, and August Belmont—were New York bankers or financiers. On the other hand, Bull and Belmont were involved in Northern Pacific matters and served on that company's board of directors; they had at least some knowledge of the area.[23]

Bull's first report to M&StL stockholders in 1895 was upbeat. The company was "without any floating debt whatever" and had $276,360 cash in the treasury. William Crooks pledged that the property was in good order, and the master mechanic promised that the motive power fleet was in excellent condition. Five thousand tons of steel rail were on order, and a new roundhouse at Cedar Lake had been authorized. Bull was especially enthusiastic over the potential of M&StL's service territory and the industry of its people. His optimism was the more notable given the continuing trauma attending the panic of 1893.[24]

All factors considered, M&StL really was in pretty good shape. But where was it going? What was its destiny? Bull offered no hints, and the past gave little clue. The road had been independent earlier, then tied to Northern Pacific, then independent again before linkage to Rock Island. Now again it stood alone—and was in the hands of distant persons whose motives were unknown.

There was no gainsaying the importance of agriculture to M&StL's fortunes. Indeed, much of Minnesota's soil, especially in the southern third of the state and in the west, proved marvelously productive for tillers of the soil. And many of those same farmers were embracing crop rotation and diversification of crops as means to avoid soil exhaustion and dependence on a single commodity. Of course, Minnesota remained the country's leading producer of wheat, but increasingly farmers were turning to oats, corn, hay, barley, rye, flax, potatoes, and alfalfa. The latter crop, pioneered along M&StL near Carver and Excelsior, reflected another dimension of the "new agriculture," dairying, with attendant establishment of creameries. Yet another shift to diversification was reflected in livestock numbers—cattle, sheep, and especially hogs—which in turn resulted in the establishment of St. Paul Union Stockyards in 1887, which attracted Swift & Company, a major meat packer that opened a nearby facility a decade later.[25]

Similar changes came more slowly to South Dakota, which still shuddered in the wake of the panic and the collapse of the great boom of the 1880s, but came even earlier to Iowa. In general terms, the movement of the wheat culture and then the rise of the corn-hog culture, plus the rotation of diversified crops including oats, barley, rye, flax, and hay, moved through Iowa on an angle from southeast to northwest, suggesting even earlier changes in neighboring Illinois. Iowa had ranked second in wheat production at the end of the 1860s, but was not among the top six by the end of the century; it was, however, number one or two (alternating with Illinois) in production of corn during the last forty years of the nineteenth century. Moreover, Iowa farmers fed more beef cattle than those in any other state save Texas, and in 1899 Iowa claimed more dairy cattle than any other state. It also led in butter production, with creameries located in ninety-seven of ninety-nine counties. Iowa's industrial establishment was predictably tied to agriculture, a fact mirrored by growing meat packing centers at Sioux City, Ottumwa, Cedar Rapids, Waterloo, Fort Dodge, and Mason City, as well as in nearby Omaha, Sioux Falls, and Austin and Albert Lea.[26]

Such patterns were reflected in M&StL's traffic volumes and in its mix. For the decade of the 1890s, revenue tonnage averaged 1,178,223 per annum, and among commodities lumber and grain alternated in the highest two positions throughout. Coal slumped badly after 1886, as did flour, but tonnage in all commodity groups was higher in 1899 than in 1890. The number of ton miles more than doubled, from 77,087,412 in 1890 to 156,379,613 in 1899, and freight revenues rose from $1,101,910 to $1,860,257. All of this was especially impressive given the panic of 1893 and that M&StL's route miles during the decade increased only marginally.[27]

One great disappointment, however, was the sharp decline in locally mined coal. M&StL's Iowa extension had been predicated, in part, on bringing a large and regular tonnage of coal to fuel-starved Minnesota. With ample justification, for nearly one-fifth of Iowa was underlain with coal of commercial value—"wonderful carboniferous treasurers," as one booster had styled it—and, in fact, from 1880 to 1930 coal mining ranked only behind agriculture as the state's major industry. Although Iowa's coal was of at least average value, its beds were of irregular thickness and slope and were neither continuous nor contiguous. When one of those disconnected basins tailed out to a thickness that would no longer permit economic production, the mine shut down. That was the case for some, and then most, of the mines served by M&StL in Webster County south of Fort Dodge. Craig Coal and Standard Coal opened several mines at or near Kalo during the 1880s, to the great delight of M&StL management, which rejoiced at the prospect of significant northbound tonnage. But production petered out as the veins narrowed, and, for that matter, some shipments were hardly compensatory, moving only to Fort Dodge, just a few miles distant. Better reserves lay across the Des Moines River from Kalo at Coalville, but these were tapped by rivals Illinois Central and Chicago Great Western. Webster County's production peaked at 249,100 tons in 1893, but held steady at about 135,398 tons per year during that decade.[28]

The mines farther south held greater potential, but they did not prove inexhaustible either. For a while, though, Angus was an extremely important coal camp, a hub of activity for the Iowa mines scattered nearby in Boone, Greene, and Dallas Counties. Perhaps three thousand persons—two thousand of them miners working for Climax, Eagle, or any of several other companies—called Angus home at its apex. James J. Hill and associates were early and important players in this region, with substantial coal-bearing lands and Climax Coal Company as well. In 1883, however, C. H. Pettit of Minneapolis, representing several personalities who at that time controlled M&StL, had sought to acquire these several properties and threatened to establish new mining operations in competition. Hill's group responded instead by selling their assets to St. Paul, Minneapolis & Manitoba, in which they were principals, to supply locomotive fuel. That arrangement lasted only briefly. When the Washburn crowd sold its M&StL holdings to Rock Island interests, R. R. Cable increased the rates from Angus to Minneapolis, and Hill quickly determined to secure Manitoba's coal elsewhere. It was an ugly omen.[29]

Meanwhile, Angus boomed. Switch engines

prowled to spot empties, pick up loads, and make up trains. The roundhouse, servicing power for M&StL and Des Moines & Fort Dodge alike, was always busy. So were the saloons—perhaps eighteen of them on "whiskey row," where booze was dispensed to miners, who seemed to live by a simple code: live hard, drink hard, and die hard. When Methodists put up a church and installed a preacher whose views on alcoholic consumption were contrary to their own, miners set the place afire, torching the nearby jail for good measure. After that hilarity, however, matters went downhill. When a strike broke out in 1884, strikebreakers were imported from Minneapolis over M&StL; a riot ensued, and the militia was summoned from Des Moines to restore order. Angus was never the same. Moreover, the coal field was being depleted. Climax shut down early in 1886; Eagle and Standard followed in 1887, with Keystone ending production in 1889. Smaller operators persisted, though, and a new mine was opened at the northeast edge of nearby Rippey in 1888. Production at Angus temporarily spurted in 1892, and mining persisted at Angus and Rippey into the next century. But the bloom was off. The Angus Exchange Bank failed in 1893, and two years later the town's population was down to 493. Abandoned lots were sold for taxes and reverted to farmland.[30]

M&StL's tonnage in coal ebbed and flowed according to production at Kalo, Otho, Berkeley, and Angus, but also according to the demand for fuel for its own locomotives and the length and depth of winter in its service area. The annual average volume ran about 92,000 tons during the 1890s, much of it loaded online. Nevertheless, stockholders were told bluntly that the mines served by M&StL were inadequate to meet demand. M&StL did receive considerable coal loaded at stations on Burlington, Cedar Rapids & Northern, as well as lake coal moved from Duluth by St. Paul & Duluth.[31]

Passenger business followed a very bumpy path during the 1890s; it was jostled and bruised by the panic of 1893 as well as by crushing competition from larger roads, but trended upward. Boardings improved by only 8 percent, from 500,449 in 1890 to 657,077 in 1899, but passenger miles nearly doubled to reflect longer average hauls (37.9 miles). Revenues from all sources—tickets, mail, and express—rose from $375,328 to $547,574 during the same period—a marvelous increase of 63 percent.[32]

While not as important as freight in generating revenue, passenger operations nevertheless contributed a full 40 percent of all receipts in 1888 (by comparison, the figure at BCR&N for that year was 28.5 percent) and for the 1890s was nearly a quarter of the road's gross revenue. Indeed, the "gay nineties" in many ways represented the belle epoque of passenger service on M&StL, which included splendid trains as part of the "Albert Lea Route," full participation in the excitement at Lake Minnetonka, commuter operations, and a constant blur of promotional excursions, plus the mundane but absolutely essential regimen of delivering local service, mail, and express.[33]

Rock Island, BCR&N, and Burlington continued participation with M&StL in through service to St. Louis, as did BCR&N and Rock Island to Chicago. M&StL asserted that the Pullman sleepers on those trains were "models of elegance" and that "dining car service is not surpassed by the finest hotels in the land"—"all meals are served at 75 cents each." Two daily trains in each direction plied the line from the Twin Cities through Albert Lea and Cedar Rapids to West Liberty, splitting or combining there to complete service to or from Chicago and St. Louis. For its part, Chicago, Burlington & Quincy offered two routes from Burlington, Iowa, to St. Louis—via Monmouth, Illinois, or more directly along the west bank of the Mississippi River. The Cannon Ball (with Chicago and St. Louis cars to Albert Lea) remained M&StL's premier train. The cooperation and even interdependence seen among participants in the Albert Lea Route was typical of the time, and for M&StL, with its highly abbreviated route, was essential. The same was true for BCR&N, and, if it were to have even so much as a toehold in the Northwest, would be true for Rock Island as well. But for CB&Q, which in 1890 gained 98.3 percent of cousin Chicago, Burlington & Northern's stock and thus acquired its own St. Paul–St. Louis line, the Albert Lea arrangement must have been problematic. Still, CB&Q had a financial stake in BCR&N and did not wish to endanger a heavy interchange of business with the Cedar Rapids

Figure 6.2. In 1888 passenger revenues from all sources (including tickets and mail) contributed a full 40 percent of M&StL revenues. Pictured here, American Standard (4-4-0) engine 8 is in charge of a Lake Minnetonka train at Tonka Bay, Minnesota, near the Lake Park Hotel. Author's collection.

road at Burlington. For that matter, CB&Q picked up 37.2 percent of revenues on the Albert Lea route's St. Paul–St. Louis traffic via Burlington, while BCR&N took 42.6 percent and M&StL pocketed the remaining 20.2 percent.[34]

During the fall of 1895, passenger service to the southwest was improved when M&StL and Rock Island joined in an overnight operation to Des Moines and Omaha, with through coaches, a smoking car, sleepers, and a diner. This resulted in the usual hoopla and grand claims of impeccable service, and also in the following promotional poem, penned by some long-forgotten author.

Their Bridal Tour

They were pelted with shoes
As they entered the train,
When she smoothed out her skirts,
Lo! the rice dropped like rain;
They were Omaha bound
On the M. & St. L.,
'Twas their bridal tour, too,
As you quickly could tell.

The snug stateroom was theirs:
From the ceiling to floor,
There was richness employed
Which they'd ne'er seen before;
And they sat side by side,
To observe and admire,
Though each secretly knew,
That 'twas time to retire.

For, please bear it in mind,
They were scarce three hours wed,
And embarrassment came
With the mere thought of bed
So they talked of the car,
And the rare taste displayed,
And each thought: "When we start,
Then we'll have our berths made."

So they waited and talked,
(For all know very well
There is much to admire
On the M. & St. L.)
And they just had agreed,
That the train had no flaw,

When a brakeman came through
And yelled out: "Omaha!"

For so smooth was the track,
And so short was the line,
And so easy the car,
And the fittings so fine,
That the train had pulled out
And had made its full run,
'Ere the happy pair knew
That their tour had begun.

Rates varied according to competitive pressures and political whim, but for most of the 1890s M&StL charged 3 cents per mile in Minnesota and Iowa, 4 cents in South Dakota. Sleeping car fares from Minneapolis or Albert Lea to Chicago were $2.00 for a double berth ("will accommodate two persons," said Rock Island), and $7.00 for a drawing room ("entirely separated . . . contains one section and a sofa which can be made up into a double lower berth"). For passengers needing to change stations at St. Paul, Albert Lea, Britt, Des Moines, Fort Dodge, Ogden, or Watertown, "omnibus" companies charged 25 cents one-way. At larger stations, Fort Dodge for example, patrons could avail themselves of streetcar lines that passed nearby.[35]

Rates for special trains were unpublished and subject to negotiation. Such trains were as diverse as that of November 7, 1888, which was operated on behalf of the *Minneapolis Tribune* to deliver special editions reporting the results of the general election that unseated President Grover Cleveland. The special reached Waseca at 7:00 a.m., passed Britt at 10:48, and steamed triumphantly into Fort Dodge shortly after noon, pleasing large crowds eager for news at every station en route. A few months later M&StL advertised a special train to Washington in celebration of Benjamin Harrison's inauguration. Other special trains took Minneapolis public health officers and city councilmen to the "quarantine hospital" in 1889 and a trainload of Grand Army of the Republic (GAR) veterans to their annual encampment at Boston in 1890; the GAR's "headquarters train" with "a well stocked commissary" went to Louisville in 1895, and several trains were used for its 1897 encampment in St. Paul. In 1896 M&StL advertising played on the fact that several men aspired to the Republican presidential nomination, noting that "Politicians are Divided as to the Candidates But are Agreed on the M&StL Road" when urging the public to book passage aboard its special train to the St. Louis Republican Convention on June 13.[36]

Special car movements also were part of the passenger department's smorgasbord. Throughout most of the 1880s and 1890s M&StL operated what it called "Phillips' Celebrated Weekly Tourist Car Line," leaving St. Paul and Minneapolis for Los Angeles every Thursday. Patrons were assured "the escort of gentlemanly conductors" aboard cars "completely furnished with carpets in the aisle, upholstered seats, clean linen and blankets for berths, and cooking ranges in separate compartments." M&StL likewise operated buffet sleepers with limited meals to Hot Springs, Arkansas (via St. Louis), during the winter months.[37]

As the largest city on-line and the company's headquarters, Minneapolis predictably served as the hub for passenger promotions. M&StL teamed with the Minnesota Experimental Farm during December 1893 in sending a delegation westward over the Watertown line to hold "farmer institutes" at Fairfax, Echo, and Clarkfield, among other Minnesota locations, and three years later it used three trains to bring farmers from stations on that same line to visit the state's Experimental Farm at St. Anthony Park. Eager excursionists from St. Paul and Minneapolis headed for the State Saeagerfest at Jordan in 1889, and the same year three hundred Foresters from Albert Lea took the cars to Minneapolis. Almost two thousand persons in three trains from the line above Fort Dodge arrived in Minneapolis for a jolly day of sightseeing during August 1895, and a few days later another train originating at Madison brought a large group from western Minnesota for a Sunday outing. The list was nearly endless. A delegation of commercial men from Watertown arrived in Minneapolis to "look the place over," and a "party of prominent Boston capitalists" passed through the city en route to Watertown. A group from the Evans & Hoey company came in over M&StL rails and went west on Northern Pacific. Some travelers came to Minneapolis to shop—for instance, at Donaldson's Glass Block Store, which in 1895 announced a "Leather Goods Sale" after M&StL delivered a carload of those goods on February 28—while others came for social events or for dramatic, athletic, or musical performances. In 1896 M&StL even sold joint theater–round-trip rail tickets to enthusiasts from nearby locations—Excelsior, for example—for $1.00.[38]

Special excursion rates on regular trains were infinite. Some of these were for trips to Waseca for the Minnesota Chautauqua assembly and to Hanley Falls for the meeting of the Norwegian Lutheran Association. Still others, for off-line gatherings, were issued on behalf of the Catholic Total Abstinence Association, the Sons of Veterans, the Travelers Protective Association, and the Seventh-Day Adventists. Harvest excursion tickets were authorized to various locations in the West and Southwest, and homeseekers' excursion tickets were available "to all points between Redwood [Minnesota] and Watertown [South Dakota]."[39]

The Chicago World's Columbian Exposition of 1893—the "White City" as it came to be known—provided a chance to visit that bustling and brawny city, but also through the exposition to be exposed to "ancient Rome and Greece" as well as "marvels of the modern world." Through its Rock Island connection, M&StL boasted, travelers could leave trains at Englewood and, after a five-minute ride "on electric line," be on the exposition grounds. Furthermore, puffed M&StL, it was the only road from the Northwest with this arrangement.[40]

It was the rare occasion when M&StL could brag of having any kind of unique arrangement. Competition and pressure from larger roads was a constant, even more so now with the road's independent status and relationships with BCR&N and Rock Island that were at once restless and tenuous. Burlington, Milwaukee, Omaha–North Western, Wisconsin Central, and even Chicago Great Western (CGW) had better routes to the Chicago market, friendly St. Paul & Duluth was threatened by Great Northern's new Eastern Railway of Minnesota for traffic via Duluth, CGW and North Western had lines connecting the Twin Cities and Des Moines, Burlington had its own outlet to St. Louis, and CGW at one point teamed with Iowa Central and Wabash for through cars to St. Louis, while Milwaukee joined with Iowa Central for service to Peoria, Illinois, and Kansas City. And typically, where there were passenger arrangements, freight agreements followed.[41]

Freight was not much of an issue regarding M&StL's interest at Lake Minnetonka, although carloads of beer occasionally found their way to the Lake Park Hotel for special picnics. But competition there was always part of the equation. Great Northern had a profound presence at the north end of the lake, and its Lafayette was clearly the most impressive of the many hotels; Milwaukee had arrived later and was in direct competition with M&StL on the south shore; and an electric line soon was on the scene. Nevertheless, M&StL was a major player at this famous watering place throughout the 1890s, carrying trainloads of patrons who looked forward to refreshing days of bathing, boating, fishing, and sailing, or to extended stays at Lake Park Hotel, set among impressive stands of oak, maple, and elm, with a twenty-two-horse stable, roller skating rink, billiard parlor, bar, and dance pavilion only a few steps from M&StL's Tonka Bay depot and telegraph office. M&StL held a half interest in the hotel but had no financial stake in the *City of Saint Louis,* the fine old sidewheel vessel that W. D. Washburn once had owned, which remained in service through 1898.

The attractions at Minnetonka were many and varied; so, too, were the people who came to visit. Croquet and tennis lured some, while others admired boat races, and still others anticipated performances by the Lyceum Company, which "occupied the boards" at the Lake Park theater. And there was yet another timeless attraction. "They say the number of pretty girls at Minnetonka this season is unprecedented," gushed one Minneapolis newspaperman in 1890. "The hotels swarm with them, and at the hops their elegant costumes are the cynosures of all eyes," he concluded with a nearly audible sigh. All of this created a great demand for transportation, to which M&StL responded by scheduling (in addition to regular through runs for Winthrop and Watertown) four trains in each

Figure 6.3. Chicago's Columbian Exposition of 1893 offered M&StL a tantalizing opportunity to sell excursion business. Author's collection.

direction for the 1889 season, eight in 1896, and five in 1900. Furthermore, M&StL ran a nearly endless stream of special excursions to Excelsior and Lake Park—for the Railroad Porters Association, United Typothetae, Minneapolis Engine Company No. 7, the Scandinavian Church of Christ, Mt. Zion Hebrew, the Knights Templar, and the Gustavus Adolphus Society, to mention but a few. M&StL also involved itself in an interesting "reverse commute" in 1895 when it arranged to carry passengers from Minnetonka to Minneapolis for a lecture at the Metropolitan Opera House by the popular Mark Twain.[42]

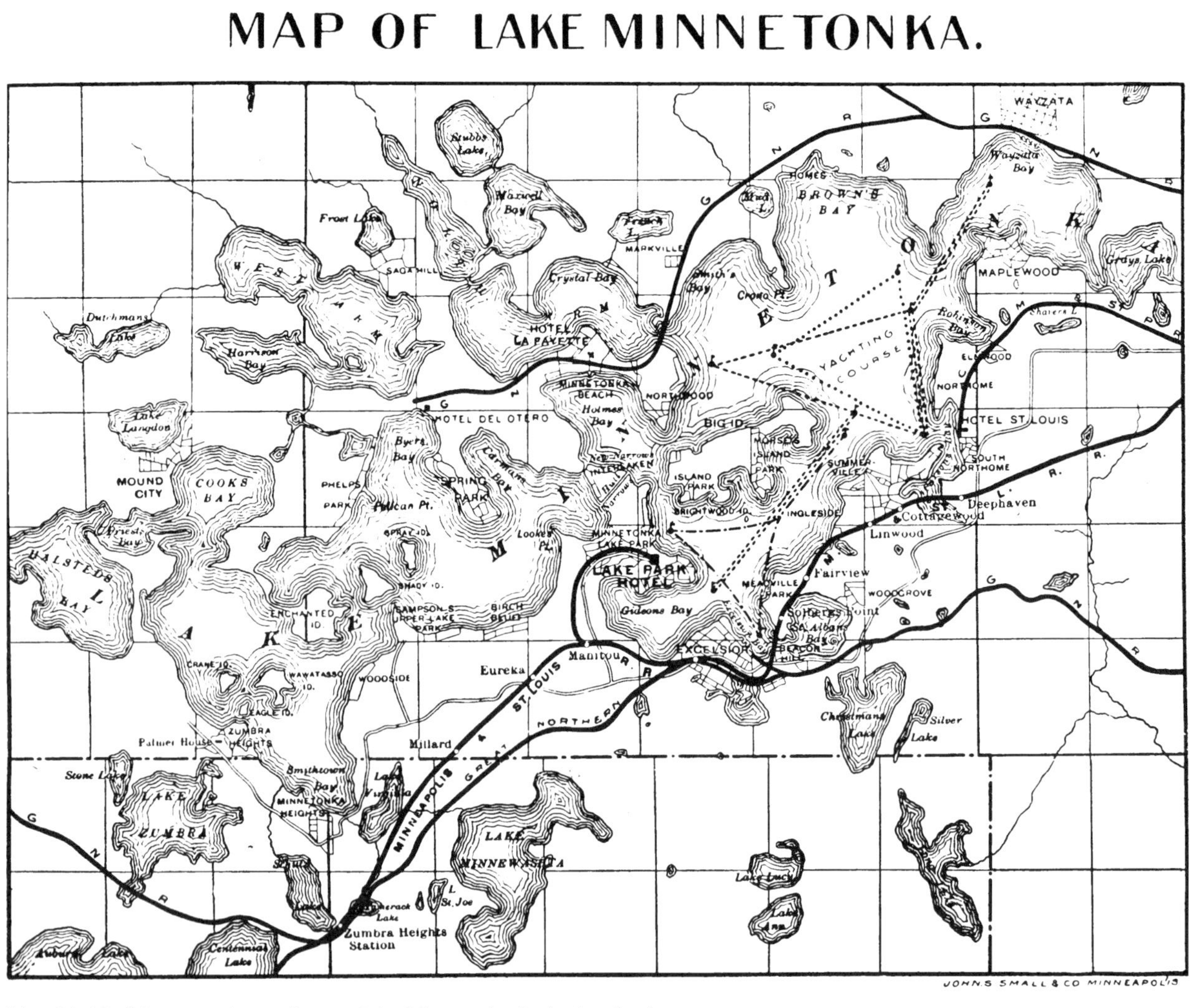

Map 6.1. M&StL was a primary player at Lake Minnetonka. Author's collection.

In 1895 four specific groups required special trains to the lake. Ever mindful of the advantages of publicity, M&StL hosted Twin Cities newspapermen and their families on a special from St. Paul to the lake, where guests enjoyed a ride on the *City of Saint Louis* and music by the New York Opera Company. Another twelve hundred persons attended a picnic and series of athletic contests hosted by the Ancient Order of Hiberians and the Daughters of Erin, and at the end of the summer entire trains were required for the Modern Woodmen of America's annual logrolling contest and picnic at Tonka Bay. Then there was the excursion and charter trip on the *City of Saint Louis* for the Concatenated Order of Hoo Hoo. Made up of lumbermen and railroad managers, this organization required an initiation fee of $9.99 and annual dues of 99 cents, restricted its membership to 9,999, and met at 9:09 p.m. on the ninth day of the ninth month of the year with the black cat (with its nine lives) as its official symbol. Surely Hoo Hoo Day on the M&StL was one to be remembered.[43]

M&StL no doubt looked at the Lake Park Hotel and attendant investments in and about Excelsior with a view toward making profits—but also as a means of establishing bragging rights. In 1895 the company built an engine house and installed a turntable at Excelsior in support of commuter and excursion traffic, and a year later expended a considerable amount on tables and swings at the Lake Park picnic grounds, extended the hotel's dock, dug a new well, and built a new powerhouse and electric plant. At mid-decade, the Lake Park Hotel was carried on M&StL's books at $15,000, growing to $17,859 in 1900. But it lost money every year—$11,549 in 1897 alone. M&StL held on, nevertheless, and by the end of the century Lake Park was able to break even.[44]

Not nearly as important as Minnetonka but still significant in M&StL's passenger calculations was Lake Waconia, about thirteen miles west of Excelsior, which competed for tourist dollars as best it could. For years the masthead of the *Waconia Patriot* declared Waconia the "Paradise of the Northwest," and the attractions of Lake Waconia and the amusements at its Coney Island were worthy indeed. From late May into September, passengers in large numbers unloaded at the Waconia depot or at Coney Island, 1.7 miles east, and headed for picnic grounds, baseball games, or theatrical performances, rented rowboats, went fishing, or merely lounged. The steamer *Niagara* met trains and conveyed passengers to hotels. M&StL advertised special trains to the "Coney Island of the West" and conducted thither a stream of groups—the grocery clerks of St. Paul, the Murphy Temperance Society, the Chaska Literary Society, the People's Party of Carver County (with Ignatius Donnelly as speaker), and the United Order of Horseshoers among them. M&StL especially praised the pleasures of Waconia in local newspapers on the line west as far as Watertown, South Dakota.[45]

M&StL predictably focused on traffic to and from Minneapolis and St. Paul; this matter, in turn, was wrapped up in station facilities at the road's two primary locations. Back in 1883 M&StL had entered into a contract with Northern Pacific by which joint operation was pledged between Minneapolis and St. Paul as soon as NP completed its "A Line," 9.5 miles, most of the intervening distance. This was not accomplished until 1886, however, and on February 8 M&StL began use of the joint line with freight service into NP's Seventh Street facility in St. Paul. Passenger operation was delayed briefly, though, because M&StL had been ejected from St. Paul Union Depot, which likely reflected the powerful hand of James J. Hill and his antagonism toward NP and M&StL. Meanwhile, NP arranged temporary passenger accommodations in the basement of its general office building nearby. M&StL's W. H. Truesdale was not optimistic that NP would soon wrench M&StL into St. Paul Union Depot. He was right. Consequently M&StL leased property from NP and established its own depot at Broadway and the foot of Fourth Street, about four blocks from Union Depot.[46]

A curious sidebar to the M&StL-NP contract of 1883 gave M&StL rights to provide passenger service for intermediate stops between Minneapolis and St. Paul. NP duly constructed "first class standard passenger stations" at University Avenue, Prospect Park, St. Anthony Park, Hamline, Warrendale, Como Avenue, and Rice Street, but no similar stations were constructed by M&StL on its tiny portion of the Minneapolis–St. Paul thoroughfare. M&StL began commuter service during the early spring of 1886 with hourly service, but by 1888 trimmed that service to eight daily turns plus five daily through trains in each direction. However, during State Fair season each summer, M&StL ran trains on ten-minute headways to accommodate the demand. But other than those few days each year costs ran ahead of revenues. The same was true for Milwaukee, which in 1888 dispatched an astonishing sixty-two daily passenger trains between St. Paul and Minneapolis, and for Manitoba, which ran trains every thirty minutes over its "great four-track line." In 1889 the *Minneapolis Tribune* joined other forces in denouncing the "injustice of a 50 cent round trip fare" (2.5 cents per mile) and demanded a 35-cent tariff (1.42 cents per mile). A political move soon was afoot to legislate such low commuter rates. Another important variable was the bicycle craze of the 1890s and, more important, the expansion of streetcar lines, including one completed in 1890 that reached from Hennepin Avenue in Minneapolis to downtown St. Paul. The increased frequency of streetcars and very attractive fares (20 cents per round trip, 1 cent per mile) quickly drew traffic from the steam railroads; in fact, revenue passengers on the Twin Cities Rapid Transit would double in the period between 1899 and 1903. The steam roads responded by cutting their passenger service, but there was no profit in it anyway. M&StL threw in the towel effective October 1, 1892.[47]

Americans in M&StL's service area no less than others elsewhere embraced or were embraced by the steamcar civilization. Yet without question railroads and the trains they operated upset the status quo, challenged traditional conventions, and led to considerable head shaking. For instance, there was the question of the character of certain of the railroads' regular customers, vaudevillians and traveling salesmen in particular, as well as those who simply hung around depots or were otherwise attracted to railroad property—not to mention railroaders themselves. It was one thing to have itinerant salesmen stop over at the American House in Jordan (Hilgers Sisters, proprietresses), or the fashionable Hotel Broz, a couple of blocks from the depot on Main Street in New Prague, where they could be carefully monitored, but quite another in a larger community with bigger and less personal hotels—like Albert Lea and the Winslow House, standing astride M&StL's yard. The Winslow, a combination depot, restaurant, and hotel, always was busy—well-known for 40-cent steak dinners, sleeping rooms with "bed bugs in high carnival throughout the second and third floor," and general high jinks. It was at the larger stations, too, according to the popular refrain, where "baggage smashers" did their best to destroy or disable passengers' luggage and salesmens' display trunks. But mischief also found its way to smaller locations such as Jordan, where in 1892 a female passenger's trunk was stolen by "a couple of toughs." Nor was railroad property safe. Local "gentlemen" from Gaylord made off with M&StL's velocipede in 1886 in order to play a ball game in Green Isle, stopping at Arlington "for the usual refreshments." The Gaylord newspaper subsequently reported that M&StL officials took a dim view of such misappropriation.[48]

Moving a growing volume of freight and passengers during the 1890s required more personnel and equipment. Employee numbers increased slightly, from 996 in 1890 to 1,126 in 1896, while the freight car fleet jumped from 1,930 in 1890 to 3,084 in 1899. The bulk of the freight roster was composed of boxcars along with gondolas, flats, a few livestock cars, and assorted others. The passenger car inventory grew to fifty-seven by decade's end, up from thirty-one in

Figure 6.4. The Winslow House in Albert Lea was a perennial favorite. Author's collection.

1890, mostly coaches but with two business cars and the other cars for head-end business (mail, express, and baggage). Surprisingly, the locomotive roster grew by only one, to sixty-eight, and remained pedestrian in the extreme—American Standard 4-4-0s except for a handful of 0-4-0 and 0-6-0 switchers.[49]

M&StL's humble stable of equipment and tiny employee numbers reflected the disciplined management of the late Truesdale administration, the realities of life in receiver's court, the hard times of the 1890s, and the cautious approach of New York owners who, in the main, must have been pleased with the road's performance. The operating ratio for the decade was an admirable 58.93, and despite the depression the road earned net operating income every year while keeping the plant in good repair. Payment of interest on bonded debt remained current after the reorganization, and dividends on stock began in 1896 with $1.049 million paid out over the years between 1896 and 1899. There was, however, one serious cautionary note: M&StL's equity and debt per mile of road, high since its expansion during the early 1880s, jumped to an alarming $60,887 in 1897 before turning downward. (BCR&N's, by stark comparison, was about $20,000 per mile for the 1890s.)[50]

The numbers looked good for the most part, but the New York owners still had given no signal as to their long-term intentions. M&StL started somewhere of importance, but went to no place in particular. Its tiny route structure could not support independence, and as the panic of 1893 ended the giants again awakened to imperial conquest. Would the New Yorkers merely gussy up M&StL for marriage? Would they milk the property for all it was worth and then throw the carcass to the jackals? Would they expand M&StL as a means of goading the giants into bidding for the pesky smaller road? Or would they chart a strategic course designed for long-term independence? Whatever the cards in that hand, they would be played by Edwin Hawley, named president of the road in 1897.

Chapter 7
The Little Harriman

Edwin Hawley "was one of the few men I knew who had a natural poker face. It was pale and cameolike, and when he talked he hardly opened his lips."
—Bernard M. Baruch

Edwin Hawley's life was reminiscent of the popular Horatio Alger stories contemporary with his own time. The beginnings of Hawley, referred to as "the little Harriman" during the early twentieth century, were nevertheless humble. Born in 1850 at Chatham, New York, he left home at age seventeen and headed for New York City. He took the first job offered—as messenger boy for the Erie Railroad. Hawley subsequently moved to Chicago, Rock Island & Pacific as clerk and contracting agent. His personal characteristics took hard form: he worked, he watched, he studied, he learned, he kept silent. And he invested, buying railroad stock that he considered undervalued.[1]

Luck was with him at Rock Island, where he came to the attention of those in charge of the California Fast Freight Line, to which Hawley moved next. At California Fast Freight he learned more about the railroad business, and there he met Collis P. Huntington, of Southern Pacific (SP) fame. Indeed, Hawley soon found employment at SP, assuming responsibilities in New York as assistant general eastern agent and then, in 1890, assistant general traffic manager. Internally and among a few outside SP, Hawley was also known as one of Huntington's chief aids and confidants. Even fewer, perhaps only Huntington himself, knew that Hawley was doggedly pursuing his own ends—saving every penny he could, even salvaging mutilated postage stamps from correspondence, and investing in SP and other rail stocks.[2]

Hawley seemed a riddle. Friend Bernard M. Baruch recalled that Hawley "was one of the few men I knew who had a natural poker face. It was pale and cameolike, and when he talked he hardly opened his lips." Hawley tended to be a loner, but he was not without friends. Indeed, by the mid-1890s Hawley spent nearly every Saturday afternoon and evening playing poker with the likes of John Muir (railroader and broker), L. C. Weir (president of Adams Express), John W. "Bet a Million" Gates and A. A. Housman (brokers), George Crocker (son of SP's "Big Four" Crocker), Charles S. Mellen (president of New York, New Haven & Hartford and then president of Northern Pacific), Daniel Sully (Wall Street investor), and James B. "Diamond Jim" Brady (plunger extraordinaire). Many of these men also joined together in assorted business ventures and investments; Crocker, Mellen, and Weir served on the Minneapolis & St. Louis board of directors.[3]

There is no record of how Hawley fell in with William Bull and others during M&StL's reorganization. Perhaps it was M&StL's stock that he "bought cheap" and then held. In any event, Hawley's was a rising star among those in the railroad industry as well

Figure 7.1. Edwin Hawley—"the little Harriman." Author's collection.

as on Wall Street. Despite his position as vice president and then president at M&StL, Hawley remained connected with Southern Pacific in New York and was one of its significant shareholders.[4]

One of the prickly issues confronting Hawley was the strategic relationship of M&StL and Rock Island, on one hand, and M&StL and Wisconsin, Minnesota & Pacific (WM&P), on the other. Rock Island, after all, owned the entirety of WM&P's debt and equity, but M&StL leased and operated WM&P's disconnected parts—the line from Red Wing to Eagle Lake via Waterville as well as the line from Morton to Watertown, connecting M&StL's own line between Hopkins and Morton with Burlington, Cedar Rapids & Northern at Watertown. In 1886 *Railroad Gazette* reported that M&StL would expand WM&P about forty miles to Mankato, Minnesota, a well-established and thriving community on the Chicago, St. Paul, Minneapolis & Omaha's St. Paul–Omaha line, and then up the Minnesota River valley to New Ulm, smaller but likewise vibrant. Since 1879 Mankato had preached the gospel of a tap road east to M&StL at Waterville, and in June 1887, with ten miles of new track from Eagle Lake, WM&P fulfilled that dream. But WM&P was at the heart of Rock Island's quest for a northwest passage to Pacific tidewater—a quest that ended during the late 1880s; further construction up the Minnesota valley from Mankato became problematic, although it was often and carefully considered. Late in 1889, WM&P's corporate secretary dryly recorded that the road declined "for the present time" to build on to New Ulm. As always, M&StL, the lessee, could recommend, but Rock Island, the lessor, made decisions on such strategic matters.[5]

From an operational point of view, WM&P's west end was simply an extension of M&StL's Hopkins–Morton line; the Red Wing–Mankato segment was known as M&StL's Cannon Valley Division, or locally simply as "The Valley." The public was unaware that these disconnected pieces of railroad were other than M&StL's or that the real owner was Rock Island. One passenger train in each direction plied the Valley line, but in 1890 M&StL also advertised "solid through trains from Mankato and St. Paul and Minneapolis." Waterville, where the Valley intersected M&StL's main line, was a busy hub, with Valley trains moving to and from M&StL's depot. Nearby stood the handsome Ealing House. Excursionists flocked to Waterville and its environs, attracted by the beauty of Lake Tetonka, by performances of the Andrews Opera Company, and by a splendid racetrack for trotters and pacers. WM&P boardings increased by 56 percent between 1885 and 1899, but its passenger miles nearly doubled. In freight, grain dominated outbound commodities, while lumber, coal, and cement were the primary inbound billings. Heavy movements of stone originated near Mankato, and stoneware and clay sewer pipe from Red Wing added to the Valley's traffic mix.[6]

It was inadequate. WM&P's earnings rose from $181,784 in 1885 to $292,702 in 1895, but beginning in 1888 the road was embarrassed by net loss from operation; interest on bonds went unpaid. During the summer of 1893, Metropolitan Trust of New York foreclosed, and W. H. Truesdale was appointed receiver. On November 16, 1893, the Wisconsin, Minnesota & Pacific *Railway* was sold to United States Trust of New York in the interests of Rock Island, and on April 24, 1894, it was reorganized as the Wisconsin, Minnesota & Pacific *Railroad,* with Rock Island's R. R. Cable as president but with continued operation by M&StL.[7]

During the mid-1890s Rock Island's system map was a curiosity, showing, as it did, two disconnected line segments in Minnesota. The circumstance was all the more bizarre after Rock Island lost M&StL to the Bull-Hawley group. The environment was ripe for rumor. In 1894 *Railroad Gazette* once again predicted that the Valley would be lengthened to join M&StL's Pacific Division, but a year later, after Chicago Great Western's A. B. Stickney toured the line, the *Minneapolis Tribune* repeated a story that Stickney wanted to acquire not only the Valley but all of M&StL. Stickney's real motives in 1895 are unknown, but M&StL did, indeed, want to link the Valley with its own western appendage. That would not happen, however, because M&StL's relationship with Rock Island continued to cool. In the end, M&StL and Rock Island reached a compromise of sorts. As 1899 unfolded, M&StL turned its back on the Valley but arranged to purchase WM&P's Morton–Watertown segment, taking ownership on February 20. Stickney's Chicago Great Western took the Cannon Valley line, beginning operation on June 1 and retaining the Wisconsin, Minnesota & Pacific corporate shell. This news was antiseptically reported to Rock Island shareholders, who, if they looked carefully, noted a significant loss on the road's investment in WM&P.[8]

Disposition of the Cannon Valley line had a curious sidebar that involved a hearty and lengthy campaign by the prosperous little city of New Ulm to gain a second railroad; its first had been Chicago & North Western (née Winona & St. Peter), which had officially introduced itself to New Ulm on February 22, 1872. New Ulm was strategically located as a commercial and milling center and was heavily populated with German Americans who enthusiastically saw to the establishment of several breweries. Eager to secure railroad competition, in 1882 the community had passed a bond issue in an unsuccessful effort to entice Cannon Valley westward, and had passed another bond proposal in 1891 for a "paper railroad" that failed to be born. Congressman and future Minnesota governor John Lind was among other New Ulm leaders who chafed at the absence of competition and decried the lack of direct linkage with Minneapolis and St. Paul. Indeed, in 1887 Lind had urged construction of a plug line from New Ulm to Winthrop as a means of satisfying New Ulm's needs. Nothing came of that effort, but in 1895 Lind tried again, leading a delegation to meet with M&StL representatives, who were receptive but asked for concessions. There followed incorporation of the Minneapolis, New Ulm & Southwestern Railroad, with a board of directors reflecting New Ulm's milling and brewing industries and a pledge of free right-of-way through the city plus a small bonus of $9,000. M&StL said the New Ulm road would be "operated independently," but in fact M&StL purchased all of its bonds, and in 1899 it would purchase the road outright.[9]

Given M&StL's relationship with Rock Island in 1895–96, there is ample reason to believe that the New Ulm–Winthrop line was more than a plug—likely even an integral section of a broader design to expand the Cannon Valley line from Mankato to M&StL's Pacific Division at Winthrop. The idea of linking Cannon Valley and M&StL's western line was hardly new, and Rock Island maps for 1896 did show anticipated construction up the Minnesota valley to New Ulm and on to Winthrop. For that matter, M&StL's capital expenditures at New Ulm were registered under "Mankato [Cannon Valley] Division." But events proved otherwise, and in 1900 Chicago & North Western would seal off any opportunity by building its own line from Mankato to New Ulm.[10]

In any event, John Lind's dream was about to become reality. Construction was easy for the thirteen miles south from Winthrop to and through the new villages of Lafayette and Klossner, cuts and fills were few, and for the most part track was merely thrown down on a superficial grade. The remaining six miles were much more challenging, however, requiring nineteen pile trestles and a 194-foot descent down the rugged ravine of Fritsche Creek and a 1,227-foot pile trestle and a through lattice truss bridge over the Minnesota River before ducking under C&NW and into New Ulm. Chief Engineer William Crooks had ordered Pacific fir from Washington for the Minnesota River structure, and bridge men were a busy lot during the first six months of 1896. There was impatience but also anticipation at Winthrop, where the editor of the *Winthrop News* wrote: "Almost before we know it we will be whirling away to the city of breweries, and then when we are quenching our thirst, and only then will we realize how fast the world moves." Finishing touches remained, but on July 4, 1896, residents of New Ulm rejoiced in "a double-decked holiday," celebrating not only the nation's birth but also inauguration of operation by the new railroad. Virtually the entire place turned out, and two special trains—one from the Twin Cities and the other from nearby Winthrop—brought additional throngs. Two days later regular service began with one daily-except-Sunday freight and one mixed train in each direction. By September M&StL was running one passenger train daily from St. Paul to New Ulm, and a turn from New Ulm to Winthrop met the road's day trains on the Pacific Division. One important question remained: What was implied by the word *Southwestern* in *Minneapolis, New Ulm & Southwestern*? *Railroad Gazette* suggested a possibility. M&StL, it said, would extend the New Ulm line "to connect with roads to the Missouri River."[11]

Meanwhile, the difficult and unsettling panic of 1893 was giving way to recovery and optimism. A "splendid little war" with Spain in 1898 vented a surge of patriotism (M&StL started the Twelfth Minnesota Infantry Volunteers on its trek to Camp George H. Thomas in Georgia) and planted the United States firmly among the world's imperial powers, while American industrial output now exceeded the capacity of the domestic market to absorb all production. This, in turn, obliged the youthful nation to find opportunities abroad. And the era of heroic entrepreneurship was in full flower. Edwin Hawley was increasingly a member of that class.[12]

Hawley had an innate capacity to make money—a characteristic that Collis P. Huntington found marvelously attractive. The two men were increasingly close. At the same time, however, Hawley went his own way, joining, for example, Jesse Lewisohn, C. S. Mellen, and "Diamond Jim" Brady in a pool on Iowa Central stock. Then, late in 1900, Huntington died suddenly, and for a while Hawley was in control of SP through both his own stock and influence he had with the Huntington heirs. Hawley soon pledged his own shares to railroad titan Edward H. Harriman and openly urged sale of the estate's stock to Harriman-controlled Union Pacific. It was done. Harriman rewarded Hawley with a seat on SP's board of directors, and in the process Hawley's name was presented to a much wider audience.[13]

Meanwhile, Hawley responded to growing national self-confidence by studying means to expand M&StL's dominion and carve out a broader strategic niche. Late in 1898 or very early in 1899, he decided to lengthen the New Ulm stub southwestward, keeping his own counsel as to the ultimate destination and exact route. This was shrewd, for it set off competition among existing communities for the route, allowed friendly associates to make plans for townsite options, and tended to flush out the intentions of competitors or potential competitors. Three routes were considered over a thirty-five-mile swath leading generally toward Council Bluffs, Iowa. In the Hawkeye State, Spirit Lake gloated that the extension would surely tap that community, if for no other reason than to share the heavy seasonal passenger trade that was the reward of any road serving that well-established resort area. Estherville, sixteen miles to the east, discounted such arguments, while Spencer, south of Spirit Lake and southwest of Estherville, fully expected to gain the line no matter which of these aspiring communities it came from. A half county beyond, Sioux Rapids had long solicited north–south service and now pinned its hopes on M&StL. Other locations—Storm Lake, for instance—fidgeted and hoped for the best. Hawley continued his tight-lipped approach, but at least some winners and losers became apparent when M&StL purchasing agents appeared at various locations—St. James, 26 miles from New Ulm, and Storm Lake, another 109 miles to the southwest. Moreover, L. F. Day

(*L* was Day's actual first name, although he was referred to as "Larry"), who had replaced A. M. Moehler as general manager, announced, "We shall eventually reach Omaha, but probably not this year."[14]

Hawley's motivations were at once tactical and strategic. M&StL needed more traffic—originated locally or handled "overhead" by M&StL as an intermediate carrier. Line expansion into new territory would accomplish the former, and pushing into Council Bluffs and/or Omaha to meet Union Pacific and other roads might satisfy the latter. The line would pass through glaciated plains typified by deposited drifts or wind-blown loess soils that were beautiful for agriculture. Two decades earlier an Omaha predecessor had claimed that "Southwestern Minnesota and northwestern Iowa had the soils of the river bottoms and the climate of the mountains. A few years, therefore in this section, makes the poor man rich and the sick man robust." An overdrawn, account, no doubt, but that part of the world was truly blessed with good soil. In the 1890s Iowa dominated in corn and hog production as well as in cattle and horses—and prosperity in that state was real, if uneven. William C. Brown, president of New York Central, would say: "The state of Iowa has grown from a wilderness to a great agricultural and industrial commonwealth in the allotted life of man." True enough. Government land offices had been closed long since, but Thomas & Bradford of Storm Lake, for example, offered "a large list of farms" in that region, while several real estate firms at Estherville advertised "wild and improved lands" around that place. Timber was scarce, found only along creek and river bottoms, but so much the better for M&StL, which could wheel vast supplies of lumber from Minneapolis. The new route also had sure appeal for Minneapolis wholesale merchants as well as manufacturers of everything from agricultural implements to oil-based paint.[15]

Timing was important. Milwaukee had purchased a line from Des Moines to Fonda with intentions of pushing it on northwestward to Spencer along with a branch from Rockwell City to Storm Lake—connecting its existing primary horizontal arteries from Chicago at Herndon and Spencer, and in the process linking Iowa's capital city with two important county seats in northwest Iowa. Rock Island had similar aspirations in the region, using leased Des Moines & Fort Dodge through Angus to Gowrie, Iowa, and construction by a puppet northwestward to Burlington, Cedar Rapids & Northern's Sioux Falls and Watertown line at Sibley. Iowa Central also was rumored to have designs on South Dakota by stretching its Story City branch northwestward through Callender; others said Iowa Central would add to its Algona branch by building to Spirit Lake and beyond. Farther north, C&NW was busy planning a new line from Mason City that would intersect another North Western line in southern Minnesota. And there were reports that both Illinois Central and Chicago Great Western wanted lines from Fort Dodge to Council Bluffs. Hawley needed to act quickly lest his road be sealed off with a strange-looking stub dangling from M&StL's Pacific Division at Winthrop.[16]

Activity quickened. On February 14, 1899, M&StL stockholders ratified the board's recommendation to acquire Minneapolis, New Ulm & Southwestern and to issue bonds adequate for payment on that property plus construction as far as Storm Lake, 158 miles from Winthrop. A decision as to routing followed in the spring, and by May the company began acquiring right-of-way, most of it by warranty deed. Construction contracts were let in segments—with Johnston Brothers & Faught of St. Elmo, Illinois, for example, getting the northernmost chunk, and John Scott & Sons of St. Louis the southernmost. Subcontractors were grading at various locations by June.[17]

Engineering challenges ranged from modest to significant. Much of the route was across flatlands, often marshy, but it also bisected numerous streams and creeks, necessitating extensive excavation and bridgework. Getting out of the Minnesota valley immediately south of New Ulm would require deck-plate girder spans over the Cottonwood River (871 feet) and the Little Cottonwood River (858 feet), plus several pile trestles—some of them lengthy—even then saddling the line with a 1.3 percent grade. At Estherville entrance to the Des Moines River valley from the north would be easy, but exit would take a steel span over the river as well as shelving on the west escarpment of the valley, plus a very unusual (in the prairies) horseshoe curve to gain the lush rolling countryside beyond. The Little Sioux River at Spencer would demand another steel span and a lengthy pile trestle, but from south of Greenville to beyond Sioux Rapids, about ten miles of rough, hilly country, another crossing of the now much broader and deeper valley of the Little Sioux, along with numerous gullies and ravines carved by anxious tributaries, would demand extensive cuts and fills in addition to lengthy and expensive pile trestles and a substantial open-deck steel trestle at Sioux Rapids, to be installed by the well-known Phoenix Bridge Company. (One source estimated that eight hundred carloads of timber and ancillary materials went into bridges and trestles between Spencer and Sioux Rapids.) Having escaped from the clutches of the tyrannical Little Sioux, the line would be mostly straight and flat across fertile farmland for the final seventeen miles into Storm Lake.[18]

Construction started at each end of the extension. Bridge builders erected lengthy temporary pile trestles to get the road out of New Ulm, while a steel bridge gang toiled on the permanent structure. At Storm Lake a crew put in a track that connected with Illinois Central to receive material and then threw down an elementary yard as preemption against the designs of Milwaukee Road, hurrying toward the same objective. Material and contractor crews were fed to job sites from existing lines of railroad at St. James, Sherburn, Estherville, Storm Lake, and later Spencer and Sioux Rapids. The focus was on the north end of the project, with substantial construction camps at New Ulm, St. James, and Estherville—accompanied by occasional chaos at those locations when men had too much drink or when race became an issue (several laborers were black).[19]

Meanwhile, the Iowa & Minnesota Land & Townsite Company, with offices in the prestigious Lumber Exchange at Minneapolis, set off a series of campaigns to launch the new communities of Searles, Hanska, LaSalle, Echols, Ormsby, Monterey, and Dunnell in Minnesota, as well as Huntington, Raleigh, Langdon,

Figure 7.2. One of the most substantial of several bridges and trestles on the Southwestern was over the Little Sioux River at Sioux Rapids, Iowa. Author's collection.

Greenville, Cornell, Rembrandt, and Truesdale in Iowa. Indeed, only St. James, Sherburne, Estherville, Terril, Spencer, Sioux Rapids, and Storm Lake were established places on the new line. The pattern was the same at each new location. The townsite company secured a block of land and, as M&StL's "Omaha Extension" was nearing completion, held "a special town lot sale." The one at Ormsby on October 24, 1899, was typical. Located twelve miles south of St. James and twenty miles above Sherburn "in one of the finest agricultural districts in southern Minnesota," Ormsby had "a splendid opening for all classes of business," the townsite company announced, then declared: "We want live, energetic, wide-awake businessmen to locate in this town where a prosperous future is assured." The surrounding area, the company continued, was settled by "fore-handed" farmers, "about equally divided among Germans, Scandinavians, and Americans"—"well out of debt and in a position to pay for what they purchase." Terms of sale: "50 per cent cash, balance three and four months, 6 per cent interest." Each new community was neatly laid out, with "Railroad Avenue" often paralleling M&StL's tracks.[20]

Graders were followed by bridge crews, track gangs, construction trains, pioneer trains, and finally regularly scheduled service. A construction train entered St. James from the north on December 1, 1899, but bad weather and tardy delivery of rail slowed progress above Estherville. Track gangs from the south had passed into Minnesota early in November, and finally, on December 21, a construction train from St. James steamed slowly into Estherville. The track was not ballasted, but winter's icy grip would hold gauge adequate for "irregular freight service." To the south work was slower, owing to lack of rail and severe bridging obstacles. By December a crossing of Milwaukee was effected and an interchange track installed at Spencer, but it was not until March of 1900 that pioneer service reached Terril, about midway between Estherville and Spencer, and Scott & Son's mules were turned out to pasture until frost left the ground. Trestlework continued, however, and the telegraph line was completed, depot construction commenced, and bridge material and steel were delivered at Sioux Rapids over the recently completed connection with C&NW. By April Scott & Sons opened a camp at Willow Creek near Cornell to prosecute work in both directions. Late in June the first train passed over the new bridge at Sioux Rapids and proceeded on to Storm Lake to pick up more material. But the line north from Estherville had been opened to scheduled service on June 1, and at long last, on August 19 the entire Southwestern extension to Storm Lake was in business. In some cases, however, agents had not yet been assigned to stations, and much remained to be done to get the track ballasted and surfaced. Two "boarding trains" and 120 men were moved from Sherburne to Sioux Rapids to work behind trains bringing gravel loaded by "The Irishman," a great steam shovel, from the pit near Willow Creek above Cornell. It was an impressive show, with up to two hundred cars loaded daily, handled by two switch engines, and dispatched from a temporary telegraph office at the pit.[21]

The line gave birth to fourteen new villages and punched a surge of adrenaline into the seven existing communities. "Spencer is Jubilant," cheered that city's newspaper when M&StL announced its coming. At St. James a local banker erected the Park Hotel, a splendid edifice located between M&StL and Omaha stations, while Storm Lake produced several new buildings, the elegant Bradford Hotel among them. Rembrandt sported three buildings early in 1900, and a post office was ordered for Monterey late in 1899. Every new town was fleshing out—especially Hanska, Monterey, Dunnell, Greenville, and Rembrandt. Hanska sprouted a dozen businesses, including Torgrimson & Synsteby, which handled seeders, drills, harrows, and other machinery eagerly acquired by farmers from the surrounding countryside. Ole and Anun Halvorson, from Clarkfield on M&StL's West End, were two reverse migrants, establishing themselves in the hardware and implement business at LaSalle. Yet however rapid the growth at these new locations, the townsite company still had plenty of property to dispose of; another round of auctions was scheduled to correspond with the opening of the "new Omaha extension." Investors, said the townsite company, "can and will double their money on every lot they buy inside six months." Moreover, the surrounding countryside was rich, with "immense

Figure 7.3. Monterey, Minnesota, was one of sixteen new townsites spawned on the Southwestern. Business there was good. Author's collection.

crops this year and crop failures never known." Those who bought one or more lots during the campaign of August 1900 were promised reimbursement of ticket expenses to and from the site.[22]

Regular train service was an instant hit. On June 1, 1900, M&StL instituted double daily passenger service between Minneapolis and Estherville, with one of those sets extended to Storm Lake on August 19. Freight schedules included a daily local in each direction. Trains served shippers and travelers, of course, but also railroad employees. Louis E. Chambard arrived at Hanska on the first northbound passenger train to become agent at that place—serenaded, as he got off, by the Lake Shore Band. M&StL's passenger department quickly instituted fishermen's excursions to Minnetonka and half fares to the Minnesota State Fair. A $2.50 round-trip rate to Minneapolis emptied Monterey and filled the train on Sunday, June 17. Two months later M&StL hosted a special train for Minneapolis jobbers, stopping at each station for the Minneapolitans to see and be seen in a shrewd campaign to create symbiotic relations.[23]

That Minneapolis jobbers would be thrilled with 154 miles of new railroad tied directly to the interests of their city was certainly understandable. Moreover, that sixteen new townsites could be made to sprout in already settled country seemed prima facie evidence that the line from Winthrop to Storm Lake was justified by local needs alone. But every inch of that line ran through country honeycombed with appendages of the Chicago roads and hotly contested by them. M&StL obviously would seek the longest possible haul, to Minneapolis, and do everything to create an adhesive linking Minneapolis to this hinterland. But the longest potential haul was only 234 miles—from Storm Lake, a community served additionally by two Chicago roads. Of the twenty-four stations south of Winthrop, nine were competitive points, every one with a Chicago road; the average distance between these competitive points was a mere 17.1 miles. On the entire line, Terril, only 14.7 miles from Estherville, was farthest removed from an alternative rail line. The likelihood that M&StL could control all traffic to its own advantage was nil; much business to and from stations between Winthrop and Storm Lake was certain to be short haul, interchanged to or from intermediate carriers of Chicago persuasion. In sum, local business alone was unlikely to justify this expansion.

What were Hawley's motives? As early as 1898, the new line was referred to internally and in public as the "Omaha Extension." At one point there was even talk of running through trains to Omaha via Storm Lake and Sioux City, and repeated news stories promised that the road would ultimately get to Omaha—but not in 1900, said one report, "owing to the excessive price of steel and ties." For that matter, M&StL maps for 1900 showed a prominent dotted line from Storm Lake through Denison to Council Bluffs. Surely Hawley would soon show his strategic hand, or at least another card in that hand, by completing the remaining 100 miles of road to the Missouri River.[24]

America was patently vibrant at the turn of the century. In 1901 was established United States Steel Company, America's first billion-dollar corporation, and the same year railroad chieftains James J. Hill and Edward H. Harriman fought a high-stakes dual that resulted in the creation of Northern Securities, a holding company, into which were poured neighboring Northern Pacific and Great Northern. There had been a burst of similar if less spectacular activity following the Spanish-American War. Within two years' time at least forty thousand miles of railroad were transferred to companies owning other lines. Of course the pattern was hardly new; consolidations, joint ownerships, and mergers were, and long had been, as elemental to American railroading as ties and spikes.[25]

But what did the accelerating consolidation movement mean for M&StL? The big were getting bigger; the small were in danger. The old question was again appropriate: where did M&StL fit in? Some observers thought they knew when Hawley and friends gained stock control of Iowa Central Railway, an orphan road to the south whose predecessors had played various parts in M&StL thinking from the beginning. Iowa Central owned an L-shaped main line from Mason City through Hampton, Marshalltown, and Oskaloosa that crossed into Illinois with a bridge at Keithsburg and continued on through Monmouth to Peoria, with Iowa branches from Mason City to Northwood, Oskaloosa to Albia and Hocking, Hampton to Belmond, Minerva Junction to Story City, Grinnell to Montezuma, and New Sharon to Newton (with a stub to Lynnville)—510 miles in all. Hawley became president of Iowa Central on June 20, 1900; associates who were on M&StL's board of directors took a majority position on Iowa Central's board at the same time. L F. Day, M&StL's vice president and general manager, assumed a vacancy in that position at Iowa Central, but the rest of the local management stayed in place. The executive offices of both companies were in Hawley's Southern Pacific quarters at 349 Broadway in New York—an arrangement unthinkable in a later time.[26]

When Hawley took control of Iowa Central, it had but a single physical link with M&StL, at Corwith, Iowa, sixty miles southwest of Albert Lea and forty-four miles northeast of Fort Dodge, and only a recent one at that, since Iowa Central's Belmond Branch had been stretched northwestward through Corwith to Algona a few months earlier, in 1899. More important, of course, at Albert Lea M&StL was removed by only seventeen miles from Iowa Central's upper extremity at Northwood, Iowa. Rails had spanned that gap in 1877, but ownership and operation of the line from Manly through Northwood to Albert Lea was confused because Iowa Central had built and owned but leased the eleven-mile segment from Manly to Northwood to Burlington, Cedar Rapids & Northern; BCR&N had built, owned, and operated about four miles of the road to the state line; and BCR&N had built, M&StL owned, but BCR&N leased and operated the remaining thirteen miles of the road into Albert Lea. For BCR&N the Manly–Albert Lea segment was integral to its main line from Burlington to Albert Lea, but Iowa Central's operation to Northwood as a stub from Mason City was modest in the extreme. Hawley understandably wanted to link M&StL and Iowa Central to take advantage of potential traffic advantages (northbound coal, for instance, and southbound lumber), but the Cedar Rapids road was increasingly under Rock Island's thumb; tinkering with the status quo risked further alienation between Rock Island and M&StL. Relations already were tense, made even more so by Hawley's recent assertive sortie with the M&StL into western Iowa. If Hawley pressed completion of the Southwestern to Council Bluffs, traffic agreements with Rock Island for western business via Des Moines were sure to be obviated. Even if Hawley did not play that card, M&StL had increased its reach to Storm Lake and connection there with Illinois Central, an Edward H. Harriman–controlled road of great standing.[27]

Burlington, Cedar Rapids & Northern, locked between M&StL and much larger Rock Island—indeed, pivot for the "Albert Lea Route"—found itself at the vortex of a rapidly changing railroad landscape in the upper Midwest. Chicago, Rock Island & Pacific and Chicago, Burlington & Quincy, in addition to persons directly connected with those roads, had assumed control of BCR&N back in the 1870s; the board's executive committee had two representatives from each camp, with BCR&N's president the fifth member. While CB&Q's Charles E. Perkins and his lieutenants kept a careful watch on BCR&N, Ransom Cable and Rock Island were much closer. Indeed, Cable's style was to expand Rock Island's domain through stock control or lease; BCR&N mirrored this approach. And Cable willingly gave reign to local management; the long tenure of BCR&N's president, C. J. Ives, reflected as much.[28]

There had been and continued to be predictable pulling and hauling among the Albert Lea Route's family members. Ives was irritated during 1895 when M&StL and Rock Island upgraded their passenger service to Omaha via Des Moines in a way that drained California business away from BCR&N's long-mile route through West Liberty. M&StL's A. L. Mohler assured Ives that "the close alliance between your line and ours" was in no danger and that M&StL had "no desire whatever to break up old relations with you." Five years later Ives complained that CB&Q was favoring its St. Louis–St. Paul line through Illinois and Wisconsin over the Albert Lea Route. Not so, said Burlington's Howard Elliott. "We maintain a through passenger line with your company and M&StL, and aim to make it a high grade, first class and the best line between St. Louis and St. Paul; I think we have succeeded." Nevertheless, irritations increased in frequency and in intensity. BCR&N gave up trackage rights over M&StL between Madison Junction and Forest City, Iowa, building its own line and becoming a competitor at Forest City; three years later, when a BCR&N surrogate projected a spur off this line to the northwest, M&StL belligerently tried to prevent a crossing at grade southwest of Forest City near Hayfield. More important, Iowa Central got into a serious fuss with BCR&N over the jointly operated route from Manly to Northwood, and in 1896 even threatened to build its own sixteen-mile line on to Albert Lea.[29]

Iowa Central's grievance was as long as it was meritorious. Thwarted in its aspirations to reach M&StL, the road had languished at Northwood since 1871. The eleven-mile portion from Manly had been leased to BCR&N in 1877, and the road then had excused itself from service on that stub, as there was not sufficient business to justify two carriers. But residents

Figure 7.4. The Albert Lea Route—and its long association among M&StL, BCR&N, CRI&P, and CB&Q—would soon unravel. Author's collection.

of the county had voted public financial support for construction of the lines, the matter flew to the courts, Iowa Central lost, and the railroad had been forced to reestablish operation; however, under the provisions of the lease, "receipts from such service accrued to the lessee," BCR&N. Small wonder that Iowa Central wanted revisions in the contract. BCR&N, however, was well satisfied and balked when asked for concessions. Indeed, it played tit for tat, threatening late in 1896 to put down its own track parallel to Iowa Central from Manly to Northwood. Iowa Central's Russell Sage countered, saying: "I do not believe the increased volume of business would justify going on and building parallel lines." But BCR&N persisted, saying it would abrogate the lease a year from that time. Iowa Central then considered selling to BCR&N its line from Manly to Northwood, but even if it did so it would remain saddled with the court decision and would have to lease trackage rights from BCR&N to maintain service to Northwood. Meanwhile, M&StL received pressure from BCR&N to sell its property south from Albert Lea to the Iowa boundary. In September 1897, Iowa Central and BCR&N papered over their differences with a new ten-year contract, but it settled nothing.[30]

Matters got ever more complicated in 1898 and 1899. Iowa Central's fortunes improved, its stock value moved upward, and BCR&N's New York office advised C. J. Ives in Cedar Rapids, "The eyes of several railroads are doubtless turned toward it [Iowa Central]," significantly adding, "as are our own." Indeed, maps were prepared with BCR&N's route superimposed on Iowa Central's; they showed dramatic compatibility. At the same time, BCR&N was quietly studying acquisition of St. Paul & Duluth and openly asked CB&Q if it would dispose of any property in Minneapolis that could be used for terminals. The answer from Burlington was "No," but its George B. Harris did not slam the door on working with BCR&N in the Twin Cities. By late 1899 it was clear that BCR&N—with clear and certain backing from Rock Island—was about to launch itself directly into the Twin Cities market—and possibly move on to Duluth. In partial anticipation of this, Rock Island completed a second main track from Chicago to connection with BCR&N at West Liberty, 221 miles away.[31]

Meanwhile, a nearly constant barrage of reports in 1897 through 1901 had Illinois Central gaining control of M&StL. Prosecution of M&StL's Southwestern extension in 1899–1900 fueled some of this speculation because at the same time IC was hurrying toward Council Bluffs–Omaha with a new artery from Tara, just west of Fort Dodge. The Southwestern tapped IC's Sioux City line at Storm Lake, and, if lengthened, could be made to connect with IC's Omaha route at Denison. Moreover, shortly after IC's Omaha line entered service in January 1900, M&StL and IC initiated a new through Minneapolis-to-Omaha passenger operation via Fort Dodge; M&StL dropped its earlier arrangement with Rock Island through Des Moines.[32]

Rumor and reality became one, blurring any distinction as to which was more important in causing or propelling events. BCR&N's treasurer in New York telegraphed C. J. Ives on December 23, 1899, saying that Clarence Day & Company had informed him that "if we wish to negotiate for control of St. Paul & Duluth . . . he [Clarence Day] is now ready to talk." A few weeks later BCR&N surveyors were at work variously above Albert Lea; Rock Island Chairman Ransom Cable told Ives that a final location would be determined after the surveys were studied. Chicago Great Western interjected that BCR&N could save considerable money by using its line north from Manly. "We could give your traffic . . . first class service, and do it cheaper . . . than if you ran your trains into St. Paul and Minneapolis direct," said CGW. And in May 1900 Burlington's Charles E. Perkins suggested that BCR&N build to meet Winona & Southwestern at Osage, Iowa, acquire that road to Winona, Minnesota, and use CB&Q into St. Paul. It was a poor idea. In any event, Winona & Southwestern soon fell into CGW's orbit. Ives and Cable did, however, carefully consider the option of using CGW elsewhere, part of it the old Wisconsin, Minnesota & Pacific recently given up by M&StL, from Faribault through Randolph to St. Paul. Hearing of that prospect, Jules M. Hannaford of Northern Pacific suggested that NP could provide terminal space in the Twin Cities for BCR&N and could handle its trains between St. Paul and Minneapolis. Hannaford added that NP was now "in the market for Duluth business strong . . . since we have purchased the St. Paul & Duluth road."[33]

BCR&N was not alone in missing an opportunity to acquire that historic line to Duluth. M&StL, at least when A. L. Mohler was around, had plotted to acquire the Duluth road and, using the old Minneapolis & Duluth (leased to St. Paul & Duluth) plus M&StL's existing line to Winthrop and constructing the Southwestern Branch to Omaha, hoped to create a single-line operation from the Head of the Lakes through Minneapolis to the Missouri River. BCR&N also failed to bag Iowa Central, although it bought stock in the road, as did principals of both BCR&N and CRI&P. "It is a pity that we could not have awakened our friends to a realization of how important it was to us to acquire Iowa Central," moaned BCR&N's representative in New York upon hearing of Hawley's success in gaining control of the Iowa road. "This makes it very necessary for us to protect ourselves between Albert Lea and St. Paul," he brooded, adding: "I wish we could have our own line to and terminals in that city."[34]

Illinois Central was a constant variable in all of this. That company had long since taken control of a prize horizontal road in Iowa from Dubuque to Sioux City along with branches to Sioux Falls, Cedar Rapids, and Onawa, and now a very important route to Omaha. In addition, IC held the little-used line from near Cedar Falls to Lyle, Minnesota, on the Iowa border just south of Austin, which in 1899 it proposed to bend to the northwest, "to Albert Lea . . . there to meet the Minneapolis & St. Louis Railroad." Nineteen miles of road were constructed in 1900, to Glenville, six miles south of Albert Lea on M&StL's line leased to BCR&N, and land was acquired for right-of-way into Albert Lea. IC was in a powerful bargaining position, and BCR&N quickly agreed to "joint use" of the track from Glenville to Albert Lea; M&StL and BCR&N further agreed to grant yard and terminal privileges to IC at Albert Lea. Its first regularly scheduled passenger train left that town on December 3, 1900.[35]

M&StL now met Illinois Central at three locations—Albert Lea, Fort Dodge, and Storm Lake, with the prospect of another meeting at Denison. (Iowa Central met IC at Peoria, Ackley, and Albert Lea.) This added fuel to speculation that M&StL, and maybe Iowa Central, shortly would pass to IC. Strategic advantages were clear. M&StL could provide access to Minneapolis and St. Paul, long desired by IC, from the east via Cedar Falls and Albert Lea, and from the west by way of Fort Dodge and Albert Lea, while the Southwestern presented opportunities to and from Sioux City. However, in April 1901 Hawley announced that negotiations with Illinois Central had been called off because M&StL was earning 11 percent on its common stock and Hawley wanted a guarantee of more than four percent annual dividends, which was all that Illinois Central had offered. In the end, Harriman called the shot, seeming to want M&StL but not M&StL and Iowa Central together.[36]

As these negotiations rolled forward, BCR&N pressed northward in 1900, reaching Owatonna, thirty-three miles from Albert Lea with track parallel to M&StL but fifteen miles east of it. BCR&N continued dickering with CGW for means to enter St. Paul and with NP for routing between St. Paul and Minneapolis. NP would allow BCR&N use of its "B Line" for freights and its "A Line" for passengers, with BCR&N "making its own terms for the use of M&StL track" as part of the NP-M&StL joint operation of the "A Line." M&StL's cooperation seemed doubtful, however, given the direction of all of this, and in April 1901 BCR&N told NP that it would use Chicago, Milwaukee & St. Paul between St. Paul and Minneapolis as well as Milwaukee's passenger station in the Mill City. For that matter, BCR&N chose to use CM&StP instead of CGW from near Faribault. With construction of seventy-five miles and trackage rights of forty-six miles BCR&N would have its own route from Albert Lea through St. Paul to Minneapolis.[37]

To the south, negotiations among Iowa Central, M&StL, and BCR&N produced a new "reciprocal joint trackage arrangement" governing the line from Manly to Albert Lea. Effective July 1, 1901, Iowa Central would operate its trains into and out of Albert Lea; Illinois Central would remain a tenant between Glenville and Albert Lea.[38]

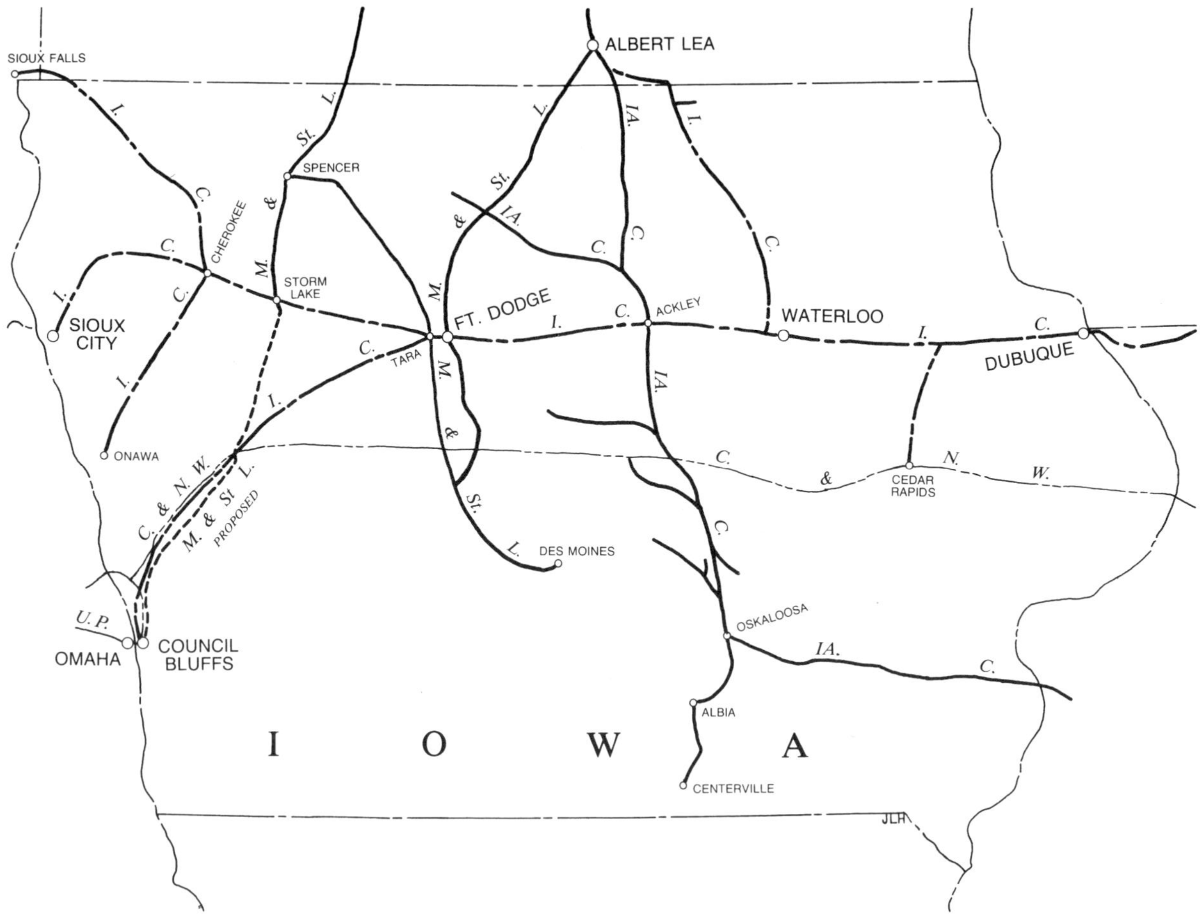

Map 7.1. Harriman was intrigued by strategic advantages offered by M&StL, but was not interested in Iowa Central. Author's collection.

This entire scene was played out against the backdrop of startling changes at Rock Island that in 1901 swept out much of the historic power structure and replaced it with one of dubious purposes—the Reid-Moore syndicate. Ransom Cable hung on as chairman, but he was mostly window dressing. The new team had made millions in other industries and set out to duplicate their earlier fetes at Rock Island. A salient example of CRI&P's now aggressive posture came close at hand. "The new owners are very busy in the affairs of Rock Island," BCR&N's emissary in New York wrote to C. J. Ives on April 16, 1902. He noted further that Rock Island recently had acquired an important Oklahoma road, "issuing bonds to pay for it." But he could not explain why BCR&N stock "should have been so rapidly advanced" and seemed not to sense that immense change was about to surround him. A month later the same man was boxing up certificate books and other corporate material, taking only a short break to tell a desperate C. J. Ives that "the present management are very reticent as to their plans . . . and I am asking no questions." Indeed, a few days earlier, on June 1, Rock Island had leased BCR&N; in 1903 it would issue more stock and acquire virtually all BCR&N equity on a one-to-one basis. Important players in this development were CB&Q, Charles E. Perkins, and others close to BCR&N, who sold their holdings at $160 per share. CB&Q, after all, had its own St. Louis–St. Paul line, and, although it would continue to operate through trains between those points with new owner Rock Island, Burlington's interest was tepid. For that matter, CB&Q itself was now owned in equal parts by Northern Pacific and Great Northern and was no longer the proud and powerful independent property that it long had been.[39]

So BCR&N disappeared from the pages of the *Official Guide,* the "Albert Lea Route" arrangement among CB&Q, BCR&N, and M&StL was sundered and undone, and Rock Island was spread across the letter boards of cars on the first passenger train from Minneapolis over the new line to Albert Lea. The date was November 2, 1902. Rock Island freight service commenced on January 25, 1903, and Rock Island ended all use of the former joint facility at Albert Lea in August.[40]

Elsewhere, loss of the long-friendly St. Paul & Duluth was a serious blow. M&StL ranked second behind much larger Milwaukee among the Duluth road's interchange partners, and since 1895 StP&D had used M&StL terminal facilities in Minneapolis. In addition, StP&D held the lease on M&StL's former Minneapolis & Duluth to White Bear Lake, Minnesota. All of this produced revenue for M&StL. But StP&D had found itself terribly squeezed. Omaha had its own line from the Head of the Lakes to St. Paul, and James J. Hill, despite his stern injunctions against duplicating existing lines, had indulged in just that practice by creating the Eastern Railway of Minnesota, which in a staggered construction program had finished a line parallel to StP&D all the way to the Lakehead in 1899. This clearly harmed StP&D and greatly irritated powerful Chicago, Milwaukee & St. Paul, which first tried to capture the Duluth road for itself and then seriously considered throwing down its own tracks in an already crowded corridor. It was Northern Pacific, of course, that finally ended St. Paul & Duluth's independent status by purchasing the road and all of its property effective July 1, 1900. NP, to be sure, had held the line during the early 1870s, had smarted ever after at its loss during the panic of 1873, and had looked diligently for ways to reclaim it, but in 1893 also had considered a new St. Paul–Duluth route for itself from Anoka through Cambridge to Sawyer, on its original main line west of Duluth. Milwaukee, which had done heavy business with StP&D, was mollified by NP with trackage rights all the way to Duluth. At any rate, passage of St. Paul & Duluth to Northern Pacific produced a mere shrug from the *Commercial & Financial Chronicle,* which said, "The event serves to emphasize the prevailing tendency towards the elimination of smaller and weaker roads."[41]

Northern Pacific was certainly not one of the smaller and weaker roads. On the other hand, it did suffer its share of indignities, including a siege of receivership that began in 1893, followed by humiliating control through an alliance of J. P. Morgan & Company and arch rival James J. Hill, and then a fearful tussle between Morgan and Hill on one side and Edward H. Harriman and Kuhn, Loeb on the other, in which NP was a central player. In 1890 NP had seemed to have perfected its route structure by leasing Wisconsin Central, gathering up terminal facilities in Chicago, and basking in a single-route highway all the way from Lake Michigan to Puget Sound. But the bargain was a bad one, and the Wisconsin Central lease was jettisoned. Reorganization followed in 1897, and by the end of the century NP's regained vigor was manifest in its acquisition of St. Paul & Duluth.[42]

M&StL was hardly disinterested in NP's fortunes. The two roads cooperated variously—for example, in the joint line between Minneapolis and St. Paul. And what a busy thoroughfare it was—eighty-four scheduled trains a day in 1897 by NP and M&StL plus tenants Wisconsin Central, Soo Line, Chicago Great Western, and St. Paul & Duluth over portions or all of that joint route. Of the eighty-four trains, fourteen were M&StL's—ten passenger and four freight. M&StL tonnage to and from St. Paul increased by only 4,036 in 1899 over 1895, and it commanded only 5.2 percent of the total. Nevertheless, M&StL remained properly committed to a presence in Minnesota's capital city. It had no such loyalty to Duluth, however. Any hope of establishing an independent avenue to that city had long since vanished, and, with the passing of friendly St. Paul & Pacific, M&StL's business to and from Head of the Lakes would move by one of the big railroads—Omaha, Great Northern, NP, and eventually Soo. And NP's acquisition of St. Paul & Duluth rendered redundant to M&StL the former Minneapolis & Duluth to White Bear Lake. NP, having inherited the lease of that property through acquisition of StP&D, forced the issue by canceling the contract with M&StL on September 4, 1901, and then purchased the line outright on November 29, 1901.[43]

Edwin Hawley was an infrequent visitor at M&StL and Iowa Central; rather, he studied and planned in his New York office. This was done at Hawley's Southern Pacific quarters until March 1, 1902, when he gave up his salaried position at SP and moved his business activities to 25 Broad Street, occupying space on the thirteenth floor with a clear view of Governor's Island, the Statue of Liberty, and the majestic Hudson River. Frank H. Davis, SP's assistant treasurer and a friend, left at the same time; together they formed the financial house of Hawley & Davis, with Hawley as senior partner taking a seat on the New York Stock Exchange. Hawley did not sever all ties with SP, however, retaining positions on SP's board of directors and on its executive committee.[44]

The young firm of Hawley & Davis was quickly in the thick of railroad events. "A syndicate composed of Edwin Hawley and his friends," announced the *New York Times* on March 27, 1902, had acquired Colorado & Southern, which itself held a majority position in Fort Worth & Denver City. At almost the same time, Hawley joined with John W. Gates in a pool that briefly controlled Louisville & Nashville (L&N); these important holdings in L&N were sold only a few months later at an immense profit. Then in 1903 Hawley was approached by Benjamin F. Yoakum—president of St. Louis & San Francisco, one of those who had joined Hawley in gaining control of Colorado & Southern, and recently elected to Rock Island's board—who told Hawley that Rock Island had designs on Chicago & Alton (C&A or Alton) and wondered if Hawley & Davis would undertake a quiet campaign to acquire C&A stock for Rock Island's account. Hawley agreed; in due course Rock Island came to have a controlling interest in Chicago & Alton. But this was at the expense of Edward H. Harriman, who with powerful others had reorganized that property in 1899 and 1900 and believed they had a firm hand on the company. Hawley proved otherwise. Harriman was stunned, then turned wrathful, even more so when he learned that Hawley's firm had handled the transaction. When the two men met at a business meeting in June 1904, Harriman upbraided Hawley in the presence of others, charging him with duplicity. Hawley said that he had seen the matter as a routine business opportunity, told Harriman that his conduct that day had been discourteous, and stomped off to his office, where he immediately penned a letter of resignation as director of Southern Pacific. Then, as if to add insult to Harriman's Chicago & Alton injury, Hawley joined the board of George Gould's Western Pacific, then in the process of irritating Harriman by building a new line alongside SP from the Bay Area to Salt Lake City.[45]

Hawley was hitting his stride. By 1905 he was a force to be reckoned with within the railroad industry and on Wall Street. If the past was prologue, it appeared that Hawley watchers would not have long to wait before his next move. They were not disappointed. In 1904 he quietly and skillfully crept into Rock Island's camp and scampered back with 145-mile Des Moines & Fort Dodge under his arm. Rock Island had leased the Iowa road since 1887 and recently had completed a 109-mile angular spur from Gowrie, on Des Moines & Fort Dodge (DM&FtD) twenty miles southwest of Fort Dodge, to Sibley, in northwest Iowa, on BCR&N. The Reid-Moore syndicate may have been distracted by larger matters; it certainly was asleep at the switch when DM&FtD stock became available. But Hawley was wide awake, and eagerly picked up this plum for M&StL's benefit. It was a good fit. M&StL ran its passenger trains to Des Moines over DM&FtD from Angus, Iowa, the two roads shared terminal facilities and interchanged traffic at Angus and Fort Dodge, and there were other potential benefits.[46]

Bewildered Rock Island stockholders were told only that the lease of DM&FtD had expired on December 31, 1904, and "as of midnight on that date the property was relinquished and restored to the owners." Important issues remained. DM&FtD had a track that paralleled Rock Island from Des Moines to Valley Junction, four miles west; DM&FtD and CRI&P agreed to pair these and operate them jointly. Rock Island's Gowrie–Sibley line was now a disconnected orphan; DM&FtD granted Rock Island trackage rights of 66.7 miles from Valley Junction to Gowrie. DM&FtD stubbed at Des Moines; Hawley secured trackage rights for Iowa Central to use Chicago, Burlington & Quincy from Oskaloosa to Des Moines, establishing in the process a through route from Des Moines to Peoria. Matters on the north end seemed more problematic. *Railroad Gazette* advised that work had begun on an eleven-mile construction project to link DM&FtD at Ruthven with M&StL's Southwestern at Terril. If Hawley was employing a ruse, it worked. M&StL secured operating rights over Milwaukee's Iowa & Dakota track from Ruthven to Spencer, 12.5 miles, and connected there with the Southwestern.[47]

Edwin Hawley had succeeded in uniting disparate parts—M&StL, DM&FtD, and Iowa Central—into an organized unit even if each company retained its own corporate identity. All of it would take effect January 1, 1905.

Chapter 8
The Newest and the Best

The NORTH STAR LIMITED*—a New Train Between St. Paul–Minneapolis and St. Louis. Electric Lighted Sleepers and Chair Cars. Dining Service.*
—Minneapolis & St. Louis advertisement, 1902

Even as Edwin Hawley and friends looked for new worlds to conquer, L F. Day had a railroad to run. And it was a larger, more complex operation in 1905 than it had been a decade earlier, when Minneapolis & St. Louis had operated only 370 route miles of line. It had grown to 662 miles after completion of the Southwestern to Storm Lake, and to 799 miles with lease of Des Moines & Fort Dodge.

Minneapolis remained M&StL's headquarters city, its operating hub, and because of the road's well-known presence in the milling district, M&StL still played an important role in delivering wheat and hauling away flour. By the turn of the century Minneapolis was the country's undisputed flour milling center; output increased from 9,349 million barrels for the 1892–93 crop year to 16.505 million barrels in 1902–3. Much of this was for export—4.7 million barrels of it in 1900, fully one quarter of all flour shipped from the United States for that year. M&StL handled 4.5 percent of Minneapolis flour billings in 1901 and 5.8 percent in 1902, well down from earlier glory years, but still very important to the company's financial health.[1]

Among Minneapolis millers, Washburn Crosby and Pillsbury were the two that dominated. Not all Minnesota flour was milled in Minneapolis, of course. About four hundred flour and grist mills dotted the state in 1901. One of the best of the state's "country mills" was Eagle Roller Mill Company at New Ulm. Also in that community was New Ulm Roller Mill. Together they had an annual capacity of four hundred thousand barrels, and both were known as producers of high-grade flour. Among several other Minnesota country mills on M&StL were Jordan Flouring Mills—"45 pounds of good flour for one bushel of wheat"—at Jordan, and Franklin Roller Mills—"Wheat Crisps, Better Than a Spring Tonic"—at Franklin. Additional flour millers along M&StL lines in Minnesota were at Arlington, Carver, Clarkfield, Dawson, Echo, Fairfax, Gaylord, Gibbon, Hanley Falls, Madison, Montgomery, New Prague, New Richland, Norwood, Twin Lakes, and Waseca. In South Dakota, a mill at Watertown provided revenue, and in Iowa M&StL gained traffic from flour mills at Estherville and Humboldt and from Great Western Cereal Company at Fort Dodge.[2]

Wheat, of course, was elemental to the flouring business. Production varied from year to year according to the vagaries of weather, blights, and insects. In 1895, for example, farmers around Gaylord expected to get twenty-two bushels per acre. After threshing, area farmers might have chosen sale of their grain to Pacific Elevator Company among three grain handling firms bidding for business at Gaylord. Pacific had elevators on M&StL at several locations across the road's West End to Watertown, South Dakota—among them Victoria, Waconia, Young America, Norwood, Hamburg, Green Isle, Arlington, Gaylord, Winthrop, Gibbon, Fairfax, Franklin, and Morton in Minnesota, and Revillo, Strandburg, and Watertown in South Dakota. Great Western Elevator Company likewise had line elevators on M&StL. Nearly absent along M&StL rails at this time were farmers' or cooperative elevators, although a cooperative wheat marketing association had been organized at Dawson, Minnesota, in 1885. By 1900 only one farmers' elevator held a lease from M&StL, at Hazel Run, Minnesota. Whether billed from a line elevator, an independent, or the one cooperative, wheat from M&StL stations in many cases was consigned to Minneapolis, which by the twentieth century far outstripped rivals Chicago and Duluth in annual receipts. In 1902 M&StL handled 7.1 percent of 88.7 million bushels, ranking sixth among carriers delivering wheat to Minneapolis—well behind leaders Great Northern and Milwaukee, both of which had far more route miles and much broader penetration of wheat producing districts.[3]

Lumber and other wood products, always a staple in M&StL's traffic mix, continued to flow in prodigious volume from mills now located primarily north of the Falls of St. Anthony in Minneapolis. Local millers there produced 307.1 million board feet in 1896, 493.0 million board feet in 1899, when Minneapolis became the leading lumber market in the world, and 465.2 million board feet in 1902. Most of this was construction material—lumber, shingles, and lath—and most of it was headed for traditional marketing areas west of the Mississippi River, but as production waned in Wisconsin and Michigan, billings also went east. Demand throughout M&StL's service domain remained high, much of it supplied at the retail level by line yards. During the late 1890s and into the next century M&StL usually stood behind Chicago, Milwaukee & St. Paul and Chicago, St. Paul, Minneapolis & Omaha in Minneapolis billings, handling about 16 percent of lumber shipped from that city.[4]

There were no surprises for M&StL in terms of tonnage and revenue by commodity during the 1890s and into the decade following. Grain and lumber amounted to nearly 50 percent of all tonnage (25.0 percent and 23.8 percent, respectively) for the period 1890–1899. Flour, coal, cement, and merchandise followed in order. Revenue tonnage, revenue ton miles, and revenue dollars grew handsomely during the 1890s but fell flat during the first half of the new decade. M&StL typically was a net exporter of tonnage throughout this period, usually originating two cars of freight on-line for every car received from other roads. Principal connections to Duluth were St. Paul & Duluth and then Northern Pacific; to Chicago, Burlington, Cedar Rapids & Northern and Rock Island, then Illinois Central; to St. Louis, Burlington, Cedar Rapids & Northern and Burlington, then Iowa Central and Wabash; and to Omaha, Rock Island, and then Illinois Central.[5]

Table 8.1. M&StL revenue and tonnage, 1890–1905

Year	*Revenue tons*	*Revenue ton miles*	*Freight revenue*
1890	882,615	77,087,412	$1,101,910
1900	1,605,383	174,564,187	$2,117,553
1905	1,967,599	184,140,096	$2,021,993

Source: *M&StL annual reports, 1890–1905.*

Information on shipments to and from stations is elusive and anecdotal. Minneapolis, which did not tire in its claim that it was the greatest jobbing, manufacturing, and wholesale center in the "whole Northwest," received or dispensed everything from school suits, waistcoats, shoes, and fall hats to pickled lambs' tongues, ginger ale, and Colorado peaches and Muscatine melons in season. In general, Iowa stations were most reliant on agricultural produce for outbound tonnage, while building materials and general merchandise typified inbound lading; business at Minnesota stations tended to be a bit more diversified. For instance, in 1892 Waconia shipped 545 cars of freight, including 125 of wheat and 400 of wood (fuel, likely destined for markets in Minneapolis and St. Paul), and received 91 cars, including 40 of lumber, 25 of beer, and 12 of brick.[6]

Freight train service was spartan. Waconia-bound cars, for example, were likely handled on a way freight that plied the line from Cedar Lake to Morton; a through freight also was assigned to that route. Beyond Morton to Watertown, a thrice-weekly local sufficed in each direction. Two through freights and a local worked the division from Cedar Lake to Albert Lea; locals only were assigned from Albert Lea to Fort Dodge and Angus, as well as from Winthrop to Estherville and Storm Lake and on leased Des Moines & Fort Dodge. (Extra trains were called as needed.) Number 96, covering 99 miles from Hopkins, Minnesota, to Albert Lea in five hours and fifty minutes, was M&StL's "hottest" freight in 1904—not impressive, but probably typical of scheduled freight operations at the time.[7]

M&StL's passenger service during these years could hardly be classified as a poor cousin, however. Boardings more than doubled between 1890 and 1905, passenger miles more than tripled, and the average distance traveled rose from 27.6 miles to 38.1 miles. Revenue per mile slid from 2.30 cents in 1890 to 2.02 cents in 1900 and to 1.88 cents in 1905, but total income from passenger offerings (tickets, mail, express) nearly tripled. During the 1890s, passenger income represented about 35 percent of all revenue, but in 1905 contributed an astonishing 51.6 percent.

Table 8.2. M&StL passenger service, 1890–1905

Year	*Number of passengers*	*Number of passenger miles*	*Total passenger revenue*
1890	500,449	13,831,892	$ 375,328
1900	755,816	29,759,191	$ 730,983
1905	1,216,937	46,391,032	$1,044,668

Source: *M&StL annual reports, 1890–1905.*

M&StL properly honored its various agreements with others in the Albert Lea Route consortium until Rock Island entered St. Paul and Minneapolis over its own line late in the fall of 1902. To that time the Cannonball remained the company's top train and was advertised accordingly. And M&StL joined with Burlington, Cedar Rapids & Northern Rock Island, and Chicago, Burlington & Quincy in other ways to maintain at least a semblance of solidarity. In 1900 M&StL worked with BCR&N to carry the "Miss Coghlin" theater company from Albert Lea to Cedar Rapids and in 1902 with Rock Island to carry passengers on special excursions to and from Minneapolis on behalf of the National Baptist Anniversaries, the Fraternal Order of Eagles, and the National Education Association. But relations were tense. BCR&N and Rock Island were irritated at a serious imbalance of westbound patrons over eastbound, feeling that M&StL was not doing its fair share to hold up the bargain. Matters only worsened after BCR&N disappeared into Rock Island during the summer of 1902.[8]

Illinois Central, of course, was the new kid on M&StL's block. IC entered Albert Lea in November 1900, and it initiated passenger service to and from Chicago through Waterloo on December 3. But IC's more immediate interest in working with M&StL was to put traffic on the Chicago road's recently completed (January 28, 1900) appendage from Tara to Omaha. New IC-M&StL working agreements went into effect almost immediately thereafter, with service through Albert Lea and Fort Dodge over what IC labeled the "Omaha and Minneapolis and St. Paul Short Line." M&StL gleefully concurred. Together they ordered up a day train equipped with Pullman buffet-parlor cars and coaches, and a night train with Pullman vestibule sleeping cars and coaches plus a Pullman tourist sleeping car to and from Los Angeles with connections at Omaha, Colorado Springs, and Ogden, Utah. The cost of a double berth from Omaha to St. Paul was $2.00. M&StL handled the trains 223 miles to and from Fort Dodge, IC the remaining 141 miles. IC also supplied station facilities at Fort Dodge, used jointly by the two roads beginning November 10, 1901. M&StL understandably combined its Des Moines and Omaha service, with the result that trains between St. Paul and Fort Dodge were long and heavy, especially the night trains, often requiring double heading.[9]

More richly recalled was M&StL-IC service to and from Chicago to replace that portion of the old Albert Lea Route package. But the historic arrangement with BCR&N and Rock Island could not be breached until Rock Island saw itself safely into St. Paul and Minneapolis. Meanwhile, early in 1901 IC increased its Chicago–Albert Lea offerings to twice daily, while Iowa Central coordinated schedules with

Figure 8.1. Train 2, shown here at Montgomery, Minnesota, handled a through coach to Omaha via Fort Dodge, Iowa, and Illinois Central. Author's collection.

M&StL at Albert Lea on June 8, 1901, to promote through service to and from Peoria over its own line and to St. Louis with Wabash from Albia, with Iowa Central simultaneously if awkwardly honoring its commitments with Milwaukee for joint operation from Minneapolis to St. Louis via Mason City and Albia. Iowa Central soon broke off its traffic arrangement with Milwaukee, however, and M&StL dickered successfully to gain access to St. Paul Union Depot effective August 1, 1902, abandoning the nearby and homely facility that had been provided by Northern Pacific. Meanwhile, M&StL's Anson B. Cutts, in charge of passenger operations, told a friend at the *Minneapolis Journal* that M&StL would pay $25 to the person who supplied the best name for the company's new premier train to Chicago and St. Louis. The resulting news story brought in about one thousand recommendations; out of those L F. Day and Cutts selected North Star Limited.[10]

M&StL said its new "luxurious train" would "challenge comparison"—it would be "palatial." IC promised that service would be "first class in every particular." M&StL announced that the train would be made up of new cars—"all broad vestibuled and built to Pullman's latest and best models"—including two sleepers (one standard and one compartment) plus a chair car and a buffet-library for Chicago, and a sleeper and coach for St. Louis (with a diner on IC to and from Chicago). A reporter from the *Minneapolis Tribune* got a sneak preview and gushed that the cars were "elegantly furnished throughout, the mahogany furnishings being particularly rich. In the buffet-library car is everything that a passenger might enjoy, books, magazines, stationery and every article arranged to give the greatest convenience possible." November 2, 1902, was the appointed day for debut; 7:35 p.m. was the appointed hour for departure. Out of the shabby Minneapolis station at Washington and Fourth Avenue North strutted M&StL's shiny entry; out of Milwaukee's depot a few blocks away steamed Rock Island's new contender. M&StL asserted that the North Star Limited was the "Newest and the Best," but Rock Island shook its head in disagreement, claiming that its time to Chicago was "faster, its line shorter, track better and trains handsomer than any other line to the south." Newspaper accounts suggest there was early support for the North Star, which was "crowded to its fullest capacity" on the first run and "loaded when it left the station" a week later. A. B. Cutts was ecstatic, but not everybody shared his exuberance. North Western reminded the public that its "20th Century Trains" between Chicago and Minneapolis were "electric lighted inside and out," Chicago, Burlington & Quincy said flatly that it had the "Best Line to Chicago and St. Louis," and Milwaukee, "The Fast Mail Line," even claimed that M&StL had pirated the North Star name from one of its trains that long had served "the copper county." Cutts would have none of it. "It is certainly very surprising to find that you have a train by this name, and careful scrutiny of the *Official Guide* fails to reveal anything of the kind; if you are making use of the title," he told Milwaukee, "it is done so quietly and secretly that nobody seems to have discovered it." Minnesota was the "North Star State," he affirmed, not Wisconsin or Michigan. "Our name is appropriate," Cutts concluded. "This name has been finally decided upon and will continue to be used by us."[11]

The North Star Limited was M&StL's queen, but it was not the sole attraction. During this period M&StL ordered three trains in each direction between St. Paul and Albert Lea; IC put on three between Albert Lea and Waterloo; Iowa Central scheduled two from Albert Lea to Albia; and, Wabash had two daily offerings on its Albia–St. Louis leg.[12]

Figure 8.2. Anson B. Cutts relished promoting M&StL's North Star Limited. Author's collection.

American railroads large and small saw the St. Louis Fair of 1904 as a right and proper justification to drum up business among discretionary travelers. Campaigns to boost the exposition and rail service to it were extraordinary. The North Star was no more than launched in November 1902, for instance, when A. B. Cutts began a vigorous awareness campaign, pointing out that the St. Louis fair would be twice as large as Chicago's splendid Columbian Exposition in 1893, and that North Star patrons could get "a full view of the grounds and buildings" from the cars. He was right. Of all St. Louis railroads, Wabash was most actively associated with the fair; its line was adjacent to the grounds, and it built a special if temporary station just outside the gates. When the extravaganza finally opened, Wabash ran a fleet of shuttle trains to and from Union Station downtown, and in the end Wabash handled more fair passengers than any other single road. Cutts was in his element. M&StL offered round-trip excursion fares of only $12.98 from St. Paul, Minneapolis, and nearby stations. The cars bulged with persons anxious to see South Dakota's "Corn Palace," Minnesota's "Butter Exhibit," a plethora of agricultural wonders in the "Iowa Building," and other marvelous sights. A delegation from St. Louis was in St. Paul and Minneapolis during the fall of 1904, reminding potential fair-goers that the exposition would soon close and urging a late dash to enjoy the spectacle. Cutts lowered the tariff to $10; that brought the desired response. On November 14, for example, two hundred additional passengers boarded the North Star, requiring more sleepers and coaches than usually assigned. When the gates finally closed in St. Louis, 19.7 million persons had passed through—a splendid showing.[13]

For Anson Cutts the St. Louis fair was a dramatic opportunity to put patrons on M&StL's passenger cars, but in his fertile mind there was a constant flow of lesser opportunities. During the 1890s he had inaugurated the company's marvelously successful "popular excursions," patterned to move people to any number of events and programs at almost any place on the system. Other carriers admittedly engaged in the same practice, but from about 1890 to 1917, no road in the upper Midwest was more energetic or effective in this regard. "Those in search of health or recreation can do no better than to take an outing to one of the resorts on the M&StL," Cutts admonished in 1900. He was thinking of Waterville, Waconia, and Excelsior, of course, and to make the point he offered half rates to those destinations on Sundays from all stations on the property. Half-rate fares also were made for the Republican State Convention in Minneapolis and for the Minnesota State Fair. In Iowa Saturday night excursions rumbled down the track from Fort Dodge to dances at Kalo, and early in the fall of 1900, nearly five hundred persons from Storm Lake, Rembrandt, Sioux Rapids, and Spencer boarded a Minneapolis-bound special, with school suspended so that teachers and students alike could enjoy the "educational experience." Another special train carried Minnesotans to the Democratic National Convention at Kansas City in 1900 for rail fare plus $6.00 in sleepers "including two nights on the track at Kansas City." In 1901, the modern Woodmen Picnic at Estherville, featuring a contest among twenty brass bands and a speech by William Jennings Bryan, prompted M&StL to send a special train up the line from Storm Lake. During the next year five carloads of excursionists from stations on the Southwestern and from west of Winthrop were forwarded to Duluth through St. Paul, and in 1903 eager partisans flocked to cars on the Watertown line when President Theodore Roosevelt visited Minneapolis. Out in South Dakota, however, railroad commissioners took a dim view of Sunday outings, citing "the interests of railroad employees" who should have a day of rest, as well as the "need to keep sacred the American Sabbath," recommending a law "against the running of trains on Sunday, except the main line through trains, and especially against the advertised Sunday excursions in the state or out of the state." A. B. Cutts would have frowned on such a statute.[14]

Jordan, on the main line twenty-four miles south of Hopkins, became a premier destination for excursionists from the Twin Cities, especially after Schutz & Hilgers improved its dance pavilion and park across from the brewery. The Ironmolders gathering in August 1902 drew about one thousand persons; "both hotels had their hands full waiting on the hungry," reported the local newspaper. A few weeks later, 580 tickets were sold to Herman Sons, who came to enjoy the Jordan Cornet Band, a waltzing contest, and athletic events including a tug of war and a boys' shoe race. In 1903 two trains were required to carry to Jordan the St. Paul Eagles, two more the Meat Cutters' Union. Later on four hundred persons appeared for the Minneapolis & Jordan Brewers' Union Picnic, and two thousand enjoyed Cigar Makers' festivities.[15]

Cutts was constantly alert to opportunities for "popular excursions," but he counted on regular patronage aboard scheduled trains—passengers like Gottlieb Schultz of Revillo, who went to the hospital in Minneapolis when he became ill; young women and their female chaperone from Leland, off to Clear Lake for a week's vacation; and Carrie Nation, the temperance advocate, who passed through Montgomery on her way to Waseca. Cutts also courted massive movements and special accounts—two trainloads bearing the Third Battalion of the 8th U.S. Infantry en route to Manilla in 1900, for example, and the same year a chapel car movement from Jordan to Corwith, "where the condition of sinners will be improved," according to the *Jordan Independent,* and later other Iowa miscreants would be dealt with at Valley Junction, Greenville, and Langdon before the car returned to Minnesota locations including Ormsby. In 1902 M&StL moved "California Exhibit" cars to Winthrop, and delivered the Winthrop band for a concert at Spencer. And every Wednesday M&StL dispatched a sixteen-section tourist car from the Twin Cities to Los Angeles "via the Santa Fe route"; another car departed on Thursdays using "the Scenic Line through Colorado and Salt Lake," with tickets costing "$32.90 and through berth rate of only $6."[16]

M&StL handled passengers of other types, too, but they produced no revenue. Hoboes, tramps, and bums always were a part of the landscape during this era, often appearing in great numbers at junctions such as St. James where a hobo jungle sprang up between M&StL and Omaha properties. Locals usually tolerated such places, but when drunken hoboes undertook a nocturnal serenade—and neighborhood dogs took up the chorus—they lost their sense of humor. The situation was much the same at Sioux Rapids, where the mayor ordered a "get tough policy" and the editor of the newspaper growled that "the duty of every citizen" was "to refuse to feed a tramp." Indeed, he said, "tramps are certainly enemies to the prosperity of the country and it is treason to give aid and comfort to the enemies of our country." Itinerants and drifters certainly did give M&StL and other roads reason for concern. One company official counted fifty-seven men riding on a single M&StL freight train; he noted further that passenger trains on the Watertown line often had tramps riding the tops of cars. Tragedy could follow, as it did for one nineteen-year-old who tried to board a moving train at St. James, but missed the grab irons, fell under the wheels, and lost both legs. Nevertheless, a certain mystique built up around those who beat their way across the country, and at the turn of the century a couple of enterprising entrepreneurs at Britt convinced "The National Tourist Union" to select Britt (where M&StL's Albert Lea–Fort Dodge line intersected Milwaukee's Iowa and Dakota line) for its annual gathering. Thus was born Britt's annual hobo convention, a celebration that has survived to this day.[17]

Still others found M&StL a useful if unwitting transportation medium. Several Winthropites in 1903 "borrowed" M&StL handcars for a seven-mile trek to Lafayette to attend a ball game, and in 1901 men who had robbed the bank at Greenville, Iowa, broke into M&StL's tool house and stole the company's handcar for their getaway. The same year thieves burgled the depot at Cornell, Iowa, absconded with two barrels of beer, liberated a handcar from the tool house, and pumped themselves nearly to Sioux Rapids. Section men later retrieved the handcar, but neither thieves nor beer ever was found.[18]

Edwin Hawley likely never heard of tramps riding atop M&StL coaches or thieves running off with handcars. Those sorts of issues were left to local managers from L. F. Day on down. Those same managers, however, were responsible for sending a steady stream of statistical data to New York, where Hawley carefully studied what he received. M&StL's business numbers for the period from 1900 to 1905 were mixed. Day was effective in keeping expenses under control; the operating ratio reflected as much, averaging a commendable 57.53. But the best that could be said of net operating income was that it stayed steady, at about $1.4 million. M&StL's interest on debt amounted to $919,257, and its debt and equity per mile stood at $44,037 (BCR&N's in 1902 had been $18,096). The company paid dividends each year, hitting $500,000 in 1902 and 1903, but dropping to $350,000 in 1903 and $200,000 in 1905. The market value of the company's common stock reflected this, plummeting from a high of $110 per share in 1903 to only $40 in 1904 before gyrating wildly if generally upward in 1905. Freight revenue, or the lack of it, was the culprit—only steady over the entire six-year span, showing no propensity for growth during a period of national prosperity and good feeling. M&StL had been the first among Hawley's railroad collection, and he had a sentimental attachment to it. But what did shrewd business judgment say to him? Should he hold it? Should he get rid of it? Should he expand it? Edwin Hawley no doubt pondered all of these options as he gazed soberly out of his office windows at 25 Broad Street.[19]

Chapter 9
IT WILL BE A HUMMER

We have excellent crops, rich farmers, good land, everybody making money, country settling rapidly.
—THOMAS A. WAY, 1907

ON SATURDAY, JULY 16, 1904, THE CREW OF THE Minneapolis & St. Louis "Passenger Extra 7 East" at Spencer must have exchanged expressions of mixed wonder, bemusement, and anticipation. They were in charge of Edwin Hawley's inspection tour, had right over all other trains, and had been given two hours and forty-three minutes to get Hawley to Winthrop, 117 miles distant over mostly dirt-ballasted railroad, which would require speeds of nearly sixty miles an hour between some stations. Another crew at Winthrop would receive similar orders to whisk Hawley to Minneapolis for a connection there for Chicago and then home to New York City. "Have Auditor Scott meet us on arrival with any mail or telegrams," L F. Day wired the Minneapolis headquarters. "Mr. Hawley will not leave station and will not want carriage." None of this implied a cavalier attitude toward M&StL on Hawley's part; it was simply his style. He eschewed publicity, avoided the press, hated crowds, and delegated full authority to L F. Day to manage M&StL and Iowa Central. His greatest comfort came in New York, in analyzing, studying, contemplating, biding his time, and only then moving with deftness and determination.[1]

Just as Hawley stalked opportunity, so did others stalk him. "I have the opportunity of controlling the Minneapolis & St. Louis and Iowa Central," J. P. Morgan wired James J. Hill on January 3, 1903. "The only way I can get it [M&StL and Iowa Central] is that Hawley is short and must have relief," Morgan confided. He would be pleased to "take it [M&StL and Iowa Central] either for CB&Q [Chicago, Burlington & Quincy] or Northern Pacific . . . or jointly." Hill huddled with Charles S. Mellen, once a member of M&StL's board of directors but now president of Northern Pacific, itself controlled by Morgan-Hill interests. Mellen would be pleased to have M&StL for NP, but saw no value in Iowa Central. Nevertheless, he thought Iowa Central might be acquired in the package and then at a judicious moment spun off to Chicago, Milwaukee & St. Paul. Morgan pressed the issue, saying that "these properties must go together," reminding Hill and Mellen as to the acute value of M&StL's Minneapolis terminal properties, and holding over them the awful specter of arch rival Edward H. Harriman. "What would be the result if the Illinois Central or Union Pacific [both Harriman-controlled roads] should get these terminals?" Morgan worried, recalling, no doubt, Harriman's recent run at Northern Pacific and the resulting Northern Securities headache. Hill was unswayed. "While we would like to control M&StL," he told Morgan, "the other line [Iowa Central] makes it impossible." But, Hawley got "relief" elsewhere and held onto both M&StL and Iowa Central.[2]

That did not end speculation as to his investments in them or his intentions for them. Alpheus B. Stickney, for instance, continued to poke about, looking for more pieces of railroad to add to his by now expanded Chicago Great Western. Among pieces recently added to that enterprise was Mason City & Fort Dodge (MC&FtD), which in 1886 had completed a line linking those towns and then passed to an ownership consortium dominated by James J. Hill and New York banker John S. Kennedy. Hill had been especially interested in lifting Webster County coal to the fuel-starved Northwest, but by 1898 local managers believed that "the future of the MC&FtD may depend on forming part of an Omaha–St. Paul line." Hill, however, had lost interest in the Iowa road, and for that matter, any Hill-sponsored sortie into Omaha certainly would have provoked immediate retaliation by Harriman. In any event, Stickney's CGW leased the Mason City company early in 1901, added a few miles of construction from Mason City to Manly, where it was joined with CGW's leg to the Twin Cities, and during the years 1901–3 added another 133 miles of new line from Fort Dodge to Council Bluffs to perfect an independent route in that diagonal corridor. Then, about the time Hawley was making his inspection of M&StL from Spencer to Minneapolis in 1904, local press reports predicted a union of Hawley and Stickney interests. If carried to fruition, the result would have been a most curious-looking route structure. It did not happen.[3]

Meanwhile, M&StL managers brooded over the company's disappointing freight earnings and contemplated means by which to improve them. Loss of independent St. Paul & Duluth to Northern Pacific had proved harmful, Rock Island's penetration of the Minneapolis–St. Paul markets clearly had hurt M&StL at its primary traffic base, and business alliances with Iowa Central were not yet matured. (In 1903 Iowa Central dispatched only two passenger trains and two freight trains south out of Albert Lea.) Expansion of route seemed the best—and maybe even the only—means to improve freight earnings. At one time or another consideration was given to lengthening the Storm Lake line to Council Bluffs, the Des Moines line to Kansas City, and Iowa Central to St. Louis. Yet any or all of these risked retribution by the great systems which, long since had laid claim to such primary gateways. Indeed Hawley, like Stickney, had missed the wave of opportunity. As eminent business historian Alfred D. Chandler observed, the great systems had taken their modern form in the 1880s; the largest systems in the early 1890s would be essentially those of the 1900s and the succeeding twenty years. M&StL's options were only two: expand or disappear into one of the larger groups.[4]

In Edwin Hawley's view, however, M&StL's disappearance was not an option. Thus he listened, and listened carefully, when L. F. Day counseled expansion to the west, beyond Watertown to the Missouri River and beyond. Yet there was good reason for caution. M&StL's revenue derived solely from South Dakota; that is, billings to and from Revillo, Strandburg, Troy, Waverly, and Watertown in that state were exceeded by expenses. In 1902, for example, the net loss was over $17,000. And the "great Dakota boom," followed by the "great Dakota bust," when long trains of uncovered wagons carried hundreds of broken and downtrodden settlers out of the state, reverberated in the collective memory. Hawley would be properly circumspect.[5]

Nevertheless, L. F. Day joined with Anson Cutts and others at Minneapolis to study newspaper reports, government tracts, and other sources dealing with South Dakota. As they did so, their eyes brightened. South Dakota was getting on its feet again with land values escalating excitingly. "Real estate is moving rapidly. Buy today; values jumping," advised one dealer in the state. Another noted that farm land was available in Codington County near Watertown for $8 to $25 per acre. "A comparison of lands in this section show favorably with Illinois and Iowa," said another. "Choice improved and wild farm lands" to the west in Clark and Spink Counties could be had "on favorable terms." Advertising of this kind reflected a new wave of optimism within the state—and justifiably so. Agricultural and livestock production, bank deposits, and average land values all increased marvelously after 1897. Farms were improved, towns sprang to life, and schools increased in number and in quality. Doane Robinson, a close observer of the Dakota landscape, proudly noted that "homesteaders occupy the region where formerly only branded steers, coyotes, and prairie dogs drifted." South Dakota, he smiled, was "distinctively the land of opportunity."[6]

Robinson likewise noted the rise of small cities, perhaps thinking of Watertown and Aberdeen. Watertown owned a favorable location in the fertile valley of the Big Sioux River and had blossomed into an important trade center. It also boasted a well-known flour mill, paint factory, foundry, machine shop, and sash and door plant, among other manufacturers. Watertown saw itself as a "hub city"; rail lines headed to it or from it in nearly all directions. But Aberdeen went further, unabashedly proclaiming itself the "Railroad Hub of the Dakotas." It, too, was a trading center of note and had a number of wholesale houses. Manufacturing was represented by a flour mill, a sash and door factory, a bottling works, and so on.[7]

Aberdeen also would profit greatly from Chicago, Milwaukee & St. Paul's decision to become a transcontinental road, gaining important terminal facilities as a result. One of the country's most aggressive railroads and one of the county's bluest of blue-chip investments, Milwaukee had in a sense rested on its oars at a crucial moment. Northern Pacific had become the first northern transcontinental in 1883, followed by Great Northern a decade later. Milwaukee managers for some years had boasted that their road, too, was ready and willing to build to the coast; they talked much, but did little. Joint acquisition of Chicago, Burlington & Quincy by Great Northern and Northern Pacific accelerated such rumblings. Not until 1906 did construction get under way, however. The Missouri was spanned at Mobridge, South Dakota, in 1908, and service to Puget Sound began the next year.[8]

Two decades earlier, during Dakota's boom, both Milwaukee and Chicago & North Western had put down a collection of secondary main lines and branches to dominate what became the eastern part of the state. Early in the new century, C&NW had augmented its service to Watertown, Aberdeen, and Pierre, South Dakota, and to Oakes, North Dakota, from Chicago with a new cutoff that crossed M&StL's Southwestern at Monterey. C&NW also pressed over the Missouri from Pierre all the way to Rapid City—as did Milwaukee from Chamberlain, almost simultaneously. Great Northern had an important presence at Aberdeen, Watertown, and Sioux Falls, and C&NW's Omaha had a modest network of lines. Rock Island had its route skirting the state's eastern boundary to Watertown, but others—Illinois Central, Soo Line, and M&StL—were bit players.[9]

As Day considered a mounting pile of data, he must have rubbed his chin, seeing a mixed picture in the country beyond Watertown. Two powerful Chicago roads, Milwaukee and North Western, were well ensconced, and St. Paul–based Great Northern could not be ignored. Neither could hard times following the Dakota boom be forgotten. But there was much that was enticing. South Dakota was clearly revitalized. Doane Robinson went so far as to call South Dakota "the proudest state in the galaxy." Moreover, the state had only 4.19 miles of railroad per 100 square miles of territory and only 72.66 miles of line per ten thousand inhabitants. There was room for expansion—for people and railroads alike. At the same time, immigration to the United States was surging, and Americans and foreigners alike continued to covet land and to embrace farming as an occupation and a way of life; in 1900, indeed, 42 percent of the country's population lived on farms. Moreover, farming was in one of its rare periods of prosperity, further driving the thirst for land. The demand was insatiable and would be met, at least in part, as the federal government redefined Indian policy to provide smaller reservations, thus freeing up more land for white settlement. Day was alert to all of what was happening—and to potential synergies. An M&StL expanded westward would surely yield a treasure trove of grain (in 1902, 48 percent of M&StL billings from South Dakota were grain), while area-milled lumber and manufactured items plus all nature of goods from Twin City wholesalers would flow outbound. In addition, coal—much of it mined at Iowa Central points—could move west.[10]

Day made the case for expansion to Hawley and then to M&StL's board. There were no dissenting opinions; Hawley gave the nod to go ahead. Subsequently, on December 18, 1905, were created two puppet companies, Dakota Construction and Minnesota, Dakota & Pacific (MD&P). MD&P was controlled by Dakota Construction, which in turn was controlled by M&StL through ownership of capital stock. MD&P was authorized to issue $6.250 million in equity and an equal amount of debt to pay for nearly 230 miles of line, which, upon completion, would be leased to M&StL for operation. M&StL, in turn, borrowed $5 million in five-year notes to aid construction, using MD&P's stock and bonds as security. MD&P's main line would be 171 miles in length, from Watertown to Le Beau, on the Missouri River about 22 miles downstream from Mobridge near the mouth of the Moreau River, which rushed down the Missouri plateau from the west; a branch would extend northwestward from Conde through Aberdeen to Leola, 57 miles. Franklin Floete, J. W. Cory, and W. S. Bemis, businessmen of Spencer, Iowa, were given the contract to acquire right-of-way and station grounds from 50 miles west of Watertown to Leola—"$350 per mile for the miles procured exclusive of station grounds." Thomas A. Way of Mason City, Iowa, gained the contract for the first 50 miles and the remainder of the line to Le Beau, organizing Dakota Townsite Company for that purpose.[11]

Area newspapers had speculated as to M&StL's intentions before Hawley made his determinations. Thereafter they wondered as to the meaning of *& Pacific* in *Minnesota, Dakota & Pacific,* and they wondered why M&StL chose Le Beau and Leola as end points. Hawley was mute regarding the *& Pacific* question and felt the answer to the other was self-evident. Le Beau had existed in various incarnations at essentially the same location for more than twenty years, had long petitioned for rail service to ensure its vitality, had become a center of interest for the cattle industry, and looked to a bright future when land across the Missouri opened to settlement. But it needed a railroad; navigation on the Missouri above Sioux City was mostly a thing of the past. Leola, too, which dated from the 1880s, had been teased by the Ordway, Bismarck & Northwestern and others, but still lacked rail service.[12]

L. F. Day was anxious to see the fruits of his dream. Construction would start in 1906, "as soon as the spring breakup" permitted. A. B. Cutts meanwhile performed reconnaissance and soon began extolling the virtues of the region beyond Watertown, seeing it as rich in potential for agriculture and grazing. During the spring and summer, graders ran ahead of rail gangs, which, beginning at Watertown on August 1, put down track across ridges and uplands in a country pocked by shallow glacial lakes. The elevation increased gradually, from 1,747 feet at Watertown to 1,804 at the crest of Coteau des Prairie, about forty-five miles west of Watertown. Beyond, after a drop of perhaps 550 feet in elevation, lay a huge expanse of attractive farm country, drainage of the James River flowing south to the Missouri. Track workers passed Conde in October, hurrying northwestward over the James River a bit more than halfway to Aberdeen, then through that city to Leola, arriving there on December 21. Yard tracks and a wye were spiked in place on Christmas Day, but scheduled trains would be delayed until well into the next year. Meanwhile, west of Conde other crews of up to fifteen hundred men scrambled to get down as much track as possible before laying up for winter. In 1907 weather conditions frustrated progress and put a pucker on Day's face, but before the end of July graders and trackmen were one hundred miles west of Conde, having passed over the Missouri Coteau at nineteen hundred feet elevation, and were moving along Swan Lake and then following the gradually descending Swan Lake Creek through the Missouri breaks to Le Beau—sixteen hundred feet in elevation. The line was thrown open to service on September 1, although considerable ballasting and surfacing remained.[13]

Some of the countryside along the 228 miles of new railroad was dotted with established farmers and stockmen. But much of it was open, and the timing was propitious. Good fortune seemed to smile; South Dakota had regained confidence. "We would rather be a blade of wheat in South Dakota than a bundle of stocks in Wall Street," jeered one newspaperman in Spink County, which M&StL now served. His frontier exuberance was justified by agricultural opportunity in the "tall grass" area from the ninety-seventh to the ninety-ninth meridian, where soils were good to adequate and where average annual rainfall ranged from eighteen to twenty-two inches. South Dakota Locating Agency at Watertown promised "wild" or unimproved farms at $8.05 to $20.00 per acre and improved farms at $23.00 to $50.00 per acre. As was so often the case in the American experience, the lure of land and the ability to work it proved irresistible. "What faith the man has who spends so many hours of careful, patient labor planting the tiny lifeless grains in the warm, moist soil," marveled one writer in *Dacotah Magazine.* But there was another lure; money could be made in the pursuit of agriculture. The territory served by M&StL's fledgling lines was "settled and occupied by rich farmers," promised Thomas A. Way, M&StL's townsite agent.[14]

This was the same Thomas Way who held the contract to acquire right-of-way for the new lines. He was indomitable—a genuine western son of optimism who rolled the dice with gusto, a salesman of the first order. An Iowa native who had lived variously at Forest City, Britt, and Mason City in that state, Way had involved himself in insurance, banking, real estate, grain elevators, and land speculation before organizing the Dakota Townsite Company in 1906 for the purpose of establishing communities along the M&StL west of Watertown. Way's approach was as simple as it was effective. He studied the territory contiguous to the new line, calculated its potential farm population and its capacity to support a town, and then determined to sell no more lots than the hinterland justified. That, he understood, would prevent inflation and leave his towns healthy. Business lots sold for $800 to $1,000 each; residential lots brought from $150 to $200. In 1906 he set up offices in the Granite Block at Watertown, and then he moved to Aberdeen, Cresbard, and Le Beau as the process unfolded. In Way's wake sprouted no fewer than sixteen new or renewed and very eager communities westward from Watertown—Yahota, Florence, Wallace, Crocker, Crandall, Brentford, Chelsea, Cresbard, Wecota, Carlyle, Onaka, Tolstoy, Hoven, Lowry, Akaska, and Le Beau. (Another company, with which Way was not associated, platted five aspiring villages on the Conde–Leola leg—Randolph, Stratford, Nahon, Richmond, and Wetonka.)[15]

Some communities along M&StL's western extensions already existed, of course, and in a few cases new townsites were located near earlier settlements. Established towns included Bradley, Conde, Aberdeen, Leola, Mellette, and Northville. Le Beau and Hoven were hybrids, so to speak. Le Beau had existed in various forms and at various locations since 1883, its fortunes never certain. Way's plat of 1907, made in advance of M&StL track gangs, was near one of the "earlier" Le Beaus, and it was impressive, with Main Street and Railway Street both centering on M&StL's terminal facilities. The circumstance at Hoven was similar in that "old Hoven," platted in 1897, found itself a half mile from M&StL's survey, giving Way an opportunity to lay out "new" Hoven. Residents at both Le Beau and Hoven had longed for railroad service and had been frustrated when attempts failed to lure steamcars. "The whistle of the locomotive would be the sweetest music a resident of the broad prairies of Dakota could hear," the Dakota Territory Railroad Commission had observed in 1885, because those melodic sounds would mark the "commencement of a new era in their lives." In 1907, such music finally came to Le Beau and Hoven. Elsewhere, "old" Cresbard moved 3.5 miles southeast to a new location on the railroad, and Launsberry disappeared when owners of the general store there moved to set up shop 3.5 miles away at Wallace.[16]

For Thomas Way, the organization, capitalization, and acquisition of land was followed by an intense campaign to lure people to his townsite creations. In this he was truly indefatigable, hiring Clayton Bailey, "a newspaperman of the first rank," to act as his "publicity man." Bailey settled for a time at Brentford and established there a weekly paper called the *Spink County Spike;* he moved later to Watertown, where he began publication of *Dacotah Magazine.* But the name of Thomas A. Way inevitably appeared on townsite advertising, and he was unquestionably the dominant force in the enterprise. In June 1907, Way invited prospective settlers to "come and examine

Figure 9.1. "Hurry Up, The Train's In!" was the inscription of the photographer on this 1911 view of the depot at Crandall, South Dakota. Several dandies and the usual gawkers assembled on the platform for the arrival of the Aberdeen Limited. Vaughn Ward collection.

new opportunities" in "new towns on new railroad in new country" in the "last 'west' east of the Missouri River"—along M&StL's line to Le Beau. "We guarantee not to overload our towns," pledged Way, adding: "We guarantee a healthy growth, but not a boom." A month later, as trackmen were laying down a mile and a half of rail per day, Way affirmed: "We have excellent crops, rich farmers, good land, everybody making money, country settling rapidly." In fact, Way was only warming up. He saved his heftiest barrage for August, as tracklayers hurried toward Le Beau. "A new town" was opened on the line "every week," said Way; five of them, he predicted, would "have 1,000 people at once." He was especially interested in recruiting parties that would build hotels, livery barns, restaurants, billiard halls, general stores, implement houses, hardware stores, and feed and flour mills. "We will sell you a lot and take pay for same when you make 20 per cent in your new business," Way bubbled. "1,000 fine business chances to be filled. 1,000 fortunes can be made."[17]

Way gave Hoven, Lowry, and Le Beau particular attention at this stage. Hoven, "in the famous Blue Blanket Valley country," was "all settled," had the "largest Catholic church in South Dakota"—was "all German"—and would "have 1,000 people soon," with "six elevators and other lines of business in proportion." Lowry, the next station west, was, Way attested, in the "best part of the celebrated Blue Blanket Valley," offered "big inducements for all lines of business," had "248 square miles of territory settled by German, Scandinavian, and American families," and was certain "to have a population of 1,000 people in a short time." Le Beau also was bound to boom. It was a "river town"; would be a "railroad division point" with a roundhouse, shop, and terminal facilities; had "natural gas" and "artisan water"; and would "ship 75,000 head of cattle per annum." Le Beau, in sum, offered "top business opportunities." It "will be a hummer," vowed Way.[18]

Fruits of Way's labors germinated as if by magic. Town building was as frenetic as Way himself. The author Ray Stannard Baker likely knew nothing of Thomas Way or of what was happening along M&StL lines west of Watertown, but he knew of such developments in the abstract and brilliantly captured the essence of the process. The town, he wrote, "lies close at the side of its parent, the railroad, as if fearing to venture out onto the open plain—a single long, wide street, the red station . . . and water tank on one side, and a row of square-front unpainted wooden stores on the other." Prominent was "the Gem Saloon." Nearby was "the post office, a feed stable, an agricultural implement emporium, a barber shop, (and more saloons), all in a row." Then, "as the town grows, they plant a brick school house—the school is always the best building in a western town . . . then a bare wooden church with silent steeple rises on a corner." Simultaneously "a side street appears, and a residential part, though it is difficult enough even for the homes to get away from" the railroad. "Earnest, strenuous, ambitious towns are these," Baker summed up, "full of ozone and energy."[19]

Baker could have been describing any number of Way's creations. When the depot at Wetonka was completed, for instance, residents there celebrated by holding a dance; a bank was established in 1908, and the Presbyterians built a cement block church shortly thereafter. Brentford's population topped 130 even as rails reached that place, adequate to support a blacksmith shop, hardware store, general store, clothing store, and small hotel. Chelsea soon after its birth claimed 200 citizens; local admirers called it "a rip-roaring western prairie town." The same might have been said of Cresbard, which in the summer of 1907 already boasted "six big elevators," a "water works supplied by two artisan wells," and "three blocks of cement walks." On its first birthday, Onaka had about 200 residents, and according to one observer was "one of the best towns on the line." Businesses there included a bank; a lumber yard; two each stores, elevators, and livery stables; plus one each meat market, confectionery, and drug store. Onaka also sported a new school house, a Catholic church, and the twenty-room Onaka Hotel. Russia's Count Leo Tolstoy saluted the infant village that took his name, urging its occupants "to be receptive to new ideas" and to say "what they think." Located on an upland crown in country nurturing the image of high plains (Missouri Coteau), Tolstoy seemed sure to prosper as the hub of a region not yet fully settled. Shortly after rail service began, it already claimed a newspaper, four grain elevators, one flour mill, a creamery, a bank, hotels, and restaurants. For its part, M&StL constructed terminal and engine servicing facilities at Conde, Aberdeen, and Le Beau. Water tanks were placed at several locations, depots at all stations (in the form of two-story structures with living quarters at Crandall, Onaka, and Akaska, likely as inducements for agents to bid on those jobs), and livestock-handling facilities and section houses (living quarters for the foreman and his family) at most.[20]

"The difference between a period of settling and a period of settling down is the difference between adventure and development" wrote one shrewd observer of the Dakota scene in 1909. Those who would do the "settling down" along M&StL's western extensions were a rich amalgam of persons native born (usually from nearby states) or recently arrived from Europe. Germans from Russia predominated in McPherson County (Leola), while significant numbers of Norwegians and Swedes were found in Brown County (Aberdeen) and Danes in Clark County (Bradley and Crocker). German stock was found in all counties served by M&StL lines, especially in Clark.[21]

In the end, M&StL would serve thirty-five communities in South Dakota. Excepting Watertown and Aberdeen, which would grow to be small cities, the rest were little towns, anchored hopefully on a windy tableland, giving an appearance of permanence. Streets were mostly deep rutted, frozen hard in winter, boiling with mud in springtime, diffusing tons of dust in the dryness of summer; hitch bars stood at streetside next to board sidewalks. Stock pens, grain elevators, lumber yards, and other structures sprang up near the depot along the "metropolitan corridor," but only a few feet beyond tie ends the loneliness of prairie plains rolled back from either side of M&StL's dirt-ballast track. No matter. Those who had come to people these towns and to settle their hinterlands were inveterately hearty, optimistic souls who took not the trouble of casting a backward glance.

M&StL's penetration into South Dakota was part of a much larger national construction pattern. As many as 41,445 miles of new track had been added to the national network in 1901–5. Another 16,563 miles were placed in service during 1906–7—"certain to go down in history as one of the most striking periods in the railway history of the Western world," according to one enthusiastic analyst. Another student of the industry concluded that "although the United States includes a vast stretch of territory, the country is well supplied with railroad facilities." That was certainly the case west of Watertown, where M&StL shared a significant domain with other and much larger carriers. Watertown had four roads—M&StL, Rock Island, Chicago & North Western, and Great Northern—and soon would receive South Dakota Central from Sioux Falls; Aberdeen likewise had four roads—M&StL, Milwaukee, C&NW, and GN. In addition, C&NW would be competitive with M&StL at Conde and Northville; Milwaukee was already in place at Bradley and Mellette and near Carlyle. On the Watertown–Leola segment, the average distance between competitive points was 28.6 miles; on the Conde–Le Beau route, the average was 28.7 miles. Was there traffic adequate to support that much railroad service? L. F. Day thought so, and he had convinced Edwin Hawley.[22]

Thomas A. Way's prediction of several towns with populations of over one thousand along M&StL's newly built lines in South Dakota proved wildly optimistic, but growth among them, uneven to be sure, was at least modestly impressive. And townsite development had not yet ended. In 1910 was born Haydenville, Minnesota, near the South Dakota boundary, between Madison and Marietta; in the same season appeared Adelaide, South Dakota, five miles west of Conde. Meanwhile, fleshing out continued at places like Chelsea, where one local entrepreneur took it upon himself to advertise in the *Minneapolis Journal* for persons who might found farm implement and general stores plus a hotel and restaurant in that aggressive if fledgling community.[23]

At the same time, Stratford quickly became the star new community on the Conde–Leola line. By 1909 four grain elevators, three lumber yards, and a cement block factory were trackside, and in the downtown area could be found two banks, two general stores, two "first class" hardward stores, two physicians, and two "good saloons," plus a newspaper office, a "small but modern hotel," a livery stable, and assorted other business houses. The town was especially proud of its "independent school district" and "new $5,000 school building." Stratford likewise sported "a well regulated opera house."[24]

Land values in the Stratford area escalated markedly following completion of the railroad, from $10 to $20 per acre to $35 and higher. It was the same elsewhere. Dakota Land Company at Hoven, Bartlett Land Company of Leola, Gunhus Real Estate in Cresbard, and Akaska Real Estate Company were especially aggressive in handling farm mortgages in the "great wheat and flax region of South Dakota." Oliver H. Craig Real Estate of Aberdeen might have spoken for all such firms, saying that 1909 would be "the boomer year in Northwest real estate values."[25]

By that same year, M&StL managers had a clarified picture as to business development along the South Dakota extensions. There were 680 identifiable freight customers, or about 2.97 freight accounts per mile of road west of Watertown. Aberdeen led with 199; Nahon had the fewest with 2. Setting Aberdeen aside, the average was 17.2 accounts per station. Shippers of grain, seed, and hay dominated, trailed closely by coal and wood dealers (whose business was often part of that of grain elevators and/or lumber yards). Accounts with grocery, dry goods, and general merchandise sellers were followed by those with purveyors of building materials and then a long list of miscellaneous businesses. Minneapolis-based lumber companies earlier had placed numerous line yards on the Hopkins-to-Watertown route, but these were conspicuously absent west of Watertown. In their absence appeared line yards owned by smaller companies—Floete Lumber of Spencer, Iowa, and Hollandsworth-Hart of Aberdeen, for example—at several locations; independent firms also dotted tracksides in many of the new towns. Grain elevators, of course, were omnipresent. Most were locally owned and operated, but Twin Cities–based Great Western, Pacific, and Security companies had line elevators at several stations; Pacific Elevator Company, in fact, had fifteen facilities along the new extensions. Eagle-Roller Mill Company of New Ulm, Minnesota, interestingly, had elevators at Aberdeen, Conde, Cresbard, Hoven, and Northville, gathering wheat for its hungry flour mill at New Ulm and providing, in the process, handsome line-hauls for M&StL.[26]

M&StL managers noted seventy livestock shippers strung out over the new lines, but most of these were piddling accounts compared to a handful of very large customers at Le Beau. And it was the expansive "boot and saddle" territory around Le Beau that gave M&StL its only contact with the "cow country West" and its sole flirtation with the romantic West of Hollywood films. Thomas A. Way seemed to anticipate as much as anyone what he often called "The City of Promise," holding onto his own assets and franchises at Le Beau after he sold to local banks all his remaining lands at Carlyle and Onaka, for example, and even after he looked elsewhere for other worlds to conquer. In 1908 and 1909 Way confidently predicted a population of three thousand for Le Beau, and, putting his money where his mouth was, promised to take payment for residential lots only "when the town has 3,000 people." The townsite itself was bounded by the Missouri River on the west and was laid up against the railroad on the east, with ten bold streets and six proud avenues, the depot immediately beyond the intersection of Main Street and Railway Street.[27]

The catalyst for Le Beau's glory years was clearly the cattle trade. This, of course, was part of a much broader pattern, which had begun at the end of the

Figure 9.2. M&StL's facilities bounded Le Beau, South Dakota, on the east, the Missouri River to the west. Author's collection.

Civil War with long drives of cattle from South Texas that sent to slaughter steers from Abilene, Texas, and Ellsworth and Dodge City, Kansas, among other places, but which simultaneously spread the cattle kingdom throughout the Great Plains with astonishing swiftness. For example, an entire trainload of Montana cattle was billed "for transportation east" from Bismarck, Dakota Territory, in midsummer of 1880. "This will be the inauguration of large shipments of Montana stock over the Northern Pacific," *Railway World* correctly forecast. These animals were likely bound for Chicago, where Nelson Morris, Philip D. Armour, Gustavus F. Swift, A. A. Libby, and John Cudahy already had established themselves among titans of meat packing. A vast web of rail arteries from the West brought in raw material (live animals), and an equally impressive web of lines sped the finished product (dressed meat) by a steady stream of refrigerated cars to eager markets in the East. In short order Chicago had become the "Great Bovine City of the World."[28]

Movement of the cattle culture into what became South Dakota initially had been hindered by the absence of rail routes and by the fact that much of the region remained "Indian country." Nevertheless, by the end of 1884 about eight hundred thousand head were in and about the Black Hills district, and little by little federal legislation opened up more reservation lands to leasing by cattlemen. Among those who watched with great interest was Murdo Mackenzie, who in 1890 had become general manager of the Scotland-based Matador Land & Cattle Company, which owned substantial operations in Texas. Under Mackenzie's talented leadership, Matador expanded into Kansas for short-term fattening, and in 1892 into South Dakota, near Belle Fouche, for an experiment in "double wintering"—to see if range animals could tolerate harsh northern climes and to see if holding them on northern grass would produce satisfactory gain. The answer came in 1894, when four-year-old Matador steers from South Dakota netted $35 per head on the Chicago market—the best average price the company had ever received. The experiment was an obvious success, and Mackenzie was predictably eager to expand Matador's Dakota theater.[29]

Mackenzie and others in the cattle trade soon urged the adoption of federal policies to create grazing districts on portions of the public domain unsuited to agriculture, as well as more grazing leases on Indian reservations. The focus turned to the Standing Rock and Cheyenne River Reservations, which lay west of the Missouri River and at least thirty miles above C&NW's projected line from Pierre to Rapid City. Indeed, no rail lines touched either reservation; the nearest was at Evarts, about sixty-five air miles north of Pierre and thirty-five miles south of the North Dakota boundary, on Milwaukee's line jutting west from Aberdeen. Mackenzie, representing Matador, and Burton C. Mossman, range manager for Hansford Land & Cattle Company, another Scotland-based firm better known as Turkey Track, chose the Cheyenne, splitting nearly a half million acres of leased land at 3.55 cents per acre. The leases—Matador on the north, Turkey Track on the south—were divided by a neutral zone or strip, really a horizontal chute from the 102nd meridian eastward to the Missouri River, that Matador, Turkey Track, and other ranchers could use to move cattle to and from their respective leaseholds.[30]

What captivated the black-bearded Mackenzie was Cheyenne's ocean of hills covered with grass—fattening grass, tallow-making grass—plus an abundance of sunshine and water. To these essential elements in 1904 he added others—cattle, men, and horses. Mossman did the same, each man committing to graze not more than one steer per thirty acres. Evarts became the entrepot, according to one account "the wildest of all wild cow towns." In any event, cattle moved across the Missouri to and from Evarts on a flimsy pontoon bridge or aboard a Milwaukee-owned ferry.[31]

As always, the cattleman's trio of enemies included the elements, thieves, and hard times. The first of these hit soon. A nasty late snowstorm in May 1905 claimed many cattle, and the "big winter of 1906–1907" left cowhands with ugly memories of "white hell." Carcasses of dead animals littered gullies and river bottoms the following spring. Some operators simply folded, turning their leases over to others. Mossman, for instance, picked up White River Cattle Company's Sword & Dagger rights, and with others formed the Diamond A, a formidable enterprise that then assumed Turkey Track's operation in South Dakota. Diamond A at one time or another ran as many as forty thousand head. Matador, with grizzled Murdo Mackenzie at the helm, was equally impressive. And when the year 1907 ended, Mackenzie and other Cheyenne Reservation cattlemen had ample reason to smile: South Dakota steers had averaged $45.44 on the Chicago market, up $9.60 over 1906.[32]

The Cheyenne Reservation cattlemen had another very good reason to smile. M&StL had reached the Missouri River in time to participate in the 1907 shipping season, and Le Beau offered an alternative to Evarts just as M&StL offered competition to Milwaukee. In addition to expansive livestock-handling facilities at Le Beau, which were enlarged and improved in 1908, M&StL established pens to hold thirty-five hundred animals on the west bank, across from Le Beau, to which point cattle could be driven and held before transit to Le Beau aboard the *Scotty Philip,* a steam-driven ferry.[33]

And Le Beau blossomed—nay, it boomed. One writer in 1908 called it "one of the most promising cities in the West, . . . because every person spares neither time nor money to push the city along." The business district was robust and included two banks, a couple of cafes, a drug store, a general store, a dry goods merchant, plus offices for physicians, dentists, and attorneys. Moreover, the "Idle Hour" billiard and pool parlor ("amusement resort") featured cigars and soft drinks, while saloons and other emporiums of pleasure and amusement required no paid advertisement. And the Hotel Le Beau—"steam heat . . . no dogs allowed in rooms . . . $2.00 per day"—provided "cuisine the best on the StL extension." Or one could check in at the Arcade Hotel, where everything was "new and first class" at competitive rates—"25¢, 35¢, 50¢, and up." The Le Beau Business Men's Association looked out for commercial interests, while Baptists and Presbyterians divided responsibility for community morality. Cultural needs could be met at Zimmer's Opera House, and news was disseminated by the *Le Beau Phenix,* with Edward McBride, "an earnest and active Republican," publisher and editor. Near

Figure 9.3. The *Scotty Philip* looked ever so much like a floating stockyard. Author's collection.

the tracks were two lumber yards, a grain elevator, a livery and stable, quarters for the City Dray Line, and M&StL's various facilities.[34]

Le Beau almost immediately eclipsed Evarts. In fact, rail service to Evarts ended in 1907, and Chicago, Milwaukee & St. Paul was abandoned two years later; business buildings were even lugged overland to enjoy new life at Le Beau. That did not mean, however, that Milwaukee vacated the field; rather, it encouraged cattlemen to use Glenham or stations immediately west of Mobridge on what had become its transcontinental line. Still, M&StL claimed a marvelous portion of livestock moving to and from the great leaseholds. In a general sense, stocker cattle moved to the range in the spring, while slaughter cattle were billed out in the fall. For Matador, the process was threefold: yearlings from the home ranch in Motley County, Texas, moved to the Alamositas division in the Texas panhandle, and then northward for double wintering (two winters, three summers) on the Cheyenne spread. Animals had to be "dipped" to rid them of ticks, lice, and scabies before leaving Texas and again at Le Beau prior to movement across the river. The process, time consuming and unpleasant for man and beast alike, required cattle to swim through long vats containing a mixture of lime, sulfur, and hot water or a nicotine solution of tobacco and hot water.[35]

The year 1908 gave M&StL managers the first full twelve-month period to gauge the impact of livestock traffic from Le Beau. In July a late-season train of twenty cars brought two-year-olds for Turkey Track, and eleven cars of mixed slaughter cattle headed for South St. Paul. A month later two carloads of horses moved to South St. Paul, and then the fall rush began. Double-headed trains of twenty to thirty cars left daily with Turkey Track steers consigned to Chicago Union Stock Yards. At the end of September, M&StL's Anson B. Cutts accompanied Murdo Mackenzie and other Matador officers and directors who had come to Le Beau aboard a special train to inspect local operations and to witness the first twenty-two carloads of Matador cattle dispatched to Chicago. Shipping ended on November 16, when Turkey Track, Diamond A, and Matador each shipped a trainload. In the aggregate, twelve thousand animals had been billed out in 1908, with approximately the same number received; the estimated gross value was $1 million. For M&StL it meant about one thousand carloads. Matador accounted for only 20 percent of the total, sending most of its animals via CM&StP at Wakpala, three stations and fourteen miles west of Mobridge. But prospects were excellent for a much greater move in the next year through Le Beau. If so, said the *Le Beau Phenix,* "Le Beau will lead all other cities in the United States in the number and value of its livestock business."[36]

The Matador company had reason to be pleased with its Dakota operations. Matador managers knew, and grudgingly admitted, that northern ranges produced better gains of greater quality and that four- and five-year-olds from Dakota graded better at Chicago than range beef from Texas. That meant greater profit. Moreover, Matador's reputation for quality was enhanced by five ribbons it won in competition at Chicago in November 1908. Its prize-winning show animals had traveled east over M&StL from Le Beau.[37]

There was great expectation in Le Beau as 1909 dawned. In January Matador received fifteen hundred sacks of cottonseed to be used as winter rations for livestock, but business on the railroad was slack until the shipping season began early in May. During that month 5,670 animals in ninety-three cars arrived during one week, but in June fourteen trainloads of twenty-five cars each arrived in just seven days. Before it was over, forty-five thousand head were branded, run through dipping tanks, and transferred to the far side of the Missouri by the *Scotty Philip.* In the fall a like number would be sent eastward, most of them to Chicago commission houses.[38]

If ever the sun shone brightly on Le Beau, it was during the summer and fall of 1909. M&StL, in a firm statement of confidence, appointed J. F. Knight as "Live Stock Agent with headquarters at Le Beau." At the same time, Akaska Real Estate reported active sale of quarter sections of land in the country between Lowry and Le Beau, the opera house was about to open, and ten-foot sidewalks were in place on Main Street and on Railroad Avenue to the depot. Moreover, there were rumors that M&StL would bridge the Missouri and push on west. Rumors of that type were epidemic throughout the age of railways, and many—perhaps most—were idle gossip or wishful thinking. Rumors regarding Le Beau, however, were based on fact. M&StL officials confirmed in early spring of 1909 that the company intended to extend itself to the center of Butte County above Belle Fouche, nearly to the Wyoming boundary—this in anticipation that Cheyenne Reservation, or at least a large part of it, soon would be thrown open to white settlement. Le Beau predictably was abuzz. Over at the *Phenix,* Edward McBride already had declared Le Beau "the Metropolis" of Walworth County, and now with the prospect of settlement across the river he eagerly exclaimed that Le Beau would be the "Front Door to Lands." Meanwhile, M&StL locating engineers were setting stakes to the west, and gravel ballast was being applied on the line from Lowry through Akaska to Le Beau. Before the end of July, surveyors were one hundred miles west of Le Beau, and piling, stringers, and caps littered the waterfront. "This paper stated several weeks ago that bridge work would be in full blast at this point before the snow flies," exulted Edward McBride. "When you see it in the *Phenix* it is true." Indeed, M&StL engineers had authority to bridge the Missouri. McBride could not contain himself. Surely, he concluded, the presence of the bridge gang meant M&StL actually meant to go all the way to the Pacific, with branches, incidentally, to the Black Hills, Wyoming, and elsewhere.[39]

McBride was hardly alone in advancing the idea of M&StL as a road to the coast, and Le Beau was not alone in euphoria as a reflection of that prospect. Watertown, even more than Le Beau, expected to profit should M&StL persist westward. With that thought, its leaders chartered a special six-car "good will" train to Le Beau late in July. It was great fun—and an appropriate prelude to even greater attractions.[40]

One month later President William Howard Taft signed legislation opening 2.6 million acres of land on the Cheyenne Reservation. Le Beau was designated as one of six registration points. That alone would have been adequate to ignite a local celebration, but Le Beau also was coming up on its second birthday. Double the reason for a two-day bash, September 16 and 17, featuring dancing, fireworks, music by three brass bands, athletic contests, cowboy sports, and "Doe

Figure 9.4. Opening the Cheyenne Reservation gave A. B. Cutts a marvelous chance to increase business on M&StL's West End. Author's collection.

Fisk's Great Railroad Shows." M&StL promised "excursion trains and cheap rates."[41]

As the lusty reverie of those enthusiastic festivities subsided, work commenced on M&StL's bridge and the stock shipping season began. But Le Beau was preoccupied with preparations to greet the throng of persons who were sure to appear as registrants for fourteen thousand quarter sections across the river. "The great majority of all applicants will register at Le Beau," Edward McBride freely predicted. After all, he reasoned, Le Beau was the railroad station nearest to most of the reservation. "Visitors step from the train and view the promised land 20 minutes later," he bubbled. All of this was made to order for M&StL's imaginative A. B. Cutts, who said that this surely would be the "last chance to get 160 acres of land free." Cutts authorized special trains and excursion rates of one and a half times the usual fares plus $2.00 to either Le Beau or Aberdeen (one of the other registration points) for the registration period, October 4 through 23.[42]

Attendance at Le Beau was less than Edward McBride and Anson Cutts had hoped for, but

Aberdeen thronged with aspirants expecting to be among the lucky ones chosen by lottery. The winners typically came from elsewhere in South Dakota or from surrounding states; nonlocals took perhaps 80 percent of the homesteads assigned. Many were from towns with M&StL stations to the east.[43]

Cutts saw the country west of the Missouri as an extension of "The New Empire," the James River valley and beyond, which M&StL had tapped with its line from Watertown. *Dacotah Magazine* did not differentiate, seeing all of South Dakota as "a country blessed by God and one now being developed by man with Divine consent and assistance." Others chipped in, contending that the Moreau River valley west of Le Beau, while undulating, was blessed with "rich black loam underlaid with clay" and appeared "to be well adapted to diversified farming" of the type found in eastern South Dakota, Iowa, and Illinois. One observer was more cautious, however, noting that "every region has its drawbacks . . . and nowhere does the law of survival of the fittest obtain more surely than in the land of the pioneer." This particular writer recognized that there would be casualties. Nevertheless, he persisted, while the "weak would fail and be weeded out," the "strong who come to stay" would "receive the reward always reserved for those who stick." These victors in the Darwinian struggle would make "the desert places bloom."[44]

Balderdash, sneered cattlemen. Land west of the Missouri had grass that was "right side up," as God intended. No steel plow should ever turn it. This country, simply stated, was unfit for agriculture. But Theodore Roosevelt, with whom many thought Murdo Mackenzie and other cattlemen had had a sweetheart deal, was no longer president, and William Howard Taft had taken the side of the more numerous "sodbusters." Leaseholds, at least most of them, would be extinguished over time, and cattlemen would be compelled to look elsewhere for huge tracts of grassland.[45]

The cattle culture had been good to Le Beau, but a hinterland to the west—opened up by an M&StL extension and populated with durable farmers—was even more alluring, offering the possibility of greater business volumes on a less seasonal basis and, best of all, the prospect of long-term stability. The ebullient Thomas A. Way had predicted a population of three thousand for Le Beau, but an even more sanguine prognosticator, seeing Le Beau as a "big distributing center," thought twenty-five to thirty thousand more likely. But it was not to be.[46]

Several elements combined against Le Beau. One of these had to do with the Matador Land & Cattle Company. Murdo Mackenzie had turned over management of Matador's Dakota operations to one of his sons, Dode, "a blue-eyed, sandy-haired Scot," whom one associate recalled as being "as likable and fine a young man as ever lived," adding as a serious caveat, however, "while sober." But young Mackenzie found too much time on his hands after the shipping season ended in 1909, and turned to drink and games of chance. It had no good end; Dode Mackenzie became an irresponsible drunk. He was shot and killed in a Le Beau saloon on December 11, 1909. Despite his faults, however, Dode Mackenzie was well liked. Matador hands took umbrage at his death, irritation that deepened heartily when his killer was acquitted. They boycotted Le Beau ever after. More important, no Matador cattle ever again entrained at Le Beau.[47]

A few months later a fire started on Le Beau's Main Street and quickly tore through most of the business district. Ugly fires such as this were not unusual in frontier towns made up of flimsy false-front buildings; severe conflagrations already had hit Tolstoy, Lowry, and Akaska, for example. But this one was more than suspicious in origin. The fire hose had been cut; so had telephone and telegraph lines. Bad news followed bad news. Another fire hit the town some weeks later.[48]

The lusty and gritty river town tottered uncertainly into 1910; ill fortune continued to stalk the place. In August of the previous year, editor McBride had reported in passing that M&StL's locating crew had "logged 115 miles" and had returned to Le Beau. It seemed to mean little, especially since two pile drivers had been dispatched to the bridge site. But even as that locating crew had been surveying and setting stakes west of Le Beau in the Moreau River valley, Milwaukee crews had been spiking down rails leading off from that company's new line to the coast just west of Mobridge to Trail City and branching there, one route turning west from that place to Isabel, the other proceeding south over the Moreau River and then west to Faith—essentially preempting M&StL. A full-page advertisement in the *Le Beau Phenix* taunted local readers by inviting interest in a town lot sale at Faith, approximately ninety miles west-southwest of Le Beau—"Faith being terminus of the Cheyenne Branch of the" Milwaukee Road. M&StL meanwhile had disbanded the locating crew and had removed the pile drivers and all bridge timbers, saying that its engineers had been unable to drive piling that would hold at the Le Beau crossing. Perhaps. But more likely M&StL managers recognized that Milwaukee had beaten them to the draw. They must have recognized, too, that West River country would support only limited rail service. For Le Beau, M&StL's decision had a simple consequence: it would have no hinterland to the west.[49]

Le Beau's dwindling population stumbled on, leaden-eyed, punch-drunk, reeling, yesterday's dreams dwindling. Reasons for hope were rare. The first range cattle consigned to Turkey Track for 1910 arrived late in April, and M&StL told McBride of the *Phenix* that it anticipated sending one thousand carloads of goods to Le Beau that season. A month later, however, an inspection train bearing officials of the Hawley roads and eastern capitalists derailed three miles east of town. The event, while minor, was grimly prophetic.[50]

Meanwhile, there were deep frowns under the Stetson hats of South Dakota cattlemen. Their costs of operation had escalated alarmingly over the last few years, nesters had invaded large portions of land west of the Missouri, Mother Nature turned on them with a vicious two-year drought in 1910–11, and the federal government could be expected to cancel leases as they came up for renewal. In 1902, 233,000 head of South Dakota cattle had been marketed; in 1912 the number would be 126,000, which would be down to 97,034 in 1913. During the following year the Matador lease would expire and the company would turn its northern operations to Montana and Saskatchewan. It was the same with other large outfits, most of which had already thrown in the towel or would do so shortly. The exception was Burton C. Mossman's Diamond A, including the old Turkey Track, but Diamond A cattle increasingly moved via Eagle Butte, a station on CM&StP's branch southwest of Mobridge, which Mossman described as a village of "unpainted buildings and painted women." Maybe so, but its stock pens and chutes remained active, while those of Le Beau were mostly silent.[51]

It went no better for the agriculturalists who had spilled so enthusiastically into West River country. They had clung to the delusion that the "humid belt" was working westward, ignoring warnings that favorable conditions west of the 100th meridian were transitory. What they found was a domain either indifferent or hostile to the plowman. In 1900, 43,732 persons had lived west of the Missouri in South Dakota, a figure that grew to 137,687 in 1910. But the devastation of drought in 1910–11 that lingered into 1912 hit farmers as hard or even harder than it hit cattlemen. In 1915 the census would show only 120,151 in the West River valley. Even those who turned the soil may have wondered if they had been wise to do so. This verse implies as much.

> We broke today on the homestead
> The last of the virgin sod.
> And a haunting feeling oppressed me
> That we had marred a work of God.

Burton Mossman and Murdo Mackenzie would have nodded heartily in agreement; they had always held that those grasses should have been left right side up.[52]

Le Beau suffered greatly from the collective effects of all this, its glory days ever so fleeting and ever so clearly in the past. Joy and optimism were overtaken by fear and pessimism. "In the summer of 1907," one-time resident George L. Shaw later recalled, "my mother and stepfather, George Twing, decided to move to Le Beau where he would practice law. I would also go to Le Beau and go into business for myself [hardware and agricultural implements]." Shaw was witness to Le Beau's meteoric ascent and its equally dramatic decline. "At the end of five years, in the fall of 1912, I borrowed $25 to get out of town. The score stood as follows: Liabilities, $2,800. Assets, $1,300 in unsold merchandise, $50 in uncollected accounts receivable, a wife and expected child, plus five years of business experience. It took me five more years to pay off my merchandise creditors in full," Shaw remembered. He was not bitter. Indeed, he said, "The memories of those five years at Le Beau are precious." He thought of the period as something of a transition "between the days of Calamity Jane and Wild Bill [Hickock] and the stability of the 20th century."[53]

Le Beau's sputtering flame proved patently disheartening to M&StL's managers, who late in 1911, frustrated and irritated, cancelled all passenger service west of Conde to Le Beau, offering only a triweekly freight plus a Sunday stock extra from Le Beau after the shipping season ended. Public outcry was great, however, and by March 1912 M&StL reinstituted passenger trains. It was obvious, nevertheless, that from the railroad's point of view Le Beau was a bust. The jury was still out as to the rest of the line west of Conde—and, for that matter, the entire package beyond Watertown.[54]

Chapter 10
EVERYTHING FROM CASKETS TO CORSETS

Spencer yard is blocked—not room for more than 15 cars.
—AGENT TO DISPATCHER, 1909

THE UNITED STATES UNDERWENT SIGNIFICANT growth during the first decade of the twentieth century. The service area of Minneapolis & St. Louis—and the company itself—reflected at least some of this. South Dakota's population grew from 401,570 to 583,888. Iowa's population actually dropped, however, from 2.231 million to 2.224 million, the farm population receding as it had since 1880, but the population of Des Moines jumped to 86,368 citizens. Minnesota grew nicely, from 1.751 million to 2.75 million, and Minneapolis swelled to 301,408 residents by 1910. M&StL's mileage in these three states rose from 597 in 1900 to 1,027 in 1910, representing the lease of Des Moines & Fort Dodge and new mileage in South Dakota. Passenger boardings in 1900 were 755,816, but rose to 1,372,089 in 1910; freight tonnage in 1900 was 1,605,383, nearly doubling to 3,006,219 in 1910. Both indexes mirrored rising population in the service region, a generally robust economy, and expanded route miles.[1]

While freight volumes went up impressively, especially during the second half of the decade, reflecting new route miles and to a lesser extent a healthy economy, M&StL's traffic mix underwent important shifts. The number of revenue ton miles rose refreshingly during the last five years of the decade, nearly doubling the 1900 figure, although freight revenues grew by only 62 percent by 1910 over 1900.[2]

Grain dominated loadings, and wheat led. Minnesota had been foremost among wheat-producing states in 1899, but by 1909 North Dakota had assumed the lead as the wheat culture continued its northwestwardly march. This shift in the kind of crops grown was reflected along M&StL in Lac qui Parle County, in far west-central Minnesota around Dawson and Madison, where wheat production for 1910 was only 53 percent of what it had been in 1900. During the same time, however, production of oats nearly doubled and the corn harvest increased by about 60 percent. Iowa and Illinois jousted annually for supremacy in the production of corn, much of it fed to livestock, especially swine, and the two states likewise alternated at the highest rank in the harvest of oats, some of it billed to Heath Oat Meal Mill served by M&StL at Fort Dodge.[3]

Despite these alterations, wheat, as always, moved to Minneapolis in great volume, and during the late summer hundreds of men followed the harvest to provide the labor force required by the seasonal burst. Most of the wheat was sold to elevators at the nearest towns—many of which, especially on M&StL's route to the west, were line elevators. Then, as orders came from millers, Great Western, for instance, or Pacific

Elevator telegraphed instructions to local managers at locations such as Delhi, Minnesota, and Crocker, South Dakota, to ship a prescribed number of bushels. Cars then were ordered from M&StL's agent, were subsequently spotted by an obliging freight crew, and were loaded and dispatched to the Minneapolis milling district or elsewhere. M&StL did not have a feeder system adequate to compete with the larger roads working west, so its deliveries did not match those of Milwaukee, Great Northern, or Soo Line. Still, in September 1907, a representative month, it moved over 8 percent of all wheat to Minneapolis, ranking fifth among all carriers.[4]

Minneapolis never did receive all of the wheat grown in the Northwest, of course, nor did it mill all of the flour shipped from the region. Indeed, by 1909 no fewer than twenty-one individual companies dotted M&StL tracks outside of Minneapolis. These were as substantial as Commander Mill at Montgomery, Eagle Roller Mills at New Ulm, and W. H. Stokes Milling at Watertown, or as small as Estherville Roller Mill or Echo Milling. Madison Milling began operation as early as 1893. "Madison's Best Flour," said the company, was "always good." Young America Roller Mills contended, however, that there was nothing to compare with its "Moccasin Flour." Nevertheless, for the bulk of its flour business, M&StL was much more dependent on Washburn-Crosby's "Gold Medal Flour," which was transported in forty-nine-pound cloth sacks that moved in a steady flow of boxcars from Minneapolis loading docks.[5]

Two traditional staples of the company's traffic mix, coal and lumber, were problematic. The demand for coal in the service area only increased, but by 1909 a mere eight on-line producers remained—two each at Angus and Kalo, one at Ogden, and three at Rippey—but these were far from adequate to supply demand. The balance of coal tonnage, not nearly as compensatory as one-line loadings, came via Duluth or from connecting roads such as Iowa Central or Illinois Central. For lumber, however, there was no balance to be found as production at the Minneapolis mills slumped. In 1902 not one mill worked to capacity owing to a "lack of logs," and as the supply of raw material eroded, companies long established in Minnesota looked southward to East Texas or westward to other great timberlands such as British Columbia, Washington, Oregon, and northern California. The Weyerhaeusers, long prominent in Minnesota, who in 1900 incorporated in the state of Washington and gradually moved there, provided an easy example. After 1905, Minneapolis was no longer the nation's sawmill center, although at least fifty line yard companies maintained headquarters in the city. It was on such firms that M&StL depended for a reliable flows of business. L. P. Dolliff & Company was representative, with yards at Belview, Delhi, Marietta, and five other stations, although systemwide most lumber yards were independents. For that matter, individuals occasionally ordered a carload of lumber; the blacksmith at Revillo did so, "for his own purposes," the local newspaper reported. Agents at a few stations—Waconia, Rogers, and Waterville among them—also recorded a regular flow of cord wood to Minneapolis and St. Paul markets, but those shipments declined as nearby timber stands were exhausted and as customers turned to alternate fuels. The result was a dramatic slide in lumber and wood as a percentage of M&StL's total tonnage—from 19.6 percent in 1900 to 7.8 percent in 1910.[6]

M&StL's livestock tonnage nearly doubled during the first decade of the new century, but only held steady as a percentage of all business (2.3 percent). Heavy volumes of cattle to and from Le Beau were supplemented by animals fattened on corn in Iowa and sent to Chicago slaughterhouses. Three trainloads of Montana steers bound for southern Iowa passed through Jordan in one day, as an example of the growing feeder cattle business. Other animals were destined for the Union Stockyards at South St. Paul. Promoted by the tall, red-bearded Alpheus B. Stickney and others, Union Stockyards had moved from Minnesota Transfer to its new location in 1887. Ten years later 757,229 animals (cattle, hogs, sheep, and horses) passed through its gates. Two years later the number was 980,183, and its management said that 100,000 beeves, 1,000,000 hogs, and 500,000 sheep would be required in 1900 to satisfy the trade. By 1916 St. Paul Union Stockyards would rank fifth among the nation's livestock markets. Livestock dealers and shippers were found at most M&StL stations; in a general sense those in Iowa favored Chicago, while those in South Dakota and Minnesota used South St. Paul. Many days M&StL was an "also ran" among roads delivering live animals to St. Paul, but there were impressive exceptions. On September 18, 1907, M&StL delivered 18 carloads of cattle, 26 percent of the total for that day; on December 8, 1911, it was responsible for 44 of 90 cars (48.8 percent), and on Mondays and Fridays during the first two months of 1912, M&StL brought 343 of 1,110 cars consigned (30.9 percent).[7]

All of this was at a time when railroads enjoyed a virtual monopoly on transportation. If an item required movement from one place to another, it went by rail in nearly all cases. Nevertheless, M&StL's traffic mix in 1900 was dominated by grain, flour, lumber, cement and bricks, soft coal, merchandise, and livestock—accounting for a whopping 83.5 percent. But change was afoot. In 1905 these primary commodities made up 78.6 percent of traffic; in 1910 the figure was down to 74.9 percent. Part of this was explained by the decline in lumber billings from Minneapolis, but other variables included the maturing national economy, new or expanding industries in the service area, a growth of manufacturing, a growing and mostly vibrant agricultural sector that was in the process of diversifying, and a general sense of prosperity and optimism that fostered consumer spending.[8]

A continuing push for diversification of crops and other changes in agricultural production occurred in the wake of the wheat culture's movement to the northwest. No longer would farmers in Iowa and southern Minnesota be tied to one crop or one stream of income. To illustrate the point, billings in Iowa at Corwith included corn, oats, wheat, barley, flax, potatoes, apples, butter, eggs, hogs, and cattle. In addition, throughout much of the area hay was a "natural crop" available for harvest and shipment, but alfalfa quickly became a staple, especially in support of the growing dairy industry. As farmers fully embraced the market economy, and as they pushed westward to practice extensive farming, they also more fully embraced mechanization. Regional offices of McCormick Harvesting Machine Company were established all over the country in the 1880s and 1890s. One of these was at Minneapolis, where "broken down" machines from the manufacturing plant were "set up" and distributed to franchised dealers in the field. In 1902 McCormick merged with Deering & Company to form International Harvester, a colossus that soon expanded beyond the manufacture of reapers to a full line of agricultural implements—plows, harrows, seeders, and so on. Others such as John Deere and J. I. Case quickly followed suit. Minneapolis Threshing Machine Company, with a substantial operation at Hopkins, could provide "complete steam threshing outfits," and smaller manufacturers were located at Aberdeen, Albert Lea, Fort Dodge, and Spencer. By 1909 implement dealers could be found at most stations in all three states.[9]

Figure 10.1. Livestock tonnage nearly doubled during the first decade of the new century. Eight cars of stock were on the point of this train hurrying eastward near Haydenville, Minnesota. Author's collection.

Examples of varied agricultural activities were numerous. For instance, the rise of meat packing and its expansion throughout the Midwest was linked with the open range and then with the closed range cattle industry, but also with the production of corn and swine, especially in Iowa and southern Minnesota. Other examples of a broadened agricultural base included the growing dairy trade, truck farming, and even cultivation of the lowly sugar beet. A creamery at Corwith was producing one thousand pounds of butter daily as early as 1882, and the next decade dairying and the establishment of creameries came into full bloom in neighboring Minnesota. The Hansen Creamery of Young America, established in 1890, makes the point. Business grew rapidly. By

1896 M&StL handled butter from Waconia to New York markets in refrigerator cars. The same might be said of twenty-two stations in Iowa, thirty-seven stations in Minnesota, and two stations in South Dakota, all of which sported creameries satisfying local needs and looking elsewhere for customers to take excess production. Potatoes were loaded in American Refrigerator Transit Cars at Ayrshire, Iowa; Mellette, South Dakota; and Carver, Minnesota, among other places, and onions and apples went to market from a few others. The production of vegetables for commercial purposes, especially corn and peas, escalated with the development of the automatic line canning process pioneered by Campbell Soup, H. J. Heinz, and others. In Iowa, Lake Mills Canning Factory targeted Montana and Idaho markets for its canned corn, and by 1909 other plants along M&StL were located at Arlington, Chaska, Waterville, Winthrop, Forest City, and Storm Lake. In addition, pickles by the carload (seventy-two barrels per car) left North Star Pickling Company at Jordan and M. A. Gedney Pickling Company at Chaska. More mundane by comparison, but far more important in generation of traffic, were sugar beets. They were grown experimentally and successfully near Albert Lea in 1895, and soon thereafter a substantial sugar mill was placed in operation at Chaska, taking beets loaded on M&StL at the Minnesota towns of Gibbon, Kilkenny, Montgomery, Waterville, and Young America to begin with, and at many other places later on.[10]

Agricultural produce of a very different kind, barley, was a principal ingredient in the manufacture of beer—a product central to the tastes and traditions of many who settled the upper Midwest. Not surprisingly, Minneapolis and St. Paul were home to many major brewers, but smaller operators could be found in Minnesota at Chaska, Jordan, Montgomery, New Prague, New Ulm, and Waseca early in the twentieth century. Each one required barley and hops as well as bottles, barrels, boxes, and crates, and each one, depending on the size of operation, shipped by the carload, by the barrel, or in case lots. Smaller brewers had limited sales areas, although the Union Saloon at Young America promised "New Ulm beer always on tap," and New Ulm beer could be found at Spencer, Iowa, about one hundred miles distant. Larger brewers had greater reach, of course, usually moving product to warehouses or cold storage and then to retail distribution. Theodore Hamm, for instance, was one of five brewers with branches at Albert Lea, and Minneapolis Brewing was one of three brewers that owned cold storage facilities at Sherburn. Beer warehouses also were found on M&StL at Aberdeen, Des Moines, Fort Dodge, and Watertown. Theodore Hamm reminded the thirsty at Le Beau that its beer "pleases them all in every way—Purity, Age, and Flavor." In Watertown, however, one local dealer proudly announced that he had just received "a car of the celebrated Schlitz Beer," all the way from Milwaukee.[11]

Some of this beer was likely cooled by "natural ice," harvested variously from lakes and streams along M&StL lines. During the early twentieth century ice shippers were found at eighteen locations, and most of these customers forwarded natural ice as opposed to "artificial" (manufactured) ice. M&StL itself was a customer, moving ice to Watertown, Fort Dodge, and Minneapolis for the resupply of refrigerator cars, but greater volumes went for domestic consumption. Lake Riley, between Eden Prairie and Chaska, supplied appreciable tonnage, but Lake Waconia, near its namesake community, likely provided more. Much of it went to Cedar Lake Ice Company, which had a huge warehouse covering nearly an acre adjacent to M&StL's Cedar Lake yard and shop. Sawdust, otherwise a little-valued byproduct of lumber mills, provided the packing necessary to see ice through the warm summer months.[12]

Building products such as plaster and bricks promised a larger and more regular flow of business. Gypsum, long used as a building material, is found in several states, Iowa among them, with large, high-quality deposits in that state near Fort Dodge. By 1910 seven mills near that place turned out a steady stream of plaster, and although none of the plants was served directly, cars were switched to M&StL for haulage. Clay, suitable for manufacture of bricks, was more widely distributed in Iowa and to a lesser degree in Minnesota. Given the paucity of native timber in much of Iowa, it was not surprising that clay products companies sprang up in nearly every county. By 1905 there were 302 such producers turning out common brick, face brick, paving brick, and fire brick, in addition to sewer tile, hollow brick tile, and silo tile. The industry ranked tenth in investment among the state's manufacturers. Production eventually centered around Mason City and along the Des Moines River valley from Fort Dodge through Des Moines to Ottumwa. On M&StL in Iowa, major producers were tucked away along the line from Fort Dodge to Kalo (Kalo Brick & Tile had the capacity to produce three thousand carloads annually), and the first revenue freight billed out of Storm Lake was, in fact, a carload of brick. In Minnesota, plants at Chaska offered substantial shipments of highly regarded cream-colored face brick. At Spencer, one firm manufactured cement tile and another, Straight Brothers, had six kilns and a large drying house for clay brick, drain tile, and hollow block. Other plants were near Albert Lea, Jordan, Monterey, and New Ulm. In all, during the 1900s M&StL served twenty-eight brick and tile works plus fourteen producers of cement block and tile.[13]

Drainage tile was in particular demand. A large area of wetland (swamps and sloughs), the result of late glacial activity, ran from the Dakotas and southern Minnesota across Iowa and Illinois into Indiana and Ohio. In Iowa, the most poorly drained areas were those served by M&StL, especially around Forest City through Fort Dodge to Gowrie, and from around Ruthven to Fort Dodge. Early agriculturalists bypassed these areas, used them for grazing, or cut the natural hay. But with the advent of steam-powered dredges and inexpensive tile, the rich, soggy soil could be made productive of cereal grains and row crops. "Drain tiles pay their costs every two years and last forever," said one manufacturer. For M&StL, the prospects were marvelous. In the short run, the road would haul drainage rigs and a monumental tonnage in tile manufactured by on-line plants—not to mention inbound coal to fire the kilns necessary in the manufacturing process. In the long run, a far greater volume of agricultural bounty would clearly boost annual loadings at several stations once the land was drained. The matter became public policy in many counties, where drainage districts were created to raise taxes and let contracts for ditching. The entire issue could be seen in microcosm around Monterey, Minnesota, where the process had begun as early as 1886, but where it would not be completed until well into the next century.[14]

In addition to major commodities in carload lots, there was a plethora of miscellaneous freight that in the aggregate was impressive. Kerosene and other refined petroleum products initially moved in barrels or drums, but as demand grew these products were more often found in tank cars. Oranges from California arrived in season, and each spring saw emigrants heading for new homes. "IC just gave us 3 cars emigrants and stock for Minneapolis," the agent at Storm Lake wired the dispatcher on February 8, 1909. "We also have 2 cars emigrants and stock for White, S.D. via Estherville and CRI&P [Chicago, Rock Island & Pacific]." Baled hay, mostly from stations in northwest Iowa, also was part of the traffic mix.[15]

Finally, a bewildering array of lading was billed in less-than-carload lots (LCL). In station freight houses from Akaska, South Dakota, to Waukee, Iowa, could be found everything from caskets to corsets—agricultural implements, furniture, nails, musical instruments, groceries, pumps, cigars, drugs, harness, dry goods, windmills, confectionery, sewing machines, soft drinks, and much more. Hardware stores such as G. P. Bakken at Wecota, South Dakota, or Sunde & Tungsvik at Huntington, Iowa, generated a seemingly endless volume of LCL business, receiving paints, oils, wallpaper, desks, brushes, brooms, gloves, shades, molding, wash tubs, mirrors, glass, lanterns, lamps, linoleum, pitchforks, chain, rope, and so on. LCL shipments were massed at major stations (Minneapolis, Des Moines, and Fort Dodge) and loaded into boxcars directed to larger communities (Waseca, Britt, Spencer, Watertown, etc.) or into "line cars" or "peddler cars" appropriate to service smaller towns (Manchester, Minnesota; Livermore, Iowa; Troy, South Dakota, etc.). Entire carloads of LCL for a particular station were set to the house track behind the depot for unloading later by station help, but otherwise the peddler car was opened at way stations and items to or from that location were wrestled off the car or out of the freight house by the train crew, with inspection and itemization done by the agent, as was the mountain of paperwork. All of it was ritual in the railroad business during the age of modal domination.

By the end of the first decade of the twentieth century, M&StL ran expedited freight trains to and from principal destinations—Minneapolis, Albert Lea, Fort Dodge, Des Moines, and Watertown. The most impressive of these were numbers 95 and 96, both labeled St. Louis Chicago Time Freight between Minneapolis and Albert Lea. These and other expedited trains handled time-sensitive lading of various types; for example, flour was typical for number 96. But most of M&StL's business was performed by homely locals such as number 49 (Fort Dodge–Estherville) and number 51 (Estherville–Winthrop). Their consists for one day (December 31,1910) offer a representation of way freight duties and commodities handled at that time (see Figure 10.2). Local business was good—too good on occasion. "Talk about business at LaSalle," exclaimed the *Hanska Herald* for March 8, 1907. "The side track is full of coal, elevators full of wheat, stockyards full of hogs and cattle and the thing is up to Agent Grasshoff to get cars." LaSalle was not unique. "The passing track and house track are full from one end to the other," complained a conductor at Spencer in 1909. "About 2 or 3 hours work to do here and no room," he drolly concluded. A few days later saw little improvement. "Spencer yard is blocked—not room for more than 15 cars," the agent telegraphed the dispatcher. And two more trains were headed for Spencer at that moment.[16]

Passenger business was similarly strong. Revenue from all sources (tickets, mail, and express) rose significantly, from $730,983 in 1900 to $1,470,809 in 1911, representing 25.5 percent of all revenue in 1900 and 28.9 percent in 1911 after ballooning to 33.9 percent in 1905. M&StL reflected national patterns in most categories for those years.[17]

M&StL's marquee passenger operation was, of course, the North Star Limited, which, the company said, was the "Newest and Best Limited Train between the Twin Cities and Chicago and St. Louis," with "Combination Stateroom and Open-section Sleeping Car, Buffet-Library-Smoking Car and Free Reclining Chair Car" to and from Chicago, and "Pullman Sleepers and Chair Cars" to and from St. Louis. Illinois Central added a diner between Chicago and Freeport, and Wabash provided dining service between St. Louis and Moberly. M&StL charged $8.75 for chair cars from Minneapolis to Chicago, $11.50 to St. Louis, another

No. 49

1 merchandise Estherville
1 merchandise Spencer
1 merchandise Ruthven
1 empty stock Pioneer
Pick up at Tara from Des Moines
1 merchandise Estherville
1 merchandise Spencer
2 merchandise Spencer
1 merchandise Ayrshire
3 company coal Spencer
5 company coal Estherville
1 company coal St. James
2 company coal Gilmore City
2 empty stock Mallard
5 empty stock Plover
1 empty stock Gilmore City
2 empty stock Curlew (from Rolfe)
1 empty boxcar Watertown (from Plover)
1 cement Curlew
1 rye Spencer
2 corn Minneapolis (from Curlew)
Pick up at Spencer from south
1 refrigerated merchandise
3 corn Minneapolis
1 barley Minneapolis
1 scrap iron St. Paul
2 hay Minnesota Transfer
1 corn Richmond, Va.
1 hay Minneapolis

No. 51

4 merchandise way (en route points)
1 hay Minneapolis
1 hay transit (to be sold en route)
1 hay Minnesota Transfer
1 hay Carlyle, S.D.
6 corn Minneapolis
1 corn transit
1 flax Minneapolis
6 wheat New Ulm
1 stucco Ormsby
2 oats Minneapolis
1 stucco Hanley Falls

Figure 10.2. Consists for trains 49 and 51. Train 49 originated out of Fort Dodge, and 51 originated out of Estherville, Iowa.

$3.00 for a double berth or $11.00 for a stateroom in the Pullman. M&StL's buffet cars were open to sleeping car passengers without charge; coach passengers ordering meals were not charged for seating, but those who simply ordered drinks or a cigar and wanted to linger had to ante up a 35-cent seat charge. A second set of trains on these runs had similar equipment, operated on somewhat slower schedules, and went unnamed. Among the roads operating these trains (M&StL, Illinois Central, Iowa Central, and Wabash), M&StL was clearly the most aggressive in advertising. Illinois Central's position was especially curious, since it advertised its Seminole Limited from Chicago to Jacksonville in the Twin Cities, but failed to mention the M&StL-IC route from St. Paul and Minneapolis to Chicago.[18]

Illinois Central was, however, more energetic in promoting service between the Twin Cities and Omaha—a day train with coaches and a parlor-cafe car, and a night train with coaches and a sleeper. These trains were integral to M&StL's St. Paul–Des Moines service: IC's Omaha cars set out or added at Fort Dodge, M&StL's own coaches on the day train and its "high back coaches," chair cars, and "Brand New Electric Lighted Wide Vestibuled Pullman Drawing-room Sleeping Cars" on the night train going through to Des Moines. The night trains were always heavy, occasionally running in two sections on the weekends, often exhausting the food supply. "Please get me six dozen eggs and have them at the depot for no. 4," a Pullman conductor once wired the agent at Waseca in anticipation of the morrow's breakfast needs as the train steamed toward Des Moines.[19]

Passenger offerings on the West End were increased in September 1907, when service was established to Aberdeen and Le Beau, with mixed trains between Aberdeen and Leola. Then on May 22, 1910, the day train from St. Paul to Watertown was extended to Aberdeen, supplementing the Aberdeen Limited, the night train that made connections with the Leola mixed at Aberdeen and the local passenger run from Le Beau at Conde. A touch of elegance attended the Limited, with its "Pullman vestibuled sleepers (individual electric lights in every berth)." Other improvements also commenced on May 22, 1910, when the Waconia local was extended to Winthrop and New Ulm. Known locally as the Wooden Shoe, the New Ulm accommodation was at once a local and, at least between Minneapolis and Waconia, a commuter train.[20]

Passenger business west of Minneapolis through Excelsior remained important, but it was changing. The great hotels at Lake Minnetonka were gone or in decline, seasonal "cottagers" were more evident, and the area was increasingly suburban, with permanent residents. The number of station stops immediately west of Hopkins—Minnetonka Mills, Deephaven, Cottagewood, Linwood, Fairview, Solbergs Point, Excelsior, Manitou Junction, Wildhurst, Eureka, Zumbra Heights, and then on through Victoria to Waconia—mirrored this. So did M&StL's service—six local trains to Minnetonka points during the summer of 1900 to meet seasonal demand, and two trains to Excelsior (plus through runs to the west) during the winter of 1904 to handle volumes not affected by seasonal swings. Two examples are adequate to illustrate the change. J. H. Reem of Cottagewood commuted to his job as a barber in Minneapolis, and Hazel R. Patriece of Deephaven used M&StL trains to get to and from a high school in Minneapolis. Fares were reasonable: 50 cents one way, or $9.00 for a 50-ride ticket.[21]

M&StL still catered to seasonal business, of course, and in the first five years of the new century spent lavishly to make its facilities at Minnetonka points attractive and efficient. In 1902, for example, a new pavilion, sidewalks, and "arc" lighting were authorized at Tonka Bay. And the depot was painted. Three years later the water tank, pump house, and depot at Excelsior were repainted (the depot had been painted only five years earlier). M&StL, as it had for years, scheduled extra trains to accommodate demand on the Fourth of July. "Large, roomy cars, and seats for all," promised the Passenger Department in 1907. But the bloom was off. The great steamers were gone from the lake, replaced by smaller craft. Gone, too, were the Hotel St. Louis and the Lafayette. M&StL carried the Lake Park Hotel on its books with a value of $17,859, but the enterprise typically turned in net losses. Early in the new century it was disposed of to Thomas Lowry, the Twin Cities streetcar magnate, who earlier had taken a half interest in the place and would continue to operate it through 1911. For that matter, Lowry pushed his streetcar network to Lake Minnetonka in 1906, and on October 1, 1907, M&StL threw in the towel, leasing its 1.4-mile Tonka Bay branch to the Minneapolis & St. Paul Suburban Railroad, which electrified the line, giving it access to Wildhurst and the Lake Park Hotel.[22]

M&StL's Anson B. Cutts was likely saddened by what had come to pass at Lake Minnetonka, but he was undaunted. A North Carolinian by birth, Cutts had graduated from Middle Georgia Military College, and in 1884 took a clerk's job with Chicago & Alton. He moved west, working for Omaha and then Great Northern before signing on with M&StL as general passenger and ticket agent in 1894. It was the irrepressible Cutts who dreamed up M&StL's famous "little man" caricature—a happy, jaunty fellow whose head, arms, and legs protruded from his round, M&StL-logo body as he scampered quickly and confidently over a landscape served by "The Road That Runs." Charles L. Bartholomew, a well-regarded cartoonist at the *Minneapolis Journal*—and a regular customer on M&StL trains to and from Lake Minnetonka—drew the little man at Cutts's request. It adorned M&StL flyers and leaflets for perhaps a dozen years, and it appeared on the road's wall calendar for 1908, which the *Official Guide* called "one of the striking calendars of the year."[23]

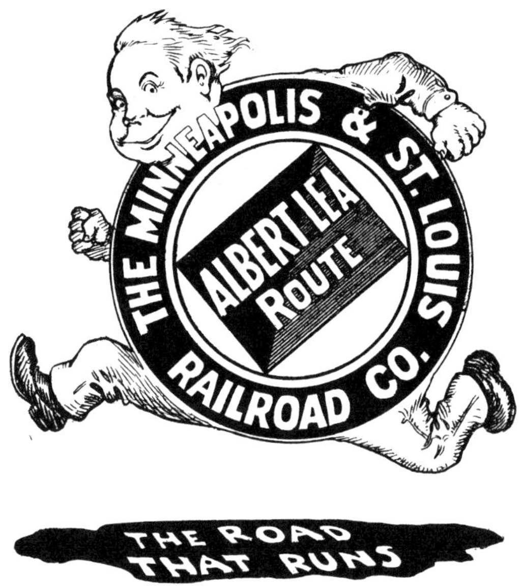

Figure 10.3. Charles L. Bartholomew created the "little man" caricature for the M&StL at Anson Cutts's request. Author's collection.

Cutts did not have an enviable task at M&StL. The road faced intense competition. "We did lots of Chicago business," Cutts recalled, "but had to steal it from North Western, Milwaukee, and Burlington which were much shorter and better equipped." The same could have been said of St. Louis trade where M&StL–Iowa Central–Wabash had to contend with Burlington Route, Burlinton–Rock Island, and even Diamond Jim Steamers. It was no different from the Twin Cities to Des Moines (Chicago & North Western, Chicago Great Western, and Milwaukee–St. Paul & Des Moines via Mason City), Fort Dodge (Chicago Great Western), Aberdeen (Milwaukee and Great Northern), and Watertown (Great Northern). Still, said Cutts, "they knew we were in the game."[24]

Cutts was ingenious in promoting popular excursions (much to the chagrin of the Western Passenger Association, whose other members in 1907 wanted to kill them) and in soliciting all sorts of special movements. The "Popular Excursion" of October 13, 1906, to Minneapolis and St. Paul from Des Moines and intermediate stations up the line to Fort Dodge was typical, with round-trip coach fares from Des Moines, $4.50; "double berth accommodating two people" in tourist sleeping cars an additional dollar. What to do in the Twin Cities? Visit area lakes or Minnehaha Falls, "see the largest flour mills in the world," tour the state capitol in St. Paul ("erected at a cost of over $4,000,000"), or head to the many theaters. In October 1906 the weary conductor on one crowded extra train from Watertown turned in 1,013 tickets purchased at West End stations. The state fairs of Iowa and Minnesota and even off-line county fairs were always appropriate targets. Extra trains were ordered from Spencer to the Buena Vista County Fair at Alta (via Storm Lake and Illinois Central) and from Perry to the Union Sunday School Picnic at Valley Junction, and a Des Moines Booster Train was ordered to Spencer and a speech there by Champ Clark (Democrat-Missouri), speaker of the U.S. House of Representatives. Another Cutts favorite focused on civic responsibility. "Visit the Legislature" was his routine admonition whenever the solons were in session. A special train from Iowa destinations to Des Moines on March 22, 1907, featured $2.00 round-trip tickets from Mallard, $1.50 from Gowrie, and $1.25 from Dana. And Cutts sold a special train to the Watertown Knights of Columbus for initiation proceedings at Aberdeen late in 1907.[25]

Other special movements were innumerable and included excursions from Watertown to Yahota, a summer resort at the outlet of Lake Kampeska, and the usual stream of groups heading from the Twin Cities to Waconia. These included seven hundred rambunctious (locals thought them riotous) *Minneapolis Journal* newsboys in 1907 and presumably more decorous Brown & Bigelow salesmen in 1911. Jordan's Schutz & Hilgers Park remained a popular destination for excursion groups, in the summer of 1907 drawing the Blacksmiths of Minneapolis, the German Benevolent Societies, and the Colored Elks of Minneapolis, among others. A growing prohibitionist sentiment stalking the countryside forced the Sunday closing of Jordan's several saloons, which threw a damper on Sunday excursions, but many groups circumvented do-gooders by scheduling Saturday outings. Extra coaches were added to regular trains when the State University of Iowa played Minnesota in football at Minneapolis, when Spencer hosted the Northwestern High School Annual Field Meet, and when the South Firemen's Association held its annual meeting at Watertown. Traveling shows and theater groups were regular customers, heading for places like Le Beau after the opera house opened there in 1909 and to Cresbard and Carlyle in 1910. Terry's Uncle Tom's Cabin Company, consisting of thirty-seven persons occupying one sleeper with paraphernalia in a single baggage car, was received at Watertown on August 20, 1909, and played at Boyd, South Dakota, New Prague, Minnesota, Pilot Mound, Iowa, and fourteen other M&StL locations before delivery to Chicago & North Western at Ogden, Iowa, in mid-October. And special runs were made to Humboldt, Iowa, for sports fans to watch Humboldt native and legendary wrestler Frank Gotch train for his world heavyweight championship bout with George Hackenschmidt, the Estonian strongman known as the Russian Lion. (Hundreds of fans in Humboldt waited impatiently at the telegraph office on April 3, 1908, for word from Chicago's Dexter Park Pavilion as to the outcome; they were not disappointed when news came.)[26]

The vast majority of M&StL patrons, of course, were not excursionists or ticketed on special movements, but were those who traveled on regular trains and whose comings and goings mostly went unrecorded. They were on business, on vacation, heading for medical attention, off to see a friend, or perhaps bitten by wanderlust and moving on to take up new lives at Moose Jaw, Medicine Hat, or in the Salmon River Valley of British Columbia. Occasionally, however, travel plans were documented. On August 27, 1908, the *Le Beau Phenix* recorded that "Mr. and Mrs. Left Hand departed on the M&StL for a honeymoon" and that "four reservation children" had left by train for the Indian School at Flandreau, South Dakota. In July 1907 Senator Robert M. LaFollette (Republican-Wisconsin) stepped off the cars at Watertown to deliver a rousing two-hour discourse on the nation's woes before a packed house at the Methodist church. The wrestler Frank Gotch during his career confronted challengers at Luverne, Forest City, Des Moines, and Fort Dodge, as well as in Minneapolis and St. Paul, taking the train from one place to another for his matches. Catholic services were administered at Chelsea, Cresbard, Carlyle, Tolstoy, and Lowry, South Dakota, by a circuit priest using M&StL to get him from one place to another. Merchants headed to distant metropolitan centers on buying trips, and in the fall of 1908 cattleman Cap Mossman took his wife and baby to Kansas City to avoid the vicissitudes of a Dakota winter. In June 1909, a resident from Hanska took himself to Minneapolis for surgery, and a physician from New Ulm used the cars to Hanska to consult with the local doctor on a difficult case. Fugitives and perpetrators likewise rode the rails. During the summer of 1910, the sheriff at Spencer asked for the arrest of three men in Sioux Rapids; "Bring them up on the first train," he obliged the marshal at Sioux Rapids. A year earlier an M&StL conductor had wired another marshal, this one at Ruthven, Iowa, asking him, "Please lock up man by name of Kiley who stole a pair of red oxford shoes and 2 pair of mittens." The man had purchased a ticket and ridden the freight up from Ayrshire.[27]

Neither a thief nor a perpetrator—not usually, at least—the traveling salesman, "drummer," or "knight of the grip," was nevertheless a mysterious if omnipresent fixture in the passenger trade throughout this period. Most such salesmen were in the employ of wholesale houses whose businesses had expanded with the railroad; their number nationally increased by a factor of six between 1880 and 1920. Armour & Company, the meat packer, alone employed four thousand. Minneapolis and St. Paul together put five thousand "knights of the grip" on the road in 1915; Des Moines claimed five hundred. Fort Dodge's Green-Wheeler Shoe Factory had five men out on the road "drumming up business," and Jordan's Herder Cigar Factory employed one fellow who worked several stations along M&StL lines. In a general sense, all of these salesmen traveled through the hinterland, unpacking trunks and sample cases in small communities so that local merchants could inspect goods without having to "go to market" at large manufacturing and distribution centers "back east." The drummer usually was a "live wire" who, as Meredith Willson pointed out in the *Music Man,* had to "know the territory." He also seemed to know the latest slang, the latest song, and the newest dance, was attired in the latest style, was known as a ladies man, knew the most recent gossip from the diner or the smoking car, and of course could tell the best jokes. He was a "sport," a "bird of passage." He also was a link to the great outside world—a man who knew of and trafficked in the finest hotels and eateries around his circuit. Lac qui Parle Hotel in Madison, Minnesota, was one of these. Salesmen from the Twin Cities tried to work their way west from Hopkins to be in Madison on Friday so that they could stay the weekend at the hotel, moving on into South Dakota the following Monday. The kitchen was known for "Royal T-Bone Steaks," and the dining room for waitresses attired in crisp white uniforms.[28]

Nearby stood M&StL's, depot, where the drummer had arrived, where his trunks had been unloaded, where he wired his orders back to headquarters, where he purchased a ticket for his next destination, where his trunks were reloaded, where the goods he had sold to local merchants would one day soon appear. The depot was the focal point of the community during the steamcar civilization—the funnel through which people, goods, and information passed, the prism through which country folk and small-town America looked to the outside. The depot was one of the few buildings where the lights burned all night; it set the tempo for the entire community. Yes, the railroad company held legal title to the building, but the depot belonged emotionally to the townspeople. The company's agent—the "depot agent" as he was universally called—was a pillar in the community, and the fact that he was also a telegrapher only gave him greater prestige. He was, in the era before long-distance telephonics, the first person in the community to "get the latest news," and he was the keeper of "standard time," courtesy of Western Union.[29]

There clearly was a mystique about the depot, with its tobacco-smelling office, its clattering telegraph instruments, and its dark and dingy freight house. There was an excitement about the place—a great lure for those who saw that "city life" began at the country depot, and a great fear for those who likewise recognized that fact, but were frightened by it. "Train time" always resulted in considerable milling about, hack drivers and draymen appearing as if by command, passengers heading toward the platform, the generally curious simply taking it all in. But even after train time there were curious attractions in and about the depot area. Considerable comment derived at Le Beau, for example, when a nine-button rattler was killed in the depot. More benign were regular meetings of the Bachelors' Club in the depot at Wecota, South Dakota. Elsewhere, in 1899 M&StL acquired a wood-frame hotel hard by the depot at Morton, Minnesota—this for the convenience of railroaders and the public alike. There one could stay the night or get a "bucket of hot mud and a sinker" (coffee and donut) at the restaurant. Near the depot at Estherville stood Billy Baker's store—sleeping rooms on the upper floor, cafe at ground level—where a steaming bowl of Billy's oyster stew was guaranteed to revive circulation even in the harshest of January blizzards.

Still other attractions were near at hand in tool houses where M&StL trackmen stored their velocipedes, curious contraptions that proved tempting beyond the pale. A Roman Catholic priest at Onaka, South Dakota, "borrowed" one of these and pumped his way to celebrate mass at Chelsea—36 miles one way—and two men at Monterey, Minnesota, commandeered an M&StL handcar to attend a Masonic Lodge meeting at Sherburne—7.7 miles one way. Bank robbers at Monterey likewise made "unauthorized use of company property" by stealing the company's velocipede to make their getaway. Other villains broke into the depot at LaSalle and robbed a local store but failed in escape when M&StL's velocipede, which they had taken from the tool house, could not get traction on snow-covered rail.[30]

Other thieves were drawn to M&StL freight houses, which sheltered LCL shipments but also more highly valued items handled by express. "Between the hours of 5 and 11 p.m. there was stolen from freight house 2 kegs of whiskey," the agent at Sioux Rapids wired Minneapolis headquarters early in the century. Distilled spirits, wine, and even beer in small lots were among a profusion of items handled by express companies during this time. Express business dated from 1839, when an enterprising railroad conductor on an eastern road hit upon the idea of carrying small parcels, money, and valuable papers from place to place. Wells Fargo & Company was among others attracted to the business. Suffice it to say that express companies and railroads grew up together. On M&StL, American Express and then United States Express Company held the contract until 1906, when it was awarded to Adams Express. Revenue deriving from this trade was a mere $1,462 in 1875, still only $23,930 in 1892, but rose to $113,931 in 1911. Liquid spirits were an important part of the traffic mix for express companies, but the array of items handled was increasingly impressive. Precious metals, specie or paper money, dressed game and fowl in season, Coca Cola syrup in cases "containing six dozen single pints," fresh fruits and vegetables, baked goods, cheese, fresh milk and cream, cut flowers, and even race horses in carload lots were expedited by passenger trains under contract between express companies and railroads. Newspapers were yet another example. In 1901 an Estherville rag experimented with a pre-printed supplement that arrived each day on the down train from Minneapolis, but more typically express messengers looked after the timely dispatch of major dailies (in bulk) from St. Paul, Minneapolis, and Des Moines.[31]

Among the very best of express company customers were mail order houses—Montgomery Ward, the first of them beginning in 1872, and then the even more aggressive Sears, Roebuck & Company, which began business in 1887. The 31-page Sears catalog of 1891 grew to nearly 1,200 pages in 1908 and offered a very clear reflection of the tastes and desires of the American people at that time. Sears offered customers a simple formula: low cost, wide choice, guarantee of satisfaction, and prompt service. Its catalog—"the silent salesman"—presented everything from accordions to windmills, boric acid to yarn. And for M&StL there was an important personal connection. Richard W. Sears, a Minnesota native born in 1863, learned telegraphy and entered the employ of M&StL as an operator working vacancies at locations such as Lake Mills, Iowa, transferred to the general office in Minneapolis, but soon found himself at North Redwood, Minnesota, as agent. When a local jeweler rejected a shipment of watches, Sears obtained permission to acquire and dispose of them on his own. He did so, made a quick profit, and in 1886 left M&StL to go on to bigger and better things.[32]

If railroads provided the conduit for delivery of goods from Sears, Roebuck and other firms large and small, they also provided the means to order from them. Urgent matters might go by telegraph, but the vast majority of messages were handled by the United States Post Office Department, which in turn contracted with railroads to haul the mail. M&StL's involvement dated from 1874; en route sorting of mails by postal clerks in M&StL Railroad Post Office (RPO) cars began in 1882 and included car lines to Angus and Watertown. Revenue increased accordingly, from $2,050 in 1874 to $23,114 in 1882. Later authorizations included St. Paul & Des Moines (RPO designations identified head-out and terminal points) in 1886, St. Paul & Storm Lake on October 24, 1900, and both St. Paul, Watertown & Aberdeen and

Conde & Le Beau on November 26, 1907. In 1911 M&StL earned $130,531 for handling federal mails.[33]

Railroad Post Office car routes on M&StL were part of an extremely intricate national web that connected major metropolitan hubs with every village and hamlet—and after full implementation of Rural Free Delivery, begun late in 1896 and gradually accomplished, every nook and cranny of the country. M&StL RPO cars attached to passenger trains heading into or leaving from St. Paul Union Depot fed or received first-class (letters) and second-class (magazines and newspapers) mail to or from "all lines diverging." Additional points where mail was delivered or picked up in substantial volume included Minneapolis (where M&StL had its own station), Albert Lea (where Illinois Central and Iowa Central utilized M&StL's station), Fort Dodge (where M&StL used Illinois Central's facility), Des Moines (where after August 1905 M&StL shared Union Station with Milwaukee, Wabash, Chicago Great Western, Burlington, and Des Moines, Iowa Falls & Northern), Watertown (used also by Rock Island), and Aberdeen (a handsome edifice used by M&StL alone).[34]

With expanding volumes of traffic offered to M&StL, the Hawley management team was compelled to put more money into plant and equipment. A major grade reduction between Hopkins and Chaska early in the century allowed M&StL to move trains "loaded to their full capacity," and other campaigns in 1909–10 widened cuts, ballasted track, and raised sags at several locations. In 1907, 114 miles of main track were relaid with seventy-pound (per yard) rail, and in 1910 the two main tracks from Railway Transfer through Cedar Lake to Hopkins were relaid with eighty-pound steel.[35]

Terminals and structures likewise received attention. Yard tracks were rearranged, and a fifteen-stall roundhouse was erected at Albert Lea in 1903. Multiple improvements and additions were authorized at Morton to create a crew change point, and the same was true

Figure 10.4. Hawley and his managers ordered periodic betterments to track, including ditching and surfacing near Waseca, Minnesota. Author's collection.

at Winthrop to accommodate business coming off or flowing to the Southwestern. Substantial investment was required at Fort Dodge to meet business needs, and even more was required there, in Des Moines, and elsewhere when Des Moines & Fort Dodge came under M&StL's umbrella in 1905. A "general overhaul of the depot" was mandated at Waukee, the Perry structure was remodeled, and stock pens were authorized for Minburn and Pioneer among other stations. Elsewhere, rooms were repaired and screens applied to windows at the Winslow House in Albert Lea, the depot at Forest City was "enlarged and improved," and the depot at Norman literally was picked up and moved a half mile to Emmons. An outhouse was built at Kilkenny when the agent there requested such a luxury in 1907, but a similar facility at Burnside that was "decayed and blown to pieces" merely needed "renewal." Machinery-unloading platforms were constructed at Cresbard, Sherburne, Spencer, and several other locations. Bridge crews renewed structures between New Ulm and Sioux Rapids, while paint gangs spruced up depots all the way from Storm Lake to Winthrop in 1904–5. Brick depots appeared at Hopkins and Dawson, and a 160-foot transfer platform was erected at Winthrop.[36]

Capital investment also flowed to rolling stock and motive power. Substantial expense derived from converting to automatic couplers from primitive link and pin coupling as well as from applying air brakes to all rolling stock. On August 5, 1907, M&StL stopped accepting cars without air brakes, at the same time sending "all foreign non-air cars . . . in the direction of home." For its own account, M&StL owned 3,068 freight cars in 1900 with an average capacity of 24.4 tons; ten years later it had 4,224 cars averaging 29.1 tons in carrying capacity. Boxcars predominated, at 87 percent of the total. The passenger car inventory similarly increased, from 65 cars in 1900 to 92 in 1911. Most of these were coaches, although by 1911 M&StL also owned 34 head-end cars (to handle baggage, mail, and express), two office cars, two buffet cars, and one cafe-observation car. Additions also swelled the motive power inventory. In 1900 M&StL owned 78 locomotives averaging 17,310 pounds in tractive effort; by 1911, however, the road's locomotive fleet increased to 110, with tractive effort averaging 23,350 pounds. American Standard types (4-4-0) bulked large, 51 of them, with duties shared by 0-4-0s (2), 0-6-0s (11), 2-6-0s (28), 4-6-0s (8), and 2-8-0s (17).[37]

There was little enough in any of this that was impressive. Indeed, since the Hawley management had taken over the railroad in the mid-1890s, M&StL's expenditure for plant and equipment ranged from prudent to parsimonious. By 1911 a mere 15.1 percent of main track boasted eighty-pound rail; seventy-pound was the norm, and forty miles of main track was still fifty-six-pound. And only about one-third of the main track had seen gravel ballast. Rolling stock and motive power were adequately maintained, and bad-order ratios were in the acceptable range, but the locomotive stable was filled mostly with tiny, elderly, and inefficient power. Indeed, the fifteen Mogul (2-6-0) locomotives ordered in 1900 represented the first road power heavier than the road's venerable 4-4-0s, and the Consolidation engines (2-8-0) only recently had arrived.[38]

Edwin Hawley and his managers did agree to periodic betterment bursts—the Chaska hill project of 1902–4, impressive track allocations in 1910, five hundred boxcars in 1904 to make up for Des Moines & Fort Dodge's inadequate car supply, and ten Consolidation locomotives in 1911—but on the whole they were chary about making substantial investments. Why? One reason was the increasingly unsettled political scene. The shift from a rural and agrarian society to one that was urban and industrial only accelerated in the new century. And the pace and degree of this change unnerved many Americans, frightened more, and radicalized some. Grangers and others earlier had brought about state regulation of railroads and in 1887 the passage of the Interstate Commerce Act. Railroad managers and investors thought it all a bad dream, one that surely would go away. But the antimonopolists, the populists, and then the Progressives would not go away. Their message resonated mightily with the average citizen, who, whatever the true merits of the matter, nevertheless demanded more and more departure from laissez-faire economics. Railroads were the easiest target. They held a nearly modal monopoly. They touched everybody in one way or another, because this, nobody could deny, was still the age of railways. Teeth—long

Figure 10.5. M&StL's motive power inventory was less than impressive, with no really heavy locomotives. Moguls like 93, shown here with a caboose hop at Morton, Minnesota, handled many of the freight assignments. Author's collection.

and sharp—were added to ICC's statutory authority. The Elkins Act of 1903 stiffened penalties against rebating, and the Hepburn Act of 1906 gave ICC the authority to set "just and reasonable" maximum rates as well as legal power to check railroad books. The Mann-Elkins Act of 1910 further empowered ICC in the matter of establishing reasonable rates and, strange to say, placed on carriers—not the government—the responsibility for demonstrating the reasonableness of proposed rates.[39]

All of this regulation gave the federal government power to establish de facto price ceilings with no convenient or expeditious way for railroads to respond to escalating costs. They remained capital and labor intensive and captive to huge fixed plants, and now found themselves tied by law to a governmental bureaucracy that would establish maximum rates; at the same time these railroads were subject to the market in terms of labor, material, fuel, equipment, bank loans, and all other necessities of business. In sum, railroads could not pass on their increasing costs except after lengthy bureaucratic procedures subject to political whim or pressure. Squeezed by price control and inflation, they increasingly sought outside sources of capital through sales of equipment trusts, stocks, and bonds.[40]

Additional antirailroad public policy was manifest at the state level, reflecting populist and then progressive instincts. On the far left stood those advocating government ownership and operation of transportation and communication devices, but many more Americans wanted only government control of rates plus regulation of working hours and conditions. Railroad attorneys made the case that such laws would deprive owners of property without due process of law, rebelling in part against powerful state railroad commissions such as those in Minnesota and Iowa that had assumed authority to fix maximum rates on intrastate traffic. An Iowa case in 1897 found that rates were set so low that there was no reasonable return on investment, and the same year another case in Minnesota established that the reasonableness of a rate set by the railroad commission was subject to judicial review lest owners be deprived of property without due process. But these matters hardly were settled.[41]

In 1906 Minnesota reduced intrastate rates on merchandise freight, and on May 1, 1907, moved to institute a maximum rate of 2 cents per mile on intrastate passenger fares. Other reductions followed in tariffs on freight—grain, coal, lumber, livestock, and other commodities—to show the political muscle of rural and small-town constituencies. Suits were brought against the railroads by individual shareholders demanding that they not accede to unwarranted governmental intrusion, and a temporary injunction forbade the state's attorney general to enforce the rates. He did so anyway, and in 1908 was rebuked by the United States Supreme Court. Nevertheless, the issue remained alive, working its way through the judicial process, with M&StL shareholders taking active roles, and it would not be resolved until 1913.[42]

In the end, the court did *not* rule on the reasonableness of these intrastate rates—a matter that universally irritated railroad managers and owners early and late. Nationwide, they pointed out, the number of ton miles increased by 9.4 percent in 1910 over 1907, but freight revenues grew by only 3.7 percent, and payrolls jumped by over 6 percent. Observers in the financial community blamed legislation unfriendly to business for the panic of 1907. The Hepburn Act of 1906, they pointed out, was especially onerous, because it made rate increases so very difficult to obtain. That kicked in a multiplier. Railroads found themselves with trimmed profits, which made investors skittish about railroad stocks; this, in turn, deprived the carriers of the huge sums necessary for plant improvement and expansion.[43]

Officially, M&StL's irritation with handicapping laws in Iowa and Minnesota was muted, although its shareholders were active litigants in both states. In 1910 and 1911, however, company representatives became markedly vocal. Inadequate rates had forced M&StL to abandon a proper high standard of maintenance; without higher rates the road would continue on a "downward slide of condition," the road's general manager told the Interstate Commerce Commission in 1910. A year later M&StL's president reminded shareholders that "the trend of railroad rates has constantly been toward a lower level—the result of competition, increased operating efficiencies the consequences of modern equipment," and an ever-improving "science of railroading." He thought it more than ironic that "while operating costs during the past ten years have been steadily increasing, rates of transportation have been gradually decreasing." To make his point he offered examples from M&StL's experience (see Table 10.1). "With no provision for the vast additional sums required for further improvements and extensions, the outlook is not encouraging," he somberly concluded.[44]

Table 10.1. Intrastate passenger and freight rates

Year	*Average rate per passenger mile*	*Average rate per ton mile*	*Taxes*
1900	2.019 cents	1.145 cents	$107,932
1910	1.884 cents	1.050 cents	$225,278

M&StL and the other carriers had ample cause for complaint. The heavy hand of government restricted their initiative, their income, and their potential income, while the market controlled costs. And labor was increasingly restless and demanding. M&StL held the high ground on the rate matter, but it—like the rest of the industry—left itself open to legitimate criticism by not moving energetically and enthusiastically to make railroading a safer work environment. One thoroughly exhausted conductor wired the dispatcher to say, "Myself and crew have been up 39 hours with 3 hours sleep and you have laid out work enough for 12 hours more. We had better tie up at Montgomery until daylight." In 1909 another exasperated conductor complained, "We have put in 16 hours everyday for the past two weeks," when told he could not have a day off. "Do you think we are made of iron?" he wondered. A week later the agent at Spencer reported that "Brakeman Bowman got two fingers crushed on right hand at Greenville tonight . . . company surgeon amputated the fingers." Such messages, sad to say, were not infrequent. A federal law regulating hours of service instituted on March 4, 1908, was designed to promote safety, but managers saw it as an act of government usurpation. As applied to telegraphers who handled train orders, the law prohibited duty beyond nine consecutive hours in continuously operated offices or thirteen hours in single-shift offices. Most of the latter were way stations, where work assignments were changed to twelve hours (one hour for meals). All of this threatened to escalate labor costs, so M&StL lowered wages on a pro rata basis to "fairly conform to the reduction in the hours of labor." Telegraphers likely thought M&StL's response spiteful, but the argument used in enacting this legislation had related solely to safety (not increased wages), and M&StL frankly found itself with little wiggle room in terms of income versus outgo. It would do what it could to contain labor costs, but labor-management relations suffered accordingly.[45]

Company-community relations were at issue in Minneapolis, where M&StL skirmished with nabobs of Kenwood neighborhood, several of whose homes stood on a bluff above the Cedar Lake yard and shops. Matters reached a fever pitch in 1910, when M&StL sought to expand operations very modestly, provoking a city council order to desist and then the arraignment of M&StL's general manager for violation of an antismoke ordinance by switch engines working in the yard. This followed complaints from the Kenwood set that smoke and gasses from M&StL's yard and shop were killing stately elms and maples in their neighborhood; that their household furniture, curtains, carpet, and even food were being destroyed; and that their wash could not be hung out to dry without being ruined. Moreover, said angry residents, nocturnal slumber was impossible because of "the ceaseless whistlings, the jarring of heavy cars, and ringing of engine bells," which, they claimed, made them "ill and fretful." Kenwood residents and city officials urged that M&StL move all operations to Hopkins, only a few miles distant, and local managers put the idea before Hawley, whose response, if any, is not recorded, although he may have asked whether M&StL or public monies would be used in such an expensive relocation. And he may have asked why the Kenwood set had chosen to build their expensive and handsome homes right above the valley holding M&StL's facilities. In any event, tempers cooled in this early example of a "not-in-my-back-yard" mentality that in a later time would become epidemic.[46]

One can only speculate as to the overall thoughts of Edwin Hawley regarding M&StL in this period. He kept his own counsel, as usual; even at board meetings the laconic Hawley had little to say. But it was at M&StL that he had made his first mark; his investments in it had been made propitiously. He had prospered accordingly, and his reputation had soared. Then in 1907, the compact, gray-eyed Hawley struck again, handling the sale of Rock Island's interest in Alton after the federal government talked ominously about antitrust action and after Rock Island determined that Alton was not the bonanza investment that had been expected. Hawley toyed with the idea of acquiring control of Alton for Iowa Central, but L F. Day who as vice president oversaw management of Iowa Central as well as M&StL, counseled against the notion. In the end, Rock Island sold its interests in Alton to Toledo, St. Louis & Western (Clover Leaf), with Hawley handling the transaction.[47]

That was only the beginning of the story. Clover Leaf, with a straight-shot line from Toledo to St. Louis (and access to Detroit through jointly owned Detroit & Toledo Shore Line), now had 53.5 percent stock control of Alton, having issued ten-year bonds in the amount of $11,527 million to Rock Island in payment. One financial observer dryly reported that Clover Leaf's ownership was "very much the same as that of Minneapolis & St. Louis"—part of the "Hawley Group," as he put it. Indeed, Hawley was on the board at Clover Leaf, as were Hawley friends and sometime M&StL board members William A. Read, Henry B. Huntington, James V. Wallace, F. H. Davis, and Theodore P. Shonts. The last named had been born in Pennsylvania, grown up at Centerville, Iowa, graduated from Monmouth College in Illinois, been involved in the affairs of Iowa Central, with Hawley and others had secured control of Clover Leaf, and in 1905 been appointed chairman of the Isthmian Canal Commission by President Theodore Roosevelt. The president appreciated Shonts's "technical executive abilities," as one historian observed, although his brusque, authoritative manner irritated almost everybody. Another writer simply said: "What he has to do, he does; what he has to say, he says." Curiously, Shonts actually looked much like Roosevelt—pince-nez, mustache, bulldog facial expression, and all. In any event, Shonts left the Canal Commission in due course and became tightly associated with Hawley, who in 1909 named him president of Clover Leaf, Chicago & Alton, Iowa Central, and M&StL. During his time on the Panama project Shonts had come to appreciate the talents of William G. Bierd, a native of Baltimore who had been in railroad service with several companies before his appointment to run the Panama Railroad. A brief stint at New York, New Haven & Hartford had preceded Bierd's appointment in 1910 as vice president and general manager of M&StL, where he replaced the attractive and suave L F. Day, whose health had failed.[48]

"I buy a railroad just as an individual buys a piece of real estate," Hawley told a writer from the *Saturday Evening Post* in 1909. Perhaps that explains the enigmatic look of the core Hawley roads on railroad maps for the years 1907–12. M&StL and Iowa Central made an end-to-end connection at Albert Lea, but Iowa Central touched only a Chicago & Alton branch at Peoria, and Clover Leaf met Alton only at East St. Louis. Traffic synergies, though grandly ballyhooed, were, except for M&StL and Iowa Central, more fiction than fact.[49]

Not connected in any physical way to the other Hawley roads was Colorado & Southern, which the "Hawley crowd" had picked up at a bargain price and then disposed of to Chicago, Burlington & Quincy in 1909 at a most handsome profit. Neither was the splendid Chesapeake & Ohio (C&O), which fell under Hawley's control in 1909. But C&O quickly gathered up a derelict road that gave it independent entry to Chicago as well as direct links to both Chicago & Alton and Clover Leaf. Only a few months later, Hawley and friends took control of Missouri, Kansas & Texas—with which Clover Leaf and Alton both made head-to-head connections at St. Louis and with which Alton connected at Kansas City. After this hectic shopping spree, Hawley's name was predictably on the lips of fellow railroaders, politicians, investors, and journalists. "I have played a lone hand and stuck to my job," Hawley told one writer. "I have done two things: I have worked and I have waited. Most people do not realize what a good thing it is to know how to wait. Many things come to you. It does not pay to get restless," Hawley explained. To be sure, Hawley had patiently hunched over the roll-top desk in his New York office, alternating between close examination of financial reports and maps and study of the tape flowing out of his nearby stock ticker. Hawley's keen eyes searched constantly for opportunity, his face showing

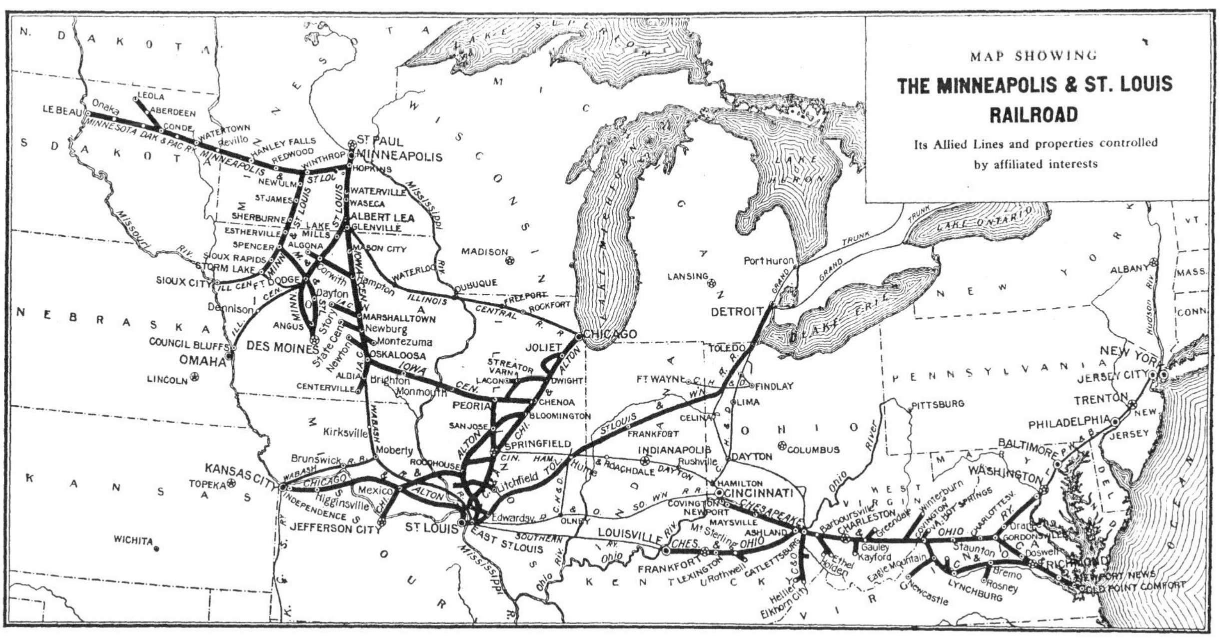

Map 10.1. This map suggests Hawley's "collection of roads." Author's collection.

no emotion, his words few, simple, and guarded. Now, however, there was no escaping the public, for a new and electric phrase had burst upon the railroad scene: "The Hawley system of roads."[50]

This curious collection of railroad companies, taken together, reached from Atlantic tidewater to the Missouri River at Le Beau, and from the Great Lakes at Chicago and Toledo to the Gulf of Mexico at Galveston. After the death of E. H. Harriman in 1909, *American Magazine* labeled Hawley "the little Harriman" and wondered if he would become the country's new "railroad king." Not so, said Hawley. "I have no ambitions and no aspirations, and I certainly do not aspire to be known or regarded as the successor of Edward H. Harriman in the railroad world," he told the *New York Times*. Yet the poker-faced and slow-moving Hawley also had an unquiet spirit that led him to team with George Gould in promotion of Gould's Western Pacific venture along with long-time friend Benjamin F. Yoakum at Rock Island, St. Louis & San Francisco, and elsewhere. The *New York Sun* dubbed him "Wall Street's new constructive genius in railroad operations," but *Railway Age* thought him a "shrewd financier rather than a constructive railway owner." Not everybody liked Hawley, of course, and in the summer of 1910 opponents and those simply jealous of him made a spirited attempt to tear down the stock values of M&StL and other Hawley roads. In Minneapolis, Anson Cutts recalled Hawley as saying at such moments: "The more I see of some men, the more I think of my dog."[51]

Cutts also remembered that T. P. Shonts and the "Clover Leaf Crowd" brought new attitudes to the management of M&StL. Despite his infrequent visits to the property, Hawley had invested not only his money in M&StL, but also his "personal pride and interest," as one intimate associate recalled. Shonts and those who came to dominate the affairs of Clover Leaf, Alton, Iowa Central, and M&StL had a more detached view. Indeed, Shonts centralized as much authority as he could in Chicago, although each road kept its own general manager—Bierd at M&StL, for example. This dry-eyed, unemotional perspective led Shonts and his team to take a very hard look at M&StL as a stand-alone entity. Hawley was disposed to pay dividends, "providing dividends with the first dollar that was not absolutely needed for expenses," as the *New York Times* put it. His stewardship at M&StL reflected as much, with the road paying $4,229,583 in dividends between 1896 and 1910. Capitalization per mile of road was down dramatically, from an awful $62,673 in 1896 to a tolerable $29,929 in 1911, but the operating ratio was up from 56.0 to 69.7, and in 1911 interest on bonded debt would be nearly $1.40 million, more than twice that of 1896. Then there was the troubling need to constantly refinance short-term notes secured by Minnesota, Dakota & Pacific securities used in building the lines west of Watertown. These arrangements had been predicated on the assumption that the Dakota extensions would be self-supporting within five years. Sad to say, however, earnings from South Dakota were far short of expectations, and bankers were becoming anxious about the matter. Another perennial headache was shippers' propensity to short haul M&StL, using it for only minimal haulage. Examples abound—cattle from Texas to Le Beau routed via Northville, South Dakota, giving M&StL less than a hundred-mile haul instead of billed via Des Moines and/or Minneapolis, or corn from Rembrandt, Iowa, to Chicago diverted to Chicago & North Western at Sioux Rapids or to Illinois Central at Storm Lake, giving M&StL only a few miles of haul. M&StL's route structure and the interlacing of its entire service area with lines of powerful Chicago roads militated against any easy remediation—the matter becoming all the more serious as M&StL became increasingly dependent upon on-line customers for its freight business. Finally, inadequate monies were being invested in plant, equipment, and rolling stock. This inevitably affected performance; a rising operating ratio was the prime indicator. Average tons per train was another index by which M&StL's record was embarrassingly shabby and reflected Hawley's devotion to paying out dividends rather than cutting down grades or buying heavier and more efficient locomotives. That, in turn, ultimately affected the bottom line; gross revenues had grown acceptably, but net was palid by comparison.[52]

Still other threats to M&StL's well-being came from debilitating traffic alliances among competitors or even merger of those competitors—not to mention the prospect of new roads or new lines. For some years Soo Line had looked at Chicago Great Western as an appropriate means by which to gain entrance to Chicago, but instead it look a ninety-nine-year lease on Wisconsin Central effective April 1, 1909. Northern Pacific raised eyebrows two years later when it forged an agreement with Chicago & North Western by which Northern Pacific's famous North Coast Limited used Chicago & North Western between Chicago and St. Paul—this despite the fact that Northern Pacific and Great Northern jointly owned Burlington, which had its own Chicago–St. Paul artery. Many railroaders wondered: was there more to this than met the eye? To the south, a paper outfit, Des Moines & Northern Iowa, threatened to build a Des Moines–Minneapolis thoroughfare if Great Northern would give it access to Minneapolis from Hopkins, and upstart Des Moines, Iowa Falls & Northern did inch upward from the Iowa capital with an attractive line that reached Mason City in 1909. Milwaukee instantly concluded a traffic alliance with that road to create a St. Paul–Des Moines irritant, but the Iowa road soon fell into Rock Island's orbit and posed a serious threat to M&StL's business in that corridor. To the west, local proponents talked often of a short line from Watertown to various points on Lake Kampeska, but nothing ever came of it. Elsewhere, an electric railway between Des Moines and Perry drew off M&StL traffic after completion in 1906, and Fort Dodge, Des Moines & Southern, another but much more impressive "interurban" line completed in 1907, offered profound competition between Fort Dodge and Des Moines. The "Dan Patch Air Line" proposed an electric railway from the Twin Cities to Dubuque, did complete a line from Minneapolis to Northfield, and eventually became the Minneapolis, Northfield & Southern. The Iowa Railroad proposed an electric line from Waterloo through Story City to Perry, but perished before construction. So did the grandiose Minneapolis, Kansas City & Gulf Electric Railway, which promised but failed to deliver "a double tracked" route from Minneapolis to Galveston.[53]

M&StL itself was a player of sorts. In 1907 there had been active rumors that it would become a "Coast Road," and certainly Hawley approved but then cancelled plans to bridge the Missouri River at Le Beau. A year later *Railway Age* reported that Chicago & North Western would extend itself by thirty miles from Gettysburg and join M&StL in a bridge project at Le Beau. The report was bogus. But in another year the *Le Beau Phenix* and other newspapers forecast that M&StL would extend the Leola branch to Ashley, North Dakota, and in fact M&StL did run a preliminary survey beyond Leola. The intent remains unclear, but perhaps it was related to an astonishing scheme to build a vertical-axis thoroughfare from Winnipeg to Corpus Christi. What resulted was the Midland Continental Railroad, which eventually placed seventy-two miles of track in operation in North Dakota and showed Leola on its projected southward path. Other reports had M&StL in support of an electric railway to be built from Pierre to Le Beau (nonsense) and with plans to complete a diagonal line from Aberdeen to Pierre (a glimmer of truth). In fact, M&StL did authorize its Minnesota, Dakota & Pacific puppet to acquire stock of Duluth, Pierre & Black Hills, the brainchild of A. W. Ewart of Pierre, which had done some grading. M&StL managers seriously considered completing that part of it from Cresbard to Pierre, but as red ink increased from operations west of Watertown (net deficit of $157,677 in fiscal year 1911), that project was euthanized. At Watertown, a connecting track was built to the recently completed South Dakota Central, up from Sioux Falls, rumored to be a "Hawley road" and reportedly in the mood to build a line eastward from Sioux Falls to Spencer, Iowa. M&StL did work out preferential traffic arrangements with South Dakota Central, and the matter continued to percolate.[54]

For M&StL, strategic matters and financial issues became tightly intertwined during the second half of 1911. The immediate concern was maturation of troublesome short-term notes (MD&P) early in 1912; it was a matter of very considerable worry to Edwin Hawley. Enter now Newman Erb, a man greatly interested in aligning himself with Hawley and a person backed by Frederick H. Prince, a Bostonian well known in investment circles. Hawley talked at length with Prince during the summer of 1911, and ultimately agreed to Erb's entering the M&StL picture if both he and Prince would commit to substantial acquisition of M&StL and Iowa Central securities. It was done, through Hawley on the New York Stock Exchange, and Newman Erb was forthwith elected to the boards of M&StL and Iowa Central, as well as to the presidency of each, T. P. Shonts stepping aside.[55]

Newman Erb proved to be an erratic leader, but he put his mark on M&StL immediately. Born in Germany in 1850, Erb emigrated to the United States, was educated at St. Louis, passed the bar examination in 1872, was associated with a number of railroads, and came to M&StL after a brief stint as president of Wisconsin Central. In August 1911 New York news tickers bristled with reports that Erb was behind plans for M&StL to build northward from Watertown or perhaps Leola to make connection at the international boundary with either Canadian Northern or Grand Trunk Pacific, that another M&StL line might protrude northwestward from Minneapolis to Emerson, Minnesota, (on the border south of Winnipeg), that Iowa Central would build from Centerville, Iowa, to St. Louis, and that M&StL and Iowa Central might then merge and make "Minneapolis *and St. Louis*" a reality. If it all came to pass, Hawley would have, with Missouri, Kansas & Texas at St. Louis, a system stretching all the way from Canada to the Gulf of Mexico. M&StL's W. G. Bierd and Chief Engineer R. G. Kenly were reported to be at Winnipeg and at various places in northwestern Minnesota on reconnaissance, while General Counsel George W. Seevers did meet with state officials in St. Paul and Des Moines to enlist political support. Still other stories had M&StL planning to extend itself from Storm Lake to Omaha and maybe even on to connection with Missouri, Kansas & Texas at Kansas City, in addition to building a modest extension westward from Leola to Mound City, South Dakota. Why do any of it, Erb was asked? Because, he said, M&StL suffered from intolerably short hauls, a problem that would be remedied by lengthening the system. He admitted that another reason for M&StL's anemia was its "small average train loads," which he promised to increase, but he did not say how.[56]

In any event, Newman Erb convinced Hawley that at minimum they should put Iowa Central together with M&StL. The two roads had worked together harmoniously on traffic matters, Iowa Central passenger time tables carried M&StL advertisements regarding South Dakota's "New Empire," M&StL occasionally borrowed Iowa Central locomotives, and solicitation for traffic by the Hawley roads had been pooled since 1909 with headquarters in Chicago. That pooling of efforts had not implied an imminent merger of the several Hawley roads, but rather had been an experiment "for mutual cooperation in the delivery of business to an allied line," a plan to be given "a fair trial." Results were unimpressive. Late in 1910, seeing that combined benefits for M&StL–Iowa Central were not at all those of Alton–Clover Leaf, a decision was made by senior management "to operate the four roads in two groups instead of one." Erb felt that even this was inadequate, and in September 1911 a plan was undertaken to arrange a lease of Iowa Central to M&StL. Then Erb gradually moved Hawley to the notion of consolidation—an end-to-end merger. The two roads already had a shared management and advantageous traffic alliances, and there would be very few if any duplicate facilities. None of this, however, was adequate justification for amalgamation. Erb instead was thinking primarily of M&StL's debilitating short-term notes. Merger with Iowa Central, he argued, would create a good talking point for selling a new issue of bonds that would, at least in part, allow payment of those notes. Hawley, who with Erb and other associates owned over 75 percent of M&StL's stock, agreed; meetings were arranged to execute Erb's plan.[57]

Events moved swiftly. Iowa Central would sell all assets to M&StL; M&StL would take on Iowa Central's debt, but Iowa Central would kick in $2.5 million "additional money." One share of M&StL common stock would be exchanged for two shares of Iowa Central common, along with one share of M&StL common and nine shares of M&StL preferred stock for each ten shares of Iowa Central preferred. M&StL would authorize $75 million in new Refunding and First Mortgage Extension Five Per Cent Fifty Year bonds and $2.5 million for first lien on the lines west of Watertown, retiring Minnesota, Dakota & Pacific bonds. Existing shareholders of both companies who chose to subscribe would receive, said Dow, Jones & Company, "a bonus of five shares of preferred stock for every $1,000 bond." Additional issues would discharge obligations that came due later and also be available for line expansion. J. S. Bache & Company of New York would underwrite the issue. Then, at 12:01 a.m. on December 20, 1911, the two roads were merged in terms of operations with the creation of three divisions—Eastern, based at Oskaloosa; Central, based at Minneapolis; and Western, based at Watertown. (Legally the two companies were not combined until January 1, 1912.) Traffic moved without a hitch through Albert Lea, where, after all, the two roads had shared facilities for more than a decade, and on January 16, 1912, M&StL reconfirmed another connection with the former Iowa Central by trackage rights over Rock Island between Des Moines and Oskaloosa.[58]

Mergers were as much a part of railroading as ties and spikes, locomotives, and cars. Southern Pacific's Collis P. Huntington referred to combinations as "a natural tendency of railroad corporations" to "secure the largest possible amount of tonnage and transport it with the least expenditure of money." Bankers such as J. P. Morgan defended consolidations as necessary and useful to achieve economies of scale, to end ruinous competition, to effect economies, to improve efficiencies, and to increase profits. Others during the Progressive Era saw them differently, fearing the rise of corporate leviathans and huge concentrations of wealth. But the national economy was strong in 1912, optimism was great, and few eyebrows were raised by Hawley's success in putting Iowa Central together with M&StL.[59]

With Iowa Central under its belt, M&StL boasted a route structure of 1,586 miles in four states—South Dakota, Minnesota, Iowa, and Illinois. What was the nature of the Iowa Central property, and what was its record? This old verse, of unknown origin, implies much.

> If you are looking for an office,
> And not prepared to die;
> Don't stop at Oskaloosa,
> Because it's on the Hook and Eye!

"Hook and Eye" was Iowa Central's nickname, of course, and the author of this ditty seemed to know that it was a poor old road devoid of baubles, bangles, or cotillions. But Iowa Central's history was long and important, linked to M&StL's earliest instincts, and its own earliest ambitions predated even M&StL.

Chapter 11

Struggling among the Titans

The facility and economy with which traffic can be handled over [the Peoria] gateway make it an important center for railroads having terminals there . . . and to shippers for the interchange of business between the trunk line territories and the West and Northwest.

—Newman Erb, 1912

The new year of 1912 seemed auspicious enough. The national economy was strong, the Dow Jones Industrial Average remained steady, and immigration to the United States continued apace. But not all news was good, sad to say. The country, and indeed the world, was stunned in April when the British liner *Titanic* went down in the Atlantic with heavy casualties on its maiden run. Closer to home, M&StL experienced its own loss when Edwin Hawley died suddenly on February 1. In Minneapolis, W. G. Bierd ordered that all work at M&StL stop for three minutes at 1:00 p.m. on February 3 out of respect for Hawley, whose funeral in New York City would begin at that moment. When the estate was finally settled it would pass to a trust whose beneficiaries were siblings, a niece, and two nephews—one of whom, Walter S. Crandell, had long been associated with the Hawley & Davis firm. In this way Hawley would be represented in M&StL affairs for many years to come.[1]

As to Hawley, the man, and his character, there was nearly unanimous agreement. Bernard M. Baruch referred to him simply as a "sound man," Greenville M. Dodge as "the finest and squarest of men." And William B. Davids, long associated with Hawley & Davis, said that "Hawley never did a crooked thing." As to Hawley, the railroader, however, reviews were mixed. One writer reminded readers that when he died in 1912, Hawley was "a dominant figure in railroads and high finance," but *World's Work* unflatteringly called Hawley "'The Stormy Petrel' of the railroad world," adding: "There has hardly been a conflict in the last ten years in which Ed Hawley failed to ride with the foremost." Early in the century Hawley had been called "Wall Street's new constructive genius in railroad operations," but by 1911 the *New York Sun* wondered as to Hawley's sagacity when he seemed to go about "buying railroads as a boy buys marbles." Neither could *Railway Age* make sense of "the Hawley system," which in 1909 it had unkindly labeled as "a gathering . . . of roads with . . . curious dissimilarities." *Age* did not quarrel with Hawley's "selection of independent roads," because they were "good ones," but cautioned, "It remains to be seen what use he will make of them." By the time of his death, however, the position of *Railway Age* had hardened. "It was as a speculative banker that Mr. Hawley earned the position in both the railway world and the financial world which he occupied at the time of his death," said its editor. "Mr. Hawley was a shrewd financier rather than a constructive railway owner," he added sourly. Specifically, *Age* concluded, "The Alton, the Clover Leaf, the Minneapolis & St. Louis, and the

Iowa Central were not well managed from a railway man's point of view." Hawley, who had always seen himself as a railroader, would have disagreed. "Good service on the rails is the first consideration," Hawley had said emphatically in 1909. "That was one of Mr. [C. P.] Huntington's rules. I stand by my properties, I never skin them; and I believe all railroads should be built up." W. D. Davids, who had worked closely with Hawley and known him well, likely summed him up best. "He was only human," said Davids. "He could not do the impossible merely by waving a magic wand. He made mistakes, like any other human; but his errors were greatly outnumbered and outbalanced by his successes."[2]

In one area there was no doubt: Edwin Hawley had been behind the curve in fashioning, or in trying to fashion, a great system of roads. The huge enterprises of the twentieth century had taken their modern form in the 1880s. Indeed, the largest systems of the 1890s were essentially the same ones that were the largest in the first two decades of the next century. Hawley, as a consequence, had faced formidable odds in his quest for a "Hawley system."[3]

For all of this, nobody knew exactly what Hawley had had in mind for the future. He had been patently reticent; he had rarely tipped his hand. Instead he had typically kept plans concealed in his well-guarded mind, mulling, studying, analyzing until he was absolutely ready to act. He had, of course, intimated desires to foster a transcontinental system, although instead of an east-west amalgamation, he rather more likely considered a vertical-axis combination across the nation's midsection. Whatever his true goals, they were interred with his remains at Chatham, New York.

Nevertheless, Newman Erb audaciously contended that "Hawley had comprehensive plans under way at the time of his death for the development of the railway properties in which he was interested." These plans, Erb continued, "were known to his friends and I believe they will be carried on without interruption." As to M&StL specifically, Erb said, "Mr. Hawley had relieved himself of the handling . . . by placing the work entirely in my hands." Brave words. But the matter of the Hawley estate was greatly perplexing and would be for some time. That reality sent a profound shudder through the board rooms of all companies in which Hawley had been dominant.[4]

Meanwhile, Erb plunged ahead. He clearly understood M&StL's dilemma. To be successful in the long run, the road had to increase the length of its hauls and had to become more efficient in handling freight by increasing the number of ton miles per train. Both needs would require substantial capital, of course, but Erb argued that it took money to make money. Central to Newman Erb's thinking was implementation of Hawley's hopes for a transcontinental road from the Canadian border to the Gulf of Mexico using M&StL and Missouri, Kansas & Texas as existing centerpieces. Erb sought financial support for an M&StL extension to Canada, but found bankers uncertain. Potential financiers then turned to Chicago Great Western's respected S. M. Felton as an independent adviser in the matter. Felton's views, sad to say, are not a matter of record, but they must have been at least mildly supportive of Erb, because in the summer of 1912 Erb saw to incorporation of the Minneapolis, St. Louis & Canadian Railway, which gained authority to build from Watertown up to the international boundary. New York's powerful J. S. Bache & Company was among others in financial support; construction was promised shortly. Erb was busy elsewhere at the same time. In November 1911, Erb and Hawley had developed plans to extend Chesapeake & Ohio's reach westward from Atlantic tidewater by domination or acquisition of Hocking Valley, Ann Arbor, and Pere Marquette, which, through the latter's cross-lake ferries, would stretch all the way to the western shores of Lake Michigan. Erb subsequently took a large investment position in Green Bay & Western, which had a line from the ferry connection with Pere Marquette across Wisconsin to the Mississippi River at Winona, downstream from St. Paul and Minneapolis and tantalizingly close to M&StL. Turning his attention again to the West, Erb sought control of South Dakota Central, whose line ran northward from Sioux Falls to Watertown, and M&StL maps soon showed that route as part of its own. There was more. Early in 1913, Erb studied plans to drive an M&StL line south from Peoria through the southern Illinois coal fields to the Ohio River.[5]

Erb's enthusiastic aspirations ran contrary to a general malaise in financial circles, however, with the result that these and other plans were forced into abeyance. Hopes for promoting M&StL securities faced additional problems. Generous reciprocity legislation in Canada had failed, and that clearly put a damper on Erb's dreams for a new line northward to some Canadian connection. And there was general skepticism as to the viability of the newly combined M&StL–Iowa Central. That skepticism only increased with the reading of M&StL's dreary performance in 1912.[6]

Undaunted, Erb turned his attention to improving M&StL's property. "Quaker sag," just to the north of Oskaloosa, was obliterated with heavy excavation to lower grades at that location, and a substantial line relocation eased grades and curvature near Searsboro. Additional yard tracks were installed at Albert Lea and Mason City while a new yard and a seventeen-stall roundhouse took shape at Oskaloosa. Bridges were renewed and strengthened, permitting dismissal of watchmen as well as allowing greater loads. "We have rattle snake coal and too many slow orders is why Engine 147 can't make the time," the engineer of a Peoria-bound passenger train had told the dispatcher on one occasion. Erb had little ability to improve the quality of coal fed into M&StL fireboxes, but he was in a position to do something about slow orders. Heavier rail (nearly sixty-two miles of eighty-five-pound steel in 1914 alone) was put into the track, and gravel by the trainload was poured from pits near Manchester, Deephaven, and Grand Junction, among other places, to provide much-needed ballast. Train performance was improved and safety enhanced by interlocking plants at crossings with other roads at Hopkins, Montgomery, St. James, and elsewhere. Twelve new Consolidation (2-8-0) locomotives were ordered in 1912, and fifteen Mikado (2-8-2) locomotives were authorized in 1915; five more 2-8-2s and ten 0-6-0s followed in 1916. Collectively this new power "added materially to the paying trainload, with a corresponding reduction in the cost of train operation." Indeed, M&StL's average tonnage per train moved up, from only 294.2 in 1910 to 427.7 in 1916. The road's inventory of motive power also peaked in that year—152 locomotives for freight, 33 for passengers, and 27 assigned to switching. In 1916 M&StL additionally had 142 passenger cars (unchanged since the merger) and 7,819 freight cars (down from 8,060 in 1912, but because of acquisitions and betterments the average age per car was lower and aggregate carrying capacity was higher).[7]

"It is the increase in tonnage and decrease in train miles that spells revenue for the stockholder," said a plain-speaking writer for *Moody's Magazine* in 1916. Newman Erb certainly concurred, his many improvements to M&StL in 1912 through 1916 reflecting as much. But other betterments, arrangements, and agreements were likewise required. New brick depots were erected at Humboldt, Minburn, and Albert Lea, while warehouses were built or purchased at Minneapolis for lease to major shippers such as Gamble-Robinson and Universal Carloading. An arrangement with the city of Minneapolis in 1916 gave M&StL access to municipal water terminals on the Mississippi River (a development that would bear fruit in the future), and Cedar Lake shop forces converted two chair cars into combination cafe and chair cars for use in St. Paul–St. Louis service. At St. Paul, M&StL leased a large freight house with three tracks holding twenty-three cars each from Northern Pacific, which performed the switching. And, where possible, M&StL entered into joint agency agreements—with Milwaukee Road at Mason City Junction, Pickering, Hedrick, and Capron; with Rock Island at all stations between Albert Lea and Manly plus four others elsewhere; with Atchison, Topeka & Santa Fe at Nemo, and so on.[8]

Given its circumscribed route structure, M&StL of necessity turned to solicitation of interchange or overhead business, such as freight moving from Pennsylvania to Washington or from Oregon to Ohio. M&StL was hardly alone in such enterprise. "You have an enormous tonnage in the Northwest . . . lumber, fruits, salmon and other products . . . that to a certain extent you control the routing of," S. M. Felton of Chicago Great Western reminded Northern Pacific's Howard Elliott in 1913. "You could throw to us a reasonable amount of your controllable business," Felton urged. Indeed, he continued, "without your support as a feeder, we cannot hope

Figure 11.1. Despite improvements to property made by Hawley and then Erb, much of M&StL's road was laid with light rail that restricted the use of newer and heavier power. That was evident between Spencer and Storm Lake, Iowa, where this crew posed before the day's work began. Author's collection.

to exist." It was the same for M&StL. Soon after merger with Iowa Central, M&StL began daily package car service with Illinois Central to Chicago (the third morning delivery) by way of Albert Lea, with Chicago & Alton via Peoria, and with Burlington Route via Monmouth. More intriguing were package cars to and from the Northeast on Delaware, Lackawanna & Western and those of the Kanawha Dispatch from Norfolk and Lynchburg, Virginia. Cars from the latter arrived in or left Peoria over Cleveland, Cincinnati, Chicago & St. Louis, one of nearly a dozen carriers serving that city. "The facility and economy with which traffic can be handled over this gateway make it an important center for railroads having terminals there," said Erb, "and to shippers for the interchange of business between the trunk line territories and the West and Northwest." Others pointed to unholy congestion at Chicago, with its attendant expense and delay to both lading and rolling stock. The Peoria Gateway, by comparison, was the route of least resistance. Erb enthusiastically sought to upgrade the line between Oskaloosa and Peoria while directing M&StL traffic representatives at twenty-seven locations around the country to focus on the Peoria Gateway as an important means of boosting "through interline traffic." It proved a sound strategy; such business increased nearly 15 percent in fiscal year 1913 alone.[9]

Figure 11.2. Freight volume increased, and with M&StL's undulating main-line profile, double heading with any available power was routine. A diminutive American Standard and a much larger Consolidation had just taken water at Gifford, Iowa, and were getting a roll on heavy tonnage. Author's collection.

At the same time, however, circumstances on the West End were more problematic. There was no more talk of building beyond the Missouri River, and if there ever would be extension to Canada, it would be from Watertown and not Leola. The bloom clearly was off at Le Beau, and a crop failure in 1911 west and northwest of Conde was comprehensive; M&StL hauled in seed grain free of charge for the 1912 season. Catastrophic fires hit Le Beau, Akaska, Cresbard, and Tolstoy in 1908, and the next year a prairie fire burned a swath thirty miles long and fifteen miles wide that stopped just short of Cresbard. Revenues suffered accordingly. By the summer of 1913, Nahon, Richmond, and Wetonka on the Conde–Aberdeen leg, and Adelaide, Chelsea, Wecota, Carlyle, Onaka, and Akaska were made "prepaid stations," that is, without agents. (Agency status later was restored to a few.) Bridge and building crews who hated servicing the turntable at Le Beau because the pit was full of rattlesnakes were relieved when business at that town fell off to the point where the table was removed in 1914 (sent to replace the one at Cedar Lake), and a wye was installed there to turn engines. Frontier regions always were characterized by cheery optimism, but sufficient time on the land had soberly demonstrated that as M&StL's mileposts extended beyond the ninety-eighth meridian the prospects for profitable agriculture on an annual basis became more marginal. The reduction of yearly rainfall by only an inch, or a shift of greatest precipitation from spring and summer to fall, could mean the difference between a fine crop and a burned field. "The sun shines on Dakota the same as on Godly people," wrote one wag; "discrimination is more noticeable in the matter of rainfall," he caustically concluded.[10]

None of this implied the categoric end of colonization in South Dakota or elsewhere in the American and Canadian West. In 1913, fifty-one carloads of farm machinery, household goods, and livestock belonging to Iowa farmers en route to Minnesota came off the Southwestern at Winthrop. In March 1913, a farmer from near Gibbon left with a carload of goods for northern Minnesota, but a week later another party from Illinois arrived in Winthrop with two carloads of household goods, machinery, and the like to take up residence on a nearby farm. Saskatchewan lured others from along M&StL lines in the next few years, but South Dakota still held a sparkle. "Many new settlers are being attracted to the low priced lands tributary to your lines in South Dakota," M&StL shareholders were told in 1916, "and special attention is being given to the introduction of better methods of, and more diversified farming."[11]

Midwestern agriculture was, in a general sense, quite healthy during the first two decades of the twentieth century. For that matter, so too was the general economy, except for a blip in 1907 and another in 1914, when the Great War began in Europe. Minneapolis, St. Paul, Des Moines, and Peoria all were growing nicely, fed, so to speak, by the vibrant prosperity of their respective hinterlands. An amazing national growth in manufacturing was explained in part by a resilient outlands economy that swallowed up large chunks of industrial production. In rural areas, mortgage indebtedness increased, but this was more than matched by sharp increases in crop prices and land values. All of it was reflected at M&StL's way stations, except for those blemished by drought conditions in South Dakota. Boyd, in western Minnesota, might be considered typical. In 1916 its citizens and those in the surrounding countryside supported four each churches and grain elevators; three each hardware stores, implement dealers, and restaurants; two each banks, general merchandise stores, lumber yards, meat markets, and physicians; and one each newspaper, hotel, flour mill, and drugstore. Elsewhere, a business journal in Des Moines correctly declared that "business depends on buying power," and continued, "Iowa's people are prosperous and have power."[12]

Agricultural prosperity was reflected especially in M&StL traffic statistics. The road's freight mix remained essentially as it had been before merger with Iowa Central, with grain, flour, lumber, cement, coal, merchandise, and livestock making up nearly 74 percent of all tonnage in 1915. But revenue tonnage and revenue ton miles were up handsomely in 1916 over 1912 (see Table 11.1). Freight revenues also advanced smartly, from $5.7 million in 1912 to $8.3 million in 1916. Passenger numbers were not as impressive (see Table 11.2). Total passenger revenues advanced very modestly, from $2,061,652 in 1912 to $2,393,764 in 1916, dropping from nearly 26 percent of system revenue in the former year to under 22 percent in the latter.[13]

Table 11.1. Tonnage and ton miles

Year	*Tonnage handled*	*Ton miles*
1912	4,747,163	755,890,137
1916	6,502,405	1,060,812,922

Table 11.2. Passenger service

Year	*Passengers carried*	*Passenger miles*	*Average distance carried*
1912	2,366,727	84,129,559	35.5 miles
1916	2,457,856	92,842,539	37.8 miles

Anson B. Cutts remained in change of M&StL's passenger service. In 1913 he thanked local agents for their good efforts in the year previous, but wondered: "Don't you think we can do a little better in 1913?" It was vintage Cutts. "Please don't let any business get away," he admonished. Cutts was, as always, at his best in promoting special movements and special trains. In 1913 M&StL operated a tourist sleeping car from St. Paul to Los Angeles (M&StL–Wabash–Santa Fe) during the Christmas season, and special movements during that era were arranged for the Chicago Ladies Orchestra (Winthrop to Dawson and elsewhere), Royal Palm Southern (Winfield to Peoria), the Methodist General Conference Committee (for its Minneapolis convention), and the St. Olaf College choir (to and from Forest City, Lake Mills, Albert Lea, New Richland, Waseca, and St. Paul). Three cars were required for the New Ulm Amusement Company to transport its tent show, motion pictures, and vaudeville numbers from place to place. The Minnesota State Fair of 1913 warranted reduced fares from stations on the Southwestern as distant as Storm Lake, and Cutts's trademark "popular excursions" remained a staple. One of the more unusual excursions in 1914 featured special trains off the Newton, State Center, Story City, Algona, and Montezuma branches bound for Minneapolis and St. Paul, with rates extraordinarily attractive—$4.00 from points on the Newton branch, for example. Another dollar purchased double bedroom space one way in a Pullman tourist car. Rates from stations on the Southwestern in 1913 were equally attractive for a special train taking football fans to Minneapolis for a contest between the University of North Dakota and the University of Minnesota. Opportunities seemed endless. Special trains took Turn-Verein performers from New Ulm to Young America, racing enthusiasts from Winthrop to New Ulm to watch the pacers; St. Paul West Side Turners to Carver for their annual outing; citizens of Gaylord to neighboring Gibbon and Green Isle to lobby for the award of the county seat to Gaylord; funlovers to Watertown when the circus showed there; dog fanciers to Wetonka from Aberdeen to attend the All-American field trials; and members of the Norwegian Church from New Richland to Albert Lea for a church meeting. In a year that Marshalltown High School fielded an undefeated football team, a showdown contest was arranged with Mason City's similarly powerful gridiron group, and M&StL put on a special train for the game (which was played to a tie). And several sections were required in 1916 to move the First Regiment of the Minnesota National Guard to active duty along the Mexican border.[14]

A much greater volume of passengers used regularly scheduled trains to meet routine transportation needs. College students were regular customers, as were traveling salesmen representing any number of businesses—grocery houses, meat packers, and retailers of clothing, implements, rugs, and carpet, to mention only a few; most of these drummers represented wholesale offices in Minneapolis, St. Paul, Peoria, Des Moines, Fort Dodge, and Aberdeen. M&StL delivered the new pastor for Salem Lutheran Church at Lake Mills; took the thirsty from areas already blighted by the prohibition urge to Sherburn, where they restocked; and handled "town team" players and fans from station to station for ball games and dancers and merrymakers to the new Lakeside Club pavilion at Waconia. Marshalltown High School regularly sent its basketball team on the cars to contests at Grinnell and Oskaloosa, and Grinnell College ordered Pullmans when its football team traveled to games in St. Louis. A family from Berwick, Illinois, preferred shopping in Galesburg, using M&StL to Abingdon,

Figure 11.3. The irrepressible A. B. Cutts sold all nature of excursions, including this one from Marshalltown for picnickers headed to Clemons Grove, Iowa, on September 2, 1912. Author's collection.

the People's Traction cars to Galesburg, and reverse routing in return. A man from Winthrop went to Aberdeen for an indefinite stay, and a woman traveled to Fort Dodge to see relatives. Students from the tiny village of Troy, South Dakota, used M&StL for a six-mile ride to Strandburg in order to attend high school; a bandmaster from New Ulm took the train once a week to give lessons at Echols; church groups from Hanska utilized Sunday trains for picnics and songfests; and residents of Ormsby, Echols, and LaSalle often headed to St. James for a few hours of shopping, visiting, or loafing. The relationship between smaller and larger stations was the same elsewhere. In one nine-month period that was likely representative for the time, 65 percent of all local tickets sold at Wallace were to persons bound for Watertown, twenty-four miles distant, with a 36-cent one-way fare. And, as always, the railroad provided means of transportation for which it was only partially or never compensated. Women from LaSalle walked the track to and from Ladies Aid meetings held at outlying farms, and five young blades from Winthrop "took advantage of a nice day" and walked to Gibbon, but with sore ankles and blistered heels anted up the fare for a return on the train. Elsewhere, a Sunday school teacher and her class walked the track from Sioux Rapids to Cornell, five miles, but returned by way of the afternoon train. At Leola, hoboes crowded the jungle at the west edge of town in July 1914, and every train brought more. But the railroad looked the other way because those same men represented an itinerant labor force necessary for the annual harvest.[15]

M&StL's passenger offerings were fully developed by 1915. Three trains in each direction operated between St. Paul and Albert Lea and on to Oskaloosa, two from Oskaloosa to Peoria, and two from Oskaloosa to Albia, Iowa. Triple daily service was available from Albert Lea to Des Moines, and three trains ran from St. Paul to Winthrop, one heading south to New Ulm, two running on westward to Watertown, and one continuing to Aberdeen. A single set sufficed on the Winthrop–Storm Lake run and on the Fort Dodge–Ruthven route, although the latter ran through to Estherville, giving Spencer–Estherville stations two sets. The Conde–Le Beau, Aberdeen–Leola, and Fort Dodge–Angus legs and all of the Iowa branches featured homely locals or mixed trains, some seeing twice-daily service in each direction. The Van Noy Railway Hotel & News Company had news privileges on M&StL trains and operated lunch counters, news stands, and dining and parcel rooms at various points.[16]

M&StL's premier trains remained the Aberdeen Limited to South Dakota, variously named numbers 3 and 4 between St. Paul and Des Moines, and of course the North Star Limited. Competition in each of M&StL's major avenues was perpetually intense. Milwaukee's offerings to Aberdeen were part of that road's transcontinental operation, and high-speed, elegant service was the norm. Burlington touted its "Mississippi River Scenic Line—Where Nature Smiles Three Hundred Miles" between Chicago and the Twin Cities in a corridor where competition was always acute. Rock Island, North Western, and Great Western all were stern rivals for Des Moines business, and Rock Island and Burlington combined for double-daily service to St. Louis, while Chicago, Burlington & Quincy sported its own independent offerings. Nevertheless, the North Star maintained its heady presence, although Illinois Central proved a less than sterling partner. In fact, in 1912 that road turned its back on M&StL and partnered with CB&Q for a special train from Minneapolis to New Orleans and connection there with a steamer to Panama. The joint M&StL-IC service between St. Paul and Omaha dwindled and the through sleeper discontinued in 1911, but the two roads maintained close connections at Fort Dodge for patrons who were willing to change trains. By 1914 the North Star designation singled out only M&StL-Wabash service to and from St. Louis, along with through cars from IC and Chicago moving between St. Paul and Albert Lea on other trains.[17]

These were the salad days of Pullman service on American railroads. M&StL's participation in the sleeping car trade was never great compared to that of larger roads, but sleepers were in the consists of major trains from the early days of association with Burlington, Cedar Rapids & Northern and Rock Island. By 1915 M&StL joined with Pullman on five overnight routes.

St. Paul–Des Moines	Trains 4/3
St. Paul–Fort Dodge	Trains 4/3
St. Paul–Watertown	Trains 15/16
St. Louis–St. Paul	Trains 5/6 (North Star, with Wabash)
Chicago–St. Paul	Trains 7/4 (with IC)

The contract with Pullman called for M&StL to pay 1 cent per car mile on lines earning less than $6,000 per annum, 2 cents per car mile on lines earning less than $5,000. Small wonder there was pressure to sell Pullman space at M&StL's city ticket agencies, fashionably located at 402 Nicollet in Minneapolis and at 512 Walnut Street in Des Moines. And small wonder that locomotive engineers assigned to trains handling Pullman cars took an opportunity to "open 'er up" when possible. But M&StL's physical plant did not invite this—with the exception of the "race track" between Waseca and Albert Lea, a thirty-two-mile stretch of nearly tangent track with light grades and a splendid roadbed.[18]

"Mobile hotels [passenger trains handling sleeping cars] dart across the country in a stream of light at aeroplane speed on a nonstop schedule," wrote one observer of the railroad scene in 1915. It was not likely he was thinking of the North Star Limited or of the Waseca–Albert Lea "race track," but his reference to an "aeroplane" is instructive and implied much, although few persons at the time envisioned the impact that "flying machines" eventually would have on public transport. Neither did most persons, save a few visionaries, perceive the astonishing impact that motor vehicles would have on the life and time of the American people—and on the nation's railways.[19]

"The horseless vehicle" had burst upon the western world late in the nineteenth century. The first gasoline-powered automobile built in the United States, a contraption of Charles and Frank Duryea, bicycle and toolmakers of Chicopee, Massachusetts, appeared in September 1892; one month later, William Morrison of Des Moines rolled out his invention, an electric auto. In Minnesota, the first motor vehicle may have been cobbled together at Franklin in 1899 by George Forsyth, a flour miller, and Olaf Nelson, a blacksmith. At the turn of the century, only four thousand such vehicles were found in the country, but as one contemporary observer noted, "Potentially . . . [the automobile's] . . . utility is unlimited." After all, he said, "The automobile solves the problem of a portable power adapted to the needs of personal and commercial transportation without the supplementary inconvenience and expense of oats thrice daily, or the limitations of steel tracks and prescribed routes of travel." Another chipped in: "The train is a service. A motor car is a servant." In 1895, Crisham & Winch of St. Paul had proudly advertised a full line of "Traps, Broughams, Family Carriages, and Sleighs," and in St. Louis Park were found busy factories belonging to the Minneapolis Jarless Spring Carriage Company and the Thompson Wagon Company ("We build the only Concord Buggy made west of New York"). But much had changed by 1912, when the *Minneapolis Journal* of February 18 contained a full forty-page supplement celebrating the Annual Automobile Show staged in that city. William Howard Taft had ridden to his presidential inauguration in a carriage; four years later, in 1913, Woodrow Wilson chose an automobile.[20]

Indeed, in the twinkling of an eye the automobile would transform the American landscape, its culture, and its economy. In 1905 only 799 motor vehicles were registered in Iowa; four years later there were already 7,000 autos registered in neighboring Minnesota. By 1916, Iowa registered 145,134 autos; Minnesota tallied 180,400 a year later. Ancillary industries and businesses appeared instantly. By 1909, there were 190 motor vehicle dealers at M&StL stations. Mauer Sales Company at Spencer sold Paige-Detroit automobiles; Mueller & Aab were agents for Stoddard-Dayton and Maxwell brands at New Ulm. Colby Motor Company of Mason City built and sold its own models, and auto repair shops and filling stations could be found in every small village. Ford's Model N, a "Runabout," was available for $600 in 1907, but a year later Ford introduced its famous four-cylinder Model T—the "Universal Car"—which ranged in price from $590 to $900 depending on appointments. Seventy-four manufacturers were represented at the Minneapolis Auto Show in 1912; $2 million in sales were registered there in only eight days.[21]

America's love affair with the automobile was immediate, if uneven. "The automobile is something new in our lives," a Methodist minister at Fort Dodge warily pointed out. "It is not a thing of evil, but it could be put to an evil purpose." He was mollified only when his wife noted, "The automobile also can be used to bring people to church who live too far away to walk." When A. B. Cutts took a delegation of newspapermen to Chicago in 1902 to show off the resplendent North Star Limited, the group was met by Illinois Central representatives who loaded their guests into automobiles for a tour of Chicago. Neither Cutts nor the newspapermen uttered as much as a peep of surprise as to the use of automobiles instead of horse-drawn carriages, as the auto was already a routine fixture in their minds. But the place of the automobile in the transportation galaxy was not yet complete. In 1911 and 1912 the *Minneapolis Journal* featured an automobile section in its Sunday editions, but it was found in the Dramatic and Social portion of the newspaper, not with transportation or business. Young sports at Winthrop formed an Auto Club whose members "toured the streets" of that community—again suggesting that the automobile was not yet taken seriously for transportation. But Thomas A. Way used a bright red Pope-Toledo touring car to visit and promote his townsite enterprises on the Le Beau line (where an irritated bull once assumed a most bellicose attitude toward his horseless carriage), and, curiously, Le Beau's first recorded death came as the result of an overturned automobile. Elsewhere, a farmer with a new Ford became flummoxed at a grade crossing near Hanska when a freight train surprised him; he tried desperately if unsuccessfully to stop his machine by yelling, "Whoa, whoa there!" a command that had been perfectly effective in driving his team of horses.[22]

This farmer and all who purchased motor vehicles became instant members of a powerful special interest group demanding new and better roadways. In 1902 the state of Iowa began to reverse the historic tradition of local control over roadway construction and maintenance. Three years later Minnesota created a state highway commission to help establish an efficient and widespread system of roadways. Minnesota businessmen and farmers were quick to join in lobbying for a state road from Mankato to Minneapolis, while kindred spirits at Lake Mills, Iowa, urged a "Des Moines–Twin Cities Short Line" highway by way of Albert Lea; in South Dakota an organization was born to promote "an interstate highway" from Yellowstone Park to Minneapolis, parallel with M&StL's line all the way to Minneapolis. The first rural concrete pavement in Iowa was a short stretch near Eddyville in 1911, and the first full mile of concrete highway in the state was laid west of Mason City in 1912; by the end of 1918 it was extended to Clear Lake—the state's "first interurban concrete highway."[23]

Railroaders were first bemused by the intruder and then perplexed. "W. E. Lyman left by train for Aberdeen," reported the *Le Beau Phenix* in 1908, "where he expects to purchase an automobile before returning." It was the same at Lafayette eight years later, when five men took the train to Minneapolis, returning soon with five new autos. "They were compelled to do some pretty substantial road work at certain places before they could get through," the local newspaper reported. Railroad managers were perplexed, but many of them asserted that good roads would encourage immigration, help farmers diversify their operations, and lead to a more stable flow of traffic. Indeed, it became nearly an article of faith among railroad managers that a direct and measurable relationship connected the condition of roads and the volume of rail traffic.[24]

The motor vehicle soon proved a mixed blessing for the railroads, however. One automobile dealer shipped two hundred carloads of Buicks in four trains from Lansing, Michigan, to Minneapolis during 1912, producing very substantial revenue for participating carriers. Two carloads of Fords were delivered to Winthrop in 1913, and several carloads of International trucks arrived at Jordan in 1915. These were hardly isolated examples of a growing volume of business. M&StL built a wooden platform for unloading autos at Minneapolis in 1909; others soon were provided at Storm Lake, Ackley, and Newton, and even at tiny locations such as Union and Oakville, during the years 1911–15. M&StL acquired its own automobile-carrying boxcars in 1916 and more of them in subsequent years. But there were also disturbing contraindications. In 1914, ten thousand persons swarmed Waconia for the Band Tournament there, many arriving on special trains bulging with patrons; two thousand automobiles parked on all the side streets likely delivered even more. By 1916 there was clear reason for concern. Moreover, just as the automobile was eroding short-haul passenger traffic, the truck was eating into short-haul and less-than-carload freight. And a tiny jitney operation had begun in Minnesota's iron ore country—the earliest predecessor of Greyhound."[25]

Frowns increasingly appeared on the faces of railroad managers. Advocates of more and better highways were not simply interested in providing opportunities for tinkerers and the rich and famous to entertain themselves with newfangled pleasure vehicles. "The auto truck and the automobile are blazing the way for better highways and reduced freight and passenger rates—as the railroads will no longer have a monopoly of transportation," said one bitterly candid report from Redwood Falls in 1912. Railroaders found themselves at once squeezed between growing public impulses to promote tax-supported highways sure to enhance modal competition and other public impulses to shackle railroads' ability to compete. Equity holders and managers alike chafed at the new environment of private ownership and government control. Labor militancy added another sulfurous element. "No business can be conducted to best results if its managers are prevented from deciding what they will pay for material . . . and what they will receive for its product," M&StL's T. P. Shonts had pointed out in 1911. "Labor organizations seek to control the cost of railroad operations and government officials determine income derived from operations," complained an obviously vexed Shonts. The courts recognized the legal principle that government-set rates should not deny a fair return on investment, but railroads rarely succeeded in sustaining that right. The Minnesota Rate Case, long in litigation, illustrated the point. The Supreme Court ultimately upheld the state of Minnesota against Great Northern and Northern Pacific and in favor of M&StL—but only because the court found M&StL

less favorably situated and less prosperous than the larger roads. For M&StL the Minnesota case was but a Pyrrhic victory, because it was forced by competition to reduce rates anyway to meet the court-mandated lower rates established for its railroad competitors.[26]

Matters only worsened with passage of the Hepburn Act (1906) and the Mann-Elkins Act (1910), which greatly strengthened the Interstate Commerce Commission. Unfortunately, such government involvement put a distinct chill on investors, who increasingly shied away from railroad issues, with the result that railroads had to pay more for capital. That, in turn, caused a growing malnutrition among the nation's railroads and, much worse, drove the spirit of enterprise from the railroad sector. Simultaneous if conflicting demands for increased and faster service along with better equipment, higher compensation for labor, and cheaper rates for transportation were a prescription for disaster. In 1914 Newman Erb estimated that heavy-handed government regulation since 1906 had wiped out $6 billion in the market value of railroad securities. "There is a tendency by both the National and State Governments . . . to press further upon the railroads lower freight and passenger rates and increased expenditures," Erb complained. "This tendency, with the unrestful condition of labor, is retarding the prosperity of the country's transportation systems and must more or less affect their ability to keep pace with the development of the country, and respond effectively to the demands which are ever to be made upon them for new extensions, additional equipment and further improvement in service.[27]

By late 1915, one-sixth of railroad mileage in the United States was in the hands of receivers—and this, ironically, was in a period of general prosperity. Fewer miles of railroad were built in 1915 than in any year since 1864, and more miles of railroad were in receivership than ever before. In 1916 four operating craft brotherhoods demanded federal legislation mandating an eight-hour day without reduction in wages, and to avoid a threatened nationwide strike, Congress passed and President Woodrow Wilson signed into law the Adamson Act, giving labor what it wanted. However meritorious from a safe practices standpoint, Adamson added monumentally to operating costs without providing means for offsetting increases in revenue. It also emboldened other labor organizations to take advantage of liberal support in the nation's capital at a time of manpower shortages. Industrial wage disputes had entered politics.[28]

All of this was context for M&StL's private circumstance in the period between its merger with Iowa Central in 1912 and America's participation in the Great War five years later. On August 9, 1915, M&StL purchased Des Moines & Fort Dodge (under lease since 1905), and a year later entered into a consolidation agreement with Iowa Central & Western (the Algona Branch from Belmond), by which that company ceased to exist. These twin acquisitions boosted the road's capital and debt per mile to over $42,000, adequate cause for concern. Dividends had not been paid since 1910, and 1916 common stock traded in the $26–36 range, well down from a high of $42 in 1911, and far from $84 in 1906 and $110 in 1903. Nevertheless, the operating ratio for the years 1912–16 averaged 70.58, respectable compared to the country's largest railroads at the time.[29]

American route mileage peaked in 1916 at 254,036, and the great systems were essentially in place. There was a flurry of reports in 1912 that Chicago & North Western and Northern Pacific would combine to create a huge Northwestern Pacific, but such a marriage would have been difficult in the extreme given the existing political climate. Trustbusters already had undone E. H. Harriman's handiwork in combining Southern Pacific with Union Pacific and were presently seeking to take Central Pacific from parent Southern Pacific. In this stultifying atmosphere Newman Erb's enthusiastic aspirations for an expanded M&StL simply evaporated. And M&StL increasingly was penned in. Rock Island by now had purchased or controlled lines and had built others to complete an enviable route from Minneapolis through Des Moines and Kansas City to the Gulf of Mexico, effectively cutting off similar dreams by Hawley and then Erb. For that matter, in 1915 Missouri, Kansas & Texas, once part of the Hawley system, succumbed to a passel of short-term notes that put it in receivership. That same year, however, and into the next, Wall Street insiders predicted an amalgamation of M&StL

and Canadian Northern or Grand Trunk, but those roads had their own problems and soon would disappear into mammoth Canadian National, a Crown corporation. Neither did other rumors of M&StL's combination with Soo Line come to fruition. M&StL, it was increasingly clear, was not going to become one of the great systems, nor , it seemed, was it going to become even a part of a great system. It would remain a modest-sized regional road struggling among the giants. Nothing new in that.[30]

Yet soldiering on as an independent was problematic. Financial arrangements resulting from the merger of M&StL and Iowa Central had eradicated some but hardly all of the irksome short-term note frustrations that continued to plague the company. Over the years 1912–16, M&StL paid $10,431,815 in interest , or an annual average of $2,086,363. In good years this burden could be shouldered, but in 1914 the road incurred a net deficit and failed to settle interline accounts with connecting roads; this, in turn, greatly frustrated the board of directors and sent a fright through the investment community. New short-term 6 percent notes were floated, but they were bid down, signaling unattractiveness. Maturation of these and other notes on February 1, 1916, prompted a movement that resulted in an unusual reorganization without receivership. Owners of M&StL stock surrendered their holdings and paid $20 per share in cash for a new $78 par value issue. This "voluntary" reorganization brought in funds adequate to pay off short-term notes and other debt, left the company's bonds undisturbed, and reestablished M&StL's credit. Hayden, Stone & Company and J. S. Bache & Company ramrodded the transaction, in the process landing Charles Hayden on the board as chairman. He was joined by Jules S. Bache and others from New York who had been part of the underwriting syndicate. The Hawley estate was represented by F. H. Davis, Hawley's former partner and a member of the directorate since 1896; the earlier era also was represented by Henry E. Huntington. Newman Erb stayed on the board, but stepped down as president, succeeded by Edward L. Brown, formerly vice president and general manager at Denver & Rio Grande.[31]

With some of its financial liabilities removed, M&StL had a new lease on life. But the road still suffered from inadequate length of line hauls, was much too dependent on agriculture for its livelihood, had inadequate motive power and too much of a roller-coaster profile to efficiently handle tonnage per train mile, and had stock and debt per mile ranging from $42,000 to $45,000 per year. And there was another issue. "The earnings of a road must be plowed into the property so as to create an equity in it for the welfare of those who hold its mortgage securities and afford security for future evidences of its indebtedness," contended Theodore Prince from the New York Stock Exchange firm of that name. Had Erb adequately met those stringent conditions during his stewardship since 1911? And would the new management see the need and/or be able to meet that need? On these questions the jury was out—and would stay out for some while.[32]

Chapter 12
Sweet and Sour

We left Fort Dodge for Albert Lea
Just as happy as any crew could be
The train was short and the engine small
But that was all she was able to haul

Humboldt was the first place in sight
The goon was out with a big red light
Clean out the yard he says to me on an order from H. E. E.
And if it was not for the law
We would be there still.

—A rhyme that circulated among Minneapolis & St. Louis trainmen in the early twentieth century

Good crops and a robust national economy spelled attractive numbers for Minneapolis & St. Louis in 1916 and 1917. Interline freight business grew nicely, the average length of haul increased to nearly 170 miles, and in 1917 revenue tons reached 6.6 million, the highest in company history to that time. The numbers of passengers carried and passenger miles were down slightly, but system revenues from all sources were the greatest yet achieved. M&StL's operating ratio stood at 68.89, compared to 68.31, the average of all Class One railroads (those earning over $1 million in revenues per year). Substantial combination depots were erected at Wayland and Storm Lake, Iowa, and at Green Isle, Minnesota, to replace others consumed by fire, and more new eighty-five-pound rail went into the track, mostly between Hopkins, Minnesota, and Peoria, Illinois—all positive statements of permanence and stability.[1]

Over in the passenger department, the irrepressible Anson B. Cutts continued to work his magic, pointing with pride in 1916, for instance, to $30,818 generated by his "popular excursions." Some of those trains were headed for Clear Lake, Iowa, not an M&StL station, but a dozen miles west of Mason City on Mason City & Clear Lake, an aggressive traction road with which Iowa Central and then M&StL connected. Entire trainloads of exuberant excursionists bound for Clear Lake's famous Oaks Hotel, the White Pier dance pavilion, or other attractions were interchanged at Mason City. Elsewhere special trains were ordered to take St. Paul policemen to Waconia in 1916, bank workers boarding the "Dakota Bankers' Special" of 1917 across M&StL's western lines, and Iowa Governor W. L. Harding and other mourners to Humboldt for the funeral of legendary wrestler Frank Gotch in December 1917. Barnum & Bailey likewise used M&StL that year to reach New Ulm, Spencer, Fort Dodge, Marshalltown, and Mason City; in conjunction with these engagements, M&StL always promised "popular excursions" to meet the needs of circus fans from outlying communities. Most passengers, of course, were not aboard special trains, but rather availed themselves of the company's regularly scheduled service, especially on the North Star Limited to St. Louis and the Capital City Limited between St. Paul and Des Moines. The latter train was the road's speediest in 1917, covering 99.4 miles between Albert Lea and Hopkins, Minnesota, in 153 minutes—averaging 42.66 miles per hour—and making only one stop, at Waseca. In season, M&StL also handled the Minnesota State Fish Car to on-line lakes, where milk cans full of pike fry were dumped to replenish the supply of game fish.[2]

Accumulating clouds on the horizon tempered optimism, however. The Interstate Commerce Commission, now greatly strengthened, had become at once prosecutor, judge, and jury—paradoxically often proclaiming policy that was harmful to the industry it was designed to regulate, but also in many instances to the very consumers it was supposed to protect. There were other clouds of an even more ominous nature. Events growing out of the assassination of Archduke Franz Ferdinand on June 28, 1914, quickly escalated into the Great War—World War I, as it would eventually be called. A Europe at war soon craved American production; industrial and agricultural activity swelled traffic on the nation's rails. That swell only increased when the United States itself declared war early in April 1917. The railroad industry moved immediately to deal with new challenges by creating the Railroads' War Board, pledging to support the war effort by running the country's manifold independent carriers as a "continental system," by organizing car pools, and by eliminating duplication of services. But problems were great. War traffic tended to move only in one direction, east, and when Atlantic port facilities and ocean transport proved inadequate, rail cars simply piled up as unintended warehouses. A severe car shortage was the predictable consequence.[3]

The industry's performance in 1917 was nevertheless impressive—9 percent more ton miles and 12 percent more passenger miles than had been produced in 1916. But problems persisted and even worsened. Federal law and federal bureaucracy were at the heart of the matter. Unification of operation to promote efficiency was suspect under antitrust legislation, and car pooling was prohibited under ICC provisions. Congress was reticent to change positions on either issue, the needs of war notwithstanding. At the same time, the ICC was unwilling to authorize increased rates to compensate for increased costs of labor and material. Under the circumstances, railroads were reluctant to seek capital to expand plant, and when they did, bankers were reluctant to lend. Gridlock was at hand. President Wilson, to complete mobilization of the country's resources required by war, took possession of the railroads by means of a proclamation issued on December 26; control passed to the United States Railroad Administration (USRA) and to William G. McAdoo, director general, effective noon December 28, but for accounting purposes on January 1, 1918. Congress then passed and President Wilson signed into law the Railroad Control Act, which provided that the federal government would make annual compensation to the carriers on the basis of net operating income for the three years preceding June 30, 1917. It also promised adequate maintenance of property during the time of government operation. Regional federal directors were appointed to oversee general operations, with local federal managers assigned to on-the-job responsibilities, but final authority rested in Washington with the tall, thin-lipped, long-nosed McAdoo.[4]

At M&StL, Edward L. Brown had no more than unpacked his bags than he was gone, replaced as president by homegrown William H. Bremner, who himself was obliged to resign and then was appointed federal manager over M&StL. That was only the beginning of change. From the forceful and ambitious McAdoo came orders to terminate immigration and agricultural development efforts, to discontinue solicitation of traffic, and to trim advertising. Bremner and other railroad managers must have looked at each other in quizzical disbelief. The ICC and antitrust law were summarily put on the shelf, USRA's sweeping authority superseding them. ICC and antitrust had obliged railroads to compete with one another; USRA now obliged them to cooperate.[5]

Cooperation meant change, and for M&StL change meant unraveling the distinctive passenger program so skillfully knitted together by Anson Cutts. USRA-mandated consolidated ticket offices at Des Moines and Minneapolis cost not only M&StL's individuality but also its identification by the traveling public. On April 1, 1918, Illinois Central, likely at USRA's behest, quietly dropped all through car arrangements via Albert Lea, effectively pulling the plug on M&StL's historic association in the Twin Cities–Chicago passenger trade. Illinois Central still operated trains into Albert Lea, of course, and patrons could make platform connections just as they did at Fort Dodge in the Omaha trade, but it simply was not the same as through service. A much happier change was made at Minneapolis on May 11, 1919, when M&StL began use of Great Northern's new and modern Union Station on Hennepin Avenue, finally rid of the shabby nearby "temporary" facilities it had utilized for more than two decades.[6]

American railroads had handled more passengers in 1916 than ever before, but those records were eclipsed in 1917, then fell again in 1918. This was not replicated at M&StL, however, when the number of revenue passengers in 1917 was nearly 10 percent short of the 1916 number, and the number for 1918 was 9 percent below that for 1917. Cutts blamed snowstorms, war conditions, and the disappearance of his "popular excursions," but he admitted also that "local passenger travel was considerably reduced through the use of automobiles." Still, M&StL boarded two million passengers in 1918, and Cutts even found a way to justify a special train from Hanska and New Ulm to the Twin Cities for the Sons of Hermann. Military movements were a necessary and predictable part of the mix. Recruits bound for Europe to make the world safe for democracy were loaded at most stations—Leola and Forest City, for instance—and entire trainloads were mustered at Minneapolis and then shipped to St. Louis (M&StL-Wabash). One doughboy recalled that the train that took him to St. Louis was devoid of dining service; stops were made at Iowa stations, however, where the Red Cross put aboard sandwiches, coffee, and milk. Locomotives equipped to supply steam heat often were in short supply, and when Atchison, Topeka & Santa Fe once delivered four sections of "artillery trains" at Nemo, M&StL carmen had to scramble to find Baker heaters adequate to keep the men warm, as no passenger locomotives were available. Other military moves went via Perry and the Inter-Urban Railway that served Camp Dodge, near Des Moines.[7]

Figure 12.1. Recruits from McPerson County board the cars at Leola, South Dakota—off to make the world safe for democracy. Author's collection.

Military freight in substantial volume also moved to Camp Dodge through Perry as part of the war effort, but M&StL predictably made its greatest contribution to the campaign by hauling heavy tonnage in products related to agriculture. Grain, flour, livestock, and packing-house products made up more than a quarter of all tonnage in 1917 and nearly a third in 1918. Coal held steady, but billings in cement, lumber, and all building materials slumped as a result of wartime restrictions. So did traffic in motor vehicles, likewise a reflection of production restrictions caused by war. The growing enthusiasm for prohibition explained the loss of revenue from transporting alcoholic beverages. "Effective April 14, 1917," said M&StL management, "all agents in Iowa will refuse to deliver shipments of intoxicating liquors to anyone except actual permit holders." In Minnesota, the issue of prohibition got mixed with anti-German and "100% America" hysteria, especially at New Ulm, a well-known brewing community, where a substantial portion of the German-American population came under scrutiny by the state's "watchdog of loyalty," the infamous Minnesota Commission of Public Safety. State prohibition laws, like those in Iowa, were, of course, merely forerunners of the Eighteenth Amendment, passed by Congress late in 1917 and ratified in 1919, which shut down the breweries at New Ulm and all others—in the process denying M&StL shipments of barley, hops, and bottles inbound to the several on-line breweries that it had served, as well as shipments of outbound cases and barrels of beer. Even earlier, on August 12, 1918, USRA's William McAdoo, President Wilson's son-in-law and a man often referred to as the "Crown Prince," had perfunctorily declared, "The sale of liquors and intoxicants of every character in dining cars, restaurants and railroad stations under Federal control shall be discontinued immediately."[8]

Meanwhile, government spokesmen exhorted American farmers to ever-greater production; "Food will win the war" became the great domestic rallying cry. Farmers no doubt responded to this patriotic calling, but they also responded to another instinct: self-interest. Farming was profitable; a dramatic surge in demand from the international market made it even more so. Farmers plunged ahead with gusto. The incentive was patently clear in the market. At Winthrop, for example, wheat traded at $2.62 per bushel on May 10, 1917, up from $1.71 just before America formally entered the war in April. Indeed, market prices for grain and fiber more than doubled during the years 1915–20 compared to 1910–14. It was the same for livestock. Cattle prices in 1910 averaged $24.54 per head, rising to $52.64 in 1920; hogs averaged $9.05 in 1910, $20.00 in 1920. Between 1914 and 1918, agricultural profits in constant dollars more than doubled.[9]

In a well-ordered world, general prosperity in a railroad's service area would be reflected positively in that company's traffic statistics and income account. Such was not the case, however, for M&StL. Passenger boardings had peaked in 1915, moving downward in the next three years and spiking upward only in 1919; passenger miles also drifted downward after 1915, although they lifted nicely in 1919. Total passenger revenue rose modestly each year, reaching $3,131,675 in 1919, still 23.4 percent of total revenues. Freight tonnage in 1917 was slightly above the year before, but actually went down in 1918 and would do so again in 1919. Operating revenues went up each year, but so did expenses—dramatically in 1918, and staying very high in 1919. This was instantly and alarmingly reflected in M&StL's operating ratios: 66.28 in 1916 and 71.50 in 1917, but up to 94.73 in 1918 and 97.61 in 1919.[10]

M&StL's circumstances under USRA leadership were hardly unique. Yet government control did have a particularly harmful impact on M&StL, as later events would show. M&StL and all other roads were clamped solidly in a vise, with powerful labor interests that had a most sympathetic ear in the Wilson administration on the one side and on the other side an equally powerful block of agricultural and industrial shipper groups that effortlessly convinced the government to deny rate increases. The accelerating wages mandated by USRA were an especially perplexing problem. For average hourly earnings of American railroad workers, officers excepted, the index number (1915 = 100) stood at 129 late in 1917, at 198 a year later, and at 225 early in 1920. The inability to offset such rapidly escalating costs with an equal increase in the revenue stream was immediately apparent in the operating ratio not only at M&StL, but among its larger neighbors as well (see Table 12.1). M&StL's great handicap was its inability to hold remunerative Minneapolis–Peoria bridge or overhead traffic that it had solicited before the advent of USRA—this because of USRA's generally understandable policy of saving car, ton, and train miles by funneling traffic to the shortest routes. (Whether or not this was the best plan in terms of expediting lading was another question.) But the knife did not cut evenly. Omitting Rock Island from among several carriers handling cross-country traffic via Chicago and Minneapolis, for example, would have marginal impact on that road, because it could reallocate motive power and rolling stock to other of its primary arteries; for M&StL, however, there was no such option, because it had only one primary artery.[11]

Meanwhile, the war went on, sucking life and treasure from all parties. The United States raised, trained, and deployed an army, ready in 1918 to bear the full weight of combat in Europe, while at home "Americanization" continued apace. In Iowa, the governor issued a proclamation restricting oral communication to English; at Hanska, Minnesota, students buried "Kaiser Bill" in effigy on Main Street; and at Redwood Falls a mob halted a Nonpartisan League parade because "Leaguers" were perceived as less than patriotic at best and troublemakers at worst. At Waseca, intense patriotism took the form of singing "America the Beautiful" in every household each evening at 7:30. But then, after fifty-one months of combat, it was over, the result of an armistice. Assigning winners and losers in what many Americans had hopefully expected would be the "war to end all wars" proved difficult, however, and a confused world almost immediately began stumbling toward World War II.[12]

Table 12.1 Operating ratios of selected area roads, 1916–20

Road	*1916*	*1917*	*1918*	*1919*	*1920*
Chicago & North Western	66.46	72.75	86.02	85.66	94.82
Chicago, St. Paul, Minneapolis & Omaha	65.25	73.76	84.11	84.08	88.98
Chicago, Rock Island & Pacific	68.14	74.07	86.21	86.95	94.63
Chicago Great Western	69.74	76.32	93.02	87.24	110.00
Minneapolis, St. Paul & Sault Ste. Marie	55.82	66.49	82.49	80.65	90.66

War raises people to the highest pitch of energy and sacrifice; when it ends, a letdown is almost inevitable. That was the case at home in America as 1918 passed to 1919. There was, of course, the euphoria of troops' returning; the last combat division sailed from France in September 1919. But war's reality was underscored at places large and small as citizens gathered on station platforms to receive the remains of fallen warriors coming back from Europe. And America's involvement in an international war had proved unsettling, the end of hostilities through an armistice was ambiguous, and the conduct of the war itself had been so grisly that many concluded that Western civilization must itself be deeply, inherently flawed. Progressivism was on the wane; a "return to normalcy" had great appeal.[13]

It was in this milieu that a strenuous debate occurred regarding the disposition of the nation's railroads. At issue was the proper relationship of private to public power in American society. In 1917 President Wilson had promised that the country's railroads would be returned to their owners as soon as the "emergency" had passed, but one month after the armistice, the phenomenally forceful and ambitious William G. McAdoo proposed continuing government operation for another five years before returning properties to individual companies. More frightening by far were the notions of Glenn E. Plumb, an Iowan representing labor, who vigorously advocated the purchase of railroad properties by the federal government, the creation of a national operating corporation, and the lease of these lines to it. Others joined the fray. The Interstate Commerce Commission (frozen out of power by USRA), the National Association of Owners of Railroad Securities, the National Industrial Traffic League (a shippers' organization), and proponents of the scientific management of railroads all opposed nationalization, but wanted additional regulation of one sort or another. Another Iowan, Senator Albert Cummins, chairman of the Interstate Commerce Committee, would be at the vortex of these debates and would have a hand in any forthcoming legislation. Indeed his task, not easy, would be to frame a plan of economics that would be solid but capable of political passage.[14]

Cummins, a Republican, had the advantage of dealing in a Congress controlled by his party, although Woodrow Wilson, a Democrat, would hold the presidency until March 1921. "The greatest problem of your company, like so many other railway companies, is to obtain needed capital for expansion of its facilities," M&StL's Charles Hayden told stockholders in 1920. "Under private ownership, this can only be done by fixing rates so that railway securities will offer to the average citizen, as an investor, an attractive investment." But what were the odds of getting compensatory rates? Anything but good. If managers could not control the income side of the ledger, they had but one alternative: control the expense side. Only by driving down the operating ratio could there be salvation for "our insolvent railroads," one dry-eyed if pessimistic observer wrote, pointing in great anxiety to a distressing industrywide average of 90.89 early in 1919—far from the 60 to 65 that would yield 35 to 40 percent of operating revenue for taxes, fixed charges, dividends, and surplus and would be adequate to attract capital investment.[15]

Senator Cummins fully engaged himself in the art of the possible. He recognized that there was unequal earning capacity in the family of railroads, and this led him to counsel "a series of consolidations which will merge weak roads with strong ones, to the end that the resulting systems, and they will be comparatively few in number, may do business on substantially even terms." Railroad consolidation would be a hallmark of what became the Esch-Cummins Bill. Pulling and hauling added other important elements, which included returning railroads to their owners, creating a Labor Board with authority to arbitrate labor disputes, establishing 5.5 percent as a fair return on the aggregate value of property, allowing the pooling of traffic if that was found to be in the public interest, and variously strengthening the ICC. Esch-Cummins reflected shipper interests more than railroad interests, but given the political landscape of the time, it was about all that railroaders and investors could hope for. Indeed, M&StL directors thought that Esch-Cummins, or the Transportation Act of 1920, "was the most constructive railroad legislation that has ever been passed by Congress." It was signed into law by President Wilson on February 28, 1920.[16]

"The Minneapolis & St. Louis Railroad Company today resumed control and possession of its property and we are free to give our time and attention to the interests of the corporation," exclaimed an ebullient William H. Bremner on March 1. "There has been a close relation between the officers and employees of this railroad and I hope this will continue and become even closer," said M&StL's president. What of the future? "The outlook for the Minneapolis & St. Louis is bright," Bremner exclaimed. Indeed, a surge of optimism spread across the system. Off-line traffic offices were reestablished at Chicago, New York, San Francisco, and eight other locations—all touting the "Peoria Gateway," changed without ceremony in May 1918 from the historic "Albert Lea Route" after the through car arrangement in passenger service ended with Illinois Central. From American Locomotive Company came five sparkling 4-6-2s for service on the North Star Limited and fifteen 2-8-2s that supplemented twenty similar machines already assigned to freight duties. Cinder ballast was authorized for most of the Iowa branches, and in 1921 M&StL would begin using Rock Island instead of Burlington to move trains between Des Moines and Oskaloosa.[17]

In the passenger department, Anson B. Cutts quickly reopened city ticket offices in St. Paul, Minneapolis, and Des Moines, and renewed his old campaign to lure patrons to "popular lake resorts" such as those at Waterville, Waconia, and Excelsior, Minnesota. In 1921 M&StL joined eight other roads in proud use of St. Paul's marvelous new Union Depot, and in the same year moved from Peoria's Union Station to Rock Island's facility nearby.[18]

Freight presented a mixed picture. Tonnage bounced up by nearly one-third in 1920 over 1919, but lost half of that gain in 1921, pushed upward a tad in 1922, and then surged to a historic high of 7,311,139 tons in 1923. The road's traffic mix was still tied tightly to agriculture, which represented 29.40 percent of all traffic in 1920; but the percentage was not greatly different that season from that at other

Figure 12.2. The arrival of newer and heavier power still left M&StL short. A 2-8-0 and a smaller 2-6-0 head a very long train of farm tractors from a plant at Hopkins, Minnesota. Photograph courtesy of the Minnesota Historical Society.

granger roads (Chicago & North Western, 23.07; Chicago Great Western, 35.50; Omaha, 34.60). New cement plants at Valley Junction, Iowa, as well as scattered lumber yards, feed mills, bulk oil stations, and assorted other small customers plus expanded tonnage through the Peoria Gateway augured well.[19]

But in fact all was not well. The year 1920, one close observer of the industry said, provided "the greatest traffic in railway history; the greatest operating revenues; the greatest operating expenses; the greatest wage aggregate; the greatest taxes; and the smallest net operating income in more than 30 years." Marvelous rate increases authorized by the ICC in 1920 mostly evaporated when special interest groups favoring agriculture got the tariffs knocked down on hay, grain, and grain products and when carriers voluntarily reduced their rates to stimulate business as the country slumped into a postwar depression that began late in 1920 and lasted until 1923. And the Transportation Act of 1920 that returned the railroads to their owners had ominously reaffirmed the authority of the ICC, seeming to replace the direct and powerful one-man federal control of McAdoo at USRA with what one observer caustically labeled "indirect, halting, defective and inefficient federal control by a commission of eleven quasi-judicial deliberators." But in its wake USRA had saddled the industry with a 16 percent larger work force and a payroll expanded by a startling 86 percent.[20]

The postwar depression was striking for its brevity but also for its severity; prices, employment, and wages fell sharply. The impact can be understood only in context. During the late nineteenth century and the early twentieth century the productive capacity of the American economy increased at a rate greater than that during the Industrial Revolution. And the United

States became a dominant world power, its population and national income three times larger than those of Great Britain. During the period from 1914 through 1919, the volume of domestic manufacturing production rose by 26 percent, and the wages paid industrial workers more than doubled. The chemical industry, which had started in the 1880s, was greatly stimulated by World War I, the new synthetics industry was also sparked by the war, and the output of light metals such as aluminum and magnesium experienced a meteoric rise, with that of aluminum more than doubling between 1914 and 1920. But the automobile industry stood above all others. Sales of passenger cars had tripled between 1914 and 1917, then dipped sharply in 1917–18 because of government restrictions, but surged after the war to reflect pent-up demand. In 1922 neighboring Chicago & North Western reported handling 23 percent more automobiles and 38 percent more trucks than a year earlier. Ancillary industries such as rubber goods and petroleum refining boomed similarly. An important corollary was the concentration of manufacturing in and about cities; not surprisingly, the Census of 1920 showed that for the first time more Americans lived in urban areas than in rural environs (farms or in towns of twenty-five hundred or fewer persons).[21]

In any event, the economy had been unstable when the conflict ended; it was precarious as 1920 approached. The downturn began in January and reached a trough during the summer of 1921. By then industrial production had fallen to only 65 percent of the recent high, and unemployment had grown from 1.4 percent to 11.7 percent. The faltering economy had a shattering impact on several of the newer industries and producers and on a number of old-line firms as well. J. Ogden Armour lost control of the huge family-owned meat-packing business bearing that name; Sears, Roebuck was saved from default only when its president drew on his personal fortune to cover accounts; and even General Motors had to write down the value of its bloated inventories.[22]

The agricultural economy was particularly devastated after spectacularly prosperous years before and during the war. Good times, sad to say, had stimulated too much optimism, unleashing too much expansion, extravagance, and speculation. A correction had been inevitable; it came when the war ended abruptly at the end of 1918. Within a year the bonanza export market disappeared, and the blazing agricultural prosperity turned to deep depression. Farm income in Iowa crested at nearly $1 billion in 1919, but dropped by a third in 1921. The value of farmland and farm buildings in Iowa had more than doubled in the years 1913–19 and had risen by 75 percent in Illinois, but at least a third of that value vanished in the first half of the 1920s. The same was true for implements and machinery, which skidded in value during the years 1920–25. Nationally, wheat prices dipped from about $2.20 per bushel in 1919 to $1.01 in 1921. This was reflected at Winthrop, where wheat brought $2.44 a bushel in January 1920 but only $1.18 in September 1921; flax dropped from $4.77 to $1.72. Swine producers fared no better. The price of hogs crested at $16.69 per hundred weight in 1920, but plummeted to $7.63 when federal price supports were abandoned in 1921. A startling loss of capital investment, high mortgage rates, escalating taxes, rising operating costs, and depressed commodity prices afflicted farmers to one extent or another in all four states of M&StL's service area.[23]

The circumstances for cattlemen were no less troubling. Per capita consumption of red meat had gone down even before the war, and "meatless days" at home during that conflict only accelerated the decline. A growing domestic population plus demand from the government during the war kept prices up, however, and cattlemen enjoyed real prosperity. But prices headed down in 1918 and kept going down, the result of changed consumption habits and collapse of the export market. The case of South Dakota producers was typical. The cost-price squeeze that they found themselves in was exacerbated during the winter of 1919–20, when heavy, wet snow blanketed the grass until May, forcing the use of expensive hay to keep cattle alive, and this even as market prices went down further.[24]

For M&StL the movement of livestock reached all-time highs as a percentage of tonnage in 1919 (4.76) and as revenue tonnage in 1922 (291,713). Stocker cattle still moved in trainload lots, although by this time most shipments on M&StL were smaller consignments, such as twenty-five carloads of cattle from Rockwell in January 1912 and seventy-two cars of cattle and hogs from Hanska in the year 1916. "Effective at once and until further notice be advised stock yards at Keithsburg will not accept stock account yard full and not able to get stock cars," the dispatcher alerted agents on the Oskaloosa–Peoria line in a message that at once belied railroad frustrations in handling live animals but also pointed up the dependence on rail of such business in those years. To face this apparently growing but unpredictable demand, M&StL invested heavily in new or expanded livestock facilities at thirty stations between 1912 and 1922—especially in Iowa, which ranked second among states in cattle numbers and first in swine.[25]

Of the states served by M&StL, South Dakota was most seriously affected by economic dislocations following the war. During the period 1914–18, however, prosperity had reigned. Onaka was typical. There was great activity around that town. Surrounding rangeland was plowed and turned over to planting, although animal husbandry still flourished. Crops were good. But long-term prosperity proved elusive. At Adelaide, five miles west of Conde, the lone store building was jacked up and moved to Brentford in 1920; grain elevators were carted off to other towns. When Carlyle failed, its stock pens and water station were retired, but the depot and other buildings were moved two miles east to Norbeck, a new creation where M&StL crossed a Milwaukee branch. Catastrophic fires hit Cresbard in 1918 and 1920, Wecota in 1919, and Norbeck in 1922. The same winds that drove those conflagrations also tore at topsoil recently exposed when rangeland had turned to cropland. Twenty of South Dakota's sixty-seven counties experienced their greatest populations during the years 1910–29. Population shifts in South Dakota were actually a microcosm of broader trends. After peaking in 1917–18, America's farm population began to decline, and as farmers left, the small towns they supported also dwindled.[26]

Adjustments and alterations also occurred in lumbering and flour milling, two industries historically important to M&StL's fortunes. In 1919 the last lumber mill at Minneapolis shut down; thereafter lumber products billed to M&StL destinations or "roller cars" (whose contents usually were owned by brokers, sold en route, and subject to diversion) moving overhead would derive from mills elsewhere in Minnesota or increasingly from the Pacific Northwest, then be handed to M&StL at Minneapolis or Minnesota Transfer. In flour milling, the years 1909–20 saw Minneapolis mills at their height; peak production was reached in 1916, when they turned out 18.5 million barrels, perhaps one-sixth of all domestic volume. After 1920, however, production slumped, several factors combining in explanation. Favorable milling-in-transit rates long had worked in favor of Minneapolis, but pressure from other milling centers forced the ICC to broaden those privileges to Chicago, Milwaukee, Kansas City, and elsewhere. Additional factors included the rise of Buffalo as a milling center, inadequate supplies of high-grade wheat in some seasons, competition from southern Minnesota millers (Eagle Roller Mill at New Ulm, Everett Aughenbaugh & Company at Waseca and New Richland, and New Prague Flouring Mill among them), a decline in per capita consumption of wheat flour, and a shift away from home baking to commercial baking. Nevertheless, flour and lumber made up 13.8 percent of all M&StL traffic in 1919, 12.25 percent in 1922—tonnage especially important in the long-haul traffic mix to Peoria.[27]

Of the several problems facing M&StL and all other railroads in the wake of the USRA experience and the Transportation Act of 1920, none loomed larger than labor conditions—the size of the work force, wages, and work rules. Woodrow Wilson, gentle by nature and humanitarian by inclination, had taken a generally favorable attitude toward labor, and that posture was well reflected in McAdoo and USRA. The results were predictable: labor's power during the Wilson years grew tremendously. USRA, arguing with merit that railroad workers were being squeezed by increased costs of living and courted openly by munitions works, ship yards, and other industries that paid better, had determined to raise wages across the board in order to retain railroaders and keep the trains running. At the same time, McAdoo instituted rules and regulations affecting conditions of employment that were uniform for all roads under his control; these were adopted without reference to local conditions or individual companies. Among other effects was a dramatic increase in the number of workers required, with all employees covered by national agreements drawn with individual unions representing specific crafts and jurisdictions. In sum, in 1920 railroads were saddled with many more workers who were much better paid than they had been in 1917—and they were segregated rigidly by craft to restrict employer flexibility. (At M&StL, the number of employees in 1920 was 13 percent over 1917; compensation had risen by 125 percent.) Then in 1920 the Labor Board, established as part of the Transportation Act, granted a substantial wage increase to nearly all rail employees. The ICC tried to offset these additional expenses and to secure a 5.5 percent return on the property of carriers by authorizing sizeable rate increases, but depressed business conditions left the railroads with high rates and little traffic. To this the ICC responded by lowering rates, especially on grain and livestock, but for the railroads that had the effect of increasing business while decreasing gross revenues. Managers shook their heads. The only solution, they concluded, was to bring down operating costs, and, since the most significant operating expense was wages (60 percent of the total in 1920), managers quickly turned to that area.[28]

Workers understandably were unwilling to give up their recently won gains, but managers were determined to cut the labor bill; strikes were certain. The worst occurred in 1922, when shopmen responded to wage reductions and changes in work rules with a nationwide walkout effective July 1. In the Twin Cities, approximately ten thousand shopmen left their jobs, seven hundred of them at M&StL's Cedar Lake facility. Not all employees departed their work stations, and as the strike continued others returned, but a majority did leave, and they did stay away. Managers and clerks from the general office downtown soon found themselves in overalls and engaged in the tasks necessary to service engines and cars. M&StL and its president, William Bremner, initially kept a low profile and delayed hiring replacements "because of the desire to give former employees every opportunity to return to service." Bremner also resisted a temptation to seek an injunction against strikers, saying with a mixture of pride and relief that "there has been no disorder in any way, shape or form in Minneapolis [on M&StL]." Bremner did, however, join other railroad presidents who insisted on a "stand pat" position when workers said they would return to work only if the roads would restore their seniority—meaning, in effect, displacement of any who had been hired in the stead of strikers. Ultimately the shop strike of 1922 ran its course. In February 1923 members of the Federated Shop Crafts called off the strike, but by that time many carriers, including M&StL, had signed agreements with new organizations that were much weaker. Were there winners? Many men lost both their jobs and their pensions, fissures erupted among the several crafts—especially between the operating crafts and the nonoperating crafts—and were hard to paste over, and a spike was driven between labor and management. For the companies much-needed revenue had been lost during the strike, some business was lost to competition when trucks stood forth to demonstrate their versatility during this time of national trial, and the government even considered the use of aircraft to move the mails. Arguing that there were winners in this conflict would be a challenge at best.[29]

The circumstances for M&StL during the strike were varied. Violence was not visited on the company, as was the case elsewhere, and animosities before, during, and after the strike were not as deep or as protracted as at some properties. Feelings at Peoria were likely the hardest, but at Oskaloosa and elsewhere the worst that happened was that those on strike did not talk to those who stayed on the job. Nevertheless, Bremner was forced to admit that "the effect of the strike on the equipment and particularly the motive power was . . . very bad . . . and the deterioration of the locomotives necessarily brought about a serious handicap to economical and efficient operations." On the positive side, M&StL did succeed in getting control of its labor costs—an issue that loomed even larger for it than for other roads.[30]

Unfortunately for M&StL, labor costs were only one of several thorny problems that it faced in the early 1920s. Thin net earnings provided a double whammy, providing inadequate monies for betterment of plant and frightening lenders, who either denied M&StL's requests or provided capital only at very steep rates. M&StL did find money to acquire over four hundred acres of land in Humboldt County, Iowa, underlain with rock useful in the manufacture of cement or for crushed stone, and a very modest campaign to install tie plates and "anti-creepers" (track anchors) was begun. But rail on several lengthy line segments—Spencer to Storm Lake, Fort Dodge to Ogden, Tara to Ruthven, and Conde to Le Beau—remained so light that only tiny Moguls were permitted as motive power. When snippy residents of the Kenwood district in Minneapolis during 1922 urged support for a curious but abortive $75 million project to electrify all freight terminals in the city, M&StL managers could only groan at what that undertaking would have done to its profit and loss statement. In another area, in 1922–23 Northern Pacific fortunately was responsible for appreciable line changes and a new bridge over the Mississippi River on the route it shared with M&StL between Minneapolis and St. Paul.[31]

Unhappily for M&StL, storm clouds in ominous abundance gathered about it. The USRA experience in many ways proved disastrous, although the negative impact had not been immediately apparent. The inability of the road in those years to solicit business for its own account and the denial of serious advertising cost the company not only in revenue but also in loss of identity among the public. This was especially serious in the matter of bridge traffic for the Peoria Gateway that had been won at great effort over the years and, once lost, was hard to regain. And the company's physical plant and its financial condition were frankly not as strong in 1920 as before USRA. This was partially explained by USRA's controversial "test period" formula, under which M&StL earned $2.8 million per annum, which was adequate to meet fixed charges but little else, despite the road's understandable need for cash to satisfy principal payments or equipment trusts, additions, betterments, and the like. In sum, USRA had left M&StL in an emaciated condition in 1920.[32]

Troubles compounded. Frank Davis, who had been deeply involved with M&StL since the dawn of Hawley's time, died in 1921, and Charles Hayden was lost to the cause when Newman Erb, who long had been a thorn in Hayden's side, took it upon himself to file a complaint against Hayden's simultaneous association with competing Rock Island. To the growing vacuum of superior leadership and devoted interest were added other issues and concerns. M&StL needed to more firmly establish the assets of the franchise in the minds of the public, an obdurate ICC was even more tightly in the saddle, net earnings were in decline, and modal competition was increasing. Indeed, the number of revenue passengers and revenue passenger miles for the nation's railroads peaked in 1920 and then trended downward. At M&StL, revenue passengers declined by 18 percent in 1922 alone, then went down another 12 percent in 1923—"due principally to increased competition of automobiles and motor busses, made possible through the continued development of hard-surfaced highways," said a crestfallen A. B. Cutts.[33]

M&StL's collective problems loomed starkly in hard, cold numbers. Between 1916 and 1923, operating revenues mounted by 66 percent, but operating expenses rose by nearly 100 percent. In 1920 M&StL sustained a loss of over half a million dollars from operation—the operating ratio hemorrhaging at 103.97, up alarmingly from 66.28 in 1916. Costs were better contained in 1921 and 1922, with the operating ratios 91.20 and 94.18, respectively, but fixed charges more than consumed net operating profits.[34]

William H. Bremner boldly asserted that the problem was one of faulty public policy wherein rail rates were fixed by the ICC and wages determined by the Railway Labor Board—"making it impossible for any railway company to operate at a fair profit" and forcing the roads to neglect maintenance of equipment "to an alarming degree simply because they are unable to afford it." Indeed, "new capital," Bremner said flatly, "is no longer being added to the business, and railroads are deteriorating." That carriers clearly had their problems was indicated by the operating ratios of M&StL and selected neighbors (see Table 12.2). Net income for all Class One railroads in 1921 was less than in 1915, and less than half of what it had been in 1916. Hard numbers and dry-eyed analysis of them shook the industry to its foundations, but of course some roads were healthier than others. Among M&StL's neighbors, Chicago Great Western, like M&StL, earned inadequately in 1920 to cover fixed charges, while Omaha, Chicago & North Western, and Soo Line experienced that trauma in 1921. A year later railroad bonds amounting to $109 million were in default, and most rail securities were trading lower than before the war (M&StL common stock ranged between $26 and $36 in 1916, between $4.50 and $14.75 in 1921). Business then picked up, however, and many Class One carriers regained strength and confidence. By October 1922, anguished shippers even complained of car shortages.[35]

Table 12.2. Operating ratios of selected area roads, 1920–23

Road	*1920*	*1921*	*1922*	*1923*
Chicago & North Western	94.82	89.17	81.58	82.60
Chicago Great Western	110.00	88.43	87.82	83.31
Chicago, Milwaukee & St. Paul	97.94	87.18	82.57	79.59
Chicago, Rock Island & Pacific	94.63	81.33	80.33	80.46
Chicago, St. Paul, Minneapolis & Omaha	88.98	86.69	80.20	82.91
Great Northern	91.23	79.45	76.98	72.25
Minneapolis & St. Louis	103.97	91.20	94.18	86.46
Minneapolis St. Paul & Sault Ste. Marie	90.66	93.30	77.36	76.23
Northern Pacific	89.30	82.12	75.62	78.79
All Class Ones	94.38	82.71	77.32	77.77

In 1922 giant Southern Pacific ordered fifty 2-10-2s from Baldwin Locomotive Works, which would erect those machines at its Eddystone plant outside of Philadelphia. Baldwin dispatched the first twenty of them to the West Coast in what it ballyhooed and the public celebrated as the "Prosperity Special." One year later a Philadelphia newspaper used the term "Prosperity Special" as a metaphor describing a rebounding national economy and a reawakened railroad industry. "May it run in sections, split no switches, find no soft track, and keep a sharp eye on the semaphores," an editorial writer wished. William Bremner likely never saw this hopeful missive, although he certainly would have embraced its spirit. And Bremner would have nodded in agreement with a less optimistic writer at the *Nation* who pointed urgently at four ornery elements that continued to plague the nation's railroads: "a rate-reducing electorate, an efficiency-investigating and economy-demanding public, a railroad-stock-scorning financial public, and a management-grasping employed staff."[36]

Bremner knew that M&StL faced yet another imposing enemy: a stubborn depression in the agricultural sector of the economy, which showed no inclination to join the rapidly improving general economy. "The repeated crop failures of previous years, on top of low prices obtained for what was harvested caused a very severe business and agricultural depression in our territory," sighed neighboring Soo Line. "Many farmers were so discouraged that they made no effort to retain their farms, so that the number of foreclosures and vacant farms was constantly increasing." It was much the same in M&StL country, especially in western Minnesota and South Dakota.[37]

Nevertheless, M&StL's gross revenues in the first four months of 1923 exceeded those of the same period in 1922, and by year's end the road had handled more freight than ever before (7,311,189 tons). Net operating income was $2.236 million, and the operating ratio was down to 86.46. But bonded indebtedness, fixed charges, and other debt, along with taxes, spelled more red ink—$1.21 million in 1923, $4.21 million in the three-year period 1921–23. M&StL had been slow to settle various charges since March 1920; for example, it owed Great Northern for use of its Minneapolis passenger station and was very sluggish in settling interline accounts. Bremner was embarrassed. "I am sure that you realize how repugnant it is for me to trespass on your good nature," he told GN, but then continued, "I cannot say that we are in a position to put this account on a current basis," adding editorially, "The stronger roads ought to be somewhat lenient with their weaker sisters." Great Northern and others were, in fact, remarkably restrained. "We have been handling a very heavy tonnage since the first of the year," Bremner announced on February 13, 1923, "but unfortunately for us about 25% of our interest charges, as well as certain payments on the principal of equipment trust notes, fall due between January and March 1st, which makes our burden in the first two months of the year a rather heavy one." Heavy indeed. M&StL's financial position was intolerable. On July 26, 1923, the Minneapolis Steel & Machinery Company filed a creditor's bill in the United States District Court asking for appointment of a receiver. The request was granted in the form of William Bremner. M&StL needed Edwin Hawley or a man like Edwin Hawley, but he had been gone for more than a decade, and those who followed him, though dedicated and talented—had not the same incentive to keep M&StL a going concern. "They acted more like men who had a bear by the tail, and were ready to let go when the bear became obstreperous," said W. B. Davids, a long-time Hawley associate and M&StL director. "It was not their brainchild, and they lost no prestige."[38]

To be fair, however, the circumstances facing M&StL in 1923 were very different from those that had confronted Hawley three decades earlier. Indeed, M&StL's current distress derived from diverse, multiple, and cumulative problems that defied easy and immediate solution. Among them were the following:

- A curious route structure that proved vulnerable to both rail and vehicular competition.
- A physical plant and motive power inventory that were inadequate to provide the most efficient operation.
- Malnutrition and inattention by USRA, along with a loss of traffic and identity.
- Inadequate traffic density.
- Alterations in lumbering and flour milling.
- The shopmen's strike of 1922, which had resulted in loss of revenue and undermaintained motive power and rolling stock.
- A five-month coal miners' strike in 1922 that had deprived the road of revenue and boosted operating costs when fuel had to be purchased from distant nonunion mines.
- The continuing drag on the system by the lines west of Watertown, South Dakota.
- Cumbersome and counterproductive regulatory laws that failed to fix on ICC or state commerce commissions any responsibility for their acts.
- The rise in gross earnings by 50 percent for the period 1916–23 mirrored against the rise in operating expenses of 100 percent in the same period—and the unlikelihood that this problem would be remedied to any great extent in the future.
- Inability to earn a fair return, which had set off a train of problems—the inability to perfect adequate financing, which had led to huge increases in unfunded debt (short-term notes), which itself resulted in painful shortages of working capital.
- The rise of modal competition, which had been aided by public policy devoted to subsidization.
- Decline in passenger revenues.
- The stubborn agricultural depression, which showed no signs of easing.
- The absence of determined leadership among principal owners and the loss of talented managers.

Chapter 13
Hard Times in Good Times

Down between the railroad tracks,
Our busy restaurant stands.
The viaduct is over it,
And the vinegar works close at hand.
—Stone's restaurant, Marshalltown, Iowa

"Failure to participate in the growth of our national traffic is usually a sign of some serious trouble," said a plainspoken analyst at Moody Investor's Service in 1923. Such was the lot of M&StL. "Our financial difficulties have been brought about by general conditions affecting the northwest railroads," William Bremner told *Railway Age* when asked about the receivership. "In the last two or three years we have not shared in the prosperity which has accrued to the southern and eastern roads." There was more to the story, of course, including a recalcitrant Interstate Commerce Commission and obdurate state regulatory bodies that remained wedded to the do-good mentality of the late Progressive Era and proved unable or unwilling to redress legitimate problems faced by the railroad industry. Iowa's Senator Cummins understood that "the present policy of private ownership under public control" could not "endure unless the railways, taken as a whole [were able to] earn the cost of their maintenance and operation"; he continued to promote public policy that would "take this railway system of ours as it is and make it competent to render the constantly increasing service which the welfare of the country requires." But death soon would claim Cummins, and other public figures proved inadequate by comparison.[1]

There was no reason to be optimistic about an early end to M&StL's woes. The road cried out for capital investment, but inadequate earnings—and a lack of prospects for future earnings—put off potential investors. Moreover, M&StL had borrowed $2.4 million from the federal government during the U.S. Railroad Administration years, but had not been able to repay that loan, and likelihood of early settlement of it was nil. In addition, the company had run up a whopping $6.5 floating debt that would be impossible to satisfy expeditiously—and this debt would probably have precedence over the several mortgages. Finally, there was the stubborn agricultural depression, which showed no ebbing.[2]

Farm prices plummeted in 1920, stabilized the next year, but were flat through 1929. Foreign markets went slack, and domestic demand fluctuated. Consumption of cereals declined by about one-third, while meat consumption remained constant. Prohibition dried up demand for barley and hops, changing styles and synthetic fabrics reduced the need for wool, and the move from horse-drawn vehicles cut requirements for hay and oats. A predictable ripple effect flowed from these collective changes. All too often money was rashly borrowed or rashly loaned, with the unfortunate consequence of failure, foreclosure, or bankruptcy for borrower and lender alike. In all, five thousand banks failed during the 1920s, most of them in grain-producing states. Iowa, sad to say, led the nation in bank failures from 1921 through 1931, with an average of eighty-seven per year. Failures of farmers and banks sent an immediate tremor through small towns and even county seats. The loss of a bank meant not just the loss of investment and deposits but also the loss of potential capital locally applied. The net result was fewer shoppers in stores, fewer students in schools, and fewer persons paying the bills.[3]

To William Hepburn Bremner fell responsibility for leading the company in these curious and often contradictory times. Born at Marshalltown on October 24, 1869, Bremner attended the University of Iowa, where he was a member of that school's first football team in 1889, earning his "I" the next year. He graduated in civil engineering, but soon returned for a law degree. Bremner set up practice in Des Moines, serving as city solicitor from 1902 to 1908. In 1909 he accepted a position in M&StL's law department at Minneapolis and moved rapidly through the chairs to become general counsel on November 1, 1916. Frank H. Davis of the Hawley interests saw executive talent in Bremner, and in 1917 Davis succeeded in pushing him forward as president following the brief and unremarkable stewardship of E. L. Brown.[4]

Bremner was not an operating man, but was a fine lawyer. A. B. Cutts remembered him as "short, pouchy, very friendly but quiet." Others recalled Bremner as big hearted—one of "nature's noblemen." He should have been a senator, one person thought. Bremner was never a gambler, but he loved to play poker—with a 10-cent limit—and he remained interested in athletics. His office in the Transportation Building at Minneapolis faced west, and when the summer sun warmed those environs beyond endurance he simply walked out and went to a ball game; it was also his way of alleviating stress. Bremner believed fully in the need for a culture at M&StL that would boost the morale of company employees, and he did all he could to that end. Small wonder that "Bill" Bremner was admired and respected by all hands.[5]

Bremner probably made it to the company's highest office on his own merits, but the path admittedly was uncluttered by an abundance other internal candidates. William G. Bierd—thin, hardworking, partial to lengthy and detailed reports, and of a commanding and pleasant personality—was a great favorite as vice president and general manager. But Bierd had gone off to Chicago & Alton as president in 1914, succeeded by the equally talented and respected Clarence W. Huntington, who for the previous dozen years had been general superintendent of the Central Railroad Company of New Jersey but earlier had been general superintendent at Iowa Central. Unfortunately, however, Huntington got caught in a power struggle and personality clash between Newman Erb and Charles Hayden, got demoted, and left M&StL to become president of the Virginian Railway. Other officers who left the road for better opportunities included Charles S. Lake, who became assistant to the president at St. Louis Southwestern, and Ross S. Marshall, who eventually served as senior vice president at Chesapeake & Ohio. In March 1920, Bremner brought in colorless but solid Elliott E. Nash from Chicago & North Western to handle operating responsibilities. Nash was aided by capable and loyal Ritchie G. Kenly, chief engineer since 1909, and, among others, Jerry Moynihan, who, when he retired in 1928, would have forty-seven years of service at M&StL, all but two of them as superintendent of the Railway Transfer, where he labored endlessly and effectively to prosper the company's interests.[6]

M&StL also suffered talent loss when Walter L. Ross, vice president of traffic (sales) for the Hawley Roads, departed for greener pastures (he eventually became president at New York, Chicago & St. Louis), and when S. G. Lutz left in 1914 to become general traffic manager at Chicago & Alton. Lutz was succeeded by Frank B. Townsend, who at the age of seventeen had taken a job in Iowa Central's accounting department and, after military service in the Spanish-American War, became traveling freight agent and in 1911 was named general freight agent at Minneapolis. Townsend had an uncanny ability to cite cases and statistics when appearing at rate hearings before the ICC and earned the title "little czar of transportation" in dogged battles against rate policies designed to discriminate against Minneapolis and M&StL. Townsend,

Figure 13.1. M&StL's profit margins were as thin as track ballast on the West End. Bremner (second from the left on the observation platform of the *Twin Cities*) was joined by officers and directors on an inspection trip during the mid-1920s. M&StL photograph, author's collection.

who had emerged as a rough-and-tumble regimental sergeant major in the Forty-ninth Iowa Volunteers during the Cuban war, was an ideal man to fight M&StL's traffic battles in the tumultuous 1920s.[7]

Townsend and his forces had to be nimble in dealing with an increasingly competitive landscape and in responding to changes affecting M&StL's traffic mix. Grain, flour, lumber, cement, soft coal, merchandise, and livestock had made up 83.55 percent of all system tonnage at the turn of the century. By 1920, however, these primary commodities made up only 70.10 percent of tonnage, dropping to 60.65 percent in 1925, and would account for 52.93 percent in 1930. Townsend could point to additional miscellaneous small shippers located trackside each year of the 1920s, but M&StL was unsuccessful in attracting any really large new customer. In Minneapolis, for example, Townsend was exasperated when M&StL could not maximize its strategic advantages between Cedar Lake and the milling district, an area rich in warehouses and distribution centers, "lack of funds" frustrating his dreams. Townsend was especially disappointed that he could not lure year-round traffic in fruits and vegetables because M&StL lacked heated warehouse facilities in Minneapolis; shippers understandably resisted changing routings to favor M&StL only in the warmer months.[8]

Despite hard times, or perhaps because of them, M&StL continued to fund its Agricultural Development Department, which actively proclaimed policies of constructive diversification—"better cow, sow, and hens"—for farmers and was particularly active in western Minnesota and South Dakota. Another interest of M&StL's Agricultural Development Department was expansion of sugar beet production, which would result in more tonnage moving to and from large mills at Chaska, Mason City, and Belmond. Beet production increased in popularity, with dumps springing up at several stations in Minnesota and northern Iowa. In 1928 and 1929 M&StL moved American Beet Sugar's "Crop Improvement" car from place to place in a cooperative educational endeavor calculated to win more farmers to beet planting. Small wonder. In 1929, for example, M&StL handled 3,253 cars of beets, coal, pulp, sugar stone, and fertilizer to and from the Chaska facility alone.[9]

Food products were increasingly a factor in M&StL's traffic picture. The Jacob E. Decker & Sons packing plant at Mason City received hogs and cattle and provided handsome revenue in Iowana brand meats dispatched to an on-line distribution center at Minneapolis and off-line centers in Texas, as well as to brokers and jobbers at principal eastern cities. H. M. Noack & Sons at Arlington, Minnesota, billed "White House Brand Poultry" in addition to eggs and butter. Eggs moved from Winfield and many other stations, and assorted milk products flowed from seven stations in Minnesota's Freeborn County (Albert Lea) alone. Local freights handled refrigerator cars on specified days of the week to accommodate small butter producers at Echo and LaSalle among others while larger customers, such as the creamery at Winthrop, loaded out ten thousand pounds weekly in one car. Volumes of locally produced fruits and vegetables declined, but shipments of potatoes from the Red River valley and apples from Washington's Yakima and Wenatchee valleys increased to local stations, moving overhead. Especially impressive was the growing number of canneries along M&StL lines. Corn was packed at

Arlington and Chaska as well as at Gifford, Grinnell, Lake Oskaloosa, Perry, Storm Lake, and Story City; tomatoes at Brighton, Lake Mills, and Oskaloosa; and pumpkin at Brighton. Catsup was manufactured at Brighton; sorghum at Victoria and Waconia; sauerkraut at Brighton, Chaska, and Victoria; pickles at Chaska and Des Moines; and vinegar at Des Moines and Marshalltown. Marshall Canning Company—Headlight Brand—had plants at Marshalltown, Hampton, Ackley, and Roland. On December 28, 1927, Marshall billed an entire trainload of its "Brown Beauty Beans" in URTX refrigerator cars marked with M&StL's logo in a promotion that showcased that company and the railroad as well. Western Grocery Company, wholesale distributor of Marshall Canning and other products using the "Jack Sprat" label, owned or supplied several branch offices, most of them on M&StL, at Albert Lea, Mason City, Marshalltown, Minneapolis, and Oskaloosa.[10]

As always, grain and flour were M&StL mainstays, accounting for a quarter of all business during the decade. In 1924 M&StL billed flour from twenty-two stations—fourteen in Minnesota, six in Iowa, two in South Dakota—and in 1927 Minnesota led all states in flour production. But the place of Minneapolis among milling centers continued to erode; Buffalo assumed top rank in 1929. An important aside: in 1923 Minnesota's Washburn Crosby created a new division to manufacture Softasilk cake flour and Wheaties, a ready-to-eat breakfast cereal, later adding Kix and Cheerios and other packaged products such as Bisquick. All of this helped counteract the dwindling demand for baking flour, and in 1928 Washburn Crosby metamorphosed into General Mills, the world's largest miller.[11]

Livestock, as a percentage of all traffic, had peaked at 4.76 in 1919, but held steady at roughly 4 percent throughout the 1920s. Chicago & North Western assigned its eastbound train 254 "to handle all time freight and stock including that from M&StL at Sioux Rapids," and M&StL ran a daily "Chicago Stock" train from Oskaloosa to Peoria, plus Saturday stock trains in South Dakota eastward from Akaska or Hoven. In Iowa, barefoot boys on the Story City and Newton branches perched on stock yard fences to watch railroaders load animals and to hear the pant of the locomotive eager to highball out of town with stock extras. Up in Minnesota, LaSalle dispatched 265 carloads in 1923, and Winthrop billed 459 cars in 1929. The exercise was not always compensatory, however. A howling blizzard caught a northbound freight with 23 carloads of cattle at LaSalle in January 1929, and despite the best efforts of railroaders on their behalf, several animals died and others suffered heavy shrinkage before a snow plow opened the line a day later. Claims were substantial. Nevertheless, M&StL improved and/or added capacity at twenty-five stations during the 1920s, and in 1929 ordered three hundred stock cars—the first acquisition of rolling stock in years. On the other hand, M&StL retired or reduced capacity at fifteen stations.[12]

Coal was a regular and important contributor to the traffic mix, furnishing over 30 percent of tonnage in 1920 and averaging nearly 21 percent for the decade. Coal produced on-line was only one-third of all coal handled in 1924, reflecting the competition of "lake

Figure 13.2. On December 28, 1927, Marshall Canning at Marshalltown, Iowa, billed an entire trainload of its "Brown Beauty Beans." Vaughn R. Ward collection.

Figure 13.3. Output from on-line coal mines near Albia, Iowa, held steady until 1923 and then tilted downward. Much of it was consumed by M&StL itself and moved in crude gondola cars such as those on this train crossing new trestlework near Carver, Minnesota. M&StL photograph, author's collection.

coal" moving via Duluth-Superior; vacillating rail rates on coal from Illinois, Indiana, and Kentucky; and diminished fields in Iowa. Indeed, production from Mahaska County (Oskaloosa) mines had peaked in 1897 and turned sharply downward after 1900; mines in Monroe County (Albia) reached maximum output in 1912, held steady until 1923, and then slumped. The value of coal mined in Iowa reached its apex in 1920 at nearly $31 million, but skidded thereafter, losing about two-thirds of that value by the end of the decade.[13]

Miscellaneous freight was diverse in nature and impressive in the aggregate. The long-promised Municipal River Terminal in Minneapolis, which M&StL alone would serve, was slow to develop and yielded no traffic in the 1920s. But shingles, lath, and poles from lumber yards and facilities at or near Minnesota Transfer, plus linseed oil, paint, machinery, and other manufactured goods, provided a rich lode of business from the Twin Cities; Des Moines provided brooms, candy, caskets, crackers, drugs, furnaces, hog feeders, paint, pumps, soap, water tanks, and more. The Quaker Oats plant at Fort Dodge was a fine customer, Maro & Rodenborn of that community shipped gloves, and the Gypsum City Bottling Works provided soda pop. Overalls and jackets came from Oskaloosa; feathers from Farmington; carriages and wagons from Monmouth; washing machines from Peoria, Grinnell, and Newton; and paper, steel wire, and Caterpillar Tractors from Peoria.[14]

The growing volume of cement billings, mostly from substantial plants at Des Moines, Gilmore City, Mason City, and Valley Junction, had its ironic side. In 1920 cement accounted for 4.13 percent of M&StL tonnage, increasing to 6.86 percent in 1929. Much of this was consigned to "road paving programs," especially in Iowa. "We have six contractors' 'set ups' at various points," Bremner bragged in 1927. But he was hardly a Pollyanna, knowing full well that paved roads for motor vehicles would only exacerbate competitive pressures; but hefty revenues from cement business was at least a short-term elixir.[15]

It was much the same with traffic in motor vehicles. There was no ignoring the centrality of the Detroit–Pittsburgh axis during the boom economy of the 1920s, especially in 1928 and 1929. Nor could Bremner gainsay important revenues deriving from transport of set-up automobiles, petroleum products, tires, and tubes. Indeed, in 1900 M&StL handled 9,511 tons of petroleum products, chiefly illuminant, but in 1929 it handled 287,824 tons, mostly gasoline to fuel motor vehicles. Minneapolis had become a major distribution center for automobiles, and in 1921 M&StL constructed a new auto unloading facility at that place. Unloading platforms also were built at Fort Dodge and Ruthven during the decade. Most vehicles arrived from the great assembly plants of Detroit, but some came from Ford's new facility in St. Paul.[16]

Given the blistering general economy and Frank Townsend's bulldog tenacity in pursuing business, one might expect that he could have wiped his brow and smiled in satisfaction at M&StL's traffic figures. That was not the case. Tonnage reached a historic peak in 1923 (7,311,189), but in 1929 the figure was slightly less than that recorded in 1920, and the annual average for the decade was about 6,730,000 tons. Townsend and crew must have concluded that getting business for M&StL was much like pouring water into a bucket filled with holes: the more poured in, the more flowed out.[17]

It was not for lack of aggressive instinct that M&StL turned in a disappointingly static performance during the "prosperity decade," but for lack of capital to make better and more efficient plant and equipment, a stubborn agricultural depression, continuous pressure from the larger roads, and a growing modal competition that regulatory agencies and other public authorities were unable or unwilling to properly factor in when formulating transportation policy. In 1927 E. D. Luce blustered about extending his wobbly Minnesota Western from Gluek to Dawson and Madison, but nothing ever came of it; the era of railroad construction was over in the upper Midwest. But the era of gigantic highway construction had only begun.[18]

The Federal Highway Act of 1921 required that states design a system of interstate and intercounty roads for which federal dollars might be made available. In 1919 Iowa already had established a 6,500-mile state road system; Minnesota established a similar trunk highway network of 6,877 miles a year later. Costs were staggering for the time, $30,000 per mile in the 1920s, paid for usually by license fees, a gasoline tax, state-issued bonds in some instances, and federal aid on occasion. By the end of the decade, Iowa had 2,317 miles of paved road; communities and farmers living off the main arteries stayed "in the mud" or supported campaigns to gravel local roadways. In Minnesota the *St. James Plaindealer* reported at the end of 1924 that one could "travel over gravel roads to every village in the county with the exception of Echols."[19]

The use of motor trucks during the Great War greatly excited those who advocated their use in commercial transportation, but in the mid-1920s the place of over-the-road trucking was not yet ensured. There was not so much as a tad of ambiguity as to the impact of automobiles. Ownership of an auto was no longer a class distinction in the 1920s, as had been the case earlier. By 1920, 407,578 automobiles were reported in Iowa. Illinois registered 504, 250, Minnesota 300,166, and South Dakota 112,589. The Ford Motor Company was turning out 9,000 cars daily, its famous Model T selling for only $290. In 1929 the automobile industry produced a record 4.5 million passenger cars; nationwide registration reached 23.1 million.[20]

Railroad managers could understand the charm of the automobile, and they recognized the freedom and independence it gave travelers; they were utterly at a loss, however, to understand why passengers left trains for motor buses. But buses often could provide more frequent and flexible service, and they could do so at a fraction of the cost of local passenger trains. Intercity buses initially engaged in short-haul operation, averaging about thirty miles, but in the late 1920s a few companies began long-distance service. In 1927, 85,636 motor buses were employed on 635,609 miles of route, carrying 2.52 million passengers. "Greyhounds travel over 70,000 miles each day," claimed that company in 1928.[21]

In 1923 the nation's railroad carriers transported approximately the same number of passengers as they had in 1912; the ICC later found that boardings on Class One roads declined by nearly one-third between 1920 and 1926. This dramatic shrinkage was almost totally in local traffic; sleeping car and parlor car numbers increased by over one-fourth during the same period. M&StL's passenger record tended to mirror the national experience. Boardings in 1923 (1,139,239) were about what they had been in 1907; in 1929 (458,246) they replicated those of 1895. The average distance traveled moved up from 38.1 miles in 1920 to 58.4 in 1929, so passenger miles did not decline as rapidly, but total passenger revenue dropped by two-thirds and comprised only 10.41 percent of M&StL's operating revenue in 1929.[22]

The bloom clearly was off M&StL's passenger operation; even the irrepressible Anson B. Cutts was gone, having resigned at middecade to take up another line of work. But the trains still ran—most of them, at least—and continued to set the tempo in communities throughout the service area. Young boys from Hanska purchased tickets for a ride to New Ulm to see the "war tank" on display there; a woman at Berkeley used M&StL to visit cousins at Ogden, returning the next day; the Brentford and Mellette boys' basketball team used M&StL's morning train to reach the Cresbard game site, returning on the afternoon train; M&StL continued to issue time tables promoting service between the Twin Cities and Lake Minnetonka and Waconia (although only through trains to and from the west now called at the dozen stops between Hopkins and Waconia); and the road still advertised its North Star Limited—"through sleeping cars, diner, chair cars"—to St. Louis, with connections there for New Orleans, Hot Springs, and "points in Florida and Texas." The North Star continued to do "very well" through 1926, said M&StL, but in 1927 fewer tourists headed for Minnesota resorts and fewer "commercial men" worked "the territory." Volume was off. Demand on M&StL's Aberdeen train likewise remained strong, although in 1928 competitive bus service on the leg from Minneapolis to Watertown began to erode sales. The Des Moines trains were especially vulnerable both to rail competition and to the increased popularity of automobiles and buses. In 1929 sleepers still plied the lines to St. Louis (with Wabash), Des Moines, and Aberdeen, but the Aberdeen and Des Moines cars were in jeopardy. Excursions generated $50,000 in revenues for 1924; one of the more memorable of these was from Aberdeen into Minneapolis for the Minnesota-Illinois football game and the dedication of Memorial Stadium. One passenger recalled that the crowded train was "alive" all night, but excursionists were ready for a full day in the city—breakfasting at a fashionable hotel, seeing the sites, watching the game (Illinois, with Harold "Red" Grange and "his ten assistants" was heavily favored, but Minnesota pulled an upset, 20–7), eating dinner, and then going back to the depot to line up at the gate with hopes "for the best seats home." Excursion revenues in 1925 were down to $40,000, and the Minnesota-Butler game on November 13 drew mostly yawns despite M&StL's attractive fares—$3.68 round trip from Hazel Run, for example, or $1.45 from Green Isle.[23]

Marshalltown provided a microcosm of change and continuity. The Thompson Hotel, located near the tracks, once known as the Bowler House and/or Bachelor's Inn, a fashionable place in earlier days, had fallen on hard times as fewer passengers found need for overnight accommodations between trains. But Charles Duell, proprietor of the depot news stand and self-appointed station master, still "called trains" and hailed taxicabs for persons needing them. And nearby, under the viaduct down by the vinegar works, was Stone's Restaurant, a venerable institution begun in 1887 as Stone's Lunch Room. Passengers and railroaders alike flocked there for a quick piece of pie or a full meal. For regulars Stone's offered meal tickets: twenty-one meals for $3.00. Packed lunches—usually baked ham or roast beef sandwiches and trimmings—were available for 35 cents. Stone's also provided sleeping accommodations upstairs: an "outside" room with a window for 75 cents, an "inside" room with no window for 50 cents.[24]

Revenue from handling mail during the decade went up nicely, from $290,186 in 1920 to $805,854 in 1929. The Post Office Department maintained Railroad Post Office routes on most M&StL lines, although assignments on the Algona Branch were trimmed back to Corwith in 1920 and ended altogether in 1922; similar service on the Story City Branch terminated in 1917. In addition to an endless stream of letter mail, clerks also sorted newspapers and magazines (everything from *Colliers* and the *Saturday Evening Post* to *Police Gazette* and *Wallaces' Farmer*). After 1913 Parcel Post was also found in mail cars, experiencing a two hundred–fold growth in its first ten years.[25]

Much of Parcel Post's success came at the expense of the express companies, which, like the Railway Mail Service, blanketed the country with a highly integrated system, finally under one flag, Railway Express

Agency, incorporated in 1928 and owned by eighty-two participating railroads. Express tariffs were monumental in what they covered—precious jewels, bank deposits, baked goods, dry goods, and fresh fruits and vegetables, to name only a few. "Have 72 cases of eggs for Chicago," wired the express messenger on train 10 heading for Monmouth on March 19, 1917. "Please arrange for trucks to handle same [in transfer to the nearby Chicago, Burlington & Quincy depot]." Bulk copies of the *Minneapolis Journal* (an afternoon paper) were dropped off at Troy, South Dakota, around 5:00 a.m.; the *Minneapolis Tribune* (a morning paper) arrived about 5:30 p.m. In 1925 creameries at seventy-six M&StL stations relied on express service, and bakeries at Conde, Des Moines, Fort Dodge, Marshalltown, and Monmouth, among other towns, utilized express service to reach a wider customer base, as did cigar manufacturers at Watertown and St. James and ice cream makers at Peoria and at Newton, Hampton, Forest City, and Brighton. Live frogs shipped in wooden crates and covered with wire mesh were billed to eastern markets from Troy, where they had been caught by enterprising individuals and youngsters recruited by the Ladies Aid of the Congregational church. Express was tailor-made for the burgeoning film industry. Minneapolis became a major distribution center, dispatching hexagonal metal cases of movie film to local destinations on intricate schedules so that they could be shown on a precise day at a given time. In that way Charlie Chaplin, Greta Garbo, and Al Jolson came to swank theaters in Peoria and Des Moines and even to hamlets like LaSalle, Minnesota, and Callender, Iowa, where movies were shown in the humble town hall or even outdoors in the summertime. Express receipts for M&StL held steady at about $250,000 per annum during the 1920s.[26]

Not all newspapers moved by mail or express. For several years the conductor on the up from Des Moines threw off a daily paper at Raleigh where it was retrieved by Saul, a handsome collie dog, who dutifully carried it to his master, M&StL's section foreman at that outpost. And not all that was carried aboard M&StL was legal. As prohibition closed in, innovative means were developed to meet the needs of the thirsty. The "news butch" on M&StL's day train to South Dakota, for instance, typically carried booze to "customers" in Watertown, and at the height of "the great experiment" an M&StL freight train carrying a car of "fish oil" (actually liquor) billed to Peoria was hijacked near Eden Prairie. Railroaders including the crew must have been in on the deal, because the car of "fish oil" conveniently developed a "hot box" at a location where the cargo could be unloaded onto waiting trucks as trainmen attended to overheated journals.[27]

Meanwhile, efforts to reorganize the company went nowhere. M&StL posted net operating profits of $15,857,047 for the decade, and the operating ratio for the 1920s was 90.42. Fixed charges, however, resulted in a bleak net deficit of $14,702,998 for that ten-year period, a surplus earned only in 1920. Under the circumstances, Bremner had few opportunities to cut down grades or ease track curvature, acquire modern rolling stock and more efficient motive power, invest in plant such as the heated warehouses greatly needed in Minneapolis, or even advertise the assets of the franchise. Bremner and Nash were restricted to the greatest economy, husbanding meager resources and expending them to greatest advantage. There was no room for nostalgia. Cold eyes looked at the line to Le Beau where now only two families lived and where gaping rows of basements and unused concrete sidewalks bore testimony to a fleeting, hectic era only a few years back. In 1923 M&StL had received $467 in freight revenue and $2.00 in passenger receipts on the 12.38-mile line from Akaska to Le Beau against expenses of $7,939. Le Beau by now was a nonagency station; its water tank had been moved to Akaska, where a wye had been installed; and trains were already originating and terminating at that station. ICC approval for abandonment was pro forma, coming in 1924; after the summer sun had browned the hills and dried the streams, dismantlers got at their melancholy business of tearing out the most westwardly piece of M&StL's *& Pacific* dream. Elsewhere, there had been no such expansive dreams, and there were no protests against M&StL's abandonment of 10.46 miles of the State Center Branch in Iowa from Van Cleve to State Center. The only intervening station was Malta, but it had been abandoned in 1915 and its population scattered. The final train ran on August 22, 1925; the tracks were removed shortly, with service remaining from Newburg to Laurel and Van Cleve.[28]

In 1927 M&StL was forced to pare mileage even further, although in this instance abandonment was not the result. Fifty years earlier, in a joint agreement among M&StL, Burlington, Cedar Rapids & Northern, and Rock Island, BCR&N had put up the money for M&StL's line reaching down from Albert Lea to the Iowa boundary (12.34 miles), but granted an Iowa Central predecessor (owner of the line from Manly to Northwood) the right of entry to Albert Lea should ever it wish to reach that place. Iowa Central did so early in the new century, of course, and Illinois Central likewise used this track to Albert Lea from Glenville, Minnesota. After Rock Island acquired BCR&N in 1902, the Manly–Albert Lea section was operated jointly by Rock Island and Iowa Central, later by Rock Island and M&StL. But a crucial corollary in the original agreement gave BCR&N, or its successor, the option of acquiring the Albert Lea–State Line leg at any time until June 1, 1927. Rock Island exercised the option and assumed ownership on that date. Joint operation continued, with Rock Island doing the dispatching and owning the Northwood–Albert Lea segment, M&StL owning the Manly–Northwood portion.[29]

At least, Bremner may have concluded, M&StL was relieved of having to maintain a very busy piece of track. Other cost reductions were more mundane, and included moving the city ticket office in Minneapolis to less fashionable surroundings at 15 Washington Avenue South, finding a tiny office space in downtown Des Moines after the consolidated ticket office was dissolved there, moving passenger operations from Des Moines Union Station to the nearby Rock Island facility, and, "on account of a heavy deficiency in earnings," terminating passenger service in 1924 between Fort Dodge and Angus on the original line, substituting a daily-except-Sunday turnaround mixed train from Fort Dodge.[30]

Yet it was not possible for M&StL to "save its way" into prosperity; spending nothing at all on improvements was never an option. The company had been approached by Baldwin Locomotive Works in 1915 with a proposal for 2-10-2s that would have had appreciably more tractive power than Mikados with substantially lower driver axle loading. M&StL did not yield to Baldwin's pitch, although 2-10-2s would have been an appropriate palliative to the hill-and-dale profile from Hopkins to Peoria. By middecade the road had 157 freight locomotives with an average tractive effort of 34,350 pounds, plus 40 passenger locomotives (including 17 weary 4-4-0s) and 25 switchers. A comprehensive study in 1926 determined that recently acquired 0-6-0s, 4-6-2s, and 2-8-2s alone could be "considered efficient, well designed, and modern"; only 105 locomotives in the entire fleet had superheaters. A resourceful mechanical department urged scrapping the most decrepit of the bunch, converting a few Moguls into 0-6-0s, and tinkering creatively with a majority of the inventory. Despite well-reasoned arguments, however, little was done in modernizing M&StL's motive power; the report was tucked away for future reference. It was the same in other areas. Passenger and mail cars were equipped with steel underframes, and the passenger fleet (cars for passenger, mail, baggage, and express service) was ever so gradually fitted out with electric lights. The track was improved by 99.2 miles of new rail installed in the period 1923–29, including 25.4 miles of hundred-pound steel in 1929, all of it on the main line; lighter rail was cascaded mostly to the Albert Lea–Des Moines line, a smaller amount relaid between Hopkins and Winthrop. In the aggregate, this track improvement was far short of needs. Such was the case with tie plates and track anchors, which were applied mostly on the main line, very sparingly elsewhere. A significant bridge renewal program between Revillo and Leola was carried out in 1925; a large icing platform was constructed at Fort Dodge; mechanical coaling stations (usually replacing antiquated trestle-type coalers) were installed during the decade at Corwith, Grand Junction, Olds, Oskaloosa, Middle Grove, Montgomery, and Winthrop; a gas engine replaced the windmill at Lynnville; new stucco depots were erected at Leola and Valley Junction; depots at Dawson and New Prague were outfitted with toilets; lights for depots and platforms were authorized for Belview, Hanley Falls, Conde, Nemo, Ollie, and Rippey; and for the

Figure 13.4. GE-2 took up duties on the Southwestern. M&StL photo, author's collection.

car shops at Marshalltown and the engine house at Watertown. Machinery platforms were constructed at a dozen stations; a few motor cars were purchased for section men; gas engines were provided for handcars in a few instances; mail carts were provided at Chelsea and Waukee, agents at Albert Lea, Albia, and Bartlett (Peoria) were awarded typewriters; the agent at Mason City got a new velocipede; and a Chevrolet sedan (later replaced by a Dodge coupe) was made available for senior managers at Minneapolis. Paint crews were unheard of; not one structure was authorized for paint during the entire decade.[31]

Bremner could coax money out of the court overseeing receivership matters only if he could show absolute need to maintain operation or if he could clearly demonstrate savings from an expenditure. Indeed, proving a cost benefit was M&StL's entree into the use of gas-electric cars for passenger service. Other roads had experimented with such technology; in 1918 Rock Island had run off 126,437 motor car miles, and in 1924 Bremner had talked wistfully of "rail-riding buses" that M&StL might use in competition with vehicular transport. Industry orders for "rail motor cars" totaled 1,056 in the years 1922–28. In 1929, 169 of them were ordered, 3 for M&StL. Self-contained seventy-five-foot cars were built by St. Louis Car Company and fitted out with a 300-horsepower Electro-Motive engine, each one fitted out with a fifteen-foot mail compartment, a twenty-two-foot baggage/express section, and seating for thirty-two persons. To differentiate them in numbering from steam locomotives, each one took a *GE* prefix, viz GE-1, GE-2, and GE-3. And each one was named for a primary community on the route to which it would be assigned: GE-1, *Peoria,* handled trains 19 and 20 between Oskaloosa and Peoria; GE-2, *New Ulm,* handled trains 28 and 29 between Winthrop and Storm Lake; and, GE-3, *Oskaloosa,* was responsible for trains 9 and 10 between Mason City and Oskaloosa. Each "GE car" would spell a more labor-intensive steam train as well as the ancient locomotives and cars assigned to them, and each would make one round trip daily, except Sunday. In addition, the Shoppers Special between Keithsburg, Illinois, and Peoria would be terminated, leaving only the Oskaloosa–Peoria local on that line segment. GE-1 introduced the new era, entering service to Peoria on December 27, 1929.[32]

Chapter 14
SOLDIERING ON

Since its very inception there has been something about this road that made men want to stick to it and fight for it, with the result that today it is one of the . . . closest knit railway organizations in the country.
—*THE RAILROADER* (OCTOBER 1931)

THE MARVELOUS "BULL MARKET" THAT HAD TYPIfied Wall Street trading since 1924 came crashing down on October 24, 1929, when sell orders exceeded the ability of the New York Stock Exchange to execute those orders. There had been earlier indicators of instability, and many stocks were selling wildly at odds with actual corporate assets, and some speculators shrewdly began to sell. In any event, a serious correction was a foregone conclusion; the only question had been when it would happen. Yet despite the crash in October, William H. Bremner made no mention of it in the company's 1929 annual report, nor did his words in that document suggest any hint of serious hard times for the entire country. Bremner rather seemed preoccupied with the independent difficulties of Minneapolis & St. Louis, now moving wearily into the seventh year of receivership.[1]

M&StL was not alone among railroads suffering financial embarrassment during the 1920s. Seventy-nine roads operating 22,786 miles of line headed for the courts during the decade. Among those were Chicago & Alton and even giant Chicago, Milwaukee & St. Paul, both of which continued to operate while they sought reorganization, but tiny Chicago, Peoria & St. Louis was not as fortunate. In 1923 that road secured Interstate Commerce Commission permission to cease operation and sell its properties for junk or to sell to those who might buy line segments. The path at M&StL was like that of Alton and Milwaukee. Protective committees were formed by holders of various bond issues; a similar committee, dominated by persons representing the Hawley interests, was instituted to look after rights of stockholders. Not surprisingly, investment analysts rated the company's securities as only speculative. Buyers took note. In 1926 M&StL stock traded drearily at between 4⅞ and 1⅜ per share.[2]

Reorganization attempts went nowhere. In 1924 consulting engineers Coverdale & Colpitts correctly concluded that M&StL's plant and equipment were inadequate—urging, among other things, immediate acquisition of twenty locomotives, ten second-hand passenger cars, and seventeen hundred freight cars. Nothing doing, said the federal court overseeing M&StL's receivership. In 1925 Coverdale & Colpitts trimmed that request to five locomotives and "between 1,000 and 2,000 new freight cars." Nothing doing, said bondholder committees. Further confusing matters was the federal government's contention that $2.309 million owed it in loan payments or overpayments on guarantees after federal control had priority even over the road's mortgages—a serious issue not cleared up until 1930, when the Supreme Court ruled against the government. Meanwhile, in 1928 Howard S. Abbott, United States master in chancery, recommended to the district court that M&StL's property "be administered and sold and the net proceeds thereof distributed in a manner to be determined by the court." Bremner shrugged. "I suppose that eventually the road will be sold and reorganized. . . . There will be no immediate sale," he predicted.[3]

In reality there was pathetically little that Bremner could control. Even matters pertaining to personnel policies and company employees often were beyond his ability—or any railroad manager's ability—to master. In 1926 the Railroad Labor Board was abolished, replaced by the Railway Labor Act, which the brotherhoods hailed as railway labor's "Magna Carta," since it guaranteed rail employees the right to organize and bargain collectively. The act also placed the federal government squarely in the negotiating process through mandatory federal mediation in the event of failed private efforts between carriers and unions; it also authorized the president of the United States to appoint emergency boards to review matters and stave off strikes should federal mediation be unsuccessful.[4]

Public policy likewise governed rates, as had been the case for several years, with the result that carriers typically took requests to regulatory bodies en masse. In 1925 roads operating west of Chicago, Peoria, and St. Louis made a determined effort to secure a general increase in tariffs that would allow a 5.75 percent return on the value of their properties. Bremner was one of the industry's lead advocates in these proceedings, a sign of the respect that his peers had for him, but industry leaders also wished to showcase M&StL as an example of what could happen to other roads if the ICC did not deliver the rate of return promised under the Transportation Act of 1920. "Unless the Minneapolis & St. Louis Railroad Company can be assured of a sufficient income to permit it to be properly equipped and to operate in an efficient manner, a large industrial as well as a large agricultural population, will be seriously inconvenienced," Bremner solemnly forecast if M&StL were to be wiped from the scene. And, he implied, there was the simple matter of justice. "The stockholders and bondholders and creditors of this company are entitled to consideration and should not be compelled to longer devote their money to the service of the public without any compensation whatsoever." Two years later found the ICC still dithering over the matter. Bremner must have shaken his head in wonderment, telling the regulatory body that had M&StL "been permitted to charge the same rates in 1922 as in previous years it would have shown a $2 million surplus and would not be in receivership today." But even now, predicted an emboldened Bremner, "if rates are increased to a point where we will be able to obtain credit, we can put through" an improvement program including reduced grades and ballasted track as well as new equipment. The commissioners listened, but would not be hurried. "Your receiver is very hopeful that the Commission will grant some relief," Bremner mistily reported to M&StL security holders. But as so often happened, his hopes were misplaced.[5]

Optimism and pessimism alternated among those directing M&StL's affairs, leading predictably to vacillation regarding appropriate strategy. During fleeting flits of optimism (usually when there was at least a possibility of increased rates), managers and owners thought hard about M&StL as a stand-alone company; when frustrated, as was more often the case, they pondered how M&StL might be marketed to a larger road. Sale or merger of the property, they knew, was compatible with tenets of the Transportation Act of 1920, which, among other things, gave the Interstate Commerce Commission authority over railroad combinations and even obligated the commission to provide a comprehensive plan for amalgamation of the country's carriers. In doing so, ICC was required to preserve competition and maintain existing routes and channels of trade while arranging systems that would earn essentially the same rates of return under a system of uniform tariffs.[6]

The regulatory agency had no enthusiasm for this task, but it had no choice, and over the 1920s spewed forth three plans, each one viewing M&StL differently. The first, devised by Harvard University's William Z. Ripley, proposed twenty-seven systems, most clustered around one or two principal roads. Ripley placed most of M&StL with system number 14, which included

Chicago, Burlington & Quincy, Northern Pacific, Denver & Rio Grande, Western Pacific, Chicago Great Western, and portions of M&StL. Ripley's report was written on behalf of ICC, but the commission's own "tentative plan" in 1921 differed in detail—seeking especially to "minimize dismemberment of existing lines or systems." In the ICC's tentative plan of nineteen systems, M&StL found itself intact and arranged with Chicago, Burlington & Quincy and Northern Pacific along with Chicago Great Western and Spokane, Portland & Seattle. The ICC invited comment before rendering a final plan; it was not long in coming, but concrete action, as opposed to blather and complaint by carriers and bureaucrats alike, was halting at best.[7]

Yet a few intriguing ideas surfaced. Early in the 1920s and running into the next decade, leaders of Great Northern, and to a lesser extent Northern Pacific, sought merger of their roads with jointly owned Spokane, Portland & Seattle. But Ripley had placed Great Northern with Milwaukee Road and had placed Burlington—like Spokane, Portland & Seattle (SP&S), owned jointly by GN and NP—with Northern Pacific. The ICC's tentative plan went along with those configurations. This caused indigestion, especially at Great Northern. As early as 1922, GN's talented Ralph Budd came to the view that Ripley and the ICC had merely promulgated suggestions, had enunciated nothing carved in stone, and with that in mind Budd began low-key studies to gauge public response to a possible combination of GN, NP, and SP&S. NP's Howard Elliott was nervous, fearing the wrath of an irritated ICC if such an application were made. Consequently he preferred to follow the Ripley-ICC plans for merger of NP and Chicago, Burlington & Quincy. That would mean taking on weak sisters Chicago Great Western and M&StL. But Elliott was philosophical. "There is no question, no matter what consolidation is made, the stronger roads will have to take over some of the weaker ones." Budd, by comparison, cautiously favored GN-NP-SP&S as a package, and Minneapolis shippers whom he consulted supported that view—but only, they firmly pointed out, as long as hometown M&StL was added. Budd hedged, wanting to think about it. By 1924, however, he had come around to Elliott's view that any "consolidation of three roads like ours" that ICC might approve would carry "an obligation to include a fair proportion of the so-called weak railroad mileage in the territory." Between M&StL and CGW, Budd thought M&StL "would suit us better in some respects, particularly because it has excellent freight terminals in Minneapolis . . . and because it parallels the Burlington for quite a distance in Iowa, where one line could be used. On the other hand, the Chicago Great Western . . . would offer a better Twin Cities–Kansas City line than we now have." In the end, Budd predicted, the greatest difficulty in taking either M&StL or CGW would be "determining the price that ought to be paid for them."[8]

During the spring of 1927, Budd quietly ordered an exacting study of M&StL; it was accomplished jointly by GN and NP personnel who were brutally dry-eyed. Evaluators studied M&StL's combination with every one of its major connecting carriers to test which ones might prove the best from any number of angles. In the end they found only four logical scenarios: M&StL with Chicago & North Western, M&StL with Illinois Central, M&StL with Wabash, and M&StL with GN-NP-SP&S.

Having narrowed the field, GN-NP evaluators then put each of the finalists through further grueling analysis. Chicago & North Western was rejected because merger of M&StL with it would obviate competition at too many communities where those roads met (which was anathema to the ICC); Wabash was ruled out because it did not "appear to have sufficient strength" to carry out acquisition; and Illinois Central (M&StL's leading interchange partner, with junctions at six locations and the evaluators' favorite "from the view of maintaining present routes and channels of trade") failed because the ICC had signaled earlier that Illinois Central should not be extended farther into northwest territory. By process of elimination, then, the evaluators concluded that "absorption of Minneapolis & St. Louis by [GN-NP-SP&S] has more apparent advantages than any of the other combinations suggested."[9]

William Bremner's views on all this varied over the decade. Early on he favored M&StL's inclusion with NP and CB&Q, provided M&StL could secure a satisfactory price, but as Ralph Budd perfected plans to include M&StL as part of Great Northern Pacific, which is what a combined GN-NP-SP&S would be called, Bremner's ardor cooled. This likely reflected pulling and hauling among M&StL stockholder and bondholder groups, or he simply may have disagreed with one nationally known academic who labeled M&StL a "permanently weak line"—a "cancer"—and truly believed that M&StL could, with adequate capital infusion, make it as a stand-alone carrier. In any event, when Budd and the managers at NP went ahead with a formal application to create Great Northern Pacific, Bremner was moved to argue that this merger would "not carry out the proposal of the Transportation Act of 1920."[10]

M&StL, of course, was motivated to seek its own advantage. But its best advantage was not apparent even to those who were in charge. Making the strong stronger and the weak weaker, as M&StL counsel said was being attempted in this application, was certain to harm M&StL by diverting essential traffic—especially lumber products and produce from the West presently received from GN and NP at Minnesota Transfer—to CB&Q, which Great Northern Pacific presumably would continue to own should the application be approved. Budd worried about restless Minneapolis shippers who were disposed to M&StL's interests, and during the proceedings he made a casual proposal to Bremner to include M&StL in Great Northern Pacific—adding, as an aside, that if M&StL came into the fold, he contemplated "no change with reference to M&StL." Bremner was obligated to pass along Budd's proposal to the court as well as to stockholders and bondholders, all of which turned thumbs down, and Bremner himself absolutely refused to believe that Great Northern Pacific would continue M&StL as a self-contained entity within the larger whole. He was right. Budd intended to carve up M&StL, its southern lines going to CB&Q (which earlier had made an independent study of acquiring M&StL) and the remainder to Great Northern Pacific. "We feel that one of the large advantages in taking over the M&StL," Budd told Hale Holden, CB&Q's president, "would be the fact that one line between the Twin Cities and Chicago [M&StL-IC] would be eliminated and that by taking it [M&StL] over, the business would to a large extent go to the Burlington." It would also rid the Twin Cities market of a "serious competitor" [M&StL], which, Budd told Holden, Minneapolis shippers favored because "it gives the best deliveries of any line from the East . . . through Peoria." It was a curious if candid admission of Chicago's horrible congestion and delay to lading and the efficiency of M&StL's Peoria Gateway by comparison.[11]

In 1928 Great Northern Pacific merger hearings continued in Washington, where Budd and NP's Charles Donnelly presently made a formal offer to acquire M&StL for $20 million in long-term 3 percent bonds or $15 million in 4 percent bonds. "I am of the opinion," said Budd, "that owners of the securities of Minneapolis & St. Louis will do better to make a sale to some large system than to put more money into it . . . [and] certainly they would get more by selling it as a whole than they would to have the property broken up and sold piecemeal." Budd then joined Bremner on an inspection of principal lines in April. He was depressed at what he found. From Des Moines he wrote to Walker D. Hines, a friend and an attorney representing the company, saying, "The whole property is like a railroad of 20 or 25 years ago." Budd was astonished and dismayed that there had not been, "during the receivership, the expenditure of money usually expected to be put into property during such a period." Budd also was bewildered at Bremner's unalterable contention that M&StL could go it alone. Budd did not believe that would be a remote possibility—even with an infusion of $5 million that Bremner thought adequate, or with $7 million that Budd though more likely was needed. "I am more strongly than ever of the opinion that he [Bremner] is mistaken," Budd told Hines, "and that there is no hope of independent operation."[12]

Matters creaked along to a curious resolution. Final arguments were heard in the merger application, and members of the Interstate Commerce Commission retired to deliberate. M&StL throughout had taken the position that Great Northern Pacific would restrict competition and that M&StL would be harmed irreparably. Meanwhile, early in 1929 Ralph Budd, worried in particular about M&StL's lines west of

Figure 14.1. Ralph Budd was surprised that M&StL had not spent more on maintenance, given its receivership since 1923. Indeed, bridge and building crews like this one at Dawson, Minnesota, on the road's West End were on spare rations. Author's collection.

Watertown, withdrew Great Northern Pacific plans to include M&StL. Then, at the end of the year, tipping its hand in the Great Northern Pacific matter, the ICC announced its "final plan" for consolidation of the nation's railroads into limited systems, placing GN and NP together, making Burlington the centerpiece of another system, and now including M&StL with Illinois Central. Two months later the ICC found the proposal for Great Northern Pacific compatible with the Transportation Act of 1920 and in the public interest—but conditioned its merger approval on the willingness of GN and NP to divest themselves of jointly owned and very lucrative CB&Q. "No," came the anguished and clipped response of the two northern roads, and the status quo was maintained.[13]

Consolidation efforts under the Transportation Act of 1920 proved a monumental bust, showering distinction neither on railroad owners and managers nor on politicians and bureaucrats. In fairness, however, the matter was not simple. The age of railways had passed, but that reality had not adequately settled in on the public or its policymakers or even on railroaders, most of whom remained captives of the past. Furthermore, owners of stronger railroads were understandably reluctant to see their investments diluted through merger with weaker roads. And despite industrywide improvement in earnings—an average of 4.48 percent on property investment in 1923, about 5.25 in 1926—in 1927 railroad stocks typically traded at levels lower than in 1906, investors finding greater attraction in autos, steel, copper, electricity, and so on. Some observers even argued that the nation's railroad network had been overbuilt. To be sure, more miles of line had been abandoned than had been built during the last decade, and entire roads, most of them serving mining or timber industries in areas where resources had been exhausted, had perished. But in general, collapse and abandonment of complete systems was as yet unthinkable.[14]

Throughout all of this William Bremner comported himself with honor and respectability. He clearly had obligations of trust to M&StL security holders, to the various protective committees, and to the federal district court overseeing the road's receivership. That he effectively discharged these difficult and often contradictory responsibilities was not questioned. Neither was there any doubt that Bremner had keen feelings toward other important M&StL stakeholders—the communities served by the road, its customers, its suppliers, and especially its employees.

The number of persons employed by the company ebbed and flowed, driven by several factors. In 1882 an average of 2,888 persons had been on the payroll, reflecting active construction projects that season, but in 1889 the average was only 881, mirroring M&StL's financial plight at the moment. After merger with Iowa Central, employee numbers climbed predictably, and in 1919 stood at 5,757—suggesting not only an expanded service area but also a general growth in business. It likewise suggested the powerful influence of the United States Railroad Administration. Numbers dropped to 4,804 in 1922, to 4,745 in 1929, and they would have been lower had Bremner been able to secure capital to make the property more efficient by purchasing newer and larger locomotives, by cutting down grades, and so on. But Bremner found no such money—which, in a curious way, may have given him relief, for he frankly had not the stomach to let people go.[15]

It is not trite to say that, to a greater or lesser degree, a sense of family had characterized the corporate culture at M&StL from not long after the Iowa Central merger in 1912. That kindred sense seemed only to deepen as the company experienced hard times. William G. Bierd had noted as much before he left for Chicago & Alton: "When family is poor they all stick together," he observed in admiration of esprit de corps at M&StL. Bierd was hardly a Pollyanna. Of course there was a degree of tension between workers

Figure 14.2. William Bremner did not have the stomach to cut off employees and did what he could to shore up employee morale. This section gang on the West End was lucky to have a motorized car; many still used handcars. Author's collection.

and supervisors. M&StL employees, in the same way as other railroaders, were motivated to join unions to seek better compensation and a safer workplace as well as to counter feelings of eroding self-worth and dignity. But in the main, tension between labor and management was muted at M&StL compared to most other roads.

M&StL's management often initiated loyalty-enhancing programs, but in other cases employees themselves took the lead. During the late 1880s M&StL conductors and engineers at Minneapolis played "a match game of ball for the benefit of the railway reading room," and in 1895 M&StL players won the pennant in the Twin Cities "Railroad League." A year later clerks from the general office were among "local amateur wheelmen" engaged in a race sponsored by the company from Deephaven to Minneapolis. Even during the stressful 1920s receiver Bremner arranged for funding to construct a grandstand at the M&StL employees' baseball park at Marshalltown, and at the end of the decade the Minneapolis & St. Louis Railroad Quartet from Minneapolis had "gained a statewide reputation as real entertainers." In 1924 General Manager Elliott E. Nash, entirely at his own expense, hosted an evening at the Minneapolis Armory for all Twin Cities employees. The main feature was "a motion picture of the guests at their daily work." Nash, who had written the script and directed the filming of this silent reel, was intent on boosting sagging morale, reminding all hands that M&StL was a worthy enterprise, that every person had a stake in the company, and that every employee had a positive role to play in its success. "There is no progress without labor," Nash summed up. "We need our railroad and our railroad needs us."[16]

M&StL booster clubs, however, were categorically the provenance of employees who, of their own volition, held picnics, Christmas parties, and other events without any kind of financial support from the company—a fact that differentiated the M&StL booster club experience from that of other properties. M&StL booster organizations provided essential psychological nourishment for employees working for what many outsiders considered a down-and-out organization. "Think—Boost—Act" was the motto of the M&StL groups, whose members put this into effect by soliciting new traffic, by using up or using to the maximum extent all material and equipment, and by getting trains over the road with reliability. And, of course, they had the motivation of self-preservation; a healthy employer was the best job insurance. The first club was formed at Monmouth in 1921; others followed at Marshalltown, Fort Dodge, Oskaloosa, Albert Lea, and the Twin Cities. "Our railroad" was a term often on the lips of booster club members; few, if any, were actual holders of M&StL securities, but each member, make no mistake, was a stakeholder—and it showed.[17]

William H. Bremner was greatly moved by what he saw in these clubs. He was asked to be a guest at one of their meetings and took the opportunity to offer a brief address. "When I look out over this great throng of families, I realize the grave responsibility resting on the railroad to take care of them," he said. Bremner, of course, was really saying, "*I* have the great responsibility for these people." He went on: "No large employer can or should try to evade this responsibility." In fact, Bremner was solemnly promising himself and those in the audience that *he* would never shirk that responsibility. It was vintage

Figure 14.3. Receiver Bremner found cash to build the M&StL employees' ball park at Marshalltown, Iowa, because it further solidified loyalty and because he simply thought it was the right thing to do. Vaughn R. Ward collection.

Bremner—belying ever so clearly his core value as M&StL's senior steward.[18]

Bremner's values were matched by those of others at the company of lesser rank who ordinarily might not have attracted attention. "Loyalty" was the single word that the *Railroader* for October 1931 chose in explaining why M&StL had prevailed "when so many other roads gave up the struggle." Since its very inception there had been "something about this road that made men want to stick to it and fight for it, with the result that today it is one of the . . . closest knit railway organizations in the country." In this instance, the *Railroader* had in mind a particular person, A. E. Smith, the road's comptroller and assistant secretary, whose "life centers on hard won experience and loyalty to the road that gave him his chance for success . . . [a man] . . . never too busy to make a friend for his road." The same might have been said of Roadmaster James Teyro, who on May 31, 1931, retired after fifty-one years' service at M&StL in maintenance of way. The company scraped together enough cash to publish a "short story" on Teyro—"a simple recital of one plain, honest man's life which has been entirely devoted to one job," as the company put it. "Outside of his loyalty and faithfulness, Jim is . . . an authority on track building, and has made himself a court of last resort on everything pertaining to his work," wrote Bremner. "Everything good come to you, old friend," said the receiver. "We love you, Jim, and Mrs. Jim, too," echoed Elliott Nash. "He is a thoroughly good man," affirmed Ritchie G. Kenly, M&StL's long-serving chief engineer. "He never told a man under him to do a job he would not do himself . . . [he] . . . has always been the kind of man that men liked to work under and to work with," recalled Superintendent Robert E. Ryan.[19]

The era of the boomer railroader was about over, with "homers" now dominating the ranks. Seniority rosters showed names of men employed for decades—the senior telegrapher in 1931 had hired out in 1878—and multiple generations of some families—Lanphier, Elder, Dorn, Dallman, and Severson, to mention only a few. It was, for the most part, a man's world. Men ruled in train and engine service, in the mechanical and maintenance of way ranks, in bridge and building gangs, in the shops, and in the officer corps. There were few exceptions. Women found employment in the general offices as secretaries and stenographers, wives of bridge and building foremen sometimes accompanied their husbands as cooks for the gang, and there were a handful of female station agents. One of these, Mrs. M. D. Rutsen, left the South Dakota Central to become agent at Boyd, Minnesota, where she tutored a young Manford J. Reintan in station accounting and telegraphy. Reitan eventually became a chief dispatcher for M&StL.[20]

One of the best-known M&StL employees, at least west of Hopkins and on the Southwestern, was Henry Severson of Winthrop. A brakeman and then conductor in passenger service, Severson also was an accomplished ventriloquist with an enlarged sense of humor. On one occasion a lumberman from Wood Lake who was returning home from Minneapolis became concerned by cries from a person he thought to be "riding the rods" (on the undercarriage of the passenger car). "PLEASE stop the train and let me off," came the plaintive cries from below; "I can't hang on much longer." The lumberman frantically reported this to Severson, but the conductor said surely the man could hang on a little longer until the train stopped at Arlington. The lumberman took exception to the conductor's hardheartedness, but at the station stop Severson told the lumberman that he had looked under the car and found nobody. Then, as the train started up, Severson looked out and saw a shabbily attired fellow walking away from the depot and suggested that he might have been the vagrant riding under the car. The irate passenger was not humored, writing a letter to the Wood Lake newspaper accusing Severson of wanton disregard for human life. On another occasion, a newly married couple on their honeymoon to the Twin Cities boarded the train at Monterey. Soon thereafter Conductor Severson began meowing like a cat and then proceeded up the aisle looking for the origin of those sounds. When he got to the bride he told her that she could not bring a cat with her on the car. The woman blushed, protesting that she had no cat. But Severson stood his ground, saying that he knew a cat's meow when he heard one, and nearby passengers nodded their heads, saying they too had heard meows. Severson looked about, found no cat, and then glanced up to the luggage rack, where he espied the couple's suitcase. Perhaps the cat was in the suitcase, Severson suggested. The bride again denied that she had a cat, but the conductor demanded that the woman open the luggage and release the poor cat. Strange to say, no cat was in the suitcase. On another trip passengers were startled when Severson loudly ordered a woman to come into the coach from the vestibule—company rules forbade riding out there. "I don't have to," came the sassy reply from the phantom woman outside. Severson shrugged and rolled his eyes when passengers turned in their seats to see what was happening. Regular patrons recalled Severson quacking like a duck until passengers began looking about, trying to locate the wayward bird, discovering instead their genial conductor, a broad if mischievous smile spread across his face. He also was renowned for fierce "cat and dog fights" staged aboard the cars. When Severson married the manager of Winthrop's depot lunch room in 1932, the local newspaper noted—perhaps with tongue in cheek—that Severson enjoyed "a wide acquaintance in this locality."[21]

It was Severson and his fellows who were called upon to deal with accidents and acts of God that are, unfortunately, a predictable part of railroad transportation. Mosquitoes humiliated an M&StL passenger train and its crew at Badger in 1907, stalling the train on slippery rails for two hours and inflicting themselves on 120 humorless passengers. Railroaders could do little about the mosquito pests, even less to prevent a tornado in 1919 from ripping the deck off "Horseshoe Bridge" two miles north of Sioux Rapids, Iowa. Out in South Dakota, the James River, usually a sluggish stream with very modest fall per mile and a low-lying flood plain, proved obstreperous for several years, with special trouble near Stratford and Mellette. In those cases track was underwater or washed away, and nothing could be done until the river subsided. In other cases, railroaders could respond to an immediate crisis. Early in the century came this message: "95 delayed 15 minutes at Marsh putting out fire on roof of depot," wired from the conductor of that train to the dispatcher in explaining his tardiness. In 1927 an awful fire at Searsboro destroyed much of the downtown, but damage would have been greater had it not been for draining water from the tenders of a northbound passenger train and then a freight.[22]

Derailments and collisions nearly always resulted from mechanical failure or human error. Two Iowa Central extra trains met head on east of Marshalltown in 1883 when a dispatcher issued faulty train orders, and a failed bridge at Steamboat Rock resulted in a spectacular pileup in 1912. Several persons were injured at Minneapolis in 1896 when a streetcar motorman failed to stop at a crossing and hit an M&StL freight train broadside; sixteen years later an engineer at Oskaloosa was scalded to death after a collision between a passenger train and a freight train whose crew had "attempted to make Oskaloosa station on too short time." Chaska Hill, between Chaska and Eden Prairie, was the scene of another head-on meeting between an Omaha freight and an M&StL freight. The fireman on the M&StL train was crushed to death; misunderstood orders was the cause. Sad to say, five persons—two enginemen and three passengers—were killed at New Prague in September 1906 when a freight locomotive failed to get in the clear and was hit by a passenger train. An even nastier accident occurred on July 3, 1920, near Arnold, south of Livermore, when the locomotive tender on a northbound passenger train derailed shortly before a trestle over Bloody Run Creek, tumbling cars into the ravine with the loss of eight lives and injuries to thirty. More often death or injury came to persons who were trespassing on company property, trying to board or leave its moving trains, or those who were victims of grade-crossing accidents.[23]

Snow was the perpetual seasonal enemy. The winter of 1880–81, for example, proved long, stormy, and disagreeable. Snow in February held fast an M&StL passenger train north of Hartland and then entrapped five locomotives and crews attempting rescue. Seven days were required to extricate passengers, crews, and equipment; the story was featured in the far-off *New York Times* of February 18. Storms in January 1886 shut down service on Des Moines & Fort Dodge for several days, and another in March 1887 plugged M&StL. "Pedestrians who happened within three blocks of the railroad track at 11:00 o'clock last

Sunday night as the snow plow passed up the road say that snow fell for five minutes after the infernal machine was out of sight," reported the editor of the *Jordan Independent,* stretching credulity just slightly. "A real live snow plow is a curiosity to which distance lends charms," he concluded in reestablishing veracity. Apparently M&StL was clearing the line with a plow mounted on a locomotive pilot or was employing some kind of elementary "bucker" or "wedge" plow, because steam-powered rotaries had not yet made an appearance in the upper Midwest. M&StL was not long in acquiring such equipment, however, allocating $15,399 for a Leslie Rotary Plow in 1889 and taking delivery early in 1890. Management told shareholders that the device would "fully protect the line and save the cost of the plow several times over in a winter such as we are likely to have in any year."[24]

M&StL's rotary was put to a stern test early in the new century. In February 1905 it opened the line from Winthrop to Storm Lake and then, "so there won't be any delay," detoured eastward over Illinois Central to take up plowing M&StL lines out of Fort Dodge. In 1909 the "X-1," as the rotary was labeled, was back on the Southwestern, which was closed for a week, according to the *New Ulm Journal.* Among other troublesome places, long cuts between Spencer and Sioux Rapids were filled with five to six feet of snow. "Get 5 men with picks and shovels and meet snow plow at Greenville," the section boss at that town was told by the Roadmaster. "Pay 15 cents per hour and their board away from home." A year later X-1 made at least two trips to Le Beau—in January and March. In the latter case the line had been closed in February after a freight got stuck two miles west of Akaska (and was freed by an extra from Le Beau and fifty shovelers recruited from the countryside) and then closed again for two weeks. When the rotary arrived on March 3, it was followed by a passenger train bringing a huge backlog of mail and express to the local populace, which turned out in enthusiastic greeting.[25]

Storms were unrelenting during the next decade. The North Star Limited was snowbound near Hampton early in 1912, and the line between Marshalltown and Manly was closed again two weeks later. In 1915 two train crews and several section men left Winthrop with the rotary en route to Storm Lake. The *Winthrop News,* which kept a close eye on M&StL, reported that snow was "four feet on the level in many places." On March 16, 1916, train 3, the up passenger train from Des Moines, double headed out of Fort Dodge, became stuck north of Emmons and did not reach Albert Lea until March 19.[26]

But the blizzards of 1917 were doozies, remarkable for their frequency and ferocity. Storms late in January plugged the West End all the way to Le Beau as well as the Southwestern to Storm Lake. No trains moved west of Minneapolis for two days, but on January 31, X-1 started out for Watertown, reaching there on February 2, doubled back to Winthrop, and then began clearing the line toward Iowa. Meanwhile more storms bludgeoned South Dakota; the rotary was withdrawn from the Southwestern, which then received piecemeal attention. Opening the West End developed into a saga. X-1 cleared the twenty-four miles of track from Watertown to Wallace in one day, but another seven days were required for the next eight miles to Bradley. X-1 suffered under the strain, broke down, and was returned to Cedar Lake for repairs, but M&StL was able to borrow from Great Northern a similar plow, which punched through from Bradley to Crocker (7.5 miles) in another week. Two 2-8-0s shoved the rotary, but their collective tractive effort was insufficient between Wallace and Crocker, where twenty cases of dynamite per day were necessary to loosen packed ice, snow, and dirt. Even then the going remained tough. Conde, just 17.5 miles distant, remained seven days away. Lighter Moguls replaced Consolidations at Conde, and the relief train pressed on. The Great Northern machine failed at Hoven, but was replaced by a healthy X-1, which finally struggled into Le Beau on March 7. There was no time to rest. M&StL had used wedge plows (three of which were acquired in 1916–17) to attack snow on the Southwestern, but new storms necessitated use of a Rock Island rotary south of Estherville. Then one or two storms weekly in March created drifts that were, according to one account, "mountain high in cuts," and X-1 spent much of the month working between Winthrop and Storm Lake. "The winter of 1916–1917 was the most severe experienced in many years," shareholders were

Figure 14.4. M&StL's rotary was busy on the Southwestern and on the West End in 1917. It drew a crowd of gawkers at Monterey, Minnesota. Author's collection.

advised. Indeed New Ulm, for example, had received eighty-eight inches of the white stuff, and removing it from M&StL rights-of-way had exacted a frightful toll on men and machines. X-1 had taken a beating, but nothing like that taken by one of the wedge plows, which simply broke in half when thrust into packed drifts near Crocker.[27]

Other ornery storms visited M&StL's service area in the 1920s, but none were as vicious as those of 1917. In 1927 the up train from Storm Lake was trapped in twelve-foot drifts north of LaSalle, and the one hundred or so passengers and crew were obliged to trudge back to town, where provisions soon ran short. Two hundred loaves of bread and a quarter of beef were sent overland from St. James, Minnesota, to alleviate the problem, and when wedge plows failed, X-1 opened the line after it had been closed for nearly a week. A year later the rotary also found itself employed in clearing the line to Watertown.[28]

By 1930 M&StL had the cumulative experience of six decades. Its owners, managers, and employees had been tested by the storms of nature, assaulted by giant railroads and more recently by vehicular competition, hammered by well-intentioned but misguided public policy, pummeled by vagaries of the national and international economy, and even kicked around by dumb luck. Surely, they must have believed, they had stood up to every possible exigency. Indeed, they had soldiered well in the past, but nothing, they quickly discovered, had prepared them for the vicissitudes of the Great Depression.

Chapter 15
Mean and Ugly

Rain, Rain, Come Today, Before We're Dried and Blown Away.
—*Florence Forum,* September 28, 1933

Hoopla surrounding the fabulous Foshay Tower and its dedication on August 30, 1929, in downtown Minneapolis had seemed an appropriate exclamation mark with which to end the "Prosperity Decade." Minneapolis, now grown to a population of 464,356 and ranking fifteenth among American cities, rejoiced in the Foshay building, patterned after the Washington Monument, and Minneapolitans eagerly turned out to hear *The Foshay Tower Washington Memorial March,* which had been composed by the famous John Phillip Sousa and was played by his equally famous band. In fact, however, the closing of Minnesota's largest lumber mill at Virginia on October 9 was a more appropriate metaphor for the end of that curious and often contradictory decade.[1]

Shutting down the Virginia & Rainy Lake mill was unrelated to the stock market crash (an adequate timber supply to propel the mill had been exhausted), just as the crash did not precipitate the Great Depression. The depression resulted rather from multiple causes, including the crash. The agricultural sector had been unhealthy for a decade, as had the soft coal industry, both crucial elements of the national economy. In addition, normally conservative bankers had grown intoxicated by good times, especially in the last half of the 1920s, and often had required inadequate security or otherwise made "bad loans," in the process creating a shaky banking industry. The cost of living was essentially constant during the same period, unemployment was negligible, and labor productivity in manufacturing rose by nearly three-quarters, but hourly wages increased by less than 10 percent. America simply was producing more than it could consume—a monumental problem exacerbated by high protective tariffs that dampened international trade and diminished capacity to sell American products abroad. Finally, domestic economic distress became part of a devastating worldwide depression.[2]

In any event, the crash of October 1929 seemed to usher in a nasty new era, and many Americans dated their memories of hard times from it. Soon thereafter industrial production plummeted, unemployment rose, and consumer demand slumped. Domestic manufacturing in 1932 was half of what it had been in 1929; the gross national product for 1933 was 54 percent of that for 1929. The powerful Detroit–Pittsburgh axis was thrashed. Sales of motor vehicles in 1929 hit 4.6 million; the figure in 1933 would be a mere 1.3 million. It was much the same elsewhere. American Locomotive Company had built an average of six hundred locomotives per year during the 1920s; it sold but one in all of 1932. Business failures in 1932 reached epidemic levels; unemployment in the nonagricultural sector reached 25 percent, perhaps higher. Not surprisingly, the country's banking system mirrored, and in some ways caused, trauma in other portions of the economy. Indeed, bank suspensions—9,765 of them in the five-year period from 1929 through 1933—deepened the nation's economic malaise. Of 1,764 banks in Illinois, 572 failed during the first three years of the 1930s; in Iowa it was 442 of 1,252, in Minnesota 184 of 1,041, and in South Dakota 151 of 386. For several months there was not one open bank in all of Sibley County, Minnesota (Green Isle, Arlington, Gaylord, Winthrop, and Gibbon).[3]

The depression in industry and commerce was quickly manifest in agriculture, already smarting after a decade of difficulty. Exports of grain and meat fell off due to shrunken demand abroad in conjunction with counterproductive tariffs; domestic consumption fell, too. In 1932 gross farm income nationwide was but 40 percent of what it had been in 1929. Commodity prices provided a useful barometer. A farmer near Kanawha took fifty bushels of shelled corn to town, where he tried to sell it for $5.00, but there were no takers, and that evening he returned home with his corn, unable to secure even 10 cents a bushel. Livestock producers fared no better. Steers brought $9.50 per hundred weight at South St. Paul on January 1, 1931, but only $4.00 on December 31 of that year; hogs went for $7.75 per hundred weight and $4.00, respectively. Foreclosures by lending agencies were predictable, but prices realized because of severely diminished market value often threw them into bankruptcy; that, in turn, ruined others. As one observer recalled, it took faith, fortitude, and patience to be in farming. It was no less true for businessmen in small towns dependent on the producing countryside as well as industries and workers tied in any way to agriculture.[4]

Quirky Mother Nature soon added insult to injury. Summers during the 1930s in most of M&StL's service area proved dry, hot, and windy. Indeed, portions of Iowa and Minnesota as well as all of South Dakota unfortunately found themselves in what would be labeled the "dust bowl." June of 1933 was abnormally hot, rainfall sparse. It was merely a prelude to 1934. High winds for two days in April swept dirt into the atmosphere and caused serious damage in southern Minnesota between Waseca and Albert Lea, among other places. Temperatures soared in May, rains stopped, and burning hot wind whipped viciously across grain fields. Drought gripped most Minnesota counties west of Hopkins and along the Southwestern. Farmers near Madison plowed under crops, and the Madison Milling Company shut down production because blown dust had infiltrated the plant and contaminated the flour. To the east, Lake Minnetonka was nearly nine feet lower than its high water mark. Iowa was worse off. In May the *Des Moines Register* reported "parched pastures and failing water supplies"; in July twenty-one Iowans died of oppressive heat within four days. The *Estherville Daily News* worried about serious erosion of topsoil by high winds, with dirt settling in grader ditches, drifting along fence rows, and even covering posts.[5]

Conditions in South Dakota made Iowa and Minnesota look pristine by comparison. South Dakota's population had grown to 692,349 by 1930, and throughout the previous decade M&StL had continued to portray it as a "land of sunshine and opportunity" to which tenants should go to "find a home for your family," landowners to procure "a farm for your boys." The company said the soil in counties served by its lines "will raise anything . . . natural to temperate climate." As late as 1932, M&StL advertised "homeseeker excursion rates" to South Dakota. Nevertheless, a trend away from small villages and hamlets such as those found on M&StL west of Watertown had begun as early as the second decade of the new century. Hard times among farmers and stockmen in the next decade accelerated that trend. Bank failures became routine during the 1920s; before the decade was out, banks at Wecota and Wetonka, among other places, were gone, and with them the essential elixir of commerce. In sum, conditions were precarious in most of M&StL's South Dakota service area even before the onset of the Great Depression and its ugly twin, the dust bowl. Grasshopper infestations, drought, and crop failures hammered the state. Many of South Dakota's rural population could conclude only that the place was wild, dirty, and thankless. Beginning in 1933, dust storms became the routine. Above the masthead of the *Florence Forum* for September 28, 1933, was the plaintive cry: "Rain, Rain, Come Today, Before We're Dried and Blown Away." It was a desperate plea unanswered—except by the wind, which seemed angry at any vertical object. During 1934 alone, seventy-three "dusters" hit the state. In 1930 and 1931, M&StL installed 388 sections of snow fence in a valiant if not particularly successful effort to keep cuts between Conde and Akaska free of dirt. Revillo, well to the east near the ninety-seventh meridian, remained determined to put the best face on things. Its commercial club invited relocation to Revillo—a place that had "every conceivable enterprise not generally found in smaller towns"—just as it urged agrarians to settle in the countryside near town, "where you can make farming pay." The depression could be turned to advantage, said the commercial club. "Investments in land can be had at lowest prices ever offered. . . . We have the soil, you have the opportunity." But it was a tough sell. In 1931 Minnesota newspapers reported the arrival of nearly destitute farmers who had returned to their native state after several years in South Dakota, defeated by depression, drought, and grasshoppers. A year later civic-minded persons around Winthrop contributed to the South Dakota Relief Fund, which donated feed and hay to several stricken areas; at Zearing, Iowa, the American Legion collected a carload of corn for shipment to South Dakota to benefit livestock producers.[6]

Hard times cut unevenly, of course. The "Century of Progress" celebration to honor Chicago's centennial opened on schedule in 1933; interurban cars at Mason City, Iowa, still screeched around sharp downtown curves en route to Clear Lake, and Jacob Decker & Company spewed forth a seemingly endless stream of meat products, but dust from cement plants on the north edge of town was sporadic depending on the ups and downs of construction demand. Foreclosure

Figure 15.1. Track crews such as this one at Wallace, South Dakota, built and maintained snow fences that during the "Dirty Thirties" did double duty, stopping snow in winter, dirt in summer. Author's collection.

notices appeared regularly in local newspapers. At the *Winthrop News,* Editor C. C. Eaton spoke for all on January 14, 1932, when he said, "Old Man D. Pression could please us now by moving on," urging his readers, however, to keep a stiff upper lip. "It is time for us to look up, not down." By summer he needed a dose of his own tonic. "The panic is now dragging wearily toward its third birthday," he woefully recorded.[7]

Circumstances did not improve in 1933. As that year ended, Eaton thought matters could hardly worsen. "It ought to be easy for 1934 to be a better year than 1933," he said in a measured mixture of exasperation and hope. Twenty-five miles west, at Franklin, Hansen Lumber and Franklin Mercantile both folded up shop and the local bank failed. In South Dakota, Revillo dared to stage its jubilee on September 6 and 7, 1934, with baseball contests against neighboring Marietta and Strandburg, as well as speeches, concerts, and a "big dance" with music by Larry's Rhythm Kings of Dawson. Ironically, however, the August 30 edition of the local newspaper promoting all of this also contained a prominent advertisement for yet another "As I am quitting farming" sale. In Iowa a spectacular fire in 1931 added to depression woes at Spencer, where much of the downtown was leveled. Telephone service was lost during the inferno, and when flames routed the Western Union operator from her office, she retreated to M&StL's tower, where she telegraphed the outside world for assistance. "Please accept our heartfelt sympathies," an M&StL representative wired Spencer's mayor. "If we can be of any service, especially in expeditious handling of any particular material or foodstuffs, kindly let us know as we want to help all we can," he promised. Among other things, M&StL delivered soft drinks "on all trains," because the city's water supply had been contaminated.[8]

Railroaders were no less flummoxed than others by the stock market crash and the depression that followed. Late in November 1929, *Railway Age* editorialized that "the fundamental economic conditions of the country have changed but little," suggesting that "a mild recession in business" had been occurring since late summer. In fact, however, in 1930 American railroads hauled only as much freight as they had in 1920. That was only the beginning of bad news. In 1932 they handled 646 million tons, earning $2,451 million; in 1929 they had hauled 1,339 million tons and had taken in $4,826 million. Passenger revenues were worse: $874 million in 1929, $377 million in 1932. Carriers cut operating expenses by nearly half and reduced dividends by almost three-quarters, but their taxes fell by less than a third, and bonded interest actually rose. An aggregate net income of $897 million in 1929 melted into a deficit of $139 million in 1932. Fifty-eight roads operating 43,681 miles of line entered receivership in the six-year period from 1929 through 1934.[9]

Economic dislocation of this magnitude and scope was immediately part of the political landscape. President Herbert Hoover and fellow Republicans hoped to aid the commercial and industrial areas with the Reconstruction Finance Corporation (RFC), a bank of last resort that essential but down-and-out companies might turn to. Hoover was fond of predicting that prosperity was "just around the corner," but 1932 proved so devastating that many normally conservative citizens were radicalized. In November voters turned out Hoover and the Republicans, embracing instead Franklin D. Roosevelt and what he and fellow Democrats called a "New Deal."[10]

Roosevelt acted with dispatch when he took office in March 1933, immediately shutting down the nation's banks for one week to stem the tide of panicky withdrawals. The psychological impact of this and other New Deal nostrums was immediate. In the next year devastating drought moved the federal government to purchase 8.3 million cattle from producers whose feed bins were empty and their pastures bare. Condemned cattle too weak to ship or unsuitable as food were destroyed; the rest were dispatched to packers at South St. Paul and Albert Lea, among other places, where they were processed into meat products used by relief agencies in aiding needy families or were ground into fertilizer. Another matter of public policy bearing on railroad fortunes was the fall of prohibition with ratification of the Twenty-first Amendment on December 5, 1933. Even before, in March, Congress had changed the legal definition of an intoxicating beverage from 0.5 to 3.2 percent alcohol, and with that decision breweries had reopened, at least some of them. Along M&StL lines, breweries were reestablished at Peoria, Chaska, Jordan, Minneapolis, Montgomery, New Ulm, and St. Paul. Inbound lading, as before, included barley, hops, and bottles, with outbound billings of kegs and cases, now mostly in carload lots.[11]

Nothing was of greater interest to those concerned with M&StL matters than what the new Democratic administration in Washington had in mind as to overall railroad policy. In September 1932, Franklin Roosevelt, as part of a nationally broadcast campaign speech at Salt Lake City, had declared that preservation of the railroads was essential to the well-being of the entire nation, as well as to the protection of investors and employees. Railroaders everywhere took heart, and in Washington, after Roosevelt's election but before he took office, Congress began work on transportation issues and new rules for railroad reorganization.[12]

What emerged in the first half of 1933 was Section 77 of the Bankruptcy Act, the Emergency Transportation Act of 1933, and Jesse Jones, an expansive Texas banker, who was to head a much more aggressive Reconstruction Finance Corporation, which soon would become not only the nation's largest bank but also its largest single investor. A reorganization plan under Section 77 required Interstate Commerce Commission approval and then passed to the judge before whom the case had been commenced. The judge could accept or reject the plan, but if accepted, it would bind all security holders and claimants. The Transportation Act included amendments to the Interstate Commerce Act that made it an objective to eliminate duplicative rail service if this could be accomplished without decreasing employment below the level of May 1933 (with the exception of normal attrition), and that promoted financial reorganization of carriers primarily through reduction of fixed charges. To carry out these provisions, the president of the United States was authorized to appoint a federal coordinator of transportation; Roosevelt chose Joseph B. Eastman, a well-regarded Interstate Commerce Commissioner. Finally, the ICC was ordered not to approve RFC loans to carriers it believed were in need of reorganization.[13]

Did these new variables have any positive bearing on M&StL's plight? Not necessarily, and certainly not immediately. On March 22, 1932, M&StL receiver William H. Bremner had made application to the RFC for a loan of $3.899 million to cover preferred claims, receiver's certificates, and principal on specific bonds. RFC personnel did not perceive that these monies would go for any "broad program looking to the lifting of receivership," and they were miffed that M&StL's Reorganization Committee had given the impression that it was unwilling to attempt any reorganization unless RFC would lend all funds necessary. The request was denied. Bremner returned to RFC in 1933 with a very different request, for $1.027 million to pay vouchers for indebtedness plus principal and interest on four equipment trust obligations. This action brought a peculiar and very hostile response from Phillip J. Roosevelt, chairman of M&StL's Reorganization Committee, who said that Bremner's request should not be honored, that there was no reasonable expectation that the debt could ever be paid, that further borrowing could "only postpone, and cannot avoid, the inevitable consequences of the present inadequate earnings." Roosevelt concluded that the "Committee is fully cognizant that the consequences of denial of the Receiver's application may be cessation of operations." M&StL, said Phillip Roosevelt, had become nothing more than "a charitable enterprise for the purpose of paying wages and taxes that are not now being earned." In sum, "The Reorganization Committee believes that it is unfair, unlawful, and contrary to the public interest to postpone through prior lien borrowing the time when operations must cease, thereby consuming what little value remains in the property for the investor." But Roosevelt, as it turned out, did not speak for all members of the committee. William P. Hawley, M&StL company's vice president, himself chairman of one bondholder protective committee and representative of the Edwin Hawley estate, publicly and vigorously opposed Phillip Roosevelt's contention that "no loans should be made except in connection with a reorganization." RFC bureaucrats were bewildered, and properly so; they said "No" to M&StL once more. These curious vacillations pointed out, among other things, a huge fissure in M&StL's reorganization camp, one long rumored, and it likewise showed the wretched position of William H. Bremner, who now felt called upon to deny that M&StL was about to suspend operations.[14]

If there was a happy note anywhere for M&StL, it certainly was not apparent. In 1930 the district court had studied a petition to authorize the sale of portions of M&StL covered by each of the mortgages, but it had been denied. Appeals followed. Then, on May 11, 1934, the court did order the sale of properties piecemeal, but there were no bidders at auction on September 5, and the matter was postponed. Meanwhile, Bremner got permission from the court to scrap 21 locomotives and 1,633 cars; this was to be done at Minneapolis and the proceeds divided among three hundred employees who had been getting little if any work because of hard times.[15]

Bremner as receiver and Elliott Nash as chief operating officer were under tremendous pressure to trim costs, just as J. A. Lucey as chief traffic officer was under the gun to gather as much business as possible. In 1929 M&StL operated four time freights (trains handling time-sensitive lading) from Cedar Lake to Albert Lea, three from Albert Lea to Peoria (another from Monmouth to Peoria to handle Santa Fe tonnage from Nemo), with the same number of trains in the reverse direction plus locals to take care of business on the main line. Time freights likewise moved from Cedar Lake to Morton, from Albert Lea to Des Moines, and from Des Moines to Estherville, again with equal numbers of reverse movements as well as locals and extras as needed on all line segments, with mixed train service in South Dakota between Conde and Akaska, Aberdeen and Leola, and on all of the Iowa branches. Passenger operations were similarly impressive. Three trains moved from St. Paul and Minneapolis down to Albert Lea, with two proceeding to Albia, one to Peoria; three trains also headed west to Winthrop, one bending off on the Southwestern to New Ulm, the other two continuing on to Watertown, one pressing beyond to Aberdeen; two trains as a continuum from St. Paul moved through Albert Lea and on to Des Moines, joined between Fort Dodge and Des Moines by one that also served the line from Estherville and Spencer; another worked the Winthrop–Storm Lake leg. Again, equal service was offered in the reverse direction. Lucey predictably argued that all of it was necessary to protect existing business and attract new customers. But the depression was unyielding; business was dwindling, and cuts, however painful, were essential.[16]

Dreary numbers told the tale. In 1923 M&StL tonnage had peaked at 7,311,189; in 1929 it was down modestly to 6,910,349. During the next year volume slipped to 6,222,222, but in 1931 sank to 4,998,200, and in 1932 to a miserable 3,666,781—only 53 percent of 1929 business. (In 1911, before its merger with Iowa Central, M&StL had handled 3,043,626 tons of freight.) Passenger numbers were grimmer yet. Peak business had occurred back in 1915, when M&StL had carried 2,574,797 passengers, generating 93,386,576 passenger miles. Then the bottom dropped out. In 1930 M&StL served only 296,984 patrons (19,972,510 passenger miles), and in 1932 a paltry 150,017 (9,805,122 passenger miles). Distasteful traffic figures were matched by sour financial numbers. In 1929 M&StL posted a net operating profit of $2.9 million and an operating ratio of 80.55; in 1932 its net operating income dropped to $409,082 but the operating ratio climbed to a frightening 94.79. And of course there was no surplus; the road failed to cover its fixed costs in all years after 1920.[17]

Nash had no choice but to curtail service. Late in 1931 he removed all scheduled freight trains between Watertown and Aberdeen, substituting extras as needed. In April 1932 he reduced time freight service between Cedar Lake and Albert Lea by half and by one-third between Albert Lea and Peoria. In 1931 the Des Moines–Estherville time freight was trimmed back to Spencer, and it was removed altogether two years later. With the passenger service operating ratio leaping to 199.3 in 1932, passenger offerings predictably took an even greater drubbing. The Des Moines–Estherville train was peeled back to Spencer in November 1930, and the sleeper from St. Paul to Fort Dodge was removed; the Watertown sleeper perished a year later. For that matter, passenger service to Aberdeen was ended in June 1933, mixed trains west of Watertown sufficing thereafter. Other schedules were juggled and reduced to eliminate train miles. This often was driven by Nash's desire to take maximum advantage of M&StL's growing inventory of gas-electric cars, the first of which, a self-contained car, had gone to work between Oskaloosa, Iowa, and Peoria very late in 1929. Two sister cars, GE-2 and GE-3, the *New Ulm* and *Oskaloosa,* arrived shortly thereafter to take up duties between Winthrop and Storm Lake and between Mason City and Oskaloosa. To these were added later in 1930 four seventy-five-foot, 400-horsepower units with thirty-foot mail compartments plus thirty-foot baggage-express sections that were capable of toting trailing storage and passenger cars. Built by St. Louis Car Company and powered by engines from Electro Motive Company, these four were GE-25, GE-26, GE-27, and GE-28—named *Albert Lea, Fort Dodge, Des Moines,* and *Watertown,* respectively—and were assigned to the two train sets between St. Paul and Des Moines, and to one set between Albert Lea and Albia. In 1931 came four more, GE-4, unnamed, a self-contained unit assigned to Minneapolis–Winthrop–New Ulm chores; GE-29, the *Montgomery,* added for the Des Moines pool, to which responsibility was added the Des Moines–Spencer run; and GE-30 and GE-31, unnamed but like GE-29 equipped with Railroad Post Office and baggage sections, which were placed on the two sets of Watertown trains. The "GE cars," as they were called, released twenty-five lightweight and weary steam locomotives, could be operated without a fireman, proved reliable, and cost $0.3056 per mile to operate compared with $0.6628 per mile for steam engines, saving the company about $300,000 per year. Local observers took a mixed view of the new machines, snickering at their anemic "musical horns," and poking fun at the "puddle jumpers," which were said to "howl along the rails where once puffed the old coal burners"—especially when they came out second best in collisions with motor vehicles, "requiring the old reliable steam engine to be called out to pinch hit for the new tangled locomotives of today." But M&StL was proud of its "Fast Gas-Electric Passenger Trains," as M&StL's agent at Storm Lake phrased it in a local newspaper advertisement. "Only two cents a mile," added the agent at Winthrop in another ad—$1.33 to Minneapolis, 38 cents to New Ulm. "Travel in comfortable coaches and avoid congested highways," he urged.[18]

M&StL's trauma in the passenger-carrying trade was hardly unique. Passenger traffic nationwide decreased in 1931 to the lowest level since 1904, with the result that passenger revenues dropped to $551,054,000, about 24.5 percent below the 1930 level. The twin villains, said William Bremner, were the "depression and the popularity of highway transportation." Like other roads, M&StL fought back with low rates—$1.75 round trip to St. Paul from Winthrop for the Minnesota State Fair in 1932, and "2¢ per mile" between Fort Dodge and Des Moines to meet competition from Fort Dodge, Des Moines & Southern ("the results of which were not satisfactory due to unfavorable economic conditions"). The road could not count on heavy patronage from excursions or special movements as in the past, but M&StL did host itself with a special train to Waconia for employees in 1930, and in the same year ambassadors from Florence, South Dakota, chartered a special car to visit numerous locations on M&StL lines in Minnesota and Iowa to tout their community, its nearby Medicine Lake, and the prospect of building a lakeside sanatorium to take advantage of the lake water's rumored healing powers. In summertime M&StL typically handled migrant laborers from the Southwest to work on farms at Wood Lake or elsewhere Minnesota and in Iowa, but "owing to labor conditions of the time" that revenue stream was cut off and not matched by new sources such as the Civilian Conservation Corps. Revenue for M&StL also was curtailed when the Post Office Department removed mail from mixed trains on the Iowa branches in favor of star routes (using trucks).[19]

In 1933 M&StL's passenger operating ratio hit an intolerable 205.8; Bremner could do nothing but admit that more difficult decisions were necessary. He took a deep breath and swallowed hard; M&StL would exit the St. Paul market. This would save road crew wages and switching performed by St. Paul Union Depot, and would allow cancellation of the lease for three tracks and retirement of all M&StL facilities at Northern Pacific's St. Paul coach yard. Service to St. Paul ended on June 10, 1933.[20]

Other cost-cutting measures varied in scope and dimension. Station platforms at many locations were shortened or even retired as demand for passenger service ebbed, and forty-five pieces of passenger equipment and over one thousand freight cars were retired between 1932 and 1934. When trolley service to Tonka Bay on Lake Minnetonka ceased in March 1932, 1.45 miles of line leased to the streetcar company since 1907 was surrendered, and the historic line was taken up shortly thereafter. M&StL joined with Chicago & North Western to establish a joint agency at Wright, Iowa, in 1930, but labor restrictions foiled a similar venture with Great Northern at Hanley Falls, Minnesota. Nor did anything materialize after an exhaustive consolidation study was made by M&StL and all other roads at Aberdeen. In Iowa low-demand joint agencies with Rock Island at Abbott Crossing and Givin were reduced to custodial service, but attempts in Minnesota to close agencies at Carver and Manchester failed. Off-line traffic representatives were trimmed to forty-six in 1935 (from fifty-nine in 1929), and contract employees and managers alike took a 10 percent and then a 20 percent pay cut. The number of employees shrank from 4,745 in 1929 to 3,200 in 1934; the total labor bill fell from $8.0 million to $4.5 million.[21]

Of course it was impossible to "economize" the railroad into prosperity. Monies had to be spent routinely to maintain service, and betterments were greatly to be desired. But after Bremner was slapped down early in his receivership when he supported the recommendations of Coverdale & Colpitts, advisers to the Reorganization Committee, that the company purchase new motive power and rolling stock, he became cautious when it came to advocating serious programs of improvement. Incrementalism suited him. For that matter, getting money for anything significant was arduous business. For every substantial expenditure receiver Bremner was obliged to provide a detailed petition to the court, with copies sent to no fewer than eighteen parties representing various classes of creditors and other interests of the property. Objections came as a matter of course, hearings were ordered, and the judge might approve or not. Still, by 1931 Bremner could take pride in a main line from Minneapolis to Peoria, which had been laid with eighty-five-pound to hundred-pound steel that was adequately tied and underlaid with cinder or gravel ballast and with bridges that had been strengthened as they came up for renewal in anticipation of heavier locomotives later on. Five hundred boxcars were ordered in 1930, several passenger cars were converted to "trailers" for service behind GE cars, mechanical firedoors were applied to more than fifty locomotives, and boosters were authorized for Mikados 629 and 631.[22]

In 1934 a blend of economy and improvement took form on the Peoria line. Chicago, Burlington & Quincy, which years before had picked up narrow-gauge lines that had bedeviled Iowa Central in the Brighton-Coppock area and then standard-gauged them to provide difficult competition in a zone of parallel operation between Oskaloosa and Winfield, now wanted to vacate that field. This was good news for M&StL because it would no longer have to divide business, and it presented an opportunity to acquire parts of the CB&Q line that were better engineered than M&StL's. This was the kind of arrangement that seemed to have an attraction for everybody, including Bremner, the court, M&StL debt and equity holders, CB&Q, and even the ICC. When the last Burlington train steamed out of Oskaloosa on September 29, M&StL already had permission to purchase two line segments—30.5 miles from Martinsburg to Coppock and 14.5 miles westward from Oskaloosa to Tracy. The latter would give M&StL access to another CB&Q

Figure 15.2. Looking east at St. Louis Park, Minnesota. Bremner pointed to a main line that had mostly eighty-five-pound rail and was ballasted with either cinders or gravel; adequate, no doubt, but the property certainly had a threadbare appearance. M&StL photograph, author's collection.

line to Des Moines over which M&StL would have trackage rights, allowing cancellation of the current Oskaloosa–Des Moines arrangement with Rock Island. To the east, M&StL obtained a much-improved profile with lower grades, less curvature, and fewer bridges, and offered "new" service to the communities of Pekin, Linby, Packwood, Woolson, and Veo. Moreover, CB&Q was able to rid itself of an unremunerative branch, and a smile was put on the faces of government bureaucrats who loved voluntary coordination. The losers were the villages of Ollie and Richland, which M&StL now bypassed and from which rails would be removed in 1936.[23]

Bremner was totally without control or ability to influence other instances regarding M&StL's single stem from Oskaloosa to Peoria. In 1924 Muscatine, Burlington & Southern (successor to Muscatine North & South and known euphemistically as Many Bumps & Sores) abandoned its line from near Muscatine to Burlington, which included trackage rights over M&StL from Elrick Junction to Oakville, in the process denying M&StL those revenues as well as valuable interchange business. Farther east, the romantic-sounding Fulton County Narrow Gauge, which crossed M&StL at the Spoon River community of London Mills, Illinois, and had become part of CB&Q's empire early in the new century, had been standard gauged, but suffered during the depression and fell to the wrecker's torch in 1934. This left London Mills and its environs solely to M&StL—fortuitously, as it later developed. As a curious footnote, in the 1920s London Mills had been seen as the connecting point by promoters of the ill-starred Jacksonville & Havanna and Chicago, Springfield & St. Louis, which together had wanted to fashion a latter-day through route between Minneapolis and St. Louis. Nothing was perfected during the depression years, though, and for M&StL it was only the latest of dashed dreams in that regard.[24]

Back in Minneapolis there was no sympathy in 1934 for parvenu residents of Kenwood, who again sought to have M&StL yards and shops removed from Cedar Lake to Hopkins and wanted M&StL to reroute its two main tracks north of Cedar Lake along Great Northern's line. The 750 M&StL employees who would be affected by a move to Hopkins, residential and commercial interests along Great Northern's line, Great Northern itself, and others who would be asked to pay for a project benefiting only the Kenwood nabobs took a uniformly contrary view. The issue did not go away, however, and took on new energy when Kenwood leaders dreamed of using "relief laborers" paid by Washington New Dealers in a way that would reduce the burden to local taxpayers. Nothing happened, but the denizens of Kenwood continued to feel victimized by the railroad and its assorted ilk.[25]

Elsewhere M&StL was seen in a more positive light. In 1930 the road pledged to furnish feeder cattle or lambs to reliable farmers to be finished in their feed lots, and the road also was willing to loan money directly to farmers to purchase livestock. "This is done solely to encourage livestock raising and feeding" along M&StL lines, said the company's agricultural development agent. Two years later M&StL happily delivered several carloads of feed to Clarkfield, where it was given to needy persons in the area. And as the drought deepened, in 1934 M&StL handled hay and feed at two-thirds the normal rate and billed "grasshopper bait" (bran or sawdust laced with toxin) at half rate. M&StL also joined with the *Minneapolis Journal* in sponsoring local youngsters from on-line communities for the 4-H Club week held at the University Farm in St. Paul. The road took pride in delivering a carload of McCormick-Deering cream separators to Gaylord in 1933 because the delivery showed that McCormick-Deering and its dealers "have confidence in the future," and when Winthrop staged its jubilee in 1931, M&StL dispatched a special train from Minneapolis bearing Bremner and other officers plus the famous M&StL quartet. A full-page M&StL ad in the *Winthrop News* reminded readers that "History Links the Railroad with the Upbuilding and the Prosperity of Winthrop and the State," and that the road employed twenty-nine persons in the community with an aggregate annual payroll of $54,656. "We respectfully ask for your whole-hearted support and the routing of your freight and passenger business via M&StL," said Vic W. Munsell, the company's agent. In other cases, however, M&StL's best intentions went awry. When in 1931 the road donated twenty elderly boxcars to start a boxcar colony for the purpose of housing Spencer's poor, other residents of that community stormed the city council, fearful that such a colony might become a permanent part of that place. The council passed a resolution condemning the measure, M&StL shrugged and retreated, and the idea of a boxcar colony perished.[26]

Transients and vagrants certainly were an issue during the Great Depression. Many of them set up flimsy villages named "Hoovervilles," mocking President Herbert Hoover. Some were moving from place to place looking for work; others had given up; still others had no intention of working. Most were harmless; some were not. Collectively they created a problem for railroads whose trains typically provided "free" transportation in "sidedoor Pullmans" (boxcars) and on whose property they frequently congregated in "hobo jungles." One of the largest of these was under the Chicago Great Western bridge near M&StL's yard at Fort Dodge. Train crews and track workers often overlooked the presence of these trespassers, taking a "there but for the grace of God go I" approach, but exceptions occurred when one group provoked the other or when damage to property or loss of lading was involved. It was one thing for hard-pressed local residents or transients to scavenge coal that had fallen to the company's right-of-way from locomotive tenders or coal-carrying gondolas—or even from around coaling stations where locomotive firemen "accidentally" overfilled tenders so that a quantity of fuel would litter the ground; it was another matter to steal coal from company bins or from cars en route to customers or to destroy property. At Storm Lake, desperate residents frequently helped themselves to M&StL coal at the engine house, and finally a company detective went out to investigate. He told the section foreman to turn his back on persons who were gathering up fuel by the sack but to report larger thefts. Perhaps it was the same special agent who apprehended a thief in Des Moines who was loading his truck full of coal from a car in M&StL's yard; the thief got away, but the police confiscated his truck. Ice that M&StL had purchased to supply refrigerator cars at Fort Dodge disappeared with regularity from the storage shed in hot weather; company personnel chose to look the other way. And boxcars stored at Albert Lea were set upon in 1932 and largely dismantled before discovery by railroaders; their elements had been magically transformed into parts of corn cribs, coal bins, garages, and even houses around the area. Two years later, boys from South Minneapolis "bummed" their way westward, but cold forced them off the train at Winthrop, where they stole an automobile and headed toward California—only to be apprehended in Iowa.[27]

In 1934 those holding certain of M&StL bond issues again urged a reorganization using money to be borrowed from the Reconstruction Finance Corporation. Judge Wilbur E. Booth in Minneapolis took the matter under advisement, but cautioned that he would make no decision until the RFC made a thorough study of the road—an examination that had been started a year earlier by RFC's John W. Barriger III. Much of the effort behind this request had come from F. J. Lisman, long a student of M&StL's circumstance, who represented one class of bondholders and had replaced Phillip Roosevelt as chairman of the Reorganization Committee. Barriger and Lisman were convinced at this point that M&StL could be reorganized and made profitable as a stand-alone company if a new management team could be assembled and if RFC would provide cash to rehabilitate and modernize its plant—saying as much to Jesse Jones, head of the RFC, who asked the ICC for concurrence. But the regulatory body saw no prospect of a profitable M&StL, and the idea stalled. Jesse Jones, likely at the prodding of Barriger and Lisman, meanwhile had come to the conclusion that, at the very least, M&StL had to have new leadership—an operating man—if any money ever was to flow from RFC. Thus began a quiet search for such a person, but it proved hard going; talented men who were approached turned away offers to work at M&StL.[28]

At the same time, however, M&StL's cash flow became a more immediate concern, with wages and salaries occasionally in arrears and fear internally on the part of some that the road would have to cease operation unless government aid was immediately forthcoming. Surviving data do not suggest that matters were at the crisis level. Rather it seems that one or more of Bremner's subordinates, seeing him as living on borrowed time and soon to be expelled, tried to sabotage him by passing inflammatory information, misinformation, rumors, and half truths to creditors, especially local creditors, who hired D. C. Noonan, a former operating officer of the company, to snoop around and report back. In the end, Noonan repeated rumors regarding purchase of locomotive coal from off-line sources instead of on-line mines, sweetheart deals in the purchase of boiler compound, excessive salaries for managers, and general malfeasance on the part of Bremner's senior team. Everett M. Dirksen, then a member of Congress from Illinois, even got into the act, asking that the House Judiciary Subcommittee investigate "slipshod, haphazard operation" at M&StL. No such investigation ever was performed, and no formal charges ever were levied. All of it was a sordid reflection of these very unhappy times.[29]

If these unsavory events represented some means of levering RFC into quick action to save M&StL, they failed, for the law did not permit direct loans merely to stave off impending cessation of operation. Yet Barriger and Jones were frightened, and they determined that every effort should be made to ensure continuation of service on M&StL lines out of respect for communities, customers, and employees alike. This could be accomplished, they ultimately reasoned, only by requesting that another carrier take over and operate M&StL. Barriger then patiently and privately met with the president of every major road that M&StL connected with, asking whether, under the right circumstances, his road might be receptive to such a proposition. "Yes," was the nearly unanimous response, but only if M&StL lines could be acquired reasonably, RFC provided financing, ICC approved the purchase, and considerable latitude could be given in abandoning what for that particular carrier was unattractive mileage. The problem was that lines of M&StL that were attractive to one carrier had little or no utility for another. This posed a dilemma—one that could be understood only in the context of transportation needs in the 1930s, the vicissitudes of the Great Depression, and political reality. These considerations led Barriger to a new approach—"multiple consolidation" wherein several roads might bid for chunks of M&StL so as to maintain service and jobs to the maximum extent possible. Barriger and Jones floated the idea before a parade of senior railroad managers who streamed regularly to Washington in search of RFC aid or to influence transportation policy in one way or another. The concept was received favorably, but because there still were important social and political ramifications as well as financial and economic ones, in October Jones took the matter to President Franklin Roosevelt, who gave tentative approval, saying, however, that RFC should also consult with Minnesota Governor Floyd B. Olson, a live-wire radical from the Farmer-Labor Party whose favor Roosevelt courted. Olson embraced the multiple consolidation concept and pledged his support. Barriger then began construction of a formal proposal that soon would go to interested carriers.[30]

How much of this was known to Lisman, Bremner, Judge Booth, or others associated with M&StL is not clear. They appeared to be ignorant, even believing that RFC was about to approve a newly drafted loan application that included the name of a prospective candidate to lead the company or at least serve as co-receiver—Lucian C. Sprague. In fact, M&StL board members assembled in October to adopt resolutions required in Chapter 77 proceedings for reorganization. Even as they were gathered in New York, however, a telegram arrived from Jesse Jones denying M&StL's application, requesting that all independent reorganization efforts stop, and announcing his preference for dissolution of M&StL and division of its lines among competing roads.[31]

That depressing news certainly threw a crowbar into the flywheel of reorganization. Bremner glumly returned to Minneapolis to carry on as receiver, Sprague was told that his prospective position at M&StL had evaporated, and government bureaucrats and railroaders elsewhere began plans to carve up the road. Then the unexpected happened again: William Hepburn Bremner died on December 12, 1934. There was deep mourning among company personnel, who remembered the cheerful and optimistic Bremner as one who had steadfastly protected their interests. Indeed, said the general chairman of M&StL telegraphers, "all employees held him in high esteem on account of his genial and kindly disposition toward all." Bremner was sixty-five years old at the time of his death and had served as president since 1917.[32]

Bremner's sudden passing put the Reorganization Committee into turmoil as to managerial leadership. Elliott Nash, the road's chief operating officer, and J. A. Lucey, its chief traffic officer, both had resigned late in 1933, and the venerable and capable J. P. Houston, who followed Nash, died only a few months later. The internal cupboard was bare, and several outsiders had shunned the opportunity to come to the road even in the past, when reorganization of M&StL as a stand-alone entity had been at least a possibility. Why would anybody want to come now, only to be present at the road's dismemberment? Nevertheless, Sprague, earlier endorsed by the committee, was again contacted, and again he said he was available. Hawley interests were not keen on Sprague, however, and Edward C. Delafield, chairman of one bondholder group, held out for two receivers. Judge Booth's decision was to appoint Lucian Sprague and John Junell as co-receivers. It was effective on January 1, 1935.[33]

Chapter 16

FREY AND DISMEMBERMENT

No trains were moving Monday night on the M&StL and all service on the road today is annulled.
—*Marshalltown Times-Republican*, February 4, 1936

Once upon a time there was a railroad whose name was M. N. Saintell. He lived many years in the states where he was born. He was a peace-loving railroad, always minding his own business and never trying to get anyone else's.
—Harry E. Bloom, M&StL clerk, 1936

John Junell was a prominent and wealthy Minneapolis attorney and likely a friend of Judge Wilbur E. Booth, who was overseeing the receivership of Minneapolis & St. Louis. Born at Indiana, Michigan, in 1886, Junell graduated from the University of Michigan law school in 1907, and, except for service as a naval aviator in the Great War, had practiced in Minneapolis since 1911. His clients included several short-line railroads, and he represented Chicago Great Western in Minnesota. As M&StL's co-receiver he was essentially window dressing, there to appease the Hawley interests and a bondholders' group led by Edward Delafield.[1]

There was never any doubt that between two equals the other M&StL co-receiver, Lucian Sprague, was more equal than John Junell. Born at Serena, Illinois, on September 29, 1882, Sprague attended public schools, studied mechanical engineering and business by correspondence, and hired out as a call boy with Chicago, Burlington & Quincy. He became successively a telegraph operator, fireman, and locomotive engineer at Burlington before signing on as an air brake instructor for International Correspondence Schools and then moving to Great Northern, where he was supervisor of air brakes. In 1915 Sprague became general mechanical inspector for Baltimore & Ohio, leaving there in 1917 for Chicago Pneumatic Tool, where he was sales manager. Uintah Railway hired Sprague as superintendent in 1922 and promoted him to general manager in 1924, then to vice president in 1927. During the years 1929–31 Sprague was on his own as a consulting engineer in New York City; in 1931 he was named executive representative for Missouri-Kansas-Texas, based in St. Louis.[2]

There was utterly no reason to envy Sprague his job at M&StL in 1935. He was following William Bremner, who had been popular with the company's rank and file, who looked askance at the newly arrived outsider. That was only the beginning. There was no unanimity among bondholder and stockholder groups as to the ultimate disposition of the road, Judge Booth had sent mixed signals as to his views of the company and its fate, most financial investors and virtually all railroad managers elsewhere saw M&StL as fatally afflicted with systemic disease, the road's physical plant and equipment were in questionable repair, principal customers were uncertain as to M&StL's ability to be a reliable performer, and in Washington John Barriger and Jesse Jones at the Reconstruction Finance Corporation had fully agreed to a policy of dismembering Minneapolis & St. Louis.

And the Great Depression showed only modest and reluctant signs of abatement.

Gross farm income for the nation dropped from $13.646 billion in 1929 to $6.286 billion in 1932 and inched up to only $6.905 billion the next year. The number of meat animals slaughtered in April 1935 was the smallest per month in over twenty years, although later in the year swine producers did receive $11 per hundred weight, the highest paid since mid-1929. Grain prices were mixed, wheat gaining slightly in local markets, oats and corn dropping sharply in 1935. President Franklin Roosevelt's New Deal had not lifted the country out of hard times, but government nostrums did help. Only one bank in Minnesota failed during 1934 after the Federal Deposit Insurance Corporation was implemented. And the Civilian Conservation Corps provided opportunities for unemployed young men; sixty-three from Minnesota's Brown and Sibley Counties (New Ulm and Winthrop) boarded the afternoon train from Gaylord on April 20, 1935. At Spencer, one newspaperman reported a new attendance record for the famous Clay County Fair, which, he thought, suggested that the country had marked a turning point in its economic recovery. Minnesota's Governor Elmer A. Benson was hardly as sanguine. "I am convinced that nothing short of social ownership of key industries can save us," he gloomily exclaimed. "Capitalism as we know it is doomed."[3]

It was against this uncertain backdrop that proponents of M&StL's dismemberment got about their business. On October 19, 1934, Ralph Budd, now president of Chicago, Burlington & Quincy after leaving Great Northern, hosted a meeting with fellow presidents of Milwaukee Road, North Western, and Illinois Central, along with representatives from Great Northern, Wabash, and RFC for the purpose of studying maps and other data to determine what companies might be interested in M&StL line segments. When they finished, every piece of track was placed with one or more prospective owners, including roads not even represented at the meeting; Wabash demurred ultimately, however, saying that it only wanted to protect the Albia gateway in one way or another. Before the year was out a memorandum of understanding was drafted among the roads represented at Budd's meeting (plus late entrant Chicago Great Western) whereby they agreed to create a new corporation, with participating roads taking stakes on a pro rata basis. They further agreed that the new corporation should bid $6.5 million for M&StL's property, that RFC should finance the entire package, and that Great Northern, Northern Pacific, Soo Line, and others should be added to membership if they wished.[4]

Dismemberment plans matured over the next several months. By summer 1935 the agreed price was advanced to $7.2 million, and RFC agreed to loan that amount to Associated Railways Company, a creation of North Western, Burlington, Great Western, Milwaukee, Rock Island, Great Northern, Illinois Central, and Soo Line; George W. Hand of Chicago & North Western was to act as president. "The plan seems an equitable solution of an unhealthy railroad situation in a particular territory," beamed RFC's Jesse Jones. In the end, he said, the public would enjoy service better "than can possibly be furnished by an impoverished road." In September Associated Railways rolled out its plan—previously approved by RFC, of course—and placed it before the ICC. C&NW would take 140 miles of bits and pieces and with Illinois Central jointly the 99-mile main line from Hopkins to Albert Lea; Burlington would assume the line from Tracy through Oskaloosa to Peoria, 197 miles; Milwaukee or Chicago Great Western would accept 429 miles of route including Mason City to Albia; Rock Island claimed 92 miles and with C&NW jointly 21 miles from Northwood to Mason City; Great Northern was interested only in the 47 miles from Hanley Falls to Marietta. Associated would either retain M&StL's Minneapolis terminals or convey them to a consortium of roads serving that city in a form similar to that of Minnesota Transfer. Under the plan, if adopted, 507 miles of route would be abandoned—168 in South Dakota, 55 in Minnesota, 284 in Iowa, but none in Illinois. Included on the junker's list was the entire line from Albert Lea through Fort Dodge to Angus.[5]

The response to all of this among the several parties interested in M&StL's welfare varied from shock and

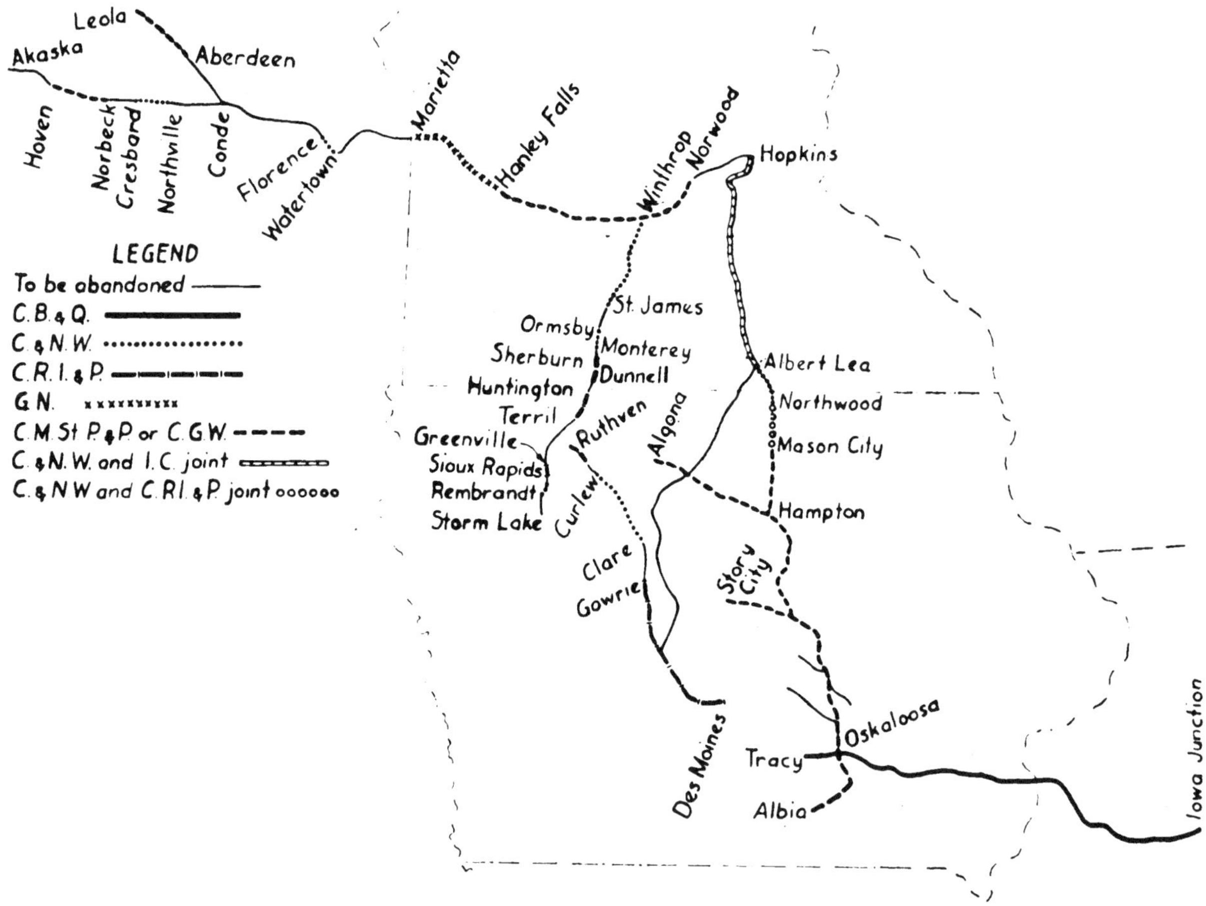

Map 16.1. Under Associated Railway's plan, 507 miles of M&StL routes would be abandoned. Author's collection.

anger to fear and disorientation. Frank M. Tompkins, long the company's secretary in New York with ties back to Edwin Hawley, wept when told of the road's possible dismemberment. The positions taken by the Reorganization Committee were not nearly as clear-cut; in fact, they were bewildering. In September 1934, F. J. Lisman, chairman, had told Ralph Budd that he supported "piece meal disposition of M&StL," but two months later the committee itself contended that the road would receive better terms if it was reorganized and then sold. Labor organizations did not equivocate. A. L. Gardner, general chairman of M&StL's telegraphers, raised the ugly specter of M&StL employees' standing in "bread lines" should Associated prevail. "It is entirely wrong to confiscate the property and leave numerous communities without any rail service and turn a couple of thousand employees out of their jobs," Gardner exploded. A mass meeting to acquaint the public with the Associated Railways proposal was held in the Community Hall at Sully on September 25; business interests and others from the Iowa towns of Newton, Lynnville, Taintor, Kilduff, New Sharon, Sully, and Grinnell were represented. Gardner engineered similar meetings at Akaska, Conde, Humboldt, Britt, Luverne, Madison, Excelsior, and Minneapolis, among other places. Politicians, too, were energized. The Iowa legislature passed a resolution protesting dismemberment, and in the United States Senate, South Dakota's rustic conservative Democrat William J. Bulow introduced a resolution to direct both the Interstate Commerce Commission and the Reconstruction Finance Corporation to defer any approval of sale, reorganization, or dismemberment for one year, to the end that the road should finally be reorganized "in a manner fair and equitable to all concerned."[6]

It is unlikely that Lucian Sprague ever sided with any policy designed to dismantle M&StL; rather he labored as diplomatically as he could—restricted, of course, by his responsibilities as co-receiver—to bring opinion around to reorganization of M&StL as a stand-alone property. He was aided mightily in this by influential Walter W. Colpitts of Coverdale & Colpitts, advisers to the Reorganization Committee, and even by the bright, volatile, but terribly impolitic Philip J. Roosevelt, who back in 1933 had concluded that M&StL be scrapped. Now, many months later, Roosevelt thought M&StL was "as good a little single-track road as you are likely to find." Sprague also won over M&StL employees. Just days after his appointment as co-receiver, Sprague had ordered out an inspection train and personally took the throttle of spritely Ten-wheeler 229 leaving Waseca. After the operator at Otisco reported that the train was by that station, the dispatcher at Cedar Lake quickly tapped out an order for the operator at New Richland, six miles distant, to "throw the board" (change the train order signal to red) against the onrushing special and then to copy a message for the conductor and engineer sternly telling them that their train was running too fast and that from now on they were to "observe time table speed." When the train screeched to a stop, Superintendent R. E. Ryan burst into the office, grabbed copies of the message from a very nervous young telegrapher, and then walked out to make delivery to the conductor and engine crew. Sprague read the message, said he did not know they had been going that fast, grinned, and threw the message out the window. This story, or versions of it, got out quickly to rank-and-file employees, who breathed easier, seeing Sprague as one of their own kind.[7]

Sprague recognized that he also had to win the support of other important constituents—fellow managers within the company and within the industry, on-line communities, shippers, opinion makers, and politicians. He was active on several fronts simultaneously. In John W. Devins, Sprague found a crusty but competent general manager. Devins had started with M&StL in 1912 and had worked in office and yard capacities before being named trainmaster, superintendent, and then acting general manager. Sprague, in fact, retained most M&StL managers, but he did bring in Herbert W. Ward from the Omaha to head up the Traffic Department (sales) and William L. Trout, whom he had known at Uintah, as general master mechanic. Sprague understood that Ward's sales force would have to do the "heavy lifting" in seeking and retaining traffic, but promised that he would spend at least one-third of his time drumming up business for the road. And he was good at it. John W. Barriger recalled Sprague as a person with "lots of charisma, a good salesman." Sprague also was good with the public, and in Barriger's estimation, the "public made him look good." Indeed, Sprague was the toast of the town at Aberdeen, New Ulm, Des Moines, and other locations as he made his way around the system.[8]

Sprague's task, however, was freighted with difficulty. He had to get disparate forces singing M&StL's song. To do that he had to demonstrate that M&StL traffic was increasing in a way that implied future profit as a stand-alone entity; he had to assure every employee and every manager that their jobs were secure in the short term and in the long run; he had to convince every community that M&StL had a particular commitment to that place; and at the same time he had to wring more efficiency out of the operation. It was not possible to do it all at once—or ever. Sprague and Trout dreamed of modern motive power (2-6-6-4s) that would expedite tonnage over the Peoria Gateway and at the same time eliminate helper districts and reduce labor expense, but requisite capital was nowhere to be had; nor was there money adequate to quickly elevate Cooper's ratings on all main-line bridges to support such heavy machines. M&StL would have to make do with existing power—shopped only by cash infusions derived from junking 43 locomotives, 1,568 freight cars, and 39 passenger cars in 1935–36—and undertake only routine improvements to its track and structures. Sprague, however, proved to be an adept cheerleader—he was, frankly, full of himself—and his abiding self-assurance translated rapidly into improved morale among the company's diverse constituencies, which increasingly bowed their backs to save M&StL—"Maimed & Still Limping," as some called it, while others said that its trains were regular only in arriving at "Midnight & Still Later" and that its existence was "Miserable & Still Limping," or would be merely one of "Misery & Short Life," and old hands joyfully recalled M&StL's running "little man" character and chortled that M&StL was indeed the "Road that Runs—for Coal and Water."

Even as they laughed and poked fun at the old road, they also came to defend it, taking an increasingly proprietary interest. It was "their" railroad. Lucian Sprague was a most adroit performer in mobilizing such sentiments.[9]

Sprague recognized the crucial importance of generating support for an independent M&StL from every on-line community, but he quickly concluded that most available money would have to be pumped into the Minneapolis–Peoria main line if the road was to have any chance of survival; that meant cash-starved M&StL would have to take an extremely dry-eyed look at all of its other lines, measuring them against their profitability vis-à-vis required improvements and, candidly, against their scrap value. Sprague also may have anticipated the very significant abandonment proposals made by Associated and wished to make a preemptive strike, showing that he, too, could make hard choices, but that his were far less draconian. And certainly the growing reality of vehicular competition eating away at local revenues was a factor in his calculations.[10]

Abandonment always was larded with great emotion, yet it was not the jolting issue that it had been earlier. The nation's railroad network had been shrinking since 1916; abandoned mileage hit 1,183 in 1918, for example, and 6,353 for the five-year period 1930–34. The Interstate Commerce Commission, which ruled in these matters, weighed benefits of service against the costs of providing that service (past and probable earnings); in the end it approved 87 percent of all applications for abandonment during the 1930s. It was in that environment that Sprague sought and gained permission from the district court to seek abandonment of the following five line segments, all in Iowa, aggregating 125.7 miles.

Kalo Junction to Angus	44.0 miles
Algona to Corwith	15.1 miles
Newburg to Van Cleve	16.1 miles
Grinnell & Montezuma Junction to Montezuma	13.6 miles
Spencer to Storm Lake	36.9 miles

The ICC scheduled hearings on each application.[11]

Meanwhile, competitive pressures eased not one bit. In fact, the depressed economy likely worked to increase them. In 1930 paving was completed from Des Moines through Dallas Center to Perry, and across the state of Iowa a thousand miles of concrete was laid in that season alone. For the first time it was possible to travel from Des Moines to every one of the state's ninety-nine county seats on improved road. By 1938 over 5,000 miles of Iowa highways would be paved and more than 35,000 miles of roadway graveled. In Minnesota, 250 miles were paved in 1931, including one leg serving Gaylord, Winthrop, and New Ulm. The Federal Highway Act of 1934 only increased such construction. And even earlier, in 1930, the nation had boasted 600,000 miles of surfaced highway, nearly three times the total rail mileage; investment in highways and motor vehicles was $35 billion, $10 billion greater than in rail.[12]

Americans clung wistfully to their automobiles—the depression notwithstanding. In 1931 the fifty millionth automobile rolled off an American assembly line; five years later auto companies were selling more cars than in any previous year save 1928 and 1929. Six-passenger Studebaker cruising sedans were available at Fort Dodge for $665; $510 would fetch a Ford V-8 sedan at Winthrop; and, Hudson 6 Touring Broughams could be had at Grinnell for $925. "Mr. & Mrs. R. L. Teslow of Spencer drove to Minneapolis to visit Mrs. Teslow's mother, and W. H. Van Sickle and daughter left Greenville by auto to pick up and return relatives from Kewanee, Illinois," reported the *Spencer News-Herald* for July 2, 1931. It was all too typical; travelers were forsaking rails even for longer-distance trips.[13]

Jitneys—buses—too were making deep inroads into passenger traffic. In 1927, 85,163 motor buses were employed over 635,609 route miles carrying 2.525 billion passengers. Buses could and did offer frequent and flexible service, and in territory offering light traffic were able to provide a better public utility at a lower cost than railroads. For example, by 1933 Northland Greyhound advertised twice-daily departures on a route serving the Minnesota towns of Gaylord, Winthrop, Fairfax, and Redwood Falls—over a publicly owned and maintained highway that paralleled M&StL, on faster schedules, and with tariffs of only 2 cents per mile.[14]

In 1933 the domestic population was about two-thirds greater than it had been in 1900, but in that depression year intercity travel per capita was approximately 800 percent greater than in 1900. Railroads hauled a greatly diminished portion of those miles. The decline was demonstrable across M&StL's system, but no more dramatically than in Illinois between Monmouth and Peoria, as table 16.1 shows. Collapse of business on the Peoria line can be explained not by reduced train miles, which were constant, but only by the depressed economy, and even more by desertion of passengers to autos and buses.[15]

More threatening to railroads by far was the growing presence of trucking in the fabric of American transportation, particularly in short-distance haulage and in the movement of livestock, milk, household furniture, and less-than-carload freight (LCL). One-fifth of all livestock entering Kansas City was delivered by truck; one-fourth of Omaha receipts arrived that way. At South St. Paul, one-fourth came by truck in 1930, up from only 2 percent in 1921, but in 1932 more than one-third were truck-delivered. The trend was irreversible. For M&StL, livestock tonnage slumped from 207,110 in 1930 to 52,306 in 1936; LCL dropped from 166,619 to 69,373, both indexes reflecting mostly modal competition.[16]

Table 16.1. Passenger tickets and revenue along the Peoria Line, 1929–33

*Station**	*Tickets 1929*	*Revenue 1929*	*Tickets 1933*	*Revenue 1933*
Peoria	3,643	$6,138	413	$818
Farmington	2,474	$1,161	196	$148
Middle Grove	1,154	$ 465	78	$ 33
London Mills	1,718	$ 993	187	$108
Abingdon	2,430	$1,826	245	$234
Berwick	1,415	$ 698	97	$ 84
Monmouth	3,238	$3,601	322	$497

**All these stations in Illinois.*

All those associated with M&StL must have felt that the gods were everlastingly against the road. Even the weather proved contrary—contrary in the extreme. Drought hit Iowa in 1930, South Dakota in 1931 and 1933, both states and much of Minnesota in 1934 and 1936. Dirt storms blotting out the sun swept over western Minnesota during the spring of 1931 but were nothing compared to the awful "black blizzard" in South Dakota on Armistice Day 1933. "Star Dust" and "Stormy Weather," popular tunes of the time, took on a warped meaning across much of the upper Midwest and abroad the Great Plains. "We had storm windows," recalled one South Dakota housewife, but "the dust was so thick on the bedspread you couldn't tell what color it was." The wife of the lumberman at Revillo remained watchful every Monday—fearful that a dust storm would roll out of western skies before she could retrieve her washing from the outdoor clothesline. In 1934 the *Winthrop News* observed that "April showers this year have been showers of dust instead of the usual liberal precipitation at the hands of old Jupiter." Drought was an open invitation to grasshoppers, which mowed brazenly through crops, deleafed trees and bushes, and even devoured corks out of bottles. "They ate everything that had survived the drought," reported one distraught farmer near Conde. Chinch bugs and seventeen-year locusts plagued southeast Iowa around Oakville, and in 1934 no water ran in Minnesota's Cannon River at Waterville. Forage crops and grain withered in brutal heat.[17]

As often happened, sizzling summers were followed by frigid winters. That of 1935–36 was a corker. A former employee died along the track near Oskaloosa during a Christmas Eve snowstorm, and a reading of 19 degrees below zero a few nights later at Spencer was the lowest in the state. It was merely a prelude. January proved nasty, cold, and snowy. A storm late in the month plugged the Southwestern. Peterson's Cut, long, shallow, and on a curve southwest of Raleigh, was level full; so was another long cut north of Sherburn—one laced with minor water springs that kept track in a permanent semisoft condition but in the winter put a sheet of ice over the rail beneath the snow pack. Locomotive 470 and the snow plow it was driving were off the track and buried in snow there on January 27; M&StL borrowed Rock Island's wrecking crew from Estherville, but the task of rerailing was lengthy and arduous. Nearby Monterey recorded fourteen days of below-zero temperatures in January—with minus 30 degrees the coldest. Fort

Dodge, among other places, observed the most frigid January in twenty-five years. A freight train was nearly buried in snow on a siding at Dillon and the crew gave it up, drawing fire and abandoning locomotive and train alike. In the consist was coal "for the relief of the Marshall County poor." Not far away, M&StL's section foreman at Laurel, died of a heart attack in the waiting room after clearing snow around the property.[18]

Frey, the Norse god of weather, now unleashed his full fury. Blizzards with depressing gray skies, snow, and killer winds lasted for days; clearing brought sun dogs, those silent, invincible sentinels of bone-numbing cold temperatures. As February arrived, a resident of Storm Lake claimed to have seen a bluebird, a sure sign of spring, but if so the bird was a false prophet. A three-day storm, "the worst in years," pasted Storm Lake, all of northwest Iowa, and much of the Midwest during the first week of the month. Schools at Greenville and Cornell, among other places, were closed and would stay closed because of snow and a shortage of fuel. Coal was rationed at Spencer; Storm Lake even imposed a "fuel embargo." Another storm hit before the line from Spencer could be cleared. Estherville authorities pleaded with M&StL for use of the company's coal reserve, and the road issued all that could be spared. Company coal also was released at Rembrandt. Conditions were no better elsewhere around the system. Huge drifts near Arlington blocked the route west of Hopkins; the agent at Klossner reported a drift three thousand feet wide and up to eight feet deep covering the track south of that village on the Southwestern. Two locomotives and a plow on the first train up the Laurel Branch in three weeks became entrapped; fierce winds shut down the main line at Eldora; Roland (on the Story City Branch) saw no M&StL train for nearly two weeks because of a fourteen-foot drift over the track east of that town; and church services at Union, Liscomb, and Albion, among other places, were cancelled in order to conserve fuel. The headline of the *Des Moines Register* for February 9 was comprehensive: "ALL IOWA PARALYZED IN STORM." Hampton, Mason City, and Fort Dodge were among many Iowa communities without rail service for days. Marshalltown joined a long list of cities and towns reporting serious shortages of eggs, milk, and coal; Marshalltown's Lennox Furnace Company shut down, giving its coal supply to Hotel Tallcorn. William Penn College at Oskaloosa closed for lack of fuel, and public buildings were opened in many communities for families unable to heat their homes. In South Dakota, farmers in the Watertown area burned hay and even fence posts as fuel.[19]

Digging out was slow, painful, expensive, and continuous. A locomotive driving a plow through packed drifts north of Langdon broke drive rods; the badly disabled and thoroughly entrapped engine blocked all attempts to clear the Southwestern. Near Chapin, a broken rail derailed a caboose carrying snow shovelers, injuring fourteen men. Meanwhile, the fuel crisis deepened. Guards were posted in the yards at Marshalltown to protect company coal, and shipments bottled up there because of line blockage. Families moved in with neighbors at Kanawha, on the Algona Branch, in order to conserve fuel, and local authorities implored M&StL to open the line and move coal stranded at Hampton. The Commercial Club at Forest City organized a crew of 150 shovelers to help clear drifts near Leland so that fuel could be brought in from Albert Lea. Managers of the elevator and lumber yard at Moorland donated their coal supplies to the area's needy; local farmers burned corn in lieu of coal. Other farmers near Rolfe cut down trees in their groves and picked corncobs out of pigpens for fuel. The public library at Marshalltown locked its doors for lack of coal, and the Iowa Liquor Commission announced that all stores in the state would open for only six hours each work day until the fuel shortage ended. At Spencer, coal billed to Greenville and Cornell idled in the yard, finally delivered to those villages by bobsled. The Spencer–Storm Lake line remained utterly snowbound, crews and equipment committed elsewhere, but M&StL customers at Storm Lake were switched occasionally when Illinois Central was able to substitute. By February 15, service was restored between Fort Dodge and Des Moines, and the line from Fort Dodge to Spencer had been opened. Plover was among other stations between Fort Dodge and Spencer that had seen only two freight trains and no passenger service since February 3. But all efforts

Figure 16.1. Digging out near Dunnel, Minnesota, on the Southwestern—a scene repeated endlessly in most of M&StL's territory during February 1936. M&StL photograph, author's collection.

to free the Southwestern failed; the disabled locomotive remained marooned between Langdon and Terril. Snowfall ebbed, but vicious winds drove snow into cuts newly cleaned. M&StL's Minneapolis–Des Moines route was open for one day and then blown shut again. *A Mid-Summer's Dream* played at the Spencer Theater, taunting natives who may have smiled grimly at the irony. By February 20 the line from Fort Dodge to Spencer was open again, and a plow inched down toward Storm Lake, only to be rebuffed short of Rembrandt and forced to retreat to Spencer in the face of yet another blizzard. It was no better in South Dakota, where many communities remained isolated; Watertown recorded below-zero temperatures for thirty-seven consecutive days.[20]

Eventually, however, winter was forced to retreat. Iowa reported nearly normal temperatures late in February; the worst cold wave in 117 years had ended. The Newton Branch, embargoed by snow for three weeks, was opened on February 20. Three days later M&StL marshaled equipment and crews—two engines and a plow—for another attempt to free the long-marooned double-headed plow train on the Van Cleve Branch. This generated considerable interest at Laurel, where a Sunday gathering watched the campaign west of town and, the mission at last successful, the curious but victorious return train—four locomotives, two cabooses, a plow in front and another trailing. Schools at Newburg reopened after three weeks, at Searsboro and Gilman after four weeks. "There she comes," exclaimed an old codger at Latimer when the plow train arrived there with highly prized coal incident to clearing the Algona Branch. The Fort Dodge–Spencer artery, closed again, was reopened on

March 2, and in the next several days M&StL organized an all-out assault on the Southwestern, where no through trains had been seen since February 3. On March 3 a double-headed plow train burst through stubborn snow barriers to reach Rembrandt, where the town's residents turned out en masse to see the first train in exactly a month. The plow train entered Storm Lake that evening, turned the next day, and then headed back to Spencer and on to extricate the entrapped locomotive north of Langdon. That was accomplished on March 7. The next day, locomotives 470 and 473 coupled, with 405 trailing as the "pull out engine," left Winthrop with a borrowed rotary plow, and moved slowly southward. (M&StL's venerable X-1 was unavailable, a victim of recent easy winters that likely seduced management into ignoring maintenance and overhaul. It was now terminally infirm, already written off the books, and soon headed for the scrap yard.) M&StL hired local men to break the ice crust on a twenty-three-foot-high drift in the Haakon Evjen cut near LaSalle—a successful strategy, as it turned out. At St. James curious residents gathered to see the first M&StL train in over a month, but they became mesmerized by the smoke-belching, roaring rotary and failed to realize until too late that it was lofting skyward snow chunks and ice missiles that soon would rain down upon them without mercy. Thirty-eight miles down the line, the Estherville Chamber of Commerce arranged to have the local high school band on hand to greet the train when it shambled into that community on March 10. The next evening, the rotary broke through to Spencer, and the Winthrop–Storm Lake line was finally open to service. No fewer than six locomotives and crews had earned their rest in Spencer that night.[21]

The ornery winter of 1935–36 finally surrendered. It had been one for the record books. That February in Minnesota was the coldest in over one hundred years—the average temperature was zero. Total snowfall at New Ulm was 85.85 inches; by March snow averaged three feet on the level across southern Minnesota. In Iowa, the average snow across the state was 48.90 inches, up substantially from the normal 30.00 inches. "When some stripling in future years starts complaining about cold and snow," observed the *Winthrop News,* "the scornful will remind: 'You should have lived through the winter of 1936.'" At M&StL, the bill for removing mountains of snow and ice came to $117,153 (up from $25,625 in 1935), but that was only part of the story. The company lost substantial revenue when trains did not operate at all, when cars stalled in yards accumulated per diem charges, and when overtime claims mounted. Freight trains often required double heading, and passenger trains routinely featured steam in support of the GE cars. Moguls 309, 315, and 322, for example, took turns leading GE cars up the line from Fort Dodge to Spencer in February and March. Before the year was out, Sprague got court permission to scrap fifteen wedge plows beaten up by the recent winter and to build eleven new plows out of ballast cars.[22]

As winter eventually turned to spring, the Interstate Commerce Commission began to hand down decisions on M&StL's five abandonment requests. In the first of these, ICC allowed M&StL to end service on the Algona Branch for eight miles between St. Benedict and Algona, but demanded that M&StL continue to offer on-demand carload operation from Corwith to St. Benedict. The last M&StL train rumbled out of Algona on April 3, 1936. The next request, regarding the line from Spencer to Storm Lake, was more complicated. Passenger revenues on that line segment were negligible and carload business remained substantial, but out-of-pocket losses

Figure 16.2. Engines 502 and 229 stood in for the regular GE car on train 7 at Mason City, Iowa, on January 18, 1936—dramatically increasing the costs of operation of that train but absolutely necessary due to dreadful weather conditions throughout the area. The thermometer stood at a frigid 20 degrees below zero when William F. Armstrong made this photograph.

from operation were not offset by revenues accruing to the remainder of the system from traffic deriving from or destined for the line. Of immediate concern to M&StL were the many bridges that required substantial and expensive renewal, but the regulatory agency brooded about the inconvenience to on-line communities in the event of abandonment. The latter concern was partially obviated, however, when Milwaukee agreed to acquire and operate the lower portion of the route in order to maintain rail transport to Truesdale and Rembrandt. That tipped the scale. The final M&StL train steamed up the line to Spencer on Saturday, April 25; the first Milwaukee train pulled into Rembrandt on the April 30 and turned on a newly installed wye. The American Legion post purchased the depot at Sioux Rapids, a Fort Dodge firm salvaged the bridges, and Hyman-Michaels of Chicago dismantled the track—all of it except two miles for Rock Island to use to reach Greenville from its Gowrie–Sibley branch, an arrangement that lasted only into 1938, and then that track, too, disappeared. Thus perished Southwestern's ultima Thule and what might have been Edwin Hawley's dream of reaching Omaha or even Kansas City.[23]

Other cases were more straightforward. The "Mud Line," the original main line from Fort Dodge to Angus, fell next—at least that part of it from Otho to Berkeley, thirty-six miles. Coal mines near Otho and Ogden long since had played out, and M&StL's remaining customers consisted mostly of grain elevators, plus a few bulk-oil stations and coal yards. Out-of-pocket loss had been incurred every year since 1929. The final through train passed over spindly rails on May 22, although "call-basis" service from Kalo Junction to Otho obtained into 1937, and from Angus to Berkeley into 1938 before those short stubs also were scrapped. Next came the old Grinnell and Montezuma, or "G&M," which had been promoted back in 1875 by Josiah B. Grinnell and ever since had provided trains that bumped back and forth between Grinnell and Montezuma over a 13.6-mile branch. Carloads dropped to a mere 350 in 1934, 53 of which contained, ironically, highway construction material. Businessmen and others at Montezuma organized in opposition to abandonment, but to no avail. The last train to that village—dubbed the "Monte Flyer" by local wags—ambled over the branch on August 1 at about fifteen miles per hour, only a caboose bobbing along behind Mogul 332. A small crowd gathered in respect at Montezuma; aboard the caboose on the return leg was the wife of the conductor, riding on a pass, and two ticket holders, one of them Mayo Harris, who had ridden the first train into Montezuma sixty-one years earlier. The ICC, however, turned back M&StL's request to tear out the Van Cleve Branch. Nevertheless, by the end of 1936 M&StL's receivers could report that 94.5 miles of uncompensatory route had been excised.[24]

These several abandonments put a hard edge on already emotionally charged hearings staged by the ICC regarding Associated Railways and its campaign to dismember M&StL. Indeed, the Associated Railways proposal was a vitally important case for any number of constituencies, pitting an old order, so to speak, against a new order. The old order celebrated the historic importance of railroads in opening up the country and in making it productive. "There is but one point in the state [Iowa] that is fourteen miles from a railroad line," the *Des Moines Leader* had bragged in 1896. This classic example of Midwestern boosterism then was overlaid with successive coats of prairie populism, legitimate claims of symbiotic relationships between railroads and their service areas, the needs and desires of labor, and an understandable fear of change. Producers and carriers were "intimately and inseparably bound together" Iowa's Railroad Commission exclaimed at one point. "The people and stockholders are partners in the ownership of the road; in a measure that railway belongs to the public." It was an ancient logic that in the mid-1930s had a profound resonance with many M&StL advocates in their campaign against Associated. And, chimed in labor, "cutthroat competition" as practiced by contemporary industry and reflected in the Associated case was an evil that ought to be curbed; social welfare should not be ignored. Moreover, said the Railway Labor Executives' Association, "consolidation . . . is contrary to progress." And there was the obvious and crucial connection between, on the one hand, main roads and principal arteries, and, on the other hand, short-line railroads and branches that originated or delivered nearly 50 percent of transcontinental traffic. The health of one, the argument went, was the health of the other.[25]

The new order did not categorically reject the old, but it did take positions contrary to that order. The industry suffered from overinvestment, had too much capacity, and, as Pennsylvania's W. W. Atterbury said, "needless multiplicity of routings," all of which reflected "a public policy for years that had needlessly enforced excessive and wasteful competition." Many of the country's roads could not maintain themselves alone, went the notion, although some of their lines might find application as parts of larger systems. In Washington, the recently appointed federal coordinator of transportation, Joseph B. Eastman, reflecting the views of the Roosevelt administration, was prepared to encourage amalgamation and unification in specific local situations. Burlington's Ralph Budd would go further. He recommended folding the country's several hundred operating roads into about twenty in a way that would "eliminate a tremendous amount of overhead organization, would enable the traffic to be concentrated on the most favorable routes, using the best parts of the lines as they now exist, and would automatically bring about the most desirable types of coordination of terminals, coordinated under a few strong ownerships." What about labor's interests? "Economies in railroad operation are bound, in large part, to be labor-saving economies," admitted Joseph Eastman, but it would be "cruel and inhuman to discard faithful employees like worn-out crossties." Thus, said Eastman vaguely, it was essential to "work out a program which will afford reasonable protection to labor without stifling progress." Associated Railways was a microcosm of the new order—praised by supporters, condemned by critics, but studied assiduously by both.[26]

Hearings began in Minneapolis on April 6, 1936. Chicago Great Western dropped out of Associated's plan, its president saying that Great Western did not "care to be a party to depriving . . . communities of services and facilities which they now enjoy," and announced its opposition to Associated, while Wabash reminded those present that it merely wanted to protect the Albia gateway if Associated's plan was accepted. RFC's John W. Barriger III argued that M&StL had to "eat itself up" because of its palpably thin traffic density—probably the thinnest in the United States, he opined, without giving any evidence for that view—and he presented wide-ranging testimony to demonstrate that leaving M&StL as a stand-alone property was hopeless. Challenged as to his credentials by an opposing attorney, Barriger was asked if he had ever managed or operated a railroad. "No," he replied, then added a bit of levity: "I never laid an egg either, but I can tell a good one from a bad one." George W. Hand, Associated's president, asserted that his plan was the only one that would permit continued operation of any significant part of M&StL. As to employees, Hand said rather indefinitely that the six railroads making up Associated would retain as many of them as possible. Illinois Central, which planned to utilize M&StL's Albert Lea–Hopkins leg with Chicago & North Western, said it would be happy to take over M&StL's Minneapolis freight house and participate with five other Twin Cities carriers in joint ownership of M&StL's Minneapolis terminals and its line from the milling district through Cedar Lake to Hopkins. Illinois Central had no interest in the Cedar Lake shops, however, and neither did any other road; nor was there interest in shops elsewhere.[27]

The prospect of dismemberment, significant abandonment of line, and termination of service to numerous communities, and the very live prospect of serious job loss, had the effect of energizing disparate groups to a common defense. South Dakota Republican (and former M&StL passenger conductor) Fred H. Hildebrandt of Watertown became chairman of an unofficial group of congressmen from Iowa, Illinois, Minnesota, and South Dakota who opposed dismemberment, while F. K. Gage, an attorney and prominent civic leader from Fairfax, Minnesota, headed up what was called the M&StL Executive Defense Committee, which soon sought money to secure legal representation and to mount a public relations campaign. The committee thought this would require $50,000, a daunting figure in view of the depressed economy. Minneapolis businessmen coughed up $1,500, contract employees and company officers chipped in, and so did communities; Marshalltown, for example, promised $2,000. Tiny Callender contributed $100.

Farmers from around that village offered cash or, more likely, chickens, eggs, corn, or seed; merchants assessed themselves $5.00 each, but most turned over groceries, furniture, electric appliances, and even a garden plow. Farm goods and merchandise alike then was auctioned off on Callender's main street, and the resulting $100 was wired to the Defense Committee. Gage's group hired talented counsel, sent speakers on an endless round of engagements all over the system, and churned out a wave of news stories calculated to show M&StL in a positive light, to demonstrate how dismemberment would harm communities and individuals, and to mobilize public opinion against Associated Railways. M&StL itself entered the public relations fray, boasting of improved earnings, growing customer satisfaction, and physical betterments, and showing L. C. Sprague as a "can-do" manager. W. F. Lewis, himself a member of the Executive Defense Committee and head of M&StL labor organizations opposing Associated, echoed company claims. Newspapers picked up the theme. The *Minneapolis Star* editorialized that "given a little more time, M&StL could be profitably reorganized and taken out of receivership." At Madison, the *Independent Press* urged immediate action. "Now is the time to act. There is yet time to save the road." A mass meeting of M&StL employees at the Radisson Hotel in Minneapolis elicited support from employees, who pledged financial aid for legal counsel and promised to lobby customers and politicians. A special train chartered by supporters of the company passed over the Albert Lea–Fort Dodge leg, which Associated planned to abandon, in a calculated effort to mobilize opposition on that part of the system. Iowa's Governor Clyde L. Herring smelled something foul in RFC's willingness to finance Associated's plan "to disarrange our transportation system" and declared his opposition to carving up M&StL. "The M&StL plan has many of the earmarks of an experiment," Herring complained. "We object to being the subject of that test."[28]

M&StL advocates won a temporary delay in further ICC hearings, and in May 1936 attention then focused on Washington, where Minnesota Senator Elmer A. Benson (Farmer-Labor) had succeeded in getting the Senate to establish a subcommittee of the Committee on Interstate Commerce for the purpose of investigating M&StL's possible dismemberment. In fact, it was a public forum for M&StL partisans, chaired by Minnesota's Henrik Shipstead (Farmer-Labor), with William H. Dieterich (Democrat-Illinois), Harry S. Truman (Democrat-Missouri), and Benson as fellow members (Louis Murphy, Democrat-Iowa, sat in on most sessions and was an active participant). The tall, silver-haired Shipstead, a former dentist, purposefully and skillfully focused on only a few themes:

1. M&StL was reviving and needed only more time to reorganize.
2. Associated's plan would put 2,600 of M&StL's 3,200 employees on relief.
3. Forty-eight communities in Iowa, South Dakota, and Minnesota would be isolated and without rail service if Associated's plan were approved—and Associated would surely seek even more abandonments later on.
4. RFC, an agency of the government set up for the purpose of economic reconstruction, was duplicitous in sponsoring dismemberment of M&StL—perfectly willing to loan money to Associated to carve up M&StL but unwilling to loan money to M&StL to effect its own reorganization plan.[29]

Shipstead called on both sides to provide testimony, but proponents of M&StL's independence outnumbered opponents by a ratio of 14 to 1. Lucian Sprague proved to be a splendid witness. Chest out, brimming with confidence, eyes twinkling mischievously under bushy dark eyebrows, Sprague said, "I certainly do believe that" when asked by Senator Shipstead if he thought M&StL could be operated as one system "under normal conditions and a proper management." New York banker Philip Roosevelt, President Franklin Roosevelt's distant cousin, scathingly indicted the Roosevelt administration in a mix of righteous snarl and biting scorn, calling RFC's denial of loans to M&StL and sponsorship of Associated's plan to bury the road tantamount to "abetting a robbery" of M&StL owners. Shipstead was indignant at some of what he heard from banker Roosevelt. The

RFC, he huffed in an interview with the *Minneapolis Tribune,* had been created "for the purpose of lending funds to distressed industry to help industry carry on through the depression and keep men employed." But RFC's dismemberment plan for M&StL, Shipstead growled, was "a perversion of that policy." In Minneapolis, the *Tribune*'s headline for May 22 was bald: "RFC BLOCKS M&STL REORGANIZATION." Jesse Jones, RFC's formidable chairman, burning with rage at what Philip Roosevelt had said and at the way he had said it, continued to back Associated's plan, saying: "The country is overstocked with railroads now; it would be better if there were fewer." But he did allow, when Shipstead pressed him, that he would "look at any bondholders' reorganization plan . . . if reasonable." When the subcommittee wrapped up its work at the end of May, M&StL advocates could claim a moral victory. They had put the RFC on the defensive, and they had scored a public relations success. But the struggle was hardly over.[30]

Philip J. Roosevelt took up the challenge of laying a new reorganization plan before the RFC, Jesse Jones rejected it, and Roosevelt sent forth another volley—both Roosevelt and Jones handing copies of letters and documents to the press in obvious and vigorous attempts to sway public opinion—while Senator Shipstead urged both men to find middle ground. *Time* was bemused by Roosevelt's "resilient scheme" and by the caustic and belligerent repartee of both Roosevelt and Jones, but in fact Jones and RFC had been backed into a defensive posture.[31]

Meanwhile, ICC hearings on Associated's dismemberment plan resumed in Minneapolis and then moved out to Fort Dodge, Newton, Grinnell, Albert Lea, Spencer, St. James, Aberdeen, Selby (off-line, near Akaska), and Watertown, where testimony would be taken as to abandonment of line segments proposed by Associated. A predictable pattern of testimony ensued: except for the Hopkins–Albia line, all other M&StL routes would be abandoned or reduced to branches or stubs that the Associated roads eventually would kill; business at communities devoid of rail transport would wither and die, with the communities themselves perishing in time; precious jobs would be squandered; M&StL was coming back, it was a "going concern" and needed only more time to be fully reinvigorated; no, M&StL was a hopeless case, ill maintained, unable to go it alone, and the only reasonable prescription was euthanasia for the company and parceling out of its few valuable parts to stronger concerns. The Iowa hearings were volatile, which was understandable given that Iowa would shoulder the brunt of Associated's abandonments. The circumstance of Callender, one of the communities that would be bereft of rail service should Associated have its way, was typical. Mayor Clifford K. Ferguson (also M&StL's station agent) bluntly told the ICC that loss of the railroad would be "disastrous" to business in his town. Ferguson's assessment was corroborated by the town's banker and owners of local elevators and other businesses. Larger places, too—Aberdeen, Albert Lea, Fort Dodge, and Watertown—would see their status as trade centers erode under Associated's scheme. Peoria weighed in, pointing to the importance of the Peoria Gateway, and boldly asked the ICC to dismiss the Associated plan if M&StL could be shown to have a chance of survival as a stand-alone company. Final hearings were held late in July at Minneapolis. "The committee is not out of the woods yet," noted F. K. Gage of Fairfax. He was correct. There was no reason to breathe easier, although Jesse Jones did announce that a thoroughly competent engineer would be retained by RFC to render an unemotional independent study of M&StL's physical condition—apparently in response to Philip Roosevelt's amended and revised reorganization proposal, Shipstead's pressure, contradictory testimony at both the Senate and the ICC hearings as to M&StL's physical shape, and the state of Iowa's determination to appeal any Associated victory to the Supreme Court. And public opinion had moved in M&StL's favor. "When it is pointed out, as Harry Hopkins did at the mayor's convention in Washington, that the key to recovery is the problem to providing steady employment to workers," said the *Minneapolis Star,* "it would seem that the best social ends, as well as practical ends, would be served by keeping the M&StL intact and allowing it to continue operations." All parties filed final briefs that fall, and the hearing officer began the lengthy task of preparing a recommendation for the ICC to consider.[32]

Considerable heat and even a bit of light had been generated at the ICC hearings, but none of it compared to the wrath of the weather god Frey that dreadful summer of 1936. From Peoria to Leola a blazing sun beat the crust of the topsoil, pounding the ground's surface and beating it into powder; everywhere in the distance danced devilish and mocking heat mirages. "You'll Never Hear Us Complain About a Hot Summer Again," had been the caption over a cartoon in the *Des Moines Register* of February 11 showing a fierce-looking and mean-spirited Old Man Winter running off with the state's coal pile and grocery reserve. And the heavy snow cover provided during the winter of 1935–36 had seemed to drive off the moisture deficiency of several years. So thought prognosticators. "There was water everywhere" that spring, recalled one man near Rolfe. Then, late in March, most of M&StL's western Iowa service area was ripped by tornadoes, hail, and even a dusting of Oklahoma topsoil. Drought returned with a vengeance. In central South Dakota west of Watertown, less than nine inches of moisture fell in all of 1936—about half of normal. Eggs were fried on a sidewalk at Aberdeen when the temperature hit 115 degrees; Aberdeen had registered a temperature minus 50 degrees the previous winter. M&StL's entire service area was blistered in July, with fiery temperatures above 100 degrees for over a week; the *Register*'s cartoonist had ample reason to change his mind about hot summers. By mid-July forty-four Iowans had succumbed to heatstroke, but more than that had perished in the Twin Cities alone. Terrible hail storms knocked out crops around Langdon and Spencer, and grasshoppers were thick at Ayrshire and Curlew. Sweet corn grown near Lafayette, Gibbon, and Gaylord under contract for Minnesota Valley Canning failed, and potato fields west of Arlington were plowed under. Northwest Iowa harvested about half a corn crop and was thankful for that.[33]

The winter of 1936–37 gave early indication of repeating that of 1935–36. Mogul 309 again found itself assisting the regularly assigned GE car on the Fort Dodge–Winthrop assignment, turning at Spencer when the line to the north was blocked, but winter's wrath was mostly directed to South Dakota, where the line to Akaska often was plugged. Aberdeen received an amazing 110 inches of snow in the 1936–37 season. But over the system at large, the winter of 1936–37 fortunately proved less spectacular than its immediate predecessor.[34]

Where did M&StL stand after the terrible trials of the mid-1930s? There was no clear picture. Sprague's energetic and enthusiastic persona had shrewdly and skillfully won over and had certainly pumped energy into the spirits of company employees at all levels; so, too, had fear and the survival instinct sent adrenaline pouring through their bodies. Physically the company was in better shape. The number of cross ties installed in 1936 reached 350,788, compared to 245,186 in 1935 and up from 192,390 in 1934; several main-line bridges also had been renewed and strengthened. The rolling stock inventory remained much the same, although sixty-five new hopper cars had been added, several locomotives had been shopped, and the road also had found money to purchase a used seven-passenger La Salle automobile for executive use. And despite ugly weather conditions that escalated the costs of operation and reduced agricultural production, M&StL increased its revenue movement by 853,827 tons in 1936 over 1935 and boosted its net operating revenue to $1,841,010 from $847,980 the previous year. It paid its bills on a timely basis and by now had cancelled pay reductions ordered in 1933. Nevertheless, the "Misery & Short Life" moniker remained tightly clamped around its neck, and considerable pessimism surrounded not only M&StL but the industry at large. Several neighbors, including Milwaukee, North Western, Rock Island, and Great Western, were in Chapter 77 proceedings or soon would be, and Great Northern and Northern Pacific avoided the courts only through RFC loans or juicy dividends paid by jointly owned and relatively prosperous Chicago, Burlington & Quincy. "Many adverse forces operating against the rejuvenation of the railroads are chronic—they cannot be cured," asserted railroad-focused Poor's Publishing. "The competitive pressure against the railroads from other forms of transportation is irresistible . . . inflexibility is their [the railroads'] fatal weakness." Ultimately, Poor's concluded somberly, "Historical precedents are against the rejuvenation of a great industry which has been out-moded." Federal Coordinator of Transportation Joseph B. Eastman would not go that far, but he continued his vigorous campaign of cooperation and coordination as an essential remedy to reduce "waste and unnecessary expense . . . owing to the fact that the railroad system of the nation is in the hands of many separate and independent companies." At the same time, organized labor, with strong support from powerful politicians, urged government ownership of the nation's railroads. It was a strange chemistry into which the M&StL issue was poured. And an ugly recession within the Great Depression was about to further cloud the horizon.[35]

Chapter 17
Reason for Hope?

On the Akaska run I used to enjoy sitting on the step box on the rear platform of the single coach it handled, riding with the sway of the car as it passed over the joints, at times looking ahead toward the engine and seeing the middle of the tender as the baggage-mail car swayed to one side and the coach to the other side. It was seldom dirty back there as the speed of the train was such that dust was not disturbed to any great extent.

—Manfred J. Reitan to the author, June 20, 1973

Near the end of August 1937, the stock market experienced a shudder and business across the country showed signs of slackening. By fall the market was demoralized; prices would not bottom out until April 1938, and then only after losing about two-thirds of the gains registered since their nadir in early 1933. Business dropped over the same precipice. Industrial production fell by one-third in only nine months, showing no symptoms of recovery until May 1938. Several small railroads entered receivership in 1937, and larger ones including Erie and Soo Line followed in 1938. Mild optimism that had been creeping across the land for the last few years turned sour; the "recession" of 1937–38 was one of the sharpest short-term economic downtrends in national history.[1]

The Great Depression did not greatly alter the industrial landscape of the Minneapolis & St. Louis service area, but the face of agriculture was modified rather considerably during the 1930s. Minnesota ranked seventeenth in the value of manufactured products at the end of the decade, down from fifteenth position in 1930; Iowa ranked nineteenth, down from seventeenth. South Dakota was static at forty-third, and Illinois held onto third place. In agriculture, Iowa continued to lead the nation in the value of hogs, cattle, and corn, although the market fluctuated greatly. Farmers at the same time turned to hybrid seed corn and disease-resistant wheat, which increased productivity. They also began to plant soybeans in substantial quantity. The Des Moines Chamber of Commerce was a champion of diversification of crops to include soybeans, and in 1937 enticed M&StL to move a Soybean Exhibit Car to dozens of stations in the four-state territory. Yet despite hard times, farmers continued to embrace mechanization; wholesale purchases of farm machinery averaged $408 million annually from 1935 through 1939. And the recently established Rural Electrification Association promised to expand electrical service to farms and ranches—a development sure to further enhance productivity and improve the quality of life in rural America. In the aggregate, by 1940 American agriculture was able to produce greater quantities of food and fiber at more efficient rates than ever before—and with fewer persons needed in the process.[2]

Meanwhile, M&StL's fate remained frustratingly confused as all hands awaited a decision from the Interstate Commerce Commission on Associated Railways' plan for the road's acquisition and dismemberment. The sharp recession of 1937–38 strangely worked in M&StL's favor as renewed fear of rising unemployment and long bread lines gripped the country. In Minneapolis, Special Master in Chancery Howard

Strickland Abbott donned his topcoat and gray fedora, picked up his briefcase, and, as he had done so many times before, headed for Cedar Lake, where he pulled out a pile of documents, adjusted his pince-nez, and began to read descriptions of M&StL property long on the block. He was at it for two hours, pausing only briefly for a puff on his cigar. "I now offer for sale upon such terms and conditions designated in said final decree of foreclosure," he droned. Abbott finally finished, and looked up. "Any bids?" There were none. For that matter, there were no bidders. Only M&StL personnel were around, and they paid him no heed; by May 1937 he had been there for that performance seventeen times.[3]

In Washington, at the same time policymakers and government functionaries were under intense pressure to preserve railroad jobs all over the country—pressure that came from employees themselves, organized labor, elected officials, and commercial groups from communities large and small. Currents were mixed and swift. The Railway Labor Executives Association now even more vigorously advocated government ownership of the railroads, and ICC's chairman went so far as to float the idea of a single national railroad system. Burton K. Wheeler (Democrat-Montana), pugnacious chairman of the Senate's Interstate Commerce Committee, introduced a bill to create United States Railways, which, he hoped, would take the industry out of the hands of bankers, who, he contended, currently controlled the country's carriers. For his part, Jesse Jones at the Reconstruction Finance Corporation favored merging all roads into a few large ones—five east of the Mississippi, five west.[4]

It was in this environment that C. E. Boles of ICC's Bureau of Finance and hearing officer in the Associated case pored over data and proceeded to write his report. A tip as to his inclinations came in August 1937, when the ICC signaled a willingness to review the reorganization proposal that had been put forward in 1936 by Philip J. Roosevelt but rebuffed by RFC. Eyes brightened in Minneapolis and around the system. Then, two months later, Boles recommended to the commission in a four hundred–page document that Associated's scheme be denied, arguing that, among other things, Associated's proposal to carve up M&StL was contrary to ICC's own plan of consolidation, which would place M&StL with Illinois Central, and that M&StL's Peoria Gateway long had relieved pressure on congested Chicago. The implications of all of this sank in quickly. Soon appeared protestations by roads making up Associated Railways and complaints by certain of M&StL's security holders. But ICC took a hard line when Associated attorneys and others asked to present new information on the case. ICC said that argument had to be confined narrowly to the issue as originally presented and to the Boles report. Associated, as a consequence, could not introduce new evidence prepared by engineers employed by Jesse Jones and the RFC.[5]

That study, universally referred to as the Boatner Report, prepared late in 1936 by V. V. Boatner and A. J. Hammond of Chicago, was devastating. Although likely reluctant to do so, Sprague had had no choice but to cooperate fully with RFC and its investigators, and so M&StL had made GE-31 and a coach available to Boatner and crew, who made a daylight inspection of the entire system. Then the party retreated to Chicago to compose its report. Boatner categorically refuted the testimony of Sprague and Devins at the ICC and Senate hearings that M&StL had been or was being adequately maintained. "Physical condition of railway plant and appurtenances is poor," said a plainspoken Boatner in the opening sentence. He pointed accusingly to "much deferred and under-maintenance of ties, ballast, rail, tie plates, anchors, and other accessories." What about M&StL's laudable safety record? "This is due," said Boatner, "in measure to light traffic with light power, to slow time and to the efficiency of management and men." Moreover, the freight car supply was "inadequate," the passenger fleet was "elderly," shops and engine houses were "poor," the road was afflicted with "much unprofitable mileage," and the road's competitive position was "inferior." To continue independent operation under the present circumstances would "appear only to maintain an uneconomic and unsound transportation situation in the area." If, however, M&StL should choose to go it alone, all Iowa branches, everything west of Watertown, and the Southwestern between St. James and Spencer should be jettisoned. Especially intriguing was Boatner's suggestion that M&StL acquire a dozen 2-10-4s with a tractive effort of 84,000 pounds, similar to those employed by neighboring Chicago Great Western, to iron out the pesky profile of the line between Hopkins and Peoria with its several heartbreaking helper districts. (RFC's John W. Barriger had testified at the Minneapolis hearing that M&StL was "a mountain railroad in a prairie country.") Finally, Boatner believed that with an upgraded main line and modern power, two crew changes—at Monmouth and Marshalltown—could be eliminated for through trains. In the end, however, Boatner did not advocate putting money into M&StL. His reasoning was simple: "There is now more transportation in the territory than is needed . . . there is little to justify placing so much new capital into a run-down plant."[6]

But the ICC had ruled that no new evidence was permissible, and by the time RFC's Jesse Jones released Boatner's report to the public, the commissioners already had ruled against Associated Railways. In a split decision dated June 13, 1938, the commissioners argued that existing routes and channels of commerce would be disrupted by Associated's plans, that some two thousand employees would lose their jobs, that abandonment of lines would destroy investments in grain elevators and other businesses, that several communities would be denied rail service, that competition would be damaged, and that Associated's proposal did not accord with ICC's final plan for coordination. Burlington's Ralph Budd, really the architect of the Associated plan and its most ardent supporter, nevertheless had been pessimistic all along. As early as January 1935, Budd had written: "In my opinion the opposition of communities and of labor union leaders will prevent abandonment and absorption of lines."[7]

In Minneapolis and everywhere along the road, there was first relief at the news and then euphoria. Talk of a celebration filled the air, ripening quickly. An "M&StL Victory Jubilee" was scheduled at the Minneapolis Auditorium for July 21–23; nearly sixty thousand admission tickets—actually ribbon badges on which was imprinted: "M&StLRR: We Are Here To Stay"—were distributed in sixty communities where M&StL employees were located. The main floor of the auditorium was transformed by a railroad motif with replicas of stations, dining cars, and locomotives. The *Winthrop News* was like many on-line newspapers in urging local citizens to head for the celebration—"to have a little fun, enjoy ourselves, and to join with the city of Minneapolis in the great M&StL Victory Jubilee." M&StL provided special trains ($1.50 round-trip from Winthrop or Gaylord); over one hundred Gaylordites, including the thirty-member American Legion Junior Drum & Bugle Corps, joined the lively throng. The celebration began on Thursday, July 21, with a three-block handcar race over downtown streetcar tracks; crews were composed of mayors from M&StL communities. A luncheon at the Hotel Radisson sponsored by Minneapolis interests and the M&StL Defense Committee preceded opening festivities at the auditorium, where speakers, including Senator Henrik Shipstead, recalled with pride M&StL's historic relationship with Minneapolis and commended M&StL's aggressive and progressive management, and the crowd danced the night away. Thousands more poured into the city on Friday for the M&StL fete. Twenty-two bands and drum and bugle corps marched from the post office down Nicollet to Seventh Street and then down Hennepin Avenue to the West Hotel. Montgomery had the distinction of sending two musical groups plus a delegation of young girls attired in Bohemian costumes to distribute "kolachy" pastries, a local favorite. Marchers and others then repaired to Nicollet Park for a double-header ballgame between the Minneapolis Millers and the Toledo Mudhens. Saturday was given over to tours of Minneapolis manufacturing plants, broadcasting stations, and other attractions. "The Club Car Jamboree" at the auditorium ended that evening with the crowning of Loella Braun as queen of the M&StL Jubilee; her attendants were chosen from a group of M&StL employees. The *Minneapolis Journal* covered it all in a "Special M&StL Jubilee Edition."[8]

As part of the festivities, mayors from M&StL communities had sung "I've Been Workin' on the Railroad," a sure hit at this celebration, and truly, as the words of that popular tune implied, mayors and other civic leaders had done much to help M&StL in its darkest hour. The company, too, had been "workin' on the railroad." Boatner's dry-eyed appraisal of

M&StL's condition in 1936 had been accurate enough, but in 1935, and even more in 1936, 1937, and 1938, Sprague had begged and/or cajoled Judge Wilbur Booth and the bulk of M&StL bondholders into a series of expenditures designed to make the company more efficient and reliable. Sprague sold for scrap a few more weary locomotives and inaugurated a step-by-step program to modernize the road's Mikados with additional air pumps, enlarged sand domes, superheaters, mechanical stokers, and other improvements both practical and cosmetic. Leased stock cars, used and new boxcars and gondolas, and two new Russell snow plows were added. Right-of-way fences were rebuilt systemwide, while main-line bridge renewal and strengthening was accelerated, as was the tie program. Heavy relay rail went into the busy Iowa Manly–Northwood segment shared with Rock Island: nearly one hundred miles of main line received gravel ballast. And general offices were provided in the fashionable Northwestern National Bank building at Minneapolis. All of this was well and purposefully broadcast to media that took note of M&StL's perky attitude.[9]

M&StL had managed to dodge the Associated bullet and had reestablished itself in the minds of employees and other constituencies, including shippers, but it still faced the knotty problem of reorganization. Here, too, an occasional favorable gust of wind went into the road's sails. Late in 1937 Jesse Jones had continued to say that he "did not see how the railroad could operate profitably as an independent system," but six months later the exceedingly bright but often maladroit Philip Roosevelt resigned as chairman of the road's general reorganization committee, to be replaced by the shrewd and politically savvy Walter W. Colpitts of the respected engineering firm Coverdale & Colpitts, which the Reorganization Committee had employed as advisers. (In an unrelated development, John Junell resigned as co-receiver at about the same time.) In October 1938, RFC's John W. Barriger returned to the M&StL property for a second look. Back in 1933, M&StL had rolled out wheezy Ten-wheeler 214 to tote Barriger over a neatly groomed but visibly malnourished property. This time, however, shiny and recently shopped Ten-wheeler 228 sped Barriger over a much-improved roadway. Soon thereafter, Jones revealed that studies were under way to determine the possibility of M&StL's reorganization, but he promised nothing.[10]

Matters began to jell. Jones softened his position, promising $5 million if a plan were approved by the federal court and by the ICC—suggesting, curiously, that any reorganization be effected through a division of the property. Colpitts put together such a plan, calling for two roads, one (Minneapolis & St. Louis Railway Company) owning the Minneapolis–Peoria line and all Iowa branches, plus the legs from Albert Lea to Des Moines and from Hopkins to Watertown, and the other (Minneapolis & St. Louis Railroad Corporation) owning only the leg between Winthrop and Tara and everything west of Watertown. The second road would be owned outright by the first. RFC money would go to improvements ($2,978,000) and purchase of all present properties ($2,022,000). Preferred creditors and certain bondholders would receive second mortgage 4 percent bonds; other bond-

Figure 17.1. When RFC's John W. Barriger returned to the M&StL late in 1938, he found it much improved. Barriger is at top right, Sprague at lower left. John W. Barriger collection, St. Louis Mercantile Library.

holders would get stock in the first company; holders of general claims and stockholders of the current company would get nothing. The court gave its assent, and the matter went to the ICC, where hearings were scheduled.[11]

No reorganization plan likely satisfies all parties; this one provoked genuine hostility. Most bondholders agreed to the plan or sought minor concessions, but stockholders, labor, and numerous communities took aggressive exception. M&StL Corporation clearly would be a weakling that owner M&StL Company could abandon with little notice. Another issue involved closing the Cedar Lake shop and moving all locomotive work to Marshalltown—an idea that Marshalltown greatly applauded but Minneapolis roundly condemned (ironically, given the eruptions against M&StL over many years by the Minneapolis suburb Kenwood). Many opponents—several leaders of the M&StL Executive Defense Committee and others who so recently had valiantly labored against dismemberment—felt badly betrayed and now launched hostile missiles against Sprague, Colpitts, and M&StL. The ICC promised a decision in 1940.[12]

Whatever the outcome in Washington, M&StL managers again determined to trim the size of the system. In 1939 M&StL succeeded in lopping off the top 6.8 miles of the Van Cleve Branch, now abbreviated as the Laurel Branch, and late in 1938 the court gave management the authority to seek abandonment of the entire Story City Branch and the Lynnville stub of the Newton Branch, although Sprague did not act on that authority. Nevertheless, before the decade was out, M&StL trimmed 138 route miles in Iowa, 17 percent of all abandonments in that state during the 1930s.[13]

But it was on the South Dakota lines west of Watertown that Sprague's eyes were now tightly riveted. These always had been problematic. As early as 1875, General W. B. Hazen had forecast "disappointment and misery" for farmers who ignored his contention that rainfall west of the hundredth meridian was inadequate "for successful agriculture." The novelist O. E. Rolvaag later spoke to the fearful vacancy of the same country in *Giants in the Earth*. "Monsterlike the Plain lay there—sucked in her breath one week, and the

Figure 17.2. Stepping through the weeds just east of Story City, Iowa. The court gave M&StL permission to seek abandonment of the entire Story City Branch, but Sprague did not exercise that option. William F. Armstrong photograph.

next blew it out again," he wrote. "Man she scorned; his works she would not brook. . . . She would know, when the time came, how to guard herself and her own against him!" Only the short stretch from Lowry through Akaska to Le Beau lay beyond the hundredth meridian, of course, and generally normal to nearly normal rainfall had peppered the area served by M&StL during the years 1907–14. Above-normal precipitation favored the region just as the Great War stimulated demand for wheat and other agricultural produce; the amount of land in South Dakota farms grew by one-third between 1910 and 1920, and the value of farmlands and buildings more than doubled. But the next two decades proved devastating. "So you are the next victim of this prairie dog and rattlesnake country," was the less-than-cheerful exclamation of the conductor as Manford J. Reitan stepped off the cars to take the agency at Onaka in 1923. Rainfall in M&StL's service territory was below average (17.3 inches per annum) three of the last five years of the 1920s and eight of ten years during the 1930s—the longest stretch of dry weather since weather records had been kept. In 1940 South Dakota's farmlands and improvements would be worth only about half of what they had been in 1910. By 1935 nearly 40 percent of the state's population was on relief rolls—the greatest percentage of any state—and the largest proportion was in the central section, that served by M&StL. Searing wind, a scorching sky, and heat-warped light followed by bone-numbing winters combined with the long and deeply depressed economy to produce an unprecedented exodus of rural residents; the state's population dropped by 7.2 percent during the "Dirty Thirties," but its rural/farm population fell by 21 percent. The average farm size grew to 545 acres in 1940 from 434 in 1930, but there were fewer persons on those farms and thus fewer to support nearby trade centers.[14]

Comptroller G. A. Anderson seemed to find only dreary, unpromising numbers to place on Sprague's desk. Every county touched by M&StL lines in South Dakota except Codington (Watertown) and Brown (Aberdeen) had reached its greatest population before 1940, and not one of the many townsites given birth in 1906 and 1907 along M&StL lines had ever lived up to the billing projected by Thomas A. Way and others. West of Conde, the best stations were Hoven and Cresbard, but in 1935 their meager populations were only 370 and 298, respectively. On the line up to Leola, the circumstances of Wetonka were typical. As the 1930s ended, Wetonka was down to one store, a cafe, two grain elevators, and a few other small enterprises. M&StL's expenditures on these lines were governed accordingly. In 1925 four bridges between Northville and Akaska had been rebuilt, but thereafter the company mounted no systematic program of renewal, patching track structure only as required to maintain safe operation.[15]

Not every year produced disappointing agricultural production, of course. In 1937 John Devins had predicted "about 40% of a crop" in the wide expanse from Watertown through Conde to Cresbard ("not much west of there"), and according to time-honored custom M&StL began to stockpile boxcars in anticipation of the rush. When farmers delivered grain to elevators and as wheat rattled down spouts into the cars, M&StL ordered out doubled-headed Moguls westward from Conde to distribute empties and pick up loads. Cars from only two or three stations produced tonnage trains for the diminutive 2-6-0s—such as 315 and 309, coupled at Tolstoy on November 11, 1939—which turned over their burden to larger Consolidation locomotives at Conde. East of Watertown, at Troy, in late summer and fall local residents were treated to spectacular displays of heavy black smoke, eardrum-splitting exhaust, and wildly urgent whistling as wheat extras pounded through that town in valiant attempts to "make the hill" east of town—sometimes successfully and sometimes, to the delight of townspeople who got to see the show again, not.[16]

An interesting sidelight developed on M&StL's West End as the road sought to trim costs of operation. Late in 1936 the road discontinued its daily-except-Sunday mixed train (or "hog and human") service between Aberdeen and Leola, providing instead delivery of mail, express, and less-than-carload lots of freight by truck on the original frequency supplemented by train operation twice weekly. A half-year later M&StL purchased a truck line and its franchise and then two trucks to provide delivery of mail, express, milk, cream, and LCL on the Conde–Akaska line with Aberdeen as the hub of operation.[17]

Track maintenance, to be sure, could not be deferred indefinitely. Bridges between Tolstoy and Akaska needed attention, and the brittle sixty-pound rail west of Wecota would have to be replaced in a few years. Could such serious expenditures be offset by increased revenues over time? The record of recent years did not provide encouragement. On the Conde–Akaska line, for example, the number of carloads handled to, from, or between carriers dropped from 2,035 in 1934 to only 728 in 1938; the number of passengers fell from 626 to 67. Daily-except-Sunday mixed trains ended on December 26, 1935, and were replaced by a triweekly offering that surprisingly held the Railway Post Office authorization until January 26, 1938, when once-weekly scheduling went into effect. Thenceforth mail went west of Conde in closed pouches aboard M&StL trucks. The line into South Dakota from the east, by contrast, was not in jeopardy. Heavy trestlework west of Revillo had undergone renewal during the mid-1920s, although several of those bridges continued to require regular and expensive attention. Late in 1937, Sprague talked with Great Northern's C. O. Jenks about a new three-mile cutoff from near Revillo to Great Northern's line at Albee or Labolt that, with Great Northern trackage rights, would allow M&StL to abandon about thirty-five miles of high-maintenance route into Watertown. Sprague seemed agreeable, but at that time the Associated Railways issue clouded matters, and nothing ever came of the idea, although it did surface again later.[18]

Senior managers had a difficult decision to make. Should M&StL's West End be severed incrementally or altogether, in one whack? The answer seemed to come on May 18, 1939, when M&StL attorneys emerged from Wilbur Booth's court with permission to seek abandonment of everything west of Watertown. Three weeks later, however, those same lawyers filed documents with the ICC seeking to drop only the route west from Conde and the top portion of the Aberdeen line to Leola. Surviving information does not reveal why Sprague and company opted to compromise. Perhaps their motivation was politically inspired, for the people of South Dakota, especially Aberdeen, had been close allies in the recent campaign against dismemberment. In any event, S. W. W. Carr and others who had been active in saving M&StL from Associated now found themselves in opposition to M&StL's own abandonment attempts. "We still have a country of wide open spaces compared to the more densely populated districts," said Carr. "We need what service we have."[19]

The Conde–Akaska case involved a significant 103 miles of route, but issues there were more clearly defined than in the Aberdeen–Leola application. Passenger demand west of Conde had essentially evaporated, and freight traffic was down appreciably, with only marginal hope of recovery should dust bowl and Great Depression conditions ever pass. Tonnage was comprised mostly of grain, livestock, coal, gasoline, oil, and lumber; of these, grain was the most important and the least susceptible to competition—lignite, in fact, was trucked in from North Dakota pits. North Western and Milwaukee branches intersected at three locations, and the population in the entire zone tributary to the line was under eight thousand. Deficits from operation of the line were not offset by revenues accruing to the system as a whole; net system deficits aggregated $92,468 over five years—intolerable given M&StL's financial condition. The axe fell on June 15, 1940, when the ICC authorized abandonment. M&StL earlier had promised to retain truck operation to Akaska and soon leased bulk cargo rights to Dakota Transfer, a Conde-based firm that eventually acquired a fleet of small trucks that moved grain from elevators all along the line from Akaska to Conde for reloading at the latter into boxcars—one of the earliest truck-rail arrangements to guarantee shippers all-rail rates. Revenue rail operation ended on November 18, 1940, when the final melancholy train rumbled into Conde with a few cars of wheat and ghosts of an earlier, happier era not so many years earlier, when eager farmers arrived to turn the soil, the sound of carpenters' hammers proclaimed the opening of a dozen new townsites, trainloads of cattle moved to and from that boisterous river town called Le Beau, and the nation's consciousness had been directed ever westward toward the sunset. Iron inflexibilities of low or erratic rainfall, short and often tempestuous growing seasons, and wild extremes of temperatures eventually had quashed the optimism and faith of many a soul, driving them from this marginal short-grass country. Soon the wreckers would come with their cutting torches to unbolt the rail and tear out ties, leaving only memories of an era so very interesting and yet so very brief. What would Edwin Hawley have thought?[20]

The Leola issue was more complicated and involved, among other variables, the little remarked Mound City & Eastern Railway. Early in the century M&StL had entertained several plans to move beyond Leola and did, indeed, run a sophisticated survey beyond Mound City, about fifty-five miles to the west. Other companies, too, had considered lines in the area, but no construction followed. In 1917 Julius Rosholt of Minneapolis badgered Great Northern for an extension of its line from Forbes, North Dakota, to Mound City or, as an alternative, from Forbes to Leola. GN declined, citing "unsettled conditions," but Rosholt persisted over the years, pestering M&StL, Great Northern, Milwaukee, and especially Soo Line. Frustrated, in 1927 Rosholt floated a trial balloon for a line that would pivot on Eureka, already served by a branch off of Milwaukee's transcontinental line, with one leg to Mound City on the west and another to a new townsite northwest of Leola, to be called Long Lake. Ralph Budd, then at Great Northern, called it "unnecessary railway construction," and William Bremner agreed, saying that M&StL would not aid the project, but neither would it oppose. Budd fretted that if Rosholt's line was actually built, some major road would have to take it over. Budd had it right. Rosholt was willing to build the road, but then he wanted it leased; what really intrigued him was potential profit from townsite development. Matters took concrete form later in 1927, when Rosholt modified his plans to build the Mound City & Eastern over a route from

Leola to Mound City and filed the necessary papers with the ICC, which approved the project partly on the grounds that it would provide "a comparatively large volume of traffic" to M&StL at Leola—traffic that would, said the ICC, "be of material help to that struggling carrier."[21]

Construction was delayed by Rosholt's death in March 1928, but began, haltingly, in 1929, only to be stopped forever by hard times a mere eighteen miles northwest of Leola at the new community of Long Lake. On March 25, 1932, Mound City & Eastern was sold to satisfy claims of $230,381. The road limped along, nevertheless, with motive power supplied by a curious gasoline engine contraption capable of dragging five or six cars over spindly former interurban rail, making two or three trips per week except in winter, when the road frequently shut down. In 1937 M&StL had agreed to lease its Aberdeen–Leola line to Mound City & Eastern, and the ICC concurred the next year, but the agreement was not executed; in 1939 the short line sought abandonment of its tiny operation. That was accomplished in 1940.[22]

Flummoxed by the Mound City & Eastern experience, in 1939 M&StL determined to lop off the thirty-mile line up from Aberdeen, but it was stopped cold as the result of spirited campaigns by Leola interests that greatly impressed the ICC. When fully alert to the prospect of abandonment, business leaders in the McPherson County capital formed a Civic Club whose members signed a pledge to ship all of their freight by M&StL, none by truck line or gypsy truckers, and sent copies of their agreement to every wholesale house with which they did business. The results, said a very happy M. W. Lothringer, M&StL's agent, were "most gratifying in that our business into Leola practically doubled, even during the slack month of January." Soundly rebuffed in this abandonment tilt, M&StL managers readjusted their thinking, put on a happy face, and announced triweekly mixed train operation to Leola (supplemented by truck service).[23]

In 1938 the nation's Class One railroads incurred their greatest net loss since 1932, provoking another spate of articles, prognostications, and commentary on the plight of and questionable prospects for the railroad industry. But the following year proved better. At M&StL, net income was less in 1937 than in 1936, owing primarily to failed crops, but the company showed a nice increase in 1938 to buck the national trend, and in 1939 its net income stood at nearly $1 million ($2.8 million for the period 1936–39). M&StL's operating ratio during the last four years of the decade was a tolerable 80, compared to the industry average of 74. Scheduled freight service was lean: two through freights between Minneapolis and Peoria, one train sufficing elsewhere, mixed trains assigned west of Watertown and on the Iowa branches. Employee numbers dropped from 4,497 in 1930 to 3,200 in 1934 and 2,793 in 1939; average wage costs varied little—$1,609 in 1930, $1,760 in 1939. The average employee was gray or graying at the temples. No bridge and building carpenters were hired during the 1930s, no carmen were hired at Cedar Lake, and only ten carmen were hired at Marshalltown; one telegrapher gained employment between 1931 and 1938, and for the central part of the system, from Minneapolis through Albert Lea to Des Moines, no brakemen were promoted to conductor and no firemen were promoted to engineer. It was the same on the eastern section from Albert Lea to Peoria, where no brakemen were promoted during the decade and none were hired from 1926 through 1936. Yes, M&StL's was a senior work force. And loyal. When Joseph J. Thomas retired in 1934, for example, he had been in M&StL engine service for sixty-one years; fifty years with the company was not unusual in most of the crafts.[24]

As the decade ended, there was a discernable springiness in the step of M&StL personnel. The company remained tethered to the courts, to be sure, but the property had been trimmed to its profitable parts; its track structure, rolling stock, and motive power were vastly improved; and customers had come to see M&StL as a more worthy and reliable transportation partner. Overhead business, an exacting barometer, was up nicely. Judge Booth had approved equipment trusts for procurement of boxcars, hoppers, and automobile cars; programs for bridge renewal, tie replacement, and relay rail—especially on the main line—were now routine, as was the modernization program for certain classes of locomotives, especially the Mikados. And in 1938 and 1939 M&StL decided against new fireboxes and other betterments to a few elderly switchers, instead embracing the fledgling diesel-electric movement; it acquired seven units, six from Electro-Motive Corporation and one from American Locomotive Company, which were dispersed to the Middle Yard at Minneapolis and to Albert Lea, Oskaloosa, Peoria, and elsewhere. Sprague likewise convinced Booth to approve conversion of the office car *Twin Cities* into car 100 and acquisition of a more recent-vintage car with a steel underframe that was soon improved and rolled out as the "new" *Twin Cities.* And a Cadillac sedan was purchased for the executive department to replace the company's venerable and stately but aged LaSalle.[25]

The better days that had come to M&StL were part of a larger context. Out in the countryside there were glimmers of hope. Weather conditions had moderated, and demand for agricultural products turned upward to bring hope not only for farmers but for depression-riddled towns and villages as well. "Prosperity for the farmer means prosperity for the merchant," wrote the erstwhile editor of the *Winthrop News.* The National Industrial Conference Board estimated that 9.5 million Americans remained out of work in 1939, but that did not dampen the mood in New York City, where on April 30 the gates to the World's Fair were opened with ceremonies in a vast enclosure called the "Court of Peace." The emphasis was on modern miracles of invention, in keeping with the "World of Tomorrow" theme. Yet that world was severely and irrevocably shaken a few months later, when Adolph Hitler set Europe ablaze with still another war. At Des Moines, the *Register* devoted its entire front page for September 1 to the dramatic news of Poland's invasion. One month later, the *New York Times* spoke of "long term uncertainties occasioned by the outbreak of war in Europe" and speculated that for America's railroads "the present trend indicates substantially increased earnings until the war ends or until this country becomes a participant." The *Times* cautioned, however, that "eastern carriers of manufactured goods and such raw materials as coal and ores" had a better chance of profiting than western and southern roads, which were tied more tightly to agricultural tonnage. In Minneapolis, Lucian Sprague must have pondered all of this at his desk in the Northwestern Bank Building, but there was no way of knowing what a European war might do to or for M&StL, or how it might bear, if at all, on ICC deliberations regarding the reorganization proposal.[26]

Figure 17.3. Mikado 605 had taken coal and water at Hampton, Iowa, and had train 94 under way again. M. B. Cooke photograph, author's collection.

Chapter 18
FREE AT LAST

In the final analysis, the weight of evidence is that railroad net earning power has been permanently impaired and that only in exceptional cases can it be restored to anything like former record high levels.
—*POOR'S MANUAL,* 1938

THE YEAR 1940 PROVED A WATERSHED. IN Europe, Hitler gobbled up and occupied a huge expanse from Norway through France, while a monumental air war raged over England. Instincts of isolation tugged mightily on American heartstrings, but President Franklin Roosevelt did all he could to prepare the country for a war he thought inevitable. Congress grudgingly concurred, enacting the first peacetime draft, nodding in approval when Roosevelt called the National Guard to federal service, and authorizing major military appropriations. At the same time, calls for increased industrial and agricultural production surged across the long rusty marketplace. The iron grip of the Great Depression loosed and then broke.

Railroad managers, traumatized by hard times and by recurring threats of nationalization during the depression, mostly took defensive positions as the demand for transportation increased. They hesitated even in 1940, as the industry rang up higher total operating revenues than in any year since 1930—much of it war related. At about the same time Congress passed and the president signed into law the Transportation Act of 1940, which broadened the authority of the Interstate Commerce Commission over some waterborne commerce and pledged "fair and impartial regulation of all modes of transportation . . . to recognize and preserve inherent advantages of each." Important to the railroads, the ICC was relieved of the duty, imposed in 1920, to promulgate a national consolidation plan for railroads—a matter of some significance in M&StL's reorganization efforts. Industry purse strings were loosed. It was a good thing.[1]

American industrial and agricultural production surged. During the period from 1939 through 1941, sales of automobiles rose by 35 percent; production of steel ingots reached 97 percent of capacity as early as February 1941. By the fall of that year, cement plants were running at about 80 percent of capacity, soft coal mines at 96 percent. Agricultural productivity likewise increased, as did profit margins for farmers. Unemployment lines shrank, and labor rates escalated; concerns over inflation were heard in board rooms and in the halls of Congress.[2]

The federal government obviously was a principal player in all of this. The defense program began in earnest during 1940, and the Lend-Lease Act of 1941 dramatically increased that activity. Even as the demand for domestic industrial and agricultural activity leapt upward, Selective Service drew off large numbers of able-bodied men. The armed forces grew from 822,000 in November 1940 to 2,071,000 a year later. The events at Pearl Harbor a few weeks later dramatically accelerated patterns of change already under way. "UNITED STATES AT WAR!" declared the bold and ominous headline of the *Des Moines Register* for December 8. In a matter of days, an unprecedented demand for transportation was placed on the country's railroads.[3]

M&StL stood to gain from all of this. The Sprague-Devins plan for improvement, accepted grudgingly at first by the district court and the Reorganization Committee but then aggressively applauded, continued in 1940 and beyond, with the result that the company proved to be not just a willing participant in the industry's war effort but, more important, a competent player. Additional gravel ballast, track anchors, and tie plates went into the main line, cuts were widened, and new or used rail was purchased. Several automobiles were acquired for traffic representatives, and the freight car fleet was expanded by the purchase of used boxcars and gondolas and new covered hoppers. Shopmen at Cedar Lake continued to improve the road's 600s with mechanical stokers, feedwater heaters, trailing truck boosters, increased fuel capacity for tenders, additional air pumps, and cross-counterbalanced main disc driving wheels. A couple of Mikados even were gussied up with stainless steel jackets, and the sole surviving Pacific, 502, was snatched from the bone yard, run through the shops, and dolled up to become the darling of the motive power fleet and Sprague's favorite stallion. Several of the newer Consolidations likewise received improvements. M&StL also took delivery of three more 1,000-horsepower diesel-electric switchers, one each from Baldwin and Electro-Motive in 1940 and one from Alco in 1941. Two 380-horsepower units came from General Electric in 1942. Air conditioning was installed on the "new" office car *Twin Cities,* and a rakish clock measuring 81 feet by 181 feet, with bright red neon letters above and on the side reading "Fast Freight Service—On Time" and below "Minneapolis & St. Louis Railroad," proudly decorated the skyline above the Minneapolis freight house—the latter for "advertising purposes," unheard of at M&StL for ages, it seemed.[4]

One dimension in which M&StL was severely limited in what it could provide the war effort was passenger service, where Lucian Sprague and John Devins had cut power and equipment to the bone and had pared regular offerings to the fewest possible. The final runs of the Wooden Shoe, essentially a commuter operation to Minneapolis from New Ulm (which

Figure 18.1. Mikado 620 was gussied up with a stainless steel jacket. M&StL photograph, author's collection.

Figure 18.2. The sole surviving Pacific, 502, was snatched from the boneyard, put through the shop, and used for revenue service and special movements. Sprague's darling headed a director's special at Iowa Junction (Peoria), Illinois, on June 12, 1941. Paul H. Stringham photograph.

served incidentally Lake Minnetonka and the western suburbs of Minneapolis), took place in mid-January 1935 after lengthy proceedings. Nevertheless, despite management's stern measures, M&StL's passenger operating ratio during the mid-1930s hovered at the dismal 200 level.[5]

Under the circumstances, discontinuance of the road's proud North Star Limited had been necessary if traumatic. In 1929–30 cafe-chair cars 856 and 857 were converted into cafe-lounges *Marshalltown* and *Mason City,* respectively; M&StL advertised "unsurpassed meals Table d'Hote and ala carte service." The menu was genuinely impressive: $1.50 would fetch a broiled steak, grilled lamb chops, or loin pork chops, among other entrees, including all the trimmings—even dessert. With head-end cars, chair cars, the cafe-car, and a sleeper (*Circumnavigator Club* or *Propeller Club*), the North Star remained a popular item through 1931. But in 1932 M&StL had to admit that the depression was especially hard on through business: "During the greater part of the year there were but a few traveling salesmen of eastern firms in the territory, and summer tourist travel from the South to summer resorts in Minnesota was very light." The next year proved no better. By early 1934 the North Star was M&StL's only steam-powered passenger train; 500s were assigned from Minneapolis to Oskaloosa, where smaller power made the Albia turn as the Pacific was made ready for its northbound trip. That soon changed with assignment of GE cars, replacement of Pullman's eight-section buffet-lounge cars with twelve-section sleepers, and reshopping of the *Marshalltown* and *Mason City* into trailer cars, with kitchens converted to smoking rooms, coach seats installed in the dining section, and wicker chairs placed in the parlor area. But the end was in sight. On May 30, 1935, without notice or comment, M&StL terminated sleeper and lounge service and dropped the North Star designation except briefly on the leg between Minneapolis and Albert Lea. So ended, without a whimper, a romantic and elemental institution long a part of the M&StL landscape.[6]

Other alterations in passenger offerings were more routine. By mid-1937 schedules had been rejiggered so that the portions of the system from Minneapolis to Albert Lea, from Minneapolis to Winthrop, and from Fort Dodge to Des Moines alone enjoyed twice-daily service—and that only by supplementing the overnight train from Minneapolis to Des Moines with an Albert Lea turn from Minneapolis and by running a second Des Moines train via Winthrop to serve the Southwestern, then on to Fort Dodge and Des Moines. The latter arrangement ended on August 31, 1939, when a night run was established between Winthrop and Fort Dodge and the Minneapolis–Winthrop and Fort Dodge–Des Moines segments were discontinued. This new schedule provided connections at Winthrop and Fort Dodge and was operated daily except Monday to handle Saturday's accumulation of U.S. mail, express, and Sunday newspapers. Dining car service was a thing of the past, but meals were "placed on board trains no. 7 and 8 at Mason City . . . on advance notice to conductor"; the magnificent three-story Monroe Hotel at Grinnell remained "*the* place to eat"; Stone's was the favorite at Marshalltown, and lunch rooms in or near the depots at Albia, Albert Lea, Winthrop, and Morton met local needs. Steam was gone from regular assignments, and the number of locomotives that M&StL classified as passenger power was down to five in 1941 (502 plus four 4-6-0s), although Mogul 310 stood in for or assisted GE cars in stormy weather on the main line; Consolidations did so elsewhere. During the winter, for example, the section foreman at Gardner—atop a hill and in a cut east of Watertown—kept a close eye on weather conditions and in the event of snow apprised the dispatcher, who ordered out a 400 as helper on eastbound passenger trains. Change came at certain terminals. M&StL moved out of Rock Island's facility at Peoria on June 1, 1939, starting and terminating trains at Bartlett Yard and using a connecting bus to handle passengers to and from downtown; in 1941 M&StL also moved from Rock Island's station in Des Moines to its own spartan facility a few blocks away. Also in 1941, M&StL finally disposed of its stock in St. Paul Union Depot, although its tenancy had ended back in 1933.[7]

Lucian Sprague frequently boasted that M&StL was nearly a freight-only railroad, but occasionally the passenger sector stole the show. During December 1935 grocer M. B. Erickson announced in the *Hanska Herald* that he had received a telegram from Santa Claus advising that he would arrive "with a full load of bags" aboard M&StL's afternoon train on December 23, and in 1938 and 1939 M&StL moved lengthy special trains bearing orphans and other underprivileged children from the Twin Cities to nearby Excelsior for a full day of fun sponsored by the *Minneapolis Star.* "The dear old M&StL came through in grand style," enthused popular columnist Cedric Adams. But these were exceptions. Occupancy aboard M&StL's venerable wooden coaches with their warm oak interiors had dropped steadily since 1915 (with but a few modest contradictions); only 78,537 persons boarded the cars in 1940. But rationing of rubber tires and gasoline coupled with spiked demand from the military nearly doubled the count in 1942, and it rose to nearly a quarter million in 1943. In M&StL's waiting rooms—as in the waiting rooms of all other railroads—were tacked patriotic posters urging travelers to stay home in deference to military needs. Domestic demand increased nevertheless; M&StL did what it could to accommodate that demand. For instance, residents of LaSalle took the train to Minneapolis to visit relatives, later recalling that the rigid-frame seats in the GE cars shook and "rattled a lot." Others recalled courteous and considerate trainmen. At Ruthven, Bernard Archer, badly crippled by polio, was lifted (his bed and all) into the baggage-express compartment of the GE car for periodic trips to the University of Iowa hospital. The garrulous Archer was a favorite among crewmen, who joked with him about the rocky ride and the GE's "wounded goose whistle." During the war years obliging conductors on the Watertown run held trains longer than normal at station stops so that family members could have an extra minute or two with servicemen who had been home on brief leaves. Abroad the main line between Minneapolis and Albia, full troop trains became the norm, occasionally appearing also on routes to Des Moines and Peoria. And when Milwaukee's transcontinental route was blocked, that road detoured passenger or troop trains between Aberdeen and Minneapolis. M&StL's passenger train miles were substantially if quietly reduced on March 11, 1942, however, when the road discontinued operation between Oskaloosa and Peoria, substituting mixed passenger and freight trains.[8]

Revenue from mail contracts had exceeded ticket receipts since 1932, and that pattern held until 1942, when war traffic swelled passenger sales. Yet in all seasons mail provided reliable and steady income. Railway Post Office authorizations remained for all passenger trains and even on the Peoria–Oskaloosa and Watertown–Aberdeen mixed runs. However, by now the nonstop exchanges that had been common earlier had been eliminated systemwide, with mail cranes removed at the Iowa towns of Rockwell, Geneva, Gifford, and Liscomb, among other places, and catcher arms stripped from all mail-handling equipment.[9]

Demand for freight transportation increased dramatically, not quite doubling (to 8.2 million tons) in 1943 (from 4.9 million tons in 1940); freight revenue rose from $9.179 million in 1940 to $13.885 million in 1943. Grain, flour, lumber, cement, soft coal, merchandise, and livestock made up 55.08 percent of all tonnage, compared to 52.93 percent in 1930. Less-than-carload freight tonnage remained only a small element of the traffic mix, and by this time the same could be said of livestock traffic. Losses in these twin categories were more than offset by gains in mixed lading, much of it moving overhead between Minneapolis and Peoria. Peoria, in fact, was the leading interchange point, with thirteen possible connections; Minnesota Transfer, with eight options, was second.[10]

Coal, long a staple in M&StL's traffic mix, had

gradually declined in importance as on-line mines failed, as lake coal via Duluth made inroads, and as important industrial customers such as brick and tile works, cement plants, packing houses, hotels, and residential users turned to natural gas as it became available. By 1933 tonnage was down to 545,012, slightly more than in 1911 before M&StL had merged with coal-rich Iowa Central. But also in 1933, Midland Electric Coal opened a vast strip mine near Middle Grove, Illinois, twenty-six miles west of Peoria; M&StL expected sixty carloads per day from the new tipple. Unfortunately, however, M&StL was so anemic at the time that Midland, uncertain of M&StL's viability, convinced the ICC to allow access by stronger Chicago & North Western through trackage rights from Peoria's Iowa Junction, with payment to M&StL for the use of its tracks on a tonnage basis. During the mid-1930s M&StL served nine on-line coal producers in Illinois at Maxwell, Hanna, Farmington, Middle Grove, and London Mills. To these was added in 1941 another major shipper, Fairview Collieries, at Rapatee, between Middle Grove and London Mills. Iowa's production of coal had slipped precipitously, however. Angus was little more than a memory; M&StL closed its agency there in 1933 and removed the depot in 1938. Coal still moved from nearby Rippey, but by 1940 M&StL's principal coal billings in Iowa were made at Lockman, between Eddyville and Albia; Miller Creek Coal Company's "Old Hickory" was a favorite in the Des Moines market and elsewhere.[11]

Much of Iowa's coal production had been for railroad consumption; for M&StL, the historic source was Hocking Coal Company, a wholly owned subsidiary. Located southwest of Albia, Hocking had been a mine site even before the company bearing that name was organized in 1898; Iowa Central purchased the firm in 1902. That year properties included the mine with ancillary equipment, nearly 500 acres of land, 278 dwellings, a stone building with fixtures and a stock of merchandise (the company store), an ice house, a flour house, and a barn and corn crib. M&StL acquired Iowa Central and Hocking in 1912 and opened more mines. During the 1920s, the entire output—less that used to fire mine boilers and that sold to employees—was purchased by M&StL; dividends were regular. But overproduction in the soft coal industry generally, a miners' strike in 1929, and M&StL's financial distress collectively cast a shadow over Hocking. Its total output over the years through 1929 had been 7,244,863 tons, and the company predicted that it had another 858,968 tons unmined. Nevertheless, production ended on December 31. "Under existing conditions in the bituminous coal industry, it appears that it would be most unwise to open a new mine at this time," was the drab message appearing in the annual report for 1930. M&StL thereafter acquired its coal elsewhere, some of it from on-line producers in Illinois; the main track and the maze of sidings at Hocking were taken up in 1934. Hocking Coal did not die, at least not until 1953; it just faded away, liquidating assets and selling property over time, but paying dividends until the end.[12]

However important coal, overhead, and general traffic might be, M&StL, as always, remained tightly tied to the fortunes of agriculture. That sector of the economy had been in the doldrums for two decades, but war demand sent a powerful signal to farmers to produce more food and fiber. Iowa, arguably the most agricultural of all states, found itself suddenly in the lap of prosperity. With more miles of route in Iowa than in any other state, M&StL found that only good news. In 1942 the total farm income for the Hawkeye State was nearly double that of 1939, and Iowa ranked first in production of corn, hogs, oats, horses, chickens, popcorn, value of land and farm buildings, value of farm implements, and percentage of improved farm land; it ranked second in creamery butter, soybeans, and beef cattle.[13]

Squeezing profits out of traffic volumes remained the usual challenge for M&StL managers, with regulatory agencies maintaining strict control over rates while prices for material and labor floated according to demand. M&StL's performance during the first four years of the decade was impressive, with the road earning $12,758,373 net on operations and posting an agreeable operating ratio of 71.97; a full 94.36 percent of all revenue came from freight. In 1938 the ICC had authorized freight rate increases averaging 5 percent on certain commodities, in 1942 a 6 percent general raise except on agricultural products and livestock, but it countermanded the latter in 1943 after the Office of Price Administration and the Department of Agriculture complained that the increase was inflationary and was resulting in unjustifiable wartime profits for railroads.[14]

Reports from M&StL's auditor's office widened smiles everywhere, and a generally collegial mood was abetted by the company's ongoing policy of pouring money into physical improvements and sprucing up the plant. All hands took pride in rehabilitation of the road's locomotive fleet right in the company's own shops, in shiny new diesel switchers hard at work in various yards, and in the expectation of modern, new road power that Sprague long had dreamed of. Baldwin provided blueprints and specifications for Mallet articulated locomotives in January 1935, and Chief Engineer R. G. Kenly told John Devins that several bridges between Hopkins and Albert Lea would need replacement, but that between Albert Lea and Peoria the steel bridges were in good shape and that seven thousand lineal feet of pile trestles could be strengthened over time at moderate cost. The issue simmered as the dismemberment issue was argued, but even thereafter Sprague was able to coax money only for gradual rehabilitation of the plant and existing power. At the end of 1938, bridges between Jordan and New Prague were still rated at Cooper E-40, restricting axle loading at 40,000 pounds—well off the 53,333 needed for Mallets. Nevertheless, a year earlier Sprague had publicly announced that he would petition the court to acquire 2-6-6-4s that could be operated more efficiently than with existing power, that could eliminate helper districts, and that could allow closing of "sub-terminals." Nothing happened, however, and nothing would until August 26, 1943, when the district court authorized purchase of five single-expansion articulated machines with sixty-nine-inch drivers and 75,700 pounds of tractive effort. Nevertheless, either the order was not placed or the War Production Board failed to approve it; M&StL was never witness to the great steel monsters. But, surprisingly, elderly and unremarked former M&StL 2-6-0s did play principal roles in an interesting historical drama far from home, at windswept Promontory Summit, Utah, on September 8, 1942. Scarcities of primary materials such as steel provided the pretext for giant Southern Pacific to junk a portion of the original transcontinental line in Utah where the famous golden spike had been driven in 1869; this particular part of the Overland Route had been made redundant by the newer, more efficient Lucin Cut-off. Appropriate "unspiking" ceremonies were scheduled, dignitaries appeared, and former M&StL Moguls 311 and 319, now owned by dismantler Hymann-Michaels, were juxtaposed as Union Pacific's 119 and Central Pacific's *Jupiter,* facing head to head in replication of the original event, as the first spike was drawn. Aside from these unanticipated ceremonial duties, the old warriors were assigned to power Hymann-Michaels work trains picking up the track of the rugged 121-mile line from Corinne to Lucin, Utah.[15]

Meanwhile, M&StL's reorganization rocked along over an uneven path. The Minneapolis & St. Louis *Railway Company* and the Minneapolis & St. Louis *Railroad Corporation,* often referred to as the new company and the new corporation, each formed early in 1939, shortly thereafter together asked the ICC for permission for the new company alone to acquire from the old Minneapolis & St. Louis Railroad all of its lines except those west of Hopkins and that from Winthrop to Tara, and for the new corporation alone to acquire those excepted by the new company; for permission for the new company to issue $5 million in first mortgage bonds, $3.091 million in second mortgage bonds, and 150,000 shares of common stock with no par value; and for permission for the new corporation to issue 10,000 shares of common capital stock with no par value. These collective elements were in accordance with the desires of Jesse Jones and the Reconstruction Finance Corporation, which, with ICC approval, was willing to loan $5 million; the district court already had given its concurrence, as had the Reorganization Committee. The ICC was generally sympathetic to the need for M&StL's reorganization, but frowned on the division of M&StL into separately operated corporate units. Denial came on April 9, 1940.[16]

William Colpitts waited only briefly before submitting a slightly revised plan that still offered division of M&StL, but with protection for the new corporation,

Figure 18.3. Receivership ended on December 1, 1943. A few days later this handsome Mikado roared out of Marshalltown, Iowa, with train 95—a robust symbol of the new order. William F. Armstrong photograph.

which everybody agreed was weaker than the new company, and that asked RFC for only $4 million. Hearings again were scheduled, but railroad labor called Colpitt's revisions "mere sugar-coating" for the same old "pill." This time, however, the ICC authorized acquisition and operation of the old properties by the new company and the new corporation, as well as issuances of securities; division of the properties was essentially illusory; they would be linked by joint ownership for the purposes of operation. Closure of the Cedar Lake shops and erection of new ones at Marshalltown, once demanded by RFC, was dropped as a condition, and the ICC approved a $4 million loan to M&StL from RFC. In an oblique reference to the Transportation Acts of 1920 and 1940, regulators reminded the parties that the ICC was no longer bound to group carriers within a fixed consolidation plan. The order was announced on March 4, 1941.[17]

In fact there were few qualitative differences between M&StL's reorganization plan of 1939 and that of 1940; one can only ponder what had been in the minds of commissioners. Perhaps they were caught up in a rising tide of optimism regarding the road. All receiver's certificates had been paid off by now, equipment trust obligations were current, traffic volumes were up, the operating ratio was down, and M&StL was placing snappy advertisements in *Traffic World* and elsewhere promising dependable freight service over the "Peoria Gateway line." *Railway Age* made M&StL the focus of a lengthy feature and chuckled that the road, "once pronounced hopeless by experts," now gave "evidence of vigorous life." Frankly, the publication said, "The 'doctors' were wrong." The commissioners also may have seen that Colpitts had developed a plan to bring fixed charges clearly within M&StL's earning power. That, in turn, may have allayed the fears of depression-wary investors who well recalled the profound danger that resided in a high percentage of funded debt and who had been chary of railroad securities for nearly two decades.[18]

In any event, on a dark, drizzly July 24, 1942, after forty-two failed attempts since 1934, the properties of the old Minneapolis & St. Louis Railroad Company received a bid of $2,010,000, entered by Walter W. Colpitts, chairman of the Reorganization Committee. When the United States District Court approved the deal on September 11, M&StL was near the end of receivership. Matters continued to improve. Because of exceptionally heavy wartime revenues, cash accumulated more rapidly than had been anticipated, and Walter Colpitts was able to announce that reorganization could be accomplished without any aid from RFC. The court and the ICC nodded in approval. On December 1, 1943—after twenty years and six months of receivership, one of the longest in history—M&StL proudly strode into the bright light of a new era. The cash and securities obliged under the reorganization plan were made available, and Lucian Sprague was elected president by a board made up mostly of Minneapolitans. Good news followed good news. On February 18, 1944, the New York Stock Exchange listed M&StL's 150,000 shares of no-par common stock (which traded at between 46 and 58¾ during the year), and on May 1 the company redeemed all General Mortgage Series A 4 Percent Income Bonds due in 1996 (the $2,010,000 paid for the property). As a consequence, Sprague thought M&StL might be "the only Class I railroad in the United States without mortgage indebtedness." Later in the year the *corporation* and the *company* were merged to create the Minneapolis & St. Louis Railway Company.[19]

No plan to end receivership satisfies all parties; certainly M&StL's "final solution" left bitter feelings among many groups. Creditors, including bondholders, had first claim to payment of debt in order of priority, but under the Colpitts plan, M&StL paid out only a small portion of its debt (Associated would have given more than three times as much under its dismemberment proposal). Stockholders—those responsible, or at least those theoretically responsible, for the management under which the company had failed back in 1923—were wiped out. Many of those persons were friends or heirs of friends of Edwin Hawley, or even his own heirs, certainly long-time supporters of the "old" company. They were left with nothing. In no way was the property "turned back to its owners," as is so often the assertion at the end of a receivership. In this instance M&StL bondholders who survived and hung on—previously the road's creditors—now held stock in the "new" company and were, in reality, its owners. Despite the fact that the board of the "new" company was made up principally of men local to M&StL, the vast bulk of stock was in the hands of persons living in or about New York City. Would they have the same loyalty to M&StL as the Hawley crowd of old?[20]

Chapter 19
Don't You Know There's a War On?

During the year 1945 the company handled a greater volume of traffic than in 1944, and the increase in total operating revenues was approximately 2 percent.
—M&StL Annual Report, 1945

The war experience of 1941–45 had a profound impact on the United States. Production numbers were stupendous as the economy roared into full gear. During the course of the war, factories and assembly plants churned out 80,000 landing craft, 100,000 tanks and armored cars, 300,000 aircraft, and 2.4 military trucks, consuming in the process 434 million tons of steel. From Pearl Harbor Day through 1944, American shipyards launched 4,500 cargo vessels in addition to heavy tonnage in destroyers, cruisers, battleships, and aircraft carriers. America was indeed the "arsenal of democracy," as President Franklin Roosevelt so aptly noted.[1]

The agricultural record was no less impressive. Livestock output rose by 23 percent in 1941–45, crop production by 14 percent. Farmers who in the past had good reason to worry about overproduction now were encouraged to raise all they could. It was their patriotic duty; it also was profitable. "Pullets as well as bullets are needed to win the war," puffed poultry producers. As demand increased, so did commodity prices and the value of farmland. The total farm population tilted downward, the size of the average farm tilted upward, total farm indebtedness moved lower, and overall productivity pointed higher—especially as more and more farms received electricity and as farmers were able to employ more mechanization and hybrid seed. In Iowa, for example, there were 212,318 farmers in 1940, and the cash value of their production was $561,836,688; in 1945, the number of farmers was down to 208,934, but the value of production more than doubled, to $1,232,010,705.[2]

To the nation's railroads fell the duty of providing primary transportation. The number of ton miles skyrocketed in 1942, rose again in 1943, and peaked in 1944. The bulge in passenger traffic occurred in the same years, but was even sharper; the number of revenue passenger miles in 1944 exceeded those of 1939 by 322 percent. In 1944 the country's railroads produced 737 billion ton miles, the greatest volume of traffic to that time—this in addition to 95.6 billion passenger miles, a figure twice that of 1918; 100 million meals were served aboard dining cars—nearly 500 percent more than before the war. At the peak of the war effort the carriers handled about 72 percent of commercial freight traffic and more than 74 percent of intercity passenger traffic. A significant chunk was military. Seventy-five trains and 2,700 cars were necessary to move one armored division, sixty-five trains and 1,350 cars an infantry division of 15,000 men and equipment. And most of it was handled in cars and hauled by locomotives rostered by railroads before the war began; the War Production Board was extremely parsimonious in granting requests for new cars and locomotives. Was this monstrous load of business compensatory? Tolerably. The average rate of return for the industry was 5.08 percent in 1943, 4.0 in 1944.[3]

M&StL and its service territory were a microcosm of it all. Prodigious volumes of freight necessary for the war effort and to sustain domestic needs flowed into and out of stations large and small, while the road's passenger trains were filled to overflowing. Fort Snelling in the Twin Cities served again as an induction center, and members of the Women's Army Corps took their training at Fort Des Moines. "There is presently a constant flow of war material and troops moving inter-territorially," said Lucian Sprague in 1944, "which is participated in by this company and which may be expected to continue throughout the period of the war." Local stations added billings as diverse as tin cans, containers of grease drippings, used copper, manila rope, milkweed pods, and scrap paper and metal—homely items all, but gathered enthusiastically by patriotic citizens as their part in the war effort. Forest City dispatched five carloads of scrap iron late in 1942; Winthrop hosted a countywide scrap drive a few months later; and merchants at Franklin donated prizes to residents hauling in scrap. Each example represented total mobilization. "Victory gardens" were prevalent (sometimes even inside M&StL's right-of-way fences), local post offices stayed open weekday evenings to sell war stamps and bonds, women met in school buildings to wrap bandages, and businessmen helped farmers at harvest time to ease the shortage of labor.[4]

The Railway Express Agency played its own distinctive role. By late 1943 perhaps 65 percent of its volume was war related; everything from aircraft engines to serums, antitoxins, and vaccines was expedited by Railway Express. Blood collected by the Red Cross was especially time sensitive. Inductees usually sent their civilian clothes home by express, and the army's famous "K-9 Corps" likewise moved aboard express cars. Baby chicks, especially from southern Minnesota and South Dakota, were part of the mix. Late in 1942 every inch of the depot at Winthrop was cluttered with used tires; turned in by area residents as a patriotic necessity, they were now awaiting movement by express. It was the same at most other stations. Railway Express also played an important role in bolstering morale on the home front by faithfully delivering movie films to the more than seventeen thousand theaters around the country, which thronged with upwards of 85 million attendees weekly.[5]

The number of revenue tons for M&StL reached 1.5 billion in 1945, double that of 1938, but the nature of M&StL's business—still highly dependent on agriculture—was modified by war conditions. Grain and flour still made up about 20 percent of M&StL's business, but coal led all commodities in 1944—28.6 percent of total tonnage. Lumber and cement billings were down to reflect slack construction due to war, while less-than-carload lots of freight contributed less than one percent. In fact, much of M&StL's LCL tonnage now was handled under contract with Brady Transfer and other trucking companies to wayside stations. The arrangement was faster, surer, and less expensive than peddling by local freight, although LCL in boxcars continued to flow to and from primary points such as Minneapolis, Watertown, Fort Dodge, and so on. Some patterns remained unchanged. For instance, in August 1944 the Pacific Grain Company at Winthrop, Minnesota, advertised four carloads of lump and stoker coal "on track"; three months later the Red Owl store in Gaylord offered hundred-pound bags of potatoes at $2.50 each, sold right from the car "near the depot"; and in November one entrepreneurial soul at New Ulm advertised Yakima Valley apples and pears dispensed from a refrigerator car at the Center Street crossing.[6]

M&StL's passenger offerings remained humble although absolutely essential during the transportation-short war years. In 1944 the total number of passengers carried leapt to 262,561 (from 78,537 in 1940), and it peaked at 289,372 in 1945—the highest since 1930. The number of passenger miles reflected the same pattern—25,918,183 in 1945, five times greater than in 1940 and the highest since 1929. Some of this was represented by the many MAIN (Military Authorization Identification Number) trains moving troops and their impedimenta. These grew incrementally in number from 1940 through the war years, peaking in 1944 and 1945. In one instance, battle-hardened but surprisingly undisciplined troops raided bakery boxes and other food containers loaded on baggage carts along platforms in Great Northern's Minneapolis station (which M&StL used and where it often received connecting MAIN trains) and resulted in the deeply agitated stationmaster's ordering M&StL to "get that train out of town" before more loss was incurred.[7]

M&StL's regular trains typically received less notice. Pulled by the now venerable GE cars, M&StL's passenger trains were derisively labeled "Puddle Jumpers" or "Doodle Bugs," but for many customers they provided the only transportation option. The road no longer ran commuter trains to Lake Minnetonka, but it continued to board persons needing rides to and from that area west of Minneapolis, selling "commutation fares"—twenty-five rides from Excelsior to Minneapolis at $6.53, for example. M&StL passenger offerings even provided a vehicle for courting when a soldier from Fort Snelling took his fiancée on the Friday night train to Watertown (her parents lived at nearby Vienna) and returned on the Sunday night train—getting her back in time for work and him back to the post before he was due. Another passenger who frequented the same train recalled a stop one night between stations; the conductor went forward and found the engineer asleep, his foot having slipped off the "dead man's pedal" to stop the train. Albia, where M&StL made an across-the-platform connection with Wabash, always was a busy place, with multiple four-wheeled baggage carts required to handle great volumes of mail, express, and baggage between M&StL and Wabash trains but also to and from Chicago, Burlington & Quincy's busy main line. Holidays brought an impossible surge, with mail and express (especially catalogs) stacked against the depot pending space available on the cars. Elsewhere, the run between Winthrop and Fort Dodge, which M&StL long had wanted to dump, was a casualty when the Office of Defense Transportation (ODT) ordered suspension of any train averaging less than 35 percent

Figure 19.1. Demand for transportation was immense and constant during World War II. Extra 619 had a train of mixed freight near New Prague, Minnesota. M&StL photograph, author's collection.

occupancy. The order was effective March 1, 1945, and almost immediately a bus company gained permission to operate over Iowa highways between Fort Dodge and Estherville. "Urgent requests of citizens" caused ODT to rethink its position, and the trains were reinstated on May 7, but the bus company stayed in place to offer stiff competition on the Iowa leg.[8]

The war touched M&StL in any number of ways. During 1945 the company was forced to "retire" a Buick sedan used by the Spokane sales office because "tires on automobile were badly worn and OPA [the Office of Price Administration] would not grant permit for new tires." In Minneapolis, President Sprague gained board approval to donate $3,000 to the Minneapolis War Chest Fund and to purchase $800,000 in war bonds. Out on the line, men postponed retirement in deference to the war effort and in recognition of the labor shortage. T. R. Hoit, an engineer at Oskaloosa, had fifty-four years of service when finally he "pulled the pin" in 1945; another engineer, Thomas McCarthy of Minneapolis, retired a year earlier with forty-eight years of seniority. When it could find qualified men, M&StL hired telegraphers, brakemen, firemen (especially at Marshalltown), and even a few machinists, carmen, laborers, and carpenters for bridge and building gangs. Employee numbers were remarkably steady (2,839 in 1940, 2,917 in 1945), but wage costs jumped from $4.9 million in 1940 to $7.2 million in 1945.[9]

Meanwhile, white-haired Lucian Sprague and M&StL's board tidied up corporate matters by redeeming the General Mortgage Bonds "at par and accrued interest" and by merging "all property, franchises and assets into the Minneapolis & St. Louis Railway Company for ownership, management, and operation." This, said Sprague, left the company "without any bonded indebtedness on its property." (M&StL did have $2.3 million in equipment obligations.)[10]

Figure 19.2. GE-2 had the train 18 assignment on this warm July day in 1945 near Rolfe, Iowa. William F. Armstrong photograph.

The operating income for the years 1943–45 was $5.9 million, net income $5.4 million, and the company paid out dividends for the first time since the Hawley years—$300,000 in 1944 and $600,000 in 1945. The operating ratio surged alarmingly, however, from 68.32 in 1943 to 88.27, reflecting increased wage and salary rates as well as many and varied property improvements charged to operations. The new rail program on the main line continued apace; lighter rail, eighty-five-pound and some hundred-pound, was cascaded to the Hopkins-Winthrop line in Minnesota, which in 1942–45 also was completely ballasted with gravel. Passing tracks on the main line were extended at Abbott and Union, Iowa, and at London Mills, Illinois. A snappy-looking replacement depot went up at Dallas Center, Iowa, after fire destroyed an earlier structure; a new engine house was built at Peoria when a tornado took out the elderly facility there; and water tanks at several locations were rebuilt. Bridge renewals were undertaken systemwide, long-deferred maintenance of structures was addressed (especially repairs of sills and foundations of depots), and paint crews worked up the line from Tara to Winthrop and from Watertown out to Leola. Equipment acquisitions included two additional Russell all-steel snow plows and a used sleeping car from Pullman that became M&StL's Business Car No. 102.[11]

Nothing came easily, however, given material and manpower shortages, government red tape, and M&StL's own bureaucratic sluggishness. A 141-by-70-foot canopy over the passenger platform at Des Moines proved a case in point. Begun late in 1942, and costing only $1,541.93, this small project was not completed until the summer of 1945. Approval had to come from the War Production Board, blacksmiths at M&StL's Cedar Lake shop had to cut and bend eighty-five-pound scrap rail, shopmen had to cut lumber to order, and the company's own procedures required formal authorization for even small items such as a gallon of aluminum paint to be acquired locally. All materials were on hand by late 1944, but bridge and building crews were too shorthanded and too busy elsewhere to clean up this little assignment in any expeditious way.[12]

In 1945 M&StL announced completion of its lengthy program to modernize the 600s (by now designated "MacArthur" locomotives out of admiration for war hero General Douglas MacArthur), and boasted that multiple improvements had "materially increased the tractive effort of these machines, insuring efficiency and economy in handling heavy freight trains at high speeds." A year earlier the road had bragged that it had "adequate power whatever the load." Such was better advertising than fact. By the end of 1943, M&StL owned only 101 locomotives, 97 fewer than a decade earlier, but these were to move more than twice the tonnage of 1933—certainly a tribute to the mechanical department that had made betterments to MacArthur and other types of power. (Particular pride attached to the setting of valves, so that locomotive exhaust was not a lethargic "chugga, chugga, chugga," but rather a vibrant "pop, pop, pop.") Yet heavy traffic volumes and M&StL's unforgiving main-line profile severely taxed this small and aging fleet and required massive double heading of trains using curious assortments of power—Moguls, Ten-wheelers, and Consolidations teamed up among themselves or more often with handsome 502 and/or 600s on regular Cedar Lake–Peoria freight trains (often running in two sections), and extras as needed. Steam also drew MAIN trains and had to protect work normally assigned to GE cars and to the road's dozen diesel switchers. There was consequent pressure on shopmen to keep steam in tip-top order and to add occasional improvements such as stokers for five Consolidations—450, 452, 458, 460, and 461, and to Sprague's darling, Pacific 502.[13]

In 1945 American railroads employed 45,319 locomotives, overwhelmingly steam, with an average tractive effort per locomotive of 53,000 pounds; the average at M&StL was a sorry 45,606. During the war years, the nation's carriers ordered 1,300 steam locomotives, but also 4,015 diesels. M&StL, of course, had many years of experience with gas-electric power on passenger trains, and diesel switchers had been on the property since 1938. Failures were frequent, but compared to steam, engines with diesel power proved to be in the shop less often and could be operated at lower cost. Sprague had toyed with the idea of road diesels for a long time, and his interest grew with the success of the switchers. General Electric supplied M&StL with a couple of forty-four-tonners that were adequate for light assignments at Mason City and Fort Dodge, but during the mid-1940s GE offered little else in its locomotive catalog. In 1939 M&StL had considered acquisition of a Baldwin unit for use west of Watertown, and a year later Baldwin did sell M&StL a 1,000-horsepower unit, but it had not proved satisfactory and in 1944 was exchanged at no cost for another unit that proved more reliable. Baldwin had larger units available, but M&StL placed no further orders with that supplier.[14]

M&StL turned to American Locomotive Company (Alco)—the company that had supplied much of its steam power over the years and from which M&StL had purchased three diesel switchers. What M&StL wanted was a utilitarian unit that could be employed in yard service and local road service, and that could even pinch hit when the GE cars were down. Alco had created the format for the road switcher with its RS-1 in 1941—equipped with a six-cylinder, 1000-horsepower, four-cycle engine and turbocharger that gave off a marvelously distinctive whine and that "loaded" fast, with a gritty tractive effort of 71,400 pounds. The RS-1 was exactly what M&StL wanted. An order for five of them went out late in 1943. The first arrived in Cedar Lake at 10:00 a.m. on March 11, 1944, and it was serviced and started that afternoon; shop forces added classification lights and canvas covers over radiator shutters, and also ordered top-mounted, air-activated bells from scrapped steamers to replace factory-equipped bells that "went clank, clank and could not be heard." The others drifted in over the next nine months, and as soon as M&StL made its several homemade modifications and additions, usually in one day, they entered service. Numbering followed the curious pattern begun when the first diesel arrived—designating, more or less, the month and year of arrival; thus the first RS-1 at M&StL became 244, the second 744, the third 944, and so on. There was no prescribed paint scheme; most units turned up in a different adornment from that of their predecessors. Thus was established another curiosity.[15]

But the Alcos (as the RS-1s were called on M&StL) were good power and did not have many "bugs" when delivered. On October 3, 244 proudly headed up business cars 101, 102, and the *Twin Cities* en route to South Dakota with Sprague and invited guests who looked forward to a day or two of pheasant hunting around Bradley. Then on November 1, 944 strutted her stuff with a director's special to Albert Lea, enabling "members of the board to observe the operation of the new diesel locomotive." John Devins "reported at length on the efficient operation of the new diesel locomotives" at the board meeting on April 4, 1945. Four more Alcos were ordered for delivery that year at $87,000 per copy. "Day in and day out, those Alcos took more beating than anything else," recalled Charles W. Stone, road foreman of engines.[16]

The Alcos, however, were not built for multiple-unit operation and were not designed for through freight work. The only serious supplier of such diesel power at the time was the Electro-Motive Division (EMD) of General Motors, which had sold M&StL its first diesel switcher back in 1938 and had rolled out a prototype four-unit, 5,400-horsepower FT road freighter from its new plant at LaGrange, Illinois, in November 1939. Before wrapping up an 83,764-mile demonstration in October 1940, EMD's FT 103, as it was labeled, had visited twenty railroads, including M&StL, where two of 103's four units had made a Mason City turn from Minneapolis in the winter of 1940. Company records pertaining to this demonstration trip have not survived, and of course in 1940

Figure 19.3. Alcos initially were concentrated on the West End. Extra 1144 at Deephaven, Minnesota, had a nearly solid boxcar train of wheat. M&StL photograph, author's collection.

M&StL was in no position to acquire road power—steam or diesel. Yet records certainly were made, they must have been impressive, and EMD salesmen proved solicitous of welterweights like M&StL because they saw in them means to pry open even larger accounts from diesel holdouts like giant Pennsylvania in the East. In any event, in October 1944 M&StL officials bargained with EMD for two three-unit FTs powered by sixteen-cylinder, 1,350-horsepower 567 engines. Haggling followed, and in late winter 1945, M&StL's board approved purchase at an aggregate price of $759,041.56. Why three-unit sets and not four-units? Because four-units would have required extensive and costly rearrangement of the Cedar Lake shop. Why add dynamic braking to locomotives operating in prairie country? Because M&StL's rough profile from Cedar Lake to Peoria offered mountainlike grades and because they were fairly inexpensive and required little maintenance. Numbered 445 and 545, painted in snappy green, yellow, and black with the company herald encircled by orange wings on the nose of each cab unit, the two sets were billed from LaGrange on April 30, 1945. The first, 445, arrived in Peoria on May 1, at Cedar Lake on May 3, and on May 4 at 6:30 a.m. departed with train 94. The other threesome arrived at Albert Lea on May 5, and it was polished up at the shop, taken from Cedar Lake to the nearby Parade Grounds for public inspection, and made its maiden trip to Peoria on May 16. But there were problems with both sets, and they retreated to LaGrange for adjustments. In the meantime, newly arrived Alco 645 pranced out of Cedar Lake with an officers' special at 7:00 a.m. on June 13, arriving in Peoria at 9:12 p.m.—likely testing the possibility of shortened transit time for diesel-powered freights on M&StL's 488-mile core route.[17]

Assignment of new diesel power, done randomly at the outset, evolved into patterns as more units arrived to create a critical mass. The Morton time freight drew Alcos in 1944, and that year and the next M&StL

Figure 19.4. The three-unit FTs were assigned to flagships 19 and 20. FT 545 was in charge of train 20 on this summer day as it entered the North Yard at Oskaloosa, Iowa. Robert Milner photograph, author's collection.

concentrated Alcos on regularly scheduled freights between Cedar Lake and Leola, Consolidations 405 and 419 acting as protection on the far West End, and 410, 452, 456, and even 502 handling extras between Watertown and Cedar Lake during the wheat rush. There is no doubt that M&StL wanted to place the big three-unit EMDs in expedited service between Cedar Lake and Peoria as soon as possible, but those plans misfired when they initially proved unreliable and had to be sent back to LaGrange. By fall, however, they were assigned to freight extras on test schedules designed to get eastbound tonnage out of Cedar Lake around 5:00 a.m. and into Peoria's Bartlett Yard by 10:30 p.m., leaving there around 4:00 a.m. and arriving back in Cedar Lake before 10:00 p.m.—a plan that required only the two three-unit sets for power and allowed transfer of cars to connecting roads before midnight at each terminal, saddling M&StL with only one day's per diem on this important bridge traffic. During the test period dispatchers issued train orders giving these extras rights over all other trains and obliging them to be in the clear, as inferior trains, by at least ten minutes. The plan worked well as long as the diesels stayed healthy, but if they went down or were in the shop, steam engines used in substitution could not keep the schedule because of the need to stop for fuel and water and to add helpers at some locations. In any event, M&StL would formalize the expedited arrangement on January 13, 1946, by establishment of time freights 19 and 20, carded first class like passenger trains, to become the road's flagship trains and giving sales representatives a marvelous tool to use in selling the Peoria Gateway.[18]

M&StL managers urged more expenditures for equipment and, reacting to rising wage and salary costs, simultaneously sought ways to economize. Five hundred fifty-ton steel boxcars, ten fifty-ton boxcars with aluminum superstructures, twenty-eight fifty-ton steel flatcars, and twelve steel underframe cabooses came in 1945, and a diesel shop was erected at Cedar Lake. At the same time, the company succeeded in closing several low-volume stations, particularly in Iowa, at Coppock, Taintor, Marsh, Gifford, Stilson, Wright, Freeman, and Lockman.[19]

Under Sprague's leadership M&StL spent money on public relations, community service, and traffic solicitation in ways and in volumes that would have been unthinkable a few years earlier. In 1943 M&StL sponsored a bowling team at Winthrop, and during the war years it made appreciable donations to the Mayo Memorial, Grinnell College, and Dunwoody Institute, among others. Travel to "show the flag" on-line and elsewhere was frequent. For example, Sprague and fellow senior officials were guests of the Oskaloosa Chamber of Commerce in September 1944 for a "V-Day Celebration for Oskaloosa"—really "celebrating the rise of M&StL from bankruptcy to prosperity." Sprague and entourage arrived by special train. Another one of those special trains, passenger extra 502, roared by the Hazel Run depot at 4:52 p.m. on October 9, 1945, bearing customers and friends of the company to South Dakota for a round of pheasant hunting in what already was a famous custom. In all, Sprague himself spent $27,080 during 1944 and 1945 "for promotion and traffic activities." The board approved, but thereafter requested quarterly reports on such expenditures.[20]

In Minneapolis, *The Road to Utopia* with Bing Crosby and Bob Hope played to large movie audiences early in 1945, but there seemed no road to utopia on the war front. Expectations that hostilities in Europe would be over before the end of 1944 had been dashed, and with them plans to begin transformation of the economy from wartime to peacetime. Indeed, Washington's Office of Defense Transportation warned railroads that 1945 would be the toughest year of all. By March it was clear that Germany soon would fall, and the nation's railroads braced for an accelerated east-to-west movement of men and material as the war focused on Japan.[21]

On May 8, M&StL's train 17 stopped briefly at Clare, Iowa—but it was long enough, no doubt, for the engineman of GE-2 to shout a greeting to agent D. M. Dickenson and to complain good-naturedly about having to work on V-E Day. Indeed, Germany had finally surrendered. At Forest City news of victory in Europe was received gratefully by a subdued citizenry that realized war in the Pacific would continue long and deadly. Business houses closed for the day; individual churches had services of thanksgiving at 3:00 p.m. The mood was the same elsewhere. At Winthrop, the day was observed with "the solemnity and sobriety that was typical throughout the United States."[22]

The grim business of war continued; there was no time to celebrate. Food, clothing, medical goods, post exchange items, and general subsistence materials still flowed eastward to supply the military in Europe, but the bulk of the nation's energies were riveted on the Pacific theater. The War Department, noting fierce Japanese resistance at Iwo Jima and then Okinawa, calculated that an army of nearly 7 million would be needed twelve months out to defeat Japan. At the same time it advised the railroads that about two-thirds of the force in Europe would return to this country for furloughs before heading to the Pacific. The plan would put tremendous pressure on the carriers to move men and material to the West Coast.[23]

Then, with astonishing suddenness, it was over. An atom bomb hit the Japanese city of Hiroshima on August 6. Two days later the editor of an online newspaper bubbled about Buck Rogers and an "atom smasher and harnesser" that might result in "a 'sooner' completion of the war in the Pacific." Another atomic device hit Nagasaki the next day, and President Harry S. Truman blustered that more were on the way if Japan did not capitulate. When M&StL crews went on duty at Spencer, Iowa, early on the morning of August 14, the talk was little of railroading and the day's work, much about the imminent prospect of peace. Enginemen on 457, which would take train 61 to Winthrop, agreed with their brethren on 478, headed for Fort Dodge with train 56: President Truman surely would announce Japan's surrender before they reached their respective homes that night. Such was the case; official word came at the dinner hour. Spencer received the news with unbridled enthusiasm; "shouting throngs" filled the streets that evening. At Hanska, the fire trucks were rolled out, and a band played for those who celebrated by dancing in the street. In Des Moines, streetcar operators took "a four-hour holiday" to celebrate, and Iowa's governor ordered all of the state's liquor stores closed for thirty-six hours. At Minneapolis, the siren

Figure 19.5. Chicago & North Western handled a flood of military traffic through Marshalltown, Iowa, but M&StL was also a player, as this MAIN (Military Authorization Identification Number) train indicates. Don Christiansen photograph, author's collection.

atop Northwestern Bank sounded. But there was little talk of victory; war's end was the focal point of conversation.[24]

For the railroads, the peak movement of passengers was yet to come. The military expected to reduce its ranks by about 500,000 personnel per month by year's end, with troops in Europe to be pared to an occupation force by February 1946; the same would not be true in the Pacific until summer 1946. The movement of replacement troops headed for Europe and Asia plus the glut of returnees meant that American railroads would be confronted with a demand to carry 1.25 million military passengers per month for at least a half year. (There was also a need to move prisoners of war to ports of embarkation. A large base camp for German POWs had been established at Algona, Iowa, from which they had been moved to supplement the agricultural work force at various locations, including on M&StL at Eldora, Montgomery, and New Ulm.) These would be "organized movements" only, which said nothing of movements of individual men and women in the military from place to place on orders, on furloughs, or returning to their homes around the country upon separation from the services. And it said nothing about domestic demand.[25]

In the end, World War II provided the American railroads with their finest hour. They furnished 97 percent of all domestic troop movements and about 90 percent of domestic military freight transportation. M&StL was a willing and able participant. Records do not indicate the freight tonnage that was directly or indirectly of a military nature, but the road handled no fewer than 944 MAIN trains plus uncounted individual service personnel on regular trains as they moved from place to place. Activity was particularly intense late in 1945. Between November 13 and 25, for example, M&StL handled five MAIN trains originating in the Northwest and destined for Eastern or Midwestern points. They were received from Great Northern or Milwaukee at Minneapolis and were wheeled to Illinois Central at Albert Lea or to Wabash at Albia.[26]

Chapter 20
Sprague and Prosperity

After he [Lucian Sprague] had gone back to railroading, and been promoted a few times,
he picked up a new hobby: training race horses, particularly has-beens.
Year after year his broken-down nags won purses for him.
—*Time* (November 29, 1943)

The heady euphoria of V-J Day passed quickly, giving way to confusion and frustration as America sorted through the ambiguous, fluid, and unpredictable postwar environment. The railroad industry mirrored the national mood—one of pride in wartime accomplishments, but tempered by hard memories of the 1930s and uncertainties about the future. Movement of grain continued at record levels following V-J Day, stimulated in part by programs designed to assist war-ravaged Europe. Rates on all commodities were essentially the same in 1945 as they had been at the beginning of the war; passenger rates, roughly 3 cents per mile, up slightly over 1941, were actually less than before World War I. Meanwhile the cost of providing transportation had escalated, and fuel and labor costs were certain to rise even higher as war controls came off, net operating income for the industry was nearly one-fourth lower in 1945 compared to 1944, and the rate of return on property investment averaged only 3.05 percent. Linked to these stern realities was another serious matter. Railroads needed massive infusions of capital to replace weary rolling stock and motive power, much of which had been patched and pasted simply to get through the war, with more modern, efficient equipment. All of it would be expensive; none of it could be accomplished quickly. And what did the future hold?[1]

The year 1946 was not reassuring. President Harry Truman lifted price and wage controls, the public thirsted endlessly for all kinds of consumer goods, the cost of living shot up, and increased wage rates led to even higher prices and to more cries for better wages. Inflation soared. Truman picked his way through automobile and steel strikes, but the public came to see him as outrageously pro-labor. Coal miners and railroad workers thought otherwise. Miners put a crimp in the domestic economy by striking, and so did rail labor, which had served notice by requesting increased wages. Settlements followed with all unions except for trainmen and enginemen, who threatened a strike. Truman responded by taking over the railroads in the name of the government. Train and engine crews walked off the job anyway on May 24 in a strike that lasted three days. Settlements on wage issues followed, but the strike of 1946 sent a signal that relations between labor and management in the railroad industry would be tense in the postwar era.[2]

At M&StL the strike of 1946 reduced train service by 98 percent, yard service by 95 percent; full operation was restored on May 27. Labor relations on the road were not greatly altered by the event and remained mostly positive, but Sprague pointed to dramatic changes in wage rates paid in 1946 ($8.66 million) compared to 1940 ($4.99 million), and chafed at M&StL's being subject to the bargaining positions of larger roads (general contract negotiations were not carried out by individual roads, but rather on an industrywide basis, excepting short lines). "The larger a railroad is the less inclined it will be to barter for a smaller detail that may mean a great deal to properties such as ours," Sprague argued to presidents of similar-sized roads. John W. Barriger at Monon agreed that there was "not always a community of interests" among larger roads and smaller ones when it came to "wage matters." Others were of like mind. "We agree wholeheartedly," said John M. Budd at Chicago & Eastern Illinois, and, chimed in Harold Burtness at Chicago Great Western, "the interests of the smaller roads are pretty well submerged beneath those of the larger companies." Yet there was little that Sprague and the others could do in swaying trends of negotiation at the national level; they realized as much and brooded about prospects for regional carriers. There was, said Sprague, "considerable apathy on the part of the big railroads to permit inroads of that kind and therefore the matter has been stalemated." He was not sanguine. "I don't know if you and I will live long enough to see the situation change," Sprague told Russell Coulter at Toledo, Peoria & Western.[3]

For Sprague, it was a rare moment of pessimism; at his roots he was a consummate optimist. And at M&StL nothing loomed larger than Lucian Charles Sprague—the man who, according to a growing lore, had singlehandedly saved the company and turned it around. It was an image that Sprague thoroughly relished, enthusiastically promoted, and more than occasionally embellished. The line of demarcation between Sprague the man and the company he led became confused, blurred, inexact. For the public and even for many employees, Lucian Sprague *was* M&StL. He fancied antique automobiles; in 1944 the company acquired a Stanley Steamer automobile ostensibly for purposes of public relations and advertising. Sprague also loved horses, owning and even driving champion pacers; he was secretary of the Trotting Horse Club of America, where banker E. Roland Harriman was president and where Hollywood's James Cagney was inducted as a member at Sprague's behest. Not surprisingly, the car *Twin Cities* found itself often in Louisville for the Kentucky Derby and other places fashionable to horsemen, where Sprague hobnobbed with important persons and showed the M&StL flag. He doted on his wife, Ruth (Greer Garson's double if ever there was one, according to one admiring observer), and his daughter, Geraldine, who often traveled with him on these trips, and to a lesser extent on Lucian, his son by his first wife. Family members also went with Sprague aboard the *Twin Cities* on fishing trips to Waconia but rarely if ever on the road's famous excursions to South Dakota, where M&StL officers joined shippers, friends of the company, and celebrities such as tenor James Melton in hunting pheasants near Leola, Aberdeen, Conde, Bradley, or Florence. Sprague's favorite 502 often headed the train, which was made up of a baggage car or two, the *Twin Cities,* cars 101 and 102, a diner borrowed from the Omaha, and whatever equipment could be scratched up among the larger roads in Minneapolis and St. Paul. These passenger extras had rights over all trains; grade crossings were protected by section men. "They really whizzed by," recalled the agent at Wood Lake, Minnesota.[4]

One of the most impressive of these South Dakota excursions was staged in November 1948, when a fifteen-car train took movie funnyman Frank Morgan, Hollywood filmmaker Hal Roach, and "50 top business executives" for a weekend of hunting around Conde. They were, reported the *Watertown Public Opinion,* "guests of the genial president of the M&StL, Lucian C. Sprague of Minneapolis." The hunting proved only fair, but the weather was kind, and guests clearly enjoyed Sprague's generous hospitality. Conversation among them often drifted to world affairs, the cold war, domestic business conditions, and Harry Truman's astonishing (and, most guests thought, disappointing) victory in the recent presidential election. What was the true purpose of these trips? wondered a mildly skeptical but obviously impressed writer for the *Public Opinion.* They were merely one element of M&StL's "secret" policy that had resulted in its steady growth and admirable

Figure 20.1. In 1944 M&StL acquired steam and diesel alike—a Stanley Steamer for Sprague's edification and Alcos such as 944 for revenue service. Sprague, at the wheel of the automobile, looked pleased and confident; John Devins, to Sprague's left, appeared rather more resigned. Colin W. Wright seemed to be along for the ride. M&StL photograph, author's collection.

financial condition. "We try to be tops as a freight railroad by helping the shipper sell his products and making contacts for him in areas all over the country served by M&StL," responded an expansive Sprague in his best cheerleading style. There certainly were contacts to be made on this train, with its passengers composed of the business elite from Minneapolis–St. Paul and others who represented grain, steel, banking, publishing, and transportation (even a vice president from Pan American Airways). They were, concluded the reporter, "key figures all . . . rubbing elbows, renewing acquaintances, and reviewing 'conditions.'"[5]

Sprague's favorite locomotive, the spiffy 502, was likely one of those assigned to the 1948 special, but the 502 and all of its brethren were living on short time. When it came to the issue of steam versus diesel, Sprague was coolly dispassionate. Steam required much more time for servicing, repairing, and inspecting than diesels; mass-produced interchangeable parts favored diesels; and diesels had a much more favorable availability ratio. In addition, diesels made better over-the-road time; frequent stops for coal and water were obviated. This was particularly at issue on the main line, where time freights were routinely double headed out of Cedar Lake to Albert Lea and where engines were changed at Albert Lea, Marshalltown, and Oskaloosa—aggregating five locomotives minimum for the 474-mile run and routinely consuming

Figure 20.2. Sprague and his wife, Ruth, were frequent travelers on the *Twin Cities.* M&StL photograph, author's collection.

a full nine hours en route for changing engines, taking coal and water, and cleaning fires. The numbers were unrelenting—even more so at M&StL than at many other roads, because there was no truly modern power on its roster. In any event, Sprague was unapologetic in asking the board for more diesel locomotives; the board happily complied. By the end of 1946, M&StL employed nineteen Alcos; at the end of the decade the number was twenty-seven. To these were added another General Electric forty-four-ton switcher in 1949, a three-unit F-2 freighter for main-line service in 1947, and three two-unit F-3 freighters for general service on the main line and west to Watertown from General Motors' Electro-Motive Division in 1948.[6]

M&StL's yard at Cedar Lake was the focal point in the change from steam to diesel. That venerable facility, with its roundhouse, backshop, blacksmith-boiler shop, mill and car shop, and a new diesel house, was the domain of R. C. Goebel, master mechanic. Tall, nice looking, and solidly built, Goebel had a good sense of humor and was easy to work for. "If you could not buy it they would make it," Goebel and his successor William W. Landmesser proudly boasted of Cedar Lake personnel, who had tenderly cared for M&StL's modest steam fleet and now took the same solicitous attitude toward diesel-electric power. Late in 1945 John Devins asked Goebel for a dry-eyed recommendation as to the costs versus the benefits of repairs for M&StL's steam fleet. In that study Goebel ruled out repairs adequate for more than one-year service on most of the road's remaining Moguls (four), Ten-wheelers (three), and Consolidations (twenty). Safest, it seemed, were ten 0-6-0s (numbers 80–89), eleven 2-8-0s (451–461), the remaining 4-6-2 (502), and thirty-three 2-8-2s (600–634). As more Alcos arrived, plans evolved to dieselize the line between Hopkins and Leola; water stations were retired at Excelsior, Delhi, and Dawson in 1946; coaling stations at Morton and Watertown followed a year later. But M&StL hedged its bets, arranging with Great Northern at Watertown for coal and water should the need arise, stationing a protection engine (a 2-8-0) at Aberdeen, and maintaining all steam service facilities at Winthrop. No such contingency plans were made on the line segments from Albert Lea to Fort Dodge, Fort Dodge to Des Moines, and Fort Dodge to Estherville, where Alcos replaced steam late in 1946 and early in 1947. For instance, diesels first appeared at Corwith on November 20, 1946, and at Spencer on February 15, 1947. Steam got a reprieve of sorts when snow clogged the line northwest from Fort Dodge to Estherville, but when 452 chuffed out of Spencer with train 56 on June 14, the curtain fell forever on steam locomotives in road service in and out of Fort Dodge. Steam hung on, however, at Des Moines, where an 0-6-0 protected switching assignments and where steam arrived on trains from Oskaloosa, and between Winthrop and Estherville, where Consolidation 460 regularly pulled trains 60–61.[7]

The transition on the main line and on the Iowa branches followed. Late in 1946 Moguls 330 and 333 worked the Story City Branch; two years later Consolidations 404 and 412 were assigned tasks on the Corwith Branch, and Ten-Wheeler 229 toiled up the Newton Branch. The big FTs from EMD handled trains 19 and 20, of course, but through 1948 and well into 1949 steam was assigned to trains 94 and 97, in addition to main-line locals and extras. Contraction came quickly at the end of 1949, by which time the road owned a mere thirty-eight steam locomotives. Early in 1950 steam was restricted to Winthrop and the main line, mostly between Cedar Lake and Albert Lea and between Oskaloosa and Peoria. On January 6, Mikado 625 hustled out of Monmouth with train 10, and on February 3, 633 paused at Packwood to do local work, but the handsome 2-8-2s were merely standing in for regularly assigned Alcos. Both locomotives would be consigned to junkers in a few weeks. Elsewhere, 0-6-0 number 83 toiled away at Peoria in April, but calls for steam during most of the year were rare. Only six locomotives, five Mikados and one Mogul, survived the year; the final call may have been for a 600 on a troop train in January 1951 or, curiously, for the Mogul on a branch trip. The most celebrated final bow had come earlier, however, and off-line, in September 1949, when a dolled-up 502 strutted across the stage as part of "Wheels a-Rolling," the Chicago Railroad Fair's colossal lakefront pageant. In any event, all water and coaling stations were retired by early fall of 1951, except at Albert Lea, where facilities were required to service Illinois Central power.[8]

As steam locomotives became unnecessary "for present operations of the Company," or as "they permanently became in disuse," they were disposed of—mostly to scrappers. A few lived out their lives elsewhere. Mogul 66 had gone to Bevier & Southern as early as 1943, and two 2-8-0s (452 and 457) were sold to American Crystal Sugar, where they switched cars for several beet seasons at Chaska and Mason City. A private party rescued another 2-8-0 for a proposed museum in Minnesota, and seven sprightly 0-6-0s (80, 81, 82, 84, 85, 87, and 88) went to Midland Electric at Middle Grove, where their crisp, arrogant exhausts could be heard well into the 1960s as they wrestled coal from mine to tipple. Canada's Algoma Central picked up eight of the Mikados (602, 605, 608, 613, 617, 618, 621, and 624) at bargain prices. When Algoma's president asked his purchasing agent why the 2-8-2s came so cheap, he was told: "Oh, they're dieselizing." The Algoma president looked puzzled and replied: "Don't you think we should find out why?" Sprague relished the telling of that story.[9]

The superiority of diesel over steam was indisputable. Yet not even the flintiest-eyed accountant or the most hardened industrial engineer would argue that there was a substitute for the sight, sound, and fury of awesome steel giants under steam. The whine of turbo generators; the pulsating beat of air compressors; the panting urgency of an iron steed ready for labor; the mixed smells of steam, coal smoke, and valve oil; the wail of a steam whistle distinctive to the artistry of the engineer—all of this spoke to something deep in the human soul. Of man's splendid inventions, perhaps the steam locomotive was the most humanized—its moods singularly apparent, its breathing acute and purposeful as that of any life form, its very being boasting of muscularity and self-assurance. The diesel's superiority was unquestioned, to be sure, but an important and tangible quality of railroading passed when fires were dropped for the last time on an M&StL locomotive.[10]

If Sprague's eyes lit up at the sight of shiny, new diesels, they darkened sourly under bushy eyebrows when he beheld the road's virtual museum of passenger equipment. He consistently had played down M&StL's role as a passenger carrier, and the road certainly had a limited responsibility in that area, but as World War II wound down it tugged at his ego to admit that the average age of the passenger cars in M&StL's service was nearly thirty-nine years, that some of the pieces dated from the previous century, that nearly all were fully depreciated, and that the company's master mechanic had declared that most of the roster was "obsolete," "unfit," or "should be considered for retirement." War restrictions prevented ordering new equipment when M&StL had emerged from receivership, but in mid-1944 giant New York Central was permitted to order three hundred cars, and as conditions eased Sprague was not far behind, placing a tiny booking for six stainless steel coaches with the Edward M. Budd Company at $77,250 per copy. Budd was inundated with work, however, and it was not until May 17, 1948, that the cars finally entered service—now at a unit cost of $93,718. Streamlined, air conditioned, plush in every way, the splendid new cars nevertheless looked incongruous bouncing along dutifully if elegantly behind the road's proud but shopworn GE cars on runs to Watertown, Albert Lea, Albia, and Des Moines.[11]

Not at all attractive in the way of the new Budd coaches but utilitarian and certain to earn its keep was M&StL's impressive new freight equipment. By early 1946 American railroads had 40,217 freight cars on order, swamping manufacturers. In 1945 M&StL

Figure 20.3. Passengers for the fine new Budd coach were absent, but there were mail and express for train 7 at Manly, Iowa, on this summer day in 1949. William F. Armstrong photograph.

had joined Rock Island and Chicago & Alton in an experiment with fifty-ton-capacity aluminum boxcars; each road took ten. M&StL's purpose was to use them solely for less-than-carload business from Minneapolis to St. Louis in conjunction with Wabash. During the next four years orders were more traditional but substantial—118 flats, 50 covered hoppers, 250 drop-bottom gondolas, 600 boxes, and 25 cabooses (built in company shops). At the end of the decade the road's freight car inventory stood at a modest 3,608 cars, about half the number of 1923, but with equal or greater carrying capacity.[12]

Sprague also spent eagerly on plant and structures. The main line got special attention in the four years following the war, with two hundred miles of new or used hundred-pound rail; more track anchors, ballast, and surfacing; lengthened passing tracks and spring switches with signal protection; and automatic block signals from Bartlett Yard up the hill to Maxwell, Illinois. Eighty-five-pound rail from the main line was cascaded into main-line passing tracks or elsewhere on the system—especially west of Hopkins to Watertown, which also was favored with another ballast and surfacing campaign and other betterments. Cuts were widened and ballast applied even on the Iowa branches. Snow fences in South Dakota were strengthened, and interchange capacity with Santa Fe at Nemo was increased. Depots at Boyd, Hopkins, Gowrie, and Humboldt were remodeled and modernized; handsome new "brick-block" depots were erected at Arlington, Clarkfield, Gaylord, Madison, New Sharon, Perry, and Union. A two-story office building went up at Bartlett Yard, and a fine new diesel shop was authorized for Marshalltown in 1949 and completed a year later.[13]

Aside from M&StL's fleet of new diesels, perhaps nothing of a physical nature better reflected the restored and invigorated road than its splendid new general office building at 111 East Franklin Avenue in Minneapolis. For more than a decade M&StL had been officed in the stolid Northwestern National Bank Building in the heart of downtown, but in 1947 the rent doubled and no attractive alternate space could be found elsewhere; accordingly the board authorized acquisition of lots on Franklin Avenue to be used for construction of the new building. An architect was hired in 1949; construction began in 1950, making extensive use of materials and furnishings produced in Minnesota. The $1 million dollar, 80,000-square-foot facility was completely air conditioned and would be the work home for about three hundred employees. A proud and beaming Lucian Sprague would greet hundreds of well wishers at the dedication of this handsome edifice on May 15, 1951.[14]

M&StL, of course, had owned offices at its inception, subsequently headquartered for a while in its own depot on Second Street, and thereafter moved successively, depending on its financial circumstance at the moment, to rented space in the Boston Block, the Metropolitan Life Building, the Transportation Building, and finally Northwestern Bank, where it had occupied two upper floors and space at street level. Its moves from place to place, and now into its own facility, reflected a tenacious will to live, an engaging story of accomplishment—often against great odds—and a story in which Sprague had been a central player, one that he wanted recorded and disseminated. Managers of other properties, neighboring Milwaukee and North Western among them, recently had been similarly inspired and had commissioned writers to turn out histories in book form. Fortunately for Sprague, Frank P. Donovan Jr., a prince of a man and a fine stylist, was available for the M&StL project. Born on October 4, 1909, in Pennsylvania, with a degree in English and speech from American University, Donovan had worked for the Railway Express Agency and Pacific Electric and had had his writings published in *Railroad Magazine* and elsewhere before signing on for a stint at *Trains*. Beginning at M&StL in the fall of 1948, he had an assignment at once enviable and daunting. He had easy access to company personnel and existing records plus a modest travel allowance, but company archives were scarce and Sprague wanted a book out as quickly as possible. "I only wish I had the time to spend about two years on the 'Louie' instead of just one," Donovan complained good-naturedly in a letter to Professor Henrietta M. Larson at Harvard. Company records were scant, he knew, the result of shifting financial control over the years, of moving so often from one office to another, of a 1927

Figure 20.4. Perhaps nothing of a physical nature more reflected the restored and invigorated M&StL than its new general office building in Minneapolis.

fire in a records-holding area, and of a decision to destroy records to save storage expense shortly before he had been brought on. "Outside of stock and bondholders reports and receivership records we have practically nothing," Donovan wearily admitted. In fact, the company secretary could not even provide a full run of annual reports—nothing for the years before 1878 and nothing from the entire decade of the 1880s. Nevertheless, Donovan turned out a highly readable book brilliantly entitled *Mileposts on the Prairie.* Reviews were generally favorable. The *New York Times* called it "an excellent story of a sick railroad that got well." Railroader John W. Barriger, who earlier would have dismembered M&StL, said it was "one of the finest railroad histories ever written," and historian Richard C. Overton pointed to it as "a rattling good book." For a while it seemed that Hollywood might pick up the rights to *Mileposts,* and columnist Hedda Hopper even claimed that "the colorful story of Lucian C. Sprague and the Minneapolis & St. Louis" had been purchased by Nat Holt for Paramount, but it was not to be.[15]

Sprague was never modest about his own accomplishments and those of M&StL; nor did he miss any opportunity to broadcast those attainments. *Mileposts* was a reflection of those instincts. So were M&StL's aggressive public relations and advertising campaigns. When M&StL employees from Minneapolis took first place in the 1949 American Railway Bowling Association tournament, Sprague delighted in the trophy and told team members how proud he was "of the public relations job you men are doing for our railway." The same year M&StL sponsored the Easter program of the Minneapolis Traffic Club at the Hotel Nicollet, and the company float won a third-place ribbon in the East Minneapolis Centennial Parade. Advertising in on-line newspapers and national magazines was extensive and clearly represented Sprague's inclinations. "We pledge our utmost effort . . . the same effort we devoted to winning the war . . . to make sure our service men and women are home by Christmas," read an ad in the *Arlington Enterprise* late in 1945. It sounded smug and self-serving, but it also was true. A year later M&StL promised shippers that it was making determined progress toward "ever-finer service through the years of peace," pointing to new diesel power and rolling stock as evidence of that commitment. M&StL touted soybeans as the "miracle crop" in a *U.S. News & World Report* ad and advised readers that M&StL's service area produced more than half of the domestic harvest; every month was "perfect shipping month," the company told *Fortune*'s subscribers; and in 1949, as Minnesota celebrated the hundredth anniversary of its admission as a territory of the United States, M&StL reminded readers of the *Minneapolis Tribune* that the road and the state had been "growing together" over those many years and that M&StL had long played a "lead role in Minnesota's agricultural and industrial progress."[16]

No advertising theme got greater play, however, than the Peoria Gateway, where, promised M&StL, "freight moved faster," saving "hours and even days" on transcontinental "bridge traffic" between East and West. "New equipment—heavy duty tracks—teletypewriter services" all combined for "fast, dependable freight service via the Peoria Gateway." It was not an idle boast. Reliable and adequate power plus a well-groomed main line did combine to give shippers a quality product—eighteen hours elapsed time between Cedar Lake and Bartlett on cars handled by time freights 19 and 20 and designed to make maximum utility of motive power. Tonnage on those flagship trains might be billed to or from M&StL stations, but more likely moved overhead from connections in the Twin Cities and Peoria. Great Northern and Northern Pacific were principal partners on western lading; several roads including Toledo, Peoria & Western, New York Central, and Pennsylvania vied for traffic at Peoria. Another of these, New York, Chicago & St. Louis (Nickel Plate), was the high-powered westernmost player among a collection of roads known euphemistically as the Alphabet Route, which in 1931 had developed a coordinated and remarkably efficient means of expediting time-sensitive traffic to and from New York, Philadelphia, and Baltimore.[17]

As always, it fell to the traffic department to sell M&StL's product. In 1936 newly arrived Lucian Sprague had assembled his largely demoralized sales force and put them on a five-car train for a tour of the system, inculcating them with his own enthusiasm and his basic philosophy that the way to get traffic was to help the shipper sell his goods. M&StL traffic men soon caught the spirit and began studying shipper sales and marketing problems, suggesting to customers ways they might expand their business, looking into and reporting on potential new market opportunities. It worked. *American Feed and Grain,* for example, extolled M&StL, saying that "superior customer service rebuilt this railroad" and that M&StL had "created a real reservoir of good will, of the sort that always must rate as the prime accomplishment of any successful enterprise." Sprague was relentless. In 1949 he again assembled the sales crew and again put them aboard a special train for a four-day pep talk and inspection of the road. Beyond that, he convinced the board to approve an across-the-board salary increase for all sales personnel. In the process he further cemented their loyalty to the company and to himself as well.[18]

As had been its lot from the beginning, M&StL was constricted by its own abbreviated route structure, which lay across a territory honeycombed with rail lines that offered customers a bewildering array of junction connections and routing options that might be used to avoid M&StL altogether or to short haul it. And M&StL's own territorial integrity had been breached early in the Great Depression, when Chicago & North Western had gained access from Peoria over M&StL to the rich coal fields at Middle Grove. Irked by this intrusion and arguing that the arrangement imposed "unjustified burdens" on it while accruing "large unjustified benefits" for Chicago & North Western, M&StL tried to evict the interloper in 1947, but an obdurate Interstate Commerce Commission said the matter of such agreements was "beyond its statutory power"; M&StL was obliged to go on sharing heavy tonnage in coal as a consequence. Sprague and his lieutenants likewise probed for ways to actually expand M&StL's reach, active on several fronts at once. Shortly after V-J Day, the board hired Coverdale & Colpitts to study the merits of acquiring the Illinois Terminal Railroad, which would give M&StL entry to St. Louis, among other things, and finally legitimize the company's name. M&StL representatives also poked around at Toledo, Peoria & Western, seeking lease of that road as a means to extend M&StL's bridge hauls by another hundred miles to a connection with Pennsylvania at Effner, Indiana. Even earlier, Sprague and Pennsylvania's James M. Symes, then in charge of western lines and eventually president of that huge road, had talked of M&StL's using or perhaps even leasing Pennsylvania's line from Peoria to Terre Haute, Indiana. Symes and other Pennsylvania personnel had

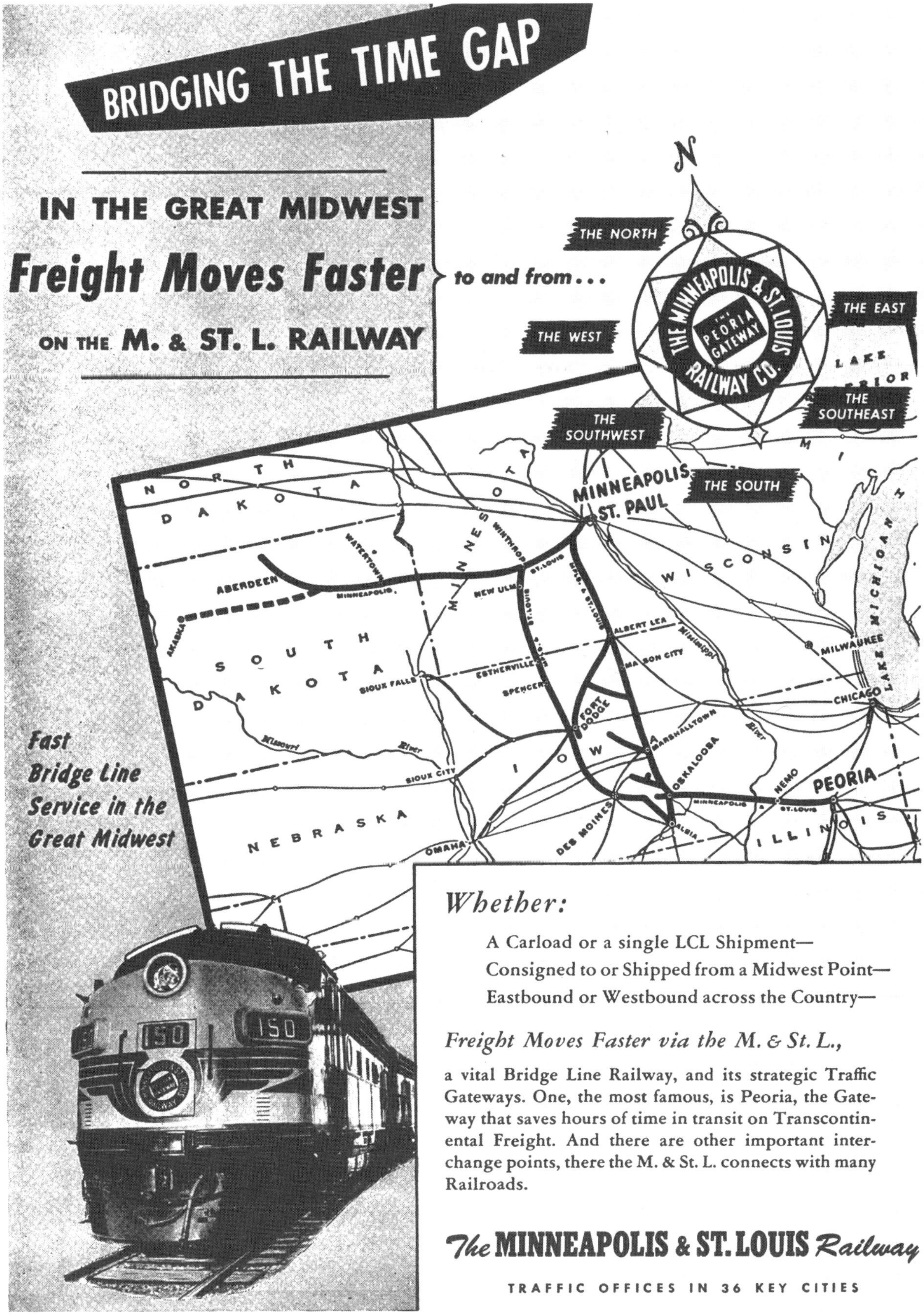

Figure 20.5. Sprague was relentless in advertising a robust M&StL in modern garb. Author's collection.

joined M&StL managers during the summer of 1945 to inspect M&StL's main line and Pennsylvania's route to Terre Haute, and in the fall of 1946 M&StL loaned one of its three-unit FTs for tests over the Peoria–Terre Haute line. Pennsylvania was impressed with the performance of M&StL's 445, but for whatever reason the two roads did not work out arrangements by which M&StL's reach could be extended to Terre Haute. Neither could any agreement be made with Toledo, Peoria & Western, and Illinois Terminal, as Coverdale & Colpitts quickly discovered, was freighted with an excess of financial liabilities. Thus perished every one of Sprague's innovative expansion efforts.[19]

These several strategic setbacks were disappointing, of course, but at the time they did not seem ominous. M&StL's feisty sales force was pulling in plenty of traffic for the longest possible hauls on time freights 19 and 20, and the postwar economy, after an early shudder, was chugging along with great demand for automobiles, housing, and all sorts of durable goods. For the period from 1946 through 1949, M&StL handled an average of 241,200 revenue cars per annum and an annual average of 8,259,209 tons; 1947 produced all-time high marks of 257,146 revenue carloads and 8,929,875 tons. Grain, flour, lumber, cement, soft coal, merchandise, and livestock produced slightly over half of all tonnage, down from 70 percent in 1920 and nearly 84 percent in 1900.[20]

Corn surpassed wheat in M&StL's tonnage in 1933 and, with only two exceptions, 1935 and 1937, held the lead in grains ever after. Barley, rye, and oats tilted for third place until they were edged out by soybeans after the war. Corn produced a surge of billings late in the fall of each year, but it was wheat that caused a rush, especially on the West End all the way to Leola. The year 1946 was typical. Dispatchers began hoarding equipment at midsummer, and sent extra trains to spot empties under grain spouts early in July. By late September the rush was over, although in some years it lasted into November. Many of these wheat billings were subject to "milling in transit" privileges, and cars headed initially to Kenwood Yard, set out there for grading by the Western Weighing & Inspection Bureau before moving on to plants at Minneapolis, where wheat was milled into flour and sent to destinations all over the country. Not all wheat billed at M&StL stations went to Minneapolis, of course; much found its way to important millers at New Prague and New Ulm and to a few smaller operators elsewhere.[21]

Coal, cement, clay brick and tile, gypsum products, and lumber also contributed significant tonnage. The number of tons of coal peaked in 1944 (2,489,955), but averaged 1,924,954 per annum during the years 1946–49, accounting for 20 to 25 percent of all tonnage, and, happy to say, much of it was loaded at Middle Grove and Fairview. Activity at cement plants located in Mason City and West Des Moines ebbed and flowed with the business cycle and with activity in the construction field, which tended to be brisk through this period. The same could be said of clay brick and tile, which provided handsome business on-line at Kalo and Sheffield, Iowa, and by connection at Mason City; of products from gypsum mills at Fort Dodge; and of the flow of lumber to M&StL points or moving overhead. The number of housing starts nationwide in 1949 was 1,349,000, up sharply from 139,000 in the war year 1944; the result was heavy demand for construction material of all kinds. For M&StL, during these years it meant 11 to 15 percent of all tonnage. Little of the lumber came from Minnesota mills, a distinct change from earlier times; it came from West Coast points that M&StL representatives solicited especially for "roller lumber looking for a home," that is, shipped before sold and "billed in transit." Most of this came from Great Northern or Northern Pacific, less from Milwaukee and Canadian Pacific–Soo Line or Canadian National–Duluth, Winnipeg & Pacific and intermediate carriers from Duluth.[22]

Food products—originating, terminating, or moving overhead—were also important in the traffic mix. Jacob Decker & Company continued to supply a regular flow of packinghouse products from its large plant at Mason City; the Wilson & Company at Albert Lea and Tobin at Estherville and Fort Dodge provided lading through connections. Cars of meat, fruit, vegetables, and other perishables needing refrigeration could be iced or reiced at Fort Dodge, Marshalltown, Oskaloosa, or Bartlett Yard in Peoria. Dried milk from the Tri-County Dairy at Winthrop needed no refrigeration. Neither did canned vegetables that spewed forth from plants at Ackley, Lake Mills, Roland, Arlington, Montgomery, Winthrop, and other stations, nor did beets moving to American Crystal Sugar mills at Chaska and Mason City and refined sugar outbound.[23]

Some traffic, prominent in the past, disappeared or became insignificant. Ice harvesting and storage facilities at Waconia burned in 1938, and although there was an icehouse at Lake Kampeska near Watertown and Cedar Lake Ice Company continued to cut at Cedar Lake and at Lake Riley near Eden Prairie, about the only ice moving on M&StL now was for its own icing facilities. Beer was still a part of the mix, but no longer in small lots from on-line brewers; now it came mostly from large firms in Milwaukee and St. Louis. LCL business was small in terms of total tonnage, and it was burdensome and not compensatory, but M&StL, like other roads, continued in the trade out of tradition and because regulators were unlikely to permit departure from it. LCL cars moved over the Alphabet Route to and from eastern cities; to and from St. Louis (via Wabash), Kansas City (via Atchison, Topeka & Santa Fe), Cincinnati (via New York Central), and Chicago (via Illinois Central); and some cars moved to principal stations such as Aberdeen and Peoria, but most LCL to on-line stations went by truck—in M&StL's own vehicles between Monmouth and Peoria and from Aberdeen to Leola and Akaska, mostly by Brady Transfer & Storage in Iowa, and by Spellacy Motor Cargo in Minnesota.[24]

Figure 20.6. Beets in season provided heavy tonnage, as evidenced by Extra 611, which was blowing through Hopkins, Minnesota, in the fall of 1949. M&StL photograph, author's collection.

One of the clearest examples of the diversion of rail traffic to highway was reflected in the receipts of livestock at major markets. Before the Great War a negligible volume of livestock had traveled by truck, but by 1930 it was around 30 percent, just before Pearl Harbor it stood at 63 percent, and in the immediate postwar era it rose to nearly 70 percent. These trends were mirrored at M&StL. During the 1930s the company had vigorously prosecuted simultaneous systemwide policies of adding pens and upper-deck loading chutes in stockyards where demand justified it and of reducing or even dismantling facilities where it did not. Upper decks were added to company-owned stock cars, and later, when this fleet was reduced, the road leased more than one hundred steel underframe cars. Loadings plummeted after 1934, however, averaging only 50,334 tons per year in the last half of the decade; the annual average ten years later, in the last half of the 1940s, was a dreary 33,415 tons. The change at Winthrop was typical. In 1931 the Winthrop Shipping Association had used M&StL exclusively for its transportation needs, but in 1938 new managers announced that the association would "operate two livestock trucks between Winthrop and South St. Paul." Four years later meager livestock loadings at that place required only a portable loading chute. Major improvements were made to livestock handling facilities at Dawson, Mallard, and Oskaloosa during the 1940s, but all facilities were removed at former principal livestock points such as Dallas Center, Grinnell, Olds, Zearing, Conde, and even Leola, where not so many years earlier the agent had crawled up the water tower on Saturday mornings to survey the horizon, looking for telltale clouds of dust that indicated cattle heading toward company pens. Based on these observations the agent had estimated the number of animals being trailed in and then telegraphed that information to Aberdeen, where an upbound train cut in adequate cars to be loaded. "I hardly ever missed the estimate," said a proud Mark F. Sharping, who as a young man had handled those responsibilities. Sharping also recalled billing wild horses from the McPherson County capital to eastern destinations. But that era was gone forever at Leola and most other M&StL stations. What livestock business remained was composed of hogs destined from local points to major livestock markets or to packing houses at Albert Lea, Fort Dodge, or Mason City; horses for slaughter at Estherville; or stocker cattle inbound from ranges in the West or the Southwest.[25]

Exotic or unusual lading was rare at M&StL. But in 1949 the road did haul potable water to Dallas Center when the town's well failed. Tank cars were loaded at the Des Moines roundhouse spout and at Dallas Center were pumped into the water tower near the depot. The railroad was happy to oblige the town's needs until a permanent solution to the shortage was found.[26]

As had been the case from the beginning of the road, Minneapolis was the focal point of traffic. In 1947 arrangements were made at the west end of Railway Transfer's property to serve a Stephens Buick warehouse that expected to see delivery of nine thousand automobiles annually. Two years later M&StL announced plans for a large produce terminal of the type desperately yearned for by generations of earlier managers. By the end of 1940s, M&StL reached 10 percent of all Minneapolis industries with sidings; in many cases it was the only carrier serving primary customers. Indeed, the line from Cedar Lake Yard to Railway Transfer was a customer-rich corridor that included a sizeable unloading platform for automobiles along Linden Avenue; significant spurs to industries and warehouses; team tracks, platforms, and derricks; R. N. Katz, Rifkin & Company, Joe Schaffer, Jacob Feinberg & Company, Armour & Company—a complex of fresh meat, vegetable, and fruit distributors; another complex with Booth Fisheries, Fairfax Produce, and Gamble-Robinson Produce; Ornes & Sons, General Electric, LaCrosse Implement, the Hudson Thurbee Company, Merchants Cold Storage, Murphy Warehouse No. 1, and National Biscuit; M&StL's "Out Freight House" between Fifth and Fourth Streets North; M&StL's "In Freight House" (full-block facilities with attending covered platforms facing tracks) between Fourth and Third; spurs to bulk plants; and, significantly, the large milling district served by Railway Transfer. To these important customers was added the Municipal River Terminal, downstream from the Washington Avenue Bridge, long advocated and finally completed during the 1930s, which was served exclusively by M&StL's Railway Transfer. Inbound coal and outbound scrap iron were early primary commodities at the River Terminal.[27]

M&StL had no sweetheart arrangements with carriers from the West at Minneapolis or Minnesota Transfer, although Great Northern and Northern Pacific were the most active interchange partners, nor was there a favored connection at Peoria, where M&StL had direct interchange with Rock Island, Toledo, Peoria & Western, and, most important, with Peoria & Pekin Union, which reached all others. Alliances with Wabash at Albia and with Illinois Central at Albert Lea were of long standing. That with Santa Fe at Nemo was little remarked but vitally important. M&StL routed an LCL car from Minneapolis via Atchison, Topeka & Santa Fe at Nemo and vigorously solicited Texas Gulf Coast and Southern California traffic, especially perishables and to a lesser extent feeder cattle, over that route. Nemo, as a consequence, was a surprisingly busy place and reflected M&StL's reliance on well-established interchange partners. During the 1940s only 21 percent of M&StL's freight traffic originated and terminated on-line; over 50 percent originated elsewhere and terminated on M&StL or originated on M&StL and terminated elsewhere. The remaining business, nearly 28 percent, bridge traffic, merely passed overhead.[28]

Persistent predictions that Americans would abandon passenger trains in favor of private automobiles in the postwar era proved painfully accurate. Short-haul business was at particular risk. Early in 1945 *Railway Age* had applauded M&StL's surprising decision to acquire new coaches, seeing in that move "the first experiment made to determine what modern equipment, operated as individual cars, can do to rehabilitate local passenger traffic." Unfortunately, however, the cars would not arrive until May 1948, long after motorists had adequate supplies of reasonably priced tires and gasoline, and almost correspondent with matched auto production and demand. This delay prevented any legitimate test of passenger loyalty at the end of the war; local passengers, the kind M&StL catered to, had made up their minds by 1948.[29]

At M&StL passenger boardings slumped from

Figures 20.7A and 20.7B. From Cedar Lake, Minnesota, to the Railway Transfer was a traffic-rich corridor. M&StL photographs, author's collection.

289,372 in 1945 (the highest since 1930) to 190,319 in 1946 and to 106,088 in 1949. Passenger miles in 1947 were only 24 percent of those in 1945. Ticket income dropped at about the same rate. There were times, of course, when trains were crowded, especially in 1946, when demobilization was finally accomplished; Georges Denzene and his wife, for example, were obliged to ride on a bench in the baggage car from New Prague to Minneapolis on the Fourth of July, and a recently discharged serviceman found the cars nearly full when he traveled to Madison after accepting a teaching position in that community. Late the next year the Auxiliary Chorus of the Hanska American Legion Post took the train to Minneapolis to give a concert and on the snow-delayed return trek amused themselves and other passengers with a song fest. But group movements of that type were rare, and the writer Frank P. Donovan Jr. was certainly the exception when he took his wife from Minneapolis to Albert Lea for Thanksgiving dinner at the station beanery ("not fancy but very good, with plenty of turkey"). The quaint restaurant in the old frame hotel next to the depot at Morton still featured an attractive menu, and conductors on the nocturnal Watertown run awakened dozing passengers so that they might get "a bite to eat" when the train stopped there. Unfortunately, however, there were fewer and fewer customers to enjoy amenities at Morton and Albert Lea.[30]

There was little that M&StL could do to increase revenues in the passenger-carrying trade and, frankly, not much that it could do in trimming costs given restrictive labor agreements. The result was predictable. Late in 1947 the company won approval to end the Minnesota leg of the Winthrop–Fort Dodge run. This prosaic but little-used operation had become essentially a vehicle for moving almost everything but passengers; the brakeman/baggageman alighted at every sleepy depot to open the freighthouse and load and unload baggage, mail, express, newspapers, company mail (including outbound cash and checks), and occasionally human remains (one regular first-class fare "regardless of the age of the deceased"). Service north of Estherville ended without fanfare on December 28, with mail and express handled thereafter along with LCL on M&StL trucks. The stub operation from Fort Dodge to Estherville was put on a daylight turnaround schedule using one car and one crew. Income was supplemented by occasional carloads of horses consigned to Estherville for slaughter and a more regular flow of dressed meat from Tobin Packing at Estherville to a connection in Fort Dodge. The daylight schedule displeased postal authorities, however, and effective April 1, 1948, mail was withdrawn from the train. It was a death sentence; M&StL urged euthanasia. Testimony showed that ticket sales provided a miniscule 3 cents per train mile, and the Iowa Commerce Commission concluded that retaining service would put the line itself in danger. Express consignments could be handled with LCL by Brady under contract to M&StL. When Conductor Levert A. Wescott stepped off the rear platform of GE-1 when it arrived at Fort Dodge on time at 4:20 p.m. Thursday, June 24, 1948, regularly scheduled passenger service ended forever on that portion of M&StL.[31]

Mail revenue exceeded ticket sales for M&StL in 1947 and was nearly double ticket revenues in 1948. It was a pattern not to be broken despite the loss of several mail contracts around the system. When passenger trains had been terminated between Oskaloosa and Peoria early in the 1940s they had been replaced by mixed trains that included Railway Post Office (RPO) authorization; postal authorities ended that contract on February 28, 1946. It was much the same in South Dakota, where a combination coach-baggage-RPO car bobbed along at the end of trains 115 and 116 between Watertown and Aberdeen. En route sorting ended there on October 15, 1948. That left three RPO routes aboard M&StL lines: Minneapolis, Fort Dodge & Des Moines; Albert Lea & Albia; and, Minneapolis & Watertown. All of these handled appreciable volumes of mail, including that to and from local stations, as well as mails received from and dispatched to connecting RPO routes. Minneapolis & Watertown, for example, connected with all other routes converging on or diverging from Minneapolis and St. Paul, with the St. Paul & Aberdeen (Milwaukee Road) at Norwood and the Willmar & Sioux City (Great Northern) at Hanley Falls. In addition, clerks postmarked letter mail handed to them at station stops and "robbed the box" (emptied the postal box) at the North Redwood depot. The latter chore posed anxiety for clerks on Minneapolis & Watertown train 13, who had to postmark and sort these "drops" before the train reached Delhi, 6.5 miles distant, where the "go back" or return pouch (containing misdirected letters or any for eastern distribution) was placed in the freighthouse for train 14. Even busier were clerks on the Des Moines run, which intersected a half-dozen major RPO routes, feeding them and being fed by them, and directly servicing forty-six communities en route. It was much the same for Albert Lea & Albia, which touched thirty cities and towns and dispatched and received connecting mail from important east-west RPO lines at Mason City, Ackley, Marshalltown, Grinnell, and Albia. Parcel Post was heavy on this route, particularly from a nursery at Hampton. Spring brought innumerable cartons of baby chicks and ducklings, and Fridays meant several pouches of registered mail containing bills and coins headed for banks so that they could cash cream checks for farmers on Saturdays.[32]

Other cuts were predictable. Mixed train service between Oskaloosa and Monmouth was reduced to triweekly frequency on July 10, 1948; nobody had protested M&StL's announcement. There were protests, however, when the railroad asked to cancel daytime passenger offerings between Minneapolis and Albert Lea, but the trains came off anyway on May 8, 1949, after M&StL agreed to shift the night runs from Minneapolis to Des Moines to day schedules. In that way the road ended the final double-daily service anywhere on the system. And on December 31, 1949, M&StL was relieved of mixed train service west of Watertown.[33]

There were times when Mother Nature or failures of men put a crimp in operations. Harsh winters were, of course, a stern reality. In December 1937 a plow train driven by a Mogul and Consolidation 470 was entrapped for a week in Creamery Cut north of LaSalle; the Mogul's fire was killed and the locomotive drained, but snow was shoveled into 470's tank and coal was fetched from town to keep up steam. It was the Armistice Day storm of 1940, however, that spread over a huge area and left vivid impressions not quickly forgotten. "Very severe blizzard over entire line, strong northwest wind, steadily colder during the day," recorded the dispatcher at Cedar Lake. The West End was plugged, freights were unable to leave terminals at Winthrop and Morton, and train 115 stalled and was snowed in between Watertown and Florence. The line to Albert Lea and on to Des Moines was blown shut and wires were down (cutting telegraph communication) beyond Merriam. Extra 611 opened the main artery between Cedar Lake and Albert Lea the next day, and Extra 479 plowed the Fort Dodge–Des Moines route, but train 57 stalled east of Ruthven and had to abandon most of its cars when water in the locomotive's tender reached a danger level, and continuing winds overtook train 60 at St. James, where engine 452 was forced to seek refuge at Omaha's engine facility. Minneapolis hotels were jammed with stranded passengers, but they were the lucky ones; several persons perished in storm-related mishaps. The Armistice Day blizzard was a reminder that serious storms could be expected any year. With that in mind, M&StL purchased steel posts and portable snow fencing to be used extensively west of Hopkins to Leola and down the Southwestern to Spencer. These measures alleviated but did not obviate the problem. In 1946 Alco 944 was stuck in snow for four days on the West End near Bradley. Two other Alcos were dispatched with a plow train for relief, but found rough going in obstinate snow-packed cuts. One location proved especially trying. Attacking this cut repeatedly at perhaps forty miles per hour yielded little success. A conductor chewing snoose (moist snuff) who was riding in the second Alco marked progress by spitting into the left-side snow bank after the bone-jarring stop of each run: the gain was about eight inches per attempt. Lines from New Ulm to Estherville and from Watertown to Aberdeen were especially vulnerable to closure and expensive snow removal. Flooding predictably followed years of heavy snowfall. In South Dakota this was especially the case in 1942 and 1949. In Iowa, in 1947 the Des Moines River caused extensive damage at Fort Dodge and Eddyville and took out the line between Fosterdale and Tracy, forcing a detour for Oskaloosa–Des Moines trains via Albia and Wabash-Burlington.[34]

The weather could prove nasty otherwise. On one occasion wind blew a boxcar off the siding at Dallas Center and propelled it without authorization or warning down the line, where it intersected an unsuspecting upbound passenger train. The resulting collision was not serious, but it jostled passengers, one of whom, astonished and a bit tipsy, jumped up and exclaimed: "It's alright folks, it's alright, lightning just struck the engine." In another instance, wind drove an occupied bunk car onto the main line at Winthrop, causing great anxiety among the occupants until one of them was able to scramble up to the top of the car and turn down the brakes.[35]

Derailments and accidents derived almost always from human error, occasionally from track or equipment failure. During the age of steam, a long, heavy train stalled in the night near Dillon, south of Marshalltown, and the engineer told a very green new brakeman to walk back and cut the train in two; they would "double in." The brakeman padded back dutifully to the middle of the train, "got the slack," and "pulled the pin" between two flats carrying long poles extending over both cars. The cargo, of course, was presently arrayed abroad the track and caused great indigestion among officials when they learned that the line was blocked. Oblique humor of sorts also surrounded light engine 608 on April 11, 1941. After helping a heavy night freight westbound from Monmouth across the Mississippi River bridge at Keithsburg and over demanding grades to Brighton, Iowa, seventy-five miles, the helper cut off and, tender first, started back in a lazy return to Monmouth. Engineer and fireman drifted into the land of Nod, however, leaving the iron steed to its own devices, which might have gone unrecorded except for a barge that approached the Keithsburg bridge almost in conjunction with wayward light engine 608. As the lift span went up to clear the barge, huge concrete counterweights came down to forcibly block rail traffic on the bridge. It was into the west counterweight that 608's tender slammed, providing an embarrassing and instantaneous wake-up for the sleepy enginemen and an indelibly memorable experience for the bridgetender, high atop this curious spectacle in his shanty. News of this did not amuse company officials. Steel beams and slides for the lift section were knocked out of line, requiring lengthy repair; 608 was trapped for the duration; and its tender was terminally damaged. Meanwhile, M&StL traffic was forced to detour over Milwaukee from Hedrick to Ottumwa, Iowa, and then over Chicago, Burlington & Quincy to Monmouth; this arrangement was later simplified by running from Maxon, near Albia, all the way to Monmouth. Bridge repairs and detour costs were extensive for the company, but engine crews, especially on double-headed time freights, delighted in seeing what M&StL's 600s "could do" when fully unnotched across Burlington's marvelous high-speed, double-track line between Maxon and Monmouth.[36]

Serious accidents involving injury and death were rare, but they were not unknown. On October 3, 1940, the crew of Extra 601 ignored a wait order and hit train 96 head on east of Morning Sun. Fortunately, no one was killed. The engineer of 601 survived the wreck but soon committed suicide. Sixteen cars left the rail near Echo, Minnesota, in July 1941 when train 75 hit a "sunkink" (a kink in the rail resulting from the sun's having heated the rail to the point of irresistible expansion), and nineteen passengers were injured when engine 226 on train 15 rammed an Omaha freight at fogbound Hopkins on April 11, 1943. An engineer died and others were seriously injured when double-headed train 96 plowed into the caboose of a local at Searsboro on January 31, 1944; another rear-ender occurred there on September 21, 1945. Nobody was hurt when GE-4 with train 17, picking its way through heavy weather east of Spencer, collided with the caboose of a standing Milwaukee freight, but the caboose stove tipped over and started a fire that consumed the caboose and damaged GE-4 so badly that it was condemned. The next year may have been the worst in company annals in terms of ugly accidents. Three 600s were involved in an altercation at Keithsburg in February, nearly new diesel 147 ran into the rear of train 20 on July 21 and was out of service for four months while repairs were made at LaGrange, and on September 21 eastbound Extra 610-627 coupled violated the integrity of train 10 at Morning Sun, leaving one dead and four injured. Except for the "sunkink" derailment, which might be blamed on Mother Nature, the rest, sad to say, were the result of human failings.[37]

It was no accident, however, that a smile swept across the face of Lucian Sprague when he reviewed M&StL's financial performance for the last half of the 1940s. The operating ratio had averaged a tolerable 81.43, while net income had averaged $1,499,680 per year, drawn down by heavy amortization charged to operating expense in 1945 and by wage increases and demoralized traffic resulting from strikes in 1946. The road had no bonded indebtedness, although new motive power and rolling stock had pushed equipment obligations from $3.9 million in 1945 to $6.5 million in 1949—all of it carrying agreeable interest rates of 1.5 to 2.3 percent. As a consequence, in 1946 M&StL had treated stockholders to a four-for-one split and continued to issue dividends—$3.3 million over the years 1944–49.[38]

Local residents long had attached nicknames or abbreviations to M&StL, and that tradition continued. Around Winthrop the road was referred to as the "Louie," at Watertown it was the "Em" or "Emmy," and at Spencer "Saint El." Old monikers such as "Miserable & Still Limping," "Musty & Stale," "Missing & Still Lost," "Midnight & Still Later," and "Misery & Short Life" were still employed by those who kidded about "their" railroad, but as the decade of the 1940s ended the old road was not seen to limp, was not musty in appearance, and certainly was not in misery. Indeed, it sparkled with vitality. M&StL, beamed a happy Lucian Sprague, was "Modern & Streamlined."[39]

Figure 20.8. Oops! M&StL photograph, author's collection.

Chapter 21
Sprague at the Throttle

Mr. Michael J. Addiego . . . speaking for himself and several other stockholders, wished to extend to the President appreciation for his outstanding accomplishments as Receiver of the predecessor company . . . and President of the reorganized company. . . . He also expressed the wish that the President be spared many more years of good health and mental vigor so as to continue in his capacity as President . . . as long as he is physically able.

—Minneapolis & St. Louis Minute Book, May 13, 1952

As the clock ran down on the momentous decade of the 1940s, America had lost much of the exuberance and self-confidence that was abroad the national landscape on V-J Day and just after, wiped away in part by growing concerns over the spread of communism and by frustration with the awesome new responsibilities that came with being a world power. Domestic discord became widespread. Labor and management shouted at one another, racism was an evil blot on the country's reputation, and another "Red Scare" was erupting. The economy wavered. Stock market averages edged upward, and the agricultural sector was strong, but industrial production was erratic and often sluggish. It was a mixed scene across the country as the calendar was turned over to January 1, 1950.[1]

The country's railroads reflected this ambiguity. In 1947 General Motors had dispatched its classy vista-domed *Train of Tomorrow* on a nationwide tour, and in the same year the *Freedom Train* had proudly begun a similar tour of the country behind a handsome new passenger diesel emblazoned *Spirit of 1776*. The year following brought spirited bows from the industry at the Chicago Railroad Fair, bows extended again for the 1949 season, but frowns crept across the faces of those in the trade press and the general media as observers and analysts pondered the state of the nation's carriers in the face of declining passenger and freight revenues even as labor demanded and got wage and benefit increases and as the companies sputtered that they would be unable to pass along costs unless they received rate increases from dilatory regulatory agencies. Net operating income for the nation's railways during first five months of 1947 had been one-third less than for the same five months in 1929. Traffic volumes were heavy, to be sure, but net profit was increasingly hard to come by—and market share was eroding. Chicago & North Western's Rowland L. Williams blamed wrongheaded public policy, and there was merit to his argument, but railroads had long since become a "mature industry," often ossified in tradition, worshiping frequently and ardently at the sacred alter of "this is the way we have always done it." Railroad labor and its leadership tended to be equally hidebound; the long-standing "us versus them" mentality of labor and management militated against cooperation to meet modal competition and common threats. By 1949 railroads were reporting surpluses of cars instead of shortages—a result of the higher-capacity newer equipment received after the war, but also because of serious inroads made by competition, especially automobiles and trucks.[2]

There was little on the surface at Minneapolis &

St. Louis that reflected national ambiguity or uncertainty as to the future of railroading. "All's Well with M&StL," declared *Newsweek* for December 18, 1950. Shippers and railroad managers elsewhere noted with admiration M&StL's efficiency over the Peoria Gateway, and financial circles took note of the road's lack of bonded indebtedness. Company stock had traded as high as $93 per share before the four-for-one split in 1946 and ranged from $11 to $28 thereafter. There were bumps and bruises in labor relations, of course, but M&StL's employee loyalty was legendary and of long duration. When steam disappeared, so did the need for boilermakers, steamfitters, blacksmiths, boiler washers, and fire knockers, but the company extended senior men to retirement and retrained and reassigned younger ones. And M&StL continued its enthusiastic advertising and public relations campaigns. In 1950 M&StL, with great hoopla, crated up a depot desk used years before by Richard W. Sears as a telegraph operator at Lake Mills, Iowa, and sent it off to the Chicago headquarters of the huge retailer that he had founded. Elsewhere the road traditionally supported the Minneapolis Aquatennial by sponsoring a company float; it also provided financial support for the Orchestral Association of Minneapolis. Four scholarships were established at the Dunwoody Institute; these were used to finance the industrial training of one boy from each of the four states served by the railroad. Total donations for such projects reached $26,979 for 1953 alone. Newspaper ads congratulated Mason City and its North Iowa Fair and Spencer for its Clay County Fair. In 1951 the company welcomed the "Red Feather Kids" for a tour of the Marshalltown diesel shop and two years later showed off the same spotless facility by hosting the initial meeting of National Railway Historical Society's Iowa Chapter.[3]

Figure 21.1. M&StL traditionally supported the Minneapolis Aquatennial by sponsoring a company float. M&StL photograph, author's collection.

M&StL's methodical program of modernization proceeded along predictable lines; the road added more track anchors, ballast, hundred-pound relay rail, culverts and fills to replace bridges where possible, steel bridge spans replacing wood at critical locations, and welded rail ends to extend the life of steel and reduce maintenance on locomotives. Other improvements likewise followed established patterns. "Bric-block" depots appeared at Waterville, Jordan, and Perry to succeed worn-out and shabby wooden structures; Armco "Steelbox" depot buildings appeared at Spencer, Kanawha, Gilman, Waconia, Excelsior, Gibbon, and Middle Grove. Communication was enhanced when another telegraph circuit was added between Minneapolis and Fort Dodge, and when the system was renewed from Oskaloosa to Peoria, although lines from New Ulm to Estherville and from Watertown to Aberdeen were retired (urgent communication to and from stations and with the dispatcher were thereafter restricted to commercial telephone). And for right-of-way grooming six fire-spewing weed burners were acquired to scorch uninvited trackside vegetation.[4]

Orders for additional motive power and rolling stock were part of the improvement mix, as was an ongoing policy of betterments to existing inventory.

Nine Alcos (some ordered in 1949) arrived on the property in 1950; three more followed in 1951 to bring the roster to thirty-five. In earlier years these would have appeared in a rainbow of paint schemes, but in 1949 the company committed to a standard policy of green and gold as its primary colors. The curious numbering system survived, however, and M&StL always insisted on its own adornments, such as distinctive front-mounted, air-activated bells. To the stable of Alcos was added a brace of F-7s from Electro-Motive in 1951 and two SD-7s from the same manufacturer in 1952. Maintenance for the nearly new diesel fleet was mostly routine, but the venerable GE cars had accumulated assorted aches and pains. GE-4, of course, had lost its life as the result of collision and fire; its sisters, GE-1, GE-2, and GE-3, were unnecessary for passenger service by 1950 and, although occasionally seen thereafter on officer specials or performing other unusual duties, they were to live out their little remaining time as undistinguished "work equipment." The larger units, GE-25–GE-31, still were necessary for standard passenger assignments, however, and shopmen at Cedar Lake looked for ways to extend their active time. In 1946 GE-27 had been subjected to an experiment using two 200-horsepower Cummins diesel engines in lieu of its well-worn 400-horsepower gasoline-fueled prime mover. The Cummins diesels were categorically inadequate. "We fought with them constantly," recalled Master Mechanic William W. Landmesser. Meanwhile, the Post Office Department urged all railroads to discontinue use of gasoline-fueled cars and finally announced that mail would be withdrawn from all runs handled by such equipment effective December 31, 1949 (subject to reasonable extension for companies furnishing definite conversion schedules). Fortunately for M&StL, Caterpillar D-397 diesel engines filled the bill. GE-26 and GE-28 were refitted in 1949; GE-25, GE-29, and GE-30 in 1950; and GE-27 in 1951. More prosaic but sure to earn their keep were seven hundred boxcars and one hundred flats, long on order, and finally delivered in 1952.[5]

Lucian Sprague, John Devins, and crew additionally continued to pursue economies of operation. During the years 1949–53, agencies were abolished at Hawley, Oak Grove, and Woolson; custodian service replaced agency service at Faulkner, Ruthven, and Story City; and a joint agency was established with Chicago Great Western at Moorland. Peddler cars for less-than-carload lots on Iowa branches and along the main line from Northwood to Albia finally ended in 1950, when M&StL was allowed to contract with Commercial Cartage for movement of LCL and Railway Express to and from stations along those lines. In South Dakota, in 1953 M&StL terminated its LCL and express truck operation from Aberdeen to Conde and along its former rail line all the way west to Akaska when rights and assets were conveyed to Mills Truck Line. (Continued were joint truck-rail grain movements via Conde.)[6]

More substantive cuts came through line abandon-

Figure 21.2. A few more diesel locomotives filtered in during the early 1950s to give M&StL motive power sufficiency. M&StL photograph, author's collection.

ments. M&StL had not sought to drop service anywhere during the recent war, but during the unsettled days of 1946, Devins recommended, and Sprague and the board agreed, that the road seek regulatory approval to end service on 50.6 miles of route—St. James to Estherville, 40.7 miles on the Southwestern; Corwith to St. Benedict, 7.3 miles; and 2.6 miles of right-angle stub from Lynnville Junction to Lynnville on the Newton Branch. In the end, M&StL backed off on the St. James–Estherville portion, the Interstate Commerce Commission denied the Lynnville request, and only the short segment from Corwith to St. Benedict on the old Algona Branch came out; dismantling was accomplished in April 1948. Floods of the preceding year had devastated the former Chicago, Burlington & Quincy route west from Oskaloosa to Tracy that M&StL used to reach Des Moines (by trackage rights from Tracy), with the result that trains thereafter were routed to Albia and then detoured over track jointly used by CB&Q and Wabash to Tracy and on to the Iowa capital city by existing agreement with Burlington. During the fall of 1947 M&StL sought and received long-term rights via Albia and then applied to abandon 5.25 miles between Fosterdale and Tracy where damage had been greatest; authority came in 1949. The same year M&StL asked to extinguish 9.5 miles of line reaching out from Newburg to Laurel, the last remnant of the State Center Branch, which had seen operation only on a demand basis. The axe fell there in 1950; dismantlers took up the line during the holiday season. Short segments were snipped off the Corwith Branch (from Denhart to Corwith, 4.3 miles) and the Story City Branch (from Roland to Story City, 5.2 miles) in 1952. The board also authorized a study to determine the profitability of all operations west of Watertown, 129 miles to Leola, but in 1952 Sprague told the board that, based on discussions with an executive of Sinclair Oil, he had come to the conclusion "that certain territory not far distant from our lines might have oil development possibilities." Abandonment studies for South Dakota were summarily placed in abeyance.[7]

During this period M&StL did expand, ever so modestly, by acquiring trackage and facilities upon abandonment by other roads—at Keithsburg, from CB&Q, and at Perry from Des Moines & Central Iowa, both in 1952, and at Watertown in 1953, when Rock Island retired from that place. In 1951 M&StL also picked up short trackage from defunct Rock Island Southern to serve various industries at Monmouth.[8]

Despite an expanding economy that developed correspondent with and was partially explained by America's involvement in the Korean conflict, there were growing concerns about the country's railroads, which often seemed trapped in an era now past—encrusted in tradition, custom, and antiquated business practice—diesel locomotives and streamlined passenger trains notwithstanding. M&StL was not exempt. There was much that was nostalgic and even vaguely romantic about depot waiting rooms warmed by coal fires in pot-bellied stoves and agents wearing green eyeshades and sleeve protectors bent over telegraph instruments. Yet that scene was an astonishing contradiction when time freight 20 zoomed by with shiny, modern locomotives on the point. For that matter, what of the caboose that trailed along behind, lighted by kerosene lamps? And despite the demonstrated utility of walkie-talkies during World War II, neither diesels nor cabooses, wayside stations nor yard offices were fitted out with two-way radios. M&StL instead chose to upgrade its telegraph system—not even adding a company-owned or leased telephone system. (It did contract with Western Union for teletype operation linking the general office with off-line traffic representatives and primary on-line points such as Des Moines, Peoria, Aberdeen, Spencer, and other stations.) It was a management problem, to be sure, but railroad labor was, if anything, just as obstinate in resisting change in an already changed and rapidly changing world.

The most graphic sign of traffic regression in the railroad industry was in the intercity passenger-carrying trade. In 1945, 891,128,000 patrons boarded trains, rolling up 91,717,226,000 passenger miles; in 1953, only 456,817,000 persons used rail transport, aggregating 31,655,134,000 passenger miles. M&StL boarded 289,372 persons in 1945, for 25,918,183 passenger miles; in 1953, only 45,148 persons entered the cars, tallying 3,409,068 passenger miles. Railroads were penned in a no-win environment. If they raised rates to cover their escalated costs, more passengers would seek alternative transport; if they did not raise rates, the flow of red ink would only increase. Moreover, the automobile touched something deep in the American psyche, offering an independence that no scheduled transport could possibly match. Short-haul, noncommuter passenger service of the type proffered by M&StL was nearly a thing of the past.[9]

The growth and expanding muscle of pipelines, waterways, and especially motor trucking (private as well as intercity common carrier and contract) was of much greater concern. Even before World War II, trucks had captured over half of livestock shipments and 40 percent of fruit and vegetable and automobile billings. Trucks, admittedly, often provided faster and more flexible service at lower rates, particularly in short-haul and medium-distance competition. Although the issue was sharply debated, truckers benefited greatly from publicly owned and maintained roadways, for which they paid only marginal portions. And while truckers were regulated under the Motor Carrier Act, restrictions on them were never as onerous as those on railroads. Regulated intercity truckers tripled their vehicle miles and more than doubled the tonnage carried in the brief period from 1945 through 1953, handling 6.5 percent of all intercity ton miles in 1945 but about 17 percent by 1953.[10]

Much of the railroad industry's distress was historic, the war years and immediate postwar boom obscuring patterns long in place. From the turn of the century through 1920, freight tonnage and collective revenues had advanced more rapidly than general business activity; thereafter rail tonnage and revenues did continue to rise in absolute numbers, but declined compared to industrial production. A bright spot for the industry was rapid dieselization, which markedly increased its operating efficiency; between 1945 and 1952 the number of gross tons per freight train hour increased by one-third. Yet wage rates more than doubled from 1939 to 1949. The same was true of costs for fuel, supplies, and taxes. And in 1949 nonoperating employees shifted from a six-day workweek of forty-eight hours to a five-day, forty-hour workweek with no loss of pay. Rate increases, as always, lagged behind increased costs, and now, more than ever, rate increases risked loss of business to other modes of transport. Operating costs absorbed more and more of gross revenue; net earnings declined accordingly. Indeed, Wall Street analysts and other observers were ever more pessimistic about

Figure 21.3. There was incongruity in a shiny, new, modern locomotive gliding by this ramshackle depot at Rockwell, Iowa. M&StL photograph, author's collection.

the rail industry. In 1952 railroads' share of intercity freight volume was down to 54.9 percent, with truckers, pipelines, and inland waterways splitting the remainder in nearly equal chunks.[11]

Where did M&StL fit in this fluid and increasingly pessimistic landscape? It certainly was not awash in red ink as were New York, New Haven & Hartford and Rutland in the East, nor was it flush with cash as was Santa Fe and Southern Pacific in the West. In the years from 1950 through 1953, M&StL turned in a mixed record despite a very strong national economy. The road's tonnage averaged 8,222,729 annually for the years 1950–52, but turned downward to 7,551,887 in 1953. Its net income hit $2,765,248 in 1950, but averaged only $1,904,978 over the next three years. And conversion from steam to diesel caused employee numbers to change little, while gross wages rose smartly. The operating ratio, mirroring rising wages, tilted upward, from 71.88 in 1950 to 77.36 in 1953. By that index alone, M&StL compared well with many of its neighbors. Despite the company's varied record over the period 1950–53, Sprague and the board pumped out $2,916,000 in dividends, and M&StL stock rose to nearly $30 per share.[12]

If Lucian C. Sprague had any qualms about a railroad industry that was going through challenging times, or if he had any doubts about himself within that industry or as M&StL's clear and singular majordomo, he certainly did not show it. His hand was as firmly attached to the tiller as ever it had been since he arrived on January 1, 1935. Yet he was around the property less and less, his icy blue eyes fixed more often on the good life than on M&StL's good. *Railway Age* for November 26, 1951 showed a photograph of Sprague and his attractive wife aboard an ocean liner headed for Europe. Sprague told *Age* that while abroad he would study the railroads of Italy and France, paying special attention to the effects of the European

Figure 21.4. This twenty-eight-foot twin-screw cruiser provided enjoyment at Sprague Island, Minnesota. M&StL photograph, author's collection.

Recovery Act on those operations. His regular expense accounts over the years included nominal items that were routine, but the board of directors also agreed to an auxiliary account in his name for "promotional and operational needs of the Company" that were expansive—$7,525 for the last four months of 1945, $18,445 for the first eight months of 1946, and $15,957 for five months in 1947, for example. Members of the board also appreciated the good life. Meetings were often but not always held in New York. The one for February 1952, for example, was scheduled for Florida at the fashionable Biltmore Hotel in Belleair. "It would not be feasible to transport the Company's business cars from Minneapolis to Florida and return," Sprague told the directors. They were to make their own arrangements and be reimbursed. But directors, managers, customers, and special guests did use business cars elsewhere and often, including over Northern Pacific to International Falls, Minnesota, where they debarked for M&StL's Sprague Island in Rainy Lake, forty-two acres of land plus improvements "suitable for occupancy in the summertime," where fishing was good and a company-owned twenty-eight-foot twin-screw cruiser was tied up at the dock, available for water recreation of all sorts. Of course office cars also went west each year for pheasant hunting in South Dakota, and were also employed for other purposes, such as a five-day trip in the spring of 1953 to show off the property for Ray Moley, founder of *Newsweek,* and for securities analysts, business journalists, directors, and others.[13]

The memorable inspection trip of April 1953 produced much intangible good will for the company and bushels of accolades for Sprague, who, in typical fashion, was "gracious to all," as a writer for *Railway Age* later reminisced, and saw to it that "every guest had a grand time." The trip also produced an article in *Newsweek* entitled "Sprague at the Throttle," with an accompanying photograph of the silver-haired, sixty-seven-year-old "stocky dynamo" who had "nursed the line back into the black" against great odds. Sprague beamed in satisfaction, greatly pleased that the story of his successful labors at M&StL had been retold once again, and for such a wide audience.[14]

Stockholders, too, appreciated what Sprague had done for the company. At the annual meeting in 1952, shareholder Michael J. Addiego praised Sprague and, as the company secretary dutifully recorded, "expressed the wish that the President be spared many more years of good health and mental vigor so as to continue in his capacity as President." Addiego then asked for a "vote of confidence in the officers, directors and management" that was "unanimously adopted." Life was good.[15]

Chapter 22
THE IDES OF MAY

Rooster today, featherduster tomorrow.
—AUSTRALIAN PROVERB

THE NEWS REACHED 111 EAST FRANKLIN AVENUE in midsummer 1953. Lucian C. Sprague was at first incredulous, then bemused, then irritated. The same was true of other senior managers and members of the Minneapolis & St. Louis board of directors, many of whom had been associated with the company since it had emerged from receivership in 1943 or even longer. They had seen the road through its darkest hours into the bright light of respect and prosperity. Sprague's role had been pivotal, and it had earned him the title "Doctor of Sick Railroads." M&StL's nearly miraculous escape from death was well fixed in railroad lore. "M&StL has always been one of the all-time miracle roads to me," David P. Morgan at *Trains* confided to writer Frank P. Donovan Jr. "The transition it accomplished in the 1930s will forever set it high in the field of recoveries." The road owned a decent operating ratio, was favored by customers, was fully dieselized, had no bonded debt, and had paid dividends constantly since 1943. It was a dramatic success story. Perhaps too good, making it an attractive target for corporate raider Ben W. Heineman.[1]

In retrospect, it is clear that those directing the affairs of M&StL should not have been surprised that the road found itself in the crosshairs of an opportunistic attacker. A proxy fight waged in an attempt to elect a dissident slate of directors was the favorite takeover device of the 1950s. Perhaps the best-known of these in the railroad industry was initiated by Robert R. Young, who portrayed himself as a doughty little David taking on Goliath in the form of sedate Wall Street clubmen who made up the directory of New York Central. Young wrapped himself smugly in the garment of a populist and waged what his opponents considered ill-bred and highly offensive guerrilla warfare of the most merciless type. In June 1954, when this bellicose corporate warfare finally ended and the votes were cast, Young captured control of New York Central, speculators and big retail houses such as Merrill Lynch siding with him instead of the establishment board. The Visigoths were in charge. At almost the same time another drawn-out, bitter proxy fight in the East surrounded the New York, New Haven & Hartford, where again insurgents wrested control. The surprise was that anybody would dabble in railroad takeovers, given the failing reputation of the industry, but that is where the action was in the first half of the 1950s.[2]

Born in 1914, Ben Heineman was a partner in the Chicago-based Swiren & Heineman law firm, which specialized in corporate matters. With an LL.B. earned from Northwestern University in 1936, Heineman first attracted attention in the railroad industry during

Figure 22.1. Alco 1050 was photographed lifting train 51 out of the Des Moines River valley from Fort Dodge, Iowa, on its daily-except-Sunday trek to Albert Lea, Minnesota. Had Sprague made M&StL too inviting? Photo by the author.

the late 1940s and early 1950s, when he negotiated an out-of-court settlement of claims brought by a group of Chicago Great Western shareholders. Heineman charged that CGW should pay dividends in arrears out of earnings instead of using those monies for debt retirement and improvements. A compromise was reached, and Heineman even wrenched an agreement from CGW to pay him $350,000 in legal fees for presenting the case against it.[3]

M&StL caught Heineman's attention early in 1953. A Chicago group he headed claimed at midyear that it owned or was identified with 140,000 of the road's nearly 600,000 outstanding shares. Observers expected a fight at the company's August 28 board meeting, but nothing happened. A few days later, however, Heineman announced that with about 25 percent of the stock his consortium wanted three directors on the board, and he expected them to play an important role in policymaking. He said, however, that his was "not a bid of control."[4]

Compromise was unlikely. Heineman's challenge was an audacious threat to Sprague's reputation and to his monumental ego. As *Business Week* observed, "Sprague has always been known as a fighter." Yet *Business Week* also warned that Sprague was "going into the ring with another fighter like himself." Heineman would be no pushover. The board considered the Chicagoan's request on September 24, but rejected it summarily, arguing that it doubted Heineman's authority to represent the number of shares he claimed. Moreover, "no advantage to the Company can be expected to accrue from the forced displacement of any members of the present board," Sprague told Heineman. "Mr. Sprague is a teller of half-truths," was Heineman's icy reply. Little time passed before Heineman upped the ante, demanding that M&StL's corporate secretary's office be shifted from New York to Minneapolis, that the board be enlarged, and that a five-member executive committee be established with two Heineman representatives—one as chairman. Sprague proffered an olive branch of sorts. "If Mr. Heineman can prove he has 10 percent of the shares outstanding," Sprague suggested, "he can call a special meeting of stockholders," adding a taunt: "We rather hope that he will."[5]

Heineman returned shot for shot. "We're trying to make peace and not rise to provocation," he told the *Minneapolis Tribune.* Heineman then accused Sprague of saying a "lot of foolish, rash, and reckless things," but added his own taunt: "We're very anxious to salvage Mr. Sprague and his management for the road." There was a caveat, however. "We don't think he is essential, but we think he is an asset to the road." The Chicago group would bide its time; it offered this warning, though: "When we've decided there is no hope salvaging the present management, we'll call a special meeting at our convenience or take appropriate action at the annual meeting." Meanwhile, Heineman urged that two internal directors, Colin W. Wright, vice president and general counsel, and John J. O'Brien, vice president and corporate secretary, leave the board; Wright and O'Brien did step down, but in a clear snub to the Chicagoans, who expected to fill those slots with selections of their own, were replaced by businessmen Archibald G. Bush of St. Paul and Joel Carroll of Elmira, New York. Investors everywhere watched all of this with an anticipation mirrored in the rising value of M&StL shares, which in 1953 traded from a low of $16 to a high of $24.[6]

Despite Sprague's bravado and the board's apparent stubborn fortitude, Heineman's attacks were having at least a partial effect. A special meeting of the board on February 27, 1954, was especially busy. Among other things, the board approved cutting nearly $500,000 out of the operating budget; authorized the use of employees of the company to solicit proxies for the upcoming annual meeting; urged an increase of company stock from 600,000 shares to 800,000, with the new 200,000 shares to be distributed as a stock dividend (assuming very probable shareholder ratification); and approved retirement for pleasant, approachable, and sincere Arthur C. Leake, who had replaced Herbert W. Ward as vice president–traffic in 1948, when Ward left to head Illinois Terminal. Leake was succeeded by Roy W. Nelson, who had begun his career in M&StL's freight claim office at the age of sixteen; his most recent assignment had been as resident vice president in New York City. The board additionally received the resignation of Max A. Lehman and A. W. Benkert, both of whom had served as members of the board since 1943, replacing Lehman with John W. Devins and leaving the other slot open. Devins also was named M&StL president when Sprague, following a well-rehearsed script, resigned. Sprague would stay on, however, as chairman of the board, authorized and requested by the board "to be available on a full-time basis for consultation with other members of the board, the President and department heads of the Company, with particular emphasis on matters relating to traffic, public relations, industrial development, and shareholder relations." His salary continued at $45,000 per annum.[7]

The Heineman team was not long in responding, announcing an open fight for control of the road on March 3. "An unfortunate situation within the management of the road has forced us to take this action," declared Heineman, presumably referring to the retention of Sprague as chairman and the elevation of Devins as president to ensure a status quo ante. "Now that the decision has been made, we expect to win." Upon that victory, Heineman promised, a new management would make "improvements in operations and returns to stockholders." What were the shortcomings or faults of the current management? At the top of the list was inadequate dividends. Beyond that, Heineman criticized Sprague for not aggressively pursuing merger of M&StL with some other property and for not vigorously wringing more net income out of operations. Moreover, the current management was "extravagant, wasteful, self-serving and inefficient" and was "using the road's funds improperly." Clearly, said Heineman, the current board did not have M&StL's best interests at heart. Collectively, he claimed, the current board members owned a mere 3,690 shares of M&StL, whereas the members of his group or their families owned 41,349. Obviously, he reasoned, a new board was required to install "a more conscientious management" and to get rid of the bunch that had allowed Sprague to run a "gravy train" for the current management.[8]

Sprague was outraged. So was the board, which on its own released a statement bluntly announcing that it would solicit proxies for the election of a board of directors "composed of those who have been familiar for many years with the operation of the road." In an oblique reference to the Chicago challengers, the board said it "has always felt that it owes a duty to the shareholders as a whole and that it should not grant practical control to any group regardless of its size." The *Minneapolis Tribune* meanwhile observed that John

Devins, "Sprague's first lieutenant in the years he was pulling the road out of bankruptcy," apparently was "trying to steer a neutral course in the controversy."[9]

Company shareholders were alerted to the annual meeting, scheduled in New York City at 2:00 p.m. on May 11. Eleven men were nominated as directors. The list included Sprague and Devins plus outsiders, seven of whom were businessmen from prominent firms in Minneapolis and St. Paul. Elbridge T. Gerry from New York represented Brown Brothers, Harriman & Company, and Joel H. Carroll was president of Carroll Motor Company. (Carroll was M&StL's largest single stockholder.) Collectively they held 21,550 shares of stock; families or firms they represented owned another 8,400 shares. Stockholders also would be asked to approve issuance of 200,000 additional shares as a stock dividend.[10]

Heineman's group proposed an alternative slate of seven businessmen and investors from Chicago and elsewhere—none from communities served by M&StL, and none of whom ever had worked in railroad management or served on a railroad board. Heineman clearly was the architect of the raid and its spokesman. M&StL's board formally responded to Heineman's "extraordinary demands" and "disparaging remarks" late in March. The board particularly questioned Heineman's complaint as to low dividends, arguing that M&StL's course had been both generous and prudent. The board likewise pointed with pride to the company's operating ratio, which compared favorably with those of other roads in the service area. As to alleged extravagance, the board noted that M&StL was greatly dependent on overhead business, that such traffic was highly competitive, and that significant expenditures were essential in that solicitation. Finally, the board challenged Heineman's credentials and his motives—"We know that Mr. Heineman has some LITTLE KNOWLEDGE OF RAILROADING," they said, damning him with very faint praise—and reminded stockholders that this "little knowledge" had come when his law firm and other attorneys had gained $350,000 for their services in prosecuting claims for preferred stock at Chicago Great Western.[11]

The return barrage was immediate and heavy with powder and shot. Heineman assailed M&StL's management as "wasteful, extravagant, self-serving and inefficient in very important areas of operation" and again charged that it was operating a "gravy train" for itself. The Chicagoan called for dividends of up to 50 percent of net income and an "end to laxness," as well as "prompt and effective consideration of merger or consolidation with other railroads" and swift termination of "wasteful salaries and expenses and unnecessary costs of traffic solicitation."[12]

Both sides hurled nasty exchanges throughout April. M&StL's Proxy Committee of Elbridge T. Gerry and John J. O'Brien reminded shareholders that the current management was the one that had brought the company back from receivership and that Heineman was baiting them with bogus charges of malfeasance. Heineman compared M&StL unfavorably with smaller Monon and with neighbor Chicago Great Western, but Gerry and O'Brien countered by noting that Monon had "about $2.2 million in total funded debt ahead of its preferred common," which was in arrears, and its Class B that paid no dividends. As for CGW, it had $31 million in funded debt, and dividends on its common stock were phantom. By comparison, M&StL had no bonded indebtedness (but a mortgage on its general office building of $887,695 and equipment issues of $7.7 million) and had paid $6.39 million in dividends since 1943 while at the same time dieselizing and pouring money into betterments of all kinds.[13]

Heineman stuck to his "gravy train" campaign, attacking Sprague head-on and the board by indirection. He said that Sprague's "shocking . . . flagrant extravagances," costing the company from $65,000 to $100,000 annually, essentially meant that he "treated M&StL's treasury as his own personal pocketbook in reckless disregard for stockholders' interests." Indeed, said Heineman, "M&StL has had one of the worst records in the country for waste in general and traffic expense." Heineman pointed particularly to monies issued to Sprague for his European trip of 1951, to horseracing expenses, to Sprague's membership in "15 select clubs from New York to San Francisco," to the cost of two Cadillacs and a private chauffeur, to Sprague's absence from Minneapolis for nearly eight months in 1952, and to Sprague Island, which, Heineman charged, had cost M&StL a full $123,984. In the end, the feisty Chicagoan growled, it was "Christmas every day" for Lucian Charles Sprague.[14]

The battering was relentless. M&StL's Proxy Committee addressed and rebutted the issues raised by Heineman in an expansive document to shareholders dated April 17. The Proxy Committee called Heineman's accusations against Sprague "one of the most vicious attacks ever made upon a loyal and faithful corporate officer." The response from Chicago was a blistering salvo attacking M&StL's failure "to keep proper records" of Sprague's expenditures and asserting that those horrendous costs "had almost nothing to do" with increasing M&StL revenues. Indeed, said Heineman, M&StL's tripled revenue stream since 1935 was due "in principal part to general increases in freight rates" and to general prosperity, not advances in traffic volume.[15]

Both sides dispatched a torrent of mail to stockholders, and both sides labored to try their cases in the media. Outside opinion varied. Professor Philip D. Jordan at the University of Minnesota followed the proxy fight with great interest and sent press reports to railroad historian Richard C. Overton at Northwestern University. "I warned [Frank P.] Donovan when he wrote his history that things were not too well at M&StL," said Jordan, "but he refused to believe me." In a guarded response, Overton said: "I am concerned about Lou Sprague, who is an ex-Burlington man, and a man I have known personally these many years. I have always thought of him as a rather free wheeler, swashbuckling type, but it never occurred to me that he would be quite so indiscreet as the clippings would indicate." Journalists had their own views. "If there is any dirty linen, it seems to me, the important thing is to get it washed," said Robert P. Vanderpoel at the *Chicago Daily Sun Times.* Robert E. Bedingfield of the *New York Times* thought M&StL's very prosperity was the real issue in this battle and considered it curious that Heineman never denied the company's financial well-being. In Des Moines, the *Register*'s Jack Magarrell thought control of the railroad now hinged on whether stockholders believed that "racetrack parties, European tours, jewelry, and Cadillacs" were "necessary business expenses." A lengthy *Register* article on April 25 attested to the strong interest Iowans had in the contest and the nervousness they felt as to the outcome. Only twenty-five persons in the state owned M&StL stock, and this a mere 1,584 shares, but M&StL had more track miles of operation in Iowa than in other of the states it served; a strong symbiotic relationship long had characterized its residents and the railroad. Principal shippers—Penn-Dixie and Hawkeye-Marquette, cement companies in Des Moines, Lennox Furnace at Marshalltown, Grinnell fertilizer manufacturer Cornland Plant Foods, and Farmers' Grain Dealers Association of Des Moines, among others—were especially complimentary of M&StL service and brooded about any change that might come with new ownership.[16]

Final shots were fired by each side through the press and letters to shareholders. Heineman urged election of his slate—"an owner management interested in increasing the values of its shares"—but Sprague recommended M&StL's current team—one "intelligently directed" by "railway-minded men." Heineman eagerly raised the possibility of merger, and Sprague agreed that "merger with one of the largest railroads in the Midwest" was a possibility. Yet, said Sprague, "if it ever becomes an actuality . . . it will be accomplished by the present management, whose entree to other railroad offices and with officers of other railroad companies is of the highest calibre." Heineman then, at the last moment, cunningly adopted a divide-and-conquer approach, saying that M&StL's obvious success over recent years was not at all due to Sprague and the board, but rather "the result of the quiet and effective work of John W. Devins, now President, and formerly Vice President in charge of operations." To drive this point home, Heineman said, "Our nominees, upon election to the board, intend to support Mr. Devins as President and Chief Executive officer." Sprague thereupon announced that M&StL's performance in the first quarter of 1954 had surpassed that of the same period a year earlier—an accomplishment, he clucked, by the "same management that has been accused of 'riding the gravy train.'" Heineman sneered that Sprague was merely offering "bait" to get badly needed votes.[17]

"Who ever thought the day would come when anybody would be fighting over the Minneapolis & St. Louis Railway?" wrote John A. Wickland in the *Minneapolis Tribune* for May 9. Only yesterday, it seemed, the road had been ridiculed and laughed off as hopeless—"Misery & Short Life," "Maimed & Still Limping," to be sure. But on the May 11, in New York City, both sides would go after it hammer and tong, and the victor would walk away with a property that Sprague loved to hail as "Modern & Streamlined." Heineman predicted "victory by a substantial margin"; Sprague refused to forecast the outcome.[18]

The meeting on May 11 proved stormy, with more than two hundred persons in attendance, many of them representing investment and brokerage houses; the proxy fight greatly excited New York financial circles. Sprague, as chairman, allowed stockholders of both sides considerable leeway to air their perspectives. Indeed, partisans of both teams spent more than two acrimonious hours asking questions, firing accusations, and shouting at one another generally. Sprague supporters yelled "Gang" and "Johnny-come-lately" at the Heineman group, which retaliated with "Sprague Island, Sprague Island." It was ugly. Sprague himself alternately chuckled and snapped replies to charges of mismanagement, denying every such accusation. One stockholder thanked Heineman for "exposing" Sprague, while another condemned Heineman for trying to "sneak" control of the road. The meeting was recessed at 5:00, no tally of votes yet available, and reconvened the next day. Sprague, who typically drank buttermilk at company-sponsored cocktail parties, may have found a need for something stronger when the results of balloting came in, for while America's favorite television program in 1954 was *I Love Lucy,* a majority of M&StL stockholders decided they did not "love Lucian" adequately to sustain his administration. Of 589,229 shares outstanding, all but 22,623 were represented by votes; in the end Ben W. Heineman was the top vote getter with 311,479. He and his slate of six fellows, plus John Devins and three other holdovers carefully selected by the Chicagoans from the Sprague board, were swept into office. In announcing the results, Sprague was probably the most composed individual in the room, showing to the public no bitterness and no regrets. "The men on this board, I hope, will have every success," he said, adding with pride, "They are taking over a fine organization." He also thanked M&StL employees, many of whom had been around since the dark days when nobody wanted the old road. A few days later he wrote to Richard C. Overton, saying: "By this time, you no doubt know I am no longer in the driver's seat on the Minneapolis & St. Louis Railway, and as I have told all of my friends, it is a baseball game that went over Niagara Falls and is probably by now a long ways down the river." Sprague said he would go fishing in Rainy Lake for about ten days "and then take up some activity that will keep me occupied and prove interesting, I am sure."[19]

Ben Heineman claimed that he had been successful in the proxy war because stockholders were tired of Sprague's managing the road as if it were his own and because M&StL paid out inadequate dividends. These were factors, of course, but hardly the whole cloth. Most shareholders were, in fact, yesteryear's bondholders, and the vast majority lived in New York (703 of them, holding 267,334 shares) and had no identification with M&StL other than as an investment. M&StL's Proxy Committee had pitched loyalty to the company, to the management that had rescued the property, to Minneapolis as M&StL's headquarters city, and to local directors who might beneficially influence traffic. To no avail. Most shareholders simply perceived that Heineman would do even more for them than Sprague. Heineman, after all, never pledged devotion to the company, its customers, its employees, or its service area; he had pledged devotion only to shareholder benefit.[20]

Sprague forces and Heineman supporters alike had sought to wrap themselves in messianic adornment, to have their beholders see them as knights of old, battling everlastingly for the right. But if there were any such selfless knights in this scenario they certainly were not plainly visible. Heineman's group had purchased M&StL stock in the open market in the finest capitalistic tradition. There was nothing wrong in that, but their arrival on the scene long after the heavy lifting had been accomplished by Sprague and crew was more than unseemly, and their purposes were transparently self-serving. Moreover, their tactics of slash and burn, and their use of half truths, insinuation, and innuendo, were less than conscionable. Nevertheless, Sprague and M&StL's board had left themselves open to attack through poor or even slipshod business practice. Nothing can diminish Sprague's marvelous record in restoring the company's reputation after what seemed an endless receivership, but Lucian Sprague in 1954 was not the man he had been in 1935 or 1945. And during Sprague's early days at M&StL the savvy and well-regarded Walter W. Colpitts had served him well as sponsor and mentor. Guiding, directing, and moderating from behind the scenes, Colpitts stayed close to Sprague and the company after receivership, but their paths later diverged and Colpitts died in 1951. Gone was his wise counsel, and by this time Sprague's energy level was down, he took himself too seriously, and he seemed to assume that the company for which he had done so much owed him a very good life. He was coasting. The company was coasting. He overstayed his time. The board should have acted to remove him or to redefine his duties before Heineman and his group did. The board also had to take responsibility for the lack of an independent audit of company books before 1953; even M&StL's vaunted lack of bonded indebtedness might be questioned because it invited a hostile takeover and because of its negative impact on federal income tax. Reasonable persons might disagree as to whether Sprague had made questionable expenditures or whether the board should have exercised greater oversight. There is no doubt, however, that both Sprague and the board could have profited from the advice of investment banker Otto H. Kahn, who at an earlier time had counseled: "A man, especially a man at the head of a great corporation, must not only do right, but he must be very careful to avoid even the appearance of not doing right."[21]

Lucian Sprague exited to mixed reviews. E. Roland Harriman, chairman of Union Pacific's board of directors, expressed "admiration for the work Lou Sprague" had done at M&StL, and historian Richard Overton thought Sprague "outgoing, sentimental, and utterly devoted to the Minneapolis & St. Louis." From St. Paul, retired businessman Julius A. Schmal spoke for many: "You personally, who brought it [M&StL] to its present success as a railroad venture, are worthy of special commendation and congratulations." At Denver & Rio Grande Western, Gayle B. Aydelott recalled Sprague as "white-haired and full of pep," a "wheeler-dealer" who "acted crazy but got things done." Ultimately, however, Aydelott thought Sprague "had his eye on himself and not the company." William K. Smith at Minneapolis-based General Mills considered Sprague "a nice man, optimistic, very generous, and a good entertainer." Smith emphasized, however, that General Mills favored M&StL not because of Sprague personally, but because the Peoria Gateway was a fine route. Nobody doubted Sprague's ability as a salesman. George L. Green at equipment supplier Pullman-Standard called Sprague a "great marketing man from a small railroad" and was especially impressed with Sprague's willingness to "put his money into people" who sold M&StL's product. James R. Sullivan, who arrived at M&StL shortly after Sprague lost control, summed it up: "Although his attackers in the 1954 proxy fight made much of the old boy's flamboyance, the fact remains that he was—in something of the Diamond Jim Brady mould—one of the railroad industry's most effective salesmen."[22]

For good or for ill, M&StL was bound to be a different place absent Lucian Charles Sprague, whose imprint had been large and long.

Figure 22.2. Lucian Sprague had succeeded in rescuing M&StL and had pumped vitality into the Peoria Gateway. Here Extra 150, with eastbound tonnage, was hurrying over the Skunk River near Brighton, Iowa, in a view that suggested the road's great confidence during the early 1950s. But ambiguity set in as Heineman took over. Robert Milner photograph, author's collection.

Chapter 23
HALTING STEPS

I believe in owner-management of railroads. Directors who are substantial investors give time and attention to company affairs. I feel that my own investment in the Minneapolis & St. Louis Railway is a good one and will become better.
—BEN W. HEINEMAN, 1955

BEN W. HEINEMAN WAS UNLIKE ANY OF THOSE who previously had directed Minneapolis & St. Louis affairs. He was no William Drew Washburn, who had seen in M&StL a tool by which to advance the broad purposes of Minneapolis interests. He was no Ransom R. Cable, head of a larger railroad who had viewed M&StL as a valuable strategic appendage. He was not a bright and talented professional manager like William H. Truesdale. He was not of a mind with Edwin Hawley, who had played a lone hand, although there were vague similarities. He was not like attorney William H. Bremner, who had seen the road only in trying times. And he certainly was unlike Lucian C. Sprague, who had come to the road as an outsider, only to become the consummate insider. During the proxy war Heineman had offered only the broadest contours of his plans for M&StL: increase shareholder value and income, end waste and inefficiency, and seek merger possibilities. He had given no indication of how or when any or all of this might be accomplished. Neither had he suggested means by which he might heal wounds opened during the fight. Employees, long devoted to the company and to the man Heineman had deposed, were understandably nervous and anxious. So were shippers, especially those on-line, but also those who profited from the Peoria Gateway as a bridge useful in avoiding Chicago. And railroaders elsewhere wondered as to Heineman, looking at him in a mix of wonder and disdain. Heineman himself admitted that "Byzantine consequences" resulted from takeovers, but he argued that they "ultimately involved questions of value and fairness to the stockholders." At the outset, then, Heineman carried portfolio only with M&StL shareholders and, given recent events, not even with all of them.[1]

In the wake of his victorious proxy battle, Heineman said he had no "spectacular plans" for the railroad. "We have no desire to change the existing organization until after a long, careful look," he declared. Heineman admitted that he was not a railroader and that he did "not know all about railroads." After the victory in New York City, Heineman, an ardent fisherman, scurried off to open the season—not in Minnesota or elsewhere in M&StL's service territory, but in Pennsylvania. A mildly hopeful but cautious *Minneapolis Tribune* concluded that company shareholders believed Heineman could do "a better job of carrying the line forward" than Sprague. "If the new management is sincere in its statement of purposes," said the *Tribune* guardedly, "it will find itself welcome as a member of the Minneapolis and upper Midwest business community."[2]

Clues as to future directions were sure to come from the board meeting to be held at Chicago on May 26, 1954. John W. Devins, long in the employ of M&StL, was reelected president, and Sprague's management team, less New Yorker John J. O'Brien, who retired as corporate secretary, was continued. The position of chairman of the board was abolished effective May 31, and with it vanished Sprague's incumbency. Amendments to by-laws created an Executive Committee (chaired by Heineman with two board members from his slate and two holdovers from the Sprague years). The board also executed the stockholders' decision at the recent annual meeting to award themselves a 200,000-share dividend and then added another 10 cents per share as dessert. In other business, the board agreed to shoulder the expense incurred by the Heineman group in its successful bid to capture the company and rejoiced at John Devins's prediction that he could squeeze "operating economies" of $1 million out of the budget in the twelve-month period beginning June 1. These economies included the eventual sale of Sprague Island, which was judged no longer a "suitable place for the entertainment of shippers." Devins likewise urged, and the board agreed to, the purchase of advertisements in on-line newspapers "setting forth certain matters relating to the policy of the new management," as well as the posting of letters to principal shippers and employees that would express "the desires of the new management to continue the good will . . . in every respect." Finally, Devins announced an inspection trip for the directors in June.[3]

That five-day trip began on June 14, with locomotive 248 and heater car 501 followed by office cars 101, 102, and the *Twin Cities.* Back from Peoria and Des Moines, the new board paid a brief visit to the road's Cedar Lake shops on June 17 and then left for Aberdeen, returning the next day. The purpose of the trip was to familiarize Heineman and the new board members with the property; Heineman made no attempt to meet shippers, employees, government officials, or media representatives. He did, however, convene the newly created Executive Committee on the evening of June 14 as the train rolled along east of Oskaloosa. The group agreed to meet monthly (with full board meetings quarterly), commissioned Arthur Anderson & Company to study the company's accounting policies, and determined to move company deposits from New York to Northwestern National Bank and Marquette Bank in Minneapolis and to Iowa–Des Moines and Bankers Trust of Des Moines.[4]

In the last half of 1954, close observers of the company would have noticed a few substantive changes, such as closing the New York office and placing funds in on-line banks. They also would have noted the creation of the Executive Committee with Heineman as chair as well as the clearly reduced function and power of the board of directors. They would have been bemused, given Heineman's earlier vociferous and caustic accusations, that he now had full faith in M&StL's managers and that he found the road well equipped with new power and rolling stock. They might have smirked when the office of chairman of the board (paying $45,000 annually) was abolished, to be replaced by the office of chairman of the executive committee (paying $24,000 annually, but not including Heineman's monthly travel and per diem expenses). And, given Lucian Sprague's unrivaled and unquestioned skill as a salesman, they would have giggled gleefully at Heineman's declaration that great focus and attention would now be given to "selling" the road to customers and the public. They most likely would have nodded in agreement, however, that company accounting practices could be improved, but would have grown pensive when Heineman and Devins turned to the matter of "attaining maximum efficiency and economy." What did that mean? they would have wanted to know. Devins already had excised $500,000 from the 1954 budget during the proxy fight, and in midsummer talked of reductions aggregating more than $1 million for the year. In June Heineman did vigorously insist on "economies" in the traffic department; a month later he demanded further "material decreases in general expense and traffic expense." Sales representatives may have wondered how they were to more vigorously solicit traffic on reduced budgets, but Devins read the tea leaves and set about slashing jobs in the general office building, cutting the sales budget, reducing supply inventories, and restricting company donations and contributions. An operating man to the core, Devins did what he could to protect capital programs: in the end, fifteen miles of rail went into the track, and a substantial bridge renewal program was concluded on the main line. Cross-tie renewal suffered, however. And local freight service was terminated between Hopkins and Watertown, between Oskaloosa and Monmouth, and between Monmouth and Peoria; freight operation between Winthrop and Spencer was made biweekly. For 1955, Devins proposed and the board approved an operating budget and additions or betterments "sufficient to maintain the railroad at its existing standard" and "adequate for foreseeable operations of the railroad." It sounded hollow—very much like William Bremner's proscriptions in the early 1930s.[5]

Heineman's provocative assertions about merging M&StL with some other property during the heated proxy battle gave predictable sprout to rumors regarding possible combinations. Having lit that fire and having fanned it, Heineman now sought to dampen the flames, calling such stories "conjectural and speculative." Ten months after deposing Sprague, Heineman told shareholders that "definite action toward this goal has been instituted," but if such was the case there was no mention of it in the minutes of the board or the Executive Committee. "Shareholders will be fully advised as promptly as the situation permits," Heineman promised, nevertheless.[6]

The year 1954 proved frankly disappointing. M&StL handled 10,731 fewer cars and 431,254 fewer tons than in 1953, earning $1.388 million less in revenue. Its total revenue was off by $1.457 million, net revenue down by $302,123. Heineman blamed the end of the Korean conflict and a "recession year for the railroad industry," arguing defensively that M&StL had experienced a "satisfactory" season, but admitting that making such a doleful report to stockholders was a painful experience. "We're not trying to pad or gloss over anything, although the temptation has been great to make a record in the past twelve months," Heineman told the media on the anniversary of his takeover. Despite unimpressive earnings, pride compelled Heineman to issue dividends in the amount of $940,000. Sober investors may have wondered what they had in Ben W. Heineman.[7]

Devins predictably was under great pressure to cut costs, but as always the path to prosperity was not simply through savings. Economies would have to be balanced by judicious expenditures. Sprague Island and its appurtenances, a great issue in the late proxy war, were sold at a considerable loss in 1955. Agencies at Bradley and Waukee were made joint with those of Milwaukee, and Devins cut $309,000 out of the budget at midyear, largely in train operation and maintenance of way. New relay rail was limited to 11.5 track miles, and the telegraph line between Marshalltown and Oskaloosa was rebuilt instead of adding a telephone line, but Devins did convince the board to approve the acquisition of forty new covered hopper cars. Devins likewise argued that the company was falling behind in industrial development; the board agreed and hired Frank E. Clawson away from the Minneapolis Chamber of Commerce to head an increased effort in that area. Whether due to Clawson's work or not, by year's end M&StL reported substantial new grain elevators in Iowa at Badger, Dallas Center, Rockwell, and Sully in addition to a dry milk plant at Clarkfield, Minnesota, and expansion of major on-line warehouses at Mason City.[8]

Devins may have had mixed emotions about serious expenditures for an integrated and mechanized accounting system recommended by Arthur Anderson & Company and implemented by Larry S. Provo, a twenty-seven-year-old accountant hired from that firm as vice president and controller when George A. Anderson, a forty-eight-year veteran, chose retirement. There was no doubting that M&StL had been using antiquated manual accounting procedures and there was no doubting that Provo forced the company to institute "responsibility accounting"; in fact, M&StL became the first railroad to do so. Devins's ill ease derived from the fact that installing International Business Machines (IBM) equipment and systemwide teletype capability would force him to fire at least one hundred loyal employees who, with him, had labored diligently to save the railroad in hard times now past. Small wonder that old heads saw Provo as "the agent of curtailment."[9]

Figure 23.1. Larry Provo, second from left, and Ben W. Heineman, third from right, took great pride in the new IBM equipment and in M&StL's "responsibility accounting." John Devins, fourth from right, seemed on guard. M&StL photograph, author's collection.

Larry Provo most assuredly was also the symbol of M&StL's future. Managers like G. A. Anderson, whom Provo replaced, typically had long tenure with the company, had grown old in its service, and were at the time of leaving. The departure of long-serving Colin W. Wright as vice president and general counsel on September 1, 1955, reflected that reality. One of the most telling raps against Lucian Sprague was that he had developed no plan for succession at the executive or subordinate levels; he had been a "one man band." Despite Heineman's castigation of M&StL's management during the proxy struggle, he had decided to retain the vast majority of its managerial ranks. But as older men chose retirement, Heineman actively sought young lions like Provo—"leaders in the railroad industry ten years hence"—and forged a program of incentives designed to stretch their talents and retain their loyalty. One of those incentives was a bonus system, and another was stock options—both radical departures at M&StL. Replacement personnel like Provo came from outside, but Heineman did not ignore talent within. Richard Musenbrock replaced Wright in the legal department, for example. Another outsider, however, was Albert W. Schroeder, who left Chicago & Eastern Illinois to sign on as vice president and general manager, a slot vacated earlier and left unfilled when Devins became president.[10]

During the fall of 1955, John Devins cautiously led M&StL into the new world of trailer-on-flat-car (TOFC or piggyback) service. Studies dated from a year earlier and curiously had focused on less-than-carload freight to and from Morton and Winthrop. When implemented on November 25, however, TOFC service was offered between Minneapolis and Peoria, with end-loading ramps at each location and five flatcars capable of handling two trailers each in dedicated operation. Draying of trailers was under contract to truckers; cars were placed just ahead of the caboose on trains 19 and 20 to expedite movement. Capital outlay was about $15,000, and Devins expected annual revenues of approximately $104,000. Meanwhile, Roy Nelson negotiated with Wabash to establish Minneapolis–St. Louis TOFC operation via Albia; that service began on December 29.[11]

During the 1950s, M&StL's four-state service area was a blend of change and constancy. In Illinois, Chicago—the nation's second-largest city—cast a huge shadow and retained a gigantic hinterland, but Peoria was hardly unimportant. Bemis Bag, Caterpillar Tractor, Keystone Steel & Wire, Hiram Walker Distillery, and Pabst Brewing were among several important shippers in and about that community that fed a dozen railroads with lines fanning out in every direction. Monmouth and Abingdon, too, featured manufacturing plants, while coal dominated at Middle Grove and Rapatee. Other intermediate stations between Keithsburg and Peoria were typically small and reflected historic dependence on agriculture. South Dakota, by comparison, was the most rural of all states served by M&StL, although manufacturing and wholesale distribution were important parts of the economy at Aberdeen and Watertown. The other stations in South Dakota were overwhelmingly small and tightly tied to agriculture that was increasingly mechanized and larger in scale, with fewer persons living on fewer farms. This, of course, was not unique to South Dakota, but rather reflected a nationwide trend. So did the use of improved seed and fertilizer to increase production, which, from M&StL stations in South Dakota, was principally wheat but also other cereal grains, flax, and corn. Iowa, in which M&StL had more route miles than in the other states, never developed a dominant port of entry, no central metropolis area—no Chicago, St. Louis, or Minneapolis. Des Moines, the capital, had led Iowa cities in manufacturers during the 1920s, but slipped thereafter and had been known in recent years more as a wholesale, insurance, and publishing center. Manufacturing and distribution were part of the scene at Oskaloosa and Marshalltown, prodigious tonnage in packing house products and

Figure 23.2. TOFC or trailer-on-flat-car service was a new approach embraced by the Heineman team. M&StL photograph, author's collection.

cement still flowed from Mason City, gypsum and clay products moved in large quantity from in and about Fort Dodge, but coal, once so prominent at Oskaloosa and Albia, was now insignificant. The bulk of M&StL's Iowa stations, from Alexander to Wayland, were small, were highly dependent on farming, and provided the company with bountiful billings in corn, soybeans, and to a lesser extent cereal grains. Of the states served by M&StL, Minnesota likely was the most balanced, almost evenly split between rural and urban population by 1950, with the value of manufacturing slightly more than that of agricultural production. Minneapolis, always central to M&StL's fortunes, boasted a population of 521,718 in 1950, and while flour milling at that site was still important, a decline that had begun earlier continued its erosion. Local stations in Minnesota, from Marietta on the west to Manchester and Dunnell on the south, continued to dispatch grain, canned goods, dry milk, and sugar beets and, like small stations systemwide, received lumber, petroleum products, coal, and LCL.[12]

Figure 23.3. The Minneapolis milling district, while not as vibrant as in yesteryear, remained a traffic jewel for M&StL. M&StL photograph, author's collection.

Every bit of M&StL's traffic, whether it derived from local stations or huge manufacturing centers or moved overhead, was subject to intense competition from other railroads or, as was ever more the case, from other forms of transport that in one way or another suckled at the public breast. For M&StL, the modal threat came from internal waterways but especially from trucks. The motor vehicle industry churned out a veritable flood of them—5,337,451 in the last half of the 1940s, 6,230,626 in the first half of the 1950s. The total number of truck registrations across the country doubled in ten years, from 5,079,802 in 1945 to 10,302,987 in 1955. After the war more trucks, with greater carrying capacity and moving over an expanded system of publicly aided hardtop roads, cut deeply into rail freight. And in some cases trucks nearly captured the market.[13]

The railroad industry was in trouble. During 1953 railroads handled 53 percent of all ton miles, down from 63 percent in 1939. In 1954 freight revenues were $7.8 billion, about what they had been in 1948; net income, however, was $683 million, essentially that of 1946. This, managers and investors moaned in unison, was after railroad companies had spent lavishly to modernize plant, motive power, and rolling stock. In 1953 the return on investment for the industry was a mere 4.19 percent; in 1954 it was only 3.00 percent.[14]

Why were the numbers sinking so fast? A cursory study might have concluded that 1954 was a blip, in large part the result of economic adjustments resulting from the end of hostilities in Korea. But 1954 was not a blip; indeed, 1954 offered a glimpse into an unpromising future. That year railroads suffered more severe declines in the levels of their operations and earnings than most other basic industries; ton miles were off nearly 10 percent, operating revenues dropped by more than 12 percent, and net income plummeted by over 25 percent. Furthermore, the decline in net would have been greater if much scheduled maintenance had not been deferred. Publicly assisted competitive modes of transportation represented a great part of the problem, but there were other serious issues. A "stick-in-the-mud" management style and tradition often was alleged, and with justification, but the heavy shackles thrown over the industry during the now-distant time when railroads had enjoyed nearly a modal monopoly had deprived the railroad companies of enterprising opportunity, which drove top talent to other endeavors. Again 1954 offers an illustration. As the economy softened, railroads sought rate reductions to hold or attract business, but regulatory wheels ground exceedingly slowly and not particularly finely. If and when reductions were granted, it was often too late; competing modes had run off with the traffic. And, once gone, that traffic was very hard to regain. Moreover, managers could do little to effectively address money-losing aspects of operation. Station closings, branch line abandonments, and passenger train discontinuances were nearly always long, drawn-out, and painful, and often they were unsuccessful when politically motivated regulatory bodies turned a deaf ear. Railroad labor likewise presented obstacles, often levering public policy to force the adoption of make-work rules and adherence to antiquated practices that hamstrung efficient operation and thwarted innovation, reduced the carriers' ability to compete, and in the end proved harmful to labor and capital alike.[15]

The upshot was that the industry found itself viewed by many as outmoded, dying on the vine, an anachronism headed for some museum of nostalgia—certainly an industry that found it difficult if not impossible to earn a reasonable return on investment and thus difficult if not impossible to attract the venture capital necessary to support a continuous program of modernization. In truth, however, railroads remained very much a part of the national landscape—in 1953 employing 1.25 million workers and purchasing $3.3 billion in supplies, material, and equipment—and some carriers—Union Pacific and Santa Fe in the West, Chesapeake & Ohio in the East, and Southern in the South—seemed quite healthy. But close at hand, sprawling Chicago & North Western had not paid a dividend on common stock since 1950; in 1954 *Forbes* referred to it derisively as the "New York Central of the West."[16]

This was the environment that M&StL and Ben W. Heineman confronted as 1955 ended. Heineman's mark at M&StL so far had been anything but spectacular. He had admitted going in that he knew little of railroading, but he was a quick study, energetic, aggressive, and determined. He also was impatient and apt to pace a room restlessly, talking rapidly, developing ideas with a lawyer's logic and fluency, constantly challenging tradition. And Heineman expressed confidence in the industry. "I like railroads," he told the trade press. "A lot of people think they're dying. I don't. I think they have a tremendous future." Heineman admitted that the carriers had been going "through a financial and physical revolution," but now, he said, "they're about to find their place in the economic picture." A ride with him into the future was sure to be interesting.[17]

Chapter 24
Days of Red and White

In December 1959, the United States Supreme Court denied our application [to acquire Toledo, Peoria & Western]. Although we are disappointed in the result, we do not believe this need have an adverse effect on our future, in earnings or otherwise.
—M&StL Annual Report 1959

John W. Devins had hired out in 1912 and worked his way through the ranks; he was without formal education, and when Heineman ousted Lucian Sprague in 1954, Devins was sixty-five years of age. Short, husky, a quick thinker and close observer of M&StL's operations and property, Devins was intolerant of poor performance, but he also had a ready wit and a merry twinkle in his eye. Mechanical Superintendent William W. Landmesser thought him "a typical Irish policeman," recalling Devins's insistence on truth: "If you ever lied to him, you were dead." Chief Dispatcher Manford J. Reitan considered Devins a "jelly bean," hard on the outside, soft within. Despite his many attributes, however, Devins was not a strategic thinker, and, unlike Lucian Sprague, he could not effectively rally employees or shippers. His reputation was tarnished with many in both groups, who saw his survival after the Heineman coup as evidence of duplicity or at least unseemly opportunism. Heineman shrewdly sought to defuse such feelings, heaping praise on Devins, calling him "one of the best operating men in the business." Some considered Devins mere window dressing, but while there was no doubt that Ben W. Heineman was the man in charge at M&StL, Devins was just as clearly in control of day-to-day business until he asked to step down as president effective March 1, 1956. The board accepted his retirement request and, in a move no doubt orchestrated by Heineman, eagerly passed a resolution declaring that John W. Devins "had been primarily responsible for the rebuilding and rehabilitation of the Minneapolis & St. Louis Railway Company to its present high standards and efficiency." It was revisionist history of the highest order and, without taking credit away from Devins's considerable accomplishments as Lucian Sprague's first lieutenant, was simply not true. But it was consistent with Heineman's grand mythology about the Sprague years.[1]

Devins's retirement, and that of C. S. Weatherill as chief engineer, set off a chain reaction of shuffling current personnel and new hires. Thirty-nine-year-old Albert W. Schroeder became president on February 9, 1956. Recently arrived from Chicago & Eastern Illinois, where he had been chief engineer and then vice president and general manager, Schroeder was a graduate of the University of Nebraska in civil engineering. His first job in the railroad industry had been in track service for Chicago, Burlington & Quincy; at Chicago & Eastern Illinois he had teamed with industry stars John M. Budd, now president at Great Northern, and Downing B. Jenks, who had gone on to Rock Island as president. Schroeder's elevation opened the way for a new vice president of operations, a position that went to William P. Coliton, thirty-six, who came from Great Northern, where he had been superintendent of the Cascade Division. A decorated veteran of World War II, the tall, handsome Coliton had begun his railroad career as a GN section laborer; he had earned a degree in economics from the University of Pennsylvania's respected Wharton School of Finance. Steven J. Owens, assistant to the chief engineer at CB&Q, arrived to become chief engineer, and James R. Sullivan, formerly supervisor of personnel development at Illinois Central, signed on as chief personnel officer. Owens, forty-eight, held a degree in civil engineering from Michigan College of Mining and Technology; he had been with CB&Q since 1938. Sullivan, forty, a native of St. Paul, had earned degrees from St. Thomas College and the University of Minnesota; he brought with him from IC eighteen years of varied experience.[2]

All of these personnel changes were concurrent with the departure of Ben Heineman from the active affairs of M&StL. Shortly after gaining control of the company, Heineman and others who had joined him also captured a Wisconsin-based manufacturer of heavy-duty trucks. Heineman was on a roll. A few months later he was associated with multiple groups purchasing large blocks of woe-enwrapped Chicago & North Western. This was followed shortly by the startling announcement that a Heineman-led group had taken options on a 43 percent interest in Wisconsin Central, recently emerged from bankruptcy, operated by Soo Line, and controlled by Soo and Canadian Pacific. Other reports had Heineman stalking Monon. Whatever the truth regarding Wisconsin Central and Monon, Heineman's sights assuredly were fixed on C&NW. His group, it became apparent, had taken "a substantial block" of its equity. By February 1956, Heineman demanded reorganization of North Western on behalf of his group; he also insisted that he have "substantial representation" on its board. North Western's financial record was "indefensible," bellowed Heineman. "Not true," came an anemic reply from C&NW. A rambunctious proxy fight seemed a distinct possibility, but—perhaps with the memory of Heineman's stunning victory over Sprague at M&StL—much larger Chicago & North Western came to heel with little more than a whimper. Balding, bow-tied, forty-two-year-old Heineman would become chairman and chief executive officer effective April 1.[3]

Ben Heineman was obliged to relinquish his membership on the M&StL board and his position as chairman of the executive committee. With that in mind, Heineman had consulted with "some of the larger shareholders" as to his successor, and they had agreed to support Max Swiren, Heineman's law partner from Chicago. His election at the next annual meeting was pro forma.[4]

When Ben W. Heineman packed himself off to C&NW, he left in his wake serious unanswered questions. Was Max Swiren a stand-in for Heineman, a mere stooge? Would Heineman lose all interest in M&StL as he wrestled with C&NW's monumental problems? The rapid departure of bright and resourceful Larry S. Provo to aid Heineman as vice president and comptroller at C&NW only underscored those questions.

Meanwhile, Roy Nelson as senior solicitor of traffic confronted the constant need to put freight on M&StL rail in an environment that was ever more competitive, always fluid, and subject as it was to weather conditions affecting crops, government policy toward agriculture, strikes in major industries, the traditional ebb and flow in the building trades and the construction industry, and vicissitudes of the business cycle. New traffic such as iron ore loaded on Milwaukee Road in southeastern Minnesota and bound for steel mills in Granite City, Illinois (via M&StL at Mason City and Wabash at Albia) brought smiles; loss of Kaiser's alumina moving overhead from Baton Rouge, Louisiana, to Mead, Washington, brought a frown. Coal typically contributed the highest tonnage, corn the most revenue. Indeed, M&StL's profit and loss statement was especially sensitive to corn—not only to aggregate production in the service area, but also to storage and movement decisions made by the government's Commodity Credit Corporation. When grain traffic went slack, Nelson and his crew came under intense pressure to produce more bridge traffic. As Nelson pointed out, however, salesmen had to scare up about three cars of bridge traffic to equal the revenue on a single car of grain loaded at an M&StL station. During the first five years of the 1950s, M&StL saw 54.6 percent of its tonnage interchanged to or from connections. This dependency on others threw into bold relief M&StL's historic problem of short average hauls and raised again the perennial question of how the road might lengthen carries. The era of expanding system domain through construction had long since passed, but merger offered a tempting alternative. And the Interstate Commerce Commission seemed at least slightly more receptive to that prescriptive than it had been earlier.[5]

Sprague had made bold strikes at territorial expansion right after the war, but without success, and then had seemed to accept M&StL's position, pursuing no ventures later. This, of course, had been one of Heineman's complaints about Sprague, and Heineman seemed of the view that M&StL's only course was to disappear into a larger system. But his perspective changed shortly after he arrived at M&StL, and he had begun to poke about with the idea of expanding M&StL itself. Even as Heineman settled in at M&StL, however, others were looking at it as a candidate for acquisition. In 1955 an active rumor that Rock Island would pick up M&StL prompted Northern Pacific to mount a very substantial study of M&StL. NP's interest was understandable. In 1953 M&StL had received 13,478 eastbound cars from NP and handed the larger road 7,583 westbound cars in return. NP analysts recognized that a substantial portion of M&StL tonnage was overhead sought after aggressively, and that M&StL often solicited traffic "as a Minneapolis Railroad and, therefore entitled to participate in traffic to and from Minneapolis in a substantial amount in order to successfully continue in operation." This, said NP, could "largely be credited to the leadership and personal efforts of former President Sprague." Increasing traffic under the new ownership, however, seemed doubtful. NP liked the idea of a through connection with several eastern roads at Peoria, appreciated the prospect of more agricultural and industrial tonnage from M&StL lines moving westbound to NP, and admired M&StL's "substantial industrial locations" in Minneapolis. Nevertheless, it feared alienating other roads with which it connected in the Twin Cities, worried greatly that CB&Q might retaliate by improving its service via Laurel, Montana, in a way that would deprive NP of longer hauls, and especially fretted that CB&Q would favor Great Northern over NP. (NP and GN, of course, jointly owned CB&Q.) In the end, NP did nothing.[6]

Meanwhile, Heineman soon fixed his attention on Toledo, Peoria & Western (TP&W), a 242-mile pike stretching from Effner, Indiana, on the Indiana-Illinois border through Peoria to Keokuk, Iowa, on the Mississippi River, with a spur to Lomax, in western Illinois, where TP&W connected with Santa Fe's main line. An ancient road with a curious past, early in the century TP&W had been controlled by giant Pennsylvania Railroad and prosperous Chicago, Burlington & Quincy. The road fell into receivership in 1917, and when Pennsylvania and Burlington failed to agree on joint ownership and division of it between them, George P. McNear of New York City purchased the company at auction in 1926. McNear took TP&W, laughed at as "Tired, Poor & Weary," out of receivership, hustled overhead traffic from Pennsylvania Railroad (PRR) on the east and Atchison, Topeka & Santa Fe (AT&SF) on the west, and, like M&StL, boosted Peoria as a gateway to avoid Chicago, turning TP&W into "Tested, Popular & Wanted." In 1948 TP&W handled 83,760 cars; by 1954 the number had increased to 110,244.[7]

Heineman was not the first at M&StL to show an interest in TP&W. Sprague had sought lease of it in 1945 and again after the death of George McNear in 1947. Heineman's dream in its fullest form was, in fact, reminiscent of a grandiose plan floated earlier by John W. Barriger to create a vast Chicago outer belt by merging or at least combining the operations of Chicago & Eastern Illinois, Monon, TP&W, and M&StL. With that concept in mind, Heineman approached the trust holding McNear stock (82 percent of the total) in June 1954, offering $69.55 per share. That proposition was rejected, but over the next months the two sides negotiated Heineman's offer upward to $100, and although the matter was vague, Heineman thought he had a deal. Heineman and associates then began to buy Monon stock—a fact that

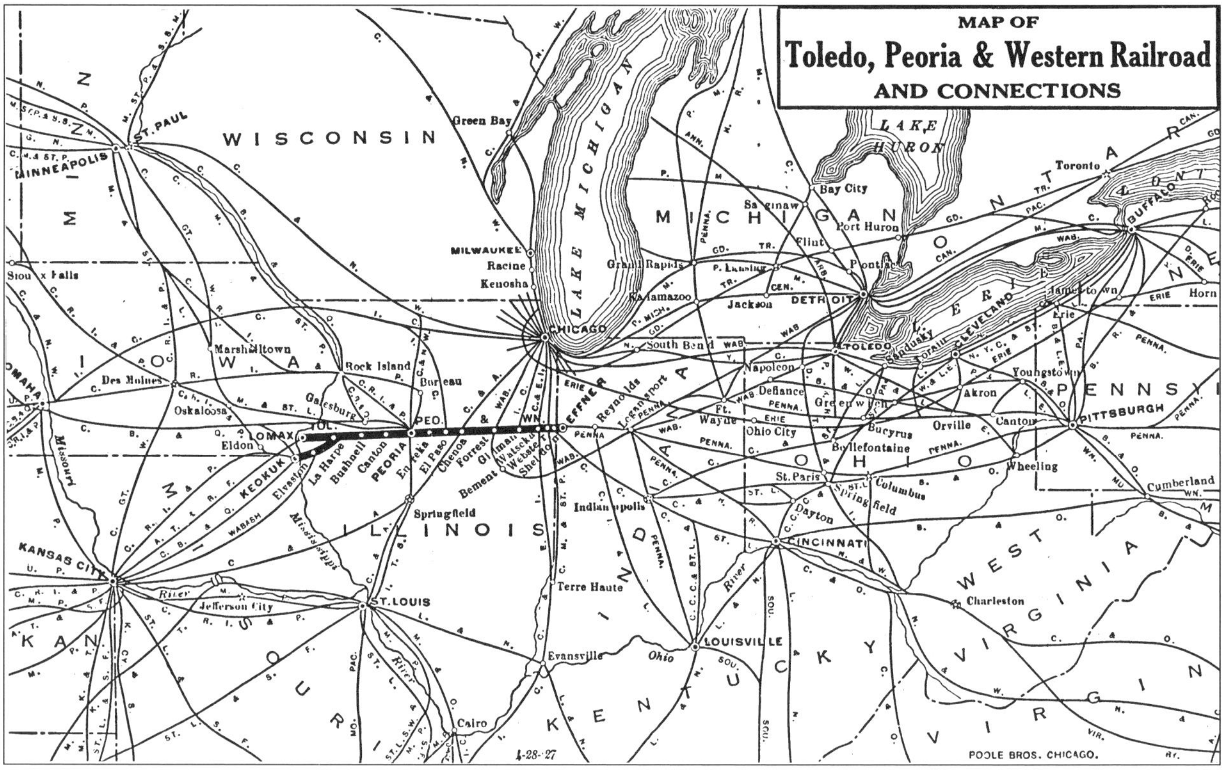

Map 24.1. An end-to-end merger with Toledo, Peoria & Western would extend M&StL's average hauls.

became known immediately and just as immediately sparked concern at Santa Fe and Pennsylvania. At the same time, there was appreciable behind-the-scenes ill ease at TP&W and among the McNear trustees; McNear's widow opposed any sale to M&StL, and one trustee exclaimed that M&StL would acquire TP&W only "over my dead body." AT&SF President Fred Gurley dispatched John S. Reed to "scout" TP&W; PRR's President James Symes sneered at the idea of linking M&StL with TP&W and Monon and promised to "take steps to stop this nonsense." In late March 1955 President J. Russell Coulter at TP&W privately told the McNear trustees that he thought the ICC would not approve the sale of TP&W to M&StL; the trustees, in turn, expressed enthusiasm for sale to Santa Fe and Pennsylvania. On April 18, Heineman was told that an agreement had been made with the two larger roads, but Heineman presently offered $133.33 per share. On June 28, though, a written agreement committed AT&SF and PRR to purchase TP&W in equal parts at $135 per share. Heineman was outraged, claiming that he had been badly treated—that Coulter and the McNear trustees had used him "as an uncompensated underwriter protecting the estate, while they were negotiating to sell it [TP&W] to the Pennsylvania and the Santa Fe."[8]

In all of this there was much that did not meet the eye. Russell Coulter, for example, was likely motivated, at least in part, by self-preservation. Elizabeth McNear, the widow of George P. McNear, may have had a strong affection for the city of Peoria and perceived that M&StL's plan would hurt and not help that community. Heineman himself assuredly was an issue. Although he could be quite charming and clearly was articulate and persuasive, he also could be assertive and brash. Moreover, the memory of his recent hostile proxy battle for M&StL was fresh. Sprague and James Symes at Pennsylvania were friends of long standing, and Symes, in fact, more than once had urged Sprague and Coulter to combine M&StL and TP&W. His views now were quite otherwise. Moreover, Heineman was at the very same time making his run at Chicago & North Western, in the process criticizing the managers and management tradition at that company but by extension the entire railroad fraternity. Leaders of the industry had not looked kindly at Heineman's early attack on Chicago Great Western, had frowned when he toppled Lucian Sprague at M&StL, and eventually would forge "an invisible ring around him," as respected securities analyst Henry H. Livingston put it. Finally, Heineman's dream of an outer belt to avoid Chicago, however meritorious, did indeed threaten companies with a vested interest in that metropolis. In a very real way, Heineman's determination to acquire Monon—not his approach to TP&W—was what tripped the trigger at Santa Fe and Pennsylvania. It was a strategic blunder of the first order. By the time Heineman and friends sold their Monon holdings late in 1955 as a peace offering, the fat truly was in the fire.[9]

Heineman was hardly going to roll over and play dead. Acquisition of TP&W by Santa Fe and Pennsylvania required ICC approval; M&StL sought and obtained permission to intervene. Indeed, M&StL sought authority to gain control of TP&W against AT&SF and PRR—a David and Goliath contest of sorts. ICC hearings were scheduled at Peoria beginning February 1, 1956. Edward K. Wheeler, outside counsel from Washington, told M&StL's board that he "was quite optimistic about . . . chances of winning the case," but as proceedings opened, Illinois Governor William G. Stratton announced his opposition to M&StL's application, and the Peoria Association of Commerce chose to side with Santa Fe and Pennsylvania. It was not good news.[10]

John Devins, Roy Nelson, and others from M&StL were rolled out to make M&StL's case, but the heavy lifting fell to Ben Heineman. It was plainly and simply in M&StL's interest to seek TP&W—"a simple geographic extension of M&StL," said Heineman—and, after all, TP&W was a company with which M&StL had for the years 1951–55 interchanged an average of 12,995 revenue loads annually, 5.9 percent of M&StL's total, accounting for 8.1 percent of its freight revenues. Heineman pointed out that M&StL was in good physical condition, well stocked with power and equipment, and financially able to shoulder the debt of acquisition. He boldly laid out his plans to eliminate duplicate facilities (Bartlett Yard at Peoria in favor of TP&W's facility at East Peoria, for example), and terminate some 256 TP&W positions. With TP&W safely under its belt, M&StL would aggressively advertise and solicit for its new and improved service to connections east of Peoria with Gulf, Mobile & Ohio, Wabash, Illinois Central, Chicago & Eastern Illinois, Milwaukee Road, New York Central, and of course, Pennsylvania at Effner, Indiana. This would give M&StL longer average hauls and in the process, Heineman maintained, "divert traffic . . . from Chicago and St. Louis gateways, mitigate further inroads by truck competition, and obtain revenue and traffic that we are not now obtaining." Amalgamation of M&StL and TP&W would, Heineman concluded, combine two small roads into a stronger, better-balanced single concern, whereas acquisition of TP&W by Santa Fe and Pennsylvania would materially injure M&StL.[11]

The positions taken by Santa Fe, Pennsylvania, their supporters, and other intervenors were essentially defensive—that M&StL simply should not have TP&W. Santa Fe's Gurley preferred to own TP&W "rather than have M&StL purchase it." PRR's Symes took the same view. Gurley, however, also feared relying solely on M&StL for Santa Fe's Peoria business (via Nemo) and wanted to strengthen movement over TP&W (via Lomax). Moreover, Santa Fe contended that TP&W better protected traffic over Lomax than M&StL did at Nemo, and, in fact, in a cost-cutting move, M&StL service had been trimmed between Monmouth and Peoria in a way that benefited TP&W and hurt M&StL. TP&W admittedly had not done well under earlier joint control (CB&Q-PRR), but Peoria interests were not eager to see loss of its headquarters (actually in East Peoria) and attendant jobs; nor did they see enhancement of Peoria as a gateway, but rather saw potential loss should M&StL prevail. Communities west of Peoria became especially agitated, worrying openly that M&StL would have no interest in the roughly hundred-mile segment out to Keokuk and Lomax, and organized labor was understandably upset at the possibility of lost jobs. Rock Island, dominant at Peoria, feared erosion of business from its strong base there, and Nickel Plate, which received from and handed significant tonnage to both M&StL and TP&W at Peoria, earnestly sought to derail M&StL's plans. So did Wabash, which fussed that heavy interchange with M&StL at Albia and Des Moines would be seriously compromised. And TP&W's Russell Coulter suggested that efficiencies could be had without corporate combination; M&StL, for instance, might secure trackage rights over CB&Q from Farmington, Illinois, to his road at nearby Canton, using TP&W into Peoria as well as its yard at East Peoria. In that way M&StL could abandon Bartlett Yard and the troublesome grade out of the Kickapoo valley to the west. Ultimately, argued Santa Fe and Pennsylvania, the best policy would be their joint ownership of the Peoria road—a maintenance of the status quo modified only by new owners who would do their best to throw traffic to TP&W.[12]

It remained for the ICC examiner to render his recommendation and then for the commission to make its ruling. Good news for M&StL came from neither; both favored the AT&SF-PRR proposal over M&StL's. M&StL vowed to appeal, but the word from Washington was a stunning blow. In fact, however, M&StL had not made a good case. Heineman needlessly had irritated and alienated the McNear family and trustees, and he had grossly miscalculated the politics of community loyalty. His acknowledgement that TP&W would cease to exist except as a division of M&StL had violated Peoria pride and frightened labor. His timing of the purchase of Monon stock and then boasting of it had been terrible. John Devins also had stumbled when he talked openly about the lack of "operational importance" to M&StL of TP&W lines west of Peoria, predictably inciting active hostility from that quarter that no amount of backpedaling could correct. M&StL also had argued that it was in marvelous physical and financial condition, but simultaneously contended that failing to acquire TP&W would be so devastating to it that the Iowa branches and all operations west of Watertown, South Dakota, would have to be abandoned. Critics failed to see the logic. And M&StL had never sought or obtained vigorous support from high-powered shippers. Neither had it gained uniform support from the states in its service area: Minnesota and South Dakota supported, Iowa abstained, and Illinois weighed in against the acquisition. In short, M&StL never had demonstrated that the public interest would be served by its acquisition of Toledo, Peoria & Western. Albert Schroeder subsequently admitted M&StL's serious miscues in a letter to the president of Peoria's Commercial National Bank. Schroeder thought M&StL should have gathered Peoria's business and political leaders and explained to them "in great detail our plans for the future of Peoria if we were successful in acquiring TP&W." That had not been done, Schroeder groaned. "If this sounds critical of the past management . . . then I cannot help it for I sincerely feel this way," Schroeder exploded in a moment of acute candor. Nevertheless, M&StL would press the issue before the courts; no early resolution could be anticipated.[13]

Success, so elusive in the TP&W case, came easily when M&StL quickly captured Minnesota Western Railway, a 112-mile short line that stretched westward from Minneapolis to Gluek on a profile approximately thirty miles north of M&StL's route through Winthrop and Morton. Begun in 1908 by real estate developer William L. Luce as the Electric Short Line Railway but known ever after as the Luce Line, the road inched out of Minneapolis to Wayzata, Watertown, Winsted, Hutchinson, and Lake Lillian before stumbling on hard times. During the mid-1920s it emerged as the Minnesota Western (curiously the name of M&StL's earliest predecessor) and appeared to take on new life—expanding through Clara City to Gluek, thirty-one miles, and planning to go on into South Dakota. In 1927 management passed to Minneapolis, Northfield & Southern (MN&S); in the next decade ownership fell to Cargill, Incorporated, although MN&S continued management under contract. On January 31, 1956, M&StL purchased Minnesota Western's capital stock for $300,000; the road's locomotives and rolling stock were not included. M&StL would operate Minnesota Western as a wholly owned subsidiary; Heineman praised the acquisition as a significant step in M&StL's "industrial development program." Direct physical connection was not possible except over a short piece of Great Northern trackage in Minneapolis so that Minnesota Western trains could gain entrance to the Railway Transfer yard in the milling district. ICC approval came in August.[14]

Minnesota Western proved a mixed blessing. It had great potential for grain gathering, especially on its

Figure 24.1. Heineman testified that failure in the TP&W case would jeopardize all M&StL operation west of Watertown, South Dakota, including service to Conde. Critics failed to see the logic. Photo by the author.

western reaches; cans moved to Hutchinson, petroleum products to several stations, and cheese was billed at Winsted. Minnesota Western's net over the years 1951–55 had averaged $93,639 annually, but a loss of $35,829 for 1957, the first full year under M&StL ownership, was depressing. Track conditions were poor, but section forces nevertheless were reduced. Train service was trimmed to triweekly; Spellacy Motor Cargo contracted to handle less-than-carload freight. By early 1958 M&StL's board was discussing the "possible future of Minnesota Western," and by summer it was studying the problem of deferred maintenance, the effect of dissolving the company, and the possibility of abandoning everything west of Hutchinson and incorporating the rest into M&StL. Nevertheless, senior managers saw potential for industrial development at Hutchinson and, to a much greater extent, near Minneapolis at Golden Valley and Plymouth. On September 8, 1959, the name of the company was changed to Minneapolis Industrial Railway to imply M&StL's long-term expectations for the property.[15]

On the merger front and otherwise, M&StL's new management team aggressively sought to make its mark. Impatient with the multiplicity of colors used on M&StL's locomotive fleet, looking for a new standard, and reflecting a national yawn at all that seemed old-fashioned, out of date, stodgy, dull, and traditional, M&StL chose a new if simple color scheme—fire-engine red and off-white—and a slightly modified corporate logo. Boxcars became "traveling billboards," with nearly seven-foot letters reading "MStL," the ampersand missing. Cars and locomotives were repainted as they came up for heavy renewal. The company's traditional but extremely curious system of numbering locomotives indicating the month and year of purchase also came under scrutiny; a long-overdue change renumbered power in a logical division according to classification and in order of acquisition. Alco 244, the first RS-1, became 200; all others followed in sequential order. Switchers took lower numbers in double digits or in a 100 series; the two SD7s became 300 and 301, the F3s and F7s became 400s, and the FTs became 500s.[16]

M&StL's stable of motive power itself came under study. The fleet was hardly elderly and certainly not ill maintained, but the road had dieselized early under steam-minded conventions. Thus, for example, the Alcos had come devoid of equipage to hook them in multiple for operation by one crew. Consequently,

M&StL remained saddled to some extent with the need to use helpers on heavy grades and even to employ double-headers with diesels. Train 95, for one, frequently required a fully manned Alco plus fully crewed F units between Monmouth and Oskaloosa. The annual wheat rush on the West End likewise spotlighted the Alco's liability. Either tonnage was left to pile up, extra trains were called, or M&StL shuffled F units or the SD7s from other assignments. But that merely shifted the problem elsewhere. The builder was approached about upgrading the thirty-five RS-1s to multiple operation and agreed to the task, but assigned a fee that management felt was exhorbitant. M&StL's Cedar Lake shops got the job instead, manufacturing controllers and doing all the wiring at a fraction of Alco's fee. "That shop could do anything," beamed a proud William Landmesser. "If you couldn't buy it, they would make it." The program began in 1955 and proceeded with groups of five or six locomotives as they came up for heavy work. Attention then turned to the three-unit FTs and the F2, until recently numbered 445, 545, and 147, which were semipermanently coupled, with the result that if one unit went down the entire trio headed for the shop. Late in 1956, Schroeder convinced the board to send these to the manufacturer, General Motors' Electro-Motive Division for the purpose of rebuilding them into popular single-unit 1,500-horsepower GP9s with multiple-unit capacity at the cost of $107,000 each—considerably less than it would cost to buy such power "off the shelf." Designed as general-purpose locomotives, GP9s also had the advantage of employing main components compatible with F7s, reducing the parts inventory, and they also could run in multiple with the F3s and F7s. The two FTs and the lone F2 moved to LaGrange in order of acquisition and emerged in 1956–57 as GP9s 600–608, painted in the new red and white livery.[17]

Schroeder and Coliton continued to refine M&StL's locomotive inventory. In 1956 M&StL sold one venerable Alco switcher (formerly D939), and later in the year and in the next year likewise disposed of its three General Electric forty-four-ton switchers, which had proved too light for company needs. By the fall of 1957 Schroeder determined to sell twenty of the Alcos and to acquire sixteen GP9s as replacements, but he was frustrated by a depressed market for used power. The board did authorize him to sell Alcos

Figure 24.2. Alcos in multiple gave M&StL flexibility and muscle when seasonal demands meant heavier tonnage. This was often the case for train 56, shown here at Gilmore City, Iowa, heavily laden in September 1959 with grain and rock. Photo by the author.

as he could, and by late 1960 a dozen of them would be scrapped on account of wrecks or sold to others. This was adequate to justify purchase of fourteen GP9s from EMD at not less than $185,980 per copy; numbered 700–713, they arrived in the fall of 1958. A year later two F7s, 408 and 409, were rebuilt by EMD at less than half the cost of new units.[18]

New and more flexible power allowed M&StL to add locomotives without additional enginemen. Two-unit Alcos were seen frequently during grain season on the West End and often between Fort Dodge and Spencer, where limestone from Gilmore City and grain from way stations produced heavy tonnage. Flagships 19 and 20 received more power and drew longer and heavier trains—often one hundred cars and over five thousand tons. The average number of cars per train systemwide increased from 42.2 in 1950 to 50.1 in 1957. Flexibility was seen graphically in the cooperation between M&StL and Illinois Central on traffic moving via Albert Lea. The two roads had a long history of mutually beneficial solicitation and movement of business through that junction, especially freight moving between Chicago and Minneapolis. Historically tonnage from one road had been set out and picked up by the other, but as early as December 1952, the two roads embraced a run-through arrangement between Cedar Lake and Waterloo using two M&StL F units, stopping at Albert Lea eastbound only to set out M&StL tonnage and pick up an IC crew, and westbound only to pick up M&StL tonnage and an M&StL crew. This arrangement obtained even after IC ended use of steam power on other trains into Albert Lea in February 1954, but on May 9, 1955, M&StL and IC began pooling power, each road effectively providing two units in turnaround service—a pattern modified when M&StL received GP9s so that run-through trains typically had one locomotive from each road. Time freights 94 and 97 on M&StL, at IC they were AC-1 and CA-1, important symbol dispatch freights.[19]

Modest alterations appeared in M&StL's traffic mix during these years. The percentage of tonnage in grains, flour, lumber, cement, soft coal, merchandise, and livestock—70.1 percent of all in 1920—dropped to 49.3 in 1955, then rose slightly to 52.6 in 1959. Livestock, of course, was a bit player—mostly stocker cattle billed to Eldora, among other places—contributing only 1,117 carloads in 1959,

Figure 24.3. M&StL's 94, Illinois Central's AC-1, was a "hot train" handling perishables and other expedited tonnage. Each road provided one locomotive for 94/AC-1, one for CA-1/97. In this instance, AC-1 was at Janesville, Iowa, in April 1960. Photo by the author.

but products of agriculture, mines, and forests made up nearly 65 percent of the total volume during the 1950s. Coal and grain tilted for first-place ranking in tonnage throughout the decade. Among grains, corn led, followed by wheat and soybeans. Cement billings, as always, varied according to construction demand, reaching an all-time high of 507,432 tons in 1959. Among M&StL's most important on-line customers were several terminal elevators, often feeding grain to the flour millers served by Railway Transfer; grocery warehouses as well as implement manufacturers Minneapolis-Moline and Massey Harris at Hopkins; International Milling at New Prague; Green Giant at Montgomery; Rilco Laminated at Albert Lea; Decker Packing, Lehigh Cement, and Northwestern Portland Cement at Mason City; Midland Electric at Middle Grove; and Penn-Dixie Cement and Hawkeye-Marquette Cement at West Des Moines. Lesser customers in the aggregate also supplied significant business at local stations. In April 1957, for example, Forest City received forty-six loads, billed eighty-seven loads, and handled 82,000 pounds of LCL. Pipe for natural gas lines and asphalt for road construction flowed in large volume to Corwith, Dallas Center, Lake Mills, and Emmons. And in 1956 M&StL donated a 15,000-pound granite block and transportation of it from Minnesota to Monmouth, where a plaque was added in honor of Wyatt Earp, the famous western marshal who had been born in that community.[20]

Train operation changed little. The flagships, as always, were 19 and 20. The run of number 20 on February 4, 1959, was typical. Moving out of Cedar Lake with units 403, 405, 406, and 410 and with eighty-seven loads, five empties, and 4,810 tons tucked between locomotives and caboose 1307, it changed crews at Albert Lea, Marshalltown, Oskaloosa, and Monmouth, picked up and set out cars at Marshalltown and Nemo, and nosed into Bartlett Yard at 11:02 p.m. Interchange cars went directly to Peoria Terminal, Rock Island, and Toledo, Peoria & Western as well as to Peoria & Pekin Union for others, including New York Central, Pennsylvania, and Nickel Plate, among several options for eastward forwarding. Pennsylvania was by this time the least favored, so slow to Terre Haute "it had difficulty getting out of its own way," recalled one M&StL officer. New York Central did a good job of getting cars to Indianapolis but then fell afoul its own problems. TP&W, too, did a good job of wheeling eastward-bound tonnage but was linked to faltering Pennsylvania at Effner, Indiana. The most reliable partner was Nickel Plate, westernmost player on the Alphabet Route. In the reverse direction, train 19 typically dropped the head portion of its train at Kenwood Yard, deposited its road engines at Cedar Lake, picked up new power (often an Alco), and hustled the hind cars to Minnesota Transfer, returning to Cedar Lake as a caboose hop. Elsewhere the "New Ulm Switch Job" handled lading between Winthrop and New Ulm and performed yeoman domestic duty at New Ulm, while Chaska and Montgomery switch runs handled heavy local business above Waseca. Trains 33 and 32 were stalwarts between Marshalltown and Mason City, the former doing local work en route to Mason City, then yielding its locomotive for the 10:30 a.m. switch engine and reclaiming it eight hours later for train 32, the "Decker Meat Express," which among its other lading contained up to twenty-five cars of meat, most of it handed off to Illinois Central at Ackley, some going to Chicago Great Western or to Chicago & North Western at Marshalltown. On the Fort Dodge–Albert Lea line, train 51 was scheduled to connect with IC manifests from Omaha bringing perishables and then hustle on to Albert Lea, where Minneapolis cars would be added to train 97. On the West End, the grain rush was traditional. "Effective immediately and continuing through July and August, all available system boxes are to be billed to Morton and forwarded," ordered Chief Dispatcher Manford J. Reitan on July 9, 1958. Two weeks later the agent at Conde advised Reitan: "SP 96983 new rye loaded here." The rush was on. Wilhelm F. Arp, the agent at Victoria, telegraphed Reitan on August 14 that Extra 407 (engines 407 and 412) had passed his station with sixty-six loads of grain—5,150 tons. The pattern was unchanged two years later. "Please place an order for 20 cars as we are 100% plugged on grain of all kinds," the agent at Conde was advised on July 29 by the South Dakota Wheat Growers elevator at Brentford, west of Conde on the abandoned line to Akaska but still advantaged by the Dakota Transfer truck-rail operation. Four days later engines 225 and 227 in multiple pitted twelve Alco cylinders and eight traction motors—2,000 horsepower of constant torque—against 2,474 reluctant tons of grain in thirty-five boxcars moved up the heavy grade through Crandall to the Choteau summit in a memorable display of thump, thump, thump, and heavy exhaust—a spectacle of sound and fury that would have done steam proud.[21]

Operating matters were the provenance of William P. Coliton, intelligent, knowledgeable, diplomatic—"one fair gentleman" recalled Road Foreman of Engines Charles W. Stone—and Frank B. Clark, general superintendent, who had begun his career as a section laborer at Eddyville, Iowa, knew the property intimately, and was regarded as "all railroad"—sober minded but fair. At the top of M&StL's leadership pole, however, was Max Swiren, chairman of the Executive Committee and formerly Ben Heineman's law partner. No mere stand-in for Heineman, Swiren was an active and aggressive chairman whose influence on M&StL's legal and financial policies was substantial and sound. Unlike Heineman, Swiren chose to work behind the scenes, did not seek publicity, and preferred that Albert Schroeder assume the role of "front man."[22]

That suited Schroeder just fine. Personable, energetic, receptive to new ideas, Schroeder met people easily; he quickly placed his optimistic stamp on the company. By mid-1956 Schroeder was clearly in harness. So was his cadre of lieutenants—a "young, hard-hitting, ambitious team"—who thrived under Schroeder's style of delegating responsibility. *Railway Age* was impressed, calling M&StL "a railway with young ideas"; Schroeder's image next to a new GP9 graced the front page of *Age* for March 31, 1958. So, too, were analysts from Hayden, Stone & Company impressed with what they found at M&StL: "Management is young and aggressive, and for a small railroad, possessed of considerable depth." Schroeder was willing to give credit where credit was due. "I think the efforts of Lucian Sprague in pulling the railroad together, in weathering the storm in the Separations Case, and emerging from bankruptcy in 1943, is a significant page in Midwestern railroad history," he boldly contended in an address to the Society of Security Analysts in 1957. He wanted to build on that legacy—"to enlarge the horizon of our progress." Schroeder forcefully contended that a "fresh approach should not be denied to any part of our activity." One part of that activity, in his view, was calling attention to the declining health of the American railroad industry.[23]

"The railroad industry today faces a crisis of proportions unprecedented since the depression of the 1930s," Alfred Schroeder told stockholders at the annual meeting in 1958. "Our situation is characterized by declining business through the general recession and purchasing restraint, substantially increased labor and material costs, and the continuing lethargy on the part of government agencies whose unwillingness to relax restrictions is throttling expansion, subsidizing our competitors, and repressing our day-to-day business opportunities." Schroeder was hardly alone in holding such strong views. At giant but stumbling Pennsylvania, James M. Symes recognized the industry's need for constant infusions of capital "if we're going to participate in this economy," but fretted that investors were made more than skittish by railroad wages that had gone up by 166 percent in the period 1939–56 while rates increased by only 74 percent over the same period. Meanwhile, modal competitors ate away at the railroads' traffic base. One Wall Street firm gloomily concluded that the industry appeared "to be in a struggle for survival," and *Business Week* called rail securities "one of the stock market's lame ducks." *Forbes* was no less pessimistic. "In a year [1956] when the rest of the economy was exuberantly setting new records, the $34 billion railroad industry remained inconsolably stalled," it moaned. Matters only worsened. In 1957 the net income for the country's Class One railroads was 14 percent below that of 1956; these roads handled 2,344,661 fewer cars, down by 6.2 percent in one year alone. Several roads failed to earn adequately to meet fixed interest and rental charges; New York, Ontario & Western simply expired. The outlook for 1958 was even worse.[24]

A few policymakers pricked up their ears. Senator George Smathers (Democrat-Florida) even admitted, "Available statistics indicate that the American railroads are heading for serious trouble." Congress agreed to listen. Railroaders complained of subsidized competition, discriminatory and often confiscatory taxes, and obsolete regulation that shackled the industry's ability to compete. Congressional response was passage of the Transportation Act of 1958, signed into law by President Dwight D. Eisenhower, which, among other things, ordered the Interstate Commerce Commission to be a bit more liberal in granting railroad requests and authorized the ICC to overrule state regulatory agencies on petitions to abandon lines or eliminate money-losing services.[25]

Railroads in the East were of particular concern. At New York, New Haven & Hartford, in August 1958 the president angrily denied that his road soon would be bankrupt, but that grim prospect became a reality. Pennsylvania's A. J. Greenough said bluntly: "Our industry must face up to the simple fact that there are just too many railroads in the country today for their own good and for the public's good." Mergers, he said, "and the consequent elimination of duplicate facilities and wasteful competition within the industry are the only solution." A more receptive ICC promised to listen carefully.[26]

It was in this pessimistic environment that Schroeder and team struggled and maneuvered. Some of Schroeder's dreams and schemes were remarkably innovative in an industry encrusted with stodginess. In 1956 M&StL commissioned one engineering firm to study the feasibility of an eighty-seven-mile "coal pipeline" along the company's right-of-way between Middle Grove and Keithsburg, while another firm considered the prospects of an oil pipeline from Minneapolis to Watertown, again using company land. A year later Schroeder told security analysts that M&StL was considering the possibility of stringing coaxial cable along major routes to provide improved communications but also to provide "television in yards or key points." This would allow dispatchers to follow train movements more closely and permit centralization of all yard functions under a single general yardmaster at one location. Schroeder's young lions also considered the merits of "pipelines or pneumatic tubes" designed to carry grain to the road's new rail-barge port on the Mississippi River at Keithsburg.[27]

Schroeder's broad aspirations for Keithsburg took concrete form in August 1956, when the Executive Committee approved an initial $150,000 (with more funds to be advanced later) to acquire land, erect a warehouse, and build a 110-by-400-foot slip for barges downstream from M&StL's lift-span bridge. A spur from the main line allowed direct loading of rail cars to or from barges or into or out of the warehouse. Schroeder indicated that International Minerals & Chemical Company would use the facility for superphosphate, and he revealed that he was talking to Wayne Grain Company and two coal companies, as well as other prospective customers. Keithsburg was, said Schroeder, "ideally located as an outlet for the distribution of products throughout the Middle West," and the new facility "symbolized the railroad's determination to broaden its traffic base so as to achieve a better balance between industrial and agricultural products in operating revenues." Advertisements went into national traffic media and on-line newspapers. The *Newton Daily News* for August 10, 1957, for example, carried an M&StL ad with a map showing Keithsburg's geographic relation to Newton. Negotiations with Federal Barge Lines and Bunge Grain focused on the exciting possibility of a 500,000-bushel elevator that could generate up to four thousand rail loads per year. Nothing happened, but in 1959 new negotiations with Standard Milling of Kansas City dealt with the prospect of a joint-venture grain elevator. This project did not reach fruition, either; M&StL simply did not have the wherewithal. By the end of 1959, M&StL's investment at Keithsburg stood at $513,429, but business was shallow—a few hundred cars of superphosphate for Iowa and Minnesota destinations and crude rubber for tire manufacturers in Des Moines. The Keithsburg venture, for all of its potential, was a singular disappointment—sadly ahead of its time.[28]

Keithsburg was only one of several places where M&StL allocated significant resources for industrial development. The crown jewel may have been on subsidiary Minnesota Western at Golden Valley, where Standard Oil opened a large warehouse in 1957, and at nearby Plymouth, where in 1959 the railroad advertised an attractive nine hundred–acre industrial park. M&StL already owned or soon acquired tracts of

Figure 24.4. Keithsburg, Illinois, offered exciting multimodal possibilities. M&StL photograph, author's collection.

land for prospective development at Aberdeen, Albert Lea, Des Moines, Fort Dodge, Marshalltown, Mason City, Monmouth, Oskaloosa, Peoria, and Watertown. Meredith Publishing and the Des Moines Register & Tribune Company picked up attractive parcels in and near Des Moines that promised very lucrative traffic in paper. Not all development was at major locations, of course, and in some cases M&StL's industrial development forces were simply blessed with dumb luck. Such was the case at Britt when three industries located there in 1958.[29]

Schroeder was able to convince M&StL's directors to make additional significant physical improvements and acquisitions, especially in the years 1956–58. The road took delivery of 1,321 new cars (boxes, flats, insulated boxes, covered hoppers, and hoppers), leased 17 additional airslide covered hoppers (M&StL had been first in the industry to use such equipment in 1953), converted 124 flats and boxes into specialized equipment, and received 32 hoppers in trade. Damage-free boxes and compartmentalized boxes were of particular utility for the on-line canning industry, 13 of the covered hoppers were assigned to brewing and malting industries on the Minneapolis–Peoria run, and bulkhead flats were of special importance to the gypsum industry at Fort Dodge. Automatic interlockers were approved for crossings at Waseca and at Marshalltown and Hedrick; a study was made to see if M&StL could profit from installation of centralized traffic control, but at no location did volumes justify such expenditure; land was purchased near Little York in anticipation of a line change; a study was commissioned to relocate the Cedar Lake shops; and telephone dispatching was extended to Marshalltown. New depots appeared in Iowa at Mason City and Forest City and in Minnesota at Echo and North Redwood (the old one where Richard W. Sears had been an operator was donated to and removed for preservation by the local historical society); a substantial and attractive new station and freighthouse at Fort Dodge was dedicated on October 29, 1959 with a luncheon for shippers, civic leaders, and company personnel. Modern engine houses were erected at Des Moines and Watertown, and the Marshalltown diesel shop was expanded and converted into a car shop. Communication was substantially improved by putting radios on locomotives and in cabooses and establishing several base stations around the system. In addition, Schroeder wanted to bring the Albert Lea–Des Moines line through Fort Dodge up to main-line standards. Heavier rail and ballast did go into the track at various locations, but the process was slowed because the main line, source of relay steel, was now completely renewed and traffic between Albert Lea and Des Moines did not justify the expense of new rail. Frustrated in that dream, Schroeder nevertheless was greatly pleased with the establishment of five truck gangs for maintenance of way scattered across the property, one system track crew, and increased mechanization of roadway work. Other improvements were aside from nuts and bolts. *The exPress,* a company publication designed to improve communication with employees and shippers, began in January 1956, and Schroeder started sending managers for refresher courses at the Transportation Center of Northwestern University and the Business School at Harvard. But belt tightening, sad to say, was required when M&StL's working capital slumped in 1959, despite an only modest capital program. Schroeder warned, moreover, that because of reduced earnings the 1960 capital program would be the leanest in several years.[30]

Lower earnings likewise served to focus attention

on the spiraling costs of doing business. Work rules, wages, and benefits—long vexing issues—became acute concerns in the late 1950s. Crafting agreements that would be equitable to labor and capital alike, that would ensure employee loyalty, and that would leave the company financially fit and able would take patience and wisdom among labor leaders, managers, and public policymakers. Patience and wisdom, alas, were not attributes found anywhere in great abundance.

Increases in wages, salaries, and benefits after a major surge early in the decade were modest until 1955, when operating crafts (trainmen and enginemen) received substantial additions that were followed the next year by similar advances for nonoperating employees. That, in turn, set off new demands from the operating crafts, and so on. New business and rate increases for M&StL were inadequate to cover the rising costs of operation, with the result that managers were forced to seek "economies" of various forms; for example, revamping its records system permitted M&StL to reduce its inventory for maintenance of way. In 1956 Schroeder told the Executive Committee that Rock Island had approached him about using M&StL for its freight trains between Albert Lea and Minneapolis; Chicago Great Western, Rock Island, and M&StL also considered joint use of track between Manly, Iowa, and Mason City. These issues never got beyond the "study stage," but Rock Island, seeking its own economies, chose to terminate use of M&StL from West Des Moines to reach its Sibley Branch at Gowrie, sixty-two miles, depriving M&StL of that revenue. The two roads did negotiate an agreement that took effect late in 1959 for coordination of operations at Beacon, Givin, and Eddyville, which allowed each company to abandon minor amounts of line; a similar arrangement permitted M&StL to use Rock Island at Estherville in a way that obviated the need for M&StL's substantial bridge over the Des Moines River. Also, the frequency of service provided by some scheduled trains was reduced—Fort Dodge to Spencer from triweekly to biweekly, and New Sharon to Newton from biweekly to once weekly.[31]

Inevitably dry-eyed analysts sought savings by cutting jobs. In 1950 wages, salaries, and benefits had taken 43.5 cents of every revenue dollar; in 1959 they claimed 56.1 cents. The matter was serious. Yet reducing costs by eliminating personnel except through natural attrition was a tricky task anywhere, but especially at M&StL, where loyalty to employees and employee loyalty were so profoundly part of the corporate culture. This remained patently evident even in the last half of the 1950s, when retirement rolls routinely showed astonishing lengths of service—engineers C. M. Sleeth of Oskaloosa (sixty-one years) and Charles A. Blankenhagen of Fort Dodge (fifty-one years); conductors Frank V. Lynch of Marshalltown (fifty-one years) and L. A. Gillander of Marshalltown (fifty years); agents S. E. Saffell of New Richland (fifty-four years) and H. E. Halverson of Conde (fifty-one years); and section foreman James Reed of Mason City (forty-nine years). These were but a few examples. Schroeder was not hesitant in praising M&StL personnel. "M&StL railroaders are doing a first class job," he said with enthusiasm in 1958. The dilemma was at least mildly apparent. On the one hand, said Schroeder, senior management had to be "concerned with day-to-day relations with our splendid organization of men and women and with the labor organizations that represent them." On the other hand, railroad management was obliged to keep costs of operation from pricing the carrier out of business. There was no easy path. "Our people have accepted reductions in force without sacrifice of morale or loyalty to their work and to the railroad." But that was hardly a true bill.[32]

Pain and tension were manifestly a part of job cuts. Labor-intensive maintenance of way was slashed when the number of sections was reduced from 115 to 60 as the company mechanized this essential activity and established roving ten-man track gangs that moved from place to place by motor vehicle. The nearly new Marshalltown diesel shop was closed, and, as with maintenance of way personnel, those with the least seniority were lopped off and those who survived had the option of "bumping in" elsewhere. It was the same at Oskaloosa when the yard there was closed and work transferred to Marshalltown during the summer of 1957. Even earlier, on January 13, 1957, the dispatchers' office at Oskaloosa, housed in the grand old Iowa Central depot, was closed; personnel retired, moved to Minneapolis, or went back on the telegrapher's roster.

Not long thereafter, the depot itself was vacated and offered to the city for community service, with the remaining offices moved to the much less attractive but functional engine house.[33]

The explosive issue of whether a fireman should be required on every unit of a multiple-unit locomotive had been more or less resolved with the practice of utilizing one person no matter how many units were employed. That begged the question, however, of whether firemen should be required at all on locomotives devoid of fireboxes. Safety issues and the tradition of firemen as apprentice engineers prevailed, but over this lengthy debate hung the incendiary term "featherbedding," a synonym for employing unneeded persons who performed no useful function. The fireman issue continued to percolate without resolution and was joined by another contentious debate over the utility of stations every few miles—manned by telegraph operators—at a time when the sale of tickets to passengers, the handling of LCL, and the billing of carload lots was greatly reduced, and in an age of telephone, teletype, and radio communication that made the telegraph seem antiquated in the extreme. This issue involved the deeply emotional element of personal pride and ego among telegraphers—"lightening stingers," persons held in awe for years by those who had not the ability to "read the wire" or to "send" and "receive." Operators were well up in the pecking order in the railroad business. Agents often were pillars in small-town America, and for decades the local depot, where the agent was undisputed master, had been the focal point of the community, a source of local pride and importance. Days of utter dependence on railroad transportation long since had vanished, and with that dependence the centrality of the depot as portal to the world. Yet the mystique lingered, its grip tenacious. Nothing except the closing or consolidation of the local school more unnerved a town's citizenry, which saw the loss of the railroad station and/or the demise of the school as the death knell of the town or at least the termination of any reasonable future. Small wonder that any attempt to end agency service often met headlong and fierce opposition.[34]

M&StL, of course, had prosecuted depot closings previously under Sprague and even William Bremner, but in 1956 Schroeder ordered a concerted effort. That year agreements were obtained to combine M&StL's agencies with those of Rock Island at Brighton, Eddyville, Livermore, and Morning Sun, Iowa, and with Milwaukee Road at Chaska and Sherburn, Minnesota. Two years later the agency at Monterey, Minnesota, was consolidated with that of Chicago & North Western at Trimont, Minnesota, and those at Farmington, Illinois, and Winfield, Iowa, with those of Burlington Route. In 1959 M&StL succeeded in combining its agency with that of C&NW at Grand Junction, Iowa, and in liquidating joint arrangements with Chicago Great Western and terminating the agency at Moorland, Iowa. A new wrinkle, "dualizing" stations—using one agent partial days at two locations—was introduced in 1956 and vigorously pushed thereafter. Successful combinations in 1957 included the stations at Liscomb and Union, Hedrick and Packwood, Gilman and Newburg, New Sharon and Searsboro, and Latimer and Alexander—all in Iowa. Neighboring Minnesota approved dualizing twenty-two stations in 1958, but that dramatic decision attracted the volatile attention of railroad brotherhoods and the state's attorney general; the matter headed for the courts, where M&StL lost. In South Dakota, Wetonka was combined with Leola in 1960, but in Iowa the dualization process stalled except for Dallas Center and Minburn. Other applications were denied by the Iowa State Commerce Commission, although in the late 1950s that same body approved closing stations at Callender, Fremont, Mallard, Plover, Oakville, Olds, Steamboat Rock, Sully, and Wayland. The anguish and dismay among proud station agents was seen in Dan N. Knight at Hendrick, whose father before him had been an Iowa Central–M&StL operator at the same location, and who, as he surveyed the scene, concluded that telegraph operators were now relegated to the status of employees in buggy whip factories "and would soon be about as useful as those once important members of society."[35]

As the decade matured, M&StL took an increasingly aggressive position on a broad range of labor issues. Schroeder was especially irritated by the need to "maintain a fireman on every freight locomotive without any necessary function for him to perform,"

Figure 24.5. Forty-year veteran James F. Holub, agent at Wayland, Iowa, received congratulations from William P. Coliton in 1956 when he billed the season's first wheat. His station would be closed not long thereafter. M&StL photograph, author's collection.

as well as the ancient requirement of "a day's pay for 100 miles of service" for train and engine crews. He likely had in mind trains 19 and 20 on the day's pay matter, because five crews were required on their fifteen-and-a-half-hour, 473.4-mile runs between Cedar Lake and Peoria—an average of 94.7 miles per crew district and something over three hours' average over-the-road duty each. James R. Sullivan, by now assistant to the president, was frequently the company's point man on these matters, speaking vigorously on "make work rules" and "sacrosanct working agreements" between unions and carriers. Ultimately, fumed Sullivan, "featherbedding" practices resulted in lower productivity, higher rates to customers, poorer service, slack earnings, and a badly deteriorated competitive position for M&StL and the industry at large. In 1959 Albert Schroeder argued that "a program for gradual elimination of featherbedding, extending over several years would be preferable to quick, drastic changes," but a year later warned that "neither the industry nor the public can support jobs rendered obsolete and useless by technological progress." The problem, said Schroeder, was "not whether to eliminate featherbedding, but how that essential step can best be accomplished." At stake was nothing less than "the stability of our industry." True. But the very term—"featherbedding"—and the free use of it understandably offended contract employees and their union leaders. Schroeder was right on the issue, wrong on appropriate technique to solve the problem.[36]

Nevertheless, productivity remained a burning issue, and, not surprisingly, M&StL managers turned steely eyes to the road's tiny passenger operation. Aside from Minneapolis and Des Moines, M&StL served no major markets, and its three remaining train sets—Minneapolis–Des Moines, Minneapolis–Watertown, and Albert Lea–Albia—were increasingly for the purpose of mail and express. The number of boardings on M&StL's "luxury air-conditioned coaches" was only 51,253 in 1950, 23,720 in 1955; ticket sales produced $90,792 in 1950, $45,587 in 1955. Total passenger revenue in 1950 was $506,811, tilting upward in 1952 and 1953 to reflect traffic correspondent with the Korean conflict, but skidded to $446,584 in 1955.[37]

Gone were the days of frequent excursions, but special movements were not unknown. On February 6, 1952, M&StL dispatched GE-30 from Minneapolis with business car 101 carrying officers and friends to the funeral of John W. Skoloda, a long-serving and very popular officer at Oskaloosa, and on May 20, 1953, shiny Alco 446 powered the Des Moines Chamber of Commerce "Goodwill Train" of heater car 501 and six heavyweight Pullmans from Estherville through Spencer to Fort Dodge and back home to Des Moines the next day. The year 1953 likewise saw a heavy movement of troop trains, three of them on the Fourth of July alone. During the next year, on May 23 M&StL hosted nearly two hundred railroad enthusiasts for a memorable trip from Minneapolis to New Ulm and back behind resplendent Alco 546.[38]

By this time, the venerable GE cars clearly were showing their age, though tenderly patched and mended by innovative maintenance personnel at Cedar Lake. Moreover, the seven cars more than met the need for five daily assignments. GE-30, long a Jonah ("car no good," William Landmesser once declared), late in 1954 suffered the indignity of being converted into a trailer car, but GE-31 took its Caterpillar prime mover to gain new life. It was clear, however, that the GE cars could not last forever. And what of the six Budd coaches now that ticket sales were so low? Into this mix was added Schroeder's predisposition to favor the Rail Diesel Cars (RDCs) introduced to the industry by Budd a few years earlier. Schroeder's will would be done. He was given authority to purchase two RDC4s, self-contained power units, each with a thirty-foot Railroad Post Office section, a baggage-express compartment, and shoe-horned seating for seventeen passengers—the modern successor, it seemed, to GE-1 of 1929. Costing $180,000 per unit, RDCs would be assigned to Minneapolis–Des Moines service (back in night operation since September 1954), would trail an aluminum boxcar for mail storage, and would replace the three GE cars, three coaches, and three storage cars currently assigned. The new arrangement would save at least $27,500 per year, promised Schroeder, and the capital outlay would be matched by salvage or sale of the present equipment. Only after the order had been placed and the on-line press notified did Schroeder dispatch Frank B. Clark and William W. Landmesser to see how RDCs performed elsewhere.[39]

Clark and Landmesser headed for Rock Island to investigate its RDC operation between Memphis, Tennessee, and El Reno, Oklahoma. They were impressed with the car's "jack rabbit acceleration" and enjoyed a flawless run, but data given them by Rock Island's diesel supervisor showed that the cost of operation per mile was greater than for the GE cars. And Rock Island pulled no trailers with its RDC. Clark and Landmesser frowned. In any event, the two RDC cars—numbered 32 and 33 and christened *Gopher* and *Hawkeye,* respectively—arrived late in January 1957, and one of them, 32, made a grand publicity

Figure 24.6. The crew of train 3 obligingly posed RDC 33 for photographer William Middleton at St. Louis Park, Minnesota, on October 28, 1958. The RDCs were terrible failures at M&StL.

tour to Des Moines. The duo entered revenue service on February 2 with accelerated schedules. They "were not a success," recalled Landmesser. Their engines and transmissions were not designed for the extra load of a trailer; failures were routine. They were not difficult to work on, said Landmesser, "but it was continuous." In March 1958 he was consulted about turning one of the RDCs into a self-contained business car, but in the end red-faced M&StL traded both units to Chesapeake & Ohio for thirty-two hopper cars. The RDCs went east on train 20 for Peoria in mid-December. Meanwhile, M&StL had sold its six streamlined coaches to Rock Island, had converted GE-25 into a weed-sprayer, and had carved out seating for twelve persons in the rear of GE-31, which was assigned to the Albia run. Three other GE cars received similar modification.[40]

Figure 24.7. M&StL operated this train on the Minnesota Western for railroad enthusiasts. This stop was at Watertown, Minnesota, on March 16, 1958. William D. Middleton photograph.

Shadows continued to lengthen over M&StL's miniscule passenger network. The number of boardings was only 23,066 in 1956, 20,848 in 1957; ticket revenues were, respectively, $54,361 and $57,222. In 1958 M&StL provided an excursion over Minnesota Western to Hutchinson for railroad enthusiasts, agreed to a short trip for youngsters at Watertown, Minnesota, during the Christmas season, and cooperated with other railroads in moving the nine-car Minnesota Centennial train to several communities around the state (including Gaylord and Dawson, among other M&StL points). During the following year M&StL handled an eight-car bankers' train to Aberdeen for the "Snow Queen Festival," a special from Minneapolis for a football game at the University of Iowa, and cars for a Christmas party put on at Hopkins by Red Owl, an important customer. But such proceedings now were very unusual.[41]

Notices went up on September 19, 1957, at Newburg and at all other stations between Albert Lea and Albia notifying the public that M&StL intended to discontinue trains 7 and 8. Regulatory agencies in Iowa and Minnesota ordered hearings. The case was not unusual. During the period from 1947 through 1957, the number of coach passengers on the nation's railroads declined from 329 million to 154 million; ticket revenues from those customers fell from $336 million to $191 million. A report made to the Interstate Commerce Commission in 1958 would forecast the end of intercity rail passenger service by 1970. Even earlier, in 1953, the Post Office Department had warned that en route sorting of mail was more expensive than terminal sorting and had begun to move first-class letter mail by air in some corridors. The message was clear: railroads could not look to the Post Office Department to "save" passenger trains. And the Post Office did not contest the removal of trains 7 and 8. Hardly anybody did. Ironically, however, as regulators retired to deliberate the fate of these trains, Meredith Willson's *Music Man* opened on Broadway. Based on memories of Willson's boyhood in Mason City, *Music Man* gently satirized an Iowa community of 1912 and proved an extremely popular valentine to the Hawkeye State. The musical's opening scenes made reference to Rock Island, M&StL's crosstown rival at Mason City, but Willson's childhood home was much nearer the Iowa Central–M&StL depot and yard—the oft-referred-to "foot bridge" was closer to M&StL track—and Willson's skillful depiction of railroads setting the tempo of American life in 1912 likely had been informed by what he saw closest at hand—the "tootin' Louie." In any event, down the line from Mason City, students at Grinnell College, mistakenly thinking train 8 was making its final run on November 30 and wanting to commemorate that mournful event by treating the crew and RPO clerks to coffee and doughnuts, flagged it down with a red lantern and a red basketball jersey. The astonished crew told the students that no discontinuance decision had been announced yet; the students laughed and gave up their treats anyway, and, as the train moved on, burst into "Sons of Old Grinnell," the school song. A few months more would pass before regulators authorized termination of passenger service that had begun nearly a century earlier. Many on-line newspapers ignored the story, although some recalled with nostalgia the days of old. School kids from Union were joined by others at Albion for a ride on one of the last runs, and the kindergarten class at Hampton boarded the final train 7 for a short ride to Sheffield. Otherwise little was noted when it all ended on May 31, 1958.[42]

Five months later trains 3 and 4 were in the same crosshairs. Although they were part of an interstate operation over a greater length of line, serving primary markets of Minneapolis and Des Moines and tapping numerous intermediate communities, trains 3 and 4 even more than 7 and 8 found utility in delivery of mail and express—a proposition not greatly challenged by protestants at hearings held in Albert Lea before an ICC examiner in December (the first such case to be heard under provisions of the Transportation Act of 1958). The trains had handled only 7,419 passengers in 1956, 5,553 in 1957, virtually all local to the line. These included two young rail enthusiasts from West Des Moines who often road train 4 into Des Moines after they finished their weekend morning paper routes. The conductor, who inevitably had closed out his paperwork, was obliged to sell them cash fares and grumpily asked why they did not ride the city bus, which, he noted sarcastically, was cheaper. On other occasions the boys rode number 3 out from Des Moines in the evening, "buying a real ticket" and keeping the conductor in a better humor. In one instance they rode all the way to Perry to watch the stream of westbound "Cities" trains on the Milwaukee Road. Daily ticket revenues for the two trains averaged \$47.55 in 1956, \$35.60 in 1957. M&StL complained of net operating losses aggregating \$99,173 for 1956–57. Managers earlier had suggested to local labor leaders that substantial savings could be achieved by eliminating the crew change at Albert Lea, running one crew through on the 296-mile run. Local union officials thought the idea "logical," but the concept was vetoed higher up in the organizations. M&StL then had filed to discontinue. The Minnesota Railroad and Warehouse Commission, in challenging M&StL, contended that the road's losses in the passenger-carrying trade were minor and easily covered by net operating income, but the Interstate Commerce Commission was "not impressed with the argument that losing operations such as these passenger trains must for all time be absorbed if the carrier's overall operations are satisfactory, or if the carrier is solvent." The trains, ruled the ICC, were not required by public convenience and necessity. At New Prague, the agent hosted Cub Scouts on one of the last trips, providing doughnuts and hot chocolate, but when the final train 3 left Des Moines on March 21, 1959, only eight passengers were aboard—four of them children on their first train ride, headed for Waukee, fifteen miles distant, each one paying 19 cents for the privilege. In a curious twist of events, the trains actually continued through April 19, giving the Post Office more time to make other arrangements, but no passengers were handled.[43]

Figure 24.8. Train 8 was living on borrowed time when William F. Armstrong captured it on film in front of the sparkling new depot at Mason City on May 10, 1958.

Given the nature of his "sharp pencil" team, Schroeder was surprisingly reticent in the matter of line abandonments. Indeed, John W. Devins had been more forceful. In a fit of rage following a losing battle with snow in 1953, he had urged that 14.5 miles of track between Monterey and Dunnell be abandoned. "Nature put it in, nature can take it out," he growled

Figure 24.9. GE-31 would meet the call for train 3 only a few more times after slumbering one afternoon at Des Moines early in April 1959. Photo by the author.

after a long-struggling wedge plow buckled in eight miles of fifteen- to twenty-eight-foot drifts north of Sherburn. The board accepted his recommendation, but nothing was done, and one of Heineman's first acts in 1954 was to rescind the decision. In 1955 Devins recommended that the entire line south of New Ulm to Sherburn be "seriously considered for early abandonment," and once more put everything west of Watertown under scrutiny. Again, nothing happened, presumably because revenues were adequate. Indeed, if data justified abandonment, during the 1950s the ICC was nearly certain to agree, approving about 92 percent of such applications. In 1957 Schroeder did alert the Executive Committee that studies were being made of the Newton and Roland branches in Iowa, and three years later the board agreed to drop the Newton Branch and its Lynnville stub. But no action followed.[44]

If curiously lethargic on the matter of line abandonment, the Schroeder crew was bold and innovative when it came to pushing competitive freight rates. General increases came from the ICC in 1958, but when the economy shuddered in the late part of the decade, and as trucks ate deeper into the traditional traffic base, M&StL and a few others sought rate reductions, especially in grain. "We're losing business to trucks because of rate hikes being made without any regard to competition," Schroeder complained. In the fall of 1957, M&StL had petitioned for and was awarded a one-year reduction on grain billed from stations on subsidiary Minnesota Western—this as an experiment to combat "the ever increasing movement of grain by truck." Loadings rose sharply. Giant Cargill Incorporated was among other major shippers applauding the move. "It looks like the dogs at their heels [trucks] have drawn blood," said Cargill.

A Pillsbury representative was equally enthusiastic. "Schroeder isn't as bogged down in tradition as most other railroaders," he said. "Too many railroaders are so concerned about getting high rates they forget they've got to get the business first." Were lower rates compensatory? Yes, said Schroeder, pointing to economies of scale. "How much do you figure it costs us to haul an extra car on a 60-car train?" he asked rhetorically. "Just a few cents compared with that first car." Finding more cars, then, was the task of Roy Nelson and the Traffic Department. "We'll deal wherever we can when it comes to rates," Schroeder promised. "We've taken a realistic view of our pricing. We know we're not the only form of transportation after the business." M&StL did not focus on grain alone. Cement from Mason City and Des Moines was extremely sensitive to rates, as was coal from Middle Grove; M&StL agreed to hold down tariffs for both. On other fronts, Minnesota grudgingly went along with M&StL's application for intrastate rail-truck rates on LCL, but Iowa refused to allow M&StL to set rates on petroleum products below those charged by trucks. Grain once more was the looming issue in the last half of 1959 and into 1960, however, as corn in particular was diverted to Duluth and eastward by water, in several instances depriving M&StL of long hauls to Peoria. Again M&StL sought and received permission to lower rates.[45]

Schroeder's approach to directing affairs at M&StL was by now as simple as it was transparent: work hard to attract new business, cut rates where possible, and keep a rib-cracking grip on expenses. All three elements were evident to one extent or another in his decision to shuffle main-line schedules and train operation and to implement his "brain child"—trains 1 and 2, "Acey-Deucy" as they were called, paired opposite 19 and 20 by a half day and carded on a fifteen-hour schedule between Cedar Lake and Peoria. Operation began from each terminal on January 28, 1959; the first number 2 was headed by three shiny, new 600s trailed by the *Twin Cities,* piggyback cars, and the rest of the train. Schroeder saw it out of Cedar Lake in an atmosphere of celebration. Operational orders called for train 1, scheduled out of Peoria at 12:30 p.m., to pick up and set out at Nemo (AT&SF interchange), Mason City (cement), and Manly (perishables from Rock Island), arriving in Cedar Lake at 5:00 a.m. Train 2, scheduled out of Cedar Lake at 5:30 p.m., would pick up at New Prague (mill products), Montgomery (Green Giant tonnage), and Nemo, with arrival in Peoria at 8:30 a.m. Connecting carriers were advised in advance about the speedier double-daily service; TP&W was especially enthusiastic. "We are extremely happy that you have added this service," J. Russell Coulter told Schroeder. "I am very much impressed with the new business we are getting since you inaugurated the new schedule on your trains 1 and 2." M&StL advertised the new trains in print media and also by an innovative "conference call" on February 3 that allowed Schroeder and Nelson to visit with shippers all over the country and to "plug" the twice-daily service. Shippers were impressed by this sales technique and by the improved service. A grain dealer from Fraser-Small was typical, promising that "the outlet and speed to the East will have first call on our business." Early reports showed trains of about sixty cars moving into Peoria, with lighter tonnage outbound but increasing as trains progressed westward.[46]

"We need to improve carloadings," said the plain-spoken Alfred Schroeder upon inauguration of trains 1 and 2. With that in mind, Schroeder and Chairman Max Swiren asked James R. Sullivan to evaluate the company's Traffic Department (sales and pricing). One of Sullivan's recommendations was to bring in management consultant Booz, Allen & Hamilton for an even broader assessment. This was done. The consultants urged modernization of Traffic's two principal functions through application of basic marketing principles and a comprehensive sales program focusing on medium-size markets, suggested a shakeup of off-line agencies, and counseled hiring persons specifically for the task of sales instead of simply promoting clerks, long the policy at M&StL. The notion of changing the Traffic Department into a market-oriented sales organization was nearly radical for the railroad industry at the time, but on some issues Booz, Allen & Hamilton merely confirmed existing knowledge—that M&StL was particularly dependent on overhead business, that its traffic expense ratio (the cost of generating

Figure 24.10. Schroeder's brainchild—trains 1 and 2, "Acey-Deucy"—came to life on January 28, 1959, when train 2 headed out of Cedar Lake, Minnesota, on a fifteen-hour sprint to Peoria. William D. Middleton photograph.

business) was frighteningly high compared to those of other roads in the region, and that M&StL, in concert with the industry at large since 1950, had seen an alarming erosion of freight cars handled, but that M&StL's decline had been greater than those of other major northwestern railroads. Nor had M&StL kept pace compared to others in the volume of bridge traffic. The consultants also confirmed that M&StL was competitive in the Minneapolis–Chicago (with partner Illinois Central) and Minneapolis–Omaha corridors, that it had a lock on Minneapolis–Peoria business, and that it was effective to the East with all connections at Peoria except for New York Central and Pennsylvania. The Executive Committee voted to act on the consultants' report, promoting Roy Nelson to senior vice president (handling large accounts) and moving Sullivan from Personnel to vice president–Traffic with the idea that he would reorganize Traffic into Sales. That transpired on July 1, 1960, with offices at thirty-three locations (six on-line) and a force of seventy-four persons plus clerks.[47]

Schroeder had an opportunity in the fall of 1959 to tell the Transportation Club of Des Moines his views on the industry and also to talk about the new approach to sales at M&StL. "The basic tenet of the marketing approach to the sale of railway services is that it recognizes the dominant position of the customer," boomed the husky-voiced Schroeder. "Translated into railroad terms this means that if they are to prosper, expand, or even survive they must recognize and act in keeping with the overriding demands of the shipping public." Indeed, the "progressive rail carrier of the future will avoid the error of spending the big end of its sales efforts trying to sell the customer a service that generally fits the railroad's operating plans but may be unrelated to the customer's needs." In advocating and nurturing this philosophy and practice at M&StL, Schroeder staked out a position well in advance of the industry. But the big, affable Schroeder really warmed to his topic of railroads in the future as he described advanced technology—the application of computers to accounting, diesel power, larger equipment, and mechanized track work—and especially when he speculated on the potential of nuclear-powered locomotives and "remotely controlled unmanned trains complete with locomotives, cars, and caboose, being guided down existing steel rails, inspected by selective-site closed television circuits."[48]

Meanwhile, the energetic Schroeder had to contend with periodic failures of current technologies, the fallibility of man, and problematic acts of God. High water at Carver in 1959 took the main line out of service for several days, during which time Peoria cars were pooled in one train and detoured, adding considerable expense, delay of lading, and demoralized connections. Unusually heavy snow and high winds entrapped train 20 near Winfield in March 1960, again disrupting service for several days; floods in South Dakota that year also caused damage. Three significant derailments afflicted trains 19 and 20 in 1958, and on February 12, 1959, train 20 derailed six cars that tore out the Morning Sun depot and provided a memorable day for the agent, who was barely hurt but greatly shaken. Fortunately, fatal accidents were rare. In one instance, train 7 ran over a man lying between the rails near Geneva, but when the train got stopped its astonished crew saw the "dead man" stalking across an adjacent field, quite unhurt. Two fourteen-year-old boys who foolishly chose to camp on the track near Minnetonka Mills were not as fortunate, dying when train 14 hit their sleeping bag on July 2, 1955. Elsewhere, GE-25, on train 4, hit a semi-trailer truck south of Gowrie on August 30, 1956, killing the driver and injuring John A. Whitman, engineer on the train.[49]

Meanwhile, Max Swiren, Albert Schroeder, and their lieutenants probed for strategic opportunities. Early in 1955 and again in 1960, studies were made with the idea of acquiring Mason City & Clear Lake, an important feeder at Mason City, and in March 1957 William Coliton, Stephen Owens, and James Sullivan gathered information on and made an inspection of Des Moines & Central Iowa (DM&CI) and Fort Dodge, Des Moines & Southern (FtDDM&S). It took little time to convince this trio that purchase of the latter two Iowa short lines "would be of substantial benefit to" M&StL, and they urged that a "serious effort be made as soon as possible to acquire them." DM&CI had exclusive entry to a large Firestone Tire & Rubber plant at Des Moines and had attractive industrial properties adjacent to its lines at several locations. FtDDM&S likewise served important industries at Des Moines and served several gypsum mills near Fort Dodge. The study team pointed out that substantial tonnage could be diverted to M&StL's Fort Dodge–Des Moines line and that all but 52 miles of FtDDM&S's 170 miles could be abandoned. For whatever reason, nothing was done to purchase any of these properties. The explanation may have been that Swiren was after bigger game. Indeed, he again was looking at Monon and eyeing Chicago & Illinois Midland. For that matter, acting possibly as a stalking horse for Ben Heineman or for a friendly investor who had a large stake in M&StL, Swiren paved the way for a Wyer, Dick & Company study that analyzed the prospects of Chicago, Milwaukee, St. Paul & Pacific's taking over M&StL. Wyer, Dick was not optimistic about this potential, and the matter died. In Chicago, at about the same time President Harry C. Murphy of Burlington Route picked up an intriguing rumor that Rock Island soon would acquire M&StL; there was no mention of it in the minutes of M&StL's board of directors or Executive Committee, but cursory studies were made. Rock Island was, of course, at that time scouting a marriage partner or partners, and one of those candidates was Milwaukee Road.[50]

The most logical strategic association of M&StL with a Chicago road was not with Chicago, Milwaukee, St. Paul & Pacific or Chicago, Rock Island & Pacific, but rather with Illinois Central. James Sullivan had come to M&StL from IC in 1956 and had remained in close contact with several friends in Chicago, including Otto H. Zimmerman, IC's vice president of operations, with whom he had several face-to-face meetings about putting the two roads together. Zimmerman needed no reminder that M&StL was a productive and profitable interchange partner at Ackley, Albert Lea, Fort Dodge, Peoria, and Tara, and that it provided a direct avenue to the Twin Cities from Chicago through Albert Lea and from Omaha through Fort Dodge and Albert Lea. Sullivan pointed out that M&StL had no funded debt and that IC could acquire the Minneapolis road "at substantially no cash outlay." Zimmerman enthusiastically carried the idea to President Wayne A. Johnston, who summarily dismissed it. Johnston, anchored everlastingly in the memory of the Great Depression, chose to "whittle down the mortgage" rather than "look outside for new business opportunity." He failed to change with the times, lacked entrepreneurial zeal, and overstayed his time. Not taking M&StL under IC's wing reflected as much.[51]

The overarching issue for M&StL throughout the period following 1954, however, was its dogged determination to capture Toledo, Peoria & Western.

As early as 1957, Chairman Swiren thought there was "a reasonable possibility that the decision of the Interstate Commerce Commission" permitting acquisition of TP&W jointly by Pennsylvania and Santa Fe "might be set aside by the Supreme Court" and that M&StL might be afforded the right to purchase it. M&StL's desire deepened as TP&W's traffic volume increased nicely each year—almost 11 percent in 1959 alone—and as the road's approval rating among shippers soared. M&StL's case failed in the federal district court, however, and the matter moved to the nation's highest court, where M&StL attorneys, led by Max Swiren himself, argued that acquisition of TP&W by AT&SF and PRR would restrain trade, violate the Sherman Act, and lessen competition or tend to create a monopoly, a violation of the Clayton Act. But the Supreme Court said that the ICC was "not so bound by the antitrust laws that it must permit them to overbear what it finds to be in the public interest," and it allowed that the ICC, not the courts, should "determine whether the proposed acquisition is in the public interest." The decision of the lower court was upheld on December 14, 1959. A month later the ICC authorized the sale of TP&W to AT&SF and PRR—permitting TP&W "to preserve its identity and continue operation as in the past" and to prove that the "ownership change is overwhelmingly 'in the public interest,'" as J. Russell Coulter put it. M&StL tried to put a happy face on this grim turn of events, but no happy face could be found.[52]

As 1959 yielded to 1960, M&StL personnel could take pride in twice-daily time freights over the full length of its main line from Cedar Lake to Peoria, in significant betterments over much of the system, in a modern car fleet with a bad order ratio of only 1.5, and in an expanded piggyback operation featuring trailers unabashedly stenciled PBQ (piggyback quick) to distinguish M&StL's modern service. All of this was spread across the pages of *Trains* for March 1959 in a laudatory article written by Frank P. Donovan Jr. The men of "red and white" had settled in at M&StL and made their mark; the atmosphere was mellow, so it seemed. On October 18, 1959, a special train left Minneapolis at noon carrying officers and directors to Aberdeen for a directors' meeting to be held at the First National Bank. The event was in keeping with Schroeder's view that official gatherings should be held variously around the system, showing the company flag, as it were. The mood was relaxed. On the leisurely return trip some of the men enjoyed a bit of pheasant hunting from the slow-moving train. The next meeting of the board was on January 28, 1960. Members received traffic forecasts, were briefed on the capital and operating budgets for 1960, took up the matter of selling a small piece of property in Minneapolis, declared a dividend for the first quarter, and they made plans for the annual meeting of stockholders, to be held on April 12 in Minneapolis. The agenda was routine, the tenor low-key. Merely routine.[53]

Chapter 25
VALHALLA

We believe that the purchase of M&StL could be considered desirable solely on the basis of M&StL earnings and our own tax position.
—BEN W. HEINEMAN, 1960.

ON THURSDAY MORNING, APRIL 7, 1960, DEpartment heads and other key personnel were assembled in the president's office at 111 East Franklin Street. Nervous banter belied a general feeling of apprehension. With good reason. Max Swiren and Albert Schroeder came directly to the point. Minneapolis & St. Louis, they announced bluntly, would become a part of Chicago & North Western if stockholders of the two companies and the Interstate Commerce Commission agreed. And, they affirmed, approval was likely. Swiren and Schroeder said that combination would not adversely affect employees and predicted that a much larger railroad would, in fact, present better opportunities for everyone.[1]

The news was astonishing. When Ben W. Heineman had taken a position with C&NW a half decade earlier, there had been no thought of combining M&StL with it. Nor had there been any indication of future association in 1956, when M&StL's pension trust acquired $20,000 in C&NW equipment trust certificates as part of a diversified portfolio. Old heads may have recalled that William H. Bremner had once asked Fred Sargent if C&NW would buy M&StL, but Sargent had replied that North Western could not do so because of its own financial anemia. To be sure, C&NW's circumstances had not materially improved thereafter. Reorganized in 1945 after a decade of receivership, C&NW had posted net losses in 1954, 1956, 1957, and even in 1959. Moody's Investor Services had noted that C&NW's working capital had declined markedly since 1946 and that "long term revenue and ton mile trends of the North Western System do not compare favorably with other railroads" in the northwest region or with "Class I carriers" at large. North Western's primary liabilities said Moody's, were three: it served a territory susceptible "to truck and other competition," it generated relatively short hauls, and it suffered from eroding passenger revenues.[2]

Nevertheless, M&StL's fate, it seemed, was hitched to C&NW's star. "By combining the operations of M&StL with those of North Western," said Ben Heineman, "the states, communities and shippers that both companies serve will obtain the benefits of greater efficiency and better service than could be provided by either company alone." Furthermore, "under combined operations we will be able to offer better freight service to points on both railroads and between major terminals," he promised. "The consolidation will result in economies heretofore unobtainable by either road." In addition, "the expanded operation of North Western will also be enhanced by the addition of M&StL's experienced and capable personnel," Heineman noted. "We intend to operate M&StL as a separate division of North Western and preserve its name." C&NW agreed to pay $3,488,320 in cash at the closing of the sale and to "assume liability for $17,441,600 in 6 per cent first mortgage bonds to be created by M&StL on its properties." In the process North Western would acquire "all property, equipment and other assets," but not the corporation itself. Schroeder indicated that M&StL would use proceeds from the sale to enter some other field of business. Max Swiren suggested that a tax loss carryover of "somewhere between twenty and thirty million dollars" would be sufficient to purchase an established business or work out a merger beneficial to M&StL shareholders.[3]

Figure 25.1. The sands of time were about to expire for M&StL. Photo by the author.

Heineman had no difficulty convincing C&NW's board and shareholders as to M&StL's value. "We believe that the purchase of M&StL could be considered desirable solely on the basis of M&StL earnings and our own tax position," he told North Western directors. But that was only the beginning. Economies of $3 million could be expected from the "elimination of duplicate field supervision, executive, accounting, traffic and station functions." This said nothing of savings "from the consolidation of yards, repair facilities, train operations, maintenance of way crews, and the abandonment of unprofitable or unnecessary branch lines." Moreover, M&StL would give C&NW access to a "number of cement plants and coal mines" plus M&StL's existing and potential industrial base at Minneapolis. Another major plum was the size and condition of M&StL's fleet of motive power and rolling stock—"relatively new" and "worth approximately $30 million"—which would greatly reduce North Western's immediate capital requirements. Finally, Heineman prized M&StL managers, who would, upon acquisition, "enable us to substitute or add competent and experienced employees to our organization."[4]

There was no debate at a special meeting of M&StL stockholders held in Minneapolis on June 28, 1960. Indeed, only twenty-seven "shareholders and others" were on hand when 590,653 shares were voted in favor, only 6,873 against. The exercise was pro forma.[5]

Acquisitions and mergers were as much a part of the American railroad fabric as locomotives and cars, of course, and M&StL's very own Iowa Central had been an amalgam of former independents or subsidiaries. The issue had been greatly confused over the years, however, by the Interstate Commerce Act as amended and by statutes involving monopoly and restraint of trade. Public policy vacillated. The federal government had encouraged merger of carriers into strong systems through the Transportation Act of 1920, but little had been accomplished until the public mind gradually changed and the railroads themselves began to clamor for combination as a cure for their collective ailments. Industry leader John W. Barriger III recently had called for "super railroads," and in 1957 Northern Pacific's Robert S. MacFarlane had predicted that the nation's railroads would merge into "perhaps 25 great systems" within fifteen or twenty years.[6]

The process, in fact, already had begun. In 1946 Atlanta, Birmingham & Coast merged into Atlantic Coast Line; a year later Pere Marquette became part of Chesapeake & Ohio and Gulf, Mobile & Ohio acquired Alton; and in 1950, Central of Georgia took control of Savannah & Atlanta. There followed a hiatus of sorts until the second half of the 1950s, when the plight of the industry frightened investors to the point where there was only the tiniest prospect of floating new issues of stocks or bonds. Merger again became the favored nostrum. Nashville, Chattanooga & St. Louis merged into Louisville & Nashville in 1957, and a year later Chicago & North Western picked up

Litchfield & Madison, while Union Pacific took control of Spokane International. Momentum increased. In 1959 Norfolk & Western acquired Virginian; in 1960 Southern gathered up Central of Georgia, and Delaware, Lackawanna & Western promised marriage to Erie. It was the tip of the iceberg. In the East, Baltimore & Ohio was talking with Chesapeake & Ohio, and New York Central with Pennsylvania; in the West, Southern Pacific looked covetously at Western Pacific. Chicago roads were eying each other nervously, and in M&StL's backyard Minneapolis, St. Paul & Sault Ste. Marie sought amalgamation with Duluth, South Shore & Atlantic and with Wisconsin Central. For that matter, Great Northern and Northern Pacific were laying groundwork to combine themselves with jointly owned Chicago, Burlington & Quincy and with Spokane, Portland & Seattle which, if approved, would create a true colossus.[7]

For M&StL the spotlight now turned to the Interstate Commerce Commission, which had jurisdiction. North Western pointed out that M&StL's balance sheet showed assets of $42,038,131, liabilities of $14,876,701, or a net worth of $27,161,430. The road's long-term debt consisted of equipment obligations amounting to $9,783,458, of which $1,051,611 would be retired in 1960. M&StL had no bonded debt, and North Western estimated the fair market value of M&StL's locomotives and rolling stock at $29,569,000, with equipment obligations of $8,652,713—a net equity of $20,936,087 or almost the exact equivalent of the total purchase price ($20,929,920) that North Western and M&StL had agreed to. M&StL's average annual net income after taxes for the period 1954–59 had been $1,732,246, while North Western had sustained average annual net losses of $885,741 over the same period. If the two companies had been combined since 1953, went the argument, C&NW would have shown a net profit in the years 1954–59. If approved now, gushed C&NW, acquisition of M&StL would "substantially strengthen North Western's cash position" and also would "provide a sound foundation to service the additional debt." Larry S. Provo invoked the obvious, terming the transaction "self-liquidating," with M&StL's contribution to C&NW's net equaling the purchase price in five years. The application went unopposed in a half-day hearing before an ICC examiner at the United States Customs House in Chicago on August 1.[8]

From April 7 onward, M&StL was very much like a ship at sea that had taken a lethal torpedo; though in the throes of death, inertia carried it forward. This was especially reflected in the company's brave attempt to reassure shippers while at the same time implementing its forward-looking sales program. Schroeder promised customers that M&StL would "continue . . . our present service to you in every possible way." James R. Sullivan likewise attempted to shore up morale among the company's understandably skittish sales representatives, but could do nothing other than admit that there would "be no easy way for us throughout the months ahead." Indeed, said Sullivan, "we face the most challenging job in our history." He reminded all hands of their goal to increase carloads by 11 percent and revenues by 16 percent in 1960—goals "now more meaningful than ever," he said, adding: "None of us should forget that this is *still* the M&StL, and we *still* have a lot to do." Moreover, he stressed, M&StL had a good product to sell. M&O Paper, for example, tested nine different routings from its mill at Kenora, Ontario, to Kansas City, and concluded that the Canadian Pacific–Soo Line–M&StL–Wabash combination was one of the two best. And Sullivan prosecuted new ventures with imagination and grit. One possibility involved "roller cement cars" and off-track delivery of cement by air-activated trucks to expand or hold M&StL's participation in that traffic by promoting on-line manufacturers. Sullivan also looked vigorously for more trailer-on-flat-car opportunities. Maytag at Newton provided outbound trailers containing washers and dryers, and Granite City Steel near St. Louis routed trailers with finished steel to M&StL. Wabash cooperated on piggybacked Ford products to Kansas City.[9]

Schroeder and company likewise continued to seek economies. Not surprisingly, the end of all passenger operations on M&StL seemed apropos as the company itself contemplated disappearance. Except for an occasional officer special elsewhere, the West End held a monopoly. Special movements for directors, securities, or analysts or for sales promotion to Watertown or beyond usually were doubled with train 13, returning on 14's schedule, as a means of containing costs. One example was the special for the company's sales team in January 1959, with locomotive 413, a heater car, one Pullman, car 101 and the *Twin Cities,* followed by the usual passenger consist—a GE car dead in tow to provide Railway Post Office facilities and three or four trailers. The sole excursion for 1960, on April 24, also was on the West End, for Minneapolis railroad enthusiasts bound for New Ulm and then returning to Minneapolis. By 1960, of course, M&StL's only scheduled service consisted of trains 13 and 14, daily-except-Sunday trains out of Great Northern's Minneapolis station to Watertown, 222 miles.[10]

Numbers 13 and 14 were essentially mail trains, although an unkind appraiser might even have labeled them mixed trains, for they handled not only passengers, mail, and express, but also less-than-carload freight and occasionally even carload freight—potatoes from Watertown or dairy products from Clarkfield for example. Diesel-engined GE cars routinely lugged three or four trailers behind their drawbars. One of these was a Parcel Post peddler car usually set out and picked up at Gaylord, another peddler on occasion for Redwood, and an LCL car to and from Watertown. Holiday "tonnage" in mail and express exceeded the capacity of the GE cars; Alcos then stood in as replacements. Railway Mail clerks found the Minneapolis & Watertown RPO a busy assignment, with mail dispatched to or picked up from thirty-three en route communities over the 9½-hour run; back in the trailing storage car, the baggageman could loaf between stations, but he was a busy fellow at each stop, moving mail, express, and baggage into and out of the car. Work at some stations always was heavy. On March 31, 1958, Clarence J. Hassinger, 13's conductor wired: "75 cases of eggs for Redwood." The baggageman must have groaned.[11]

Passengers, however, were few. The trains handled a mere 1,557 in 1958, only 1,293 in 1959. All but a few were local to the line. When train 14 left Watertown on April 21, 1960, for example, there were only two passengers aboard. One of them was William F. Armstrong, who had grown up at Mason City, and as a young lad had made a marvelous photographic record of M&StL in that area, who now was getting a glimpse of the West End. Armstrong recalled that the track was "in good condition as the ride was quite smooth

Figure 25.2. By 1960, trains 13 and 14 resembled mixed trains. Train 14 was nearly home, pausing at Hopkins, Minnesota, on April 22, 1960. William F. Armstrong photograph.

considering that the motor car is not the best rider." Armstrong likewise recalled a twenty-five-minute stop at Morton, Minnesota, "for lunch."[12]

Armstrong was referring to lunch at the trackside hotel, a two-story wood frame structure with sleeping rooms upstairs for trainmen laying over between runs and a lobby with a lunch room at ground level. Just inside the front door along one wall stood a row of wash basins, in the center of the room was a large pot-bellied stove, and to one side was the dimly lit lunch counter, behind which on shelves were deposited delightfully inviting home-baked pies and cookies; beyond was a dining room with tables and chairs. Green shades provided window covering; potted plants adorned the sills. Delectable food (German dishes a specialty) at nominal cost was as routine in 1960 as it had been since the railroad arrived during the previous century. Perhaps the hotel's most famous customer—and likely the most famous person who ever lived anywhere along M&StL lines—was Hubert H. Humphrey, a United States senator from Minnesota, eventually vice president and presidential contender in 1968. Humphrey had been born at Wallace, twenty-four miles west of Watertown, in 1911, and while his family later moved to nearby Doland, Humphrey's first long train ride had been on M&StL when he accompanied his father aboard a sleeper to Minneapolis. Humphrey was relegated to the upper berth but fondly recalled the trip as "quite an experience." Some years later, during the Great Depression, Humphrey used M&StL between Minneapolis and his South Dakota home. On these trips he eagerly anticipated the stop at Morton, where the hotel lunchroom offered a bill of fare that matched his gastronomical needs and his financial limitations: a brimming cup of coffee for a nickel and a generous ham sandwich for a dime. By 1960 the place was an ancient relic full of nostalgia, catering mostly to local trade, railroaders, and a few passengers from the night trains. Wrote one admirer, as if speaking for the old landmark: "My weathered latch-string still humbly beckons, my steaming kettle is always on, and the homey cheer of my rustic charm still reflects the happiness and peace of days long ago."[13]

The same might have been said for the trains that had stopped there for seventy-eight years. But they had lost $30,344 in 1958, $36,202 in 1959, and by late summer 1959 senior managers determined to seek discontinuance. They first talked to the Post Office Department, however, about starting and ending the trains at Hopkins to avoid $25,000 in charges at Great Northern's station in Minneapolis and over $12,000 in wages for switch crews moving equipment into and out of the station from Cedar Lake. The Post Office demurred, citing heavy costs in multiple handlings of mail. M&StL then filed the necessary papers, asking to drop the trains; the ICC scheduled a hearing, but not one person using the trains for passenger purposes appeared to protest. Approval was certain. But the Post Office made a preemptive strike by ending RPO authorization for train 13 effective May 20, 1960, and for train 14 the next day. The trains themselves limped along a few more weeks. On July 20, at 9:00 p.m., the last 14 pulled out of Watertown, business car *Twin Cities* trailing GE-27 with Albert Schroeder, William Coliton, and James Sullivan aboard, ostensibly on a "routine inspection trip," but more likely performing a farewell exercise of their own. An hour and a half later train 13 slipped out of trainsheds at Great Northern's depot in Minneapolis for the last time; it arrived "on the advertised" in Watertown at 8:00 a.m. July 21. The *Watertown Public Opinion* marked the event with extended coverage. Retired agent Ray Spooner recalled an earlier day of excursion trains from Watertown to Lake Kampeska for baseball games at a field near the outlet, special trains for performances of circuses in Watertown, and cars filled with traveling salesmen as they returned to their homes on Fridays. "Nos. 13 and 14 of the M&StL are the last of a long line of passenger trains to serve Watertown since the railroads first carved their gleaming metal signatures across the vast area of the Old West," noted the *Public Opinion* in benediction. To the east, the *Minneapolis Tribune* also took note. "Such is progress," it said dismissively. "Now the passenger trains are all but gone and the depot is no longer the center of the town's attention." True enough, however sad.[14]

There was little time in that grim summer of 1960 for Schroeder and his young crew to ponder the demise of passenger service at M&StL. Schroeder and Sullivan both had expected an upturn in business for

Figure 25.3. En route sorting of mails ended on M&StL with the demise of trains 13 and 14. The cancellation on this envelope was a sad memento of their last day of service. Author's collection.

Figure 25.4. Albert Schroeder, William Coliton, and James Sullivan (pictured left to right) made the final trip on train 14. Perhaps it was their own personal farewell exercise. *Watertown Public Opinion* photograph, author's collection.

1960, but that did not happen. Part of their optimism had been based on the dreary record of 1959; surely, they reasoned, business had to get better. Indeed, the 1959 record had been dreadful. The number of cars handled had been only 80.2 percent of those handled in 1947, the total tonnage only 84.6 percent of that year, and freight revenues were roughly those of 1951—and the figures for 1959 included those for wholly owned Minneapolis Industrial Railway, while those for earlier years did not. Schroeder, Sullivan, and shareholders could only shake their heads in disappointment as they compared the performance of 1959 with that of 1954, the year Heineman had ousted Sprague (see Table 25.1).[15]

But despite the expectations of senior managers, and despite their determined efforts, traffic and earnings slumped in 1960, the result of a general recession that much larger Milwaukee Road blamed for intensifying "the problem of underutilization of plant and equipment"—a problem hardly unique to Milwaukee but rather an industrywide issue of great concern. M&StL's net income for 1960 through June was $306,779 compared to $620,337 for the same months of lackluster 1959. July was no better; the number of revenue cars was off by two thousand compared to the same month a year earlier. Grain loaded on-line could not offset a 10 percent drop in bridge traffic. At Great Northern and probably elsewhere, eyebrows were raised

Table 25.1. Financial performance of the M&StL, 1954 and 1959

Year	*Average cars per train*	*Average tons of freight per train*	*Average distance carried (miles)*	*Average wages/salaries*
1954	32.4	1,022	198	$4,560
1959	45.5	1,106	185	$6,664

Source: *M&StL XC Minute Book, 561–62; M&StL, Ten-Year Summary of Selected Operations and Financial Data Supplemental to the 1959 Annual Report, 1–4.*

when M&StL became slow in settling interline accounts.[16]

Even the weather proved contrary. Normally docile Sand Creek near Jordan went on a wild rampage in May that took out a pier on one bridge, threatened others, and washed away 1,850 feet of roadway. Repairs, costly detours, and reduced traffic demanded "economies." Trains 1 and 2, the "Acey-Deucey" twins, never lived up to their potential, sad to say, and were truncated on July 4. Thereafter they ran only between Cedar Lake and Marshalltown; trains 19 and 20 became sole proprietors on the full run to Peoria. And, reflecting dismal earnings as well as plunging spirits among managers as they faced the prospect of M&StL's disappearance into C&NW, several large capital projects—replacement of bridges with culverts; a line change at Little York, Illinois; new depots for St. Louis Park, Minnesota, and Morning Sun, Iowa; piggyback facilities at Cedar Lake; and tie, rail, and surfacing campaigns—all were extinguished.[17]

Morale plunged. Managers in off-line offices might expect to be retained if, as expected, the ICC allowed C&NW to pick up M&StL, but many if not most others had little regard for North Western and looked elsewhere for opportunities. By late September, fourteen officers had bolted—only three of them to positions at C&NW. William P. Coliton, for example, was off to Chicago, South Shore & South Bend as vice president of operations, and Thomas J. Powers left for Pennsylvania, where he became assistant controller.[18]

Throughout these trying days of fluidity, pain, and anxiety, M&StL remained what it had always been—a homely hometown railroad, pedestrian, unassuming, plain, a work a day old road tightly tied to its many constituents as they were to it. The section foreman at Steamboat Rock, for example, religiously flashed on his house light to greet nighttime trains; trainmen returned these greetings with their electric lanterns. The routine was the same at Coppock, Iowa, where a retired water tender concerned himself with M&StL train movements; at a trackside farmstead in the Des Moines River breaks south of Estherville, where visual greetings were exchanged; and variously around the system. A white German shepherd dog regularly inspected trains just above Curlew, and at Fort Dodge, Sigreid Hearn, who lived near Illinois Central Junction, inevitably waved friendly greetings to and even provided baked goods for grateful railroaders as they waited to take trains up the hill to Tara or to switch the nearby Cargill plant. Elsewhere, men on train 61 developed a Saturday routine of buying candy in St. James and throwing it off a mile north of Hanska to the children of Elsie Smith, who on more than one occasion responded with a freshly baked cake for them. Many of the crew on that train and others employed by M&StL had come from the towns and countryside through which the road passed. Gus Dallman had hired out as a section laborer at Waconia and worked 47 years before retirement; Dallman's brothers and their sons gave M&StL 216 years of service. Two of M&StL's "really solid people," William W. Landmesser, mechanical superintendent, and Manford J. Reitan, chief dispatcher, were examples of "homegrown" men who worked through the ranks—Landmesser from Oskaloosa, Iowa, Reitan from Boyd, Minnesota. Like railroaders everywhere, they flocked to favorite "beaneries" along the line, providing them with a regular clientele. Aside from depot cafes at Albert Lea and Albia, and the hotel at Morton, Stone's at Marshalltown remained a solid favorite, as was the Canton in Albert Lea and the Oriental in Peoria. Others were less elegant. A cafe in a filling station at Belmord sufficed, as did a counter-only diner at Gilmore City and a tiny place near the depot at Estherville. In many communities options were few. Landmesser and a traveling engineer companion once found themselves hungry at Conde and trudged through snow to the town's sole eatery; en route they noticed the unmistakable tracks of a rabbit preceding them—tracks that ended near the door of the cafe. Taking stock of this, the traveling engineer

Figure 25.5. William L. Landmesser, right, was one of the "homegrown" men who worked through the ranks, becoming M&StL's respected mechanical superintendent. Author's collection.

turned to Landmesser and exclaimed: "I think I know what we're having for lunch today."[19]

Close ties and strong symbiotic relationships, long a part of the company, its people, and the road's service area, were about to be sundered. On October 13, 1960, the ICC, as expected, permitted purchase of M&StL by C&NW, concluding that "the combined properties will produce a larger, stronger company, better able to attract and hold competent management personnel." This, said the ICC, was "obviously in the public interest." Closing was scheduled for October 31.[20]

It was on that bleak Monday that Albert Schroeder and James Sullivan traveled to Chicago with papers and documents that they would hand over to Chicago & North Western in a meeting at First National Bank. At the New York Stock Exchange, M&StL closed at $32\frac{1}{8}$, up $\frac{1}{8}$. Back in Iowa, train 57 arrived at Spencer late in the afternoon; after switching chores were accomplished, the crew tied up for the evening. But not before photographs were made of the agent and crew, with Alco 227 as background. In those views were persons who made up an accurate microcosm of M&StL employees: John G. Benson, agent, whose two sons were agents at other stations; Alfred A. Severson, brakeman, whose father, uncles, and brother had served the road in train service; Max A. Sedelmeier, conductor, who had left his native Germany to enter M&StL train service in 1914; Paul K. Brubaker, engineer, World War II veteran; Peter J. Dorn, brakeman, whose father had been a long-serving bridge and building foreman and whose brother also was a brakeman; Demar C. Blankenhagen, fireman, whose father, uncle, and brothers were or had been enginemen. Collectively, these six men represented 192 years of seniority. The photographer's need finally met, the men adjourned to caboose 1140. Markers were taken down and stowed inside, a coal fire was renewed in the stove, the Aladdin lamp was lit, and (contrary to company rules) beer came out of the locker. Talk turned to railroad experiences of bygone days—of bucking snow, of memorable personalities, of weathering the Great Depression and the very real threat of M&StL's dismemberment, and of better days that had followed. Inevitably conversation turned to an uncertain future. The mood was pleasant if subdued, but with a melancholy edge. Later that evening a reporter from the *Fort Dodge Messenger* made his way to the yards in Fort Dodge to record the departure of M&StL's final train from that town—number 196 for Des Moines, in the care of locomotive 301 and Beryl H. Wiles, conductor; Edward A. Garrett and Donald R. Musselman, brakemen; Charles A. Wilson, engineer; and Raymond F. Green, fireman. It was about midnight when Conductor Wiles stood on the back platform of his caboose and the markers of 196 passed the silent old depot at Callender; Wiles stepped inside and recorded as much in his delay report. Almost simultaneously, at 12:01 a.m. on Tuesday, November 1, 1960, M&StL's properties were surrendered to Chicago & North Western and the Minneapolis & St. Louis Railway Company ceased to exist as a transportation enterprise.[21]

Figure 25.6. The agent at Spencer, Iowa, and the crew of train 57 on October 31, 1960, aggregated 192 years of M&StL service. Left to right, Alfred A. Severson, brakeman; John G. Benson, agent; Max A. Sedelmeier, conductor; Paul K. Brubaker, engineer; Peter J. Dorn, brakeman; Demar C. Blankenhagen, fireman. Photo by the author.

Figure 25.7. The train order signal at Hopkins was green when the clock struck midnight on October 31, 1960. No M&StL train would ever pass this way again. William D. Middleton photograph.

Chapter 26
UNDER A GREEN AND YELLOW FLAG

Only the land held memory of those days.
—CURTIS HARNACK, *WE HAVE ALL GONE AWAY*

OCTOBER 31, 1960, WHEN THE MINNEAPOLIS & St. Louis Railway breathed its last, was Halloween, a night of goblins and ghosts. One is left to wonder if the spirits of Henry Titus Welles, William Drew Washburn, William H. Truesdale, Edwin Hawley, and William Hepburn Bremner were about that evening, and if so, if they communed with that of Lucian Charles Sprague (who had died recently in Minneapolis) as to M&StL's fate. What might have been their line of conversation? They likely would have agreed that M&StL had fought the good fight, that the road had overcome great odds to survive so long as an independent. Perhaps they would have congratulated each other all around for their respective accomplishments in extending the company's life. Surely they would have admitted, however, that the prime element in explaining M&StL's surprising longevity had been the road's rank-and-file employees, whose loyalty and dedication over the years had been truly remarkable.

It was ironic that M&StL passed into the mists of history at a time when its financial affairs were sound, its motive power and rolling stock new and well maintained, its roadway in good to adequate shape. But Max Swiren and M&StL's directors had grown weary of pumping money into plant and equipment only to see M&StL's traffic base erode with little hope of material recovery. The loss of Toledo, Peoria & Western had been defining. Heineman's well-developed arrogance and his unwillingness to accept counsel from persons experienced in local politics and in relationships within the railroad community caused M&StL's aspirations to become a cropper before the Interstate Commerce Commission and ultimately the Supreme Court of the United States. "Had we acquired that road," Albert Schroeder asserted, "it would have been an entirely different situation." Maybe. But there were other factors. M&StL managers were surprised and dismayed at the success of the St. Lawrence Seaway in draining away lucrative long-distance grain shipments; growth of waterborne traffic on the Mississippi and the Illinois Rivers likewise ate into M&StL traffic. Schroeder and others were especially bitter about such subsidized competition. Planning for and execution of the interstate highway system only deepened their antipathy. They were equally irritated at and depressed by moss-backed government regulation, unequal and often discriminatory taxes, and labor agreements that strangled productivity. In the end, M&StL directors and other shareholders simply gave up on railroading as a profit-making venture, choosing to sell out to Chicago & North Western.[1]

Whether or not C&NW was the best place for

M&StL is a question without productive resolution. Even if Swiren and other stockholders had not chosen that moment to cash out their investments, it was simply a matter of time before the sands in M&StL's hourglass ran out. M&StL could not survive on local traffic moving from one station to another, its line hauls tended to be short, certain basic on-line industries (especially flouring at Minneapolis as well as the manufacture of clay brick and tile) were petering out, and bridge traffic would have disappeared in the approaching era of mega-mergers. The creation in 1970 of Burlington Northern, which combined M&StL's major interchange partners Great Northern and Northern Pacific with Chicago, Burlington & Quincy, certainly would have sealed M&StL's fate, because that giant enterprise would have done all in its power to keep business on its own rails. Robert W. Downing, who became president at Burlington Northern, saw M&StL as "trying to be a big railroad with low traffic density in a short haul environment where other railroads and a multitude of highway and barge operators were fiercely competing for every ton of freight." Given these collective disadvantages, said Downing, "it is little wonder that M&StL gradually lost ground and eventually disappeared into C&NW despite good management, a loyal workforce, and a considerable degree of support in the on-line business community." In any event, M&StL metamorphosed into MSL Industries, which established headquarters in Chicago with Max Swiren as president and soon purchased Universal Screw Company, a manufacturer of metallic fasteners, and Heads & Threads, importer and distributor of ferrous and nonferrous bolts, nuts, and washers.[2]

Chicago & North Western's approach to its newly acquired property was measured and cautious, perhaps on purpose, but more likely reflecting the absence of a well-designed plan of digestion. C&NW's intention had been to operate all of the M&StL lines as a unit, and that happened, but it was not until March 5, 1961, five months after the takeover, that North Western got around to issuing time table number one for its M&StL Division. By that time all former M&StL operating officers were gone, even veteran Frank B. Clark, although Manford J. Reitan and his dispatchers remained, as did the roadmasters. In the mechanical department, however, highly respected William W. Landmesser had learned that he "had no position in C&NW" only days before the takeover. Albert Schroeder's disdain for North Western had been transparent, and neither was he retained nor did he seek to be retained, going instead to Tucson (Arizona) Rapid Transit as president. Scorn among more than a few contract people was similarly evident. Merle L. Mahaffey, a fifty-six-year veteran of engine service at Marshalltown declared that he would not work for C&NW and retired on October 29, 1960. At Fort Dodge, E. A. "Red" Garrett, a brakeman, had an abiding distaste for North Western and promised to resign shortly after the takeover—a promise he kept. Many others had no choice in the matter. In Minneapolis, 112 employees in the General Office Building were advised on November 16, 1960, that their jobs had been abolished.[3]

Nervousness had been evident among M&StL personnel at all levels prior to November 1, and understandably so, because the future was impossible to predict, but naivete was just as obvious as uncertainty. Thus when C&NW moved in managers who, with arrogance and condescension, sneered at M&StL conventions, attitudes, and practices as if the road had been, at best, a wooden-axle operation, employees went into shock and dismay. "We have a knife at your back and we are going to keep it there," personnel at Fort Dodge and elsewhere were told by one new arrival, who in an instant alienated an entire body of employees who had thrived in M&StL's "lightly managed" environment. Morale sank; the stage was set for trouble. "Men who had pissed and moaned about M&StL now under C&NW found out they had been on a honeymoon before," observed one disgruntled locomotive engineer at Minneapolis. Relations between local chairmen of labor organizations and company managers, always contentious to some degree, became acrimonious and adversarial. Members of M&StL's sales team who joined C&NW likewise found a less satisfactory environment. Clifford K. Ferguson at Peoria reflected as much. "They run a railroad a lot different than we did, believe me," he said in exasperation. "They sure have a lot more red tape." Outsiders also shook their heads. "What a nice railroad M&StL had been," groaned Frank P. Donovan in Minneapolis.[4]

Train operations initially were similar to what they had been under M&StL. Trains 94 and 97 continued run-through operation with Illinois Central, and train 51 still hustled IC tonnage from Fort Dodge to Albert Lea, for train 97. Between Cedar Lake and Peoria, 19 and 20 wheeled Peoria Gateway lading, but 1 and 2 now worked through from Cedar Lake to Albia, although an early change terminated trackage rights over Wabash-Burlington between Albia and Des Moines. Regular service was cancelled on all Iowa branches, between Fort Dodge and Des Moines, and on Minneapolis Industrial, with extras operating on demand, but the old routine west of Hopkins remained in place. Service from Winthrop to Fort Dodge was curtailed by running the New Ulm switch job between Winthrop and New Ulm, and a twice-weekly "North to Alaska" assignment from Fort Dodge to Hanska, but there was nothing between New Ulm and Hanska, which gave a taste of future policy everywhere. Tonnage increasingly and predictably moved to C&NW junctions at St. James, New Ulm, Waseca, Marshalltown, and Peoria.[5]

Figure 26.1. "They run a railroad a lot different than we do," exclaimed Clifford K. Ferguson, C&NW's traffic representative at Peoria and a former M&StL man. The pedigree of the caboose in the background is clear; equally clear was the low state of maintenance of former M&StL property by the summer of 1963. Author's collection.

For C&NW, M&StL was a juicy plum. The year 1961 resulted in C&NW's highest freight revenue ever, the highest net income since 1953, and the lowest transportation ratio since 1945. "These results," boasted Ben Heineman, "were primarily the consequence of the acquisition of the Minneapolis & St. Louis Railway. The benefits thus far realized have in all respects exceeded our expectations. Others are yet to be secured," Heineman promised. Operating expenses were down, the result of "operating efficiencies" and the "continued elimination of wasteful loss producing services," he enthused.[6]

Others—shippers and employees—were less impressed. The chairman of the Minnesota Railroad and Warehouse Commission asserted that "hundreds of letters complaining" of "deteriorating, inferior service" had been received by that agency since C&NW had taken M&StL. Heineman denied those accusations, but by 1963 the Railway Labor Executives' Association was fully engaged in broadcasting the woes of shippers along former M&StL lines, who were much aroused by higher rents for track-side leases, by loss of less-than-carload freight operation, by loss or threatened loss of local agency service, by increasingly poor equipment, and, worst of all, by declines in train operation.[7]

The efforts of the Railway Labor Executives organization were not entirely selfless, of course, for the welfare of railroad employees was at stake. The Order of Railroad Telegraphers (ORT) and others had threatened a strike early in 1961, when C&NW began running trains from Marshalltown to Albia without changing crews at Oskaloosa according to agreements; the merging of C&NW and M&StL yard functions at Marshalltown had already been a thorny issue. The Brotherhoods, in effect, argued that contracts signed earlier with M&StL now were

Figure 26.2. A Fort Dodge, Iowa, crew worked all the way to Hanska, Minnesota, on what was derisively call the "North to Alaska" run. The Ormsby, Minnesota, elevator would supply a couple of cars of grain this bright January morning in 1961. Photo by the author.

binding on C&NW. No issue proved more contentious, however, than the long and bitter telegraphers' strike of 1962. ORT had been feuding with C&NW nearly since Heineman's arrival there in 1956. In this instance ORT demanded that no telegraphers' jobs or station agent positions in existence on December 3, 1957, be abolished without agreement between the union and C&NW. This, said North Western, would give ORT veto power over technological improvements, modernization, and increases in efficiency. Not even the personal intervention of President John F. Kennedy could forestall a strike as both sides dug in their heels; picket lines went up on August 30. A curious but crucial issue involved former M&StL telegraphers, who argued that their ORT contract had been signed by M&StL, that C&NW had accepted those unexpired contracts when M&StL passed to it, that ORT members on former M&StL lines were not part of the current feud between ORT and C&NW, and that C&NW had every right to shut down operations elsewhere but not on its M&StL lines. To do so, said M&StL telegraphers, was to perpetrate an illegal lockout. ORT agreed with the former M&StL employees; Iowa's Republican governor Norman Erbe saw it similarly and urged President Kennedy to end the lockout. C&NW, for its part, argued that M&StL had been so firmly integrated into North Western's operation that it could not be run independently. C&NW refused to budge. On the broader issue, C&NW and ORT both sought public support. In Chicago, where thousands of commuters were disadvantaged by the strike, sentiment tended to run against telegraphers in country stations, but in Iowa and elsewhere away from C&NW's Chicago headquarters, the public wondered why Heineman had chosen to spend lavishly on new equipment for commuter service (a losing or at very best highly marginal operation) instead of spending the same money to improve track conditions and service in the rural areas that gave C&NW so much of its traffic base. Divided as the issue was between urban and rural interests, neither side could claim a majority of public opinion. Resolution came finally on September 28, when both sides agreeed to binding arbitration, with ORT ending its strike, C&NW ending its lockout. But when the arbitration ruling favoring C&NW came down on October 8, it was clear that Heineman had won a stunning victory that would allow C&NW to rewrite work rules and abolish what it considered unneeded jobs.[8]

The lockout argument on behalf of former M&StL employees also left an indelible mark on the memories of C&NW managers. It did not help that in the fall of 1962 former M&StL locomotives still wore M&StL's colors (red and white) and logos for the most part and remained numbered according to M&StL classification; signs still identified depots and other property as belonging to "The Minneapolis & St. Louis Railway Company"; and the entire former railroad was operated as C&NW's M&StL Division. All of that was about to change, however—not immediately, but surely—as C&NW set out to fully integrate the former M&StL and to eradicate its identity and any memory of its past. "In the near future we will change all former M&StL switch locks to the standard C&NW switch locks," agents and section foremen were advised in December 1962. "This will be uniform on all installations on the former M&StL Railway."[9]

Fresh from its victory in the telegraphers' strike, C&NW earnestly pressed to eliminate station positions systemwide through a central agency plan whereby one agent was responsible for several communities. In 1963 depots at the Iowa towns of Gifford, Geneva, Leland, Corwith, Ayrshire, Badger, Rippey, Sheffield, Clare, and Emmons were shuttered; in Minnesota, those at Hanska, Jordan, Wood Lake, and Hazel Run met the same fate. This was only the beginning. Joint agencies at Winfield (with CB&Q) and even at Tara (with Illinois Central) were closed

Figure 26.3. The strike in 1962 solidified C&NW's thinking about the former M&StL. Locomotives such as 712 headed for the paint shop to exchange their red and white for green and gold. This trio of former M&StL power was about to leave Marshalltown, Iowa, with train 19. Photo by the author.

in 1966 and 1967. By late 1970, major stations such as those at Estherville, Humboldt, Albia, and Grinnell were gone; even "central stations" began to disappear. By early 1972 only those at Arlington, Winthrop, Fairfax, and Dawson remained open in Minnesota west of Hopkins; four years later only those at New Prague, Montgomery, and Albert Lea, Minnesota, and at Mason City, Hampton, and Eldora, Iowa, survived south of Hopkins on the line to Marshalltown. In 1983 those at Winthrop, Dawson, and even Watertown joined the casualty list.[10]

Operations were modified gradually. Everything west of Hopkins was given over to C&NW's Dakota Division on January 1, 1962, although train operation continued as before. The M&StL Division offices, including dispatchers, were moved to Mason City in 1963 after C&NW sold the handsome General Office Building at Minneapolis. Gross ton miles remained heavy between Cedar Lake and Marshalltown, although C&NW gradually dried up the Albert Lea gateway with Illinois Central; trains 94 and 97 disappeared, as did Minneapolis tonnage received from IC at Fort Dodge. Exotic movements were rare, although Vernon Wigfield, agent at Perry, Iowa, might have considered himself in the big leagues on December 21, 1963, when he copied orders for "C&E UP Engine 962," detouring between Perry and Grand Junction with one of the famous "Cities" passenger trains because of a problem on the Milwaukee Road. Massive floods on the Mississippi River in 1965 forced North Western to close its main-line bridge at Clinton, Iowa, and divert trains variously, including over the former M&StL main through Keithsburg until that facility, too, was put out of service by high water. Floods elsewhere in 1973 forced the diversion of C&NW trains from Kansas City over Santa Fe to Nemo and on into Peoria, and in 1981 C&NW agreed to run special passenger trains between Gowrie and Clare to celebrate Clare's centennial. Perhaps most astonishing, steam returned to what had been M&StL rail in 1976, when Southern Pacific's massive 4449 headed the Freedom Train between Perry and West Des Moines and on the main line through Hopkins. Steam also graced former M&StL trackage in 1985,

Figure 26.4. Steam returned in dramatic form when SP's 4449 headed the Freedom Train through Hopkins in 1976. Vern Wigfield photograph.

when C&NW's 4-6-0 1385 made a publicity tour from Mason City to Marshalltown.[11]

There was much in C&NW's operation of what had been M&StL during the 1960s that seemed familiar, but there were also significant changes. Before the decade was out most of the Alcos were gone, and the remaining power took on C&NW's green and gold paint. Nothing, however, more clearly signaled separation from the past than the end of Peoria Gateway service and the removal of signature trains 19 and 20 on April 11, 1968. Local trains east of Oskaloosa had become casualties under North Western's administration, and 19 and 20 had been given the impossible task of delivering through freight on time as well as handling cars to way stations. But it had not worked. Small-town customers were dismayed and irritated to see their cars speeding by in the consist of train 20, on short time to make Peoria connections, only to see them whizzing by the next day on train 19, in a hurry to make Minneapolis commitments. "They deliberately killed off business by refusing service," growled the disgusted agent at Hedrick.[12]

As it developed, C&NW had much more in mind than simply extinguishing one important train set. Business at intermediate stations between Oskaloosa and Peoria—except, of course, at Middle Grove—was by now inconsequential, the result of traditional shippers going out of business, serious inroads by water carriers on the Mississippi and Illinois Rivers, razor-sharp competition from truckers, C&NW's disinterest, or more likely a combination of these factors. In any event, local billings could not save the easternmost leg of M&StL's tiny empire; moreover, C&NW coveted the line's fairly new, heavy steel, which it could relay elsewhere. Notices appeared on depot doors in July 1970 advising locals that C&NW had filed to abandon everything east of Oskaloosa to Keithsburg. Only 360 cars had moved to stations on the line in 1969, with a mere ten cars billed out, necessitating operation of one train weekly out of Monmouth, and going west only as far as necessary to pick up or set out cars. There was no question how the ICC would rule. On October 27, 1971, the final revenue train rumbled out to Hedrick, turned, and headed back, collecting empty cars en route; the crew stopped for dinner (hamburger steaks) at Mabel's Cafe in Oakville, tying up at 7:20 p.m. in Monmouth. Dismantling began early the next January near Veo, Iowa, between Packwood and Brighton. As expected, C&NW followed up with additional abandonment requests: Keithsburg to Monmouth, granted in 1974; Monmouth through Nemo to Abingdon, granted in 1975; and Abingdon to Middle Grove, granted in 1976. Peoria to Middle Grove survived, of course, because of the mines.[13]

There followed a curious interlude during which Craig E. Burroughs of Joliet, Illinois, created the Great River Railroad, acquired the bridge at Keithsburg and

Figure 26.5. The end came for operation through Keithsburg, Illinois, in 1971. "STOP" on the concrete counterweight of the lift span now had terminal significance. Photo by the author.

twenty-eight miles of right-of-way west to Winfield, and began to lay track with the idea of shuttling covered hoppers of grain that could be unloaded directly into barges from the Keithsburg bridge, returning from the river with fertilizer. Burroughs also dickered unsuccessfully with C&NW for the Keithsburg–Middle Grove segment, which could feed from the east, but C&NW wanted the steel for its ribbon-rail needs elsewhere. In the end, Burroughs's ambitious and intriguing plan died aborning, a short line ahead of its time.[14]

The bridge at Keithsburg suffered a particularly ignominious and undeserved ending. Long abandoned and derelict, it stood as an inviting target for misdirected youths, who set afire the lift span section late in June 1981. Heat snapped the cables constraining its huge concrete counterweights, driving the east end of the span into the navigation channel and putting a pucker across faces of the U.S. Coast Guard officials responsible for marine safety and navigation. On July 5, demolition experts dynamited the damaged structure, to the great joy of a large holiday crowd. But the structure did not drop for salvage quite as expected, and the blast brought down an additional span. Perhaps it was a tribute to the bridge's designers and engineers; perhaps it was the structure's stubborn pride. After all, it alone represented Iowa Central and M&StL—mere ghosts of a departed era—at Keithsburg. Interestingly, the story was part of NBC's *Today* program on July 6.[15]

Abandonment of the former main line east of Oskaloosa, however dramatic, was not the first example of C&NW's long-term intentions. Indeed, in 1962 C&NW had abandoned lines in both directions out of the Minnesota valley at New Ulm—to Klossner on the north, 5.3 miles, and to Hanska on the south, 13 miles—effectively taking a chunk out of the Southwestern and making clear North Western's intentions of carving away at M&StL's body much as one might cut off a dog's tail one inch at a time. Another block of the Southwestern, from Estherville to Terril, was removed in 1968, and another, from St. James to Ormsby, in 1969. The same approach was employed in South Dakota, where the chunk from Revillo to Strandburg was excised in 1968, cutting the West End into two disconnected parts. The portion from Stratford through Aberdeen to Leola followed in 1969, that from Strandburg to Watertown in 1970 and from Madison to Revillo in 1971, leaving only the line from Watertown to Stratford as an M&StL remnant.[16]

Meanwhile, Ben Heineman had gone on a shopping spree, picking up mid-sized Chicago Great Western and Iowa short lines Des Moines & Central Iowa and Fort Dodge, Des Moines & Southern in 1968. Great Western had Chicago–Twin Cities, Chicago–Omaha, and Twin Cities–Omaha routes that were duplicate to those of C&NW and were immediately in jeopardy, but CGW gave C&NW a valuable entry to Kansas City via Marshalltown. All of these new additions except the Kansas City line would be subject to North Western's policy of eliminating competition, diverting traffic to surviving arteries, and deferring and then ending maintenance as traffic dried up prior to abandonment. Except for M&StL's Belmond Branch, which was pruned back from Denhart to Kanawha and severed on the other end from Hampton to Alexander in 1970—creating stubs in two directions to be served off CGW's surviving line at Belmond—former M&StL lines were not negatively affected by C&NW's additions. In fact, former CGW tonnage now found itself on the Cedar Lake–Marshalltown line.[17]

For the American railroad industry, the 1960s and 1970s could be summed up in a word: grim. Late in the 1960s, New York Central and Pennsylvania stumbled into each other's arms to become Penn Central, only to declare bankruptcy a short time later. Western giants Southern Pacific and Union Pacific jointly attempted to acquire faltering Rock Island in an endless and legendary case that fully demonstrated the innate ineptitude of the Interstate Commerce Commission. By the time the regulators finally permitted acquisition, Rock Island was in such wretched condition that both western railroads said "No thanks." In the East, several more roads headed for the courts, which resulted in a crisis adequate to involve the federal government with significant legislative medications, including an amalgamation of eastern derelicts into Conrail. The government already had entered the railroad arena with the creation of Amtrak, a national passenger company, in 1971, and during the 1970s there was serious discussion about nationalizing the country's freight railroads. That discussion was fueled in part by the rapid deterioration of Midwestern railroads—especially Rock Island and Milwaukee, but also North Western.[18]

Heineman and senior railroad managers elsewhere already were considering means by which to protect corporate assets and shareholder value and were exploring exit strategies for use if their railroads foundered or were nationalized. Southern Pacific and Union Pacific formed holding companies, for example, and Heineman saw to the creation of Northwest Industries as a means to diversify C&NW into nonrail areas. In 1970, however, Heineman seemed to weary of the railroad game and agreed to spin off railroad assets that two years later became Chicago & North Western Transportation Company, an employee-owned enterprise headed by Larry S. Provo, who had cut his teeth in the railroad industry at M&StL.[19]

Security analyst Henry H. Ivingston considered Larry Provo "a brilliant and resourceful accountant, a superb support man, the alter ego for Ben Heineman." But Provo was more than that. He was a vigorous and able leader who knew when to ask for opinions and when to give orders. At C&NW he kept his goals simple: (1) be a reliable servant for Union Pacific at Council Bluffs and Fremont on the Overland Route, (2) abandon branches, and (3) get out from under commuter responsibilities in Chicago. Provo did not live to see all of this accomplished, but his successor, James R. Wolfe, was generally of the same persuasion and energetically prosecuted the Provo model. Before the 1970s were out, C&NW was shed of commuter liabilities, had lopped off hundreds of route miles, and was Union Pacific's favored partner on overhead business into and out of Chicago.[20]

North Western was aided mightily in its own search for continued life when in 1980 bankrupt Milwaukee Road determined to pare itself into "Milwaukee II," a mere shadow of its former self, shorn of its Pacific Coast extension and its line across Iowa to Council Bluffs in competition with C&NW, and utterly without assurance of survival in any form. C&NW was even more greatly advantaged by the demise of Rock Island, which tottered into oblivion on March 31, 1980—the largest abandonment ever, 7,500 miles. Several pieces of the former Rock Island would be dismantled, but some were picked up by others for strategic purposes; the Golden State line from Kansas City to Santa Rosa, New Mexico, for instance, passed to Southern Pacific's empire. Of immediate interest to C&NW was Rock Island's splendid route from St. Paul through Des Moines to Kansas City, a luscious morsel that North Western wrestled into its system in 1983.[21]

Acquisition of Rock Island's Twin Cities–Kansas City line and other Rock Island bits and pieces quickly would have a dramatic impact on major segments of M&StL's already decimated map, which C&NW had been chipping away at throughout the 1970s. Gone by 1981 was the former Minneapolis Industrial, from Watertown, Minnesota, to Gluek (1972); M&StL's South Dakota remnant, from Watertown to Stratford (1977); and all of what remained of the Southwestern above Terril, from Winthrop to Klossner (1975), Ormsby to Estherville (1979), and Hanska to St. James (1980). The Iowa branches fell, too, one by one: Newton and Lynnville (1962–63); Roland (1981); Zearing to Roland (1977); and Belmond to Alexander (1981), leaving only twelve miles of recently rehabilitated line from Belmond to Kanawha as sole survivor of what once had been the Algona Branch. By the end of 1982, the Albert Lea–Fort Dodge line was extinct except for a tiny piece, from Humboldt to Rogerton, which survived until 1985; preceding its demise had been that of Albert Lea–Lake Mills (1976); Humboldt–Luverne, Iowa (1979); Luverne–Lake Mills

Figure 26.6. Conductor Peter J. Dorn waved farewell as the final train rumbled through Curlew, Iowa, at 4:45 p.m. on August 11, 1981. Photo by the author.

(1980); and Fort Dodge–Rogerton (1981–82). Gone, too, was the line from Mallard through Spencer to Terril (1981). The Fort Dodge–Des Moines segment was next: Grand Junction–Rippey (1984); the Fort Dodge yard and trackage rights over IC between Fort Dodge and Tara (1984); and Perry–Rippey (1989). Thereafter Perry was reached only from Des Moines, Grand Junction from Fort Dodge via Moorland and the former CGW.[22]

There was good news in 1982 for seventy miles of route—and all intermediate stations from Grand Junction through Tara to Mallard—when C&NW joined with an independent shipping association and the Iowa Department of Transportation for a massive improvement project including the addition of rock ballast and welded rail to facilitate heavily laden unit grain trains flowing to C&NW's double-track artery at Grand Junction.[23]

But such good news was the exception. More indignities were suffered on the former main line of M&StL as C&NW turned increasingly to the recently acquired Rock Island north–south route, which largely paralleled M&StL in Minnesota, was joint from Albert Lea to Manly, and then diverged, intersecting C&NW's Chicago–Council Bluffs main line at Nevada, Iowa, twenty-nine miles west of Marshalltown, before running on to Des Moines and Kansas City. Local business on the M&StL route was superior, especially in Minnesota, but Rock Island's line was better engineered and was completely signaled. C&NW chose the Rock Island line. The Manly–Mason City segment of M&StL had been scrapped in 1970 to eliminate duplicate track after C&NW took over CGW. Fourteen years later, with Rock Island's route tucked safely under its belt, C&NW sent through trains over that line and severed M&StL's former main gut between Waseca and Montgomery, five years later between Steamboat Rock and Hampton (with the line from Ackley to Geneva taken by a successor to IC). In 1990 C&NW eliminated Rockwell–Sheffield; in 1991 Hopkins–Chaska; in 1994 Maxon–Albia and Cedar Lake–Hopkins; and in 2000 Eddyville–Maxon.[24]

In all of this, the Minnesota portion of M&StL's former West End presented a most curious scenario. The line beyond Madison out to Watertown had been clipped in 1968–71, as had that on the east from Hopkins to Norwood, Minnesota, after obtaining running rights over parallel Milwaukee Road between those stations, but the twenty-one stations on the surviving 130-mile segment from Norwood to Madison had been some of the best revenue producers on M&StL—a fact that had not been lost on Lucian C. Sprague, who had poured money into the line to build it up. For whatever reason, however, C&NW chose to ignore its potential, taking heavy tonnage from it but slowing and then ending necessary maintenance. C&NW sought abandonment; permission came in 1983. Eventually, though, a local rail authority purchased the westernmost thirty-six miles from Hanley Falls to Madison and turned it over to Burlington Northern for operation; Minnesota Valley Transportation, a new independent short line, took the rest. The Hanley Falls–Madison solution proved a good one, the Norwood–Hanley Falls line more problematic, although it remained intact as the century ended.[25]

In 1995 the 4,200-mile C&NW—reduced by about 60 percent in size compared to 1972—discovered the meaning of "What goes around comes around." That year the Union Pacific colossus gobbled up Chicago & North Western in the latest chapter of the industry's mega-merger saga. Union Pacific's arrogant and dismissive attitude toward C&NW, its personnel, its traditions, and its conventions was more than reminiscent of that taken by C&NW toward M&StL in 1960. Those who had witnessed or experienced those proceedings were not moved to compassion in 1995. "My regret is that the Neanderthals handling the M&StL takeover of 35 years ago are no longer around to be crushed under Union Pacific's heel," said one plainspoken manager who had been close to all that transpired in 1960.[26]

The list of surviving bits of M&StL trackage is small. On the main line, there is a short segment through Cedar Lake, a longer one from Merriam through New Prague to Montgomery, and a longer one yet from Waseca through Albert Lea to the state boundary. In Iowa there are a series of disconnected pieces: from Northwood to Manly, Mason City to Rockwell,

Figure 26.7. Darkness had fallen forever on M&StL. Conductor Albert L. Picket checked the departure time from Angus, Iowa. Photo by the author.

Hampton to Sheffield, and Geneva to Marshalltown. The busiest part of the former M&StL is between Marshalltown and Eddyville, site of a massive grain-processing facility. Elsewhere, the spur out to Kanawha from Belmond is the token remainder of M&StL's tiny network of branches. Between Albert Lea and Fort Dodge all that remains are industrial spurs at Lake Mills, Forest City, Livermore, and Luverne. The line from Mallard through Tara to Grand Junction remains vibrant, that from West Des Moines to Perry less so. On the Southwestern, all that survives is industrial trackage at New Ulm, St. James, and Spencer. In South Dakota nothing exists; in Illinois only the stub from Peoria to Middle Grove survives. Collectively this amounts to about 330 route miles—approximately 24 percent of the M&StL and Minneapolis Industrial mileage in 1960. Nature has reclaimed much of the abandoned rights-of-way; only those persons with precise memories or active imaginations are able to identify the previous paths of the iron horse. The same might be said of M&StL's facilities. The General Office Building still stands in Minneapolis, stately as ever, but with no indication of its railroad heritage. C&NW made good use of the diesel shop at Marshalltown, and those buildings still stand, but only an industrial archeologist could find traces of the shops at Cedar Lake. Scarred footprints of a yard remain at Fort Dodge; Bartlett Yard is gone, however, as are the yards at Des Moines, Monmouth, and Watertown.[27]

"I never in my wildest imagination would have believed this would happen," exclaimed John L. Hodson in the 1980s as he reflected on the rapid unraveling of the American railroad industry as he had known it and the utter disappearance of M&StL and its successor from his native Britt, Iowa. Like many others, Hodson had a difficult time saying good-bye to that which had been familiar to him growing up. A pained look came into his eyes as he stared at the abandoned right-of-way, at the spot where the depot had stood, now gone except in his memory. Others from Conde to Kalo, Curlew to Kilduff, must have felt the same as they reflected on the age of railways—not so very long ago—when lights burned all night in the local depot, when farmers marked midday by passage of the noonday train, when railroads set the tempo of the times. M&StL had played an active role in all of this. It had been born in Minneapolis, a tool of millers and others to circumvent the power of the Chicago and Milwaukee railroads by forging an iron link with St. Louis, and although that dream was never realized, M&StL nevertheless caused the countryside to grow up around it. In other cases M&StL itself opened up an expanding countryside, giving life to villages and adjacent agricultural principalities where none had existed before the arrival of steam cars. Immeasurable opportunities were made manifest through M&StL's construction and operation—as it gave in its own right employment to thousands of persons over the years—or through the transportation of passengers, mail, express, and freight, as was its purpose. Every railroad found itself tightly tied in symbiotic relation to its service area, M&StL likely even more so because of its usual financial anemia and its restricted market area, mostly rural, in only four Midwestern states. In the end, M&StL proved a good and faithful steward of its franchise. What greater accolade could it have?[28]

> So hail and farewell
> Little railroad line!
> To progress all must bow
> Will all your siblings
> Be doing well
> Eighty years from now?
> —*Author unknown*

Appendix

M&StL Stations and Other Places Mentioned

Abbott, IA
Abbott Crossing, IA
Aberdeen, SD
Abingdon, IL
Ackley, IA
Adelaide, SD
Afton, MN
Akaska, SD
Albee, SD
Albert Lea, MN
Albia, IA
Albion, IA
Alexander, IA
Algona, IA
Alta, IA
Alton, IA
Ames, IA
Angus, IA
Anoka, MN
Arlington, MN
Arnold, IA
Ashawa, IA
Austin, MN
Ayrshire, IA
Badger, IA
Bartlett, IL
Beacon, IA
Beacon Junction, IA
Belle Fouche, SD
Belmond, IA
Belview, MN
Berkeley, IA
Berwick, IL
Bismarck, ND
Boyd, MN
Bradley, SD
Brainerd, MN
Brentford, SD
Brighton, IA
Britt, IA
Bromley, IA
Brown County, SD
Buffalo, New York
Burlington, IA
Burnside, IA
Butler, IA
Callender, IA
Cambridge, MN
Cameron, IA
Camp Dodge, IA
Capron, IA
Carlyle, SD
Carver, MN
Cedar Falls, IA
Cedar Lake, MN
Cedar Rapids, IA
Center City, MN
Centerville, IA
Chamberlain, SD
Chapin, IA
Chaska, MN
Chelsea, SD
Chisago City, MN
Clare, IA
Clarkfield, MN
Clay, IA
Clear Lake, IA
Clemons Grove, IA
Clinton, IA
Coalfield, IA
Coaltown, IA
Coalville, IA
Conde, SD
Coney Island, MN
Coppock, IA
Cornell, IA
Corwith, IA
Cottagewood, MN
Council Bluffs, IA
Cramers, IL
Crandall, SD
Cresbard, SD
Creston, IA
Crocker, SD
Curlew, IA
Dakota City, IA
Dallas, IA
Dallas Center, IA
Dana, IA
Davenport, IA
Dawson, MN
Dayton, IA
Deadwood, SD
Deephaven, MN
Delhi, MN
Dellwood, MN

Denhart, IA
Denison, IA
Dennis, IA
Dillon, IA
Dodge City, KS
Dows, IA
Doyle, MN
Dubuque, IA
Duluth, MN
Dunleith, IL
Dunnell, MN
Eagan, MN
Eagle Lake, MN
East Burlington, IL
East St. Cloud, MN
Echo, MN
Echols, MN
Eddyville, IA
Eden, IL
Eden Prairie, MN
Edina, MN
Eldora, IA
Eleanor, IL
Elk River, MN
Elkton, SD
Ellsworth, KS
El Reno, OK
Elrick Junction, IA
Emmons, MN
Estherville, IA
Eureka, MN
Evarts, SD
Ewarts, IA
Excelsior, IA
Excelsior, MN
Fairfax, MN
Fairview, MN
Faith, SD
Farmington, IL
Faulkner, IA
Faulton, SD
Flandreau, SD
Florence, SD
Fonda, IA
Forbush, IA
Forest City, IA
Fort Dodge, IA
Fort Madison, IA
Fort Ridgely, MN
Fosterdale, IA
Franconia, MN
Franklin, MN
Frazer Junction, IA
Freeman, IA
Freeport, IL
Fremont, IA
Fulton, IL
Galesburg, IL
Galveston, TX
Gardner, SD
Gaylord, MN
Geneva, IA
Gettysburg, SD
Gibbon, MN
Gifford, IA
Gilman, IA
Gilmore City, IA
Givin, IA
Glenham, SD
Glenville, MN
Gluek, MN
Gordonsville, MN
Gowrie, IA
Grand Junction, IA
Granite City, IL
Greenfield, IA
Green Isle, MN
Greenville, IA
Grinnell, IA
Hamburg, MN
Hampton, IA
Hanley Falls, MN
Hanna, IL
Hanska, MN
Hartland, MN
Hartley, IA
Hastings, MN
Hawley, IA
Haydenville, MN
Hayfield, IA
Hazel Run, MN
Head of the Lakes, MN
Hedrick, IA
Helena, MN
Hermon, IL
Herndon, IA
Hickory, IA
Hilton, IA
Hocking, IA
Hopkins, MN
Hot Springs, AR
Hoven, SD
Humboldt, IA
Humboldt County, IA
Huntington, IA
Huron, SD
Iowa City, IA
Iowa Junction (Peoria), IL
Isabel, SD
Jacob's Switch, IA
Jamestown, ND
Jordan, MN
Kalo, IA
Kampeska, SD
Kanawha, IA
Kansas City, KS
Keithsburg, IL
Kenora, ON
Kensett, IA
Kenwood, MN
Keokuk, IA
Kilduff, IA
Kilkenny, MN
Klossner, MN
Labolt, SD
Lacey, IA
LaCrescent, MN
LaCrosse, WI
Lafayette, MN
LaGrange, IL
Lake Kampeska, Dakota Territory
Lake Lillian, MN
Lake Mills, IA
Lake Minnetonka, MN

Lake Riley, MN
Lake Tetonka, MN
Langdon, IA
LaSalle, MN
Latimer, IA
Laurel, IA
Le Beau, SD
Leland, IA
Lena, IA
Leola, SD
Linby, IA
Lindstrom, MN
Linwood, MN
Liscomb, IA
Little York, IL
Livermore, IA
Lockman, IA
Lomax, IL
London Mills, IL
Long Lake, SD
Lowry, SD
Luverne, IA
Lyle, MN
Lynnville, IA
Lynnville Junction, IA
Madison, MN
Madison Junction, IA
Maine, IA
Mallard, IA
Malta, IA
Manchester, MN
Manitou, MN
Manitou Junction, MN
Mankato, MN
Manly, IA
Marietta, MN
Marquette, IA
Marsh, IA
Marshall, MN
Marshalltown, IA
Martinsburg, IA
Mason City, IA
Mason City Junction, IA
Maxon, IA
Maxwell, IL

McCallsburg, IA
Medford, MN
Mellette, SD
Mendota, MN
Merriam, MN
Middle Grove, IL
Minburn, IA
Minerva, IA
Minerva Junction, IA
Minnepolis, MN
Minnetonka Beach, MN
Minnetonka Mills, MN
Minnewashta, MN
Moberly, MO
Mobridge, SD
Moningers, IA
Monmouth, IL
Minnesota Transfer, MN
Monterey, MN
Montezuma, IA
Montezuma Junction, IA
Montgomery, MN
Moore, IA
Moorland, IA
Moravia, IA
Morning Sun, IA
Morton, MN
Mound City, SD
Mulfords, MN
Murphy, IA
Muscatine, IA
Nahon, SD
Nemo, IL
Newburg, IA
New Prague, MN
New Richland, MN
New Sharon, IA
Newton, IA
New Ulm, MN
Norbeck, SD
Norman, IA
North Redwood, MN
Northville, SD
Northwood, IA
Norwood, MN

Nugent, IA
Oakes, ND
Oak Grove, IA
Oakville, IA
Ogden, IA
Ogle, IL
Olaf, IA
Olds, IA
Ollie, IA
Omaha, NE
Onaka, SD
Onawa, IA
Ormsby, MN
Oskaloosa, IA
Otho, IA
Otisco, MN
Ottumwa, IA
Owatonna, MN
Packwood, IA
Palmer, MN
Park Forest, IL
Paton, IA
Pekay, IA
Pekin, IA
Peoria, IL
Perry, IA
Phelps, IL
Pickering, IA
Pierre, SD
Pilot Mound, IA
Pioneer, IA
Pipestone, MN
Plover, IA
Plymouth, IA
Plymouth Junction, IA
Prairie du Chien, WI
Quincy, IL
Raleigh, IA
Randolph, SD
Rapatee, IL
Red Wing, MN
Redwood, MN
Redwood Falls, MN
Rembrandt, IA
Revillo, SD

Richland, IA
Richmond, SD
Rippey, IA
Rockford, IL
Rock Island, IL
Rockwell, IA
Rockwell City, IA
Rogers, MN
Rogerton, IA
Roland, IA
Rolfe, IA
Rosebrook, IA
Ruthven, IA
Rutland, IA
Sawyer, MN
Searles, MN
Searsboro, IA
Seaton, IL
Shafer, MN
Shakopee, MN
Sheffield, IA
Sherburn, MN
Sibley, IA
Sioux City, IA
Sioux City Junction, MN
Sioux Falls, SD
Sioux Rapids, IA
Solberg's Point, MN
Spencer, IA
Spirit Lake, IA
Springfield, IA
St. Anthony, IA
St. Anthony Park, MN
State Center, IA
St. Benedict, IA
St. Cloud, MN
Steamboat Rock, IA
Stilson, IA
St. James, MN
St. Louis Park, MN
Storm Lake, IA
Story City, IA
St. Paul, MN
St. Peter, MN
Strandburg, SD
Stratford, SD
Sully, IA
Taintor, IA
Tara, IA
Taylor's Falls, MN
Terril, IA
Tolstoy, SD
Tonkawood, MN
Tracy, IA
Trail City, SD
Trimont, MN
Trivoli, IL
Troy, SD
Truesdale, IA
Twin Lakes, MN
Union, IA
Valley Junction, IA
Van Cleve, IA
Veo, IA
Victoria, MN
Waconia, MN
Wallace, SD
Waseca, MN
Waterloo, IA
Watertown, SD
Waterville, MN
Watonwan County, MN
Waukee, IA
Waverly, IA
Waverly, SD
Wayland, IA
Webster County, IA
Wecota, SD
West Des Moines, IA
West Keithsburg, IA
West Liberty, IA
Wetonka, SD
White Bear Lake, MN
Wildhurst, MN
Willmar, MN
Willow Creek, IA
Winfield, IA
Winona, MN
Winthrop, MN
Wood Lake, MN
Woolson, IA
Wright, IA
Wyoming, MN
Yahota, SD
Young America, MN
Zearing, IA
Zumbra Heights, MN

Notes

For a list of Minneapolis & St. Louis stations and other places mentioned and their states, see the appendix.

Below are abbreviations frequently used in the notes. Other abbreviations are found in the list of acronyms and shortened names near the beginning of this book.

AC	Author's Collection
AFE	Authority for Expenditure
C&NW	Chicago & North Western Secretary's Office, Chicago
ICC	Interstate Commerce Commission
JJHRL	James J. Hill Reference Library
MHS	Minnesota Historical Society
M&StL	Minneapolis & St. Louis

1. Expectancy

1. *Saint Paul Daily Minnesotan,* May 14, 1858.

2. *The Frontiersman* (Sauk Rapids, MN), April 8, 1858; Rasmus S. Saby, "Railroad Legislation in Minnesota, 1849 to 1875," *Collections of the Minnesota Historical Society* 15 (1915): 1–49; *Special Laws of the Territory of Minnesota for 1853* (Minneapolis: Hotchkiss, Staples & Jones, 1853), 27–32; *Session Laws of the Territory of Minnesota for 1855* (Minneapolis: Hotchkiss, Staples & Jones, 1855), 163–64.

3. Emory R. Johnson, *American Railway Transportation* (New York: D. Appleton, 1905), 24.

4. George Rogers Taylor, *The Transportation Revolution, 1815–1860* (New York: Holt, Rinehart & Winston, 1951), vi, 396–98; James Neal Primm, *Lion of the Valley: St. Louis, Missouri,* 2nd ed. (Boulder, CO: Pruett Publishing, 1990), 9, 49, 73, 107, 113, 165–69; William Cronon, *Nature's Metropolis: Chicago and the Great West* (New York: W. W. Norton, 1991), 26–29, 60–68, 110–15.

5. John H. Randall, "The Beginning of Railroad Building in Minnesota," *Collections of the Minnesota Historical Society* 15 (1915): 215–20; Ralph W. Hidy, Muriel E. Hidy, Roy V. Scott, and Don L. Hofsommer, *The Great Northern Railway: A History* (Minneapolis: University of Minnesota Press, 2004), 2–5.

6. St. Paul Chamber of Commerce, *Handbook of St. Paul* (St. Paul: St. Paul Chamber of Commerce, 1900), 73; Lucile M. Kane, *The Falls of St. Anthony: The Waterfall That Built Minneapolis* (St. Paul: Minnesota Historical Society Press, 1987), 9–41.

7. Kane, *Falls of St. Anthony,* 9–41.

8. Dwight L. Agnew, "Beginnings of the Rock Island Lines," *Journal of the Illinois State Historical Society* 46 (Winter 1953): 407–24; Richard C. Overton, *Burlington Route: A History of the Burlington Lines* (New York: Alfred A. Knopf, 1965), 60–61; *Yesterday and Today: A History of the Chicago & North Western Railway System* (Chicago: Chicago & North Western, 1910), 164–65; Don L. Hofsommer, "A Chronology of Iowa's Railroads," *Railroad History* (Spring 1975): 72–76.

9. Hidy et al., *Great Northern,* 318; Saby, "Railroad Legislation," 49–60; Christopher Columbus Andrews, *History of St. Paul with Illustrations and Biographical Sketches*

of Its Prominent Men and Pioneers (Syracuse, NY: D. Mason, 1890), 417–19; Isaac Atwater, *History of the City of Minneapolis, Minnesota,* part 1 (New York: Munsell, 1893), 329–30, 334–35; John C. Luecke, *Dreams, Disasters, and Demise: The Milwaukee Road in Minnesota* (Eagan, MN: Grenadier Publications, 1988), 53–73.

10. Judson W. Bishop, "History of the St. Paul & Sioux City Railroad, 1864–1881," *Collections of the Minnesota Historical Society* 10 (1905): 399–415; Andrews, *History of St. Paul,* 418–19; *Yesterday and Today,* 77; Atwater, *History of Minneapolis,* 329, 334–35.

11. *Yesterday and Today,* 61, 62, 71, 88, 165–66; Northern Pacific, Original Tracklaying Record, March 15, 1933.

12. Ellis Paxton Oberholtzer, *Jay Cooke: Financier of the Civil War,* 2 vols. (Philadelphia: George W. Jacobs, 1907), 2: 106–11, 244–45; Eugene V. Smalley, *History of the Northern Pacific Railroad* (New York: G. P. Putnam's Sons, 1883), 159–70, 186–87, 380–83; John L. Harnsberger, *Jay Cooke and Minnesota: The Formative Years of the Northern Pacific Railroad, 1868–1873* (New York: Arno Press, 1981), 70–72, 90.

13. Alfred D. Chandler Jr., *The Railroads: The Nation's First Big Business* (New York: Harcourt, Brace & World, 1965), 3–12, 21–24.

14. Kane, *Falls of St. Anthony,* 57–59; *Minneapolis Tribune,* May 27, 1867; F. H. Jackson, prep., *The Milwaukee Road, 1847–1939: A Brief Record of the Milwaukee Road from Chartering of Its First Predecessor Company to Date—August 1939* (Chicago: Chicago, Milwaukee, St. Paul & Pacific, 1939), 22.

2. Lethargy, Euphoria, and Panic

1. Thomas C. Cochran, "Did the Civil War Retard Industrialization?" *Mississippi Valley Historical Review* 67 (September 1961): 194–202; Alfred D. Chandler Jr., *The Visible Hand: The Managerial Revolution in American Business* (Cambridge, MA.: Harvard University Press, 1977), 58–78, 188–94, 240–57; Alfred D. Chandler Jr., "The Beginnings of 'Big Business' in American Industry," *Business History Review* 35 (Spring 1959): 88–101; Merle Curti and Kendall Birr, "The Immigrant and the American Image in Europe, 1840–1914," *Mississippi Valley Historical Review* 37 (September 1950): 203–30.

2. Agnes Larson, *History of the White Pine Industry in Minnesota* (Minneapolis: University of Minnesota Press, 1949), 14–19, 36, 51; Mildred Lucile Hartsough, *The Twin Cities as a Metropolitan Market: A Regional Study of the Economic Development of Minneapolis and St. Paul* (Minneapolis: University of Minnesota Press, 1925), 26–27; *Minneapolis Tribune,* August 31, 1873; *Compendium of History and Biography of Carver and Hennepin Counties, Minnesota* (Chicago: H. Taylor, 1915), 152–60.

3. Charles B. Kuhlman, "The Influence of the Minneapolis Flour Mills upon the Economic Development of Minnesota and the Northwest," *Minnesota History* 6 (June 1925): 141–54; George D. Rogers, "History of Flour Manufacture in Minnesota," *Collections of the Minnesota Historical Society* 10 (February 1905): 35–55; Paul Wallace Gates, *The Farmer's Age: Agriculture, 1815–1860* (New York: Harper & Row, 1960), 157–67; William C. Edgar, *The Medal of Gold: The Story of Industrial Achievement* (Minneapolis: Bellman Company), 17–33; Henrietta M. Larson, *The Wheat Market and the Farmer in Minnesota, 1858–1900* (Boston: Houghton-Mifflin, 1929), 68, 117; Charles Bryan Kuhlman, *The Development of the Flour Milling Industry in the United States with Special Reference to Minnesota* (Boston: Houghton-Mifflin, 1929), 117.

4. James Neal Primm, *Lion of the Valley: St. Louis, Missouri,* 2nd ed. (Boulder, CO: Pruett Publishing, 1990), 201–2, 346–47; Edgar, *Medal of Gold,* 31–32; Larson, *Wheat Market and Farmer,* 66–69; William Cronon, *Nature's Metropolis: Chicago and the Great West* (New York: W. W. Norton, 1991), 65–73, 110–15; Chandler, *The Visible Hand,* 209–13; Carlton J. Corliss, *Main Line of Mid-America: The Story of the Illinois Central* (New York: Creative Age Press, 1950), 61, 77–79.

5. *Minneapolis Tribune,* January 7, 1868; Christopher Columbus Andrews, *History of St. Paul with Illustrations and Biographical Sketches of Its Prominent Men and Pioneers* (Syracuse, NY: D. Mason, 1890), 411.

6. Emory R. Johnson, *American Railway Transportation* (New York: D. Appleton, 1905), 27; Andrews, *History of St. Paul,* 411.

7. *Poor's Manual of the Railroads, 1869–1870,* 222–28; *Cedar Falls Gazette,* July 21, 1865, November 30, 1866, and August 11, 1871; *Iowa Railroad Commissioners Report, 1896* (Des Moines: State of Iowa, 1896), 221; *Cedar Falls Gazette,* May 4, 1866, May 15, 1868, and November 12 and December 31, 1869.

8. Don L. Hofsommer, "The Grandest Railroad Project of the Age," *Annals of Iowa* 44 (Fall 1977): 118–36; *Cedar Falls Gazette,* March 20, April 27, and June 1, 1866. The Iowa Central *Railroad* should not be confused with the Iowa Central *Railway* of a later date.

9. Don L. Hofsommer, "The Railroad and an Iowa Editor: A Case Study," *Annals of Iowa* 41 (Fall 1972): 1073–1103.

10. *American Railroad Journal,* January 7, 1832; James A. Ward, *Railroads and the Character of America, 1820–1887* (Knoxville: University of Tennessee Press, 1986), 10, 93–95; *St. Anthony Democrat,* January 14, 1870; Claire Leslie Marquette, "The Business Activities of C. C. Washburn," Ph.D. dissertation, University of Wisconsin, Madison, 1940, 327–28; Isaac Atwater, ed., *History of the City of Minneapolis, Minnesota* (New York: Munsell, 1893), 330.

11. Minutes of the Minnesota Western Rail Road Constituting Minute Book of the Minneapolis & St. Louis Railroad (M&StL) to 8-28-80, August 26 and December 27, 1869 (entries are by date, not page number; hereinafter cited as M&StL Minute Book); *Minnesota Executive Documents 1872,* 1, 143–44; *Journal of the . . . Minnesota Senate* (1870), 42; *Minneapolis Tribune,* February 11, 1870.

12. *St. Anthony Democrat,* February 11, 18, and 25, 1870; *Minneapolis Tribune,* February 17 and March 6, 1870; M&StL Minute Book, April 1, 1871.

13. Atwater, *History of Minneapolis,* 335; *Minneapolis Tribune,* December 15, 1870, and February 2, July 18, and August 9, 1871.

14. *Minneapolis Tribune,* July 23, 1871; Atwater, *History of Minneapolis,* 330, 335; *St. Anthony Democrat,* January 14 and March 11, 1870.

15. *Minneapolis Tribune,* July 23, 1871; Atwater, *History of Minneapolis,* 330–35; *St. Anthony Democrat,* January 14 and March 11, 1870.

16. M&StL Minute Book, April 15, 1871; M&StL Contract File 215, August 27, 1874, Chicago & North Western Secretary's Office, Chicago (C&NW); *Minneapolis Tribune,* May 27 and 31, 1870, *St. Anthony Democrat,* November 17, 1870.

17. *Minneapolis Tribune,* July 18, August 15, and November 15, 1871.

18. *Minneapolis Tribune,* November 26 and 29, 1871; *St. Anthony Democrat,* March 11, 1870.

19. *New York Times,* October 31, 1891; *St. Paul Press,* February 16, 1870; R. I. Holcombe and William H. Bingham, eds., *Compendium of History and Biography of Minneapolis and Hennepin County Minnesota* (Chicago: Henry Taylor & Co., 1914), 216–17; Atwater, *History of Minneapolis,* 545–51; Oberholtzer, *Jay Cooke,* 2: 245; Harnsberger, *Jay Cooke,* 74; *St. Paul Pioneer,* February 17, 1871; Larson, *Wheat Market and Farmer,* 281.

20. *St. Anthony Democrat,* March 18, 1870; M&StL Minute Book, May 1 and 3, 1871; *Minneapolis Tribune,* May 2, 1871; *St. Anthony Democrat,* November 2, 1871; *Minneapolis Tribune,* July 23, 1871; Minneapolis & Duluth Railroad (M&D) Minute Book 1, 1, 3, 30, Minnesota Historical Society (MHS); Lake Superior & Mississippi (LS&M), Annual Report, 1872, 12.

21. Atwater, *History of Minneapolis,* 994–98; August J. Veenendaal Jr., *Slow Train to Paradise: How Dutch Investors Helped Build American Railroads* (Stanford, CA: Stanford University Press, 1996), 234; Marquette, "Business Activities of Washburn," 387; F. K. Bennett and J. S. McLintock, *The M&StL Railroad Co. History* (M&StL, 1921), 13; *St. Anthony Democrat,* November 30, 1871; *Poor's Manual of the Railroads, 1872–1873* (New York: Poor's Manual, 1973), 230–31; LS&M, Minute Book 2, 90, 99, MHS 136.D.11, Box 1; Edward Vernon, *American Railway Manual* (New York: American Manual Company, 1873), 531; H. T. Welles, *Autobiography and Reminiscences,* 2 vols. (Minneapolis: Marshall Robinson, 1899), 2: 139; Larson, *Wheat Market and Farmer,* 365–66; LS&M, Annual Report, 1872, 19; ibid., 1871, 10–11.

22. *Minneapolis Tribune,* September 8, 19, and 21, 1872.

23. *St. Paul Pioneer,* March 14, 1871; Francis M. Carroll, *Crossroads in Time: A History of Carleton County, Minnesota* (Cloquet, MN: Carleton County Historical Society, 1987), 108–15; LS&M, Annual Report, 1872, 9; Oberholtzer, *Jay Cooke,* 2: 334–49; Larson, *Wheat Market and Farmer,* 334–69; *St. Paul Pioneer,* March 31, 1872; E. V. Smalley, *Northern Pacific Railroad Book of Reference* (New York: E. Wells Sackett & Rankin, 1883), 86, 90, 92, 114; Oberholtzer, *Jay Cooke,* 2: 421–39, 511–14.

24. LS&M, Directors Minute Book 2, 209, MHS; Smalley, *NP Book of Reference,* 116, 118, 120, 124.

25. M&D Minute Book 1, 80, 231, MHS; LS&M, Annual Report, 1873, 9; Smalley, *NP Book of Reference,* 116.

3. Albert Lea at Last

1. Claire Leslie Marquette, "The Business Activities of C. C. Washburn," Ph.D. dissertation, University of Wisconsin, Madison, 1940, 341; *Minneapolis Tribune,* April 3, 1872; *St. Paul Weekly Press,* April 1, 1875; Burlington, Cedar Rapids & Northern (BCR&N), Annual Report, 1877, 1.

2. Railway Age, *Biographical Directory of Railway Officials of America* (Chicago: Railway Age, 1887), 39; *Executive Documents . . . State of Minnesota . . . 1873,* 2: 136, 360–61; ibid., 1874, 1: 66, 223, 226; ibid., 1875, 2: 176–78; ibid., 1876, 2: 673.

3. *Minneapolis Tribune,* June 7, 1872, November 13 and December 29, 1874; *Traveler's Official Guide* (January 1875), schedule 273; tabular data from M&StL operations,

1873–1960, derived from *Poor's Manuals,* Minnesota and Iowa railroad commission annual reports, and M&StL annual reports (hereinafter cited as M&StL tabular data).

4. M&StL tabular data.

5. Warren Upham, *Minnesota Geographic Names: Their Origins and Historic Significance* (St. Paul: Minnesota Historical Society, 1920), 81; *Minneapolis Tribune,* December 29, 1874; *Annual Report of the Board of Trade of Minneapolis, 1877,* 67–75.

6. *Minneapolis Tribune,* December 11, 1873; Minneapolis & Duluth Railroad Co. to the Holders of the first Mortgage Bonds of the Minneapolis & Duluth Railroad Co., January 30, 1874, AC; *Executive Documents . . . State of Minnesota . . . 1876,* 2: 619; *Minnesota Railroad Commission Report, 1877,* 339; ibid., 1873, 331; Richard S. Prosser, *Rails to the North Star: One Hundred Years of Railroad Evolution in Minnesota* (Minneapolis: Dillon Press, 1966), 142.

7. *Rock Island Magazine* 17 (October 1922): 34; *Chicago, Burlington & Quincy* (CB&Q), Annual Report, 1872, 66; ibid., 1875, 29; Richard C. Overton, *Burlington Route: A History of the Burlington Lines* (New York: Alfred A. Knopf, 1965), 151, 165; W. W. Baldwin, preparer, CB&Q, *Corporate History of the Chicago, Burlington & Quincy Railroad Company and Affiliated Companies* (Chicago: CB&Q, 1921), 144, 284–85, 296–99; Overton, *Burlington Route,* 174, 231–32.

8. *St. Paul Weekly Press,* April 1, 1875; *St. Paul Weekly Pioneer,* January 1, 1875; W. D. Washburn to W. D. Hale, January 12 and 13, 1877, W. D. Hale papers, MHS; First Consolidated Mortgages Minneapolis & St. Louis Railroad Company to Central Trust Company of New York, Trustee, November 2, 1894, 18, AC.

9. *Minneapolis Tribune,* April 11, 1877; Upham, *Minnesota Geographic Names,* 198–205, 300–305, 507–12, 564–67; *Minneapolis Tribune,* August 21 and October 13, 17, and 23, 1877; James E. Child, *Child's History of Waseca County, Minnesota* (Waseca, MN: Privately published by the author, 1905), 225, 291–94, 321, 324–26.

10. *Albert Lea (MN) Enterprise,* August 23, September 6 and 13, and November 15, 1877; Edward D. Neill, *History of Freeborn County* (Minneapolis: Minnesota Historical Company, 1882), 355, 377; Franklyn Curtiss-Wedge, *History of Freeborn County Minnesota* (Chicago: H. C. Cooper, 1911), 168.

11. *Albert Lea Enterprise,* November 15, 1877; *Minneapolis Tribune,* November 12–15, 1877.

12. *Albert Lea Enterprise,* September 20, 1877; *Minneapolis Tribune,* August 28 and September 11, 1877.

13. C&NW, Annual Report, 1878, 20; *Minneapolis Tribune,* November 13, 1877; *Annual Report of the Minneapolis Board of Trade,* 1877, 44; 133 ICC 18–21.

14. *Annual Report of the Minneapolis Board of Trade, 1877,* advertising section; *Traveler's Official Railway Guide* (May 1878), 425–28; ibid. (June 1878), xxxiv, 468–69; *Railroad Gazette* 11 (March 8, 1878): 130.

15. Marquette, "Business Activities of Washburn," 352–54; M&StL, Annual Report, 1878, 7–8.

16. George H. Miller, *Railroads and the Granger Laws* (Madison: University of Wisconsin Press, 1971), 150–51; *Yesterday and Today: A History of the Chicago and North Western Railway System* (Chicago: C&NW, 1910), 71, 77, 164–66; *Railroad Gazette* 5 (October 11, 1873): 413.

17. Corporate History of the Chicago, St. Paul, Minneapolis & Omaha Railway Company (April 1, 1940), 1, 8, 13–23; *Yesterday and Today,* 81, 170; Judson W. Bishop, "History of the St. Paul & Sioux City Railroad, 1864–1881," *Minnesota Historical Society Collections* 10 (1905): 399–415.

18. *Minnesota Railroad Commission Report, 1878,* 504; ibid., 1879, 22; *Minneapolis Tribune,* July 6, 11, 12, and 15, October 23, and November 8, 1878; M&StL Minute Book, August 26, 1878.

19. *St. Paul Pioneer Press,* October 24–25, 1878; *Minneapolis Tribune,* October 28 and November 1 and 2, 1878; Corporate History of the Chicago, St. Paul, Minneapolis & Omaha Railway Company (April 1, 1940), 20; *Minneapolis Tribune,* July 26 and 29, 1879, and April 21, 1880; M&StL Minute Book, July 2 and October 18, 1879.

20. Tabular data from LS&M Annual Reports, 1873–76; *Minnesota Railroad Commission Report, 1875,* 41–42; NP, Annual Report, 1876, 10–11; Eugene V. Smalley, *History of the Northern Pacific Railroad* (New York: G. P. Putnam's Sons, 1883), 295; Eugene V. Smalley, *Northern Pacific Book of Reference* (New York: E. Wells Sackett & Rankin, 1883), 147.

21. *Railroad Gazette* 2 (July 18, 1879): 39; ibid. (July 25, 1879): 404; ibid. (August 1, 1879): 421; ibid. (August 8, 1879): 433; *St. Paul Dispatch,* July 24 and August 25, 1879; *Minnesota Railroad Commission Report, 1879,* 39; M&StL Minute Book, August 2, 1879.

22. Marquette, "Business Activities of Washburn," 353.

23. Leland L. Sage, *A History of Iowa* (Ames: Iowa State University Press, 1974), 12–17, 310; John L. Larson, *Bonds of Enterprise: John Murray Forbes and Western Development in America's Railway Age* (Cambridge, MA: Harvard University Press, 1984), 162; *Iowa Railroad Commission Report, 1880,* 53; Iowa Board of Immigration, *Iowa: The Home for Im-*

migrants (Des Moines: Iowa Board of Immigration, 1870), 28–29; *Annual Report of the Minneapolis Board of Trade, 1877,* 18; *Railway World* 6 (August 7, 1880): 746; John R. Stilgoe, *Metropolitan Corridor: Railroads and the American Scene* (New Haven, CT: Yale University Press, 1983), 3.

24. Marquette, "Business Activities of Washburn," 344–50; H. T. Welles, *Autobiography and Reminiscences,* 1: 142–43; *History of Kossuth and Humboldt Counties, Iowa* (Springfield, IL: 1884), 661.

25. *Iowa Railroad Commission Report, 1896,* 227; *St. Paul Pioneer Press,* July 30, 1878, and May 1 and 29, 1879; *Lake Mills (IA) Graphic,* June 18, 1969; *Railway World* 5 (September 27, 1879): 925; Articles of Incorporation, Fort Dodge & Fort Ridgely Railroad and Telegraph Company: Miscellaneous Record, Book I, 58. Webster County Recorders Office, Fort Dodge, Iowa; ICC, *Valuation Report,* vol. 137 (1928), 812, 866, 867; H. M. Pratt, *History of Fort Dodge & Webster County,* 2 vols. (Chicago: 1912), 1: 221–24.

26. Minute Book of the Fort Dodge & Fort Ridgely R. R. & Telegraph Company, 7-28-1876/7-28-188(?), March 25, 1878 (entries are by date, not page number; hereinafter cited as FD&FR Minute Book); *Iowa Railroad Commission Report, 1878,* 259; ibid., 1879, 289–95.

27. FD&FR Minute Book; *Iowa Railroad Commission Report, 1880,* 486–91; M&StL Minute Book, July 2 and 19, 1879.

28. *Railway World* 5 (September 27, 1879): 925; *Lake Mills Graphic,* February 9, 1877; *Forest City (IA) Summit,* July 28, 1955.

29. Clyde Clarkson Way, ed., *Biography and Memoirs of Thomas Asbury Way* (privately published, 1946), 24–25; *Iowa Railroad Commission Report, 1880,* 244–46; Mortgage, Minneapolis & St. Louis Railway to Central Trust Company of New York, 1879; M&StL Minute Book, October 14, 1879; *Minneapolis Tribune,* March 20, 1880; *Britt (IA) News-Tribune,* January 26, 1949; *Corwith, Iowa "Then" and "Now"* (Corwith: Corwith Centennial Committee, 1980), 13; *Minneapolis Tribune,* June 29, 1880.

30. *Lake Mills Graphic,* June 18, 1969; *Des Moines Register,* June 24, 1973; *Corwith "Then" and "Now,"* 13.

31. *Railway Age* 5 (September 23, 1880): 503; *Railway World* 6 (August 4, 1880): 781; *Minneapolis Tribune,* August 24 and November 23, 1880; Hubert L. Olin, *Coal Mining in Iowa* (Des Moines: State Mining Board, 1965), 40, 80; James H. Lees, "History of Coal Mining in Iowa," *Iowa Geological Survey* 22 (1913): 582–83; Iowa Board of Immigration, *Home for Immigrants,* 23; E. R. Landis, *Coal Resources of Iowa* (Des Moines: Iowa Geological Survey, 1965), Table 15; *Corwith "Then" and "Now,"* 13; *Iowa Railroad Commission Report, 1880,* 574–75, 582–85.

32. St. Paul & Duluth (StP&D), Stockholders Minute Book No. 1, 1, MHS; *Minnesota Railroad Commission Report, 1878,* 576; ibid., 1879, 39; *St. Paul Dispatch,* July 24, 1879; *St. Paul Pioneer Press,* July 15, 16, and 18, 1879; *Railroad Gazette* 2 (August 1, 1879): 421.

33. *Railroad Gazette* 2 (August 8, 1879): 433; *St. Paul Dispatch,* July 24, 1879; M&StL Minute Book, August 2, 1879; *St. Paul Pioneer Press,* February 10, 20, and 25, 1880; *Railway Age* 5 (April 29, 1880): 227; *Minneapolis Tribune,* February 10 and April 28 and 29, 1880; StP&D, Stockholders Minute Book No. 1, 1, MHS; Taylor's Falls & Lake Superior, Stock Book, passim, MHS; M&StL Minute Book, March 20 and May 8, 1880.

34. *Minneapolis Tribune,* May 15 and November 5 and 10, 1880; *Dalles Visitor* (St. Croix Falls, WI, and Taylor's Falls, MN), Summer 1972.

4. Optimism and Realism

1. *Minnesota Railroad Commission Report, 1880,* 775; *Iowa Railroad Commission Report, 1881,* 146–50; FD&FR Minute Book, September 15, 1880, and April 20, 1881, C&NW.

2. Mortgage, Minneapolis & St. Louis Railway Company to Central Trust Company of New York, January 5, 1881, AC; *St. Paul Pioneer Press,* January 7, 1881; *Railroad Gazette* 14 (November 11, 1881): 640.

3. *Special Laws of the Territory of Minnesota for 1853,* 28; *General Laws of the State of Minnesota, 1869,* 340–41; *Minnesota Railroad Commission Report, 1873,* 331; *Special Laws of the State of Minnesota for 1874,* 326; *Executive Documents of the State of Minnesota for the Year 1876,* 2. 619, *Minnesota Railroad Commission Report, 1879,* 26; *Minneapolis Journal,* August 25, 1907; *Minneapolis Tribune,* November 7 and 13, 1877; *Minneapolis Journal,* January 13, 22, and 28, 1879; Mildred Lucile Hartsough, *The Twin Cities as a Metropolitan Market: A Regional Study of the Economic Development of Minneapolis and St. Paul* (Minneapolis: University of Minnesota Press, 1925), 29.

4. *Railway Age* 4 (March 13, 1879): 131; *Minneapolis Tribune,* January 28, 31, February 2, 6, and 28, April 21, June 24, and December 11, 1880.

5. Hallie Farmer, "The Economic Background of Frontier Populism," *Mississippi Valley Historical Review* 10 (March 1924): 406; C&NW, Annual Report, 1878, 11; *Railway Age* 5 (July 29, 1880): 405; *Annual Report of the Minneapolis Board of Trade, 1877,* 67.

6. *Minneapolis Tribune,* April 5, 19, and 20, 1881; *Railroad Gazette* 13 (April 22, 1881): 226; *Railroad Age* 6 (May 12, 1881): 263; Mortgage, Minneapolis & St. Louis Railway to Central Trust Company of New York, June 20, 1881, AC; *Sibley County Independent* (Henderson, MN), January 28, February 4, April 8, July 29, and November 18, 1881; *Winthrop News,* October 8, 1931; Frank Curtiss-Wedge, *History of Redwood County,* 2 vols. (Chicago: H. C. Cooper Jr., 1916), 1: 4, 233–34; *Railroad Gazette* 13 (July 27, 1881): 407; ibid. (October 14, 1881): 562; ibid. (November 11, 1881): 640; ibid. (December 23, 1881): 175; Warren Upham, *Minnesota Geographic Names: Their Origins and Historical Significance* (St. Paul: Minnesota Historical Society, 1920), 83–84, 221–25, 518–20.

7. *Poor's Manual of the Railroads, 1882,* 731–32; M&StL tabular data, AC; *Railway World* 7 (January 22, 1881): 77; *Minneapolis Tribune,* August 24, 1880, and January 18, 1881; *Railroad Gazette* 13 (October 28, 1881): 610.

8. M&StL Minute Book, March 20, 1878, C&NW.

9. *Minneapolis Tribune,* April 22, 1879, and October 2, 1880; *Traveler's Official Guide* (January 1882), 241; ibid. (February 1882), 247.

10. *Minneapolis Tribune,* June 28, July 17, August 5 and 9, and September 5, 1878; *Britt News-Tribune,* January 26, 1949; *Minneapolis Tribune,* July 12–25, 1878.

11. Agnes Larson, *History of the White Pine Industry in Minnesota* (Minneapolis: University of Minnesota Press, 1949), 111; *Railroad World* 6 (August 1880): 771; M&StL tabular data; M&StL, Annual Report, 1878, 23–31; ibid., 1879, 23–33.

12. *Railroad World* 6 (August 14, 1880): 777; M&StL, Annual Report, 1879, 16–18, 25–31; ibid., 1878, 23–31.

13. Alfred D. Chandler Jr., *The Visible Hand: The Managerial Revolution in American* Business (Cambridge, MA: Harvard University Press, 1977), 88, 120; Vincent P. Carosso, *The Morgans: Private Bankers, 1854–1913* (Cambridge, MA: Harvard University Press, 1987), 246; John Lauritz Larson, *Bonds of Enterprise: John Murray Forbes and Western Development in America's Railway Age* (Cambridge, MA: Harvard University Press, 1984), 177; James A. Ward, "Railroads in the American Context," *Railroad History* (Autumn 1994): 12–13.

14. Rendig Fels, *American Business Cycles, 1865–1897* (Chapel Hill: University of North Carolina Press, 1959), 125–26; *Railroad Gazette* 14 (March 17, 1882): 174–75; ibid. (March 24, 1882): 187; *Minneapolis Tribune,* February 12 and March 18, 1882; *Railroad Gazette* 14 (July 21, 1882): 449.

15. Frank P. Donovan Jr., *Mileposts on the Prairie: The Story of the Minneapolis & St. Louis Railway* (New York: Simmons Boardman, 1950), 69–76; *Railway Age* 6 (June 16, 1881): 330; *Official Guide* (November 1881): 253; Joyce Quinn, ed., *Lydia Ferguson Diary, 1854–1886* (Excelsior, MN: Excelsior–Lake Minnetonka Historical Society, 1981), 5; *Minneapolis Journal,* May 23, 1937; *Minneapolis Star Journal,* August 26, 1940; Kathryn H. Moody, "The Reminiscences of Lowell Henderson Moody," *Hennepin County History* (Winter 1967): 7–12; *Minneapolis Journal,* September 1, 1882.

16. James Gray, *Business without Boundary: The Story of General Mills* (Minneapolis: University of Minnesota Press, 1988), 44–45; Theodore Blegen, *Minnesota: A History of the State* (Minneapolis: University of Minnesota Press, 1963), 356–57; *St. Paul Pioneer Press,* July 15, 16, and 18, 1879; *Minnesota Railroad Commissioner Report, 1879,* 39; *St. Paul Pioneer Press,* July 15, 1879; *Railroad Gazette* 11 (July 18, 1879): 390; ibid. (July 25, 1879): 404; Karel D. Bicha, *C. C. Washburn and the Upper Mississippi Valley* (New York: Garland Publishing, 1995), 173–75; *St. Paul Dispatch,* July 24 and August 25, 1879.

17. *Railroad Gazette* 11 (August 29, 1879): 463; *Minneapolis Tribune,* October 28, 1873.

18. *Minnesota Railroad Commission Report, 1880,* 853–55; J. S. Kennedy to James J. Hill, February 26, 1881, General Correspondence, James J. Hill Reference Library (JJHRL); James J. Hill to J. S. Kennedy, April 7, 1881, StPM&M Letter Book 4: 802 (1880–81), JJHRL; *Minneapolis Tribune,* July 8, 10, 14, and 22, 1879; *St. Paul Daily Globe,* December 31, 1881; StPM&M, Annual Report, 1880–81, 506; Ralph W. Hidy, Muriel E. Hidy, Roy V. Scott, and Don L. Hofsommer, *The Great Northern Railway: A History* (Minneapolis: University of Minnesota Press, 2004), 40–41; *Minneapolis Tribune,* December 2, 1881; Hidy et al., *Great Northern,* 45–46; StPM&M, Annual Report, 1882, 11–12; ibid., 1883, 13; Chicago, St. Paul, Minneapolis & Omaha Railway Company (CStPM&O), Corporate History of the Chicago, St. Paul, Minneapolis & Omaha Railway Company (CStPM&O, 1940), 19, 22, 24, 30–31; *Yesterday and Today: A History of the Chicago & North Western Railway System* (Chicago: C&NW, 1910), 82–84; *Poor's Manual, 1882,* 727–30; Railway Age, *Biographical Directory of the Railway Officials of America* (Chicago: Railway Age, 1896), 378–79; compilation of data from annual reports of C&NW, CStPM&O, and Chicago, Rock Island & Pacific (CRI&P) for 1880.

19. Fred Taylor to the Bondholders and Stockholders of

the Burlington, Cedar Rapids & Northern Railway Company, January 17, 1877, AC; BCR&N, Annual Report, 1878, 10, 13; *Official Guide* (April 1878), 454–55; *Rock Island Magazine* 17 (December 1922): 21.

20. CB&Q, Annual Report, 1879, 24; *Iowa Board of Railroad Commissioners Report, 1879,* 104–5; *Rock Island Magazine* 17 (December 1922): 21; ICC, Valuation Docket 715, Chicago, Burlington & Quincy Railroad (1927), 240–41; ICC, Valuation Docket 152, Chicago, Rock Island & Pacific Railway (1929), 936–38; *Minneapolis Tribune,* September 6, 1879.

21. Stuart Daggett, *Railroad Reorganization* (New York: Augustus M. Kelley, 1967), 311–15; Augustus J. Veenendaal Jr., *Slow Train to Paradise: How Dutch Investors Helped Build America's Railroads* (Stanford, CA: Stanford University Press, 1996), 96–97; *Commercial & Financial Chronicle* 30 (June 26, 1880): 663–65; William E. Hayes, *Iron Road to Empire: The History of the Rock Island Lines* (New York: Simmons-Boardman, 1953), 81–82, 102–3; *Railroad Gazette* 13 (October 7, 1881): 561; Chandler, *The Visible Hand,* 134–35; Fels, *American Business Cycles,* 125–27.

22. Quoted in Richard C. Overton, *Burlington Route: A History of the Burlington Lines* (New York: Alfred A. Knopf, 1965), 169; Bicha, *Washburn and the Mississippi Valley,* 186.

23. Bicha, *Washburn and the Mississippi Valley,* 175–76; M&StL Minute Book, July 29 and October 14, 1879, and May 22, 1880; *Minneapolis Tribune,* February 14 and March 5, 1881; *St. Paul Pioneer-Press,* January 25, 28–31, and February 3, 1881; Gray, *Business without Boundary,* 40.

24. *Poor's Manual, 1882,* 732; William D. Washburn to James J. Hill, January 22, 1882, General Correspondence, JJHRL; *Minneapolis Tribune,* February 12 and 14, March 20 and 24, and April 20 and 30, 1882; CRI&P, Annual Report, 1882, 13–14; *Railroad Gazette* 14 (April 28, 1882): 262; *Railway Age* 7 (March 23, 1882): 164.

25. *Minneapolis Tribune,* May 2, 1882; *Railway Age* 7 (March 30, 1882): 169; ibid. (May 4, 1882): 248; Thomas C. Cochran, *Railroad Leaders, 1845–1890: The Business Mind in Action* (Cambridge, MA: Harvard University Press, 1953), 136; *Minneapolis Tribune,* May 3–5, 7, and 12, 1882; *Railroad Gazette* 14 (May 5, 1882): 278; ibid. (May 12, 1882): 294; ibid. (July 21, 1882): 447; *Railway Age* 7 (May 18, 1882): 276; *Minneapolis Tribune,* July 30 and November 24, 1882.

26. *Minneapolis Tribune,* September 11, 1877, July 30, 1879, January 1, 1883, and January 8, 1873; Gray, *Business without Boundary,* 45.

5. The Great Rock Island Route

1. CRI&P, "From Iowa-Minnesota State Line to Saint Paul-Minneapolis, Minnesota," in Volume E, Public Relations Department, E-14–E-15 (hereinafter cited as Volume E); Don L. Hofsommer, *Prairie Oasis: The Railroads, Steamboats, and Resorts of Iowa's Spirit Lake Country* (Des Moines: Waukon & Mississippi Press, 1975), 13; CRI&P, Annual Report, 1882, 13–14.

2. *Rock Island Magazine* 17 (December 1922): 22; Richard S. Prosser, *Rails to the North Star: One Hundred Years of Railroad Evolution in Minnesota* (Minneapolis: Dillon Press, 1966), 150, 171–72; *Minneapolis Tribune,* March 1 and May 20 and 23, 1882, and January 7 and 9, 1883; H. Roger Grant, *The Corn Belt Route: A History of the Chicago Great Western Railroad Company* (De Kalb: Northern Illinois University Press, 1984), 50–51; *Railway Age* 6 (December 1, 1881): 680; ibid. (September 28, 1882): 543; Roger Bee, Gary Browne, and John Luecke, *The Chicago Great Western in Minnesota* (Anoka, MN: Blue River Publications, 1984), 3–9; John L. Relf, *The Man Whose Dream Came True: A Biography of A. B. Stickney* (Dellwood, MN: Privately published by the author, 1992), 47–48.

3. *Railroad Gazette* 13 (November 11, 1881): 640; *Minneapolis Tribune,* November 30, 1881; *Railway Age* 6 (November 17, 1881), 656–57; *Railroad Gazette* 14 (January 1, 1882): 34; *Minneapolis Tribune,* June 13 and July 30, 1882; *Railroad Gazette* 14 (August 11, 1882): 496; StP&D Stockholders Minute Book No. 1, 29, 45–46, 49–50, MHS; StP&D, Annual Report, 1883, 23–24; *Minnesota Railroad Commissioner Report,* 1881, 62–65.

4. M&StL, Contract File 4310, C&NW; Corporate History of Chicago, St. Paul, Minneapolis, & Omaha Railway Company, April 1, 1940, 29; StPM&M and NP, General Contract, October 1, 1882, 7, 12–13, AC; *Minneapolis Tribune,* October 6 and 21, 1882.

5. *Minneapolis Tribune,* April 7, 1873; Minneapolis, St. Paul & Sault Ste. Marie (MStP&SSteM), Annual Report, 1959, 1; H. T. Welles, *Autobiography and Reminiscences,* 2 vols. (Minneapolis: Marshall Robinson, 1899), 2: 144–47; Isaac Atwater, ed., *History of the City of Minneapolis, Minnesota* (New York: Munsell & Co., 1893), 335–36.

6. MStP&SSteM, Annual Report, 1900, 5–8; *Poor's Manual of Railroads, 1887,* 816; *Minnesota Railroad and Warehouse Commission Report, 1899,* 587; John A. Gjevre, *Saga of the Soo: West from Shoreham* (Moorhead, MN: Gjevre Books, 1990), 13–19; Agnes Larson, *History of the White Pine Industry in Minnesota* (Minneapolis: University of Minnesota Press, 1949), 115; Charles B. Kuhlman,

"The Influence of the Minneapolis Flour Mills upon the Economic Development of Minneapolis and the Northwest," in *Minnesota History* 6 (June 1925): 145; *Minneapolis Tribune,* December 31, 1883.

7. Rendid Fels, *American Business Cycles, 1865–1897* (Chapel Hill: University of North Carolina Press, 1959), 127–30; *Railroad Gazette* 14 (December 29, 1882): 805; *Railway Review* (August 16, 1884): 428.

8. *Minneapolis Tribune,* December 31, 1883; BCR&N, Consolidated First Mortgage to Secure "Consolidated First Mortgage Five Per Cent Bonds," April 1, 1884–April 1, 1934, 22, 25, AC; *Minnesota Railroad Commission Report, 1884,* 586; Stuart Daggett, *Railroad Reorganization* (New York: Augustus M. Kelley, 1967), 315; *Railroad Gazette* 16 (April 4, 1884): 271; ibid. (April 11, 1884), 288; ibid. (April 18, 1884), 309; *Railway Age* 8 (December 13, 1883): 795; ibid., 9 (March 20, 1884): 189; *Minneapolis Tribune,* March 23, 1884; ICC, Chicago, Rock Island & Pacific Railway, Valuation Docket 152 (February 12, 1929), 997.

9. R.R. cable to James J. Hill, May 14, 1883, Great Northern (GN) Executive Department Vault 15 B, Box 25 C, AC.

10. *Minneapolis Tribune,* May 1, 1884; Warren Upham, *Minnesota Geographic Names: Their Origins and Historic Significance* (St. Paul: Minnesota Historical Society, 1920), 288–92, 448–54, 593–98; Frank Curtiss-Wedge, *History of Redwood County, Minnesota,* 2 vols. (Chicago: H. C. Cooper & Co., 1916), 1: 4, 232–35; L. R. Moyer and O. G. Dale, eds. *History of Chippewa and Lac qui Parle Counties Minnesota,* 2 vols. (Indianapolis: B. F. Bowen & Co., 1916), 1: 477–87, 557–65.

11. *Minneapolis Tribune,* August 1 and 14 and September 13, 1884; *Railroad Gazette* 16 (September 19, 1884): 692; ibid. (September 26, 1884): 709; *New York Times,* September 14, 25, and 27, 1884; *Railway Age* 9 (September 18, 1884): 591.

12. Upham, *Minnesota Geographic Names,* 595, 597; *Railway Age* 9 (September 1, 1884): 577; *Railroad Gazette* 16 (September 26, 1884): 709; *Minneapolis Tribune,* July 3, August 14 and 17, and October 5 and 28, 1884; BCR&N, Annual Report, 1884, x.

13. Tim Kolhei, *From Dusty Trails to Rusty Rails: The Rise and Fall of Hanley Falls, Minnesota* (Marshall, MN: Southwest History Center, Southwest State University, 1988), 4–9; Madison (MN) Centennial Committee, *Madison Historical Album* (Madison: Madison Centennial Committee, 1985), 11, 16–17; *Weekly Item* (Revillo, SD), September 6, 1934.

14. *Minneapolis Tribune,* October 5, 28, 1884.

15. Norm Cohen, *Long Steel Rail: The Railroad in American Folk Song* (Champaign: University of Illinois Press, 1981), 374–75; *Minneapolis Tribune,* July 27, 1883; M&StL, Time Table (July 1884), 3; *Official Guide* (May 1885), 244–47, 327–29.

16. *Official Guide* (June 1883), 296–97; M&StL, Time Table (July 1994), 6, 10.

17. *Minneapolis Tribune,* December 31, 1883; City of St. Paul, *Grand Opening of the Northern Pacific Railway Celebration at Saint Paul, Minnesota,* September 3, 1883 (compliments of the City of St. Paul, 1883), 66–68; Mark Twain, *Life on the Mississippi* (New York: Modern Library, 1993), 427; Christopher Columbus Andrews, *History of St. Paul with Illustrations and Biographical Sketches of Its Prominent Men and Pioneers* (Syracuse, NY: D. Mason, 1890), 422; Walter G. Berg, *Buildings and Structures of American Railroads* (New York: John Wiley & Sons, 1900), 426–31.

18. M&StL tabular data and annual reports of the railroad commissioners of Minnesota and Iowa.

19. Ibid.

20. *Minneapolis Chamber of Commerce Annual Report, 1884,* 39, 48–50; ibid., *1886,* 41–42, 117.

21. *Minneapolis Tribune,* January 9, 1883; *National Cyclopedia of American Biography,* vol. 14 (New York: J. T. White & Co., 1917), 450; Slason Thompson, *A Short History of American Railways* (Chicago: Bureau of Railway News and Statistics, 1925), 432–33.

22. *Boston Transcript,* August 5 and 11, 1886; *Commercial & Financial Chronicle,* August 29, 1885; O. H. Holt, *Dakota: Behold I Show You a Delightsome Land* (Chicago: Rand McNally, 1885), 88; *Chicago Tribune,* February 18, 1886; CRI&P, *The Western Trail,* vol. 5 (February 1886), 2; *Railroad Gazette* 18 (October 22, 1886): 732; John S. Kennedy to James J. Hill, June 28, 1886, General Correspondence, James J. Hill Collection, JJHRL.

23. *Western Trail* (a CRI&P publication) 5 (February 1886): 2; James J. Hill to J. S. Kennedy, July 8, 1886, JJH Letter Book 3-22-86/10-22-86, 268, James J. Hill Collection, JJHLR.

24. *Bradstreet's* 13/14 (April 17, 1886): 242; tabular data taken from *Minneapolis Chamber of Commerce Annual Reports, 1884–1889.*

25. *Minneapolis Tribune,* December 24, 1884; *Chicago Tribune,* February 19, 1886; *Railroad Gazette* 18 (June 25, 1886): 453.

26. G. H. Crosby, *History of CRI&P Ry Co.* (Chicago: CRI&P, 1902), 34; Richard C. Overton, *Burlington Route: A History of the Burlington Lines* (New York: Alfred A. Knopf, 1965), 196–98.

27. Charles E. Perkins to John Murray Forbes, November 1, 1883, NP President File 197-21-4, AC; *Chicago Tribune,* February 16, 1886; Map of Rock Island Lines Showing Lines Built and Acquired, April 29, 1922, AC; Daggett, *Railroad Reorganization,* 314–17; William E. Hayes, *Iron Road to Empire: The History of the Rock Island Lines* (New York: Simmons-Boardman, 1953), 127; CRI&P, Annual Report, 1889, 13–16.

28. Quoted in Saul Engelbourg and Leonard Bushkoff, *John Stewart Kennedy and the Financing of the Western Railroads* (East Lansing: Michigan State University Press, 1996), 120; quoted in *Minneapolis Tribune,* July 29, 1879; CM&StP, Annual Report, 1887, 14; Mildred Lucile Hartsough, *The Twin Cities as a Metropolitan Market: A Regional Study of the Economic Development of Minneapolis and St. Paul* (Minneapolis: University of Minnesota Press, 1925), 84–112; James A. Ward, *Railroads and the Character of America, 1820–1887* (Knoxville: University of Tennessee Press, 1986), 144; quoted in Richard C. Overton, *Perkins/Budd: Railway Statesmen of the Burlington* (Westport, CT: Greenwood Press, 1982), 48; W. M. Ackworth, *The Elements of Railway Economics* (Oxford, England: Clarendon Press, 1905), 76–77.

29. *Minnesota Railroad and Warehouse Commission Report, 1885,* 9–14; ibid., 1888, 31; *Iowa Railroad Commission Report, 1878,* 58; Leland L. Sage, *A History of Iowa* (Ames: Iowa State University Press, 1974), 204–7; *Railroad Gazette* 13 (November 2, 1888): 722.

30. Fels, *American Business Cycles,* 142; Harold E. Briggs, "The Great Dakota Boom, 1879 to 1886," *North Dakota Historical Quarterly* 4 (January 1930): 78–108; John N. Vogel, *Great Lakes Lumber on the Great Plains: The Laird, Norton Company in South Dakota* (Iowa City: University of Iowa Press, 1992), 134–37; Gilbert C. Fite, *The Farmer's Frontier, 1865–1900* (New York: Holt, Rinehart & Winston, 1966), 106–9.

31. *Minnesota Railroad & Warehouse Commission Report, 1888,* 390; *Winthrop (MN) News,* March 10, 1888; *New York Times,* January 14, 1888; *Minneapolis Tribune,* January 14, 1888.

32. W. H. Truesdale to Bondholders of the Minneapolis & St. Louis Railway Company, May 25, 1888, AC; *New York Times,* June 2 and 29, 1888; *Railway Age* 8 (June 15, 1888): 374; ibid. (July 6, 1888): 438.

6. Independent Again

1. M&StL, Annual Report, 1890, 10–11.

2. CRI&P, Annual Report, 1889, 13–17; *Official Guide* (December 1889), 318; *Rock Island Magazine* 21 (November 1926): 19–20; BCR&N, Annual Report, 1884, ix; ibid., 1888, 3; *Minneapolis Tribune,* February 25 and June 11, 1890.

3. *Minneapolis Tribune,* March 6, 1889; Agnes Larson, *History of the White Pine Industry in Minnesota* (Minneapolis: University of Minnesota Press, 1949), 229–46, 374–77; *Annual Report of the Minneapolis Chamber of Commerce, 1888,* 43; ibid., 1890, 42; ibid., 1892, 225–26.

4. *Annual Report of the Minneapolis Chamber of Commerce, 1888,* 42; *Minneapolis Tribune,* September 16, 1888, January 1, 1889, January 28, 1890, August 21, 1891; Isaac Atwater, *History of the City of Minneapolis, Minnesota,* 2 vols. (New York: Munsell, 1893), 1: 331–32; Charles Byron Kuhlman, *The Development of the Flour-Milling Industry in Minneapolis* (Boston: Houghton Mifflin, 1929), 165.

5. Minneapolis Railway Transfer Minute Book 1, March 31, 1883; *Minnesota Railroad and Warehouse Commission Report, 1904,* Entry "1," Railway Transfer Company of Minneapolis.

6. M&StL, Annual Report, 1893, 5–7; ibid., 1892, 7; ibid., 1890, 2, 8; *Railroad Gazette* 24 (April 18, 1892): 257; *Minneapolis Tribune,* November 25 and 27, 1890.

7. Lucile M. Kane, *The Falls of St. Anthony: The Waterfall That Built Minneapolis* (St. Paul: Minnesota Historical Society Press, 1987), 147; *Census of Minnesota, 1890,* 2–3; *Annual Report of the Saint Paul Chamber of Commerce, 1888,* 51, 83.

8. *American Heritage* 40 (November 1989): 11–14; Leland L. Sage, *A History of Iowa* (Ames: Iowa State University Press, 1974), 201; tabular data from annual reports of M&StL, Chicago Great Western, and CM&StP for 1893; *Report of Iowa Railroad Commissioners, 1890* (Des Moines: State of Iowa, 1890), 14; *Minneapolis Tribune,* August 2, 1890; M&StL, Annual Report, 1890, 4–5.

9. M&StL, Annual Report, 1892, 4; ibid., 1895, 5.

10. *Minneapolis Tribune,* January 25, April 6, June 10, and September 15, 1889; January 19, May 10, September 7, October 28, and November 1, 1890.

11. StP&D, Annual Report, 1888, 8, 60–61; M&StL, Annual Report, 1895, 5; tabular data derived from StP&D annual reports, 1890–94.

12. James J. Hill to John S. Kennedy, January 7, 1888; James J. Hill to E. T. Nichols, September 4, 7, 9, and 11, 1889; C. H. Warren to E. T. Nichols, September 17, 1889, James J. Hill papers, all from Letter Books and General Correspondence, JJHRL.

13. *Minneapolis Tribune,* June 18, July 10 and 11, and August 4, 1891.

14. *Minneapolis Tribune,* August 4, 1891; Watertown

(SD) City Council, "Glimpse of a Marvelous City . . . Watertown in 1889" (Watertown City Council, 1889), 16–17 and advertising following; Gilbert Fite, *The Farmers' Frontier, 1865–1900* (New York: Holt, Rinehart & Winston, 1966), 108–9.

15. *Bradstreet's* (April 26, 1890): 265; Redig Fels, *American Business Cycles, 1865–1897* (Chapel Hill: University of North Carolina Press, 1959), 159, 179–92; *Official Guide* (June 1894), xxii.

16. CB&Q, Annual Report, 1879, 19; *New York Times,* January 14, 1888; *Minnesota Railroad and Warehouse Commission Annual Report, 1888,* 30.

17. *Railroad Gazette* 23 (November 27, 1981): 850; M&StL, Annual Report, 1891, 7; ibid., 1892, 4–9; ibid., 1893, 8, 16; *New York Times,* August 13, 1892.

18. *New York Times,* September 3, 1892, and April 7 and May 8, 1893; W. S. Mellen to T. F. Oakes, November 1, 1892, NP General Manager Files 134.F.1.5, MHS; James J. Hill to W. H. Truesdale, August 30, 1892, GN President Files 479, Box 2477, MHS; *Poor's Manual, 1893,* 403–4; ibid., 1892, 153; M&StL, Annual Report, 1893, 9.

19. *New York Times,* June 7, September 1, 28, 1894; *Railroad Gazette* 26 (August 24, 1894), 588; *Minneapolis Tribune,* September 1 and October 4 and 12, 1894; *Record Containing Proceedings Held in the District Court of Hennepin County, State of Minnesota, in the Case of Henry Seibert, Trustee, against the Minneapolis & St. Louis Railway and Others, June 28, 1888 to September 1, 1892,* 2 vols. and supplements, passim.

20. *Railway Age* 6 (May 19, 1881): 272; 137 ICC 814–16; *Minneapolis Tribune,* November 3, 1894; *National Cyclopedia of American Biography,* vol. 14 (New York: J. T. White, 1917), 450–51.

21. *Minneapolis Tribune,* October 12, 1894.

22. Albro Martin, "Railroads and the Equity Receivership: An Essay on Institutional Change," *Journal of Economic History* 34 (September 1974): 685–709, esp. 689; Alfred D. Chandler, *The Visible Hand: The Managerial Revolution in American Business* (Cambridge, MA: Harvard University Press, 1977), 204–5.

23. *Railway Age* 88 (June 14, 1930): 1459; Maury Klein, *Union Pacific: Birth of a Railroad, 1862–1893* (Garden City, NJ: Doubleday, 1987), 572; *Who Was Who in America,* vol. 1 (Chicago: Marquis Who's Who, 1943), 163–64; Louis Tuck Renz, *The History of the Northern Pacific Railroad* (Fairfield, WA: Ye Galleon Press, 1980), 164–80.

24. M&StL, Annual Report, 1895, 4–5.

25. Theodore C. Blegen, *Minnesota: A History of the State* (Minneapolis: University of Minnesota Press, 1975), 390–98; St. Paul Chamber of Commerce, Annual Report, 1898, 82–84; *St. Paul Union Stockyards: 1886 Centennial Year 1986* (St. Paul: Fahey & Associates, 1986), 14–17.

26. Allan G. Bogue, *From Prairie to Corn Belt: Farming on the Illinois and Iowa Prairie in the Nineteenth Century* (Chicago: Quadrangle Books, 1963), 216–40, 285; Fred A. Shannon, *The Farmer's Last Frontier: Agriculture, 1860–1897* (New York: Harper & Row, 1945), 163, 165, 257–58; Keach Johnson, "Iowa's Industrial Roots, 1890–1910," *Annals of Iowa* 44 (Winter 1978): 163–90.

27. M&StL tabular data.

28. Jacob A. Swisher, "Mining in Iowa," *Iowa Journal of History* 43 (October 1945): 312; Iowa Board of Immigration, *Iowa: The Home for Immigrants* (Des Moines: Iowa Board of Immigration, 1870), 21; Dorothy Schweider, "Drawing the Personal Narrative into the Landscape of Iowa's Coal History," *Palimpsest* 74 (Fall 1993): 127; Donald Baker, "Operating Conditions Encountered in Iowa," *Coal Age* 14 (March 1921): 437; James H. Lees, "History of Coal Mining in Iowa," *Iowa Geological Survey,* vol. 22 (1913), 582–83; E. R. Landis, *Coal Resources of Iowa* (Des Moines: Iowa Geological Survey, 1965), tabular insert; *Iowa Railroad Commissioners Report, 1881* (Des Moines: State of Iowa, 1881), 141.

29. C. H. Pettit to J. J. Hill, February 2, 1882; J. J. Hill to E. W. Gaylord, May 15, 1882; J. J. Hill to Hamilton Browne, March 10, 1883, all from General Correspondence, James J. Hill Collection, JJHRL; StPM&M, Annual Report, 1883, 16.

30. Swisher, "Mining in Iowa," 338–39; Hubert L. Olin, *Coal Mining in Iowa* (Des Moines: Iowa Department of Mines and Minerals, 1965), 39–40; Hazel E. Drake, *History of Rippey, Green County, Iowa: A Century of Progress, 1849–1956* (Hartley, IA: Sentinel Publishing, 1956); Lees, "Coal Mining in Iowa," 579–80; Dorothy Schweider, *Black Diamonds: Life and Work in Iowa's Coal Mining Communities, 1895–1925* (Ames: Iowa State University Press, 1962), 10; CM&StP, Annual Report, 1887, 21–22; Eugene N. Hastie, *History of Perry, Iowa* (Perry: Privately published by the author, 1962), 100–107; N. E. Goldthwait, ed., *History of Boone County, Iowa,* 2 vols. (Chicago: 1910), 1: 335–37.

31. M&StL tabular data; M&StL, Annual Report, 1890, 5; *Minneapolis Tribune,* May 24, 1889; M&StL, Annual Report, 1901, 8.

32. M&StL tabular data.

33. Ibid.; BCR&N, Annual Report, 1889, 3.

34. *Western Trail* 5 (February 1886): 2; M&StL, Time Table (January 1886), 3, 6; BCR&N, Time Table (July 1887), 12, 16, 21, 26; *Minneapolis Tribune,* September 8 and December 15, 1895; CRI&P, Time Table (September 1895), 15–18; *Official Guide* (December 1889), 317, 403; ibid. (September 1894), 558–59; CB&Q, St. Louis, Minneapolis & St. Paul Time Table (July 17, 1888), 4–5; Richard C. Overton, *Burlington Route: A History of the Burlington Lines* (New York: Alfred A. Knopf, 1965), 196; *The Compendium of Passenger Rates and Divisions–July 1897–No. 23* (Chicago: W. F. Bailey, 1897), xxxviii.

35. *Compendium of Passenger Rates and Divisions,* cxxxi–cxxxiv, 220; CRI&P, Time Table (September 1895), 22; A. P. Butts, *The Story of the Fort Dodge Street Railway System* (Fort Dodge, IA: Privately published by the author, 1981), 10–11.

36. *Minneapolis Tribune,* November 7, 1888, May 4, July 30, and August 13, 1889, July 29, 1890, August 25, 1895, and June 4, 1896; *Jordan (MN) Independent,* February 8 and August 10, 1889; M&StL, Annual Report, 1897, 8; Frank P. Donovan Jr., "Passenger Trains of Yesteryear on the Minneapolis and St. Louis," *Minnesota History* 30 (September 1949): 232–41.

37. CRI&P, Time Table (June 1897), 34; *Excelsior (MN) Cottager,* January 17, 1896.

38. *Minneapolis Tribune,* March 2, August 19 and 21, and November 20, 1895, and June 9, 1896; *Excelsior Cottager,* January 31, 1896; Lucile A. Kane and John A. Dougherty, "Movie Debut: Films in the Twin Cities, 1894–1909," *Minnesota History* 54 (Winter 1995): 342–85; *Jordan Independent,* May 26, 1886; *Lake Mills (IA) Graphic,* October 4, 1899.

39. *Minneapolis Tribune,* February 23, May 16 and 21, July 18, and August 3, 1889; May 6 and 16 and June 8 and 17, 1890; January 31, 1895; August 23, 1896.

40. William Cronon, *Nature's Metropolis: Chicago and the Great West* (New York: W. W. Norton, 1991), 341–43; Phil Patton, "'Sell the Cookware If Necessary, but Come to the Fair,'" *Smithsonian* 24 (June 1993): 38–50; *Official Guide* (October 1893), xix; ibid. (November 1893), xxix; M&StL, Time Table (October 1893), 2–5.

41. *Official Guide* (December 1889), 424; *Minneapolis Tribune,* September 18, 1895; *Davidson's Minneapolis City Directory for 1895–1896* (Minneapolis: M. Davidson Co., 1895), 515.

42. *Minneapolis Tribune,* July 4, 17, 18, and 26 and August 31, 1889, May 18, June 10, July 4, 12, and 19, 1890, and July 14, 21, and 25, 1895; *Official Guide* (September 1896), 578; CM&StP, Time Table (August 1, 1890), 47.

43. *Minneapolis Tribune,* July 8 and 27 and September 1, 3, and 7, 1895.

44. M&StL, Authorities for Expenditure (AFEs) 102, 139, 195, 858; Helen Hunt Bennett, ". . . Northome," *Hennepin County History* (Summer 1961): 17–20; E. A. Holcombe to J. J. Hill, September 17, 1892, and J. J. Hill to J. C. Eliel, January 30 and February 6, 1899, James J. Hill Collection, JJHRL; M&StL, Annual Report, 1895, 10; ibid., 1897, 15; ibid., 1899, 18.

45. Waconia (MN) Heritage Association, *Waconia, Paradise of the Northwest: The Lake and Its Island* (Waconia: Waconia Heritage Association, 1986), 61–64, 73–76; *Minneapolis Tribune,* July 27 and August 8, 1889, and July 4, 1890; *Watertown (SD) Kampeskian,* June 25, 1897.

46. St. Paul & Northern Pacific, Certificate of the Fulfillment of . . . Contract . . . St. Paul & Northern Pacific and Northern Pacific, February 15, 1887, AC; Cass Gilbert Collection, MHS; M. C. Byers, Memorandum, October 8, 1913, GN President File 6092, MHS; M&StL, Time Table (October 1893), 2.

47. St. Paul & Northern Pacific, Certificate of the Fulfillment of . . . Contract; *Minneapolis Journal,* December 6, 1886; *Official Guide* (October 1886), 345; *Minneapolis Tribune,* January 2, May 6, and July 1, 1888, February 17 and 27 and September 10 and 12, 1889, December 10, 1890, and February 6, June 14, and October 16, 1891; St. Paul Chamber of Commerce, Annual Report, 1898, 65; Edward W. Solberg, "The Minneapolis Street Railway: Emergence and Disappearance," master's thesis, St. Cloud State University, St. Cloud, MN, 1999, 39; CM&StP, Time Table (May 1893), 9, 23; ibid. (June 1893), 9, 23.

48. *Annual Report of the Minnesota Railroad Commissioner, 1884,* 556–57; ibid., 1883, 185–86; *Minneapolis Tribune,* February 25 and August 25, 1895; C. B. Rogers to Frank P. Donovan Jr., February 13, 1950, AC; *Jordan Independent,* May 12, 1892; *Gaylord (MN) Hub,* May 29, 1886.

49. M&StL tabular data.

50. Ibid.; tabular data from BCR&N annual reports.

7. The Little Harriman

1. *The American Magazine* 70 (May 1910): 47; Isaac F. Marcosson, "The Coming Railroad Ruler," *Saturday Evening Post* (October 2, 1909): 6.

2. Frank P. Donovan Jr., "Edwin Hawley," *Trains* 12 (September 1952): 53; *New York Times,* March 2, 1990.

3. *New York Times,* February 2, 1912; Marcosson, "Railroad Ruler," 6–7; Muriel O. Fuller, *John Muir of Wall Street* (New York: Knickerbockers Press, 1927), 232–34;

Bernard M. Baruch, *Baruch: My Own Story* (New York: Henry Holt, 1957), 167.

4. Parker Morell, *Diamond Jim* (Garden City, NJ: Garden City Publishing, 1934), 180.

5. *Railroad Gazette* 18 (February 26, 1886): 155; *Minneapolis Tribune*, June 11, 1879; *Official Guide* (July 1887), xxv; Wisconsin, Minnesota & Pacific (WM&P), Minute Book, November 2, 1889, C&NW; *Poor's Manual, 1887*, 997.

6. Ernest H. Willman to Frank P. Donovan Jr., March 5, 1949, AC; *Official Guide* (December 1889), 420; R. L. Polk, *R. L. Polk's St. Paul City Directory, 1890* (St. Paul: R. L. Polk, 1890), 184; tabular data from various sources; Patricia Gordon Johnston, *Pretty Red Wing: Historic River Town* (Afton, MN: Johnston Publishing, 1988), 1–20.

7. *Railroad Gazette* 25 (July 21, 1893): 558; ibid., 26 (April 20, 1894): 293; WM&P, Minute Book, October 6, 1893.

8. *Railroad Gazette* 26 (October 26, 1894): 747; *Minneapolis Tribune*, September 26, 1895; *Railroad Gazette* 31 (January 20, 1899): 55, and (May 26, 1899), 362; M&StL, Annual Report, 1899, 5–6; *Official Guide* (July 1899), xxxviii; CRI&P, Annual Report, 1900, 11–12, 22; 24 ICC Valuation Reports 187, 997.

9. *New Ulm (MN) Daily Journal*, August 13, 1954; *Minneapolis Tribune*, September 15, 1889; *Railroad Gazette* 23 (February 27, 1891): 154; 137 ICC 845; M&StL, Annual Report, 1896, 8.

10. *Official Guide* (December 1896), 572; M&StL, AFE Index, Mankato Division, AC; *Yesterday and Today*, 166.

11. *Winthrop (MN) News*, March 13, 1975; *Minneapolis Tribune*, June 27, 1896; M&StL/MNU&SW [Minneapolis, New Ulm & Southwestern], Time Table No. 1 (July 6, 1896); *Official Guide* (September 1896), 578; *Railroad Gazette* 27 (November 1895): 731; *Railway Review* (August 15, 1896): 451.

12. Rendig Fels, *American Business Cycles, 1865–1897* (Chapel Hill: University of North Carolina Press, 1959), 193–208; George M. Stephenson, *John Lind of Minnesota* (Minneapolis: University of Minnesota Press, 1935), 137.

13. M&StL, Annual Report, 1912, 13; Fuller, *John Muir*, 212; Marcosson, "Railroad Ruler," 7; W. B. Davids, interview by Frank P. Donovan Jr., undated, AC; Morell, *Diamond Jim*, 181; Baruch, *Baruch*, 139; C. M. Keys, "Harriman: The Building of His Empire," *World's Work* 13 (February 1907): 8548; Don L. Hofsommer, *The Southern Pacific, 1901–1985* (College Station: Texas A&M University Press, 1986), 9.

14. *Spirit Lake (IA) Beacon*, February 3, 1899; *St. James (MN) Plaindealer*, February 21 and 28 and March 7, 14, and 21, 1899; *Watonwan County (MN) Plaindealer*, June 11, 1970; Don L. Hofsommer, *Prairie Oasis: The Railroads, Steamboats, and Resorts of Iowa's Spirit Lake Country* (Des Moines: Waukon & Mississippi Press, 1975), 105–11; *Iowa Railroad Commission Report, 1900*, 145; *Railroad Gazette* 31 (March 3, 1899): 161.

15. Earle D. Ross, *Iowa Agriculture: An Historical Survey* (Iowa City: State Historical Society of Iowa, 1951), 8–9, 61–62, 72–91; George Taylor and F. C. Taylor, *Farms and Homes in the West, Located in Northern Iowa and Southern Minnesota on the Land Grant of the Sioux City and St. Paul Railroad* (Chicago: N.p., 1876), 8; quoted in Ross, *Iowa Agriculture*, 120; BCR&N, Time Table (January 1900), 40; ibid. (September 1900), 55; Leonard K. Eaton, *Gateway Cities and Other Essays* (Ames: Iowa State University Press, 1989), 8–9.

16. *Spencer (IA) News-Herald*, March 29, April 19, 1899; *Spirit Lake Beacon*, February 3, June 2 and 9, and August 4, 1899; *Emmet County (Estherville, IA) Republican*, November 2 and December 7, 1899, and January 18, 1900; Don L. Hofsommer, "A Chronology of Iowa Railroads," *Railroad History* (Spring 1975): 78; CM&StP, Annual Report, 1900, 8.

17. *Railroad Gazette* 31 (January 27, 1899): 75; ibid. (February 3, 1899): 95; ibid. (May 5, 1899): 323; ibid. (May 12, 1899): 343; M&StL, Annual Report, 1899, 6–7, 13–14; *Spirit Lake Beacon*, March 31, 1899; M&StL, Right-of-Way and Track Maps, State Line to Storm Lake, AC; J. L. Allhands, *Railroads to the Rio* (Salado, Texas: Anson Jones Press, 1960), 206–7.

18. *Sioux Rapids (IA) Centennial*, n.d., 1955, 37, 81.

19. 137 ICC 798; *Minneapolis Tribune*, January 7, 1900; *Iowa Railroad Commission Report, 1900*, 144; *St. James Plaindealer*, July 25 and September 5, 1899; *Sioux Rapids (IA) Press*, April 5, 1900.

20. *New Ulm Journal*, August 12, 1899, and August 13, 1954; *St. James (MN) Gazette*, October 6, 1899; Shirley Knudson, ed., *History of Watonwan County* (Dallas, TX: Curtis Media, 1995), T127; *St. James Plaindealer*, August 1, 1899; *Emmet County Republican*, October 7, 1899; Iowa & Minnesota Land & Townsite Company advertising handbill, AC; M&StL, Right-of-Way and Track Maps, AC; *Spencer (IA) Herald*, October 11, 1899; *Greenville, Iowa, USA: Founded 1869–Platted 1899–Incorporated 1916* (N.p., n.d. [1998?]), v–7, 54–61.

21. *St. James Plaindealer*, December 12, 1899; *Spencer*

News, November 15 and 29, 1899; *Railroad Gazette* 31 (November 10, 1899): 701; *Emmet County Republican,* November 9 and December 21, 1899, and January 18, 1900; *Sioux Rapids Press,* January 25, March 8 and 29, April 12, June 28, July 10, and August 16, 1900; M&StL, Annual Report, 1900, 1, 12; *Spencer Herald,* March 15, July 12, and August 23 and 30, 1899, and April 25, 1900.

22. *Spencer News,* April 26, 1899; Knudson, *History of Watonwan County,* 11; C. H. Wegerslev and Thomas Walpole, *Past and Present of Buena Vista County Iowa* (Chicago: S. J. Clarke Publishers, 1909), 135; *Sioux Rapids Press,* April 19, 1900; Walter Carlson, *Happenings in Our Neighborhood,* 3 vols. (Trimont, MN: Trimont Progress, 1969), 2: 37; Hanska (MN) Centennial Committee, *Hanska: A Century of Tradition, 1901–2001* (Hanska: Hanska Centennial Committee, 2001), 106–7; John Gross, *LaSalle: Whistle-Stop on the Prairie* (Medford, MN: Privately published by the author, 1999), 17; *Storm Lake (IA) Pilot-Tribune,* July 27 and August 3, 10, and 17, 1900; Rolf E. Mosbo, *A Portrait of Rembrandt: Rembrandt, Iowa, 1901–2001* (Rembrandt: Rembrandt Centennial Committee, 2001), 7–38.

23. *St. James (MN) Courier,* November 18, 1969; *Sioux Rapids Press,* August 9 and 16 and September 20, 1900; Julia Becken to the author, November 10, 1971; *Watonwan County Plaindealer,* June 11, 1970; Carlson, *Happenings,* 38.

24. *New Ulm Journal,* August 13, 1954; *Spencer News,* November 15, 1899; *Storm Lake Pilot-Tribune,* March 30, 1900; M&StL maps, ca. 1900.

25. Don L. Hofsommer, "The Nation's Arteries," in *Rails across America,* ed. William L. Withuhn (New York: Smithmark Publishers, 1993), 90–109; Slason Thompson, *Railway Statistics of the United States of America for the Year Ending June 30, 1910* (Chicago: Gunthorp-Warren Printing, 1911), 123; Emory Johnson, *Railway Transportation* (New York: D. Appleton, 1905), 29–32; Ralph W. Hidy, Muriel E. Hidy, Roy V. Scott, and Don L. Hofsommer, *The Great Northern Railway: A History* (Minneapolis: University of Minnesota Press, 2004), 92–93; H. T. Newcomb, "The Recent Great Railroad Combinations," *Review of Reviews* 24 (August 1901): 163–74; M. G. Cunniff, "Increasing Railroad Consolidation," *World's Work* 3 (Fall 1902): 1775–80; Collis P. Huntington, "A Plea for Railroad Consolidation," *North American Review* 153 (July 1891): 272–82.

26. Iowa Central, Annual Report, 1900, 2; *Railroad Gazette* 32 (July 6, 1900): 458; *New York Times,* June 21, 1900; M. G. Cunniff, "Increasing Railroad Consolidations," *World's Work* 3 (February 1902): 1775–80.

27. Iowa Central, Annual Report, 1899, 11.

28. William E. Hayes, *Iron Road to Empire: The History of 100 Years of the Progress and Achievements of the Rock Island Lines* (New York: Simmons-Boardman, 1953), 142–46; BCR&N, Annual Report, 1896, iii

29. A. L. Mohler to C. J. Ives, September 13, 26, 1895; Howard Elliott to C. J. Ives, January 31, 1900; A. C. Ripley to C. J. Ives, October 3, 1898; A. L. Mohler to C. J. Ives, March 14, 1896, all from Albert N. Harbert Collection (MsC 434), Special Collections, University of Iowa Library (hereinafter cited as Harbert Collection).

30. Iowa Central, Annual Report, 1901, 12; Russell Sage to C. J. Ives, January 14, 1897; L. M. Martin to C. J. Ives, April 16, 1897; Albert A. Clarke to A. L. Mohler, April 28, 1897; L. M. Martin to C. J. Ives, September 21, 1897, all from Harbert Collection.

31. H. H. Hollister to C. J. Ives, August 21, 1899; George B. Harris to C. J. Ives, October 22, 1899, both from Harbert Collection; CRI&P, Annual Report, 1899, 10, 18.

32. Edward W. McGrew, *Corporate History of the Illinois Central Railroad Company and Its Controlled and Affiliated Companies up to June 30, 1915* (Chicago: Illinois Central, 1915), 236–37; *Official Guide* (June 1900), 616; Dow, Jones & Co., News Bulletin, February 16, 1898.

33. H. H. Hollister to C. J. Ives, December 23, 1899; R. R. Cable to C. J. Ives, February 1, 1900; M. J. Stohr to Robert Williams, April 14, 1900; Charles E. Perkins to C. J. Ives, May 11, 1900; R. R. Cable to C. J. Ives, July 16 and 17, 1900; J. M. Hannaford to Robert Williams, September 12, 1900, all from Harbert Collection; *Emmet County Republican,* January 18, 1900.

34. H. H. Hollister to C. J. Ives, June 27, 1900, Harbert Collection.

35. J. T. Harahan to C. J. Ives, June 2, 1900; J. F. Wallace to C. J. Ives, August 9 and 23, 1900; R. R. Cable to Robert Williams, August 27, 1900, all from Harbert Collection; McGrew, *Corporate History of the Illinois Central,* 234–35.

36. *Minneapolis Tribune,* February 21, 1888; *Fort Dodge (IA) Messenger,* May 12, 1897; *Peoria (IL) Journal,* August 29, 1899; *New York Times,* March 9, July 2, and October 2, 1901; *Storm Lake Pilot-Tribune,* August 2, 1901; *Sioux Rapids Press,* September 5, 1901; *Railroad Gazette* 33 (April 5, 1901): 238; ibid. (July 12, 1901): 492; ibid. (July 19, 1901): 508; ibid. (August 9, 1901): 568; Illinois Central (IC), Annual Report, 1899, 4; ibid., 1900, 3–4; ibid., 1901, 1–3; H. Paul Jeffers, *Diamond Jim Brady: Prince of the Gilded Age* (New York: John Wiley & Sons, 2001), 218, 277.

37. BCR&N, Annual Report, 1900, 1; C. J. Ives to J. W. Kendrick, January 3, 1901; J. W. Kendrick to C. S. Mellen, March 16, 1901; C. J. Ives to E. H. McHenry, April 19, 1901, all from NP General Manager Files, MHS; BCR&N, Annual Report, 1901, 1–2; H. H. Field, *History of Milwaukee Road, 1892–1940* (Chicago: CMStP&P, n.d. [1941?]), 205–8.

38. Edwin Hawley to C. J. Ives, April 15, 1901, Harbert Collection; 137 ICC Valuation Reports 848–51; CRI&P, Abstact to Important Contracts Affecting Operations (1965), RI Secretary's No. 2261, 20, AC.

39. Hayes, *Iron Road to Empire,* 147–70; William Z. Ripley, *Railroad Finance and Organization* (New York: Longmans, Green, 1920), 524–32; 24 ICC Valuation Report 1077–80; *New York Times,* June 5 and July 25, 1902; H. H. Hollister to C. J. Ives, April 16 and May 13, 1902, Harbert Collection; R. R. Cable and C. J. Ives to BCR&N Stockholders, June 5, 1902, AC; Richard C. Overton, *Burlington Route: A History of the Burlington Lines* (New York: Alfred A. Knopf, 1965), 165; G. H. Crosby, *History of CRI&P Co.* (Chicago: CRI&P, n.d. [1904?]), 46–47; BCR&N to Chicago, Rock Island & Pacific Railway Company, Lease, June 1, 1902, AC; *Poor's Manual, 1937,* 1310; CRI&P, Annual Report, 1903, 7–8; ibid., 1904, 7–9, 13–14.

40. *Minneapolis Tribune,* November 2, 3, 4, and 28, 1902; *Official Guide* (November 1902), xxxix; M&StL, Contract 871, C&NW.

41. StP&D, Annual Report, 1895, 8; tabular data from St. Paul Chamber of Commerce annual reports, 1890–1900; Hidy et al., *Great Northern,* 64–65, 71, 110, 117, 131, 134, 139; R. Sommer Hayes to James J. Hill, November 23, 1898; James J. Hill to C. H. Coster, September 30, 1899, both from James J. Hill Reference Library; *Railroad Gazette* 33 (May 11, 1900): 296; NP, Annual Report, 1900, 14; T. Barth, "Report on the Investigation of the Condition of the Northern Pacific Railroad . . . October 24–November 9, 1893," AC; *Commercial & Financial Chronicle* 70 (May 5, 1900): 865.

42. Hidy et al., *Great Northern,* 88–93; Renz, *Northern Pacific,* 164–68, 176–80; NP, Annual Report, 1890, 14–15; ibid., 1893, 9; ibid., 1897, 1.

43. NP/M&StL, Time Table No. 13 (August 1, 1897); St. Paul Chamber of Commerce, Annual Report, 1900, 83; M&StL, Annual Report, 1902, 9.

44. *New York Times,* March 2, 1902; Southern Pacific (SP), Official Register, Section 1, 608, and Section 5, 8, AC.

45. *New York Times,* March 2, 1902; SP, Official Register, Section 1, 608, and Section 5, 8, AC; *New York Times,* March 27, 1902; Baruch, *Baruch,* 168–76; George Kennan, *The Chicago & Alton Case: A Misunderstood Transaction* (New York: Country Life Press, 1916), 3, 8, 38; C. M. Keys, "As Many Methods as Railroad Kings," *World's Work* 10 (September 1905): 6652–59; C. M. Keys, "The Newest Railroad Power," *World's Work* 10 (June 1905): 6302–12; C. M. Keys, "Harriman," *World's Work* 13 (February 1907): 8537–52; Carl Snyder, *American Railways as Investments* (New York: Moody Corporation, 1907), 167–76; *New York Times,* June 24 and September 19, 1904; George Kennan, *Edward H. Harriman: A Biography,* 2 vols. (Boston: Houghton Mifflin, 1922), 2: 228–310; Maury Klein, *Life and Legend of Edward H. Harriman* (Chapel Hill: University of North Carolina Press, 2000), 323.

46. Hayes, *Iron Road to Empire,* 152, 175.

47. *Wall Street Journal,* May 13, 1902; *New York Times,* May 15 and June 22, 1902; *Minneapolis Tribune,* June 13, 1904; *Railroad Gazette* 37 (July 29, 1904): 48; M&StL, Annual Report, 1904, 10; CRI&P, Annual Report, 1904, 14; 137 ICC Valuation Report 789, 849, 851; *Railroad Gazette* 37 (December 2, 1904): 117; ibid. (December 16, 1904): 198; ibid., 38 (January 27, 1905): 32; M&StL, Annual Report, 1905, 5–6, 10–11; Fort Dodge & Des Moines, Contract 1045, C&NW.

8. The Newest and the Best

1. Charles Byron Kuhlman, *The Development of the Flour-Milling Industry in the United States with Special Reference to the Industry in Minneapolis* (Boston: Houghton Mifflin, 1929), 166; George D. Rogers, "History of Flour Manufacture in Minnesota," *Collections of the Minnesota Historical Society* 10 (February 1905), 53; *Minneapolis Chamber of Commerce Annual Report, 1901,* 55–56; ibid., 1902, 56.

2. *Minneapolis Tribune,* September 8, 1895; William C. Edgar, *The Medal of Gold: A Story of Industrial Achievement* (Minneapolis: Bellman Company, 1925), 210–17; James Gray, *Business without Boundary: The Story of General Mills* (Minneapolis: University of Minnesota Press, 1959), 52–62; Rogers, "History of Flour Manufacture in Minnesota," 40, 54; *Jordan Independent,* February 28, 1901; Ruby Deming, *The History of Franklin, 1880–1990* (Franklin, MN: Privately published by the author, 1990), 61, 109.

3. *Minneapolis Tribune,* December 24, 1885, and August 21, September 8 and 27, 1895; *Minnesota Railroad and Warehouse Commission Report, 1886,* 777–78; Henrietta M. Larson, *The Wheat Market and the Farmer in Minnesota, 1858–1900* (New York: Columbia University, 1926), 222,

230–33, 245; *Minneapolis Chamber of Commerce Annual Report, 1902,* 50.

4. Agnes Larson, *History of the White Pine Industry in Minnesota* (Minneapolis: University of Minnesota Press, 1949), 229–46, 376–77; *Minneapolis Chamber of Commerce Annual Report, 1895,* 48; ibid., 1901, 55–56; ibid., 1902, 56.

5. M&StL tabular data, 1890–1905; *Iowa Railroad Commission Report, 1889,* 88; ibid., 1894, 92.

6. *Carver County (Waconia, MN) News,* June 3, 1892; *Minneapolis Journal,* July 2 and September 8, 1907.

7. M&StL, Time Table No. 32 (February 28, 1904), 3–6.

8. BCR&N, Time Table (January 1900), 9, 11; BCR&N, Theatrical Notice No. 23, December 7, 1900; J. N. Farmer to Robert Williams, August 29, 1900, Harbert Collection; CRI&P, "Special Excursion Rates and General Information for Tourist Season of 1902," AC.

9. Edward W. McGrew, *Corporate History of the Illinois Central Railroad Company and Its Controlled and Affiliated Companies up to June 30, 1915* (Chicago: Illinois Central, 1915), 235–37; *Cosmopolitan* (March 1900): 88; IC, Western Lines Train Service (February 22, 1900), 7, 12; *Official Guide* (August 1905), 875.

10. *Official Guide* (April 1901), 761; ibid. (June 1902), 644–45; ibid. (July 1902), 644–45; M&StL, Annual Report, 1902, 9; Frank P. Donovan Jr., "Passenger Trains of Yesteryear on the Minneapolis & St. Louis," *Minnesota History* 30 (September 1949): 232–41; M&StL, Annual Report, 1903, 10.

11. *Official Guide* (November 1902), xxxix; *Minneapolis Tribune,* October 31 and November 1–4, 11, and 15, 1902; *St. Paul Chamber of Commerce Annual Report,* 1900, 88, 90.

12. *Official Guide* (December 1902), 642–43.

13. *Minneapolis Tribune,* November 24, 1902, and June 13 and November 15, 1904; David R. Frances, *The Universal Exposition of 1904,* 2 vols. (St. Louis: Louisiana Purchase Exposition Company, 1913), 1: 255–56, 259–60, 280, 452–58, 620–21, 627; H. Roger Grant, Don L. Hofsommer, and Osmund Overby, *St. Louis Union Station: A Place for People, A Place for Trains* (St. Louis: St. Louis Mercantile Library, 1994), 22–25.

14. *St. James Plaindealer,* May 8 and 22, June 12 and 26, and August 8, 1900; *Storm Lake Pilot-Tribune,* August 2 and October 12, 1900; *Sioux Rapids Press,* June 13, 1901; *Winthrop News,* August 14, 1902, April 2, 1903; *South Dakota Railroad Commission Report, 1902,* 18–19.

15. *Jordan Independent,* August 14 and September 18, 1902; June 11 and July 16, 1903, and July 7 and September 1, 1904.

16. *The Weekly Item,* December 3, 1897; Leland (IA) Centennial Committee, *Milestones along the Way: Leland, Iowa, 1882–1982* (Leland: Leland Centennial Committee, 1982), 85; Wilma Rugh Taylor and Norman Thomas Taylor, *This Train Is Bound for Glory: The Story of America's Chapel Cars* (Valley Forge, NY: Judson Press, 1999), 113–14; Bicentennial Committee, *Montgomery: From the "Big Woods" to the "Kolachy Capital"* (Montgomery, MN: Bicentennial Committee, 1976), 18; Ormsby (MN) Centennial Committee, *Biggest Little Town in Two Counties: Ormsby Centennial, 1999* (Ormsby: Ormsby Centennial Committee, 1999), 12; *Jordan Independent,* May 10 and August 23, 1900; *Winthrop News,* June 19 and August 28, 1902; *Minneapolis Tribune,* September 19 and November 17 and 19, 1902.

17. *St. James Plaindealer,* August 12, 1911; *Sioux Rapids Press,* May 10 and September 6, 1900, and October 17, 1901; George A. Horton, "Britt's First Convention," *Palimpsest* 70 (Summer 1970): 87–92; Britt Centennial Committee, *Recollections of Britt, Iowa* (Britt: Britt Centennial Committee, 1978), 201–5.

18. *Winthrop News,* June 25, 1903; C. H. Wegersley and Thomas Walpole, *Past and Present of Buena Vista County Iowa* (Chicago: S. J. Clarke Publishing, 1909), 98; *Spencer Herald,* November 20, 1901; *Sioux Rapids Press,* November 21, 1901; FKN to CPS, undated telegraph message from Sioux Rapids, IA, AC; *Des Moines Register,* March 12, 1967.

19. M&StL tabular data, 1900–1905.

9. It Will Be a Hummer

1. Train order number 7 to C&E [Conductor & Engineer] Engine 7 at Spencer (IA), July 16, 1904; L F. Day to D. C. Noonan, telegram, July 16, 1904, AC. Portions of this chapter appeared in Don L. Hofsommer, "Boosterism and Townsite Development along the Minneapolis & St. Louis Railroad in South Dakota," *Journal of the West* 42 (Fall 2003): 8–16, and in Don L. Hofsommer, "A Promise Broken: Le Beau and the Railroad," *South Dakota History* 33 (Spring 2003): 1–17.

2. J. P. Morgan to J. J. Hill, January 7, 1903, two telegrams; J. J. Hill to J. P. Morgan, January 7, 1903; J. J. Hill to J. P. Morgan, January 10, 1903, all from James J. Hill papers, JJHRL.

3. Ralph W. Hidy, Muriel E. Hidy, Roy V. Scott, and Don L. Hofsommer, *The Great Northern Railway: A History*

(Minneapolis: University of Minnesota Press, 2004), 63; O. B. Grant to W. C. Toomey, October 3, 1898, James J. Hill papers, JJHRL; CGW, Annual Report, 1901, 19–20; H. Roger Grant, *The Corn Belt Route: A History of the Chicago Great Western Railroad Company* (De Kalb: Northern Illinois University Press, 1984), 60–67; *Fort Dodge Messenger,* October 9, 1904.

4. Anson Bailey Cutts, interview by Frank P. Donovan Jr., undated, AC; CRI&P/Iowa Central, Joint Time Table Manly–Albert Lea, July 5, 1903; Alfred D. Chandler Jr., *The Visible Hand: The Managerial Revolution in American Business* (Cambridge, MA: Harvard University Press, 1977), 167–75.

5. *South Dakota Railroad Commission Report, 1902,* 1929; S. S. Judy and Will G. Robinson, "Sanborn County History," *South Dakota Historical Collections* 26 (1952): 170.

6. BCR&N, Time Table (January 1900), 18–24; ibid. (September 1900), 53; Doane Robinson, "Close of a Great Decade," *Dacotah Magazine* (December 1907): 88–89.

7. C. J. Bailey, "The Making of Watertown," *Dacotah Magazine* (December 1907): 1–16; C. H. Ware, "Putting the Spokes into the Hub of South Dakota," *Dacotah Magazine* (April 1908): 1–8; Commercial Club of Aberdeen, *A Souvenir of Aberdeen: The Railroad Hub of the Dakotas* (Aberdeen, SD: Commercial Club of Aberdeen, 1907), vii–viii, xii–xiii; Brown County (SD) Historical Society, *Brown County History* (Aberdeen: Brown County Historical Society, 1980), 304–8.

8. *Minneapolis Tribune,* October 12, 1902; *New York Times,* September 22, 1905; Arthur M. Borak, "The Chicago, Milwaukee & St. Paul Railroad: Recent History of the Last Transcontinental," *Journal of Economic and Business History* 3 (November 1930): 81–117.

9. C&NW, Annual Report, 1900, 25–265; *Yesterday and Today: A History of the Chicago & North Western Railway System* (Chicago: C&NW, 1910), 142, 167–68; F. Stewart Mitchell, "A Mis-Applied Response to Opportunity: The Chicago, Milwaukee & St. Paul Railway and the Great Dakota Boom, 1879–1886," *Business and Economic History* (College of Commerce and Business Research, University of Illinois, 1982), 177–88; F. Stewart Mitchell, "The Chicago, Milwaukee & St. Paul Railway and James J. Hill in Dakota Territory, 1879–1885," *North Dakota History* 47 (Fall 1980): 11–19; *Minneapolis Journal,* July 22, 1907.

10. Robinson, "Close," 88–89; Slason Thompson, *Railway Statistics of the United States of America for the Year Ending June 30, 1907* (Chicago: Gunthorp-Warren, 1908), 8; Donald J. Pisani, "George Maxwell, the Railroads, and American Land Policy, 1894–1904," *Pacific Historical Review* 63 (May 1994), 177–90; Mildred Lucile Hartsough, *The Twin Cities as a Metropolitan Market: A Regional Study of the Economic Development of Minneapolis and St. Paul* (Minneapolis: University of Minnesota Press, 1925), 174; *South Dakota Railway Commission Report, 1902,* 131.

11. Henry G. Durand, "The Railroads of Tomorrow," *World's Work* 13 (January 1907): 8465–70; 137 ICC 886–88; M&StL Contract 1257 with Franklin Floete et al., January 17, 1906, AC; Clyde Clarkson Way, ed., *Biography and Memoirs of Thomas Asbury Way* (Westchester, [no state]: Privately published by the editor, 1946), 42; *Watertown (SD) Public Opinion,* October 25, November 1, 10, 14, and 25, and December 1, 1905.

12. John N. Vogel, *Great Lakes Lumber on the Great Plains: The Laird, Norton Company in South Dakota* (Iowa City: University of Iowa Press, 1992), 79–80; Ralph E. Nichol, "Steamboat Navigation on the Missouri River," *South Dakota Historical Collections* 26 (1952): 207–21; Leola (SD) Centennial Committee, *Leola Centennial: 1884–1984* (Leola: Leola Centennial Committee, 1984), 387; *Andreas' Historical Atlas of Dakota* (Chicago: Andreas, 1884), 36, 181.

13. M&StL, Annual Report, 1906, 11; *McPherson County (Leola, SD) Herald,* December 27, 1906; R. C. Lathrop, "Watertown and West—M&StL's Final Expansion," *North Western Lines* 21 (Spring 1994), 50, 56; *Minneapolis Journal,* August 4 and September 1, 1907; *Minneapolis Tribune,* June 20, 1907; *Minneapolis Journal,* September 3, 1907; *Official Guide* (September 1907), xxxviii; Brown County Historical Society, *Brown County History,* 387–91; *Watertown Public Opinion,* July 28, August 10, and November 16, 1906.

14. *Dacotah Magazine* (December 1907): 6; ibid. (January 1908): advertising section; M. M. Dealy, "Farm Life," *Dacotah Magazine* (January–February 1909): 33–37; James D. McLaird, "From Bib Overalls to Cowboy Boots: East River/West River Differences in South Dakota," *South Dakota History* 19 (Winter 1989): 458–61; *Minneapolis Tribune,* June 30, 1907.

15. Way, *Thomas Asbury Way,* 26, 30, 32, 34, 41–44, 64; James Frederic Hamburg, *The Influence of Railroads upon the Processes and Patterns of Settlement in South Dakota* (New York: Arno Press, 1981), 310–18; Brown County Historical Society, *Brown County History,* 48–49.

16. Hamburg, *The Influence of Railroads,* 318–22; *Dakota Railroad Commission Report, 1885,* 1; Faulk County Historical Society, *History of Faulk County South Dakota 1910–1982* (Faulton, SD: Faulk County Historical Society, 334; Joanita Kant et al., *Pictorial History of Codington*

County South Dakota (Dallas, TX: Taylor Publishing Co., 1987), 18.

17. Clyde C. Way to Frank P. Donovan Jr., September 19, 1949, AC; *Minneapolis Journal,* June 30, July 30, and August 5, 11, and 12, 1907.

18. *Minneapolis Journal,* August 1, 5, and 17, 1907; *Dacotah Magazine* (November 1908): advertising section.

19. Ray Stannard Baker, "Destiny and the Western Railroad," *Century Magazine* 75 (April 1908): 892–94.

20. Leola Centennial Committee, *Leola Centennial,* 399; *Minneapolis Tribune,* June 20, 1907; Faulk County Historical Society, *History of Faulk County,* 333–37, "Golden Jubilee, 1906–1956: Church of St. John the Baptist, Onaka, South Dakota" (booklet, n.p., n.d.), 10; *Minneapolis Journal,* September 6, 1907.

21. Dealy, "Farm Life," 36; Rex C. Myers, "An Immigrant Heritage: South Dakota's Foreign-Born in the Era of Assimilation," *South Dakota History* 19 (Summer 1989): 134–45.

22. J. D. Latimer, "The Greatest Year of New Railroad Enterprises," *Review of Reviews* 34 (October 1906): 447–60; Emory R. Johnson, *American Railway Transportation* (New York: D. Appleton Co., 1905), 66; M&StL, Western Division Time Table No. 13 (April 4, 1920), 8–10.

23. Warren Upham, *Minnesota Geographic Names: Their Origin and Historic Significance,* 290; *North Western Lines* 21 (Summer 1994): 74; *Minneapolis Journal,* September 22, 1907.

24. H. R. Smith, "Stratford, South Dakota: New Town Forging to the Front," *Dacotah Magazine* (March 1909): 1–3; Brown County Historical Society, *Brown County History,* 64–67.

25. Brown County Historical Society, *Brown County History,* 64–67; *Official Shippers' Guide and Directory of the Minneapolis & St. Louis and Iowa Central Railroad* (Chicago: Perk-Hill, 1909), 2, 4, 6 (hereinafter cited as *Official Shippers' Guide*).

26. *Official Shippers' Guide,* passim.

27. *Official Shippers' Guide,* 2, 4, 50–52, M&StL, Right-of-Way and Track Map, Conde–Le Beau, June 30, 1917, AC; *Dacotah Magazine* (November 1908): advertising section; ibid. (January–February 1909): advertising section.

28. Jimmy M. Skaggs, *Prime Cut: Livestock Raising and Meatpacking in the United States, 1607–1983* (College Station: Texas A&M University Press, 1986), 50–129; *Railway World* (August 7, 1880): 751; Howard C. Hill, "The Development of Chicago as a Center of the Meat Packing Industry," *Mississippi Valley Historical Review* 10 (December 1923), 253–73; Cronon, *Nature's Metropolis,* 207–59.

29. Harold E. Briggs, "The Development and Decline of Open Range Ranching in the Northwest," *Mississippi Valley Historical Review* 20 (March 1934): 521–36; Ernest S. Osgood, *The Day of the Cattleman* (Minneapolis: University of Minnesota Press, 1926), 1–82; Lewis Atherton, *The Cattle Kings* (Bloomington: Indiana University Press, 1967), 236–40; W. M. Pearce, *The Matador Land and Cattle Company* (Norman: University of Oklahoma Press, 1964), 44–49.

30. Bob Lee and Dick Williams, *Last Green Frontier: The South Dakota Stock Grower Heritage* (Sturgis, SD: Black Hills Publishers, 1964), 229; Bert L. Hall, *Roundup Years: Old Muddy to Black Hills* (N.p., 1954), 65, 355; Frazier Hunt, *Cap Mossman: Last of the Great Cowmen* (New York: Hasting House, 1951), 233–38; Ike Blasingame, *Dakota Cowboy: My Life in the Old Days* (Lincoln: University of Nebraska Press, 1958), 15, 32–33.

31. Pearce, *The Matador Company,* 98; Hunt, *Cap Mossman,* 238; Blasingame, *Dakota Cowboy,* 115, 259; Hall, *Roundup Years,* 355.

32. Blasingame, *Dakota Cowboy,* 98, 231, 247; Lee and Williams, *Last Green Frontier,* 229–31, 241.

33. M&StL, AFE 2977; *Le Beau (SD) Phenix,* July 30 and September 17, 1908.

34. Ginny Cudmore and Jim Nelson, eds., *Timber Lake and Area, 1910–1985* (Timber Lake, SD: Timber Lake and Area Historical Society, 1989), 46–47; C. J. Bailey, "Turning the Light on Le Beau," *Dacotah Magazine* (August 1908): 115–20; *Le Beau Phenix,* July 30, 1908–June 23, 1910, passim.

35. F. H. Johnson, *The Milwaukee Road, 1847–1939: Brief Record of the Development of the Milwaukee Road from the Chartering of Its First Predecessor Company to Date—August 1939* (Chicago: CMStP&P, 1939), 26–27; Bailey, "Turning the Light on Le Beau," 118–19; Pearce, *The Matador Company,* 86; Blasingame, *Dakota Cowboy,* 35.

36. *Le Beau Phenix,* July 30, August 27, September 10 and 17, and October 1, 8, 19, and 22, 1908.

37. Mari Sandoz, *The Cattlemen* (Lincoln: University of Nebraska Press, 1958), 460; Pearce, *The Matador Company,* 112; *Le Beau Phenix,* November 5 and December 3, 1908; Sandoz, *The Cattlemen,* 472.

38. *Le Beau Phenix,* January 14, May 13 and 27, and June 10, 1909; Pearce, *The Matador Company,* 123.

39. *Le Beau Phenix,* August 20, September 24, October 27, and November 5, 1908, and April 29, May 6, 20,

and 27, June 17 and 24, July 22, September 9, and October 14, 1909; M&StL, AFE 3102.

40. *Le Beau Phenix,* July 29, 1909.

41. Ibid., September 2, 1909.

42. Ibid., September 2, 1909; M&StL, Annual Report, 1909, 14; M&StL, Time Table (September 1, 1909), 15–24; Frank J. Cory, "The Opening of the Great Land Reservations," *Dacotah Magazine* (November 1908): 1–13; Herbert S. Schell, *History of South Dakota* (Lincoln: University of Nebraska Press, 1968), 252–57; Don L. Hofsommer, "The Watertown Express and the 'Hog and Human': M&StL Passenger Service in South Dakota, 1884–1960," *South Dakota History* 3 (Spring 1973): 127–55.

43. *New York Times,* October 27, 1909; *Minneapolis Tribune,* October 27, 1909.

44. Cory, "The Great Land Reservations," 12; *Dakota Magazine* (January–February 1909): 94; Doane Robinson, "Thousands Seek South Dakota," *Dacotah Magazine* (August 1908): 1–5.

45. Sandoz, *The Cattlemen,* 465–66.

46. *Dacotah Magazine* (January–February 1909): advertising section; Bailey, "Turning the Light on Le Beau," 118.

47. Atherton, *The Cattle Kings,* 48; Blasingame, *Dakota Cowboy,* 165, 178, 275–76, 290; Pearce, *The Matador Company,* 127; Hunt, *Cap Mossman,* 256; Lee and Williams, *Last Green Frontier,* 239–41; *Le Beau Phenix,* December 16, 1909; *New York Times,* December 12, 1909; *Minneapolis Tribune,* December 12, 1909; Sandoz, *The Cattlemen,* 468–69.

48. Blasingame, *Dakota Cowboy,* 289–90; *Le Beau Phenix,* August 27 and October 29, 1908; Lee and Williams, *Last Green Frontier,* 240–41; Robert J. Hagan, "Le Beau: Old and New," M.A. thesis, University of South Dakota, 1956, 51–53.

49. *Le Beau Phenix,* August 12, September 9, and October 14, 1909; F. H. Johnson, *Milwaukee Road,* 26–27.

50. *Le Beau Phenix,* April 21 and 28 and May 26, 1910.

51. Blasingame, *Dakota Cowboy,* 291–315; Lee and Williams, *Last Green Frontier,* 250–62; Schell, *History of South Dakota,* 348; Pearce, *The Matador Company,* 140–46; Hunt, *Cap Mossman,* 268–69; Todd D. Epp, "South Dakota Ranching," *South Dakota Magazine* (November–December 1993): 16–19.

52. Gilbert C. Fite, *The Farmer's Frontier, 1865–1900* (New York: Holt, Rinehart & Winston, 1966), 110–11; McLaird, "From Bib Overalls to Cowboy Boots," 482; Schell, *History of South Dakota,* 256–57, 346; Rose Tidball, *Taming the Plains* (NP, 1976), 73.

53. George L. Shaw to Gerald L. Phelps, December 10, 1954, AC.

54. M&StL, Employee Time Table No. 12 (December 3, 1911), 9; ibid., Supplement A (March 3, 1912).

10. Everything from Caskets to Corsets

1. Paul S. Boyer et al., *The Enduring Vision: A History of the American People* (Lexington: D. C. Heath & Co., 1990), 751–88; Leland L. Sage, *A History of Iowa* (Ames: Iowa State University Press, 1974), 310–11; Theodore C. Blegen, *Minnesota: A History of the State* (Minneapolis: University of Minnesota Press), 461–69; M&StL tabular data, 1910–11.

2. M&StL tabular data, 1900–11.

3. *Minneapolis Journal,* December 15 and 16, 1911; Manual of Statistics, *Manual of Statistics: Stock Exchange Handbook, 1906* (New York: Manual of Statistics, 1906), 932–35; L. R. Moyer and O. G. Dale, eds., *History of Lac Qui Parle County Minnesota,* 2 vols. (Indianapolis: B. F. Bowen, 1916), 1: 487; *Fort Dodge Messenger,* September 17, 1897.

4. Otis H. Moore, "Handling the Grain Crop of the Great Northwest," *Dacotah Magazine* (January 1908): 61–68; *Official Shippers' Guide,* 21–27; *Minneapolis Journal,* September 1–30, 1907.

5. *Official Shippers' Guide,* 21–27; Madison Centennial Committee, *Madison Historical Album* (Madison: Madison Centennial Committee, 1985), 24–25, 140; *125th Anniversary of the City of Young America, Minnesota, 1856–1981* (N.p., 1981), 30; Montgomery Bicentennial Committee, *Montgomery: From the "Big Woods" to the "Kolachy Capital," 1856–1976* (Montgomery, MN: Montgomery Bicentennial Committee, 1976), 13.

6. *Minneapolis Chamber of Commerce Annual Report, 1902,* 131–34; Michael P. Malone and Richard W. Etulain, *The American West: A Twentieth-Century History* (Lincoln: University of Nebraska Press, 1989), 26–29; Ralph W. Hidy, Frank Ernest Hill, and Allan Nevins, *Timber and Men: The Weyerhaeuser Story* (New York: Macmillan Co., 1963), 115–16, 187; *Minneapolis Journal,* August 13, 1907; Agnes Larson, *History of the White Pine Industry in Minnesota* (Minneapolis: University of Minnesota Press, 1949), 377; *Official Shippers' Guide,* 38–40; *Weekly Item,* December 3, 1897.

7. H. H. Young, *St. Paul: The Commercial Emporium of the Northwest* (St. Paul: Pioneer Press, 1886), 106–7; *St.*

Paul Chamber of Commerce Annual Report, 1898, 74; ibid., 1900, 75, 107; Mildred Lucile Hartsough, *The Twin Cities as a Metropolitan Market: A Regional Study of the Economic Development of Minneapolis and St. Paul* (Minneapolis: University of Minnesota, 1925), 66–67; *Official Shippers' Guide,* 50–52; *Minneapolis Journal,* September 1–October 31, 1907, October 1–December 31, 1911, and January 1–March 1, 1912.

8. M&StL tabular data, 1910–11.

9. *Corwith, Iowa "Then" and "Now"* (Corwith: Corwith Centennial Committee, 1980), 20; Blegen, *Minnesota,* 390–96; Hartsough, *The Twin Cities,* 55; Alfred D. Chandler Jr., *The Visible Hand: The Managerial Revolution in American Business* (Cambridge, MA: Harvard University Press, 1977), 406–9; *Official Shippers' Guide,* 64–66; Kurt E. Leichtle, "Power in the Heartland: Tractor Manufacturers in the Midwest," *Agricultural History* 69 (Spring 1995): 314–25.

10. Chandler, *The Visible Hand,* 295–301, 391–402; John H. White, *The Great Yellow Fleet: A History of American Railroad Refrigerator Cars* (San Marino, CA: Golden West Books, 1986), 11–21; *St. Paul Chamber of Commerce Annual Report, 1889,* 84; *Official Shippers' Guide,* 90; *Corwith, "Then" and "Now,"* 106; *St. Paul Chamber of Commerce Annual Report, 1898,* 83; *125th Anniversary of the City of Young America,* 31; Waconia Heritage Association, *Waconia, Paradise of The Northwest: The Lake and Its Island* (Waconia: Waconia Heritage Association, 1981), 63; Chandler, *The Visible Hand,* 328; *Minneapolis Tribune,* September 26, 1895; *Official Shippers' Guide,* 58, 60–62; Chandler, *The Visible Hand,* 253, 295; *Lake Mills Graphic,* October 4, 1899; *Jordan Independent,* September 15, 1904.

11. Martin Stack, "Local and Regional Breweries in America's Brewing Industry, 1865 to 1920," *Business History Review* 74 (Autumn 2000): 453–63; Manfred Friedrich and Donald Bull, *The Register of United States Breweries, 1876–1976* (Trumbull, CT: Privately published by Donald Bull, 1976), 140–52; *Official Shipper's Guide,* 90–93; *Jordan Independent,* December 20, 1900; *Le Beau Phenix,* July 30, 1908; *Watertown Kampeskian,* June 25, 1897.

12. *Official Shippers' Guide,* 90–93; Eric Sloane, "Natural Ice," *American Heritage* 18 (August 1966): 83–84; John Gruber, "Harvest of Cold," *Locomotive and Railway Preservation* (January–February 1996): 20–27; Waconia Heritage Association, *Waconia,* 113–14; Stanley B. Fettl, "Ice Harvesting on Shady Oak Lake," *Hennepin County History* 32 (Fall 1977): 15–19; George W. Nassig, "Ice Harvesting, Storage, and Distribution," *Hennepin County History* 32 (Summer 1978): 14–22; *Minneapolis Journal,* December 28, 1911, and January 28, 1912. See also Joseph C. Jones Jr., *America's Icemen: An Illustrated History of the United States Natural Ice Industry* (Olathe, KS: Jobeco Books, 1984).

13. Jacob A. Swisher, "Mining in Iowa," *Iowa Journal of History and Politics* 43 (October 1945), 344–47; Charles S. Gwynne, "Early Quarrying in Iowa," *Palimpsest* 38 (May 1957): 188–95; *Official Shippers' Guide,* 44; Karl Gurcke, *Bricks and Brickmaking: A Handbook for Historical Archaeology* (Moscow: University of Idaho Press, 1987), 3–40, 84–100; State of Iowa, *Census for the State of Iowa for the Year 1905* (Des Moines: State of Iowa, 1905), 692–95; *Storm Lake Pilot-Tribune,* August 10, 1900; *Official Shippers' Guide,* 43–46.

14. William G, Murray, "Iowa Land Values, 1803–1967," *Palimpsest* 43 (October 1967): 38; Earl D. Ross, *Iowa Agriculture: An Historical Survey* (Iowa City: State Historical Society of Iowa, 1951), 123; "The Clay Industry in Iowa," *Des Moines: Spokesman for the City of Des Moines* 4 (May 1919): 12–13; Allan G. Bogue, *From Prairie to Corn Belt: Farming on the Illinois and Iowa Prairie in the Nineteenth Century* (Chicago: Quadrangle Books, 1963), 286; Walter Carlson, *Happenings in Our Neighborhood: Cedar, Galena, Trimont, Elm Creek, Fox Lake,* 3 vols. (Trimont, MN: Trimont Progress, 1970), 3: 96–101.

15. Chandler, *The Visible Hand,* 324–25; OKD to EED, February 8, 1909, AC.

16. *Hanska (MN) Herald,* March 8, 1907; M&StL, Time Table No. 12 (December 3, 1911), 1–10; wheel reports from author's collection; Conductor Kelly to FDA, October 13, 1909, AC.

17. M&StL tabular data, 1900–1911; Slason Thompson, *Railway Statistics for the United States of America for the Year Ending June 30, 1910* (Chicago: Gunthorp-Warren Printing, 1911), 79–84.

18. *Official Guide* (September 1907), 770–73; IC, Time Table, June 17, 1907, 3–4; Wabash, Time Table, September 1909), 17–18, 57–58; *Minneapolis Tribune,* July 21, 1907: M&StL, Buffet Car Regulations, July 22, 1909, AC; IC, Time Table, April 12, 1910, 21–22, 33; *Minneapolis Journal,* December 16, 1911.

19. *Official Guide* (September 1907), 772–73; IC, Time Table, June 17, 1907, 3–4; Pullman Conductor No. 4 to Agent Waseca, April 8, 1909, AC.

20. *Minneapolis Journal,* September 4, 1907; M&StL, Annual Report, 1910, 7; *Dacotah Magazine* (July 1908):

advertising section; *Watertown Public Opinion,* March 22, 1907.

21. M&StL, Time Table (Minnetonka Points), July 1, 1900; *Minneapolis Tribune,* May 24, 1896; Kenneth T. Jackson, *Crabgrass Frontier: The Suburbanization of the United States* (New York: Oxford University Press, 1985), 102; M&StL Time Table No. 32, February 28, 1904, 3; Ellen Wilson Meyer, ed., *Picturesque Deephaven* (Excelsior, MN: Excelsior–Lake Minnetonka Historical Society, 1989), 88, 107.

22. M&StL, AFEs 900, 1603, 1968, 2217, 3615; *Minneapolis Journal,* June 16, July 3, 1907; M&StL, Annual Reports, 1895–1905; Russell L. Olson, *The Electric Railways of Minnesota* (Hopkins: Minnesota Transportation Museum, 1976), 89–98; Goodrich Lowry, *Streetcar Man: Tom Lowry and the Twin City Rapid Transit Company* (Minneapolis: Lerner Publications, 1979), 68, 141, 143; Isaac Atwater, *History of the City of Minneapolis* (New York: Munsell, 1893), 336–44; Bob Williams, *Excelsior: An Historical Novel of Lake Minnetonka* (Minneapolis: James D. Thueson, 1982), 230–31; M&STL, Annual Report, 1908, 12.

23. *Biographical Directory of the Railway Officials of America* (New York: Simmons-Boardman, 1922), 151; Frank P. Donovan Jr., "Passenger Trains of Yesteryear on the Minneapolis & St. Louis," *Minnesota History* 30 (September 1949): 232–41; *Official Guide* (January 1908), xxix.

24. A. B. Cutts to Frank P. Donovan Jr., answers to questions put by Donovan, undated [1949], AC; *Minneapolis Tribune,* June 23, 1906.

25. *Minneapolis Journal,* June 29, 1907; M&STL, Popular Excursion flyer, October 13, 1906, AC; Eugene N. Hastie, *History of Perry, Iowa* (Perry: Privately published by the author, 1962), 78; *Spencer (IA) Reporter,* September 27, 1911; *Le Beau Phenix,* July 29, 1909; *Watertown Public Opinion,* October 30, 1906, and November 15, 1907.

26. *Watertown Public Opinion,* July 2 and 5, 1907, and June 6, 1979; *Dacotah Magazine* (July 1908): advertising section; *Minneapolis Journal,* August 6, 1907; Waconia Heritage Association, *Waconia,* 74; *Jordan Independent,* July 15, 1907; FDA to Agents, May 13, 1909, AC; *Minneapolis Journal,* June 20, 1907; *Le Beau Phenix,* August 26, 1909; M&StL, Transportation Order No. 64 (August 17, 1909), AC; *Hanska Herald,* February 8, 2001; Mike Chapman, *Frank Gotch: World's Greatest Wrestler* (Buffalo, NY: William S. Hein, 1990), 5, 67; Matthew Lindaman, "Wrestling's Hold on the Western World before the Great War," *Historian* 62 (Summer 2000): 779–97.

27. *Minneapolis Journal,* October 28, 1911; Chapman, *Frank Gotch,* vi, 20; *Le Beau Phenix,* August 27 and October 15, 1908; "Golden Jubilee, 1906–1956: Church of St. John the Baptist," Onaka, South Dakota (booklet, n.p., n.d.), 10; George S. Robbins, *Frank A. Gotch: World's Champion Wrestler* (Chicago: Joseph B. Bowles, 1913), 18–23, 103–21, 177, 208, 267; W. R. Rice to City Marshall of Sioux Rapids (IA), August 5, 1910; Conductor Ducharme to Marshall at Ruthven, April 17, 1909, both from AC.

28. *Jordan Independent,* April 10, 1902; Kendrick W. Brown, "Memories of a Commercial Traveler," *Palimpsest* 52 (May 1971): 225–88; *Fort Dodge Messenger,* September 17, 1897; Susan Strasser, "'The Smile That Pays': The Culture of the Traveling Salesman, 1880–1920," in *The Mythmaking Frame of Mind: Social Imagination and American Culture,* ed. James Gilbert et al. (Belmont, NY: Wadsworth Publishing, 1993), 155–77; "Drummer Accommodated: A Nineteenth Century Salesman in Minnesota," *Minnesota History* 46 (Summer 1978): 59–65; Don Marquis, "My Memories of the Old-Fashioned Drummer," *American Magazine* 107 (February 1929): 20–21, 152–54; Truman E. Moore, *The Traveling Man: The Story of the American Traveling Salesman* (Garden City, NJ: Random House, 1972), 21–39; Madison Centennial Committee, *Madison Historical Album,* 36–37.

29. John R. Stilgoe, *Metropolitan Corridor: Railroads and the American Scene* (New Haven, CT: Yale University Press, 1983), 193–211; George H. Douglas, "Down by the Depot," *Locomotive and Railway Preservation* (November–December 1992): 11–27; H. Roger Grant and Charles W. Bohi, *The Country Railroad Station in America* (Boulder, CO: Pruett Publishing, 1978), 3–10.

30. *Le Beau Phenix,* September 10, 1908; Faulk County Historical Society, *History of Faulk County South Dakota, 1910–1982* (Faulkton: Faulk County Historical Society, 1982), 261, 380; M&StL, Annual Report to the Interstate Commerce Commission for 1923, 207; Lee Deemer, *Esther's Town* (Ames: Iowa State University Press, 1980), 83; Carlson, *Our Neighborhood,* 68–69.

31. FKN to E. D. Hogan, undated [1906?], AC; "A Century of Express Service," *Railway Age* 106 (March 4, 1939): 365–68; V. S. Roseman, *Railway Express: An Overview* (Denver: Rocky Mountain Publishing, 1992), 4–9; M&StL tabular data, 1874–1911; Adams Express Company, *Official Gazette* (February 1, 1906), 44; ibid. (November 15, 1906), 1; Deemer, *Esther's Town,* 85.

32. Chandler, *The Visible Hand,* 230–33; Boris Emmet and John E. Jeuck, *Catalogues and Counters: A History of*

Sears, Roebuck & Company (Chicago: University of Chicago Press, 1950), 18–46, 100–122, 169–70; Gordon L. Weil, *Sears, Roebuck, U.S.A.: The Greatest American Catalogue Store and How It Grew* (New York: Stein and Day, 1977), 2–40; David B. Danbom, *Born in the Country: A History of Rural America* (Baltimore: Johns Hopkins University Press, 1995), 132–34, 149–50; *Lake Mills Graphic,* June 9, 1976.

33. M&StL tabular data, 1874–1911; Leo A. McKee and Alfred L. Lewis, eds., *Railroad Post Office History* (Pleasantville, NY: Mobile Post Office Society, 1972), 59; *Sioux Rapids Press,* October 25, 1900; Faulk County Historical Society, *History of Faulk County,* 336

34. Guy M. Purington, "Rural Free Delivery," *Transit Postmark Collector* 47 (January–February 1996): 28–29; Henry A. Castle, *A History of St. Paul and Vicinity: A Chronicle of Progress and Narrative Account of the Industries, Institution, and People of the City and Its Tributary Territory,* 3 vols. (Chicago: Lewis Publishing Co., 1912), 1: 233–34.

35. M&StL, Annual Report, 1904, 9; ibid., 1907, 11; ibid., 1910, 7, 10.

36. M&StL, AFEs 1744, 2363, 1649, 1618–19, 2074, 2793, 2332, 2047, 2718, 3129, 3135, 1911, 1732, 2524, 2285; *Lake Mills Graphic,* June 18, 1969; *Minnesota Railroad and Warehouse Commission Report, 1899,* 111–23; ibid., 1904, 102–6.

37. D. C. Noonan to All Concerned, August 1, 1907, AC; M&StL, Annual Report, 1911, 39–41.

38. M&StL, Annual Report, 1911, 39–41.

39. Theodore Roosevelt, First Annual Message to Congress, December 3, 1901; John F. Stover, *American Railroads,* 2nd ed. (Chicago: University of Chicago Press, 1997), 129–31.

40. Phillip Longman, "Scientific Management," *Audacity* 5 (Summer 1997): 40–49.

41. *Minnesota Board of Railroad Commissioners Annual Report, 1897,* 302–24; James W. Ely Jr., "The Railroad Question Revisited: Chicago, Milwaukee & St. Paul v. Minnesota and Constitutional Limits on State Regulation," *Great Plains Quarterly* 12 (Spring 1992): 121–34.

42. Charles E. Perkins and David C. Shepard to President and Board of Directors, April 22, 1907; Howard Elliott to Charles E. Perkins, May 3, 1907, both from NP Presidents' File 1397, MHS; *Minneapolis Journal,* September 4, 1907; *Washington Post,* March 24, 1908; U.S. Supreme Court Decision Regarding Decrees in Nos. 291, 292, and 293 (June 9, 1913).

43. Thompson, *Railway Statistics for the Year Ending June 30, 1910,* 84–85; "Railway Rates," an address by A. B. Stickney at St. Paul, February 2, 1907, AC; *Commercial and Financial Chronicle,* June 30, 1906, and August 17, 1907; *Bankers Magazine* 74 (April 1907): 506; Howard Elliott, "The Work of the Farmer and the Railroad in Minnesota," an address before the Minnesota Agriculture Society, St. Paul, January 7, 1912, AC.

44. M&StL, Annual Report, 1907, 8, 13; ibid., 1908, 8–9; *Minneapolis Journal,* July 4 and 11, 1907; *Wall Street Journal,* September 14, 1910; M&StL, Annual Report, 1911, 11–12.

45. Munson to FGA, October 17, 1909, AC; ECC to WPL, October 25, 1909, AC; M&StL, Circular No. 1, March 4, 1908, AC; D. C. Noonan to Employees Telegraph and Station Service, January 10, March 10, 1908, AC.

46. Robert W. Vincent, "The Inside History of Rock Island–Frisco Financing," *Moody's Magazine* (January 1909): 41–47; Frank P. Donovan Jr., "Edwin Hawley," *Trains & Travel* 12 (September 1952): 52–53; *New York Times,* December 30, 1906, and June 15 and 16, 1907.

47. *Railway and Engineering Review* 42 (June 21, 1902): 480–84; *Minnegazette* (Winter 1999): 22–25; *Minneapolis Tribune,* October 5–18, 1910.

48. *Minneapolis Journal,* August 24, 1907; Richard Simons, "The Clover Leaf Route," *National Railway Bulletin* 43, no. 1 (1978): 16–25; John A. Rehor, *The Nickel Plate Story* (Milwaukee: Kalmback Publishing, 1965), 119, 147, 155–58, 167–69; Taylor Hampton, *The Nickel Plate Road: The History of a Great Railroad* (Cleveland: World Publishing, 1947), 230–58; Carl Snyder, *American Railways as Investments* (New York: Moody Corporation, 1907), 689; David McCullough, *The Path between the Seas: The Creation of the Panama Canal, 1870–1914* (New York: Simon & Schuster, 1977), 462–63, 491, 503; Walter Wellman, "The New Executive of the Panama Canal," *American Monthly Review of Reviews* (May 19, 1905): 549–51; Theodore P. Shonts, "The Railroad Men at Panama," *North American Review* 199 (February 1914): 228–39; McCullough, *Path between the Seas,* 470, 533; *Biographical Directory of the Railway Officials of America* (1922), 51.

49. Isaac F. Marcosson, "The Coming Railroad Ruler," *Saturday Evening Post* (October 2, 1909), 6–7, 42–43.

50. *New York Times,* December 20, 1908; Cyrus Adler, *Jacob A. Schiff: His Life and Letters,* 2 vols. (Garden City, NJ: Doubleday, Doran, 1928), 1: 82; Charles W. Turner, *Chessie's Road,* 2nd ed. (Clifton Forge, VA: Cheasapeake & Ohio Historical Society, 1986), 131; V. V. Masterson, *The Katy Railroad and the Last Frontier* (Norman: University of

Oklahoma Press, 1952), 278–79; Marcosson, "Railroad Ruler," 7; Franklin Escher, "The Rise of a Great System," *Harper's Weekly* 53 (October 30, 1909): 28; *American Review of Reviews* 40 (November 1909): 528–31.

51. Sereno Pratt, "Our Financial Oligarchy," *World's Work* 10 (October 1905), 6704–14; *American Magazine* 70 (May 1910): 43, 46–47; *New York Times,* April 14, 1910; C. M. Keys, "The Shifting Railroad Control," *World's Work* 20 (June 1910): 13045–56; J. L. Allhands, *Boll Weevil: Recollections of the Trinity & Brazos Valley Railway* (Houston: Anson Jones Press, 1946), 258; *New York Sun,* December 24, 1911; *Railway Age* 52 (February 9, 1912): 237; *New York Times,* July 9, 1910; Anson B. Cutts, response to questions of Frank P. Donovan Jr., undated [1949], AC.

52. *New York Times,* February 2, 1912; M&StL tabular data, 1897–1911; Floyd B. Mundy, comp., *The Earning Power of Railroads* (New York: Jas. H. Oliphant, 1910), 421.

53. *Minneapolis Journal,* December 11, 1911; Don L. Hofsommer, "A Chronology of Iowa Railroads," *Railroad History* (Spring 1975): 79; *Watertown Public Opinion,* June 6, 1979; M&StL, Annual Report, 1907, 8; *Boone News Republican,* Supplement to 21st Anniversary Edition (n.d., 1910), 6; B. Campbell to L. W. Hill, March 24, 1905; E. A. Harris to James J. Hill, August 4, 1905, both from GN President Files, MHS; Hastie, *History of Perry,* 116–20, 364; *Minneapolis Journal,* June 23 and September 1 and 22, 1907; Joseph W. Gillis to Frank Hartman, March 27, 1909, AC.

54. *Minneapolis Journal,* August 4, 1907; *Railway Age* 45 (June 5, 1908): 47; *Le Beau Phenix,* March 11, 1909; 137 ICC 833; Stewart Mitchell, "About a Railroad You May Not Have Heard Of—And That Is No More," *Trains* 33 (June 1972): 20–25; H. Roger Grant, "Frank A. Seiberling and the Formative Years of the Midland Continental Railroad, 1912–1920," *North Dakota History* 43 (Fall 1976): 28–36; *Le Beau Phenix,* April 1, October 21, and November 4, 1909; M&StL Minute Book, April 13, 1909, and September 26, 1910; *Le Beau Phenix,* January 27, 1910.

55. W. B. Davids, "*Mileposts on the Prairie,* a friendly review of same by W. B. Davids" (n.d., 1951), 7, AC.

56. Dow, Jones & Co., *Electric Page News Ticker Bulletin,* no. 59, August 16, 1911; ibid., no. 6, October 18, 1911, both from AC; *Minneapolis Journal,* October 23, November 1, 2, 13, 15, 19, 22, and 24, and December 4, 1911, and January 10, 1912.

57. Dow, Jones & Co., *Electric Page News Ticker Bulletin,* no. 21, November 29, 1909; ibid., no. 66, October 31, 1910; ibid., no. 48, September 8, 1911; Davids, review of *Mileposts on the Prairie,* 8.

58. Newman Erb to J. S. Backe & Co., November 28, 1911, AC; Dow, Jones & Co., *Electric Page News Ticker Bulletin,* no. 30, December 22, 1911; *Minneapolis Journal,* December 16, 20, and 23, 1911, and January 8, 1912; M&StL, Annual Report, 1912, 5–6; Manual of Statistics, *Manual of Statistics: Stock Exchange Handbook, 1912* (New York: Manual of Statistics, 1912), 190–92.

59. Collins P. Huntington, "A Plea for Railway Consolidation," *North American Review* 153 (July 1891): 272–82; M. G. Cunniff, "Increasing Railroad Consolidation," *World's Work* 3 (Fall 1902): 1775–90; "The Trust Question," *Munsey's Magazine* 22 (January 1900): 569–74; Vincent P. Carosso, *The Morgans: Private International Bankers, 1854–1913* (Cambridge, MA: Harvard University Press, 1987), 499–508.

11. Struggling among the Titans

1. Gordon Carruth, ed., *The Encyclopedia of American Facts and Dates* (New York: Thomas Y. Crowell, 1979), 424–27; *Minneapolis Journal,* January 5, 1912; *New York Times,* February 2, 1912; ibid., January 14, 1912; *Minneapolis Journal,* February 1 and 2, 1912; *New York Times,* February 4, 1912; Isaac F. Marcosson, "The Coming Railroad Ruler," *Saturday Evening Post* (October 2, 1909), 43; *New York Times,* February 6, 9, 10, and 11, and July 28, 1912, and April 5, 1914.

2. Missouri, Kansas & Texas (MK&T), Annual Report, 1912, 2; M&StL, Annual Report, 1912, 13; Marcosson, "Railroad Ruler," 43; Bernard M. Baruch, *Baruch: My Own Story* (New York: Henry Holt & Co., 1957), 133; Grenville M. Dodge to Frank Trumbull, February 1, 1912; Jacob A. Schiff to Frank Trumbull, February 1, 1012, both from AC; O. Muriel Fuller, *John Muir of Wall Street* (New York: Knickerbocker Press, 1927), 211; *World's Work* 19 (Fall 1910): 12521; *New York Sun,* December 24, 1911; *Railway Age* 47 (October 22, 1909): 739–40; ibid., 52 (February 9, 1912): 237; Marcosson, "Railroad Ruler," 42; Davids, review of *Mileposts on the Prairie,* 8, AC.

3. Alfred D. Chandler Jr., *The Visible Hand: The Managerial Revolution in American Business* (Cambridge, MA: Harvard University Press, 1977), 167–83; William Norris Leonard, *Railroad Consolidation under the Transportation Act of 1920* (New York: Columbia University Press, 1946), 32–37.

4. *Minneapolis Journal,* February 2, 1912; *New York Times,* February 3, 1912.

5. *Minneapolis Journal,* February 14, 1912; *New York Times,* July 23, 1912; Dow, Jones & Co., *News Ticker Bul-*

letin, no. 56, May 20, 1912; ibid., no. 5, July 9, 1912; ibid., no. 40, July 15, 1912; ibid., no. 18, December 28, 1912; *Minneapolis Journal,* November 16, 1911, and January 27, 1912; *New York Times,* February 14 and 24 and August 23, 1912; *Official Guide* (June 1916), 1010; Dow, Jones & Co., *News Ticker Bulletin,* no. 32, January 3, 1913.

6. *Journal of Commerce,* December 26, 1911; Dow, Jones & Co., *News Ticker Bulletin,* no. 136, March 17, 1913; Carl Snyder, *American Railways as Investments* (New York: Moody Corporation, 1907), 433–40.

7. M&StL, Annual Report, 1913, 14–15; ibid., 1914, 13; Quagly Engr. 10 to JMS from Winfield, n.d., [1913?], AC; *Minnesota Railroad and Warehouse Commission Report, 1915,* 48–49; M&StL tabular data, 1910–16.

8. Theodore Prince, "The Rock Island: Reorganization by Anthesisia," *Moody's Magazine* (August 1916): 409–22; M&StL, Annual Report, 1915, 12; *Minneapolis Tribune,* April 21, 1916; M&StL, Annual Report, 1914, 12; M&StL, List of Officers, Agencies, Stations, etc. (July 1, 1913), 11.

9. S. M. Felton to Howard Elliott, January 11 and 23 and February 12, 1913, NP President's File 186, MHS; *Minneapolis Journal,* January 18, 1912; M&StL, Annual Report, 1912, 11; ibid., 1913, 14; ibid., 1914, 12; M&StL, List of Officers, etc. (July 1, 1913), 2–3.

10. *Minneapolis Journal,* November 30, 1911, and January 4 and 31, 1912; *Le Beau Phenix,* August 27, October 29, 1908; Herbert S. Schell, *History of South Dakota* (Lincoln: University of Nebraska Press, 1968), 182; M&StL, List of Officers, etc. (July 1, 1913), 7; John B. Allen to Frank P. Donovan Jr., March 1, 1950, AC; Dick Porter, *32 Years on the Hurricane Deck of a Freight Train* ([N.p.]: N. B. Porter, 1906), 73.

11. *Minneapolis Journal,* February 21 and 25 and March 1, 1912; *Winthrop News,* March 6, 13, and 27, 1913, September 10, 1914, and March 23, 1916; M&StL, Annual Report, 1916, 13.

12. Lucile M. Kane and Alan Ominsky, *Twin Cities: A Pictorial History of St. Paul and Minneapolis* (St. Paul: Minnesota Historical Society, 1983), 43; Don Kirschner, *City and County: Rural Responses to Urbanization in the 1920s* (Westport, CT: Greenwood Publishing, 1970), 1–5; Peter Fearon, *War, Prosperity, and Depression: The U.S. Economy, 1917–45* (Lawrence: University Press of Kansas, 1987), 8–9; L. R. Moyer and O. G. Dale, eds., *History of Chippewa and Lac Qui Parle Counties in Minnesota,* 2 vols. (Indianapolis: B. F. Bowen, 1916), 1: 557–63; *Des Moines: Spokesman for the City of Des Moines* 1 (April 1916): 4.

13. M&StL tabular data, 1912–16.

14. A. B. Cutts to Our Agents, January 27, 1913, AC; A. B. Cutts to Agents, November 18, 1913, AC; *Minneapolis Journal,* January 18, 1912; A. B. Cutts to J. J. Thompson, June 8, 1914, AC; M&StL, advertising flyers, October 23, 1913, and June 6, 1914, AC; *Winthrop News,* October 10, 1912, August 14, 1913, and July 8, 1915; T. H. Farmen to the author, March 4, 1972; *McPherson County Herald,* August 20, 1914; M&StL, Special Transportation Notice No. 435, June 17, 1914, AC; *Jordan Independent,* June 13, 1916; *Hanska Herald,* June 19, 1914; William N. Whitehall, *Ups and Downs of Iowa's Railroads* (privately published by the author, 1978), 51.

15. Whitehall, 119–20; Evelyn M. O'Day to the author, June 22, 1972; Norris D. Meachum to the author, November 14, 1972; *Winthrop News,* October 15, 1936; John Gross, *LaSalle: Whistle-Stop on the Prairie* (Medford, MN: Privately published by the author, 1999), 38; Duane E. Dewel to the author, May 19, 1965; A. P. Butts, *Walter Wilson and His Crooked Creek Railroad* (Webster City, IA: R. H. Hahne, 1976), 112–13; *Lake Mills Graphic,* June 18, 1969; Gus Dahlman, interview by the author, August 9, 1971; M. J. Reitan, interview by the author, September 14, 1995; Waconia Heritage Association, *Waconia, Paradise of the Northwest: The Lake and Its Island* (Waconia, MN: Waconia Heritage Association, 1986), 137; *Winthrop News,* August 19, 1915; *St. James Plaindealer and Courier,* July 2, 1980; M&StL, ticket stubs, Wallace, SD, September 29, 1915–June 26, 1916, AC; *Sioux Rapids (IA) Bulletin Press,* November 30, 1967; C. J. Wegerslev and Thomas Walpole, *Past and Present of Buena Vista County, Iowa* (Chicago: S. T. Clarke Co., 1909), 98; *McPherson County Herald,* July 23, 1914.

16. M&StL, Time Table, December 15, 1914; ibid., May 15, 1916, passim; *Minnesota Railroad and Warehouse Commission Report, 1914,* 543.

17. *Minneapolis Journal,* January 26 and February 1, 1912; *Minneapolis Tribune,* June 1, 1914, and July 1, 1916; M&StL, Time Table, December 17, 1911, 15–16; ibid., May 10, 1914, 16–17.

18. John R. Stilgoe, *Metropolitan Corridor: Railroads and the American Scene* (New Haven, CT: Yale University Press, 1983), 68, 210; Arthur D. Dubin, *More Classic Trains* (Milwaukee: Kalmbach Books, 1974), 93–105; Pullman Company, *Schedule of Lines: The Pullman Company,* July 15, 1915 (Chicago: Pullman Company, 1915), 135, 155, 341; *Minnesota Railroad and Warehouse Report, 1914,* 543; *Minneapolis Journal,* August 11, 1907; Peter T. Maiken, *Night*

Trains: The Pullman System in the Golden Years of Rail Travel (Chicago: Lakme Press, 1989), 8–11, 188–91, 276–81, 298–300.

19. *Railway Age* 58 (January 15, 1915): 103.

20. Carruth, *Encyclopedia of Facts and Dates,* 361, 387; Ruby Deming, *The History of Franklin, Minnesota, 1880–1990* (Franklin: Privately published by the author, 1990), 63; Edwin Wildman, "The City of the Automobile," *Munsey's Magazine* 22 (February 1900): 704–12; John B. Rae, *The Automobile Industry* (Boston: Twayne Publishers, 1984), 29–30; Jame J. Flink, *The Automobile Age* (Cambridge, MA: MIT Press, 1988), 56–72, 86–111, 135–57; Alfred D. Chandler Jr., comp. and ed., *Giant Enterprise: Ford, General Motors and the Automobile Industry* (New York: Harcourt, Brace, & World, 1964), xi–xii, 9–20; *Minneapolis Tribune,* September 11, 1895; *Minneapolis Journal,* February 18, 1912; William Leuchtenburg, *The Perils of Prosperity, 1914–1932* (Chicago: University of Chicago Press, 1958), 6.

21. Kenneth T. Jackson, *Crabgrass Frontier: The Suburbanization of the United States* (New York: Oxford University Press, 1985), 157–63; Cyrenus Cole, *Iowa through the Years* (Iowa City: State Historical Society of Iowa, 1940), 427–30; George S. May, "Getting Out of the Mud," *Palimpsest* 46 (February 1965): 96–115; *Winthrop News,* July 10, 1913, and August 16, 1917; *Minneapolis Journal,* June 23, August 26, September 1, October 22, and December 3, 1911, and February 18 and 25, 1912; *Des Moines,* 4; *Official Shippers' Guide,* 64–66; *Spencer Reporter,* June 7, 1911; R. L. Polk, *R. L. Polk's New Ulm City and Brown County Directory 1911–1912* (St. Paul: R. L. Polk, 1911), 277; Carruth, *Encyclopedia of Facts and Dates,* 367, 415, 417.

22. Hartzell Spence, *One Foot in Heaven: The Life of a Practical Parson* (New York: Grossett & Dunlap, 1940), 128–29; *Minneapolis Journal,* June 26, 1907; *Minneapolis Tribune,* November 11, 1902; *Winthrop News,* June 19, 1913; Clyde C. Way to Frank P. Donovan, September 19, 1949, AC; *Le Beau Phenix,* November 4, 1909; Julia Becken to the author, December 28, 1971.

23. Cole, *Iowa through the Years,* 467–70; Jackson, *Crabgrass Frontier,* 163–67; Arthur J. Larson, *The Development of the Minnesota Road System* (St. Paul: Minnesota Historical Society, 1966), 330–79; Rebecca Conrad, "The Lincoln Highway in Green County: Highway Politics, Land Initiative, and the Emerging Federal Highway System," *Annals of Iowa* 52 (Fall 1993): 351–89; Daniel J. Elazar, "A Model of Moral Government," in *Minnesota in a Century of Change: The State and Its People since 1900,* ed. Clifford E. Clark Jr. (St. Paul: Minnesota Historical Society, 1989), 344–46; *Minneapolis Journal,* November 30, 1911, and January 16 and February 17, 1912; May, "Getting Out of the Mud," 99; Leuchtenburg, *The Perils of Prosperity,* 185.

24. Sylvester Stewart, "The Automobile and the Railway as Transport Agents," *Engineering Magazine* 25 (July 1903), 481–87; Adams Express Co., *Official Gazette* (April 1, 1908): 538; *Le Beau Phenix,* July 30, 1908; *Winthrop News,* March 27, 1913, and May 18, 1916; *Railroad Gazette* (November 16, 1900), 761; *Railway Age* 45 (January 3, 1908): 11; Howard Elliott, "Minnesota Railways and Advertising," an address before the Minnesota Federation of Commercial Clubs, January 26, 1911, AC.

25. *Minneapolis Journal,* February 13, 1912; M&StL, AFEs 3110, 3209, 3433, 3796, 3852, 17–237; Waconia Heritage Association, *Waconia,* 75; S. M. Felton, "New Influences Affecting Passenger Traffic," *Railway Age* 61 (December 1, 1916): 997–98; *Minneapolis Journal,* October 22, 1911; Margaret Walsh, "Tracing the Hound: The Minnesota Roots of the Greyhound Corporation," *Minnesota History* 49 (Winter 1985): 314–25.

26. *Minneapolis Journal,* February 17, 1912; Carl H. Chrislock, *The Progressive Era in Minnesota, 1899–1918* (St. Paul: Minnesota Historical Society, 1971), 60, 200; *New York Times,* November 28, 1911; M&StL, Annual Report, 1913, 15.

27. "New Money for the Railroads," *American Review of Reviews* (May 1912): 627–28; "The Pitiful Plight of the American Railroad," *Current Literature* 53 (November 1912): 527–30; "Our Starving Railroads," *Literary Digest* 24 (November 2, 1912): 772–73; Benjamin F. Yoakum, "What the Railroads Need," *Harper's Weekly* 58 (March 28, 1914): 24–25; "The Public and the Railroads," *Independent* 78 (May 25, 1914): 312–15; *New York Times,* April 7, 1914; M&StL, Annual Report, 1912, 12. See Albro Martin, *Enterprise Denied: Origins of the Decline of American Railroads, 1897–1917* (New York: Columbia University Press, 1971), for a masterful treatment of this issue.

28. *New York Times,* July 17, 1914; "What Breaks the Railroads," *Literary Digest* 51 (November 6, 1915): 998; *Railway Age* 57 (December 4, 1914): 1054; *New York Times,* December 31, 1915; Walker D. Hines, *War History of American Railroads* (New Haven, CT: Yale University Press, 1928), 1–9; William Z. Ripley, "The Railroad Eight-Hour Law," *American Review of Reviews* 54 (October 1916): 389–93; Edwin J. Clapp, "The Adamson Law," *Yale Review* 6 (1916–17), 258–75; Samuel O. Dunn, "The Threatened

Strike of the Railways," *North American Review* 204 (October 19, 1916): 575–88.

29. M&StL, Annual Report, 1916, 5, 17; M&StL tabular data, 1912–16.

30. *Minneapolis Journal,* March 1, 1912; *New York Times,* January 18, 1916; *Railway Age* 58 (February 19, 1915): 350; ibid., (February 26, 1915), 390.

31. *Wall Street Journal,* January 18, 1916; Great Northern President File 6092, Box 197, MHS, passim; *New York Times,* February 1 and April 14, 1916; *Railway Age* 61 (September 8, 1916): 435.

32. Prince, "The Rock Island," 413.

12. Sweet and Sour

1. M&StL tabular data, 1916–17; M&StL, Annual Report, 1917, 17.

2. M&StL, Annual Report, 1916, 8; *Electric Railway Journal* 40 (August 10, 1912): 220; "The Electric Railways of Iowa," *Electric Traction* 19 (June 1923): 278–85; Norman Carlson, ed., *Iowa Trolleys* (Chicago: Central Electric Railfans' Association, 1975), 261–68; Frank P. Donovan Jr., "Short Line Interurbans," *Palimpsest* 35 (May 1954), 207–9; *Milwaukee Railroader* 17 (June 1987): 24; Mike Chapman, *Frank Gotch: World's Greatest Wrestler* (Buffalo: William S. Hein, 1990), 123; *New York Times,* December 17, 1917; Barnum & Bailey, "Official Route," Season 1917, AC; M&StL, Central Division Time Table no. 11 (November 11, 1917), 5.

3. Otto H. Kahn, "What American Railroads Need," *World's Work* 31 (February 1916): 451–60; Arthur Pound and Samuel Taylor Moore, *They Told Barron: Conversations and Revelations of an American Pepys in Wall Street* (New York: Harper & Row, 1930), 59–60; Richard Hoadley Tingley, "Lo, The Poor Railroads," *Current Opinion* 73 (July 1922): 11–113; John F. Stover, *American Railroads* (Chicago: University of Chicago Press, 1961), 181–86; Walker D. Hines, *War History of American Railroads* (New Haven: Yale University Press, 1928), x–xv, 1–21.

4. John F. Stover, *Life and Decline of the American Railroad* (New York: Oxford University Press, 1970), 158–73; Hines, *War History of Railroads,* 22–41; Stover, *American Railroads,* 185–97; K. Austin Kerr, "Decision for Federal Control: Wilson, McAdoo, and the Railroads, 1917," *Journal of American History* 3 (December 1967): 550–60; W. G. McAdoo, General Order No. 1, December 29, 1917; Stover, *American Railroads,* 187–97.

5. *Minneapolis Tribune,* April 5, 1917; M&StL, Annual Report, 1917, 13.

6. M&StL, Time Table, October 25, 1918, 16; *Official Guide* (March 1918), 1124–29; ibid. (October 1918), 521; *Minneapolis Tribune,* May 1, 1919; "New Great Northern Station at Minneapolis," *Railway Age* 56 (January 30, 1914): 227–33.

7. Hines, *War History of Railroads,* 41; M&StL, Annual Report, 1917, 8; ibid., 1918, 27; *Hanska Herald,* January 18, 1918; Leola Centennial Committee, *Leola Centennial: 1884–1984* (Leola, SD: Leola Centennial Committee, 1984), 86; Cyrus W. Cornelius to the author, April 6, 1988; JWD to GPM, December 17, 1917, AC; M&StL, Annual Report, 1917, 13; Eugene N. Hastie, *Hastie's History of Dallas County, Iowa* (Perry, IA: Privately published by the author, 1938), 358–61.

8. M&StL tabular data, 1917–18; JPM to All Agents, April 14, 1917, AC; Carl H. Chrislock, *Watchdog of Loyalty: The Minnesota Commission of Public Safety during World War I* (St. Paul: Minnesota Historical Society Press, 1991), 47, 133–41, 212–15; U.S. Railroad Administration (USRA), General Order No. 39, August 12, 1918, AC.

9. Leland L. Sage, *A History of Iowa* (Ames: Iowa State University Press, 1974), 250–54; Edward C. Kirkland, *A History of American Economic Life,* 4th ed. (New York: Appleton-Century-Crofts, 1969), 474–77; *Winthrop News,* May 10, 1917; Herbert S. Schell, *History of South Dakota* (Lincoln: University of Nebraska Press, 1968), 350–51; Don Kirschner, *City and Country: Rural Responses to Urbanization in the 1920s* (Westport: Greenwood Publishing, 1970), 1–4; William G. Murray, "Iowa Land Values, 1803–1967," *Palimpsest* 47 (October 1967), 461–504, esp. 461–68; Earl D. Ross, *Iowa Agriculture: An Historical Survey* (Iowa City: State Historical Society of Iowa, 1951), 138–46; Jimmy M. Skaggs, *Prime Cut: Livestock Raising and Meatpacking in the United States, 1607–1983* (College Station: Texas A&M University Press, 1986), 70–87.

10. M&StL tabular data, 1916–19.

11. *Moody's Analysis of Investments and Security Ratings: Railroad Investment* (New York: Moody's Investors Service, 1922), 899, 907; M&StL, Annual Report, 1918, 27; J. G. Woodworth to Howard Elliott, March 10, 1918, NP President File 2045, MHS.

12. Chrislock, *Watchdog of Loyalty,* 244–75; Martin Gilbert, *The First World War: A Complete History* (New York: Henry Holt, 1994), xv, 503–41; *Hanska Herald,* May 31, 2000.

13. Gilbert, *The First World War,* 519; *Hanska Herald,* May 31, 2001.

14. Glenn E. Plumb, "Labor's Solution of the Railroad Problem," *The Nation* 109 (August 16, 1919): 200–220.

15. *New York Times,* December 9, 1918, and June 6, 1919; M&StL, Annual Report, 1919, 6; Gerard C. Henderson, "Our Insolvent Railroads," *New Republic* 19 (July 2, 1919): 274–76.

16. Albert B. Cummins, "The Railway Problem," *Review of Reviews* 60 (July 1919): 61–66; James M. Herring, *The Problem of Weak Railroads* (Philadelphia: University of Pennsylvania Press, 1929), 40–43; Ari Hoogenboom and Olive Hoogenboom, *A History of the ICC: From Panacea to Palliative* (New York: W. W. Norton, 1976), 94–118; M&StL, Annual Report, 1919, 5.

17. W. H. Bremner to All Officers and Employees, March 1, 1920, AC; M&StL, Annual Report, 1920, 5–6, 16; M&StL, AFEs 21-20/23.

18. M&StL, Time Table (May 1923), 16–19; *Railway Age* 62 (May 18, 1917): 1041–44; ibid., 68 (May 21, 1920): 1442–46; ibid., 71 (December 17, 1921): 1200–1204; *Peoria (IL) Evening Star,* April 1, 1921.

19. M&StL tabular data, 1920–23.

20. Julius H. Parmelee, "Railway Revenues and Expenses in the Year 1920," *Railway Age* 70 (January 7, 1921): 129; Hines, *War History of Railroads,* 220–29; *New Republic* 22 (March 3, 1920): 6–8; *New York Times,* July 25, 1922.

21. Peter Fearon, *War, Prosperity, and Depression: The U.S. Economy 1917–45* (Lawrence: University Press of Kansas, 1987), 8–9, 15–21, 89; Alfred D. Chandler, *The Visible Hand: The Managerial Revolution in American Business* (Cambridge, MA: Harvard University Press, 1977), 488; C&NW, Annual Report, 1922, 8; *American Heritage* 40 (November 1989): 16.

22. Fearon, *War, Prosperity, and Depression,* 8–9, 15–21; Chandler, *The Visible Hand,* 456–59.

23. Kirschner, *City and Country,* 1–7; *Winthrop News,* January 29, 1920, and September 8, 1921; Skaggs, *Prime Cut,* 87; Ross, *Iowa Agriculture,* 148–54.

24. Skaggs, *Prime Cut,* 130–35; W. M. Pearce, *The Matador Land and Cattle Company* (Norman: University of Oklahoma Press, 1964), 169; *Winthrop News,* October 4, 1917; Bob Lee and Dick Williams, *Last Grass Frontier: The South Dakota Stock Grower Heritage* (Sturgis, SD: Black Hills Publishers, 1964), 262–67.

25. *Minneapolis Journal,* January 31, 1912; *Hanska Herald,* January 12, 1917; JMS to All Agents, n.d., AC; M&StL, AFE Index, 1912–22, AC.

26. "Golden Jubilee, 1906–1956: Church of St. John the Baptist," Onaka, SD (booklet), 11–12; Faulk County Historical Society, *History of Faulk County South Dakota 1910–1982* (Faulkton: Faulk County Historical Society, 1982), 331–80.

27. Marion Daniel Shuttes, *History of Minneapolis: Gateway to the Northwest* (Chicago: S. J. Clarke, 1923), 370; William G. Edgar, *The Medal of Gold: A Story of Industrial Achievement* (Minneapolis: Bellman Company, 1925), 218–23; Charles Byron Kuhlman, *The Development of the Flour Milling Industry in the United States with Special Reference to the Industry in Minneapolis* (Boston: Houghton Mifflin, 1929), 155–75; Victor A. Pickett and Roland S. Vaile, *The Decline of Northwestern Flour Milling* (Minneapolis: University of Minnesota Press, 1933), 5–15, 20–23, 34–35, 54–57; James Gray, *Business without Boundary: The Story of General Mills* (Minneapolis: University of Minnesota Press, 1954), 62–67, 82–89, 96–103, 130–35; M&StL tabular data, 1918–23.

28. Hines, *War History of Railroads,* 152–91, 226–29; *Moody's Manual, 1923* (New York: Moody's Investors Service, 1923), xxxix; M&StL, Annual Report, 1920, 4–5; *New York Times,* July 24, 1922; Samuel O. Dunn, "What Has Happened to the Railroads?" *Review of Reviews* 63 (May 1921): 501–5; *Current Opinion* 70 (June 1921): 732–36; Robert H. Zieger, *America's Great War: World War I and the American Experience* (New York: Rowman & Littlefield, 2000), 122–23; W. Thomas White, "Railroad Labor Relations in the Great War and After, 1917–1921," *Journal of the West* 25 (April 1986): 36–43.

29. *New York Times,* October 16, 1921; *Minneapolis Tribune,* July 1, 7–9, 14, 17, and 19, 1922; *Railway Age* 73 (September 16, 1922): 526; Colin J. Davis, *Power at Odds: The 1922 National Shopmen's Strike* (Urbana: University of Illinois Press, 1997), 48–79; William Z. Ripley, "Why the Railroad Strike Failed and the Coal Miners Won," *Survey* 49 (January 1, 1923): 436–38, 470–71.

30. W. W. Landmesser, interview by the author, August 19, 1992; M&StL, Annual Report, 1922, 3–4.

31. 137 ICC 785; M&StL, AFEs 181, 21-47; M&StL, Central Division Time Table No. 11 (November 11, 1917), 13; *Minneapolis Tribune,* May 23, 1919; NP, Annual Report, 1922, 11; M&StL, Annual Report, 1921, 10.

32. M&StL, Annual Reports, 1917–23.

33. *Moody's Manual, 1945* (New York: Moody's Investors Service, 1922), a14; M&StL, Annual Report, 1922, 23; ibid., 1923, 24.

34. M&StL tabular data, 1916–22.

35. *Minneapolis Tribune,* February 28, 1922; *New York Times,* May 10, 1922; tabular data from annual reports

of roads identified, 1920–23; *Wall Street Journal,* November 11, 1922; *Moody's Manual, 1922* (New York: Moody's Investors Service, 1922), xxvi, cxxxi.

36. Don L. Hofsommer, *The Southern Pacific, 1901–1985* (College Station: Texas A&M University Press, 1986), 108–11; "Clearing the Tracks for the Prosperity Special," *Literary Digest* 77 (April 21, 1923): 10–11; William Hard, "Lo, the Poor Railroads!" *The Nation* 116 (May 9, 1923): 544–45.

37. Minneapolis, St. Paul & Sault Ste. Marie (Soo Line), Annual Report, 1924, 14.

38. *New York Times,* May 6, 1923; M&StL, Annual Report, 1923, 1; C. O. Jenks to Ralph Budd, February 20, 1921; W. H. Bremner to G. R. Martin, September 20, 1921, January 16 and June 5, 1922, and February 23, 1923, both from GN President File 10,079, MHS; W. B. Davids to Frank P. Donovan Jr., May 28, 1949, AC; F. J. Lisman, "The Trouble with the Minneapolis & St. Louis," *Railway Age* 75 (August 25, 1923): 347–48.

13. Hard Times in Good Times

1. Bronson Batchelor, "Our Railroad Problem: A Glance Backward as Well as Forward," *Review of Reviews* 69 (January 1924): 48–52; *Moody's Analysis of Investments and Security Ratings: Railroad Investments* (New York: Moody's Investors Service, 1923), xxxix; *Railway Age* 75 (August 4, 1923): 227; Albert B. Cummins, "An Analysis of the Railroad Problem," *Congressional Digest* 3 (October 1923): 15–16.

2. F. J. Lisman, "The Trouble with the Minneapolis & St. Louis," *Railway Age* 75 (August 25, 1923): 347–48.

3. David B. Danbom, *Born in the Country: A History of Rural America* (Baltimore: John Hopkins University Press, 1995), 185–97; Peter Fearon, *War, Prosperity, and Depression: The U.S. Economy, 1917–1945* (Lawrence: University Press of Kansas, 1987), 28–41; Earle D. Ross, *Iowa Agriculture: An Historical Survey* (Iowa City: State Historical Society of Iowa, 1951), 154; Lester V. Chandler, *America's Greatest Depression, 1929–1941* (New York: Harper & Row, 1970), 5–55; Herbert S. Schell, *History of South Dakota* (Lincoln: University of Nebraska Press, 1968), 351–53; Calvin W. Coquillette, "The Struggle to Preserve Iowa's State Banking System, 1920–1933," *Annals of Iowa* 60 (Winter 2001): 35–59; Danbom, *Born in the Country,* 196; Boris Emmet and John E. Jeuck, *Catalogues and Counters: A History of Sears, Roebuck & Company* (Chicago: University of Chicago Press, 1950), 192–95.

4. *Minneapolis Tribune,* April 5 and May 10, 1917.

5. Frank P. Donovan Jr. to Mrs. William H. Bremner, December 28, 1950, AC; *National Cyclopedia of American Biography,* vol. B (New York: James T. White & Co., 1927), 263–64.

6. *Official Guide* (March 1914), xxx; Ross S. Marshall, *Working on the Railroad* (Cleveland: Privately published by the author, 1956), 107–21; "One of the Moynihans," *Railway Age* 86 (March 30, 1929): 736–38.

7. *Official Guide* (September 1914), xxix; Marion Daniel Shuttes, *History of Minneapolis: Gateway to the Northwest,* 3 vols. (Chicago: S.J. Clarke, 1923), 3: 814–15.

8. M&StL, Annual Reports, 1923–30.

9. M&StL, Annual Report, 1926, 24; ibid., 1928, 19; ibid., 1929, 20; *Minneapolis Tribune,* September 26, 1895; Ruby Deming, *The History of Franklin, Minnesota, 1880–1890* (Franklin: Privately published by the author, 1990), 133; "Crops after Sugar Beets," *Sugar Beet* (March 1929): 3–6, 18–19; M&StL, Annual Report, 1929, 20.

10. *Official Guide of the Minneapolis & St. Louis Railroad* (Minneapolis: M&StL, 1924), 2, 60–63; ibid., 1925, 2, 18; R. L. Polk, *R. L. Polk's Freeborn County Directory, 1921–22* (St. Paul: R. L. Polk, 1921), 388; John Gross, *LaSalle: Whistle-Stop on the Prairie* (Medford, MN: Privately published by the author, 2000), 34; *Winthrop News,* June 12, 1930.

11. Ibid., 1924, 39–45; *Minneapolis Journal,* February 11, 1927; Victor L. Pickett and Roland S. Vaile, *The Decline of Northwestern Flour Milling* (Minneapolis: University of Minnesota Press, 1933), 70; *New York Times,* August 5–7 and 15, 1926; *Minneapolis Tribune,* February 28, 1927; Charles Byron Kuhlman, *The Development of the Flour-Milling Industry in the United States with Special Reference to the Industry in Minneapolis* (Boston: Houghton Mifflin, 1929), 177–82; James Gray, *Business without Boundary: The Story of General Mills* (Minneapolis: University of Minnesota Press, 1954), 140–41, 152.

12. CM&StP, Annual Report, 1920, 7; C&NW, Northern Iowa Division Time Table No. 142 (July 11, 1920), 2, 3, 6; *St. James Plaindealer,* February 24, 1924, and January 30, 1929; *Winthrop News,* June 12, 1930; M&StL, AFE Index, passim; M&StL, AFE 28R415.

13. M&StL, Annual Report, 1924, 24; E. R. Landis, *Coal Resources of Iowa* (Iowa City: State of Iowa, 1965), tabular insert; Swisher, "Mining in Iowa," 314; M&StL, AFEs 26R364, 26R533, 27R24, 29R100.

14. *Official Guide of the Minneapolis & St. Louis Railroad* (Minneapolis: M&StL, 1924), 32, 60–63.

15. Charles S. Gwynne, "Early Quarying in Iowa,"

Palimpsest 38 (May 1957): 186–87; Swisher, "Mining in Iowa," 341–44; M&StL, Annual Report, 1927, 20.

16. Fearon, *War, Prosperity, and Depression,* 58, 95; M&StL, AFEs 12-154, 24R98, 25R550; Mildred Lucile Hartsough, *The Twin Cities as a Metropolitan Market: A Regional Study of the Economic Development of Minneapolis* (Minneapolis: University of Minnesota Press, 1925), 56.

17. M&StL tabular data, 1920–29.

18. *Minneapolis Journal,* February 1, 1927.

19. Edward Weiner, *Urban Transportation Planning in the United States: An Historical Overview* (Westport, CT: Praeger, 1999), 7–8; William H. Thompson, *Transportation in Iowa: A Historical Summary* (Ames: Iowa Department of Transportation, 1989), 71–75; Daniel J. Elazar, "A Model of Moral Government," *Minnesota in a Century of Change: The State and Its People since 1900,* ed. Clifford E. Clark Jr. (St. Paul: Minnesota Historical Society, 1989), 345; *Minneapolis Journal,* January 28, 1927; George S. May, "Getting Out of the Mud," *Palimpsest* 46 (February 1965): 96–115; *St. James Plaindealer,* December 11, 1924.

20. Victor W. Knauth, "Railway vs. Truck: A Tug-of-War in Transportation," *World's Work* 50 (October 1925): 664–68; Edward G. Riggs, "Motor Trucks vs. Railroads," *Forum* 65 (June 1921): 609–18; *Moody's Manual of Investments: Steam Railroads* (New York: Moody's Investors Service, 1941), a43–a45; Ross, *Iowa Agriculture,* 144; Kenneth T. Jackson, *Crabgrass Frontier: The Suburbanization of the United States* (New York: Oxford University Press, 1985), 161; Western Railways Committee on Public Relations, *Railroad Facts No. 7: A Yearbook of Railroad Information* (Chicago: Western Railways Committee on Public Relations, 1929), 33; Frederick Lewis Allen, *Only Yesterday: An Informal History of the Nineteen-Twenties* (New York: Harper & Row, 1931), 134–39.

21. Richard C. Overton, *Perkins/Budd: Railway Statesmen of the Burlington* (Westport, CT: Greenwood Press, 1982), 167–71; James M. Herring, *The Problem of Weak Railroads* (Philadelphia: University of Pennsylvania Press, 1929), 130–31; Greyhound, Time Table (December 20, 1928), 19; *Minneapolis Journal,* February 6, 1927; Deming, *History of Franklin,* 133.

22. *Literary Digest* 54 (January 20, 1917): 164–67; *New York Times,* August 14, 1921; "Railroads Losing Their Passengers," *Literary Digest* 86 (September 26, 1925): 22; Ralph Budd, "The Trend in Passenger Travel," *Railway Age* 84 (April 28, 1928): 1025–27; Herring, *Weak Railroads,* 131–32; "Deserting the Rails," *Literary Digest* 84 (January 10, 1025): 27; C&NW, Annual Report, 1923, 7–8; CRI&P, Annual Report, 1925, 7; GN, Annual Report, 1925, 9; Ralph Budd to Chauncey McCormick, April 18, 1928, SP Executive File 120.01, Box 22, AC; Ralph Budd, "Railways and Highways," *Railway Age* 86 (March 1929): 740–41; M&StL, tabular data, 1920–29.

23. *Hanska Herald,* December 14, 2000; *The History of Berkeley, Iowa* (Berkeley: Berkeley Centennial Committee, 1983), 7; Faulk County Historical Society, *History of Faulk County South Dakota, 1910–1982* (Faulkton: Faulk County Historical Society, 1982), 82; Bob Combs, "The Days When the Rails Ruled," *Marshalltimes* (September 1996): 38–43; M&StL, Time Table between St. Paul, Minneapolis and Lake Minnetonka and Waconia (May 20, 1927), 1–4; *Minneapolis Journal,* February 4, 1927; M&StL, Annual Report, 1926, 25; ibid., 1927, 20; ibid., 1928; 20; ibid., 1929, 20; *St. Paul Pioneer-Press,* November 13–16, 1924; Evelyn O'Day to the author, March 29, 1972; M&StL, Annual Report, 1924, 24; ibid., 1925, 25; James A. Ward, "On Time: Railroads and the Tempo of American Life," *Railroad History* (Autumn 1984): 87–95.

24. *Marshalltown (IA) Times-Republican,* September 4, 1937; Donald V. Stone, interview by author, March 5, 1966; *Des Moines Register,* June 24, 1973.

25. M&StL, Annual Reports, 1920–29; Leo A. McKee and Alfred L. Lewis, eds., *Railroads Post Office History* (Pleasantville, NY: Mobile Post Office Society, 1972), 59; John R. Borchert, "Heyday of the RPO System on the Pennsylvania Railroad," *Keystone* 32 (Winter 1999): 16–50.

26. *Railway Age* 85 (July 28, 1928): 168; H. V. Romine to Agt. Adams Express Co., Monmouth (IL), March 19, 1917, AC; Evelyn M. O'Day to the author, February 19, 1972; *Official Guide of the Minneapolis & St. Louis Railroad* (Minneapolis: M&StL, 1925), 14, 25–31, 60–63; Michael Ryan, interview by the author, August 31, 1965; Wilhelm F. Arp to the author, June 14, 1974; Evelyn M. O'Day to the author, February 19, 1972; Hartsough, *The Twin Cities,* 56–57; Margaret Thorp, *America at the Movies* (New Haven, CT: Yale University Press, 1939), 154; *St. James (MN) Journal-Gazette,* February 20, 1913.

27. *Railway Age* 87 (August 3, 1929): 352; Wilhelm F. Arp to the author, June 14, 1974.

28. M&StL tabular data, 1920–29; M&StL, Annual Report, 1924, 41; 90 ICC 630–32; M&StL, Annual Report, 1925, 43; *Iowa Railroad Commissioners' Report, 1925* (Des Moines: State of Iowa, 1925), 264; *State Center (Iowa) Enterprise,* August 27, 1925.

29. CRI&P, Abstract of Important Contracts Affecting

Operations (February 15, 1965), 20, AC; 124 ICC 610–12; 137 ICC 849–51.

30. *Official Guide* (April 1926), xxxiv; *Railway Age* 85 (July 14, 1928): 83; M&StL, "Notice!" (February 18, 1924), AC.

31. James R. Sullivan to the author, March 10 and 28, 1997, with Baldwin Locomotive Works drawings; M&StL, "Locomotive Characteristics as of June 1, 1926 with an Analysis of Proposed Improvements and Alterations," AC; M&StL, AFE Index, passim.

32. CRI&P, Annual Report, 1919, 36; *New York Times,* July 31, 1924; "Rail Motor Car Orders in 1928," *Railway Age* 86 (January 5, 1929): 109–11; "The 1929 Rail Motor-Car Orders," *Railway Age* 86 (January 4, 1930): 120–22; "Gas-Electric Cars on the Minneapolis & St. Louis," *Railway Age* 88 (February 22, 1930): 475; *Peoria Evening Star,* December 1 and 27, 1929.

14. Soldiering On

1. On the economy of the 1920s and the Crash of 1929, see John Kenneth Galbraith, *The Great Crash, 1929* (Boston: Houghton Mifflin, 1957); William K. Klingaman, *1929: The Year of the Great Crash* (New York: Harper & Row, 1989); and Robert Sobel, *The Great Bull Market* (New York: W. W. Norton, 1968).

2. Sidney L. Miller et al., *Rates of Return: Class I Line-Haul Railways in the United States, 1921–1948* (Pittsburgh: University of Pittsburgh Press, 1950), 17, 21–22, 36; *Moody's Manual of Investments: Railroad Securities* (New York: Moody's Investors Service, 1945), a24; *New York Times,* August 22, 1922, and March 22 and October 8, 1923; M&StL, Stockholders' Protective Committee Agreement, August 2, 1923, AC; *Moody's Analysis of Investment and Security Rating Books: Railroad Investments* (New York: Moody's Investors Service, 1923), lxxiii; *Minneapolis Journal,* February 10, 1927.

3. *New York Times,* March 21, April 24, and October 30, 1924, and January 6, 1925; *Traffic World* 72 (December 15, 1928): 1347; *Minneapolis Tribune,* May 23, 1928.

4. *Brotherhood of Locomotive Firemen and Enginemen's Magazine* 123 (August 1947): 135; Kent T. Healy, *Performance of the U.S. Railroads since World War II* (New York: Vantage Press, 1985), 158–59.

5. "Rating Hearings Opened in Chicago," *Railway Age* 79 (September 12, 1925): 473–77; *Minneapolis Journal,* January 30, 1927; M&StL, Annual Report, 1925, 4.

6. Michael Conant, *Railroad Mergers and Abandonments* (Berkeley: University of California Press, 1964), 49.

7. *New York Times,* January 2, 1927; William Norris Leonard, *Railroad Consolidation under the Transportation Act of 1920* (New York: Columbia University Press, 1946), 78–79, 86.

8. Ralph W. Hidy, Muriel E. Hidy, Roy V. Scott, and Don L. Hofsommer, *The Great Northern Railway: A History* (Minneapolis: University of Minnesota Press, 2004), 191–95; Howard Elliott to Charles Donnelly, October 16, 1922, NP President File 197–21, MHS; Ralph Budd to G. Griswold, July 25, 1924, GN Executive File 9825, MHS.

9. "Analysis of the Minneapolis & St. Louis Railroad Company," GN President File 12,349, MHS.

10. Julius Grodinsky, *Railroad Consolidation: Its Economics and Controlling Principles* (New York: D. Appleton, 1930), 267, 270; *New York Times,* August 5, 1927.

11. *Des Moines Tribune,* October 14, 1927; Ralph Budd to Walker D. Hines, July 26, 1927; Ralph Budd to Hale Holden, October 17, 1927, both from GN President File 12,349, MHS; Richard C. Overton, *Burlington Route: A History of the Burlington Lines* (New York: Alfred A. Knopf, 1965), 330.

12. F. S. Lisman to Ralph Budd and Charles Donnelly, December 29, 1927; Ralph Budd to C. W. Gordon, April 2, 1928; Ralph Budd to Walker D. Hines, April 3, 1928, all from GN President File 12,349, MHS; *Railway Age* 84 (February 4, 1928): 337; ibid. (March 24, 1928): 683–84; *New York Times,* March 22, 1928; *Des Moines Register,* April 4, 1928.

13. *Wall Street Journal,* April 19, 1928; *Railway Age* 85 (July 7, 1928): 63–64; ibid. (October 13, 1928): 711–13; Ralph Budd to G. R. Martin, January 10, 1929, GN President File 12,349, MHS; 154 ICC 522–89; Hidy et al., *Great Northern,* 194–95; Leonard, *Railroad Consolidation,* 172–74.

14. Samuel O. Dunn, "A Revolution in Railroading," *World's Work* 53 (1927): 419–26; H. G. Andrews, "War among the Railroads," *The Nation* 121 (August 12, 1925): 184–86; *New York Times,* October 10, 1926, and April 24, 1927; *Literary Digest* 85 (June 6, 1925): 94–95; William G. Shepherd, "Turntable," *Colliers* 81 (March 31, 1928): 8–9, 40.

15. M&StL tabular data and data from reports of the Iowa Commerce Commission, 1882–1931.

16. *Minneapolis Tribune,* August 8, 1889, July 7 and 14 and August 18, 1895, and June 11, 1896; M&StL, AFE 27R348; *Winthrop News,* August 14, 1930; *Railway Age* 76 (March 8, 1924): 566.

17. Manford J. Reitan, interview by author, August 18,

1993; Charles Dillon, "How a Western Railroad Was Humanized," *Railway Review* 78 (January 9, 1926): 113–15; "The M&StL Booster Club," *Transportation Magazine* 3 (June 1926): 8.

18. Dillon, "How a Railroad Was Humanized," 114.

19. *Railroader* 7 (October 1931): 1; M&StL, *After 51 Years* (Minneapolis: M&StL, 1931), 1, 30–33; *Hennepin County Review* 28 (May 21, 1931): 1, 8; ibid. (June 25, 1931): 1, 10.

20. Freeman Hubbard, *Encyclopedia of North American Railroading: 150 Years of Railroading in the United States and Canada* (New York: McGraw-Hill, 1981), 32–33; Benjamin A. Botkin and Alvin F. Harlow, *A Treasury of Railroad Folklore* (New York: Crown Publishing, 1953), 164–65, 312–13; M&StL Seniority Rosters, AC.

21. T. H. Farmen to the author, March 4, 1972; Albert M. Ramnes, interview by the author, January 6, 1971; Julia Becken to the author, November 10, 1971; *Winthrop News*, October 13, 1932.

22. *Minneapolis Journal*, July 17, 1907; *Sioux Rapids (IA) Republican Press*, May 8, 1919; S. S. Judy and Will G. Robinson, "Sanborn County History," *South Dakota Historical Collections* 26 (1952): 95; Wilson 95 to JMS, 1-16-??, AC; Searsboro (IA) Centennial Committee, *Roses and Thorns of Yesteryear: Searsboro, Iowa* (Searsboro: Searsboro Centennial Committee, 1970), 93–95.

23. *Railroad Magazine* (November 1942): 32–33; Robert M. P. Burnet, "Lucky Brakeman," *Railroad Magazine* (August 1941): 77–82; *Minneapolis Tribune*, October 12, 1891, and September 4, 1896; *Minneapolis Journal*, February 21, 1912; *Jordan Independent*, September 15, 1906; *Winthrop News*, July 22, 1915, and December 25, 1919; Livermore (IA) Centennial Committee, *Livermore Centennial: 1880–1980* (Livermore: Livermore Centennial Committee, 1980), 8–9.

24. James E. Child, *Child's History of Waseca County, Minnesota* (Waseca: James E. Child, 1905), 356–58; *New York Times*, February 18, 1881; *Chicago Tribune*, January 10, 1886; *Jordan Independent*, March 2, 1887; M&StL, Annual Report, 1890, 6–7; Gerald M. Best, *Snowplow: Clearing Mountain Rails* (Berkeley, CA: Howell-North Books, 1966), 106; Gene Green, "Snow Plows of the M&StL Railway: A Partial History," *North Western Lines* 23 (Winter 1996): 57–71; Paul Swanson, "The Leslie Brothers: Their Great Snowblower," *Trains* 47 (January 1987): 27–39.

25. J. Tonge to HEE, February 18, 1905, AC; *New Ulm Daily Journal*, August 13, 1954; Hanson to HEE, February 24, 1909; E. A. Kelly to N. Neilson, February 26, 1909, both from AC; *Le Beau Phenix*, January 13 and March 3, 1910.

26. *Minneapolis Journal*, January 14 and February 4, 1912; *Winthrop News*, February 11, 1915.

27. R. E. Ryan, "Notes on Snow Storm of 1917," AC; *Des Moines Sunday Register*, February 27, 1966; *New Ulm Daily Journal*, August 13, 1954; *Hanska Herald*, February 9, 1917; *Winthrop News*, March 22, 1917; Lee Deemer, *Esther's Town* (Ames: Iowa State University Press, 1980), 82; M&StL, Annual Report, 1917, 12.

28. *St. James Independent*, December 22, 1927; *Dawson (MN) Sentinel*, June 3, 1981; Jack O'Neil, interview by author, August 9, 1971.

15. Mean and Ugly

1. Lucile M. Kane and Alan Ominsky, *Twin Cities: A Pictorial History of St. Paul and Minneapolis* (St. Paul: Minnesota Historical Society, 1983), 158–59; Theodore C. Blegen, *Minnesota: A History of the State* (Minneapolis: University of Minnesota Press, 1963), 483; Frank A. King, *Minnesota's Logging Railroads* (San Marino, CA: Golden West Books, 1981), 119–20.

2. On the 1930s depression, see Broadus Mitchell, *The Depression Decade from the New Era through New Deal, 1929–1941* (New York: Holt, Rinehart & Winston, 1947); Lester V. Chandler, *America's Greatest Depression, 1921–1941* (New York: Harper & Row, 1970); Robert S. McElvaine, *The Great Depression: America, 1929–1941* (New York: Random House, 1984); and John A. Garraty, *The Great Depression* (New York: Harcourt Brace Jovanovich, 1986).

3. *Minneapolis Tribune*, October 20–30, 1929; *Des Moines Register*, October 25, 1929; Frederick Lewis Allen, *Since Yesterday: The 1930s in America* (New York: Harper & Row, 1939), 2–15; Blegen, *Minnesota*, 524; Broadus Mitchell, *Depression Decade*, 97; Peter Fearon, *War, Prosperity, and Depression: The U.S. Economy, 1917–1945* (Lawrence: University Press of Kansas, 1987), 90–97, 110, 173; Alfred D. Chandler Jr., *The Visible Hand: The Managerial Revolution in Business* (Cambridge, MA: Harvard University Press, 1977), 496; Lester Chandler, *America's Greatest Depression*, 5–29, 83, 129.

4. William G. Murray, "Iowa Land Values, 1803–1967," *Palimpsest* 47 (October 1967): 461–504, esp. 469–80; David B. Danbom, *Born in the Country: A History of Rural America* (Baltimore: The Johns Hopkins University Press, 1995), 197–202; Lester Chandler, *America's Greatest Depression*, 53–67; Fearon, *War, Prosperity, and Depression*, 101–7;

Earl D. Ross, *Iowa Agriculture: An Historical Survey* (Iowa City: State Historical Society of Iowa, 1951), 160–61; Dohn Muhm, "Comment," *Annals of Iowa* 47 (Fall 1983): 133; Jimmy Skaggs, *Prime Cut: Livestock Raising and Meatpacking in the United States, 1607–1983* (College Station: Texas A&M University Press, 1986), 140, 148, 150.

5. Vance Johnson, *Heaven's Tableland: The Dust Bowl Story* (New York: Farrar, Strauss, 1947), 147, 150, 167–73, 185–89, 195, 206–7, 214–16, 274; *Winthrop News,* July 6, 1933, May 17 and 24, June 7 and 21, July 12 and 26, and August 2 and 23, 1934; Madison Centennial Committee, *Madison Historical Album* (Madison Centennial Committee, 1985), 145; *Des Moines Register,* May 20 and July 23, 1934; Lee Deemer, *Esther's Town* (Ames: Iowa State University Press, 1980), 181.

6. Herbert S. Schell, *History of South Dakota* (Lincoln: University of Nebraska Press, 1968), 277–84, 363; M&StL, Time Table, May 1923, 5, 14–15; ibid., August 15, 1930, 9; *Minneapolis Tribune,* July 17, 1940; *Florence (SD) Forum,* September 28, 1933; M&StL, AFEs 31R42, 31R421; "Revillo South Dakota in the Heart of South Dakota's Garden Spot" (n. p., n.d. [1933?]), AC; *Winthrop News,* August 13, 1931, and March 24, 1932; Donald H. Grimm, *Community History: Zearing, Iowa* (Zearing: Privately published by the author, 1956), 205.

7. Allen, *Since Yesterday,* 123; Hartzell Spence, *One Foot in Heaven: The Life of a Practical Parson* (New York: Grosset & Dunlap, 1940), 276–77; *Winthrop News,* October 9, 1930, January 1, 1931, and January 14 and 21, February 4, March 24, and June 23, 1932.

8. *Winthrop News,* November 16, 1933; Ruby Deming, *The History of Franklin, Minnesota, 1880–1990* (Franklin: Privately published by the author, 1990), 142–43; *Weekly Item* [Revillo, SD], August 30 and September 6, 1934; *Spencer News-Herald,* July 2, 1931.

9. *Railway Age* 87 (November 23, 1929): 1177–78, 1201–3; ibid., 88 (January 4, 1930): 9; *New York Times,* November 20, 1929, and January 29, 1930; GN, Annual Report, 1930, 8; NP, Annual Report, 1929, 13; ibid., 1932, 13; CM&StP, Annual Report, 1930, 3; Soo Line, Annual Report, 1929, 14; ibid., 1930, 13; *Railway Age* 89 (October 4, 1930): 683–84; *Moody's Manual of Investments: Railroad Securities* (New York: Moody's Investors Service, 1945), a13–a24.

10. Roger Biles, *A New Deal for the American People* (De Kalb: Northern Illinois University Press, 1991), 23–24; Michael W. Schuyler, *The Dread of Plenty: Agricultural Relief Activities of the Federal Government in the Middle West, 1933–1939* (Manhattan, NY: Sunflower University Press, 1989), 1–41; Leland L. Sage, *A History of Iowa* (Ames: Iowa State University Press, 1974), 269–87; Schell, *History of South Dakota,* 282–84; Blegen, *Minnesota,* 521–29; *Des Moines Register,* November 9, 1932.

11. Edward C. Kirkland, *A History of American Economic Life,* 4th ed. (New York: Appleton-Century-Crofts, 1969), 510–13; Sage, *History of Iowa,* 288–301; Skaggs, *Prime Cut,* 142; Sandoz, *The Cattlemen,* 1958, 480; Schell, *History of South Dakota,* 289; Broadus Mitchell, *Depression Decade,* 190; Blegen, *Minnesota,* 535–36; Sage, *History of Iowa,* 301–2.

12. *New Republic* 65 (January 14, 1931): 231–32; George W. Anderson, "Salvaging Our Railroads," *Atlantic Monthly* (December 1932): 710–17; *New York Times,* September 18, 1932; Earl Latham, *The Politics of Railroad Coordination, 1933–1936* (Cambridge, MA: Harvard University Press, 1959), 1–34.

13. Herbert Spero, *Reconstruction Finance Corporation Loans to the Railroads, 1932–1937* (Boston: Bankers Publishing, 1939), 1–4, 18–41, 132–50, 163–65; *Wall Street Journal,* February 15 and May 6, 1933; Albert V. House Jr., "Post–Civil War Precedents for Recent Railroad Reorganization," *Mississippi Valley Historical Review* 25 (March 1939): 505–22; Churchill Rodgers and Littleton Groom, "Reorganization of Railroad Corporations under Section 77 of the Bankruptcy Act," *Columbia Law Review* 33 (April 1933): 571–616; Edward T. Paxton, "Railroad Receiverships and Reorganizations," *Editorial Research Reports* 1 (1933): 23–36; *Moody's Manual of Railroad Securities, 1945,* a56–a62; R. W. Harbeson, "The Emergency Railroad Transportation Act of 1933," *Journal of the Political Economy* 42 (February 1934): 106–26.

14. *New York Times,* April 6, May 4, and June 4, 1932; G. R. Cooksey to C. W. Wright, September 29, 1932; Phillip J. Roosevelt to Reconstruction Finance Corporation and Interstate Commerce Commission, February 9, 1933; Phillip J. Roosevelt to M. C. Kennedy, March 1, 1933, all from AC; *Traffic World* 51 (February 8, 1933): 323–24; ibid. (March 4, 1933): 432–33; *New York Times,* February 10–11 and 28, 1933; G. R. Cooksey to W. H. Bremner, July 17, 1933, AC; *Winthrop News,* February 16, 1933.

15. *Poor's Manual of the Railroads* (New York: Poor's Manual Co., 1934), 912–13; *Minneapolis Star,* August 20, 1934; *Winthrop News,* December 22, 1932.

16. M&StL, operating time tables, 1929–34.

17. M&StL tabular data, 1911–34.

18. M&StL operating time tables, 1929–34; *Moody's Manual of Investments: Steam Railroads* (New York: Moody's Investors Service, 1941), a78; M&StL, Annual Report, 1929, 20; Edmund Keilty, *Doodlebug Country: The Rail Motorcar on the Class I Railroads of the United States* (Glendale, CA: Interurban Press, 1982), 102–4; Alan R. Lind, *From Horsecars to Steamliners: An Illustrated History of the St. Louis Car Company* (Park Forest, IL: Transport History Press, 1978), 362–64; *Railway Age* 88 (January 4, 1930): 100–101; ibid. (February 22, 1930): 475; ibid., 90 (January 3, 1931): 102; ibid., 92 (January 2, 1932): 69; "Rail Motors Do the Job on the M&StL," *Railway Age* 92 (April 23, 1932): 689–91; *Winthrop News,* January 9, 1930, and July 23 and December 31, 1931; *Storm Lake Pilot-Tribune,* February 26, 1931; *Winthrop News,* December 7, 1932; M&StL, Annual Report, 1930, 20.

19. *New York Times,* February 10, 1932; *Waconia Patriot,* July 30, 1930; *Winthrop News,* September 25, 1930, and September 1, 1932; T. H. Farmen to the author, March 4, 1972; M&StL, Annual Report, 1930, 20; ibid., 1931, 20; ibid., 1932, 20; ibid., 1934, 19.

20. *Moody's Manual of Steam Railroads,* a78; NP President Subject File 137.D.12.4F, MHS; M&StL, Supplement to Passenger Folder Issued April 30, 1932—Change in Effect Sunday June 11, 1933, AC; M&StL, Annual Report, 1934, 12–13.

21. GN, President Files 13,919 and 14,048, MHS; *Iowa Railroad Commission Report, 1933,* 27–31; *Minnesota Railroad and Warehouse Commission Report, 1934,* 184–87; Buel W. Patch, "The Railroads and the Depression," *Editorial Research Reports* 2 (1932): 127–44; C&NW, Secretary File 480-106.

22. M&StL, Annual Report, 1930, 3–5; M&StL, AFEs 29R336, 31R327, 32R277.

23. W. W. Baldwin, *Corporate History of the Chicago, Burlington & Quincy Railroad Company and Affiliated Companies as of June 30, 1917* (Chicago: CB&Q, 1921), 203–7; *Traffic World* 53 (June 30, 1934): 1237; ibid., 54 (July 21, 1934): 92; M&StL, Annual Report, 1934, 39; 202 ICC 68–76; 207 ICC 459–60; M&StL, AFEs 34R359–65, 35R207; M&StL, Eastern Division Time Table No. 32 (September 30, 1934), 10; C&NW, Secretary File 480-106; *The History of Mahaska County, Iowa* (Dallas, TX: Curtis Media, 1984), 32.

24. 90 ICC 31–35, 117 ICC 731–33, 202 ICC 52–60; E. W. Mureen, "A History of the Fulton County Narrow Gauge Railway: The Spoon River 'Peavine,'" *Railway and Locomotive Historical Society Bulletin* 61A (August 1943): 1–71; Richard Wallin, Paul Stringham, and John Szwajkart, *Chicago & Illinois Midland* (San Marino, CA: Golden West Books, 1979), 91.

25. Albert Graber to Joseph B. Eastman, January 29, 1934; W. B. Irwin, "Twin Cities Terminal Study," March 17, 1934; W. B. Irwin, "Memorandum," November 8, 1934, all from GN President File 7502, MHS.

26. *Winthrop News,* July 3 and August 7, 1930, October 8, 1931, April 28, 1932, November 23, 1933, and April 5, May 31, and June 7 and 21, 1934; *Minnesota Railroad and Warehouse Commission Report, 1934,* 215–16; Madison Centennial Committee, *Madison Historical Album,* 146; *Spencer Reporter,* June 11, 1971, and September 8, 1977.

27. Allen, *Since Yesterday,* 60–61; *Winthrop News,* July 28, 1932, January 11, 1934; Gus Dallman, interview by author, August 9, 1971; *Des Moines Register,* March 2, 1936; Harold Hill, *Memorable Days of the Flats* (Fort Dodge, IA: Privately published by the author, 1994), 34, 42.

28. *New York News,* May 7 and June 27, 1934; *Railway Age* 96 (May 12, 1934): 709; C. W. Wright, Memorandum, November 11, 1949, AC.

29. File B1-1196-5-12, Barringer Railroad Library, St. Louis.

30. Wright memorandum; Blegen, *Minnesota,* 525, 529.

31. *Winthrop News,* September 6, 27, 1934; *New York Times,* September 19, October 12, 1934; Wright memorandum; W. B. Davids, "*Mileposts on the Prairie,* a friendly review of same by W. B. Davids" (n.d. [1951?]), 17–22, AC.

32. *Winthrop News,* December 20, 1934; *Transportation Magazine* 3 (June 1926): 8–9; *Railroad Telegrapher* 52 (January 1935): 74.

33. Davids, review of *Mileposts on the Prairie,* 22; M&StL, Annual Report, 1933, 3; ibid., 1934, 2.

16. Frey and Dismemberment

1. *Who Was Who in America* (Chicago: Marquis Who's Who, 1943), 460; *Railroad Age* 48 (January 26, 1935): 183.

2. *National Cyclopedia of American Biography: Current Volume G 1943–1946* (New York: James T. White & Co., 1946), 393; *Who's Who in America* (Chicago: A. N. Marquis Co., 1953), 2292; Henry E. Bender, *Uintah Railway: The Gilsonite Route* (Berkeley, CA: Howell-North, 1970), 141, 147, 153, 165; *Railway Age* 98 (January 26, 1935): 183–84.

3. Broadus Mitchell, *Depression Decade: From New Era through New Deal, 1929–1941* (New York: Holt, Rinehart & Winston, 1947), 226; *Winthrop News,* January 3, May 23, August 8, and December 26, 1935, and November 12, 1936; *Gaylord (MN) Hub,* April 24, 1935; *Spencer Daily Reporter,* January 1, 1936; D. Jerome Tweeton, *Depression:*

Minnesota in the Thirties (Fargo: North Dakota Institute for Regional Studies, 1981), 45.

4. *New York Times,* October 11 and 16, 1934; F. G. Dorety to W. P. Kenney, October 20, 1934; Memorandum with Respect to Disposition of M&StL Properties and Rights, Chicago, January 11, 1935, NP President File 805-46, MHS; *Traffic World* 55 (January 12, 1935): 98; Ralph Budd to Charles Donnelly and W. P. Kenney, September 29 and October 15, 1934, NP President File 805-46, MHS.

5. *Traffic World* 56 (July 20, 1935): 97; ibid. (September 14, 1935): 423–25; *Railway Age* 98 (March 2, 1935): 347; ibid., 99 (September 14, 1935): 337–38.

6. Ralph Budd to Charles Donnelly and W. Kenney, September 29, 1934, NP President File 805-46, MHS; *New York Times,* November 24, 1934; *Railroad Telegrapher* 52 (January 1935): 74; ibid. (November 1935), 857–59; *Minneapolis Journal,* October 13, 1935; *Railway Age* 98 (April 6, 1935): 551; ibid. (May 25, 1935), 836.

7. U.S. Senate, 74th Congress, Second Session, *Hearings before a Subcommittee of the Committee on Interstate Commerce,* May 13–28, 1936, 226 (hereinafter referred to as *Hearings*); Manford J. Reitan to Vern R. Wigfield, June 20, 1992, AC; Manford J. Reitan, interview by author, September 18, 1996; W. L. Landmesser, interview by author, July 7, 1990, and July 15, 1991.

8. Boone County Historical Society, *Trail-Tales,* no. 31 (1978): 18–19; *Who's Who in Railroading* (New York: Simmons-Boardman, 1940), 664; *Railway Mechanical Engineer* (August 1940): 336; John W. Barriger III, interview by author, October 17, 1975.

9. *Hearings,* 173; M&StL, AFE Index.

10. *Hearings,* 177; M&StL, Notes on Inspection Trip, January 7th to 12th, 1935, AC.

11. *Literary Digest* 60 (February 15, 1919): 27; *Railway Age* 112 (January 3, 1942): 95; James M. Herring, *The Problem of Weak Railroads* (Philadelphia: University of Pennsylvania Press, 1929), 128–29; Frank N. Wilner, *Railroad Mergers: History, Analysis, Insight* (Omaha: Simmons-Boardman, 1997), 61; C&NW Secretary File 480-106; *Storm Lake Pilot-Tribune,* March 14, 1935.

12. Eugene N. Hastie, *Hastie's History of Dallas County, Iowa* (Perry, IA: Privately published by the author, 1938), 355; George S. May, "Getting Out of the Mud," *Palimpsest* 46 (February 1965): 115; Cyrenus Cole, *Iowa through the Years* (Iowa City: State Historical Society of Iowa, 1940), 468; *Winthrop News,* December 11, 1930; Edward Weiner, *Urban Transportation Planning in the United States: An Historical Overview* (Westport, CT: Praeger, 1999), 9; Ralph Budd, "The Changing Transportation Situation," an address at Des Moines, January 7, 1931, 5, AC.

13. John Steele Gordon, "Engine of Liberation," *American Heritage* 47 (November 1996): 42–54; *Wall Street Journal,* June 19, 1996; Alfred D. Chandler Jr., comp. & ed., *Giant Enterprise Ford, General Motors, and the Automobile Industry* (New York: Harcourt, Brace & World, 1964), 4; *Fort Dodge Messenger,* January 9, 1936; *Winthrop News,* February 27, 1936; *Grinnell (IA) Herald-Register,* May 21, 1936; *Spencer News-Herald,* July 2, 1931.

14. Herring, *Weak Railroads,* 130–32; *Winthrop News,* February 9 and August 31, 1933.

15. American Association of Railroad Superintendents, *Proceedings of the Forty-Eighth Annual Meeting, May 12–14, 1942,* 244; NP President File 805-46, MHS.

16. Herring, *Weak Railroads,* 133–34; *Business Week* (November 30, 1932): 15–16; ibid. (December 30, 1933): 24; *Winthrop News,* December 31, 1931; Stuart Daggett, "Our Changing Transportation System," *American Economic Review* (March 1932): 258; *Winthrop News,* January 14 and December 1, 1932.

17. Earle D. Ross, *Iowa Agriculture: An Historical Survey* (Iowa City: State Historical Society of Iowa, 1951), 160; *Winthrop News,* April 16, 1931, and April 27, 1934; Robert D. Lusk, "The Life and Decline of 470 Acres," *Saturday Evening Post* 21 (August 13, 1938): 5–6, 30–31; Frederick Lewis Allen, *Since Yesterday: The 1930s in America* (New York: Harper & Row, 1939), 196–99, 266; Gerald W. Wolff and Joseph H. Cash, "South Dakotans Remember the Great Depression," *South Dakota History* 19 (Summer 1989): 230–36; William H. Hull, *The Dirty Thirties* (Edina, MN: Privately published by the author, 1993), 11, 20, 93–94, 189, 195, 236, 252, Michael W. Schuyler, *The Dread of Plenty: Agricultural Relief Activities of the Federal Government in the Middle West, 1933–1939* (Manhattan: Sunflower University Press, 1989), 81–114.

18. *Spencer Daily Reporter,* December 27–28, 1935, and January 21 and 28, 1936; *Storm Lake Pilot-Tribune,* January 23, 1936; *Fort Dodge Messenger,* January 7 and February 3, 1936; *Marshalltown (IA) Times-Republican,* January 23, 1936; *Grinnell Herald,* January 21, 1936; Walter Carlson, *Happenings in Our Neighborhood,* 3 vols. (Trimont, MN: Trimont Progress, 1970), 3: 89.

19. *Storm Lake Pilot-Tribune,* February 6, 13, 1936; *Des Moines Register,* February 1–11, 1936; *Marshalltown Times-Republican,* February 2 and 14, 1936; *Fort Dodge Messenger,* February 10–11, 1936.

20. *Spencer Daily Reporter,* February 11–12, 1936; *Des Moines Tribune,* February 12, 1936; *Marshalltown*

Times-Republican, February 17, 1936; *Hampton (IA) Chronicle,* February 13, 1936; *Des Moines Register,* February 11–18, 1936; *Fort Dodge Messenger,* February 14–17, 1936; *Storm Lake Pilot-Tribune,* February 20 and 27, 1936; *Spencer Daily Reporter,* February 15, 17, 19–20, and 27–28, 1936; *Winthrop News,* February 20, 1936.

21. *Des Moines Register,* February 21, 1936; *Des Moines Tribune,* February 21, 1936; *Grinnell Herald,* February 27, 1936; *Marshalltown Times-Republican,* February 22, 1936; Bob Artley, *Memories of a Former Kid* (Ames: Iowa State University Press, 1978), 92; *Storm Lake Pilot-Tribune,* March 5, 1936; *Spencer Daily Reporter,* March 9 and 14, 1936; *Winthrop News,* March 12 and 19, 1936; *Fort Dodge Messenger,* March 6 and 11, 1936; M&StL, Engineer's Register, Spencer, Iowa, March 11–12, 1936, AC; Jack O'Neil, interview by the author, August 9, 1971.

22. *Winthrop News,* February 20 and March 5, 1936; *New Ulm Daily Journal,* August 13, 1954; William J. Peterson, " Variable Winters," *Palimpsest* 42 (February 1961): 70–75; M&StL, Annual Report, 1936, 17; M&StL, AFEs 37R22, 37R23.

23. *Fort Dodge Messenger,* January 15, 1936; 212 ICC 270–72; *Spencer Daily Reporter,* February 3 and 7, March 31, April 18 and 25, July 9, August 15, and September 14 and 30, 1936; 212 ICC 441–45, 212 ICC 449–50; 212 ICC 631–32; *Storm Lake Pilot-Tribune,* April 2, 9, 16, and 30, 1936; Gus Dallman, interview by author, August 9, 1971; M&StL, Annual Report, 1936, 5.

24. 212 ICC 501–4; *Spencer Daily Reporter,* May 21, 1936; 212 ICC 575–79; M&StL, Annual Report, 1936, 5, 30; *Grinnell Herald,* August 27, 1935, and August 3, 1936; *Des Moines Register,* August 2, 1936.

25. *Des Moines Leader,* January 5, 1896; *Iowa Board of Railway Commioners Report, 1886,* 50–59; "Railroad Consolidation and the Profit Motive," *Railroad Telegrapher* 151 (January 1934): 15–17; Clarence A. Miller, "The Problems of the Short Lines," *Annals of the American Academy of Political and Social Science* 187 (September 1936): 68–71.

26. Michael Conant, *Railroad Mergers and Abandonments* (Berkeley: University of California Press, 1964), 18–21; W. W. Atterbury, "Railroad Consolidation," *Annals of the American Academy of the Political and Social Sciences* 171 (January 1934): 166–71; John Will Chapman, *Railroad Mergers* (New York: Simmons-Boardman, 1934), 30–31; Latham, *Politics of Railroad Coordination,* 108.

27. *Marshalltown Times-Republican,* March 6, 1936; *Minneapolis Tribune,* April 3, 1936; *Railroad Age* 100 (April 11, 1936): 617, 626; ibid. (April 18, 1936): 662; ibid. (April 25, 1936): 683–84; *Minneapolis Tribune,* April 7–14, 1936.

28. *Minneapolis Tribune,* April 17, 1936; *Minneapolis Star,* April 17, 1936; *Spencer Daily Reporter,* January 27, 1936; *Marshalltown Times-Republican,* January 13, 1936; *Fort Dodge Messenger,* January 30 and February 8 and 14, 1936; *Winthrop News,* February 6 and 20 (quoting the *Madison Independent Press*), and March 12 (quoting the *Minneapolis Star*), 1936; *Minneapolis Tribune,* April 1 and 6, 1936.

29. *Hearings,* passim.

30. *Minneapolis Tribune,* April 23–June 28, 1936; *Hearings,* 1–2, 78, 171–78, 297–338.

31. *Minneapolis Tribune,* May 31 and June 2 and 4–6, 1936; *New York Times,* May 30 and June 2–6 and 14, 1936; *Time* (June 15, 1936): 64–65.

32. *Traffic World* 57 (June 13, 1936): 1141; M&StL, Engineer's Register, Spencer, Iowa, July 12–13, 1936; *Spencer Daily Reporter,* July 14–15 and October 6, 1936; *Minneapolis Tribune,* July 1–31, 1935; *Variety,* August 16, 1936; *Railway Age* 101 (July 11, 1936): 88; ibid. (July 18, 1936): 131–32; *Winthrop News,* August 20 and November 26, 1936, repeating an editorial from the *Minneapolis Star; Traffic World* 58 (November 21, 1936): 1005.

33. *Des Moines Register,* February 11, 1936; *Winthrop News,* March 5, 1936; Hull, *Dirty Thirties,* 26; Ross, *Iowa Agriculture,* 160; *Fort Dodge Messenger,* March 24, 1936; John P. Johansen, "Population Trends in Relation to Resource Development in South Dakota," *South Dakota Experiment Station Bulletin* 440 (August 1954): 7; *Des Moines Register,* July 16, 1936; *Spencer Daily Reporter,* July 7–21, August 8, and October 13, 1936; *Winthrop News,* July 16 and August 6, 1936.

34. M&StL, Engineer's Register, Spencer, Iowa, February 3 and 5, 1937; *Railroad Telegrapher* 54 (April 1937): 307; *Sioux Falls (SD) Argus-Leader,* April 18, 1989.

35. M&StL, Annual Report, 1936, 3, 5; M&StL, AFE 36R505; C&NW Secretary File 480-106; Jim Holden, "Misery & Short Life," *Railroad Magazine* 19 (May 1936): 33–39; *Poor's Railroad Volume 1935* (New York: Poor's Publishing, 1935), 77–80; *Business Week* (May 23, 1936): 34–36; Joseph B. Eastman, "The Future of Transportation," *Railway Age* 100 (April 18, 1936): 655–57; "Labor Movement Once More Urges Public Ownership of Railroads," *Railroad Telegrapher* 52 (November 1935): 795–96; "Must We Take Over the Railways?" *The Nation* 143 (November 14, 1936): 566–67; Albert Shaw, "Strangling Our Railroads," *Review of Reviews* 193 (May 1936): 59–65.

17. Reason for Hope?

1. Broadus Mitchell, *Depression Decade: From New Era through New Deal, 1929–1941* (New York: Holt, Rine-

hart & Winston, 1947), p.33; *Moody's Manual of Investment: Transportation* (New York: Moody's Investors Service, 1953), a49.

2. Peter Fearon, *War, Prosperity, and Depression: The U.S. Economy, 1917–45* (Lawrence: University Press of Kansas, 1987), 213; *Des Moines Register,* February 15, 1936; *Winthrop News,* 1936–39; *Spencer Daily Reporter,* 1936; *Winthrop News,* November 5 and 18, 1937; *Des Moines Register,* March 1, 1936; *Mitchell, Depression Decade,* 220–27; Gilbert C. Fite, "The Transformation of South Dakota Agriculture: The Effects of Mechanization, 1939–1964," *South Dakota History* 19 (Fall 1939): 278–305.

3. *Minneapolis Tribune,* June 20, 1936; *Time* 29 (May 17, 1937): 78–80.

4. Earl Latham, *The Politics of Railroad Coordination, 1933–1936* (Cambridge, MA: Harvard University Press, 1959), 246; John W. Knoble, "Oh No, Day Kann Do Dat!" *Carletonian* 3–4 (May 22, 1937): Supplement 3–4; *Newsweek* 9 (January 9, 1937): 24, 26; *New York Times,* September 1, 1937; Alonzo L. Hamby, "'Vultures at the Death of an Elephant': Harry S. Truman, The Great Train Robbery, and the Transportation Act of 1940," *Railroad History* (Autumn 1991): 6–36; *New York Times,* November 2, 1937.

5. *New York Times,* August 17 and October 29, 1937; "Would Have ICC Disapprove M&StL Dismemberment," *Railway Age* 19 (November 6, 1937): 645–47; *Traffic World* 60 (October 30, 1937): 973–74; ibid. (November 27, 1937): 1210; ibid. (December 25, 1937), 1426; *Winthrop News,* December 9, 1937.

6. V. V. Boatner and A. J. Hammond, *Report on the Minneapolis & St. Louis Railroad* (Chicago, 1936), passim., Barriger Railroad Library, St. Louis; M&StL, Engineers' Register, Spencer, Iowa, October 8–9, 1936; *Minneapolis Tribune,* April 10, 1936.

7. *New York Times,* November 13, 1937; *Traffic World* 71 (February 26, 1938): 489–90; ibid. (June 18, 1938): 1407–9; 228 ICC 277–379; William Norris Leonard, *Railroad Consolidation under the Transportation Act of 1920* (New York: Columbia University Press, 1946), 241–43; *Minneapolis Journal,* June 15, 1938; *Minneapolis Tribune,* June 15, 1938; Ralph Budd to Charles Connelly and W. P. Kenney, January 12, 1935, NP President File 805–46, MHS.

8. *Winthrop News,* March 3, 1938, repeating an editorial from the *Minneapolis Star; Minneapolis Journal,* June 13, 1938; *Minneapolis Tribune,* June 19 and July 10, 13, 17, and 22–24, 1938; *Winthrop News,* July 7, 14, 21, and 28, 1938; *Minneapolis Journal,* July 27, 1938.

9. M&StL AFES; *Winthrop News,* January 7, July 17, and August 12, 1937, and December 15, 1938.

10. *New York Times,* November 13, 1937, and October 19, 1938; *Minneapolis Tribune,* June 23 and 26, 1938, and January 20, 1939; *Winthrop News,* October 6, 1938.

11. *Minneapolis Tribune,* January 20, 1939; *Des Moines Register,* February 18, 1939; *New York Times,* May 15, 1939; *Traffic World* 63 (February 18, 1939): 369; ibid. (May 20, 1939): 1128; ibid., 64 (August 5, 1939): 302; *Railway Age* 106 (May 20, 1939): 882–83.

12. *Railway Age* 107 (July 1, 1939): 50–51; ibid. (October 28, 1939), 625; *New York Times,* August 17–18, 1939; *Traffic World* 64 (August 19, 1939): 407–8; ibid. (August 26, 1939): 457; ibid. (October 28, 1939), 929.

13. U.S. Senate, 74th Congress, Second Session, *Hearings before a Subcommittee of the Committee on Interstate Commerce, May 13–28, 1936,* 177 (hereinafter referred to as *Hearings*); 233 ICC 390–94; E. S. Lynch, "Analysis of Accounting Practice in Railroad Abandonments in Iowa from 1920 to 1940," *Iowa State College Bulletin* 39 (May 7, 1941): 1–55.

14. W. B. Hazen, " The Great Middle Region of the United States," *North American Review* (January 1875): 33; O. E. Rolvaag, *Giants in the Earth: A Saga of the Prairie* (New York: Harper & Row, 1965), 241; Manford J. Reitan, interview by the author, August 11, 1991; *Minneapolis Tribune,* July 17, 1940; John P. Johansen, "Population Trends in Relation to Resource Development in South Dakota," *South Dakota Experiment Station Bulletin* 440 (August 1954): 7–8; Herbert S. Schell, *History of South Dakota* (Lincoln: University of Nebraska Press, 1968), 277–95; Douglas Chittick, "Growth and Decline of South Dakota Trade Centers, 1901–1951," *South Dakota Experiment Station Bulletin* 448 (May 1955): 18–19.

15. Bureau of the Census, United States Maps, GE-50, No. 37; Leola Centennial Committee, *Leola Centennial, 1884–1984* (Leola: Leola Centennial Committee, 1984), 399, M&StL, AFE 25R293.

16. *Winthrop News,* July 22, 1937; Manford J. Reitan, interviews by the author, August 18, 1993, and September 18, 1996; Mike Raymond, "Working on the West End," *North Western Lines* 21 (Spring 1994): 59–68; Evelyn M. O'Day to the author, February 19, 1972.

17. M&StL Bulletin 416, November 18, 1936, AC; M&StL, AFE 37R417; George LaPray, "The Dakota Transfer Company," *North Western Lines* 10 (Spring 1983): 47; E. D. Conley to All Concerned, File 1-A-10, July 14, 1937, AC; M&StL, AFE 37R304.

18. 240 ICC 329–36; W. P. Kenney to C. O. Jenks, November 5, 1937, GN President File 16,352, MHS.

19. C&NW, Secretary File 480-106; *Fort Dodge Messenger,* February 26, 1936.

20. 240 ICC 329–36; *Traffic World* 65 (March 2, 1940): 526; M&StL, Annual Report, 1940, 6.

21. Olaf Morgan Norlie, *History of the Norwegian People in America* (Minneapolis: Augsburg Publishing, 1925), 344; 137 ICC 833; Julius Rosholt to Ralph Budd, March 18, 1919; Ralph Budd to Julius Rosholt, April 15, 1919; Ralph Budd to G. R. Martin, June 29, 1927; Ralph Budd to W. H. Bremner, June 29, 1927, GN President File 8940, MHS; Julius Rosholt to C. T. Jaffray, March 4, 1927; W. H. Bremner to G. R. Martin, July 26, 1927, both from Soo Line President File 4767, MHS; *Minneapolis Journal,* March 27 and September 28, 1927, and March 29, 1928; 138 ICC 553–62.

22. G. R. Martin to Ralph Budd, August 23, 1928, GN President File 8940, MHS; *Minneapolis Journal,* August 11, 1929, and March 20, 1932; *Railway Age* 85 (September 29, 1928): 634; "Short Line Turns to Rail-Highway Operation," *Railway Age* (November 23, 1935): 673–74; 228 ICC 425–32; 239 ICC 186–90.

23. *Railroad Telegrapher* 56 (March 1939): 227; ibid. (April 1939): 244; 239 ICC 179–85; *McPherson County Herald* [Leola, SD], December 15, 1938.

24. Eliot Janeway, "What Ruined the Railroads?" *The Nation* 145 (November 20, 1937): 555–57; F. E. Williamson, "Lo, the Poor Railroads," *Current History* 48 (March 1938): 47–50; Herbert Harris, "Labor in America," *Current History* 48 (March 1938): 50–53; Edward F. Collins, "Speaking of Finance," *Nation's Business* 26 (March 1958): 68, 70; Ralph Budd, "Our Ever-Present Problem," *Vital Speeches* 4 (March 1, 1938): 301–4; *New York Times,* March 3, 1939; M&StL, Annual Reports, 1930–39, passim; M&StL, Employee Time Table No. 1 (October 2, 1938), passim; M&StL, Seniority Rosters, AC; *Winthrop News,* November 28, 1934.

25. *Monmouth Daily Review Atlas,* July 1, 1938; M&StL, Annual Reports, 1936–39, passim; *Minneapolis Tribune,* October 22, 1939; M&StL, AFE 39R553.

26. *Winthrop News,* July 29, 1937; Frederick Lewis Allen, *Since Yesterday: The 1930s in America* (New York: Harper & Row, 1939), 332–34; *Des Moines Register,* September 1, 1939; *New York Times,* October 1, 1939.

18. Free at Last

1. Eliot Janeway, *The Struggle for Survival: A Chronicle of Economic Mobilization in World War II* (New Haven, CT: Yale University Press, 1951), 181–84, 234–39, 275–76; John F. Stover, *American Railroads* (Chicago: University of Chicago Press, 1961), 200–202; Richard C. Overton, *Perkins/Budd: Railway Statesmen of the Burlington* (Westport, CT: Greenwood Press, 1982), 201–2; Broadus Mitchell, *Depression Decade: From New Era through New Deal, 1929–1941* (New York: Holt, Rinehart & Winston, 1947), 361–402; *Railway Age* 109 (September 21, 1940): 399–403; Ralph L. Dewey, "The Transportation Act of 1940," *American Economic Review* 31 (March 1941): 15–26; Ari Hoogenboom and Olive Hoogenboom, *A History of the ICC: From Panacea to Palliative* (New York: W. W. Norton & Co., 1976), 133–38.

2. Mitchell, *Depression Decade,* 384–89.

3. Mitchell, *Depression Decade,* 47, 52–53, 389–90; *Des Moines Register,* December 8, 1941.

4. M&StL, AFEs 1940–43; M&StL, Annual Reports, 1940–43, passim; M&StL, AFE 42R26; Albert J. Churella, "Business Strategies and Diesel Development," *Railroad History,* Millennium Special (2000): 23–37.

5. *Winthrop News,* March 23, June 1, and November 30, 1933, February 8 and August 16, 1934, and January 10, 1935; *Minnesota Railroad and Warehouse Commission Report, 1934,* 282–84; *Moody's Manual of Investments: Steam Railroads* (New York: Moody's Investors Service, 1941), 278.

6. M&StL, Time Table (April 30, 1932), 4; M&StL, Annual Report, 1932, 20; ibid., 1933, 20; M&StL, Locomotive Runs as of 2-8-34, AC; George A. Kelly to Frank P. Donovan Jr., November 2, 1949, AC; William F. Armstrong to Frank P. Donovan Jr., July 14, 1949, and October 1, 1951, AC; W. L. Landmesser, interview by author, June 15, 1994; M&StL, Annual Report, 1935, 19.

7. M&StL, Time Table (June 23, 1935), 1; *Winthrop News,* August 31, 1939; D. B. Ransburg to Frank P. Donovan Jr., May 14, 1942, AC; *Des Moines Register,* April 25, 1971; Manford J. Reitan to the author, May 16, 1994; M&StL, Annual Report, 1939, 6; Paul H. Stringham to the author, March 15, 1988; M&StL, Annual Report, 1941, 5–6.

8. *Hanska Herald,* December 21, 2000; *Minneapolis Star,* August 10, 1938, and July 10, 1939; Paul H. Stringham to the author, June 18, 1990; William F. Armstrong to the author, December 6, 1985; *Winthrop News,* November 5 and 26, 1936; John Gross, *LaSalle: Whistle-Stop on the Prairie* (Medford, MN: Privately published by the author, 1999), 162; Sylvia Hanschen to the author, December 10, 1971; Manford J. Reitan to the author, August 18, 1993; *Official Guide* (April 1942), 1063; Gross, *LaSalle,* 89.

9. M&StL tabular data, 1930–43; M&StL, AFEs 37R308, 42R202, 42R315.

10. M&StL tabular data, 1910–43; M&StL *Official Guide of the Minneapolis & St. Louis Railroad Co.* (Minneapolis: M&StL, 1935), 7; *Fort Dodge Messenger,* January 20, 1936; *Winthrop News,* January 23, 1936; Analysis of the Minneapolis & St. Louis Railroad by H. K. Dorgan and L. Yager (1927), AC.

11. M&StL, Annual Report, 1932, 19; ibid., 1933, 4, 19; M&StL Contract 705 (April 10, 1933), C&NW; M&StL, *Official Guide of the Minneapolis & St. Louis Railroad* (Minneapolis: M&StL, 1935), passim; M&StL, AFEs 41R330, 41R410–11; M&StL, Right-of-Way and Track Map ILL-1, 8A, AC; Jacob A. Swisher, "Mining in Iowa," *Iowa Journal of History* 43 (October 1945): 314; Eugene N. Hastie, *History of Perry, Iowa* (Perry: Privately published by the author, 1962), 109; Hazel E. Drake, *History of Rippey, Greene County, Iowa: A Century of Progress, 1849–1956* (Hartley, IA: Sentinel Publishing, 1956), 27–28; M&StL, AFE 40R159.

12. State of Iowa, *Iowa Official Register* (Des Moines: State of Iowa, 1944), 243–44; Hocking Coal Minute Books 1–3, C&NW Secretary's Office; Hocking Coal Company, Annual Reports, 1918, 1930, AC; M&StL, AFE 34R97; M&StL, Annual Report, 1953, 12.

13. Dorothy Schwieder, "Iowa: The Middle Land," in *Heartland: Comparative History of the Midwestern States,* ed. James H. Madison (Bloomington: Indiana University Press, 1988), 291; State of Iowa, *Iowa Official Register,* 1944, 237; Earl D. Ross, *Iowa Agriculture: An Historical Survey* (Iowa City: State Historical Society of Iowa, 1951), 178–81; CRI&P, *Official Directory of Industries* (Chicago: CRI&P, 1942), 36–40, 46–47; William J. Petersen, *The Story of Iowa: The Progress of an American State,* 2 vols. (New York: Historical Publishing, 1952), 1064–80.

14. M&StL, Annual Report, 1941, 6; *Moody's Manual of Investments: Railroad Securities* (New York: Moody's Investors Service, 1945), a11–a12; Kent T. Healy, *Performance of the U.S. Railroads since World War II* (New York: Vantage Press, 1985), 71; *Newsweek* 22 (September 20, 1943): 72, 74, 76; *Business Week* (February 27, 1943): 58; John Patric and Frank J. Taylor, "'Featherbedding' Hampers the War Effect," *Readers Digest* 42 (March 1943): 25–29.

15. R. G. Kenly to J. W. Devins, February 2, 1935, AC; M&StL, AFE 46-135; *Winthrop News,* August 19, 1937; Eugene L. Huddleston, "War Production Board," *Railfan & Railroad* 5 (March 1985): 43–47; *Railfan & Railroad* 11 (June 1991): 52. Curiously, Mallets did make an appearance on M&StL—in 1945, after Germany surrendered, when massive Chesapeake & Ohio 2-8-8-2s heading for new homes on Union Pacific ran light from Peoria to Monmouth for interchange to CB&Q. Bob Lunoe, "Maiden Trip: Minneapolis & St. Louis," *Railfan & Railroad* 21 (May 2002): 44–49; Don L. Hofsommer, *The Southern Pacific, 1901–1985* (College Station: Texas A&M University Press, 1986), 191–92; Don L. Hofsommer, "The Day They Repealed Promontory," *Trains* 46 (July 1986): 54–55; M&StL, AFE 41R393.

16. 240 ICC 57–89; *New York Times,* April 16, 19, 1940; *Railway Age* 108 (April 20, 1940): 711–12.

17. *New York Times,* June 14, July 3, and October 17, 1940; *Traffic World* 66 (October 26, 1940): 1025; 244 ICC 357–91; 244 ICC 395–407; *Minneapolis Star Journal,* March 11, 1941; *Traffic World* 77 (March 15, 1941): 616, 644; ibid. (April 12, 1941): 929; ibid. (October 25, 1941): 1066.

18. 252 ICC 289–319; M&StL Contract File 480-106, C&NW; *Traffic World* 68 (October 25, 1941): 1035; "The 'Doctors' Were Wrong," *Railway Age* 108 (June 8, 1940): 1000–1006.

19. *Minneapolis Tribune,* July 24 and 25 and August 22, 1942; *New York Times,* July 25, 1942; *Minneapolis Star Journal,* September 11, 1942; *Railway Age* 113 (September 19, 1942): 437, 450–51; *New York Times,* January 23, March 22, July 17, and December 2, 1943; 254 ICC 513–28; *Time* 42 (November 29, 1943): 82–83; *Business Week* (December 11, 1943), 106–7; *Moody's Manual of Railroad Securities,* a37; M&StL, Annual Report, 1943, 5–7; 257 ICC 815; *Business Week* (March 18, 1944), 69.

20. M&StL Stockholder Records, AC.

19. Don't You Know There's a War On?

1. Allan Nevins, "How We Felt about the War," in *While You Were Gone: A Report on Wartime Life in the United States,* ed. Jack Goodman (New York: Simon and Schuster, 1946), 3–27; Allen M. Winkler, *Home Front U.S.A.: America during World War II* (Arlington Heights, IL: Harlan Davidson, 1986), 14, 19–21; Harold G. Vatter, *The U.S. Economy in World War II* (New York: Columbia University Press, 1985), 11–19; John W. Jefferies, *Wartime America: The World War II Home Front* (Chicago: Ivan R. Dee, 1996), 16, 31–45; *New York Times,* January 2, 1945; John Steele Gordon, "The American Superweapon," *American Heritage* 42 (December 1991): 16–17.

2. Winkler, *Home Front U.S.A.,* 21–22; Jefferies, *Wartime America,* 58–60; Vatter, *U.S. Economy in World War II,*

52–55; Leland L. Sage, *A History of Iowa* (Ames: Iowa State University Press, 1974), 317.

3. Albro Martin, *Railroad Triumphant: The Growth, Rejection, and Rebirth of a Vital American Force* (New York: Oxford University Press, 1992), 370–72; *Official Guide* (February 1945), 14; John F. Stover, *Life and Decline of American Railroads* (New York: Oxford University Press, 1970), 184–85; *New York Times,* January 14, June 11, and October 12, 1944, and February 7, 1945; Thor Hultgren, "American Railroads in Wartime," *Political Science Quarterly* 67 (September 1942): 321–37; James E. Valle, "Railroads in the Crucible of War," *Vintage Rails* (Summer 1997): 31–42, 76–78. On the general topic, see S. Kip Farrington, *Railroads at War* (New York: Coward-McCann, 1944).

4. M&StL, Annual Report, 1944, 6; *Forest City Summit,* July 28, 1955; *Winthrop News,* June 17, 1943; Ruby Deming, *The History of Franklin, Minnesota, 1880–1990* (Franklin: Privately published by the author, 1990), 151; Robert F. Karolevitz, "Life on the Home Front: South Dakota in the World War II, " *South Dakota History* 19 (Fall 1989): 392–423.

5. L. O. Head, "Railway Express Agency Services and Problems," *Annals of American Political and Social Science* 230 (November 1943): 101–9; *St. Louis Star,* July 3, 1945; *Railway Age* 106 (March 4, 1939): 363, 365–72; *Winthrop News,* December 3, 1942; Margaret Thorp, *America at the Movies* (New Haven, CT: Yale University Press, 1939), 1–25.

6. M&StL tabular data; *Iowa Commerce Commission Report, 1943,* 151–53; *Railway Age* 114 (June 19, 1943): 1239; ibid., 104 (January 1, 1938): 100–101; *Winthrop News,* August 24 and November 2 and 16, 1944.

7. M&StL tabular data; "Troop Trains," *Life* 14 (June 28, 1943): 77–85; Manford J. Reitan, interviews by the author, August 18, 1993, and September 18, 1996.

8. H. Bill Brower to the author, November 3, 1971; Sylvia Hanschen to the author, December 10, 1971; *Official Guide* (February 1945), 14; Dan N. Knight to the author, May 11, 1978; *Winthrop News,* March 1, May 3, 10, 1945; *Iowa Commerce Commission Report, 1945,* 184–87.

9. M&StL, AFE 45-13; M&StL Minute Book, 234; M&StL, Annual Report, 1944, 7; *Winthrop News,* June 22, 1949; M&StL tabular data.

10. M&StL Minute Book, 181, 191, 229–33; *Railway Age* 116 (February 5, 1944): 334; Freeman Hubbard, "Out of the Red," *Railroad Magazine* 35 (April 1944): 46–57; *Minneapolis Tribune,* April 27, 1944; M&StL, Annual Report, 1944, 7.

11. M&StL tabular data, 1943–45; M&StL, AFEs; M&StL, Annual Report, 1944, 6; ibid., 8.

12. M&StL, AFE 43R170.

13. M&StL, Annual Report, 1945, 4; M&StL, wall calendar 1944; William W. Landmesser, interview by the author, September 11, 1993; M&StL, AFEs.

14. *New York Times,* January 2 and February 4, 1945; *Railway Age* 118 (May 19, 1945): 886–89; ibid., 120 (January 5, 1946): 88–91; ibid. (June 15, 1946): 20–21; M&StL, AFE 46-135; John F. Kirkland, *The Diesel Builders,* vol. 3, *Baldwin Locomotive Works* (Pasadena, CA: Interurban Press, 1994), 46–47, 65; Albert J. Churella, *From Steam to Diesel: Managerial Customs and Organizational Capabilities in the Twentieth-Century American Locomotive Industry* (Princeton, NJ: Princeton University Press, 1998), 75–94.

15. Albert Churella, "Corporate Culture and Marketing in the American Locomotive Industry: American Locomotive and Electro-Motive Despond to Dieselization," *Business History Review* 69 (Summer 1995): 191–229; Eugene L. Huddleston, "The War Protection Board and Diesels," *Railfan & Railroad* 5 (January 1986): 36–44; Louis A. Marre, *Diesel Locomotives: The First 50 Years* (Waukesha, WI: Kalmbach Publishing, 1995), 231; John F. Kirkland, *The Diesel Builders,* vol. 2, *American Locomotive Company and Montreal Locomotive Works* (Glendale, CA: Interurban Press, 1992), 73–90; William W. Landmesser, interviews by the author, July 15, 1991, August 19, 1992, and June 15, 1994.

16. William W. Landmesser, Work Diary for 1944, October 3, and November 1, AC; M&StL Minute Book, 262, 327; Charles W. Stone, interview by the author, August 19, 1992.

17. Preston Cook, "Electro-Motives FTs Celebrate 50 Years," *Railfan & Railroad* 8 (October 1989): 46–58; Mark Ruetter, "The Great (Motive) Power Struggle: The Pennsylvania Railroad v. General Motors, 1935–1939," *Railroad History* (Spring 1994): 15–33; J. David Ingles, "Still the Diesel That Did It," *Trains* 60 (January 2000): 46–47; M&StL Minute Book, 235, 288–89; Marre, *Diesel Locomotives,* 87–89; William W. Landmesser, interviews by the author, August 19, 1992, and August 23, 1994; Franklin M. Reck, *On Time: The History of Electro-Motive Division of General Motors Corporation* (LaGrange, IL: Electro-Motive, 1948), 131–42.

18. Landmesser, Work Diary for 1945, January 24, AC; Station Record of Train Movements and Operator's Transfer, Hazel Run, Minnesota, September 6, October 9, 1945, AC; M. Sheridan, Trip Book, 1937–46, AC; Dispatcher's Transfer Book, "East Orders," December 13–17, 1945, AC; M&StL, Time Table No. 6 (January 13, 1946), 2–3.

19. M&StL, Annual Report, 1945, 8; *Iowa Commerce Commission Reports, 1940–1945.*

20. M&StL Minute Book, 314, 339, 415; *Oskaloosa (IA) Daily Herald,* September 25 and 27, 1944; Station Record of Train Movements and Operators Transfer, Hazel Run, Minnesota, October 9, 1945, AC; M&StL Minute Book, 347.

21. *Railway Age* 118 (January 6, 1945): 1, 5; *New York Times,* March 19, 1945.

22. Station Record of Train Movements and Operator's Transfer, Clare, Iowa, May 8, 1945, AC; *Forest City Summit,* July 28, 1955; *Winthrop News,* May 10, 1945.

23. *Railway Age* 118 (May 12, 1945): 835–39; ibid. (May 19, 1945): 874–77, 907–9; *New York Times,* May 27, June 17, and July 15, 1945.

24. *Winthrop News,* August 9, 1945; M&StL, Engineer's Register, Spencer, Iowa, August 14, 1945, AC; *Spencer Times,* August 16, 1945; Hanska (MN) Centennial Committee, *Hanska: A Century of Tradition, 1901–2001* (Hanska: Hanska Centennial Committee, 2001), 407; *Forest City Summit,* July 28, 1955; *Des Moines Register,* August 14, 1945; *St. Paul Dispatch* (Extra), August 14, 1945, *Minneapolis Daily Times* (Extra), August 14, 1945.

25. *Railway Age* 119 (September 15, 1945): 452; ibid. (November 17, 1945): 789–93; ibid. (December 22, 1945): 1033; ibid. (December 29, 1945): 1058–62; Dean B. Simmons, *Swords into Plowshares: Minnesota's POW Camps during World War II* (St. Paul: Cathedral Hill Books, 2000), 89–93, 102–12; *United States News* 30 (December 14, 1945): 16–17; *New York Times,* December 17, 23, and 25, 1945.

26. John F. Stover, *American Railroads* (Chicago: University of Chicago Press, 1961), 203; *Official Guide* (January 1946), xv; M&StL, Annual Report, 1946, 10.

20. Sprague and Prosperity

1. Eric F. Goldman, *Crucial Decade—and After: America, 1945–1960* (New York: Vintage Books, 1960), 1–45; Joseph C. Goulden, *The Best Years, 1945–1950* (New York: Antheneum Books, 1976), 1–233; *Official Guide* (January 1946), xv; *New York Times,* February 12, 1946; *Railway Age* 120 (January 5, 1946): 1–2, 69–78; Kent T. Healy, *Performance of the U.S. Railroads since World War II* (New York: Vantage Press, 1985), 71; *Moody's Manual of Investments: Steam Railroads* (New York: Moody's Investors Service, 1945), a3–a12.

2. Joseph C. Goulden, *The Best Years, 1945–1950,* 120–27; *Brotherhood of Locomotive Firemen and Enginemen's Magazine* 123 (August 1947): 131–38.

3. *Railway Age* 120 (June 1, 1946): 1105; M&StL, Annual Report, 1946, 7; L. C. Sprague to H. W. Burtness et al., September 22, 1947; John M. Budd to L. C. Sprague, September 25, 1947; Harold W. Burtness to L. C. Sprague, September 29, 1947; L. C. Sprague to Russell Coulter, May 14, 1948, both from TP&W [Toledo, Peoria & Western], Executive Department, M&StL General File.

4. Nancy Ford, "Sprague of M&StL," *Railway Progress* 3 (January 1950): 30–33; M&StL, AFE 44-224; *Minneapolis Tribune,* November 4, 1940; *Time* (November 29, 1943): 82; Waconia Heritage Association, *Waconia and Its Island: Paradise of the Northwest* (Waconia: Waconia Heritage Association, 1986), 179; T. H. Farmen to the author, March 4 and 29 and April 21, 1972; Mike Raymond, "Working on the West End," *North Western Lines* 21 (Spring 1994): 59–68; W. W. Landmesser, interview by the author, July 15, 1991; M. J. Reitan to the author, July 25, 1972.

5. *Watertown Public Opinion,* November 8, 1948.

6. ICC, *Study of Railroad Motive Power, File No. 66-A-11* (May 1950), 64–68, AC; M&StL, AFEs; M&StL, Minute Book 327, 400, 427, 459, 519–20, 563–64, 737–38, 836–37, 853; Louis A. Marre, *Diesel Locomotives: The First 50 Years* (Waukesha, WI: Kalmbach Publishing, 1995), 87–90; Albert J. Churela, *From Steam to Diesel: Managerial Customs and Organizational Capabilities in the Twentieth-Century American Locomotive Industry* (Princeton, NJ: Princeton University Press, 1998), 15–19, 75–94.

7. W. W. Landmesser, interview by the author, September 11, 1993; M&StL, "Locomotive and Passenger Car Equipment-Ownership-Age-Value-Etc. 1/1/46," AC; GN, President File 16,352, Box 867, MHS; *Corwith, Iowa, "Then" and "Now"* (Corwith: Corwith Centennial Committee, 1980), 17; M&StL, Engineer's Register, Spencer, Iowa, AC.

8. M&StL, Oskaloosa Train Movement Reports 1946–48, AC; J. W. Devins to C. W. Weatherill, February 10, 1950, in M&StL, AFE 41-R-222; M&StL, Station Record of Train Movement and Operator's Transfer, Packwood, Iowa, January 6, February 3, 1950, AC; Gene Green, *Minneapolis and St. Louis in Color* (Edison, NJ: Morning Sun Books, 1996), 52; Louis Claeson, "Memories of Cedar Lake," *North Western Lines* 26 (Winter 1999): 15–22; *Railway Age* 127 (September 17, 1949): 522; Curtis L. Katz, "The Last Great Railroad Show," *Trains* 58 (August 1998): 58–67; M&StL, AFEs.

9. J. P. Lamb and Philip A. Weibler, "Moguls and Mikes: The Story of the 'Have Train—Will Haul' Line," *Trains* 21 (October 1961): 38–42; Hank Billings, "Steam Power Today on the Bevier & Southern," *Railroad Magazine* 70 (October 1959): 20–23; *Railroad Magazine* 75 (March 1974): 58; M&StL Minute Book, 428–29, 459, 791; *Trains* 19 (March 1959): 9; Dale Wilson, *The Algoma*

Central Railroad Story (Sudbury, Ontario: Nickel Plate Rails, 1984), 203; *Trains* 46 (April 1986): 4.

10. Don L. Hofsommer, "Getting to Know Her," *Railroad History,* Millennium Special (2000): 100–109.

11. M&StL, "Locomotives and Passenger Train Equipment-Ownership-Age-Values-Etc., 1/1/46," AC; M&StL, Minute Book, 237–38, 443–44, 559–62, 603–4; M&StL, Bulletin 3045 (May 15, 1948), AC.

12. *Official Guide* (May 1946), 16; *Business Week* (July 12, 1947): 48, 53–54; *Railway Age* 118 (March 3, 1945): 429; M&StL, AFE 45-186; M&StL, Annual Reports, 1946–49.

13. M&StL, AFEs; M&StL, Annual Reports, 1946–49.

14. M&StL, Minute Book, 772–75, 834–35; *Minneapolis Star,* April 8, 1949, and April 4, 1950; *Railway Age* 128 (May 13, 1950): 67–68; ibid., 130 (May 14, 1951): 102; ibid., 131 (August 27, 1951): 44–46.

15. *Railroad Magazine* 75 (April 1964): 32–33; Frank P. Donovan Jr. to Henrietta M. Larson, October 28, 1948; Frank P. Donovan Jr. to Stanley Pargellis, January 5, 1950; Frank P. Donovan Jr. to Merrill C. Wallace, August 5, 1950, all from AC; *New York Times,* July 29, 1951; John W. Barringer to L. C. Sprague, January 11, 1951, AC; *Minnesota History* 32 (March 1951): 47–48; *Los Angeles Times,* July 21, 1952; H. Roger Grant, *Iowa Railroads: The Essays of Frank P. Donovan Jr.* (Iowa City: University of Iowa Press, 2000), 1–16.

16. *Minneapolis Tribune,* April 11 and June 24, 1949; L. C. Sprague to E. H. Hanschen, May 6, 1949, AC; Traffic Club of Minneapolis, Easter program 1949, AC; *Arlington (MN) Enterprise,* December 20, 1945; *Railway Age* 120 (May 18, 1946): 248–49; *U.S. News & World Report* (May 21, 1948): 43; *Fortune* (June 1949): 88; *Minneapolis Tribune,* August 28, 1949.

17. *Railway Age* 126 (May 14, 1949): 985; ibid., 131 (November 5, 1951): 60; Taylor Hampton, *The Nickel Plate Road: The History of a Great Railroad* (Cleveland: World Publishing, 1947), 296–99; John A. Rehor, *The Nickel Plate Story* (Milwaukee: Kalmbach Publishing, 1965), 374; Julius Grodinsky, "How Consolidations Affect Movement of Traffic," *Railway Age* 84 (June 30, 1928): 1500–1503. See also Roger Cook and Carl Zimmerman, *The Western Maryland Railway: Fireballs and Black Diamonds* (Lawry Station, PA: Garrigues House, 1992).

18. *Forbes* (December 15, 1942): 14–15; *American Feed and Grain* (December 1953): 11, 35–36; *Railway Age* 127 (November 19, 1949): 215–16; M&StL, Minute Book, 800.

19. M&StL, Minute Book, 352–53, 363, 570–73; *Railway Age* 123 (October 4, 1947): 592; *Traffic World* 83 (February 12, 1949): 89; W. W. Landmesser, interview by the author, August 19, 1992; C. F. Lincoln to Queensy, October 9, 1946, AC; Mark Reutter, "The Great (Motive) Power Struggle: The Pennsylvania Railroad v. General Motors, 1935–1949," *Railroad History* (Spring 1994): 15–33.

20. M&StL tabular data.

21. Ibid; M&StL, Station Record of Train Movements and Operator's Transfer, Hazel Run, Minnesota, 1945–46, AC; Manford J. Reiten to the author, June 7, 1994.

22. M&StL tabular data, 1944–49; Samuel Rubenstein to the author, June 7, 1994.

23. *National Perishable Freight Committee Circular* 5-H, Ice Stations (March 17, 1947), 34; *Winthrop News,* December 23, 1948; *A History of Roland, Iowa, 1870–1970* (Roland: Privately published, 1970), 35.

24. Waconia Heritage Association, *Waconia,* 114; M&StL, Special Rules and Instructions No. 2 (August 22, 1949), 13; Manford J. Reitan to the author, February 23, 1999; John Gruber, "Harvesting of Cold," *Locomotive & Railway Preservation* (January–February 1996): 20–27; Healy, *Performance of the Railroads,* 122–26; *Winthrop News,* August 22, 1946, and November 6, 1947; *Iowa State Commerce Commission Report, 1947,* 201–2; M&StL, "LCL Overhead Merchandise Cars, October 29, 1949," 4; M&StL, "LCL Merchandise Freight Schedules, March 1, 1951," 1–9, AC

25. *Railway Age* 88 (March 1, 1930): 543; *Business Week* (September 11, 1937): 46–47; Jimmy M. Skaggs, *Prime Cut: Livestock Raising and Meat Packing in the United States, 1607–1983* (College Station: Texas A&M University Press, 1986), 144–46; M&StL tabular data, 1930–49; *Winthrop News,* October 8, 1931, and September 29, 1938; M&StL, AFEs; Mark F. Sharping, interview by the author, June 13, 1963.

26. Frank P. Donovan Jr., *Mileposts on the Prairie: The Story of the Minneapolis & St. Louis Railway* (New York: Simmons-Boardman, 1950), 228–29.

27. M&StL, AFE 46-163; *Railway Age* 127 (October 29, 1949): 780; Minneapolis, Northfield & Southern, "Complete List of Industries Having Side Track Facilities within the Minneapolis, Minnesota Switching District," (1948), 1–14, AC; Writers Program, Work Progress Administration, *The Bohemian Flats* (St. Paul: Minnesota Historical Society Press, 1986), 1–2, 45–47; *Winthrop News,* October 26, 1939.

28. Julius Grodinsky, *Railroad Consolidation: Its Economic and Controlling Principles* (New York: D. Appleton &

Co., 1930), 243; John B. Cruze to Frank P. Donovan Jr., August 12, 1949, AC; M&StL tabular data, 1940–49.

29. Fort Dodge, Des Moines & Southern (FtDDM&S), Annual Report, 1945, 3; *Railway Age* 118 (January 20, 1945): 183; *New York Times,* January 3, 1949; *Moody's Manual of Investments: Transportation* (New York: Moody's Investors Service, 1953), a277–a28; Richard C. Overton, *Perkins/Budd: Railway Statesmen of the Burlington* (Westport, CT: Greenwood Press, 1982), 196–99; Healy, *Performance of the Railroads,* 39–46.

30. M&StL tabular data, 1930–47; Georges Denzene to the author, March 11, 1992; Madison Centennial Committee, *Madison Historical Album,* 151; Julia Becken to the author, November 10, 1971; Frank P. Donovan Jr. to Roy Craft, November 26, 1948, AC.

31. *Winthrop News,* December 18, 1947, and January 1, 1948; *Hanska Herald,* December 26, 1947; Raymond W. Dorn, interview by the author, June 22, 1982; E. L. Crimmen to A. A. Fox, April 1, 1948, AC; *Iowa State Commerce Commission Report, 1948,* 45–49; IC, Dispatchers Sheet, Iowa Division, Cherokee District, June 24, 1948, AC.

32. Richard Thruelsen, "Postman on Wheels," *Saturday Evening Post* 219 (February 1, 1947): 32–33, 47–48, 53–56; Winfield (IA) Beacon, *One Hundredth Anniversary, 1981: The Winfield Beacon* (Winfield: Winfield Beacon, 1981), 17; Everett E. Hermanson to the author, March 5 and 31, 1972.

33. *Iowa State Commerce Commission Report, 1948,* 50; *Minneapolis Star,* April 27, 1949; M&StL, Timetable, May 9, 1949; M&StL, General Passenger Department Bulletin, January 2, 1950, AC.

34. *Watonwan County Plaindealer,* December 26, 1971; *New Ulm Daily Journal,* August 13, 1954; Hazel E. Drake, *History of Rippey, Greene County, Iowa: A Century of Progress, 1849–1956* (Hartley, IA: Sentinel Publishing, 1956), 20; M&StL, Dispatchers Record of Movements of Trains, November 11–12, 1940, AC; Shirley Knudson, ed., *History of Watonwan County* (Dallas, TX: Curtis Media, 1955), 25; *Minneapolis Tribune,* November 12–13, 1940; *Winthrop News,* November 14, 1940, and February 12, 1947; M&StL, Annual Report, 1948, 9.

35. Charles Beard to Frank P. Donovan Jr., December 4, 1950, AC; *Winthrop News,* July 3, 1948; *Perry (IA) Advertiser,* May 31, 1909.

36. W. F. Lewis to Frank P. Donovan Jr., December 4, 1950, AC; James R. Sullivan to the author, March 28, 1999; Dan Knight to the author, April 5, 1978.

37. Dan Knight to the author, May 24, 1972, and August 9, 1973; *Winthrop News,* July 17, 1941; *Minneapolis Star Journal,* April 12, 1943; *Oskaloosa Daily Herald,* February 1, 1943; *Iowa State Commerce Commission Report, 1947,* 276–79; W. W. Landmesser interview by the author, July 15, 1991.

38. M&StL tabular data, 1944–49; *New York Times,* February 12 and October 24, 1946.

39. Don L. Hofsommer, "The Watertown Express and the 'Hog and Human': M&StL Passenger Service in South Dakota, 1884–1960," *South Dakota History* 3 (Spring 1973): 126–55, esp. 146.

21. Sprague at the Throttle

1. Joseph C. Goulden, *The Best Years, 1945–1950* (New York: Atheneum, 1976), 10.

2. *Vintage Rails* (May/June 1998): 32; *United States News* 22 (February 14, 1947): 46–49; *Railway Age* 123 (August 2, 1947): 32–33; *Saturday Evening Post* (May 22, 1948): 148–50; *Business Week* (October 30, 1948): 19–20; *New York Times,* January 3, 1949; *Business Week* (March 12, 1949), 26.

3. *Newsweek* 36 (December 18, 1950): 72, 75; *Moody's Manual of Investments: Transportation* (New York: Moody's Investors Service, 1950), 610–18, esp. 614–15; W. W. Landmesser, interview by the author, October 15, 1994; M&StL Minute Book, 2291; *Railway Age* 135 (September 7, 1953): 8; Frank P. Donovan Jr. to H. C. Wigfield, October 20, 1950, AC; *Mason City (IA) Globe-Gazette,* August 3, 1953; *Minneapolis Tribune,* October 18, 1953; *Marshalltown Times-Republican,* October 9 and 15, 1951.

4. M&StL, Annual Reports, 1950–53; M&StL, AFEs 52-59, 53-91.

5. M&StL, Annual Reports, 1950–53; M&StL, AFEs 50-88, 50-194; William W. Landmesser, interviews by the author, August 19, 1992, and August 8, 1993; J. M. Hood to Member Lines Handling United States Mail, November 10, 1949, AC; Edmund Keilty, *Doodlebug Country: The Rail Motorcar on the Class I Railroads of the United States* (Glendale: Interurban Press, 1982), 102–3.

6. *Iowa State Commerce Commission Reports, 1949–1952;* M&StL Contract 1055 (October 1, 1950), C&NW; *Iowa State Commerce Commission Report, 1950,* 222–24; M&StL, Annual Report, 1953, 12; M&StL Contract 2229 (February 13, 1951), C&NW.

7. Michael Conant, *Railroad Mergers and Abandonments* (Berkeley: University of California Press, 1964), 113–19; *Railway Age* 120 (January 5, 1946): 119–20; M&StL Minute Book, 436–38, 585–87, 711–14, 848, 1099, 2004,

2012–13, 2021; M&StL, Annual Report, 1948, 9; ibid., 1952, 9; *Waterloo (IA) Courier,* December 24, 1950.

8. M&StL Contact 2229 (February 13, 1951), C&NW; M&StL Minute Book, 1080–81, 2068–69; CRI&P, "Lines Removed or Sold since January 1, 1936" (map), AC.

9. *Moody's Manual of Investments: Transportation, 1953,* a6; ibid., 1958, a7; M&StL tabular data, 1945–53; Edward M. Breecher, "Trouble on the Railroads," *Consumer Reports* 15 (April 1950): 175–78; *New York Times,* January 3, 1955; Herbert Askwith, "Railroads on the Wrong Track," *Harpers* 200 (May 1950): 75–80.

10. *Moody's Manual of Investments: Steam Railroads* (New York: Moody's Investors Service, 1945), a26–a27; ibid., 1958, a71; Stover, *American Railroads,* 210–16, 237–38.

11. *Moody's Manual of Investments: Transportation, 1953,* a9; *Harpers* 201 (August 1950): 17; *Business Week* (April 8, 1950): 86–87, 90; ibid. (February 23, 1952): 166–68, 170, 172; ibid. (October 17, 1953): 62, 64, 66, 68; *Railway Age* 135 (October 26, 1953): 13.

12. Tabular data from *Moody's Manuals,* 1950, 1953, 1958, and from M&StL Annual Reports, 1950–53.

13. *Railway Age* 131 (November 26, 1950): 49; M&StL Minute Book, 369, 444, 584, 847, 1086, 2001; M&StL, AFEs 50-75, 51-165, 51-223, 51-25; Dave Umhauer, "The Champagne Flight: Passenger Service on the Minnesota & International," *Mainstreeter* 13 (Fall 1994): 5–24, esp. 20; *Traffic World* 91 (May 9, 1953): 78–79.

14. *Newsweek* 41 (May 4, 1953): 69–70; William H. Schmidt to the author, January 22, 1994.

15. M&StL Minute Book, 2056.

22. The Ides of May

1. *Minneapolis Star,* April 1, 1949; David P. Morgan to Frank P. Donovan Jr., September 18, 1948, AC; *Minneapolis Star,* August 19, 1953.

2. *New York Times,* February 11 and April 19, 1954; David Karr, *Fight for Control* (New York: Ballantine Books, 1956), 9–41; Joseph Borkin, *Robert R. Young: The Populist of Wall Street* (New York: Harper & Row, 1969), 94–210; *Business Week* (April 10, 1954): 52; ibid. (April 24, 1954): 33.

3. *Who's Who in America,* vol. 1 (New Providence, NJ: Marquis Who's Who, 1997), 562; *New York Times,* August 20, 1949, March 29, 1950, and May 26, 1951; *Railway Age* 130 (March 19, 1951): 88; ibid. (June 4, 1951): 90; CGW, Annual Report, 1950, 1.

4. *New York Times,* August 29, September 2, October 9, 24, 1953.

5. *Business Week* (August 15, 1953): 64–68; *Minneapolis Star,* October 9, 1953.

6. *Minneapolis Tribune,* October 28–30, 1953; *Des Moines Register,* January 3, 1954.

7. M&StL Minute Book, 2272–88; *Minneapolis Tribune,* February 28, 1954.

8. *Minneapolis Tribune,* May 4, 1954; *Des Moines Register,* March 7, 1954.

9. *Minneapolis Tribune,* March 6, 1954.

10. M&StL, To Shareholders of the Minneapolis & St. Louis Railway, Notice of Annual Meeting, March 29, 1954, AC.

11. L. C. Sprague, By Order of the Board, to the Shareholders, March 29, 1954, AC.

12. *Minneapolis Tribune,* March 31, 1954; *New York Times,* March 31, 1954.

13. M&StL Management Proxy Committee to the Shareholders, April 8, 1954, AC; *New York Times,* April 10, 1954; L. C. Sprague, By Order of the Board, to Shareholders, April 15, 1954, AC; *Minneapolis Tribune,* April 15, 1954.

14. *Minneapolis Star,* April 8, 1954; *Minneapolis Tribune,* April 9, 1954; *New York Times,* April 9, 1954.

15. M&StL Management Proxy Committee to Shareholders, April 17, 22, 1954, AC; *Minneapolis Star,* April 22, 1954.

16. Philip D. Jordan to Richard C. Overton, April 10, 1954; Richard C. Overton to Philip D. Jordan, April 13, 1954, both from AC; *Chicago Daily Sun Times,* April 20, 1954; *New York Times,* April 25, 1954; *Des Moines Register,* April 25, 1954.

17. *Minneapolis Tribune,* May 2, 6–7, and 9, 1954; *Traffic World* 93 (May 8, 1954): 28.

18. *Minneapolis Tribune,* May 9, 11, 1954.

19. *Minneapolis Tribune,* May 12–13, 1954; *New York Times,* May 12–13, 1954; W. W. Landmesser, interview by the author, July 9, 1990; *Wall Street Journal,* April 24, 1995; M&StL Minute Book, 2329–45; Lou Sprague to Richard C. Overton, May 19, 1954, AC.

20. *New York Times,* June 6, 1965; Karr, *Fight for Control* 105–17; *Des Moines Register,* April 25, 1954. See also Case Study MR93, "Minneapolis & St. Louis Railway Company," done in 1955 at Northwestern University, but note that the unnamed author offers no analysis.

21. Otto H. Kahn, "Edward Henry Harriman," in *Memoirs of Three Railroad Pioneers,* ed. Stuart Bruchey (New York: Arno Press, 1981), 16–20.

22. E. Roland Harriman to Frank P. Donovan Jr., December 22, 1950, AC; Richard C. Overton to the author,

April 1, 1976; Julius A. Schmal to L. C. Sprague, May 22, 1951, AC; G. B. Aydelott, interview by the author, June 3, 1988; W. K. Smith, interview by the author, September 24, 1989; *Modern Railroads* 39 (February 1984): 28; James R. Sullivan to the author, January 20, 1990.

23. Halting Steps

1. *Wall Street Journal,* February 9, 1987.

2. *Minneapolis Tribune,* May 13 and 16, 1954; *Railway Age* 136 (May 17, 1954): 13

3. M&StL Minute Book, 2329–67; *Minneapolis Tribune,* May 26, 1954; *Railway Age* 136 (June 21, 1954): 65–66.

4. *Des Moines Register,* June 13, 1954; M&StL Executive Committee Minute Book, 1–12, hereinafter cited as M&StL XC Minute Book; *Minneapolis Star,* June 14, 1954.

5. M&StL XC Minute Book, 9, 21, 27, 32–33, 47; *Railway Age* 140 (February 27, 1956): 7; Ben W. Heineman to the Shareholders, July 12, 1954, AC; *Des Moines Register,* July 13, 1954; M&StL, Annual Report, 1954, 8; M&StL Minute Book, 2389.

6. *Traffic World* 94 (July 17, 1954): 21; *Railway Age* 137 (July 19, 1954): 13–14; M&StL, Annual Report, 1954, 3.

7. M&StL tabular data, 1953–54; M&StL, Annual Report, 1954, 3; *Minneapolis Tribune,* May 13, 1955.

8. M&StL, AFEs 54-181, 45-55, 8017; M&StL Contract 1517; M&StL XC Minute Book, 71, 128; *Railway Age* 139 (August 8, 1955): 13.

9. *Railway Age* 137 (March 28, 1955): 32; M&StL XC Minute Book, 49; M&StL Minute Book, 2421; Thomas J. Powers, interview by the author, December 16, 1982; *Minneapolis Star,* February 2 and 11, 1955; William W. Landmesser, interview by the author, August 19, 1992.

10. M&StL XC Minute Book, 95, 147; James R. Sullivan, interview by the author, December 13, 1982; *Railway Age* 139 (October 31, 1955): 8; M&StL, Annual Report, 1955, 3–4; M&StL XC Minute Book, 126–27.

11. M&StL XC Minute Book, 139; M&StL, AFEs 8216, 8217; F. B. Clarke to E. H. Garlick et al., November 25, 1955, AC; *Railway Age* 139 (December 5, 1955): 44; *Traffic World* 96 (December 24, 1955): 27.

12. David B. Danbom, *Born in the Country: A History of Rural America* (Baltimore: Johns Hopkins University Press, 1995), 233–52; Leland L. Sage, *A History of Iowa* (Ames: Iowa State University Press, 1974), 309–18; Joseph Frazier Wall, *Iowa: A History* (New York: W. W. Norton, 1978), 137–53; Dorothy Schwieder, "Iowa: The Middle Land," in *Heartland: Comparative Histories of the Midwestern States,* ed. James H. Madison (Bloomington: Indiana University Press, 1988), 276–95; Theodore C. Blegen, *Minnesota: A History of the State* (Minneapolis: University of Minnesota Press, 1963), 556–75; David L. Nass, "The Rural Experience," in *Minnesota in a Century of Change: The State and Its People since 1900,* ed. Clifford E. Clark Jr. (St. Paul: Minnesota Historical Society, 1989), 129–54, esp. 147–51; D. Jerome Tweton, "The Business of Agriculture," in ibid., 260–94.

13. Alfred D. Chandler, comp. and ed., *Giant Enterprise: Ford, General Motors, and the Automobile Industry* (New York: Harcourt, Brace and World, 1964), 4.

14. *New York Times,* January 3, April 29, 1955; *Moody's Transportation Manual, 1958* (New York: Moody's Investors Service, 1958), a6.

15. *Moody's Transportation Manual, 1958,* a9–a10.

16. Benjamin F. Fairless, "The First Freedom: Railroads Have Been Denied the Freedom to Compete," *Vital Speeches* 20 (September 15, 1954): 731–34; *Forbes* (January 1, 1954): 32–41; *New York Times,* September 21, 1955; H. Roger Grant, *The North Western: A History of the Chicago & North Western Railway System* (De Kalb: Northern Illinois University Press, 1996), 180–87.

17. *Modern Railroads* 10 (September 1955): 126–32.

24. Days of Red and White

1. William W. Landmesser, interviews by the author, August 19, 1992, and September 11, 1993; Manford J. Reitan, interview by the author, September 11, 1993; *Minneapolis Tribune,* May 16, 1954; M&StL, XC Minute Book, 155–58; M&StL, Minute Book, 2475.

2. *Minneapolis Tribune,* April 1, 1956, and September 12, 1958; M&StL XC Minute Book, 155–58.

3. *New York Times,* August 12, 1954, and March 3 and August 26, 1955; *Minneapolis Tribune,* August 26, 1955; *Modern Railroads* 10 (September 1955): 126–32; *Minneapolis Star,* September 10, 1955, and February 8, 1956; *Railway Age* 140 (February 13, 1956): 14; *Business Week* (February 18, 1956): 53–54; *Time* 67 (February 20, 1956): 82; *New York Times,* February 21, 1956; *Railway Age* 140 (February 27, 1956): 7–8; Grant, *The North Western,* 180–90.

4. *Minneapolis Star,* March 7 and May 9, 1956; *Railway Age* 140 (March 12, 1956): 11–12; M&StL XC Minute Book, 166–67.

5. M&StL XC Minute Book, 90–91; *Moody's Transportation Manual, 1960* (New York: Moody's Investors Service, 1960), 188.

6. NP President Subject File 805–46, MHS.

7. GN President File 10, 595, MHS; *Chicago Journal of Commerce,* June 14, 1926; Lloyd Rinehart, "The Tip-Up: The Toledo, Peoria & Western Story," *Railfan & Railroad* 4 (July 1983): 43–53; *Railway Age* 154 (April 1, 1963): 29.

8. M&StL Minute Book, 363, 826; George W. Hilton, *Monon Route* (Berkeley, CA: Howell-North, 1977), 198; Carl Rieser, "Ben Heinman's Very Special Situation," *Fortune* 56 (September 1957): 170–72, 268–75; "John Shedd Reed and Santa Fe's Famous Fast Trains," *Vintage Rail* (July–August 1999): 86–91; Brief of Plaintiff Minneapolis & St. Louis Railway Company, U.S. District Court of Minnesota Civil 123, No. 4-57 (February 3, 1958), 5–6, 15, AC; *New York Times,* May 28 and July 9, 1955; Testimony of Ben W. Heineman, ICC Hearing, Finance Dockets 18991 and 19086, Peoria, February 9, 1956, 26, AC, hereinafter cited as Heineman testimony; M&StL Minute Book, 2404–08.

9. Heineman testimony, 20–22; Henry H. Livingston, interview by the author, February 28, 1995.

10. *Railway Age* 139 (August 1, 1955): 13; M&StL XC Minute Book, 137–38; M&StL Minute Book, 2461; *New York Times,* February 2, 1956; *St. Paul Dispatch,* February 4, 1956.

11. Heineman testimony, 1, 4, 28, 30; Brief on Behalf of Minneapolis & St. Louis Railway, Finance Dockets 19086 and 18991 (December 31, 1956), 49, 84–89, AC.

12. Brief on Behalf of Minneapolis & St. Louis Railway, 8, 19–21, 29–30; *Business Week* (February 18, 1956): 53–54; *St. Paul Pioneer Press,* February 2, 1956; Reply to Exceptions by Certain Interveners, City of Bushnell, Illinois, et al., Finance Dockets 18991 and 19086 (February 18, 1957), 5, 26, 31–33, 40–41, AC; Statement and Analysis of Relationship between the State of Iowa and Proposals of Control of Toledo, Peoria & Western Railroad, Finance Dockets 19086 and 18991, by Atchison, Topeka & Santa Fe Railway and Pennsylvania Railroad (April 1, 1957), 19–25, AC; Testimony of J. Russell Coulter, ICC Hearing, Peoria, Illinois, Finance Dockets 18991 and 19086, February 4, 1956, AC.

13. *New York Times,* November 10, 1956, June 12, 1957; *Minneapolis Tribune,* June 12, 1957; James R. Sullivan, interview by the author, December 13, 1982; A. W. Schroeder to George Lauthy, June 26, 1957, TP&W Executive Department files; *New York Times,* December 4, 1957.

14. Richard S. Prosser, *Rails to the North Star* (Minneapolis: Dillon Press, 1966), 56, 153; Gary Lenz, "The Minnesota Western Railroad," *North Western Lines* 26 (Fall 1999): 40–55; *Minneapolis Journal,* February 1, 1927; M&StL, Annual Report, 1955, 3; *Minneapolis Star,* February 1, April 10, and August 11, 1956; GN, President File 17438, MHS; Subject File 483-14, C&NW.

15. Minnesota Western Minute Book, November 6, 1956, April 24 and August 27, 1957, January 17 and July 17, 1958, April 21 and July 2, 1959, and May 18, 1960 (entries are by date and not by page number); *Minneapolis Star,* October 16 and 27, 1956; M&StL, Annual Report, 2639–40, 2688.

16. Pierre Martineau, *Motivation in Advertising: Motives That Make People Buy* (New York: McGraw-Hill, 1957), 156; *Minneapolis Star,* June 5, 1956; *The exPress* 1 (June 1956): 1, 8; *Modern Railroads* 143 (August 19, 1957): 33.

17. Station Record of Train Movement and Operator's Transfer, Packwood, Iowa, January 1–June 30, 1950, and Revillo, South Dakota, 1955–57, AC; M&StL XC Minute Book, 209–10, 251–52; William W. Landmesser, interviews by the author, July 15, 1991, and August 19, 1992; M&StL, AFEs 8483, 8524, 8657; Louis A. Marre, *Diesel Locomotives: The First 50 Years* (Waukesha, WI: Kalmbach Books, 1995), 46.

18. M&StL XC Minute Book, 209, 361, 419, 424–25, 550–51.

19. *Trains* 19 (March 1959): 14–15; M&StL Contract 2397, C&NW; "AC-2," *Illinois Central Magazine* 51 (August 1959): 2–3.

20. M&StL tabular data, 1950–59; Annual Report of the Minneapolis & St. Louis Railway to the Interstate Commerce Commission for 1959, 512–519D; M&StL, Security Analyst Inspection Trip, October 22–24, 1956, 13–35, AC; *The exPress* 2 (May 1957): 2; *Journal of the Illinois State Historical Society* 49 (Autumn 1956): 351.

21. Log Sheet Train No. 20 Radio Initiated Brake Application Tests by New York Brake 2-4-59, AC; James R. Sullivan to the author, January 26, 1987; Frank P. Donovan Jr., *Gateway to the Northwest: The Story of the Minnesota Transfer Railway* (Minneapolis: Privately published by the author, 1954), 3–5; Joseph Pierson, "College Memories at Grinnell, Iowa," *North Western Lines* 9 (Summer 1982): 44–47; Vaughn R. Ward to the author, July 17, 1998; Chief Dispatcher's Wire to All Agents, July 9, 1958, AC; McWhorter to MJR, August 14, 1958, AC; *The exPress* 3 (August 1958): 3; Station Record of Train Movement and Operator's Transfer, Conde, S.D., August 2, 1960, AC; George Thill to M&StL Agent Conde, July 28, 1960, AC

22. Charles W. Stone, interview by the author, March 9, 2001; *Oskaloosa Daily Herald,* February 27, 1952; James R. Sullivan to the author, July 26, 1998.

23. James R. Sullivan, interview by the author, December 13, 1982; *Railway Age* 140 (April 30, 1956): 43–51; ibid., 144 (March 31, 1958): cover page; Hayden Stone & Co., "A Study of the Minneapolis & St. Louis Railway," February 17, 1957, 18, AC; A. W. Schroeder, "One Hour Off," an address to the Society of Security Analysts, New York, November 15, 1957, AC.

24. Alfred W. Schroeder, prepared remarks for M&StL's annual meeting, April 9, 1958, 5–7, AC; *U.S. News & World Report* 40 (April 20, 1956): 110–24; *Business Week* (August 11, 1956): 52–56; *Forbes* (January 1, 1957): 93–98; Edward T. Thompson, "What Hope for the Railroads," *Fortune* 57 (February 1958): 137–39, 146–48; Lawrence T. King, "Railroads in Crisis," *Commonweal* 68 (June 6, 1958): 253–55; *New York Times,* January 4, 1958.

25. E. F. Thompkins, "A Senate Objective: Rescuing the Railroads," *American Mercury* 86 (May 1958): 26–30; *Railway Age* 146 (October 7, 1957), Special Report to Congress supplement; *U.S. News & World Report* 43 (December 20, 1957): 95–97; Southern Pacific, Annual Report, 1958, 3; *New York Times,* January 6, 1959; Perry M. Shoemaker, "What's Wrong with the Railroads?" *Fortune* 62 (January 1960): 118–19, 168–76.

26. *U.S. News & World Report* 49 (November 14, 1960): 86–89; H. Roger Grant, *Erie Lackawanna: Death of an American Railroad, 1938–1992* (Stanford, CA: Stanford University Press, 1994), 72; Gilbert Burck, "A Plan to Save the Railroads," *Fortune* 58 (August 1958): 82–86; *Commercial and Financial Chronicle* 191 (April 21, 1960): 22; *Business Week* (June 25, 1960): 30–32.

27. *Railway Age* 140 (April 30, 1956): 43–44, 50–51; ibid., 143 (December 7, 1957): 60

28. M&StL XC Minute Book, 230–31, 294–95, 443–44, 477–78, 553–54; M&StL Annual Report, 1956, 3; M&StL, "The Industrial Future of Keithburg Rail-Barge Port," 1957, AC; *Railway Age* 143 (July 8, 1957): 20–21; *Newton Daily News,* August 10, 1957.

29. M&StL, Annual Report, 1956, 8–9; *The exPress* 4 (November 1959): 1; M&StL, "Industrial Properties on the M&StL and Minneapolis Industrial Railway," 1958, AC; M&StL Minute Book, 2749–53; M&StL XC Minute Book, 522–23; Board of Directors and Security Analysts Inspection of Minneapolis & St. Louis Railway, October 22–24, 1958, 14, AC.

30. *Railway Age* 142 (January 28, 1957): 27; ibid., 146 (January 19, 1959): 54; M&StL XC Minute Book, 431, 453–54, 528, 541–42, 567, 584; M&StL, Annual Report, 1956, 6, 13; *Minneapolis Tribune,* April 24, 1960; *Modern Railroads* 13 (August 1958): 75; Hayden Stone & Co., "A Study of the Minneapolis & St. Louis Railway Company," February 17, 1957, 9–10, AC; Board of Directors and Security Analysts Inspection, 7; *The exPress* 1 (January 1956): 1–4; ibid. (June 1956): 6; ibid. (August 1956): 3; ibid., 3; ibid., 4 (November 1959): 3; M&StL, Annual Report, 1959, 7.

31. *Moody's Transportation Manual, 1958* (New York: Moody's Investors Service, 1958), a33–a35; *Railway Purchasing & Stores* 51 (June 1958): 55–56, 92; M&StL XC Minute Book, 191, 231, 297, 467, 563–64; M&StL Contracts 1788 (10-2-59) and 1800 (11-17-59), C&NW; *Iowa State Commerce Commission Report, 1960,* 87–90.

32. *The exPress* 3 (October 1958): 2; *The exPress* (1956–60): passim; Alfred W. Schroeder, prepared remarks for the annual meeting, 5–7.

33. M&StL, General Superintendent Bulletin No. 6468, December 26, 1956, AC; M&StL Minute Book, 2622; *The exPress* 3 (January 1958): 4; ibid. (April 1958): 2.

34. *Locomotive Engineers Journal* 83 (March 1949): 147; H. Roger Grant and Charles W. Bohi, *The Country Railroad Station in America* (Boulder, CO: Pruett Publishing, 1978), 1–10; H. Roger Grant, *Living in the Depot: The Two-Story Railroad Station* (Iowa City: University of Iowa Press, 1993), 5–52.

35. M&StL Contracts 1593 (June 1, 1956), 1610 (September 24, 1956), 1750 (November 13, 1958), C&NW; M&StL Chief Dispatcher's Bulletin No. 221 (April 13, 1958), 27–28; *The exPress* 2 (November 1957): 1–2; *Hanska Herald,* January 9, 1958; *Railway Age* 144 (January 27, 1958): 13–14; ibid. (April 7, 1958): 9, 56; ibid. (August 25, 1958): 26; *Minneapolis Tribune,* August 24, 1958; *The exPress* 3 (October 1958): 2; M&StL XC Minute Book, 445–46; *Iowa State Commerce Commission Report, 1959,* 17, 42–64; Daniel N. Knight to the author, August 4, 1970.

36. Albert W. Schroeder, prepared remarks for the annual meeting, 6; *Traffic World* 101 (April 12, 1958): 27–29; *Nation's Agriculture* (September 1958): 12–13; *Analysts Journal* (February 1959): 1–6; *The exPress* (November 1959): 3; M&StL, Annual Report, 1959, 3; G. E. Leighty, "Are Railroad Workers 'Featherbedding'?" *Vital Speeches* 26 (January 1, 1960): 175–79; Gilbert Burck, "The Great Featherbed Fight," *Fortune* 61 (March 1960): 151–53; Guy L. Brown, "A Challenge for the 1960's," *Vital Speeches* 26 (June 1960): 500–504.

37. M&StL tabular data, 1950–55; Thomas L. Baker, "Doodlebug Junket: Minneapolis to Marshalltown," *North Western Lines* 27 (Summer 2000): 12–15; "Meeting

Postwar Competition in Passenger Service," *American Association of Railroad Superintendents Committee Reports, 1946,* 28–67; Kent T. Healy, *Performance of the U.S. Railroads since World War II* (New York: Vantage Press, 1985), 46–50; Edward M. Breecher, "Trouble on the Railroads," *Consumer Reports* 15 (April 1950): 175–78.

38. William W. Landmesser, Work Diary for 1952 (February) and 1953 (March–August); *New York Times,* August 2, 1953.

39. William W. Landmesser, Work Diary for 1950 (November 2); M&StL, AFE 54-82; M&StL XC Minute Book, 182–83; *Railway Age* 141 (December 24 and 31, 1956): 20–22; *Minneapolis Tribune,* May 11, 1956; Donald Duke and Edmund Keilty, *RDC: The Budd Rail Diesel Car* (San Marino, CA: Golden West Books, 1991), 184–85; Dennis E. Holmes, "RDCs . . . Short Lived 'Louie' Name Trains," *North Western Lines* 11 (Spring 1984): 34–36.

40. William W. Landmesser, Work Diary for 1956 (May 14–16); William W. Landmesser, interview by the author, September 22, 1992; *Minneapolis Star,* January 31, 1957; *Gowrie (IA) News,* January 31, 1957; *The exPress* 2 (February 1957): 1–2; Manford J. Reitan to the author, July 25, 1972; William W. Landmesser, Work Diary for 1958 (March 5 and December 10, 17, and 18); *Railway Age* 147 (September 7, 1959): 20–21; ibid., 143 (July 29, 1957): 28; M&StL, AFE 8530; *The Rock* 13 (Third Quarter 1986): 7; M&StL XC Minute Book, 304, 332–33, 458–60.

41. M&StL, Ten-Year Summary of Selected Operating and Financial Data Supplemental to the 1959 Annual Report, 3; *Official Guide* (February 1958), 22; *Minneapolis Tribune,* December 21, 1958; *Railway Age* 144 (May 12, 1958): 40; *The exPress* 3 (May 1958): 4; *Trains* 19 (March 1959): 17; William W. Landmesser, Work Diary for 1959 (November 6–7, December 14).

42. Notice of Discontinuance, Newburg, Iowa, September 19, 1957, AC; *New York Times,* August 24, 1957, and April 19, 1958; *U.S. News & World Report* 45 (October 3, 1958): 36–39; *Railway Age* 135 (October 26, 1953): 15–16; *Illinois Central Magazine* 43 (January 1955): 2–4; Marty S. Knepper and John S. Lawrence, "Visions of Iowa in Hollywood Film," *Iowa Heritage Illustrated* 79 (Winter 1998): 159–67; *Rocket* 17 (January 1958): 14; Meredith Willson, *"But He Doesn't Know the Territory"* (New York: G. P. Putnam, 1959), 168–77; John C. Skipper, *Meredith Willson: The Unsinkable Music Man* (Mason City, IA: Savas Publishing, 2000), 110–31, 143–53; *The exPress* 2 (December 1957): 4; *Grinnell Herald-Register,* May 22–June 9, 1958; *Marshalltown Times-Republican,* May 14 and 29, 1958; Hampton (IA) Chronicle & Times, *Pride in Our Past: A Pictorial History of Franklin County, Iowa* (Hampton: Hampton Chronicle & Times, 1996), 106.

43. Michael Conant, *Railroad Mergers and Abandonments* (Berkeley: University of California Press, 1964), 132–37, 149–51; M&StL XC Minute Book, 444–45; Michael P. Joynt to the author, December 1, 2000; *The exPress* 3 (December 1958): 2; James R. Sullivan to the author, January 17, 1990; ICC, Finance Docket 20377, March 16, 1959, 8–9, 11, 15; *The exPress* 4 (April 1959): 3; *Des Moines Register,* March 23, 1959.

44. M&StL Minute Book, 2349, 2766; M&StL XC Minute Book, 119–20, 3–7; Frank N. Wilner, *Railroad Mergers: History, Analysis, Insights* (Omaha: Simmons-Boardman, 1997), 93.

45. Kent T. Healy, *Performance of the U.S. Railroads since World War II* (New York: Vantage Press, 1985), 72–74; *Wall Street Journal,* February 17 and March 26, 1958; Albert W. Schroeder, prepared remarks for the annual meeting, 3–4; *Railway Age* 147 (August 10, 1959): 34; *The exPress* 4 (October 1959): 4; M&StL XC Minute Book, 551–53, 557, 560–62, 582.

46. M&StL, Time Table No. 14 (April 5, 1959), 1–6; James R. Sullivan, interview by the author, April 23, 1984; ibid.; James R. Sullivan to the author, February 10, 1987; A. W. Schroeder to J. Russell Coulter, January 20, 1959; J. Russell Coulter to A. W. Schroeder, January 22 and March 6, 1959, both from TP&W Executive Department M&StL General File; *The exPress* 4 (January 1959): 1–2; ibid. (February 1959): 1–3; *Railway Age* 146 (February 2, 1959): 36; ibid. (February 23, 1959): 4; ibid. (March 30, 1959): 48; Vaughn R. Ward, "Ask Me about Number One and Two!" *North Western Lines* 10 (Fall 1983): 47–48.

47. *The exPress* 4 (January 1959): 2; James R. Sullivan to the author, September 16, 1995; M&StL XC Minute Book, 534–36, 558–60, 583; *The exPress* 4 (July 1959): 2; Booz, Allen & Hamilton, Survey of Off-line Traffic Operations, Minneapolis & St. Louis Railway (July 1959), 2–6, 20–21, AC; M&StL Sales Bulletin No. 18 (July 1, 1960), AC.

48. A. W. Schroeder, "Future of Railroading," address before the Transportation Club of Des Moines, October 28, 1959.

49. Gene Green, *Minneapolis & St. Louis in Color* (Edison: Morning Sun Books, 1996), 72–77; Work Diary of William W. Landmesser, 1958 (February 3, March 1, March 15); Charles W. Stone to the author, November 15, 2000; Claire C. Earp to the author, September 15, 1977;

Minneapolis Tribune, July 2, 1955; *Gowrie News,* September 6, 1956.

50. M&StL XC Minute Book, 71, 513–14; M&StL Minute Book, 2706, 2765; S. J. Owens, W. P. Coliton, and James R. Sullivan, Inspection of Fort Dodge, Des Moines & Southern Railway–Des Moines & Central Iowa Railway, March 27–29, 1957, 1–13, AC; James R. Sullivan to the author, June 11, 1988; *Traffic World* 109 (November 28, 1959): 21; Wyer, Dick & Co., CMStP&P/M&StL—Report on Economics of Acquisition, November 6, 1959, AC; H. C. Murphy to J. M. Budd and R. S. Macfarlane, July 21, 1959, NP President File 805-46, MHS; *Minneapolis Tribune,* November 10, 1959.

51. James R. Sullivan, interviews by the author, December 13, 1982, and January 10, 1995; James R. Sullivan to the author, July 26, 1982, and September 12, 1999.

52. Conant, *Railroad Mergers,* 63–64; M&StL Minute Book, 2584–85; M&StL XC Minute Book, 513–14; *Railway Freight Traffic* 5 (August 1957): 21–23; *Railway Age* 154 (April 1, 1963): 29; ibid., 144 (April 21, 1958): 14; *Traffic World* 102 (September 27, 1958): 100; 361 U.S. 173; TP&W, Annual Report, 1959, 4; *Railway Age* 148 (March 28, 1960): 46.

53. M&StL, "Industrial Properties on the M&StL and Minneapolis Industrial Railway" (1959), 20; Frank P. Donovan Jr., "Minneapolis & St. Louis in the News Again," *Trains* 19 (March 1959): 16–19; M&StL Minute Book, 2743–44, 2755–68.

25. Valhalla

1. William W. Landmesser, interview by the author, June 15, 1994.

2. James R. Sullivan, interview by the author, December 13, 1982; M&StL Minute Book of Pension Trust Trustees, 15; *Minneapolis Tribune,* April 9, 1936; C&NW, Annual Report, 1959, 26–27; *Moody's Transportation Manual, 1958* (New York: Moody's Investors Service, 1958), 372–89, esp. 379–80.

3. *St. Paul Dispatch,* April 7, 1960; *New York Times,* April 8 and 14, 1960; *Minneapolis Tribune,* April 8, 13, 1960.

4. C&NW, Memorandum and Related Exhibits for the Board of Directors in Connection with Proposed Acquisition of the Minneapolis & St. Louis Railway Company, April 5, 1960, 1–6; Agreement for Sale of Assets Chicago & North Western Railway Company and Minneapolis & St. Louis Railway Company, April 11, 1960, both from C&NW.

5. M&StL Minute Book, 2799–2810; *Minneapolis Tribune,* June 29, 1960; *New York Times,* June 29, 1960.

6. *Railway Age* 151 (October 30, 1961): 63; ibid., 154 (February 4, 1963): 21–24; John W. Barringer, *Super Railroads for a Dynamic Economy* (New York: Simmons-Boardman, 1956), passim; *Forbes* (January 1, 1957): 94. On the issue of mergers generally, see Richard Saunders, *The Railroad Mergers and the Coming of Conrail* (Westport, CT: Greenwood Press, 1978) and Richard Saunders, *Merging Lines: American Railroads, 1900–1970* (De Kalb: Northern Illinois University Press, 2001.

7. Robert W. Harbeson, "New Patterns of Railway Consolidation," *Quarterly Review of Economics and Business* (February 1962): 7–19; *New York Times,* February 20, 1946, June 6, 1947, March 2 and November 2, 1957, October 26, 1958, February 8 and December 28, 1959, and March 20, 1960; *U.S. News & World Report* 43 (November 15, 1957): 82–86, 92–98; ibid., 48 (April 18, 1960): 90–93; *Business Week* (May 10, 1958): 30–32; ibid. (May 28, 1960): 34–38; ibid. (October 8, 1960): 62–64; ibid. (October 22, 1960): 137–38; *Railway Age* 142 (May 20, 1957): 9; ibid., 149 (October 24, 1960): 24.

8. Application, C&NW/M&StL, ICC Finance Docket 21115 (May 11, 1960), 13–16, AC; *New York Times,* August 2, 1960; *Railway Age* 149 (August 8, 1960): 29.

9. M&StL, Sales Bulletins No. 5 (January 15, 1960), No. 12 (April 14, 1960), and No. 18 (July 1, 1960); M&StL Minute Book, 2759; *Railway Age* 149 (August 22, 1960): 14–16, 30; James R. Sullivan, "Marketing and the Challenge of Private Transportation," remarks before the Dallas Transportation Club, September 13, 1960, AC.

10. William W. Landmesser, Work Diary for 1958 (January 17–18) and 1959 (January 16).

11. Ibid., 1958 (December 13); M&StL, Train Order File, Victoria, Minnesota 1958–59, AC; Hassinger to Operator Morton, March 3, 1958, AC; John R. Borchert, "The Heyday of the Railway Post Office in Minnesota," *Minnegazette* (Winter 1997): 19–34; Kent T. Healy, *Performance of the U.S. Railroads since World War II* (New York: Vantage Press, 1985), 63–66; *Minnegazette* (May–June 1985): 9–15.

12. M&StL, Discontinuance of Passenger Trains 13 and 14 in the States of Minnesota and South Dakota, February 15, 1960, Exhibit 5, AC; William F. Armstrong to the author, May 30, 1988.

13. *Minneapolis Tribune,* December 6, 1963; Hubert H. Humphrey to the author, June 16, 1972.

14. M&StL XC Minute Book, 538–39; *Minneapolis*

Tribune, February 19, 1960; Michael Conant, *Railroad Mergers and Abandonments* (Berkeley: University of California Press, 1964), 149–51; Don L. Hofsommer, "The Watertown Express and the 'Hog and Human': M&StL Passenger Service in South Dakota," *South Dakota History* 3 (Spring 1973): 126–55; ICC Finance Docket 21015, June 30, 1960; *Watertown Public Opinion,* July 14 and 21, 1960; *Minneapolis Tribune,* July 11, 1960.

15. M&StL XC Minute Book, 561–62; M&StL, Ten-Year Summary of Selected Operations and Financial Data Supplemental to the 1959 Annual Report, 1–4.

16. CMStP&P, Annual Report, 1960, 3; M&StL Minute Book, 2811–12; M&StL XC Minute Book, 604–5; M&StL, Sales Bulletin No. 23 (September 27, 1960); GN President File 10,079, MHS.

17. *The exPress,* 5 (June 1960): 2; M&StL Sales Bulletins No. 17 (June 16, 1960) and No. 18 (July 1960); M&StL Minute Book, 2817, 2824–25.

18. James R. Sullivan, interview by the author, December 13, 1982; M&StL, Sales Bulletin No. 23 (September 27, 1960).

19. Charles W. Stone, interview by the author, April 23, 2001; Don Messerly to the author, December 4, 1999; Dale L. Hearn, interview, April 14, 2001; *Fort Dodge Messenger,* November 16, 1964; James R. Sullivan to the author, December 30, 1996; William W. Landmesser, interview by the author, June 15, 1994.

20. Saunders, *Railroad Mergers and Conrail,* 83, 93, 232–33; *New York Times,* October 15, 1960; C&NW, Executive Committee Minutes, October 18, 1960, C&NW Secretary's File 480-2; *Business Week* (October 22, 1960): 137–38; *Railway Age* 149 (October 24, 1960): 34–35; ICC Finance Docket 21115 (October 13, 1960).

21. *Des Moines Register,* November 1, 1960; *Fort Dodge Messenger,* November 1, 1960; A. W. Schroeder to Chicago & North Western Railway Company, October 31, 1960, C&NW Secretary's File 480-38; C&NW, Annual Report, 1960, 2–5, 14–15, 26–27.

26. Under a Green and Yellow Flag

1. *Minneapolis Tribune,* April 8 and 13 and October 9 and 30, 1960; James R. Sullivan to the author, July 26, 1988.

2. Robert W. Downing to the author, June 13, 1989, and November 12, 1993; *Wall Street Journal,* October 28, 1960; *Railway Age* 149 (November 14, 1960): 48.

3. Don Messerly to the author, December 4, 1999; C. R. Hussey to R. W. Heron et al., November 16, 1960, AC; *Marshalltown Times-Republican,* October 31, 1960.

4. Jonathan H. Fox, interview by the author, July 18, 1990; Paul S. Green, "M&StL Memories," *North Western Lines* 24 (Spring 1997): 83–85; Clifford K. Ferguson to the author, December 13, 1962; Frank P. Donovan Jr. to C. T. Nelson, March 21, 1964, AC.

5. C&NW, M&StL Division Time Table No. 1 (March 5, 1961), passim; C&NW, Proposed Resolution, April 4, 1961, C&NW Secretary File 95–105.

6. C&NW, Annual Report, 1961, 3, 5, 7–8, 13.

7. *Railway Age* 151 (July 31, 1961): 48–49; Roger Sheedon, "Victims of Merger Fever," a report sponsored by the Railway Labor Executives Association (n.d., 1963?), AC.

8. *Des Moines Register,* March 2, 1961, August 14 and 30–31, and September 8–10 and 29, 1962; *Chicago Sun-Times,* August 31, 1962; *Chicago Tribune,* August 31, 1962; *New York Times,* September 8, 1962; *U.S. News & World Report* 53 (September 10, 1962): 103–5; ibid. (September 24, 1962): 52–54, 124–27; ibid. (October 22, 1962): 96–97; *Railway Age* 153 (September 10, 1962): 9–10, 56; C&NW, Annual Report, 1962, 3, 6.

9. R. W. Geigel to Agents, December 14, 1962, AC.

10. *Des Moines Register,* January 11, 1963; *Iowa State Commerce Commission Report, 1966,* 26–28; ibid., 1967, 27; *Albert Lea (MN) Tribune,* January 12, 1967; Iowa State Commerce Commission Docket A6-6165 (May 16, 1969); *Estherville (IA) Daily News,* December 3, 1970; Darrel W. Benson to the author, January 20, 1972; D. B. Carlisle to All Agents, October 21, 1976, AC; *North Western Lines* 10 (Fall 1983): 51.

11. C&NW, M&StL Division Time Table No. 3 (May 27, 1963), passim; C&NW Train Order No. 1, December 21, 1963, to C&E [Conductor & Engineer] UP Engine 962 at Perry, Iowa, AC; Harry B. Peterson to the author, November 27, 1972; Dan N. Knight to the author, October 25, 1973; Wilson B. Lemberger to the author, December 3, 1973; *Pacific News* (November 1981): 12–13; *Switch Lamp,* no. 7 (1975): 9–10; Dennis E. Holmes, "Iowa Central's Steamboat Rock," *North Western Lines* 19 (Fall 1962): 45–53.

12. Dan N. Knight to the author, November 24, 1971, and October 18, 1979.

13. ICC, Finance Docket No. 26231 (March 16, 1971); *Ottumwa (IA) Courier,* August 4, 1970; *Wapello (IA) Republican,* November 11, 1971; W. A. Kirkpatrick to the author, January 17, 1972; Bob Carr, interview by the author, May 16, 1972; Dan N. Knight to the author, March 10, 1972; *Monmouth (IL) Daily Review Atlas,* September 30,

1974; D. R. Freyer to All Illinois Division Employees, December 18, 1974, AC.

14. *Monmouth Daily Review Atlas,* February 8, 1973, and February 16, 1974; *Burlington (IA) Hawkeye,* October 7, 1973; *Des Moines Register,* December 10, 1973, and February 28, 1976; Craig E. Burroughs to the author, March 19, 1974.

15. *Des Moines Register,* June 30 and July 3 and 6, 1981; *Burlington Hawkeye,* July 1, 1981, and May 4, 1982; *Fort Madison (IA) Democrat,* July 6, 1981; *St. Louis Globe-Democrat,* July 7, 1981.

16. *New Ulm Journal,* February 8 and March 13 and 19, 1963; ICC, Finance Docket 24621 (December 21, 1967); ICC, Finance Docket 25402 (March 14, 1969); *St. James Courier,* November 18, 1969; C&NW, Abandonments Book reproduced by the Chicago & North Western Historical Society (hereinafter cited as C&NW Abandonments).

17. H. Roger Grant, *The North Western: A History of the Chicago & North Western Railway System* (De Kalb: Northern Illinois University Press, 1998), 210–11.

18. Don L. Hofsommer, *The Southern Pacific, 1901–1985* (College Station: Texas A&M University Press, 1986), 265–68, 276–92; Don L. Hofsommer, *Grand Trunk Corporation: Canadian National Railways in the United States, 1971–1992* (East Lansing: Michigan State University Press, 1995), 79–81, 95–111.

19. Grant, *The North Western,* 215–17.

20. Henry H. Livingston, interview by the author, February 28, 1995; Robert E. Wilcox, interview by the author, August 11, 1998.

21. Grant, *The North Western,* 231–34.

22. C&NW Abandonments; *North Western News* (February 9, 1976): 2–3; ibid. (August 15, 1977): 1; *Des Moines Register,* February 6 and 9 and September 22, 1975, July 27, 1976, July 10 and November 2, 1977, and March 2, 1983; *Lake Mills Graphic,* February 9, 1977; *Spencer (IA) Daily Reporter,* July 22 and August 14, 1981; Dennis E. Holmes, "The Loss of an Old Friend," *North Western Lines* 10 (Summer 1983): 30–33.

23. *Sioux City Journal,* November 7, 1982.

24. C&NW Abandonments; *North Western Lines* 27 (Fall 2000): 14–15.

25. Wayne E. Webb and J. I. Swedberg, *Redwood: The Story of a County* (Redwood Falls, MN: Redwood County Board of Commissioners, 1964), 376–81; *North Western Lines* 10 (Winter 1983): 30; *Journal of Commerce,* May 10, 1983; *Railway Age* 185 (October 1984): 28; *St. Paul Pioneer Press,* April 16, 1984; *Minneapolis Star Tribune,* October 25, 1985; *Clarkfield (MN) Advocate,* September 18 and October 1, 1986; *Fairfax (MN) Standard,* January 8 and 24, 1986; Charles Bohi and Leslie S. Kosma, "The Minnesota Valley," *Railfan & Railroad* 8 (January 1989): 62–67.

26. *North Western Lines* 26 (Winter 1999): 23; Grant, *The North Western,* 251–53; James R. Sullivan to the author, June 15, 1995.

27. Griffin Hamilton, "Twilight on the Marshalltown Sub," *North Western Lines* 21 (Winter 1994): 67–81; Paul Swanson, "Marshalltown Diesel Shop Today," *North Western Lines* 21 (Winter 1994): 83–88.

28. John L. Hodson to the author, December 19, 1987.

Index

Don L. Hofsommer is professor of history at St. Cloud State University. He is the author and coauthor of several books, including *The Great Northern Railway: A History; The Southern Pacific, 1901–1985; The Quanah Route: A History of the Quanah, Acme & Pacific Railway;* and *Grand Trunk Corporation: Canadian National Railways in the United States, 1971–1992.*